D1871907

CENSUS OF INDIA 1931

Census of India 1871-1951, 9 Sets In 384 Bindings (9788121258876) Rs. 700000

Census of India 1931, 28 Vols. In 52 Bindings (9788121271233) Rs. 102000

1. India - Report (9788121276153) Rs. 2820 (Vol. I, Pt. 1)
2. India - Imperial Tables (9788121276139) Rs. 3210 (Vol. I, Pt. 2)
3. India - Ethnographical and Administration Report (9788121276115) Rs. 2900 (Vol. I, Pt. 3 & 5)
4. The Andaman And Nicobar Islands - Report, Tables (9788121276078) Rs. 720 (Vol. II, Pt. 1, Pt. 2)
5. Assam - Report (9788121276054) Rs. 1340 (Vol. III, Pt. 1)
6. Assam - Tables and Administrative Report (9788121276030) Rs. 1830 (Vol. III, Pt. 2 & 3)
7. Baluchistan - Report, Imeprial and Provincial Tables and Administrative Report (9788121276016) Rs. 2320 (Vol. IV, Pt. 1 & 2 & 3)
8. Bengal & Sikkim - Report (9788121275972) Rs. 2860 (Vol. V, Pt. 1)
9. Bengal & Sikkim - Tables (9788121275958) Rs. 1660 (Vol. V, Pt. 2)
10. Calcutta (9788121275910) Rs. 960 (Vol. VI, Pt. 1 & 2)
11. Bengal, Sikkim And Calcutta - Administrative Report (9788121275934) Rs. 580 (Vol. V & VI, Pt. 3)
12. Bihar And Orissa - Report (9788121275897) Rs. 1780 (Vol. VII, Pt. 1)
13. Bihar And Orissa - Tables and Administrative Report (9788121275873) Rs. 1190 (Vol. VII, Pt. 2 & 3)
14. Bombay Presidency - General Report (9788121275835) Rs. 3620 (Vol. VIII, Pt. 1)
15. Bombay - Statistical tables (9788121275811) Rs. 3060 (Vol. VIII, Pt. 2)
16. Bombay Presidency Aden - report and tables and Administrative report (9788121275798) Rs. 520 (Vol. VIII, Pt. 3 & 4)
17. Cities of the Bombay Presidency Report & Statistical tables (9788121275750) Rs. 2020 (Vol. IX, Pt. 1 & 2)
18. The Western India States Agency, In Two Parts - The Report & The Statistical Tables (9788121275736) Rs. 2560 (Vol. X, Pt. 1 & 2)
19. Burma - Report (9788121275712) Rs. 1860 (Vol. XI, Pt. 1)
20. Burma - Tables and Administrative Report (9788121275699) Rs. 1690 (Vol. XI, Pt. 2 & 3)
21. Central Provinces & Berar - Report (9788121275651) Rs. 2340 (Vol. XII, Pt. 1)
22. Central Provinces & Berar - Tables and Administrative Report (9788121275637) Rs. 3120 (Vol. XII, Pt. 2 & 3)
23. Coorg - Report And Tables and Madras - Report (9788121275613) Rs. 2680 (Vol. XIV, Pt. 1)
24. Madras - Imperial And Provincial Tables and The Administration Report (9788121275576) Rs. 1950 (Vol. XIV, Pt. 2 & 4)
25. North - West Frontier Province - Report & Tables (9788121275538) Rs. 2300 (Vol. XV, Pt. 1 & 2)
26. Delhi - Report & Tables (9788121275514) Rs. 1180 (Vol. XVI, Pt. 1 & 2)
27. Punjab - Report (9788121275491) Rs. 2070 (Vol. XVII, Pt. 1)
28. Punjab - Tables (9788121275477) Rs. 1690 (Vol. XVII, Pt. 2)
29. United Provinces of Agra And Oudh - Report (9788121275453) Rs. 3380 (Vol. XVIII, Pt. 1)
30. United Provinces of Agra And Oudh - Imperial And Provincial Tables and Administrative (9788121275439) Rs. 3600 (Vol. XVIII, Pt. 2 & 3)
31. Baroda - Report (9788121275415) Rs. 2800 (Vol. XIX, Pt. 1)
32. Baroda - Tables (9788121275392) Rs. 730 (Vol. XIX, Pt. 2)
33. Baroda - Administrative (9788121275378) Rs. 780 (Vol. XIX, Pt. 3)
34. Central India Agency - Report (9788121275354) Rs. 1690 (Vol. XX, Pt. 1)
35. Central India Agency - Tables and Administrative Volume (9788121275330) Rs. 2260 (Vol. XX, Pt. 2 & 3)
36. Cochin - Report & Tables (9788121275293) Rs. 2460 (Vol. XXI, Pt. 1 & 2 - A & B.)
37. Gwalior - Report (9788121275279) Rs. 1470 (Vol. XXII, Pt. 1)
38. Gwalior - Tables (9788121275255) Rs. 980 (Vol. XXII, Pt. 2)
39. H. E. H. The Nizam's Dominions (Hyderabad State) - Report (9788121275231) Rs. 1540 (Vol. XXIII, Pt. 1)
40. H. E. H. The Nizam's Dominions (Hyderabad State) - Tables (9788121275217) Rs. 1510 (Vol. XXIII, Pt. 2)
41. Jammu & Kashmir State - Report (9788121275194) Rs. 2060 (Vol. XXIV, Pt. 1)
42. Jammu & Kashmir State - Imperial & State Tables (9788121275170) Rs. 1940 (Vol. XXIV, Pt. 2 & 3)
43. Mysore - Report (9788121275156) Rs. 1950 (Vol. XXV, Pt. 1)
44. Mysore - Tables (9788121275132) Rs. 1380 (Vol. XXV, Pt. 2)
45. Ajmer-Merwara - Report And Tables (9788121275118) Rs. 780 (Vol. XXVI)
46. Rajputana Agency And Ajmer-Merwara - Report and Tables and Administrative (9788121275095) Rs. 2380 (Vol. XXVII, Pt. 1 & 2)
47. Travancore - Report (9788121276092) Rs. 2960 (Vol. XXVIII, Pt. 1)
48. Travancore - Tables & Administrative (9788121275996) Rs. 1360 (Vol. XXVIII, Pt. 2 & 4)
49. Jaipur State- Report (9788121275859) Rs. 1280 (Pt. 1)
50. Jaipur State- Tables (9788121275774) Rs. 2030 (Pt. 2)
51. Mayurbhanj state- Report (9788121275675) Rs. 3180 (Pt. 1)
52. Mayurbhanj state- Tables (9788121275552) Rs. 3070 (Pt. 2)

Owing to the antiquity and rarity of this book, certain pages are regrettably absent, and readability is compromised due to the blurring of the original text. If you possess any insights regarding the availability of these missing sections, kindly inform us. Your assistance is crucial in ensuring the completion of this significant work for the benefit of future generations.

CENSUS OF INDIA, 1931

BOOK - 25: VOLUME - XV

NORTH - WEST FRONTIER PROVINCE

PART I - REPORT
PART II - TABLES

CAPTAIN G. L. MALLAM
&
A. D. F. DUNDAS

GYAN

Published by

GYAN

Gyan Publishing House
5, Ansari Road
Daryaganj, New Delhi-110002
Phone: 011-47034999, 9811692060
E-mail: books@gyanbooks.com

Distribution Network
gyanbooks.com
India, USA, Canada, UK, Australia

© Publisher

All rights reserved. No part of this work may be reproduced, stored, adapted, or transmitted in any form or by any means, electronic, mechanical, photocopying, micro-filming, recording or othrwise, or translated in any language, without the prior written permission of the copyright owner and the publisher.

ISBN: 978-81-212-7123-3 (Set) 28 Vols. In 52 Bindings

ISBN: 978-81-212-7553-8 (PB) Vol. XV, Pt. I & II

First Published, 1933

2nd Impression 2024

Printed at: Gyan Press, Delhi.

The book is sold subject to the condition that it shall not, by way of trade or otherwise, be lent, resold, hired out, or otherwise circulated without the prior publisher's written consent.

CENSUS OF INDIA 1931

CENSUS OF INDIA, 1931

VOLUME XV

NORTH-WEST FRONTIER PROVINCE

PART I—REPORT
PART II—TABLES

BY

Captain G. L. MALLAM, I. A.

and

A. D. F. DUNDAS, I. C. S.

1933

PRINTED BY THE MANAGER, GOVERNMENT STATIONERY ANDPRINTING

N.-W. F. P., PESHAWAR.

THE NORTH WEST FRONTIER PROVINCE

Scale 1 Inch = 32 Mile

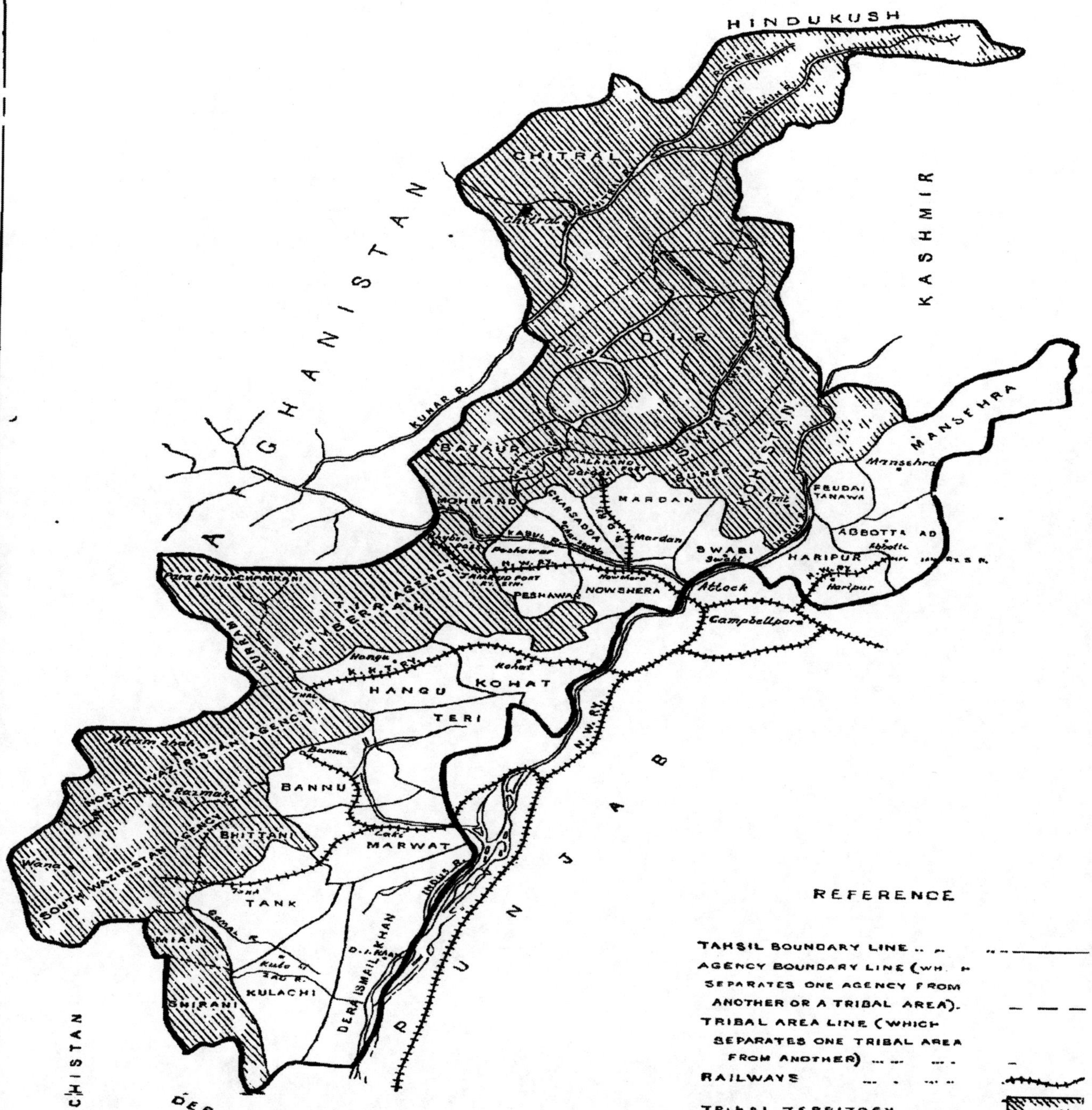

CONTENTS

PART I—REPORT

PAGES

INTRODUCTION

The present census — Previous enumerations — The scope of the present Census as compared with the previous ones — Procedure adopted for taking the Census — Code and instructions for enumeration — Preparation of Village and Town Registers — Census Divisions — Census Agency — House numbering — Training of Census Staff and preliminary enumeration — Final Census — Non-synchronous tracts — Household Schedules — Special arrangements — Attitude of the public towards Census — Provisional totals — Tabulation of results, and Slip copying — Sorting — Compilation — Cost of Census — Acknowledgments ... v—ix

CHAPTER I—DISTRIBUTION AND MOVEMENT OF THE POPULATION

Descriptive — The area dealt with — Political and administrative divisions — Changes of area — Natural divisions — The meaning of the term population — Non-synchronous areas — The actual, resident, normal and natural population — The accuracy of the enumeration — Reference to statistics — Area — Population — Density — Density of districts — Density of tahsils — Variations in population at previous censuses — The accuracy of the earlier censuses — General — Growth of population during the decade 1911—21 — The influenza epidemic of 1918 — General — Vital statistics — System of registration of vital statistics — Public health — Mortality from fevers — Plague epidemic 1921 - 27 — Agricultural conditions of the decade — Prices and wages — Extension of cultivation — The economic position of the agriculturist — Co-operative Credit Societies — Joint Stock Companies — Trade — Industrial development — Communications — Variation 1921—31 — Variation in population of districts — Variation in tahsils — Variation in density — Effect of health on variation in population of districts — Effect of migration — Pressure on resources — Definition of house — The number of houses and size of families ... 1—34

Subsidiary Tables ... ... 35—39

CHAPTER II—THE POPULATION OF CITIES, TOWNS AND VILLAGES

Reference to Imperial and Subsidiary Tables — Definition of village — Definition of town — Definition of city — Comparison of urban and rural population — The number of towns and villages — General distribution of urban population — Growth of urban population — Growth of towns classed as such since 1881 — Accretions to the urban area since 1881 — Natural growth of towns — Sex proportions in towns — Population of cantonments — Religion in towns — Distribution of urban population by religion — Peshawar City — Density and overcrowding in Peshawar City — Immigration from Peshawar rural area to Peshawar City — Distribution of rural population ... 40—48

Subsidiary Tables ... ... 49—51

CHAPTER III—BIRTH-PLACE AND MIGRATION

Reference to Statistics — Discussion confined to administered districts — General accuracy of indications — Different types of migration distinguished — Distinction is of duration — Impossibility of distinguishing by Census figures alone — General figures for the Province — Types of migration compared in regard to numbers — Natural population generally stay-at-home — District-to-district migration — Comparison of immigration with emigration, with reasons for excess of former over latter — Direction of main currents of immigration — Historical importance of immigration from the West — Connection between immigrants from Afghanistan and from tribal areas — Immigration from the West considered in groups — Decrease in immigration from the West — Figures for last two census years considered together — Other extra-Provincial migration considered — Migration between the Province and other parts of India—(*i*) Punjab — (*ii*) United Provinces — (*iii*) Other groups of immigrants — (*iv*) Other groups of emigrants — Migration between the Province and Asiatic countries outside India — Migration between the Province and countries outside Asia ... 52—59

Subsidiary Tables ... ... 60—63

PAGES.

CHAPTER IV—AGE

Reference to statistics — Unreliability of returns — Distribution of population by age-groups — Distribution by years not available — Reference to Sundbarge's theory — Population considered with reference to Sundbarge's theory — Muslim population considered by districts with reference to Sundbarge's theory — Increase in proportion of children to those of other ages — Distribution by age-groups compared with figures for 1921 — Mean age of the population — Mean age of the sexes compared — Proportions in certain age-groups for certain castes— General — Birth-rate per *mille* considered, for the decade — Variation by districts — Death-rate per *mille* through the decade — Variation by districts — Incidence of death-rate by age-periods — Incidence of certain epidemics ... ... 64—70

Subsidiary Tables ... ... 71—76

CHAPTER V—SEX

Excess of males in India compared with excess of females in Europe — Some reasons for excess of males in India — Special reasons for excess in North-West Frontier Province — Reference to statistics — Reasons for variations in excess of males to be considered Excess of male births — Infant mortality higher among males — Mortality at later ages higher among females — Effect of migration on proportion between sexes — Effect of migration illustrated by figures for districts Effect of migration illustrated by figures for religions — Same facts considered in relation to age-periods — Proportion of females in certain castes — Natural, stay-at-home, and actual populations compared — Variation in proportions since 1921 — Variation over last fifty years, considered by districts ... 77—83

Subsidiary Tables ... ... 84—87

CHAPTER VI—CIVIL CONDITION

Reference to statistics — Meaning and value of statistics — Distribution of total population — High proportion of marriages Proportion of marriages compared with records of other populations — Figures of marriage to be considered in regard to age — Proportion of married persons found in each of various age-groups — Proportion of married persons considered by religions — Lower proportions in the younger age-groups Proportion in younger age-groups lower than elsewhere in India — Decrease of proportion in last 50 years — Proportion of married population in younger age-groups by religions — Early marriage considered by castes — Proportion remaining unmarried in later age-groups — Proportion of widowed in various age-groups — Comparison with Punjab — Summary of conclusions hitherto reached — Variation in proportion of married persons by districts — Districts considered by age-groups — The younger age groups — The middle and older age-groups — Variation in distribution since previous Census — Variation among widowed by religions — Limited extent of polygamy in the Province ... 88—97

Subsidiary Tables ... ... 98—102

CHAPTER VII—INFIRMITIES

Intention of the records — Inaccuracy of the returns — Reference to statistics — Difficulty of comparisons — General tendency to decline — Comparison with census figures from 1901 — Relative prevalence of selected infirmities — Impossibility of distinguishing between varieties of mental abnormality — Comparison with other parts of India — Variation by districts from census to census — Hazara — Peshawar — The Southern districts — Early mortality among the insane — Proportion of the sexes — Classification by castes not made — Deaf-mutism — Decline in returns from each district — Variations by age — Comparison with other provinces — Statistics reasonably accurate — Causes affecting blindness — Comparison with other parts of India — Variation by districts from census to census — Distribution by districts for each sex — Proportion between the sexes — Blindness a disease of advancing age — Leprosy — Distribution by age-groups — Recorded figures only a fraction of actual — Variation from census to census — Variation by districts in last decade — Distribution by age — Prevalence among lower castes ... ... 103—112

Subsidiary Tables ... ... 113—115.

PAGES.

CHAPTER VIII—OCCUPATION

The scheme of classification — Reference to statistics — Principles of classification — Instructions to enumerators — Instructions to supervisors and others — Difficulties in the way of correct enumeration — Distinction between earners and others — Proportion of workers to total population — Distribution of workers by four main classes — Proportion of population workers in twelve sub-classes — Distribution of workers by sub-classes — Distribution not affected by any abnormal circumstances — Agriculture and allied occupations — Extraction of mineral wealth — Decline in industry — Increase in transport — Increase in trade — Public force — Public Administration — Professions and liberal arts — Persons living on their income — Domestic service — Undefined occupations — Unproductive — Main occupations by districts and natural divisions — Local distribution of subsidiary occupations — Distribution by caste — Europeans and Anglo-Indians — Low proportion of female earners — Variation since 1921 and by districts — Educated unemployment ... ... 116—128

Subsidiary Tables ... ... 129—153

CHAPTER IX—LITERACY

Reference to statistics — Method of classification — Literacy in tribal areas not estimated — Proportion of literates in total population — Trans-Frontier Posts — Hazara and Trans-Indus districts — Proportion of literacy by districts — Effect of religion on distribution by districts — Hazara and Dera Ismail Khan contrasted — Facilities in each — Peshawar — Literacy in English by districts — Literacy higher in urban than in rural areas — Literacy by age-periods — Literacy by religion — Christians — Sikhs and Hindus — Muslims — Literacy in English by religion — Effect of exclusion of figures for trans-frontier posts - Literacy by religion considered by locality — Muslims — Hindus — Sikhs — Christians — Corresponding figures for females — Literacy by caste — Males — Females — Literacy in English by caste — Literacy among Chuhras — Proportion of literacy rising — Increase during last decade — Variation in proportion of literate persons aged 15—20 — Variation by caste — Variation by districts among non-Christian population — Variation by religion — Muslims by districts — Hindus and Sikhs — Expenditure on education — Statistics of primary and secondary education — Higher education — Education among females — Obstacles to further expansion ... 154—166

Subsidiary Tables ... ... 167—173

CHAPTER X—LANGUAGE

Reference to statistics — The system of classification — Pashto — Lahnda — Method of enumeration and tabulation — Distribution of Pashto — Comparison with figures of Linguistic Survey — Pashto in the districts — Variation by districts — Comparison with 1921 General decline in proportion of Pashto speakers — Persian — Balochi — Kashmiri — Kohistani — Lahnda — Confusion between Lahnda and Punjabi — Comparison with previous figures — Growth of Lahnda and Punjabi considered together — Tendency of Lahnda and Punjabi to supplant Pashto — Figures of Linguistic Survey — Punjabi — Gujari — Urdu, Hindustani and Hindi — Gorkhali or Napali — Other Indo-European languages of India — English — Language of other families — Bilingualism — Effect of environment — Effect of requirements of business — Effect of education .. .. 174—183

Subsidiary Tables 184-185

CHAPTER XI—RELIGION

Reference to statistics — Meaning and value of statistics — Numbers under discussion - Comparative strengths — External characteristics — Distribution by districts (*i*) Muslims — (*ii*) Others — Historical reasons governing distribution — Muslims — Variations — Variations in proportion — Rate of growth by districts — Sects — Variations among Shias — Districts — Trans-border areas — Ahmadis and other sects — Hindus — Distribution by districts — Characteristics — Proportion by districts — Variation — Variation among females — Sanatan Dharam — Others — Arya Samaj — Shamsi — Sweeper sects — Sikhs — Variations — Sects — Christians — Variation and sect — Other religions ... ... 186—196

Subsidiary Tables 196-a-196-b

PAGES.

CHAPTER XII—CASTE, TRIBE, RACE AND NATIONALITY

Reference to statistics — Instructions to Enumerator — Instructions to Supervisors — Difficulty of tabulation — Caste system not rigid in Province — Musalmans — Hindus and Sikhs — Division by tribes — Caste classified by heriditary occupations — Agricultural castes — Cultivators — Cultivators and cattle rearers — Fishermen, boatmen and Palki-bearers — Barbers — Washermen — Weavers and carders and dyers — Tailors — Carpenters — Potters — Blacksmiths — Gold and silver smiths — Confectioners and grain parchers — Oil-pressers — Butchers — Leather workers — Sweepers — Traders and pedlars — Priests and devotees — Singers and dancers — Others — Distribution of Pathans — Increase in numbers — Awans — Jats — Gujars — Sayads — Aroras — Swathis and Tanaulis — Variations — Caste and tribes confined to particular areas — Reference to ethonographical glossary ... ... 197—204

Subsidiary Tables ... ... 205—206

INTRODUCTION.

This report deals with the statistics of population, both enumerated and estimated, of the North-West Frontier Province, as it was on the 26th February 1931. The Province may roughly be divided into two parts, *viz.*, the regularly administered districts within the borders of British India and the trans-border tribal tract under the political control of the Chief Commissioner* in his capacity of Agent to the Governor General. The trans-border tract is almost exclusively inhabited by various independent Pathan tribes who owe no direct allegiance to any sovereign or settled government. No statistical information regarding its internal condition or its inhabitants is forthcoming, though much literature on the subject is available, and the population data contained in the tables is based on estimates made by the Political Agents and Deputy Commissioners concerned, as distinguished from the regular enumeration conducted in the five settled districts and in the posts and military areas situated in tribal territory. This report may therefore be taken to be to all intents and purposes a discussion of the statistics of the five settled districts. Beyond giving the estimated population of the trans-border area, little attempt has been made to elucidate with regard to it the various subjects that are usually discussed in a Census Report. **The present Census.**

2. This is the third census that the Province has undergone since it was constituted in October 1901, the first having been conducted on the 10th of March 1911 and the second on the 18th March 1921.

Five previous enumerations of the districts now included in the North-West Frontier Province were conducted under the orders of the Punjab Government before the historic province of the Punjab was divided into two administrations, the Punjab and the North-West Frontier Province. The first Census in order of time was taken on the night between the 31st December 1854 and the 1st January 1855, for British Territory only on administrative grounds. It was followed by the enumerations of the 10th January 1868, 17th February 1881, 26th February 1891, 1st March 1901, 10th March 1911 and the 18th March 1921. All but the last two were carried out under the orders of the Punjab Government. In the Census of 1881, the operations were for the first time carried out on a scientific basis with due attention to detail. and a mass of information was collected on various subjects, connected with the growth of population, its intellectual and functional development, and its religious and racial distribution, by the late Sir Denzil Ibbetson whose report has since become a classic in the literature on the subject. Ever since 1881 Census Operations have been undertaken regularly every ten years and they have been conducted with the care and thoroughness which is associated with Indian Censuses. **Previous enumerations.**

3. The only changes which have taken place in the political divisions of the Province during the last decade are that in 1928 the "Malandri tract" (approximately 20 square miles) was transferred from Swat Territory (Malakand Agency) to the Peshawar District, and two transfers of small areas of unpopulated hill land took place in 1922 and 1926 respectively on the tribal border of the Kohat District, involving a nett loss to the district of four square miles. Otherwise the dimensions and boundaries of the Province are as they were in 1921. They comprise the five settled districts of Hazara, Peshawar, Kohat, Bannu and Dera Ismail Khan as well as the Trans-Frontier territories bounded on the north by the Hindu Kush mountains, on the south by Baluchistan, on the east by the borders of British India and on the west by Afghanistan. The figures for area differ with successive surveys. In 1921 the total area of the settled districts was shown as 13,419 square miles, while the tribal tract was estimated to have an area of approximately 25,000 square miles. Figures received in 1931 gave an approximate total of 14,263 square miles for the districts and 22,095 square miles for the tribal areas beyond the administrative border. Amendments subsequently received give nett reductions of five square miles in the districts and 770 square miles in Tribal Territory. **The scope of the present Census as compared with the previous ones.**

4. Captain G. L. Mallam, I. A., was Census Superintendent from the 1st April 1930 to the 8th April 1932, when he was compelled to abandon the work on transfer to Kabul. During his period of office he was deputed, in addition to **Procedure adopted for taking the Census.**

*Since 18th April 1932, the Governor.

his Census duties, as Assistant Commissioner, Charsadda from the 15th May to 6th September 1930; as Special Magistrate, Dera Ismail Khan from the 17th September to 4th November 1931, and as Additional District Magistrate, Peshawar in January 1932. From the 8th April to 27th July 1932 the Deputy Superintendent, K. Sultan Muhammad Khan, was in charge of the operations. On the 28th July 1932 Mr. A. D. F. Dundas, I. C. S, was appointed to complete the writing of the report. The difficulty of the work has thus been considerably increased by lack of continuity.

The procedure adopted for taking the census was practically the same as on previous occasions.

Code and Instructions for enumeration.

5. The Provincial Census Code, based on the Imperial Code of the Census Commissioner, was issued in two parts. Part I, concerned with the procedure for enumeration, was printed and published both in English and in Urdu; Part II, Compilation and Tabulation, was prepared only in English. Part I was issued to Deputy Commissioners and Political Agents, and Part II to Deputy Commissioners only, under whose general supervision the census operations in each area were to be carried out.

Preparation of Village and Town Registers.

6. The first step taken by the local officers was to prepare the General Village and Town registers, showing in rural tracts by Tahsils a complete list of all the villages, the number of houses and the number of workers available for enumeration, and in urban tracts the Administrative Divisions of Towns together with the approximate number of houses in each unit as well as the number of persons qualified to act as Enumerators and Supervisors.

Census Divisions.

7. Sketch maps of villages and towns were then prepared and with their help villages and towns were divided into Blocks, forty to fifty houses or the average going to a Block, and the Blocks grouped into Circles which contained ten to fifteen Blocks a piece; Circles were arranged into larger Administrative Divisions called Charges which comprised about ten Circles each. As a rule existing revenue estates and Kanungo's circles were followed in fixing the charge and circle boundaries. Boundaries were first fixed roughly and then readjusted after the completion of home-numbering. In strictly military areas no house-numbering was done.

Census Agency.

8. The Block was in charge of an Enumerator, the Circle of a Supervisor, and the Charge of a Charge Superintendent, the general supervision of the Census Operations being entrusted to the Tahsildar in the Tahsil and to the Deputy Commissioner in the District. In the trans-border territory, made up of the five agencies and the tribal tracts under the political control of the Deputy Commissioners of the adjoining districts, only the British posts and military areas were enumerated on the General Schedule, the bulk of the population of the trans-border tract being only a rough estimate from the returns maintained by the various Political Agents and Deputy Commissioners of the fighting strength of the tribes under their political control, on the assumption that there are four women and children to each fighting man; the distribution by sex being taken to be the same as for the Muslim population in the adjoining areas of British Territory.

9. Altogether 94 Charge Superintendents, 1,212 Supervisors and 14,580 Enumerators were appointed for an enumerated population of over 2 470,000 persons. In 1921 there were 125 Charge Superintendents, 1,157 Supervisors and 13,332 Enumerators. In both years the bulk of the persons appointed were officials of the revenue staff. In the case of rural areas there was no other staff available for supervision than the revenue staff. In towns and cantonments most of the staff was taken from other departments. Many enumerators both in rural and in urban areas were found from the non-official classes, and in some cases charge supervisors also were appointed from among Municipal Commissioners and leading land-owners.

House numbering.

10. After the preparation of the village and town registers, the division of the districts into Blocks, Circles and Charges, and the appointment of Enumerators, Supervisors and Superintendents, the actual operations began with house numbering and the preparation of house lists. The houses were counted

and numbers were painted in red in some conspicuous place on the door post or house wall and the limits of Blocks, Circles and Charges were finally determined.

Training of Census Staff and preliminary Enumeration.

11. The training of the staff for house numbering and the forming of blocks and circles was completed by the 15th October 1930. Further training of the staff for enumeration was carried out in the first-half of October and throughout December. Detailed instructions for the Census Staff were given in the Provincial Census Code, and those for the Enumerators were also printed on the cover of the enumeration book which was issued to each Enumerator. The District Census Officer explained the instructions for filling up the Schedules to the Charge Superintendents who trained the Supervisors ; the latter in their turn instructed the enumerators as to how the 18 columns of the General Schedule were to be filled up.

12. The enumeration book consisted of a cover, a Block List and a sufficient number of the General Schedules. The cover explained the method in which the schedule was to be filled up, the Block List gave the list of the houses in the Block, while in the General Schedule was to be entered all the information relating to the population living in the Block collected by the Enumerator From the time the Preliminary Enumeration began, up till the night of the 26th February when the final Census was to be taken, the closest supervision was exercised by the Supervisors and Charge Superintendents over the work of the Enumerators under them. The District Census Officers, the Tahsildars, Secretaries of Municipalities and other officials deputed for the pupose checked most of the entries made in the Schedule.

Final Census.

13. Preliminary enumeration in rural areas was made from the 1st to 26th February 1931, and in towns from the 16th to 26th February. The final census was taken on the night of the 26th February 1931. Entries relating to persons who had died or left the place since the preparation of the Preliminary Record, were scored through, while necessary particulars for new births and fresh arrivals were entered so as to make the final record correspond with the facts actually existing on the night of the final Census.

Non-Synchronous tracts.

14. The Census was synchronous throughout the Province except in certain areas, which were considered unsafe at night on account of the disturbed condition of the border, or where snow and long distances involved rendered it impossible for the Enumerators to visit all the houses in their Blocks by night. The preliminary record for these tracts was checked either on the afternoon of the 26th or the morning of the 27th February. The areas so treated included the Kagan Valley in Hazara and certain outlying tracts in Bannu District.

Household Schedules.

15. Special forms called the Household Schedules were distributed to the heads of European and Anglo-Indian families, who were requested to enter the necessary particulars relating to their families in the columns provided for the purpose. Brief instructions for filling up the various columns had been printed on the form and a Specimen Schedule attached thereto. The Schedules were written up on the Census night and collected by the Enumerators concerned on the following morning. The arrangement did not prove satisfactory in practice. Experience of previous years had in fact proved that it was unlikely to do so, but a sufficient number of European enumerators could not be made available. In future enumerations even more careful instructions should be printed on the schedule, asking subjects in particular to refrain from facetious entries which are not understood by those on whom the task of tabulation and compilation fall.

Special arrangements.

16. The same arrangements as in 1921 were made for the enumeration of travellers by rail or road and of persons attending fairs, but fortunately no big gatherings had to be dealt with on the Census night. Of these, railway passengers are obviously the most important. The railway Census was carried out under the direction of the Civil Authorities as a part of the district Census Operations, the local railway officers co operating with the district officers and supplying the necessary staff of Supervisors and Enumerators. All the railway stations in the Province were provided with rubber stamps and pads and the tickets of all travellers who were emumerated were stamped " Censused " to

prevent their double enumeration. This arrangement works much better than the system of enumeration-passes in the case of railway travellers, who are naturally more careful about their tickets than they are likely to be in respect of enumeration passses.

17. The incoming and outgoing passengers were enumerated by the Station Staff specially deputed for the purpose, while a special staff of Enumerators travelled in trains on the Census night and prepared enumeration record in respect of travellers who had not been counted finally before they entrained. At about six o'clock on the morning of the 27th February every train was finally enumerated at whatever station it happened to be, and every passenger whose ticket was not stamped " censused " was brought on the record. In the case of all other travellers enumeration passes were issued, when they were finally enumerated.

Attitude of the public towards Census.

18. With the political situation in the North-West Frontier Province still incompletely restored after the unsettling events of 1930, it might be supposed that the atmosphere would have been inimical to an operation requiring as an essential factor for its success the co-operation of all classes of the population whatever their political convictions. News was indeed received that the All-India Congress Committee had instructed its local bodies to boycott the Census. But no such boycott was for a moment attempted in this Province. On the contrary, all communities (and particularly the minority communities) in this Province were more than usually alive to the political significance of the present Census, and to the necessity for obtaining an accurate record of the strength of their communities.

Provisional totals.

19. On the morning of the 27th February after the Final Census was over, the Enumerators of each Circle collected the Household Schedules, if any, issued to the European and Anglo-Indian residents of their Block, totalled up the entries in their Blocks, noted the population of their Blocks by sexes as well as the total number of occupied houses on the Abstracts provided for the purpose and handed them over to the Supervisor, who, in his turn, prepared his Circle Summary from these Abstracts and sent it on to the Charge Superintendent, who compiled a similar Summary for his charge and submitted it to the headquarters of the District, tribal tract or Agency concerned, and reported direct to Peshawar by wire. Except in the case of the Malakand Agency all required totals were received by the 3rd March. The Malakand totals were delayed by snow on the Lowarai pass, but were received on the 6th March. The Provincial totals for the Province were wired to the Census Commissioner on the same date. A tabular statement showing provisional totals by districts, agencies and tribal areas was at the same time despatched to the Census Commissioner by post.

Tabulation of results, and Slip Copying.

20. The method of extracting and tabulating the information on the Schedules was the same as in previous years, namely slip-copying, sorting and tabulation. Slip-copying for Peshawar District and all trans-frontier posts was done in the central office in Peshawar ; in Dera Ismail Khan it was done at the district headquarters and in the remaining three districts in tahsils. This was the first time that slip-copying had been done elsewhere than at Peshawar. In Dera Ismail Khan the work was carried out under the supervision of the Revenue Extra Assistant Commissioner, and in the tahsils of Hazara, Bannu and Kohat under the respective Tahsildars ; Office Kanungos worked as record-keepers, and field kanungos, and in some places senior Patwaris, as supervisors. The Central Office, Peshawar, was under the superintendence of the Deputy Superintendent of the Census, assisted by two Census Inspectors. The work began in March 1931 and was completed by the 15th April.

21. The entries relating to each person enumerated on the Schedule were transcribed on to a slip measuring 4⅛″ × 2″. The colour of the paper designated the religion, and symbols of varying shapes printed on the slips the sex and civil condition (married, unmarried or widowed), the other entries in the Schedule being copied in columns provided for the purpose. Slip copying was finished by the end of the second week of April and then the next stage of Tabulation work, *viz.* Sorting, was taken in hand.

22. Sorting was carried out in the central office at Peshawar. The staff was the same as that employed on slip-copying, but was strengthened by the drafting in of a sprinkling of persons from Dera Ismail Khan and the tahsils of other districts who could provide additional local knowledge. In the making-up of boxes for sorting, twenty-five to thirty-five thousand slips were put into the two boxes on which each sorter had to work. In 1921 eight to ten thousand slips were put into each box. The slips were arranged in pigeon-holes according to the particular detail sorted for, then taken out of the pigeon hole, counted and tied up in bundles of a hundred each. Each Sorter had to sort the Slips in his boxes for all the tables in turn, a special English knowing Sorter being employed for European Slips and another for Infirmity Slips. As soon as the sorting of slips in one box was completed it was checked by the Supervisor while the sorting of the Slips in the other box was being proceeded with by the Sorter. The result of each sorting was entered in the Sorter's tickets provided for the purpose and these tickets were, after check and scrutiny, made over to the Compilers. **Sorting.**

23. The next stage was the extraction of district and area totals from the sorter's tickets and the preparation of the Tables. This stage of the operations, known as "Compilation" was entrusted to a special staff under the direct supervision of the Deputy Superintendent. The entries in the Sorter's tickets were posted in the compilation registers and two of the most intelligent compilers were told off to tabulate the results into the form of Imperial and Provincial Tables. Sorting was started on the 18th April 1931 and completed on the 31st May. Compilation was completed by the end of August. All the Imperial and Provincial Tables for the Province were submitted to the Census Commissioner for India for approval by the 3rd December 1931. **Compilation.**

24. The final charges for the printing, binding and distribution of the Census Report are not yet available, but the total expenditure in connection with the present Census is not likely to exceed Rs. 90,000. Expenditure in 1930-31 was Rs. 27,170-14-7, and in 1931-32 Rs. 46,105-5-11 ; a little over Rs. 16,700 is expected to cover the printing, distribution and other charges remaining for the current year. The total expenditure on the 1921 Census Report was given in the corresponding paragraphs of the Introduction as Rs. 42,000. This is, however, a misleading comparison, since on the present occasion the pay and census allowance combined of the whole staff has been debited to Census expenditure, while in 1921 the allowance only of the officers and staff deputed was debited to Census, while pay was debited to the departments from which the personnel was borrowed. The expenditure on printing charges has increased from Rs. 13,814 in 1921 to Rs. 18,210 in 1931, an increase of 32 per cent. This is mainly due to the revised rates of pay in the printing establishment since 1921. If the pay of the Superintendent is excluded from the total expenditure, as was done in 1921, the increase in expenditure is from Rs. 49,562 to Rs. 53,410, an increase of about 8 per cent. This increase compares favourably with the general increase of about 25 per cent. which has taken place in the pay of staff since 1921. **Cost of Census.**

25. The Census Superintendent is greatly indebted to M. Sultan Muhammad Khan, Deputy Superintendent of Census Operations. This officer was of the greatest assistance to Captain Mallam in the work of Compilation and Tabulation and held charge of the office of Superintendent from the 8th April to 27th July 1932. When the time came for the actual writing of the report, his experience and painstaking thoroughness were invaluable. The Census Superintendent wishes to thank also all Deputy Commissioners, Sub-Divisional Officers, District Census Officers and their staffs, especially Patwaris and Kanungos for their willing assistance in many arduous and tedious tasks, and in addition all those many private persons who gave ungrudging and honorary assistance. **Acknowledgments.**

PART I

CORRIGENDA TO REPORT

Chapter	Reference	For	Read
Chapter I ...	Para. 11, line 18 ...	*After* size ...	*Insert* (,) comma
	Page 5, Density ...	Para. 3 ...	13
	Page 5, Density of districts ...	Para. 4 ...	14
	Para. 13, line 2 ...	**29** ...	**129**
	Para. 13, Table North-West Frontier Province Districts.	**971** ...	**179**
	Para. 13, Bombay (including Aden).	**371** ...	**173**
	Para. 15, lines 7 and 8 ...	*After* cis and trans	*Insert* (— —) two dashes.
	Para. 17, line 26 ...	Reconsilable ..	Reconcilable.
	Para. 19, table column 4 ...	291513 ...	291523
	Page 14, line 21 ...	Was ...	Were
	Para. 22, line 2 ...	66880 ...	668,880
	Para. 23, line 7 ...	3381 ...	31,381
	Page 18, line 10 ...	*After* recorded ...	*Insert* (.) full stop.
	Para. 26, table (2) all ages ...	10·0 ...	100
	Para. 27, line 10 ...	*After* under ...	*Insert* which
	Para. 27, line 58 ...	*After* favourable...	*Insert* for
	Para. 33, line 2 ...	*After* do not ...	*Insert* (,) comma
	Page 27, line 5 ...	*Between Peshawar and Shabkadar.*	*Insert* (—) dash.
	Para. 37, Marginal heading ...	District ...	Districts.
	Page 29, line 9. ...	Name ...	Same
	Para. 43, line 5 ...	91 ...	1911
	Table 1 A. Column 6, Bannu ...	083 ...	683
Chapter II ...	Page 42 line 21 ...	26 to 19 ...	19 to 26
	Para. 54 heading of table ...	Add ...	Added
	Subsidiary-table 1 column 13, Hazara.	99 ...	199
	1-A last line column 2 ...	**2300** ...	**2830**
	1-A line 7 column 2 ...	**9604** ...	**96048**
	1-B line 8 column 6 ...	**+ 16·81** ..	**+ 1681**
	Para. 70 line 7 ...	**·6** ...	**1·6**

CORRIGENDA TO REPORT

Chapter	Reference	For	Read
Chapter III	Para. 73, line 4 ...	In ...	Of
	Para. 82, line 39 ..	*After* servants ..	*Insert* (,) comma
	Page 60 (foot note) line 2 ..	Instances ...	Instance
Chapter IV...	Para. 85, line 10 ...	VI ...	V A
	Para. 88, line 2 ..	25 ...	125
	Para. 93, table *I* (40-50 .	3 ...	— 3
	Para. 96 table Swathi column 2 ...	303 ..	393
	Para. 98, line 9 ...	1908 ...	1928
	Para. 100, line 11.. ...	23·4 ...	28·2
	Subsidiary table III Khatri column 5	102 ...	162
	V A, line 1 column 26 ...	31 ...	35
Chapter V ...	Para. 106, line 6 ...	105 ...	125
	Para. 107, line 9 ...	Religious ...	Religions.
	Para. 107, line 9 ...	Religious ...	Religions.
	Para. 113, line 1 ...	District ...	Districts.
	Page 81, line 6 ...	*After* fifteen ...	*Insert* (.) full stop.
Chapter VI...	Para. 122, line 2 ...	5 ...	Five.
	Para. 123, line 12 ...	*Before* Hindus ...	*Delete* (a)
	126, line 26 ...	Age groups ...	Age-groups.
	Page 92, line 7 ...	Sikh ...	Sikhs.
	Para. 133, table Heading column 2	29-40 ...	20-40
	Para. 140, table (1921) column 2	1,029,024 ...	1,022,024
	Subsidiary table IV all religions, column 13.	117 ...	1617
	Trans-Indus Departments column 3	68	648

REPORT ON THE CENSUS

OF THE

NORTH-WEST FRONTIER PROVINCE, 1931

CHAPTER I

DISTRIBUTION AND MOVEMENT OF THE POPULATION.

SECTION I—GENERAL.

Descriptive.

1. In the Census Reports of 1911 and 1921, and in the *Imperial and District Gazetteers* very full accounts are given of the physical and geographical features of the North-West Frontier Province, and it is therefore not considered necessary to repeat any such description here.

The area dealt with.

2. The area and external boundaries of the North-West Frontier Province have not altered since the Census of 1921. The greatest length of the Province is 408 miles; and its greatest breadth 279 miles. The Survey of India recently recorded the total area as approximately 36,356 square miles, a figure which must be assumed to be more accurate than those given at previous censuses, when survey figures were not available.

Political and administrative divisions.

3. The scheme of political and administrative divisions remains the same as in 1921. There are two main political divisions :—

(1) the Trans-Frontier area, (containing the five political agencies known severally as the Malakand, Khyber, Kurram, North Waziristan and South Waziristan Agencies and the district " Tribal Areas "), the inhabitants of which are subject only to the political control of the Chief Commissioner in his capacity as Agent to the Governor-General, and

(2) the five regularly administered districts of Hazara, Peshawar, Kohat, Bannu and Dera Ismail Khan.

The present Census is concerned with the five administered districts only, nothing more than a rough estimate of the population of the trans-frontier area (outside British posts) having been attempted.

Changes of area.

4. A few minor territorial changes have occurred since the last Census, affecting the Peshawar and Kohat Districts only. In 1928 the " Malandri tract " (approximately 20 square miles) was transferred from Swat territory (Malakand Agency) to the Peshawar District, and two transfers of small areas of unpopulated hill land took place in 1922 and 1926 respectively on the tribal border of the Kohat District, involving a net loss to the district of 4 square miles. Apart from the above, district boundaries remain the same as they were in 1921.

Natural divisions.

5. For various statistical purposes, India is divided into " natural " as well as administrative divisions. These natural divisions are distinguished mainly by their physical features, climate and rainfall. The North-West Frontier Province forms part of the main natural division, known as the " North-West Dry Area ",

which extends southwards beyond the boundary of the Province through the Punjab Districts of Mianwali, Muzaffargarh and Dera Ghazi Khan, and covers a large portion of the Western Punjab. Without disturbing the general scheme of natural divisions as applied to India as a whole, it is convenient also to sub-divide the North-West Frontier Province itself into local natural divisions, and to group the Provincial statistics accordingly. In doing so, we have made use of the same natural features as were employed in the scheme adopted at the last Census. These natural features mark the boundaries of administrative divisions, and are described as follows :—

(1) the cis-Indus district of Hazara,
(2) the narrow strip between the Indus and the hills, containing the districts of Peshawar, Kohat, Bannu and Dera Ismail Khan, and
(3) the mountainous tract between these districts and the border of Afghanistan, containing the agencies and tribal areas, which are outside the scope of the Census.

The meaning of the term Population.

6. Before proceeding to a discussion of the statistics which form the basis of this report, it is necessary to explain what is meant by the Census term "population". The criterion is the same as in previous censuses. All persons, who were enumerated as alive and present within the five administered districts and in the trans-frontier posts between 7 p. m., and midnight on the 26th February 1931, come within the definition. The population enumerated includes visitors as well as residents, civilians and non-civilians, and persons of alien as well as of British and British Indian nationality. In short, the Census population is once again the *de-facto* population.

Non-synchronous areas.

7. The Census in the North-West Frontier Province was synchronised with that of the rest of India, except in a few areas, which owing to their remoteness or inaccessibility were non-synchronously dealt with. In the Kaghan Valley in the Hazara District, the final enumeration was dispensed with altogether owing to the mountainous nature of the country, deep snow and the difficulties of travel. Again, in a few border villages in the Bannu District, where the enumerators could not move about at night with safety, the final Census was taken on the afternoon preceding the Census night. But the Census of these areas, though theoretically "non-synchronous", was actually so nearly synchronous as to be unworthy of any special consideration apart from other areas. The population returned therefore may be considered in their case also as the *de-facto* population.

The actual resident, normal and natural population.

8. The classification of the population on a *de-facto* basis is, theoretically, an accidental one and less suited to administrative requirements than a *de-jure* basis of classification by place of normal residence. In practice, however, a judicious selection of the Census night so as to avoid large scale movements of population probably secures a distribution substantially equivalent to a *de-jure* classification. Moreover a *de-facto* classification by *actual* residence has the advantage of simplicity, while a strict *de-jure* classification by *normal* residence presents innumerable complications. Normal residence, for instance, is inevitably limited, in India at any rate, to a given point of time. In the North-West Frontier Province, which is subject to extremes of climate, the normal population is affected to a large extent by seasonal migrations. The broad grazing grounds in the plain between the Indus and the hills are occupied in winter by Powindah tribes, who return to their mountain homes across the border for the summer. There are also considerable (and ever-increasing) movements of the regular population of the Province between the plains and the hills at the beginning and end of the hot weather. Considering therefore the difficulty of defining "normal residence", when it is subject to variation at different seasons of the year, it seems doubtful if even a strict *de-jure* classification would achieve much more than is actually achieved by a *de-facto* classification based on a judiciously timed Census, — namely a distribution which is normal for the Census night only. At the same time, on the basis of the information obtained from each person enumerated, various adjustments from the *de-facto* classification are possible, in order to distinguish between those details in the picture which are variable and those which are comparatively constant. Statistics of birth-place (Imperial Table VI) enable the number of immigrants, or persons born outside the area dealt with, to be deducted from the *de-facto* or actual population leaving approximately the resident population, who have not emigrated. Again, after the number of emigrants from the area dealt with has been ascertained by obtaining figures of

those persons, born in the area in question, but enumerated elsewhere at the time of the Census, then if the actual population is diminished by the number of immigrants, and increased by the number of emigrants, the result is approximately the "natural" population, that is, the population which would exist, if there had been no migration at all.

It must be remembered that these adjustments from a *de-facto* basis are only approximations, and that they give no exact indication as to how far the "actual" population represents the "normal" population which must largely depend on conditions prevailing at the time when the Census was taken. So far as the present Census is concerned, it may be said that conditions in the North-West Frontier Province, on the 26th February 1931 were normal, except in a few areas, to be noticed later on, where the figures for population were influenced to a small extent by the political situation.

The accuracy of the enumeration.

9. It is natural to claim for each enumeration a degree of accuracy no less than that attained at previous censuses. Growing experience in the organization of a Census, and the spread of education among the public should lead to increasingly accurate results. Much however depends upon the thoroughness with which the preliminary arrangements for the enumeration are made, and the degree of reliance which can be placed on the enumerators and supervising staff. While expressing my fullest confidence in the work of the staff engaged in the present Census, I will endeavour to suggest some means by which the accuracy of their work may be objectively tested. It will be remembered that the word "enumeration" covers a wide field when applied to an Indian Census — a field as wide as the 18 columns of the General Schedule, which demand a variety of personal information regarding the status, extraction and occupation of every human being. It is obvious therefore that the accuracy of the different kinds of information collected will vary with the knowledge of the persons enumerated on the subject matter of the enquiry, and with the ability of the census staff to check the answers given. For this reason it is convenient to leave remarks on the accuracy of special classes of statistics to those paragraphs in this report in which these statistics are discussed, and to deal here with the accuracy of the general figures for population only. It would be some test of the accuracy of these figures to consider in what proportion they stand to those returned at previous censuses. As will be seen later, the percentage increase in population during the decade 1921—1931, when conditions were normal, is almost identical with the percentage increase from 1901—1911, an equally normal decade. The intervening decade 1911—1921 is unsuited for the purpose of comparison, as it contains two strikingly abnormal features in the Great War and the influenza epidemic, which were directly responsible for a low percentage increase. In a Province in which there has been practically no industrial development, a comparison between the two decades 1901—1911 and 1921—1931 is not altogether unjustified and the result when considered in relation to the growth of population during the last 50 years, indicates that, taken as a whole, the figures for 1931 may be considered as reliable. While it would be idle to claim absolute accuracy for Census statistics, when this is seldom claimed for other kinds of statistical data collected in India from similar sources, yet it is impossible to do more than guess at the amount of error. In the course of a lengthy discussion on this subject in the Punjab Census Report for 1921, Mr. S. M. Jacob, I. C. S., remarks :—"As a working hypothesis, therefore, I have assumed that the mean error for the totals by religions and sexes by each territorial division is 1 per cent." The question of the accuracy of the returns for 1931 will be further discussed in the chapters on religion and sex, but in the meanwhile we consider Mr. Jacob's conclusion worthy of mention, as it is based on 17 years' intimate experience of Punjab statistics. If for the North-West Frontier Province statistics in 1931 we can claim no greater accuracy, we need admit no less.

SECTION II—AREA, POPULATION AND DENSITY.

Reference to statistics.

10. In Imperial Table I in Part II of this volume statistics are given relating to the area and the population of the North-West Frontier Province, and of its natural divisions and districts. In Provincial Table I at the end of the volume similar statistics are given for tahsils. Subsidiary Tables I and II at the end of this chapter exhibit the mean density per square mile, and classify the population according to density, while Subsidiary Table III shows variations in relation to density since 1881.

Area.

11. In area, the North-West Frontier Province is almost the smallest Province in India, only Ajmer-Merwara, the Andamans and Nicobars, Delhi, and Coorg being smaller. With a total area of 36,356 square miles, it is a little more than half the size of the Bombay Presidency (excluding Sind and Aden), about three-fifths of the size of England and Wales, one and a half times the size of the Irish Free State and about one-third of the size of New Zealand. From the statement in the margin it will be observed that the three natural divisions form 8·3, 28·9 and 62·8 per cent. respectively of the total area of the Province. The areas of districts are given in the next statement, which shows the five districts arranged according to size. Dera Ismail Khan, the largest, being just twice the size of Bannu, the smallest. The areas are those communicated by the Survey of India.

Natural division	Area in square miles
Hazara	3,009
Trans-Indus districts ...	10,509
Agencies and tribal areas ...	22,838

District	Area in square miles
Dera Ismail Khan ...	3,471
Hazara	3,009
Kohat	2,703
Peshawar	2,637
Bannu	1,698

Population.

12. The total population enumerated in the North-West Frontier Province on the night of the 26th February 1931 (including non-synchronous areas) numbered 2,471,527 persons, of whom 1,360,453 were males and 1,111,074 females. The enumerated population was the *de-facto* population in the five administered districts and in trans-frontier posts only. The general population of the trans-frontier area which was not enumerated has been estimated at 2,212,837 persons. This figure divided arbitrarily between the sexes in the same proportion as in 1921 resolves into 1,167,712 males and 1,045,125 females. Combining the estimated with the enumerated population, the total population shown for the North-West Frontier Province amounts to 4,684,364 persons, of whom 2,528,165 are males and 2,156,199 females. This total population is only slightly less than that of Scotland in 1921, while the enumerated population above is almost as much as that of Wales in the same year. When compared with other provinces in India, the total population of the North-West Frontier Province (both estimated and enumerated) stands tenth on the list out of a total of fifteen provinces as shown in the margin. Though smaller in area than her next door neighbour Baluchistan, the North-West Frontier Province has a considerably larger population.

Province	British territory	States	Total
Madras ...	46,748,644	6,754,399	53,503,043
Bengal ...	50,122,550	973,316	51,095,866
United Provinces ...	48,408,763	1,206,070	49,614,833
Bihar and Orissa ..	37,590,356	4,643,456	42,233,812
Punjab ...	23,580,851	4,910,005	28,490,856
Bombay ...	22,259,977	4,469,081	26,729,058
Central Provinces and Berar...	15,472,628	2,478,519	17,951,147
Burma ...	14,665,618	...	14,665,618
Assam ...	8,622,251	625,605	9,247,857
North-West Frontier Province	2,425,076	2,259,288	4,684,364
Baluchistan ...	463,508	405,109	868,617
Delhi ...	636,246	...	636,246
Ajmer-Merwara ...	560,292	...	560,292
Coorg ...	163,089	...	163,089
Andamans and Nicobars ...	29,463	...	29,463

The population of the three natural divisions is given in the margin. These contribute 14·3, 37·5 and 48·2 per cent. respectively to the total population of the North-West Frontier Province.

Natural division	Population
Hazara ...	670,117
Trans-Indus districts ...	1,754,959
Agencies and tribal areas ...	2,259,288 (mainly estimated)

The manner in which the enumerated population is distributed over the various administrative divisions is indicated in the margin. "Trans-frontier posts" comprise the population of all British posts (excluding "khassadar" posts) and of the bazaars immediately dependent on them, situated in agencies and tribal areas across the administrative border. In view of the imminent elevation of the five settled districts to full Provincial Status as a separate Province, care has been taken to provide separate statistics for the new Province in all Census tables under the heading "North-West Frontier Province Disrtricts". Where the total enumerated population is referred to, the heading "North-West Frontier Province Districts and Trans-frontier posts" is given, and for the total estimated and enumerated population the heading is simply "North West Frontier Province".

Administrative divisions	Papulation
N.-W. F. P. Districts and Trans-frontier posts ...	2,471,527
Districts ...	2,425,076
Hazara ...	670,117
Peshawar ...	974,321
Kohat ...	236,273
Bannu ...	270,301
Dera Ismail Khan ...	274,064
Trans-frontier posts ...	46,451

ensity.

Corrigenda to para. 13.

Page 5 *for* para "3" *read* para. "13".
In line 2 *for* "29" *read* "129".
In the table North-West Frontier Province districts *for* "971" *read* "179".
Bombay including Aden *for* "371" *read* "173".

Belgium ...	654	Bengal ...	616
England and Wales ...	649	United Provinces ...	442
The Netherlands ...	544	Madras ...	328
Germany ...	332	Punjab (British territo y) ...	244
Japan ...	2·5	N.-W. F. P. Districts ...	971
Austria ...	199	Bombay (including Aden) ...	371
France ...	184	Rajputana ...	88
Spain ...	107	Kashmir State ...	43
United States ...	32	Baluchistan (district and administered territory).	9
New Zealand ...	1 18		

Density or districts.

Corrigendum to para. 14.

Page 5 *for* para. "4" *read* para. "14".

Trans-Indus districts ...	167
Peshawar ...	369
Kohat ...	88
Bannu ...	159
Dera Ismail Khan ...	79

discussion to a brief analysis of the economic causes leading to the variations in density between different administrative divisions. In an agricultural Province, these causes must be mainly agricultural.

*Note.—As the general population of the trans-frontier area is outside the scope of the Census altogether, it will receive no further attention in this report.

No.1.

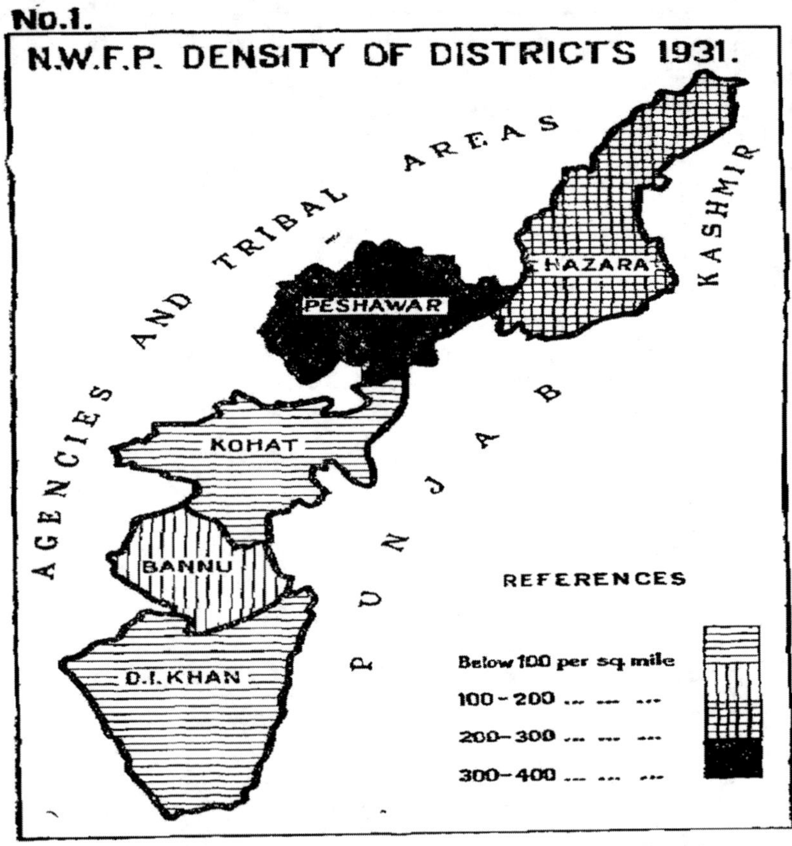

Districts		Percentage of total area cultivated	Density
Peshawar	...	51	369
Bannu ...	...	50	159
Dera Ismail Khan	...	30	79
Hazara ...	...	27	223
Kohat ...	...	19	88

To quote from paragraph 20 of the Census Report of 1921, " The climate, the customs of the people, the trading centres, the location of military stations, the establishment of industries, the means of communication, and the existence of forest reserves, all affect the growth of population, but no one of them is half so important as the nature and *extent of agriculture, which* is dependent, in its turn on the fertility and configuration of the soil, cultivable and cultivated areas, rainfall and irrigation ". In the following analysis of the agricultural factors influencing the density of the population, we would draw a distinction between (*a*) the extent of cultivation and (*b*) the intensity of cultivation in relation to density. In the marginal table the five districts are arranged according to the extent of cultivation, *i.e.* according to their respective proportion of cultivated area. The same statement contains figures for population density. It will be seen at once that, except *in the case of Peshawar, there* is no obvious connection between these two sets of figures. In Dera Ismail Khan, for instance, the percentage of the total area cultivated is higher than that of Hazara and Kohat, although the Dera Ismail Khan District supports the lowest density of population in the whole Province. But the reasons for variations in density from one district to another will be obvious as soon as figures for rainfall and irrigation are taken into consideration. We know, for instance, that in the Dera Ismail Khan District there are wide tracts of cultivable land entirely dependent for cultivation on an uncertain rainfall, while in Hazara, if the proportion of cultivated area is less than that in Dera Ismail Khan, cultivation is comparatively assured by a high and constant rainfall. Similarly, in the Peshawar and Bannu Districts, the cultivation of large areas of land is assured by an effective system of canal irrigation. It is obvious that a small area with an assured cultivation can support a higher density of population than a much larger area in which the cultivation is uncertain. We should be able therefore to establish a relationship between density on the one hand and irrigation and rainfall on the other, and this relationship should be a much clearer one than that between density and the mere extent of cultivation. Limiting our discussion first to the density of each district per square mile of *cultivated* area, figures for which are shown in the marginal statement for the last three censuses, we find that the districts fall into a geographical order from north to south. If the urban population is next eliminated, the districts, when arranged according to the density of the *rural* population per square mile of cultivated area fall into the same order. This is illustrated in the next table which also includes

District		Density per square mile of cultivated area		
		1931	1921	1911
Hazara	...	910	806	856
Peshawar	...	739	641	607
Kohat	...	463	441	498
Bannu	...	323	326	305
Dera Ismail Khan	...	267	277	302

Districts		Rural population per square mile of cultivated area	Average rainfall	Percentage of total area irrigated
Hazara	...	504	43·8	9
Peshawar	...	575	12·2	29
Kohat	...	396	16·2	2
Bannu	...	277	10·8	11
Dera Ismail Khan	...	212	9·8	4

figures for the average rainfall, and for the proportion per cent. of the total area in each district which is irrigated. We can now see distinct relationship between these two sets of figures. The Hazara District which enjoys the highest average rainfall, supports the highest density of rural population. Next in order of density of the rural population comes Peshawar District, with the highest proportion of irrigated land, but with a very much smaller rainfall than that of Hazara. Kohat District has a higher average rainfall than Peshawar, but a very much smaller area available for irrigation. Bannu and Dera Ismail Khan Districts fall naturally into order according to their average rainfall, and the proportionate area of each available for irrigation. We conclude from this that irrigation and rainfall are the most important agricultural factors influencing the density of the rural population in the North-West Frontier Province. These factors operate to afford an assured cultivation to limited areas of land, but they also promote the development of agriculture in these areas by means of intensive cultivation. There is thus a clear distinction between the *intensity* of cultivation and the *extent* of cultivation in relation to density.

Density of tahsils.

15 We will now carry our enquiry beyond the district to the next smaller administrative unit, the Tahsil. The density of the population in each tahsil is shown in diagrams Nos. 2 and 3 separately for each natural division, cis and trans Indus In the marginal table, the tahsils have been arranged, as in the case of districts in the previous paragraph, according to the density of the rural population per square mile of cultivated area. In the same table figures are shown for the average rainfall, proportionate area under irrigation and the proportionate area cultivated. It will be observed that, as in the case of districts, the tahsils group themselves in a general, though not an exact, order from north to south, and that there is a noticeable relation again between the figures for density on the one hand and those for rainfall and irrigation on the other. There is no apparent relation, however, between density and the proportion of cultivated area or the extent of cultivation. In dealing with tahsils, it will be of interest to enquire what other economic causes, besides agriculture, have a bearing on density. To facilitate discussion, we have divided the tahsils in the above table into three groups which may be distinguished by the following characteristics of economic importance:—

Tahsil		Rural population per square mile of cultivated area	Average rainfall	Percentage of total area: Irrigated	Percentage of total area: Cultivated	
Abbottabad	...	1,171	43·81	2	33	Group I
Hangu	...	1,045	24·63	3	10	
Peshawar	...	744	12·25	33	47	
Mansehra	...	730	35·61	2	20	
Haripur	...	702	27·21	5	38	
Nowshera	...	682	16·60	8	26	
Swabi	...	560	27·59	19	60	Group II
Charsadda	...	558	13·40	56	69	
Bannu	...	554	10·80	26	51	
Mardan	...	453	21·55	39	63	
Kohat	...	412	16·27	5	17	Group III
Teri	...	307	19·09	...	22	
Tank	...	237	12·51	12	30	
Dera Ismail Khan	...	220	9·80	2	34	
Kulachi	...	176	8·68	2	23	
Marwat	...	168	11·18	6	50	

No. 2.

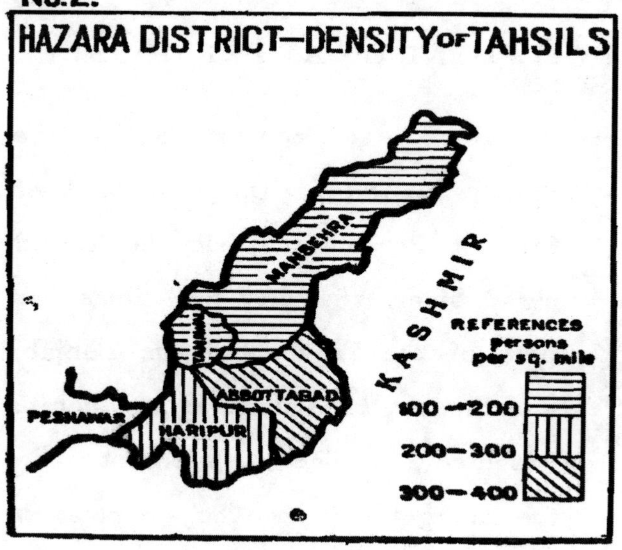

HAZARA DISTRICT—DENSITY OF TAHSILS

No. 3.

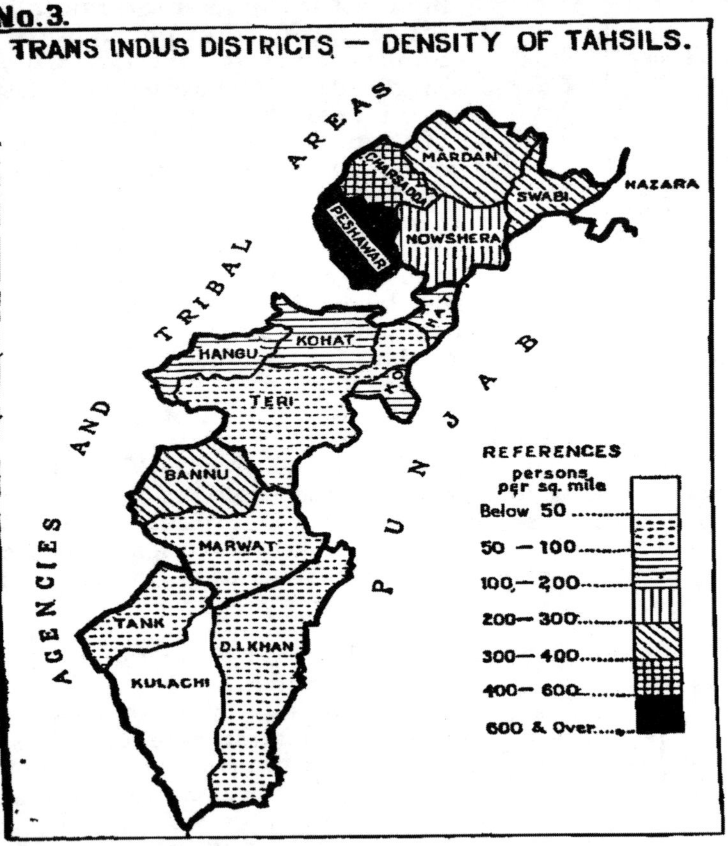

TRANS INDUS DISTRICTS — DENSITY OF TAHSILS.

(1) A marked tendency on the part of the rural population to combine other occupations with agriculture,

(2) the rural population exclusively agricultural, and

(3) the lack of economic resources either for whole-time agricultural occupation or for the combination of other occupations with agriculture.

The first group contains the whole of the rural population of the Hazara District which is known to engage extensively in domestic service and to follow a variety of other occupations in addition to agriculture. It includes also the rural population of the Peshawar and the Nowshera Tahsils where the proximity of large towns and cantonments encourages the emergence of occupations supplementary to agriculture. The Tahsils in the second group, on the other hand, possess such obvious facilities for intensive cultivation of the land, and are comparatively so far removed from the main centres of urban and commercial life, that the rural population find no inducement to engage in any other occupation but agriculture. The Tahsils in the third group, however, lack not only facilities for intensive cultivation, but also the requisite conditions for the encouragement of other than agricultural occupations. We are left therefore with the conclusion that the distribution of the population among the various administrative divisions is very largely affected by economic causes, among which the most important are those which contribute to intensive cultivation of the land. But we have noticed at the same time the existence of another factor of economic importance, which is likely in future to have an increasing influence on the density of the population in the North-West Frontier Province, and that is a tendency on the part of the rural population to combine other occupations with agriculture.

SECTION III—VARIATIONS IN POPULATION AT PREVIOUS CENSUSES.

Variations in population at previous censuses.

Year	Population (districts)	Increase per cent.	Intercensal period.
1855 ...	1,144,047	...	...
1868 ...	1,339,566	17	1855—1868
1881 ...	1,575,943	17	1868—1881
1891 ...	1,857,519	17·9	1881—1891
1901 ...	2,041,534	9·9	1891—1901
1911 ...	2,196,933	7·6	1901—1911
1921 ...	2,251,340	2·5	1911—1921
1931 ...	2,425,076	7·7	1921—1931
...	...	112	1855—1931

16. Since annexation by the British in 1849, the North-West Frontier Province has been censused eight times, the first five times as part of the Province of the Punjab, and the last three times as a separate Province. The statement in the margin shows the population

No. 4

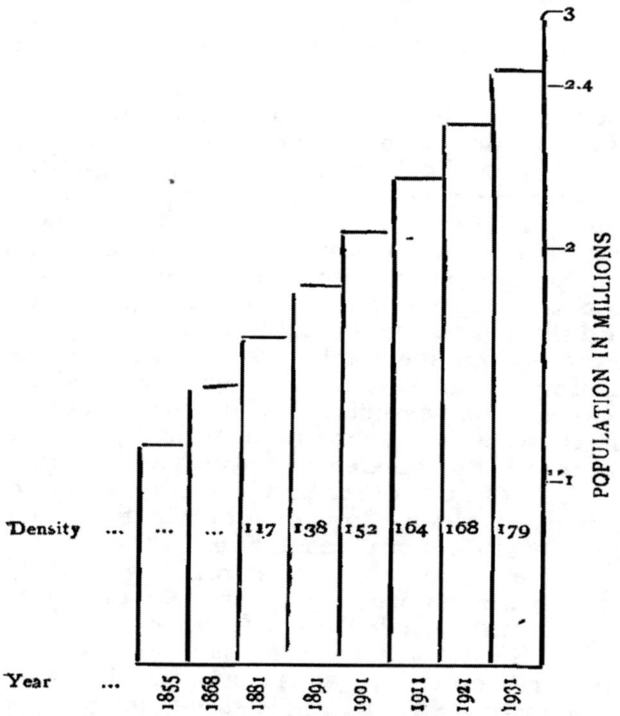

returned at each Census, and the intercensal variations. While the figures in this statement have been adjusted to allow for the main differences in the area covered by each Census, no adjustment has been made for the progressive increase in the accuracy of the enumeration at each successive Census. Such an adjustment would have to be based largely on conjecture, but it is important to analyse in some detail the evidence available regarding the accuracy of previous enumerations.

The accuracy of the earlier censuses.

17. A noticeable feature of the statement given above is the large difference between the percentage increases in population up to the Census of 1891, and the percentage increases after that Census. As recent enumerations must be deemed to be generally more accurate than earlier ones, we would be justified in regarding all enumerations prior to 1891 with considerable suspicion. The first two censuses of 1855 and 1868 are known to have been conducted with much less thoroughness and attention to detail than are required by a modern Indian Census. The third Census of 1881, though the first to be conducted on modern scientific lines has been regarded by succeeding Superintendents of Census Operations in the Punjab as less accurate than the Census of 1891. In the Punjab Census Report of 1891, a portion at least of the exceptionally large increase in the Hazara District is definitely attributed to better enumeration. With these considerations in view, we may now turn to a brief survey of the broad facts of history in their relation to the probable progress of the North-West Frontier Province during the last eighty years.

In the year 1849, when the North-West Frontier Province, then part of the Punjab, was annexed by the British, the anarchy and confusion of Sikh Rule were followed by the establishment of peace and order under a strong government, and it is natural to assume that the population at first responded to the changed conditions with an abnormally high rate of increase. The figures given above for the North-West Frontier Province, lead us to believe that this period of abnormally rapid growth lasted as long as 40 years, *i. e.* from 1849 to 1891, and that the decennial rate of increase rose from 13 per cent. in the intercensal periods 1855—1868 and 1868—1881 (13 years each) to 17·9 per cent. in the intercensal period 1881—1891 (ten years). Are these rates of increase in population reconsilable both with our knowledge of political and economic conditions in the North-West Frontier Province during the 40 years prior to the Census of 1891, and with the rates of increase recorded after that Census ?

Punjab (British Territory excluding the North-West Frontier Province)

Intercensal period		Percentage increase
1855—1868 (13 years)	...	14·1
1868—1881 (13 years)	...	7·0
1881—1891 (10 years)	...	10·0
1891—1901 (10 years)	...	7·4

A glance at the figures in the margin will show that the decennial rates of increase in the Punjab (excluding the North-West Frontier Province) up to the year 1901 never exceeded 11 per cent. and that the immediate impetus given to the growth of population by the establishment of British Rule ended in 1868, or 20 years after the date of annexation. There is little reason to believe that the progress of the population in what is now the North West Frontier Province between 1855 and 1868 differed materially from that of the rest of the Punjab, as no permanent tribal immigrations of any magnitude occurred from across the border during this period.

The history of the five districts of the North-West Frontier Province after 1868, apart from measures necessary for the protection of the frontier, may be summarised in the gradual elaboration of the public services under an organised Government, and particularly in the development of agriculture by means of canal irrigation. Nature having provided facilities for irrigation within the reach of the majority of the inhabitants, and a fairly constant rainfall, famine was almost unknown; but with a population predominantly agricultural and strongly influenced by conservative tribal customs, with very few economic resources capable of rapid development, and with the peace periodically disturbed by the depredations of transborder tribes, progress was inevitably slow. After 1868, therefore, we would expect the population to increase at a slowly diminishing rate, as peace and security gradually came to be associated with normal conditions of life. It is all the more difficult therefore to account historically for the continued rise in the rate of increase recorded by the Census from 1868—1891, and for the drop of 50 per cent. in 1901. On the other hand, our doubts as to the accuracy of the enumeratoins prior to 1891 receive further confirmation from the following facts showing conclusively that agricultural conditions in the North-West Frontier Province were actually more favourable to a rapid growth of population after the year 1891 than they were before that year. Of the three main canals under Government control in the North-West Frontier Province (all in the Peshawar District), the Lower Swat Canal was opened in 1887, but it was not until 1903 that the largest area on record (176,346) acres was irrigated by this canal. The Kabul River Canal, constructed in 1903, did not irrigate its largest area on record (51,328 acres) in 1921. Finally, the Upper Swat Canal, opened in 1914, irrigated its largest area in record (209,009 acres) in 1929. It is clear from the above that the history of canal irrigation in the North-West Frontier Province had hardly commenced by the year 1891, and that the full effect on the growth of population could only have been realised some years later.

The uneven rate of increase followed by the population of the Punjab and the North-West Frontier Province up to the Census of 1891 has been the subject of much speculation in past Census Reports, which makes interesting and informative reading We are of opinion, however, that as each new Census throws the past progress of the population into clearer perspective, the variations at the earlier Censuses, which seem to defy any historical explanation, will be increasingly attributed to the inaccuracy of the enumerations prior to 1891.

Having thus cleared the ground, we may venture the opinion that in the course of the last 80 years the decennial rate of increase of population in the North-West Frontier Province has never far exceeded 10 per cent., the maximum figure during the same period in the Punjab. If the population increased at its maximum rate between 1849 and 1868, the rates of increase between 1868 and 1891 would have to be adjusted in proper perspective with the rates recorded after the Census of 1891, which was, in fact, the first really accurate Census. We are now in a position to judge the present trend of population with particular reference to the last two decades 1911—1921 and 1921—1931, which need to be examined in more detail.

SECTION IV—CONDITIONS OF THE DECADE 1911—1921.

General.

18. The two halves of the decade 1911—1921 present a striking contrast. The first five years formed a period of general advancing prosperity under conditions favourable both to the public health and to agriculture. The Frontier, long accustomed to disturbance, remained surprisingly tranquil. Even the Great War and the outbreak of hostilities with Turkey, which created an anxious situation in 1915, left the peace, outwardly at any rate, still unimpaired. But the material advancement of the Province received a rude setback during the last half of the decade which was crowded with events among the most remarkable in the history of British Frontier Administration. As a prelude to the coming storm, the years 1916 and 1917 brought a marked decline in the public health, due to the exceptional virulence of malaria, and a succession of poor harvests, which combined with the gathering influence of the war on economic conditions,

generally, caused prices to soar. In 1918 the deadly influenza epidemic wrought sudden havoc among the population whose vitality was already weakened by ill-health in the two previous years. Accompanying this scourge came two bad harvests, and 1919 saw the resources of the agriculturist severely strained. In the same year the 3rd Afghan War broke in upon the peace of the Frontier, which had been so successfully maintained during the four trying years of the Great War. Though hostilities with Afghanistan lasted only a few weeks, they set in motion a wave of disturbance and lawlessness, which swept the full length of the Frontier and left the settled districts in a state of unprecedented insecurity and alarm. In 1920, the military operations against the Mahsuds and Wazirs in Waziristan were marked by the severest fighting in the annals of Frontier warfare. By the end of the decade the situation in this area was still uncertain, and efforts to restore equilibrium elsewhere on the border had not met with complete success. In the meanwhile the peace of the Province was being threatened from another quarter. The agitation set on foot in India in connection with the Rowlatt Bill awakened in the Pathan of the settled districts a new political consciousness, which found early expression in disloyal intrigues with hostile Afghan agents in Peshawar City; and in the creation of a general atmosphere of antagonism to Government throughout the Province. A wild and unscrupulous agitation culminated during the hot weather of 1920 in what is known as the "Hijrat" movement. Several thousands of the inhabitants of the Peshawar District, and a lesser number from the other districts, of the Province migrated *en masse* into Afghanistan, only to return a few months later after untold hardships in a state of utter destitution. This strange exodus and its tragic sequel are described in the following extract from the Provincial "Season and Crops" Report for the year 1920-21 :—

> "Owing to the mischievous agitation of certain politicians, a large "number of agriculturists left their homes for Afghanistan during the hot "weather of 1920 leaving their crops to wither for want of irrigation. These "people took considerable supplies of food-grains with them and sold the rest "at cheap rates to dealers. A few months later most of them returned penniless. "In many cases dealers were induced to return some of the grain to these "misguided people, but many more had to buy grain to live on and speculators "have been able to force up prices in consequence. The result of all this has "been that there are practically no stocks of grain in the Province either for food "or seed and the population is dependent on imports from other parts of India."

Immediately on the return of the disillusioned emigrants arrangements were undertaken by Government to resettle them in their homes and to give them a fresh start.

The events just described coincided with a severe drought, which lasted throughout the agricultural year 1920-21. In this year, the total sown area was 24 per cent. below normal, and as much as 42 per cent. failed to ripen owing to lack of rain; the total failed area was actually 44 per cent. above the normal failed area. To quote once more the "Season and Crops" Report for this year :—

> "The high prices of food-grains prevailing throughout India owing to the "failure of the rains have been accentuated by local causes. The produce of the "staple food-grains of the Province was less than half the normal. In the "tribal areas adjoining the Province the crops failed entirely with the result that "some tribes migrated almost bodily into the settled districts and the others took "all their food supplies from there, as the export of grain from Afghanistan was "restricted, if not entirely prohibited. The quantity of cereal exported to South "Waziristan alone was 1,336,532 maunds, principally wheat, while the entire "wheat crop of the Dera Ismail Khan District, whence these supplies were drawn, "amounted only to 501,297 maunds. Cotton alone has fallen in price, partly owing "to imports from Afghanistan and partly because, owing to the shortness of the "crop, the local ginning factories did not find it worth their while to start work"

Such then were the conditions under which the Census of 1921 was taken.

Growth of population during the decade 1911—1921.

19. The passage of events so deeply affecting the domestic and economic life of the Province was bound to leave its mark on the statistics of population. The rate of increase dropped from 7·6 per cent. during the decade 1901—1911 to 2·5 per cent. during 1911—1921. The vital statistics of the decade show that, although in every year, except 1918, the number of births registered exceeded the number of deaths, the net result as reproduced in the margin—was

1911—1920	Persons	Males	Females
Births ...	668,880	370,516	298,364
Deaths ...	618,451	326,928	291,513
Difference ...	50,429	43,588	6,841

an excess of only 50,429 births over deaths. The Census of 1921 recorded an increase of only 54,407 persons (47,214 males and 7,193 females) in the actual population enumerated. This comparatively small progress was due to a combination of the events described in the last paragraph but of these events, the one which far outstriped all others in the powerfull influence it exercised on the growth of population both directly at the time and indirectly on the birth-rate for many years afterwards was the influenza epidemic of 1918. The importance of this epidemic makes it desirable to give here a few essential details in regard to its effect on the five settled districts of the North-West Frontier Province.

The influenza epidemic of 1918.

20. The two statements in the margin illustrate the devastating effect of this scourge, when compared firstly with the three most unhealthy years since 1901, and secondly with each year of the decade 1911—1920. The second statement illustrates also the terrible prevalence of disease generally, and the large place which it occupies among the causes contributing to the destruction of life. But the influenza epidemic is distinguished from the general run of diseases in India by the fact that it was especially fatal to young adults, to women of child-bearing age and to women in preganancy. The marginal figures (compiled by deducting the normal figures of deaths from "fevers" from the total recorded during the epidemic) show some of the main features of the epidemic noticeable in the North-West Frontier Province. In infancy, males were more subject to attack than females, but in the higher ages there was considerably more mortality among females than among males. From the age of 15 upwards there was an almost continuously progressive increase in the death-rate, each succeeding age group (with the exception of the age-group 20—30) showing a higher rate than the one below it. 93,831 persons in all were carried away by the epidemic · but indirectly the effect on the birth rate through the loss of potential parents, was even more devastating. In the second statement illustrating this paragraph it will be seen that there was a marked drop in the birth-rate in the year 1918 and subsequent years of the decade 1911—1920, and in a later paragraph it will be noticed that this decline in the birth-rate, continued far into the following decade 1911—1930. A bird's eye view of destruction both in actual and potential life caused by the influenza epidemic can be obtained from the birth and death rate figures for the last

Year	Death-rate.	Birth-rate.	Loss per *mille*	Chief cause.
1907	33	30	3	Plague.
1918	65	28	37	Influenza.
1921	31	27	4	Cholera and fever
1924	30	27	3	Plague and fever.

Annual death-rate with main causes of death compared with birth-rate (decade 1911—1920)

Year	Death-rate from					Birth-rate
	All causes	Fever	Influenza	Cholera	Plauge	
1911	22	16·3	...	·01	1	33
1912	22	14·0	..	·5	...	34
1913	23	17·2	...	·08	·04	34
1914	24	17·6	...	1·0	·08	30
1915	22	16·6		·4	·15	29
1916	28	22·3	...	·09	·01	32
1917	28	23·0	...	...	·01	30
1918	65	18·4	42·3	01	·15	28
1919	27	20·0	·1	2·0	·001	27
1920	22	16·6	..	·001	·3	28
1911-1920	28·2	18·2	4·2	·4	·1	30·5

Death rate from influenza during the year 1918

Age	Per *mille* (1911 population)	
	Males	Females
0—1	33·08	27· 9
1—5 ...	46·17	46·64
5—10 ...	29·06	32·84
10—15	27·95	27·89
15—20	37·70	46·11
20—30	35·34	44·25
30—40	41·37	52·04
40—50	46·64	54·33
50—60	57·67	64·15
60 and over ..	73·93	80·58
Total all ages ...	40·30	45·52

Year	Death-rate	Birth-rate
1901—1910 ...	22·5	33·3
1911—1920 ...	28·2	30·5
1921—1930	22·6	26·8

three intercensal periods as given in the margin. While the death rate returned to normal during the last decade, the birth rate not only failed to recover, but continued to fall alarmingly.

SECTION V—CONDITIONS OF THE DECADE 1921—1931.

21. The decade opened on a disturbed Frontier. The border tribes stirred into active unrest by the 3rd Afghan War of 1919 had hardly emerged from the shattering experience of frontier warfare under modern conditions, and large hostile elements among them, particularly in Waziristan, were a serious menace to the peace of the settled districts. But, paradoxical as it may seem, this period of disorder brought with it a distinct, though fleeting, prosperity to the North-West Frontier Province. Although the inhabitants of the border districts are the first to suffer from any widespread tribal lawlessness, they have much to gain from the military operations which Frontier unrest calls into being. At such times, when a variety of military necessities arise, contractors reap a rich harvest and the unskilled labourer finds ready employment and a high wage. To the Pathan of fighting age, times of unrest call up memories of a princely pay earned in princely idleness, guarding with a government rifle and the prestige of his race some lonely spot on a winding frontier road. At such times, too, Police, Frontier Constabulary, Scouts and Militias open their ranks to a flood of Pathan recruits seeking adventure and honourable employment in the service, which family tradition has taught them to covet from their boyhood. General.

In the midst of this somewhat artificial prosperity the agriculturist was facing difficult times. The drought which had proved such a severe setback to agriculture during the year 1920-21 continued far into the following year, and produced a damaging effect on the first autumn crop of the decade. But thereafter climatic conditions made a rapid change for the better and for the next two years the Province enjoyed a succession of excellent harvests

In the meanwhile the situation on the Frontier was rapidly improving. In February 1922, the ratification of the peace treaty with Afghanistan was received with relief by the great majority of the clans, and by the end of that year good progress had been made with all tribes, except the Mahsuds and Wazirs, in the process of reconciliation and in the restoration of the old relations of confidence and friendship which existed before the Great War. In this year too the construction of the Khyber Railway, which had been started in 1921, was continued without serious opposition from the tribesmen in that area. In Waziristan pacification proceeded slowly but surely. In 1922 some sections of the tribe still remained aloof, if not openly hostile. Early in 1923, as part of the new "forward" policy, Razmak was occupied by troops, and a vast programme of road construction began. Since then Waziristan has never "looked back". No sooner had the roads been constructed than their civilising influence on the backward population of a hitherto inaccessible tract became rapidly apparent. During the remainder of the decade, the area of effective control was gradually extended into the heart of this inhospitable and mountainous country, and maintained by the construction of posts at strategic points garrisoned with troops and Scouts, and by the recruitment from among the tribesmen themselves of a large force of Khassadars or tribal police who co-operated with keenness and loyalty in the arduous task of road protection.

If the Mahsud and Wazir tribesmen had much to gain from the new policy in Waziristan, the harassed inhabitants of the neighbouring districts of Bannu and Dera Ismail Khan had immeasurably more. By the end of the year 1923 these two districts had passed from four years of continuous exposure to the savage depredations of trans-border raiders, into a long and hitherto unbroken period of security and peace.

While the danger from external aggression was thus happily averted, other influences were at work among the people of the border districts, which were destined to give rise to a serious political upheaval at the end of the decade. The report of the Frontier Enquiry Committee of 1922 disclosed a sharp division of opinion among Hindus and Muslims in regard to the future progress of the Province towards constitutional government, which produced a tragic sequel in the communal riots of September 1924 in Kohat. In the next year a movement advocating the immediate extension of reforms to the Province was adopted without a division in the Legislative Assembly. The year 1927 was marked by a further outburst of communal feeling, for which the agitation over the "Rangila Rasool Case" and the realization by the Muslim of his economic dependence on the Hindu, were largely responsible. Communal tension, however, soon disappeared in the general agitation over the reforms which was roused into activity again by the arrival of the Simon Commission in 1928.

When the members of the Commission reached Peshawar in the autumn of 1928, they found excellent relations existing between Government and the tribes, especially in Waziristan But the Commission's visit was hardly over, when the outbreak of Civil War in Afghanistan once more cast a gloom over the Frontier. The flight of *ex*-King Amanullah, the brief reign of Bacha-i-Saqao and the fortunes of the then Sardar Nadir Khan in his fight for the Afghan throne were followed both in the settled districts and in tribal territory with the closest interest; but, as both the tribesmen and the people of the border districts loyally identified themselves with Government's policy of non-intervention in Afghan affairs, these remarkable events passed without any serious effect on the general tranquillity of the border. Towards the end of the year 1929, however, the border districts became once more the scene of unusual internal activity. Frontier extremists, in open alliance with the Indian National Congress, began to preach a doctrine of revolution and independence, coupled with adherence to the Congress campaign of Civil Disobedience. This agitation came to a head in the serious riots in Peshawar City in April 1930, which were followed by further revolutionary outbreaks all over the Province. Repercussions among the trans border tribes of the unrest in the border districts was only to be expected. Though these were in some instances of a violent nature particularly in the case of the Afridis who, on two occasions during the following summer invaded the Peshawar District with armed *lashkars* — they were fortunately short-lived. By the autumn of 19-0 the situation had been effectively restored, and the Census was taken on the 26th February 1931 under generally normal conditions, except that a number of the leading agitators were still in jail, and the blockade of the Afridi tribe which had been maintained throughout the winter had not yet been lifted.

From the point of view of public health, the first half of the decade left much to be desired. A heavy mortality from cholera and malaria in 1921 reflected a low vitality — a probable legacy from the influenza epidemic of 1918. To the same cause we must attribute the continued fall in the birth rate to its lowest ebb in 1922. With healthier conditions in 1922 and 1923 the birth-rate started to recover rapidly but its complete recovery was impeded by ill-health in 1924, and 1925, though a healthy year, still saw no further recovery. But the second half of the decade with five years of uninterrupted good health restored to the people their normal vitality, and the complete recovery of the birth-rate in 1928 was a welcome sign that the Province was free at last from the baneful effects of the influenza epidemic.

Agricultural conditions, which had been encouraging up to the end of 1923, took an unfavourable turn in 1924, and for two years there was a run of rather poor harvests. 1926 brought some improvement, but the autumn crop of that year was severely damaged by wind and rain in August. In 1927, though the wheat crop was good, the general outturn was below the average, and in 1928 serious damage to the wheat crop from acute atrophic shrivelling spoiled an otherwise favourable year Throughout the agricultural year 1928-29 the rainfall was inadequate, and the total area harvested was 5 per cent. below the normal for the decade. The autumn and spring crops in the year 1929-30 were both good and marked a considerable improvement as compared with the preceding three years. But by this time the fall in the general level of prices of food-grains had become the outstanding feature of the agricultural situation, money was scarce owing to a movement to hold up stocks in the hope of a recovery of the market, and the deepening of the world depression, accompanied by an inadequate rainfall led to a large decrease in the areas sown both for the autumn crop of 1930 and for the spring crop of 1931. The combined outturn of these two crops was considerably smaller than that for any other agricultural year in the decade. The decade 1921—1931 thus closed under the shadow of an universal trade depression and a catastrophic fall in prices, and the outlook for the agriculturist was a gloomy one indeed.

Vital statistics. 22. Over the whole decade, the number of births registered in the five districts of the Province amounted to 603,870 as compared with 668,8-0 during the previous decade; and the number of deaths registered was 508,261 as compared with 618,451 in the previous decade 1911—1920. The natural increase (*i. e.* excess of tota births over total deaths registered) was thus 95,609 as against 50,429 in the decade 1911—1920.

The Provincial birth and death rates for each year of the decade are given in the margin with diagrams illustrating vital statistics and the natural increase in population. These diagrams should be also studied in conjunction with the description of public health during the last decade in paragraph 24 below.

Birth and death rates per *mille* of Population, 1921—1930

Year	Birth-rate	Death-rate
1921	27·0	31·2
1922	23·4	21·0
1923	27·4	23·6
1924	26·8	30·7
1925	26·6	19·6
1926	29·9	21·6
1927	29·0	21·9
1928	32·3	19·1
1929	30·6	23·9
1930	25·4	21·7

As compared with other provinces in India, both the birth and death rates in the North-West Frontier Province are low, particularly the death-rate. In 1922 the birth-rate was actually the lowest in India, and for the first four years of the decade it remained the lowest, except for Coorg. But the North-West Frontier Province birth-rate then started to recover, and in 1928 it was higher than Coorg, Burma, Bengal and Assam. The death-rate for the North-West Frontier Province was the lowest in India in 1928, and was the lowest, except for Burma in 1922, 1925, 1926 and 1927.

No. 5.

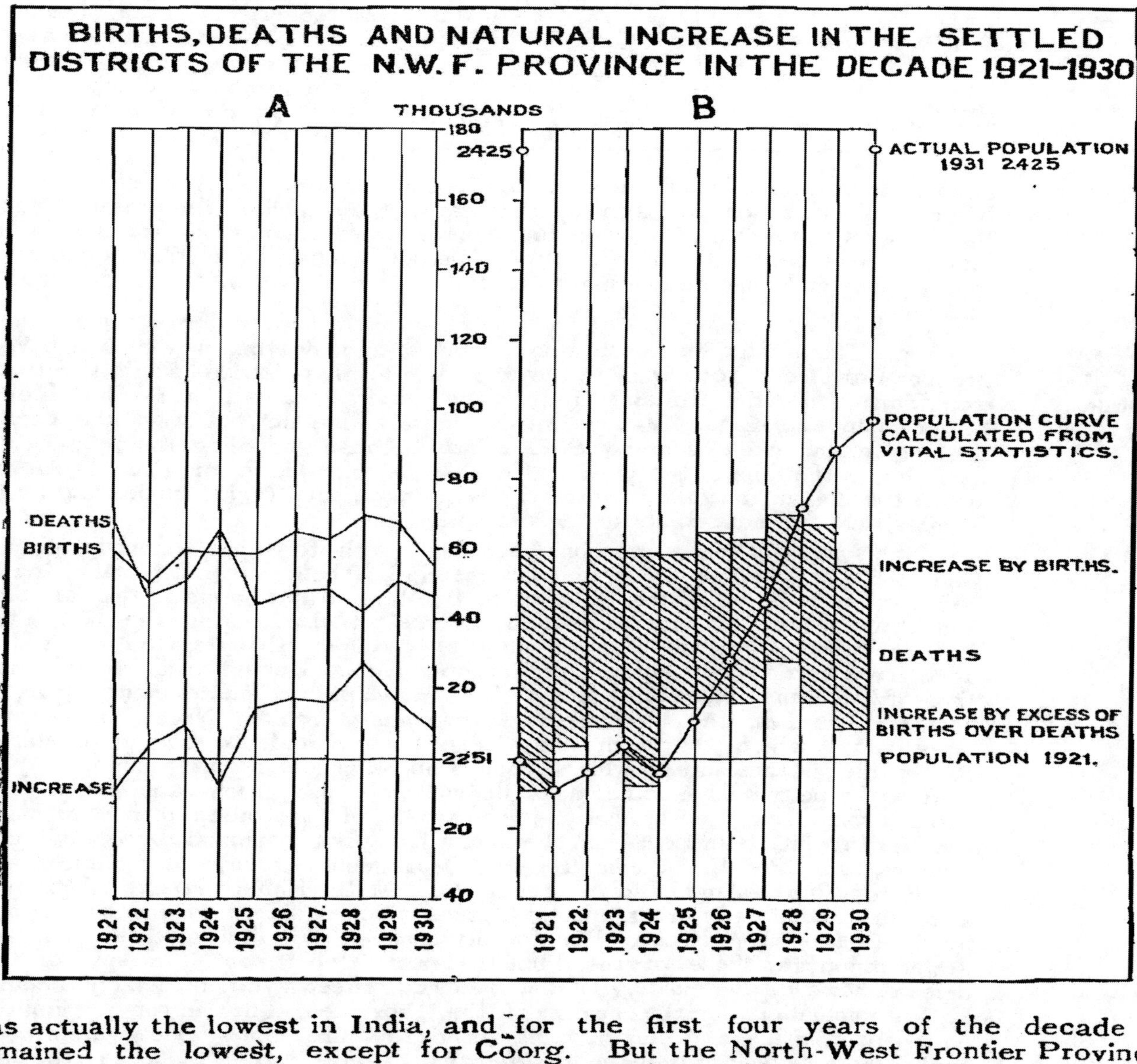

The table in the margin shows how the natural increase during the last

Natural increase, 1921—1930	Persons	Males	Females
Births	603,870	340,379	263,491
Deaths	508,261	275,460	232,801
Natural increase ...	95,609	64,919	30,690

decade is distributed among the sexes. From this table the small number of female births and deaths registered (particularly births) as compared with the male is at once obvious. This well-known feature of the vital statistics of the North-West Frontier Province has been noticed in previous Census Reports, and presents a problem which is likely to defy a complete solution until the equality of the sexes is fully recognised, and old prejudices against publishing the births of female children disappear. That these prejudices exist in their strongest form among the Pathan population of the trans-Indus districts is evident from the marginal figures which show that, in the non Pathan Hazara District (cis-Indus), female births and deaths are much more freely recorded. Moreover, in the Peshawar District, the natural increase of females during the whole decade was only 482 as compared with 12,566 in the Hazara District, while the actual increase of females in the Peshawar District, according to the Census, was 31,611. Unfortunately figures showing the balance of migration in each district are not available at the present Census, but it seems certain that the large difference between the natural and the actual increase in females in the Peshawar District cannot be attributed entirely to immigration, and must be due mainly to the failure to register the full number of female births.

Decade, 1921—1930	Number of female births to 1,000 male births	Number of female deaths to 1,000 male deaths
Hazara	869·03	900·45
Trans-Indus districts ...	739·82	825·10

System of registeration of vital statistics.

23. The area under registration of births and deaths in the North-West Frontier Province in 1921 was the whole of the five settled districts with the exception of Feudal Tanawal (Amb and Phulra States), and the Konsh, Bhogarmang and Kagan Valleys in the Hazara District. During the decade, the registration area was extended to the Konsh and Bhogarmang Valleys in 1928, but at the time of the present Census the population of Feudal Tanawal and of the Kagan an Valley numbering 57,785 persons (3,331 males and 25,404 females) was still not subject to registration.

The system of registration has been dealt with to some extent in previous Census Reports and needs only a brief description here. In most municipalities and cantonments the system is based on bye-laws framed under the Municipal and Cantonment Acts, many of which have been revised during the last decade. In these urban areas therefore it may be assumed that registration is fairly accurately carried out under proper supervision. But in rural areas and in those urban areas which are not either municipal or cantonment areas, the system is based on an old Punjab Government Circular (No. 8 of the 18th April 1892) which seems in many respects unsuited to modern conditions. Registration in these areas, which depends on periodical reports made at police stations by petty village officers is known to be far from satisfactory. That there is some lack of co-ordination in the system of registration in the North-West Frontier Province is evident from the fact that the Provincial birth and death rates published by the Public Health Department exclude cantonments and the European and Anglo-Indian community. As the Public Health Department also use a definition of urban and rural areas which is different from that adopted by the Census, there is no real conformity between the vital statistics contained in this report and those of the Public Health Department. In spite of these defects, however, the existing vital statistics do reflect with considerable accuracy normal fluctuations in the health of the Province. Their error is limited to omissions of births, and deaths, and as deaths are more widely known than births, more births are probably omitted than deaths. But, even so, the error is generally constant, and does not affect the accurate recording of periods of good and ill health.

Public health.

24 The health of the Province was maintained at a high level throughout the

decade. Of the total number of deaths recorded, 80·2 per cent. were due to malarial fever, 3·3 per cent. to plague, 1·0 per cent. to cholera, 0·7 per cent. to small-pox and 14·8 per cent. to other causes. Interest will be added to the following brief account of the health conditions of the decade if constant reference is made to the diagrams relating to vital statistics given in paragraph 22 above.

1921 opened the decade with its most unhealthy year. Malarial fever and cholera, which were prevalent in epidemic form, contributed 24·9 and 2·0 respectively to a total death-rate of 31·2, the highest recorded (apart from the influenza epidemic of 1918) since 1908. Cholera was responsible for many more deaths during this one year than during the whole of the rest of the decade. The prevalence of disease was probably due to a severe drought which lasted from the spring of 1920 to the autumn of 1921, reducing the agricultural population to a state bordering on famine ; the Province was suffering also from a low vitality since the devastating epidemic of influenza in 1918. To the same causes may be attributed the low birth-rate of 27·0. The year ended with a loss of 4 per *mille* in population, resulting from the excess of the death-rate over the birth rate.

1922 is described as an exceptionally healthy year, though the birth-rate fell to 23·4, the lowest recorded in the Province since 1893 It is difficult to attribute this low birth-rate to any exact cause beyond ill-health in the preceding year which accentuated the already reduced vitality of the population. Bumper harvests and freedom from disease in epidemic form produced a low death-rate, 21·0 the lowest for many years.

1923 proved to be another healthy year, during which the Province was entirely free from all epidemic diseases except plague, which only contributed 1·7 to a total death-rate of 23·6. In response to the cumulative effect of two healthy years, the birth-rate rose to 27·4 but, in spite of favourable agricultural conditions, hopes of rapid recovery in the fertility of the people were disappointed by ill-health again in.

1924, when plague—a legacy from the previous year—and malarial fever were prevalent in epidemic form, in spite of a moderate rainfall, an unusually high mortality from respiratory diseases was another feature of the year. The death-rate rose to 30·7, malarial fever and plague contributing 21·1 and 5·3 respectively. In sympathy with these unhealthy conditions, the birth-rate dropped, slightly, to 26·8. The result at the end of the year was a loss in population of 3·9 per *mille* almost equal to the loss in 1921.

1925 marks the return of exceptionally healthy conditions. The total death-rate was only 19·6, the lowest recorded since 1901. The birth-rate, still affected by the ill-health of 1924, remained low at 26·6. The plague epidemic of the previous year almost entirely disappeared, and the mortality from malarial fevers was unusually low.

1926 was again healthy on the whole. Cholera made no appearance at all, but malaria, small-pox and plague were slightly more prevalent than in the preceding year. The death-rate was 21·6, while the rise in the birth-rate to 29·9 showed that the Province was at last recovering its normal fertility after the prejudicial effect of the influenza epidemic of 1918.

1927, the third healthy year in succession, saw the end of the plague epidemic, the Province being entirely free from this disease for the remainder of the decade. Cholera was responsible for only two deaths, and small-pox, an endemic disease in this Province, took much less than its usual toll. The death-rate was 21·9, while the birth-rate, still on the road to complete recovery, was 29·0.

1928 was unquestionably the healthiest year in the whole decade, the Province being entirely free from both cholera and plague for the first time on record. The death-rate 19·1 was the lowest recorded since 1901 and the birth-rate 32·3—now completely recovered—the highest since 1916. These remarkably healthy conditions coincided with a small, but not an excessively small, rainfall.

1929 was yet another healthy year in respect of all diseases except malarial fevers. Heavy rains and floods in the Peshawar and Dera Ismail Khan Districts in the autumn produced conditions favourable to malaria which accounted for 80 per cent. of the total deaths. The death-rate rose to 23·9, the third highest during the decade, and the birth-rate dropped slightly to 30.6.

The health of the Province in 1930 is described as generally good, though cholera made its appearance again in slight epidemic form for the first time since 1921. The mortality from all other diseases was considerably less than that of the previous year. Both the death-rate and the birth-rate, 21·7 and 25·4, respectively, must be regarded with considerable suspicion. During the summer months political disturbances all over the Province interfered so seriously with the ordinary course of town and rural life, that in certain areas the administration was brought almost entirely to a standstill and some months elapsed before the situation was completely restored. Under these circumstances it is more than probable that a large number of births and deaths failed to get recorded.

To sum up, the decade may be described as an unusually healthy one. The number of deaths recorded was the lowest for any single decade since 1891. The recovery of the birth-rate after the terrible epidemic of influenza in 1918 was retarded by what in comparison with the rest of the decade must be considered as ill-health in 1921 and 1924; but remarkably healthy conditions during the last 6 years of the decade restored the normal vitality of the people and enabled the birth-rate to effect a complete recovery. The decade closed under conditions contrasting very favourably with those under which it opened.

Mortality from fevers.

25. As fevers accounted for 80·2 per cent. of the deaths recorded during the decade, the marginal statement comparing the mortality from fevers with canal irrigation in each district will be of some interest. In this statement the first column of figures shows the number of deaths from fevers per *mille* of the rural population during the decade 1921—1930, and the second column shows the number of acres irrigated from Government and private canals in every square mile in the representative year 1929-30. The statement shows at a glance that there is no obvious connection between canal irrigation and fever. Peshawar, with its extensive canal system, by far the most highly irrigated district in the Province, enjoys a lower mortality from fevers than any other district. Again, in Kohat District, where facilities for canal irrigation are almost non-existent, the mortality from fevers is higher than that of any other district. The conclusion is that the extension of canal irrigation has not materially affected the problem of the high mortality from fevers either one way or the other, as this problem exists in its most acute form in tracts which are not highly irrigated.

District	Fever per *mille* (rural population)	Irrigated area per square *mille* (Canal only)
Hazara ...	184	13
Peshawar ...	177	203
Kohat ...	260	6
Bannu ..	209	80
Dera Ismail Khan ..	239	16

The Plague epidemic.

25. As we have already noted, deaths occurred from plague in every year of the decade up to 1927, after which year the disease disappeared entirely from the North-West Frontier Province, until the end of the decade. The number of deaths in each year up to the year 1927 are given in the margin. From these it will be observed that the epidemic reached its peak in the year 1924, when as many as 11,463 persons died of plague alone. The large majority of these deaths (actually 10,995, of which 4,487 were males and 6,508 females) occurred in the Peshawar District, representing 1·2 per cent. of the total population of that district.

Number of deaths from plague, North-West Frontier Province (Districts)

Year		Deaths
1921	...	139
1922	...	124
1923	...	3,783
1924	...	11,463
1925	...	217
1926	...	644
1927	...	232

In view of the importance and deadliness of this disease, a further analysis of the figures for deaths from plague in the Peshawar District in the year 1924, as given in the margin, will, it is thought, be of some interest. These figures shew that females are generally more subject to the disease than males, but that the disease is less fatal to both sexes in early youth and old age than in the intervening ages.

Proportion per cent of deaths from plague in the Peshawar District in the year 1924

Age periods	Persons	Males	Females
0—1 ...	6·1	6·7	5·7
1—4 ...	9·0	8·4	9·6
5—9 ...	10·1	10·6	9·8
10 14 ...	10·7	9·7	11·4
15 – 19 ...	9·6	13·0	7·2
20 – 29 ...	13·5	13·6	13·4
30 – 39 ...	11·1	9·1	12·4
40 – 49 ...	11·4	11·1	11·7
50 – 59 ...	10·3	11·4	9·4
60 and over ...	8·2	6·4	9·4
All ages ...	10·0	40·9	59·1

Year	Kharif		Rabi		Total
	Sown	Failed	Sown	Failed	Matured
1921-22 ...	112	31	108	13	108
1922-23 ...	92	13	112	13	112
1923-24 ...	99	20	100	17	101
1924-25 ...	97	13	97	24	95
1925-26 ...	101	20	103	13	105
1926-27 ..	90	19	92	21	90
1927-28 ...	97	19	97	16	29
1928 29 ...	94	19	101	23	95
1929-30 ...	117	24	105	21	105
1930-31 ...	99	19	87	23	88

Agricultural conditions of the decade.

27. A general idea of the relative quality of the harvests during the decade can be obtained from a study of the statement below in which the sown and matured areas are shown as percentages of the average sown and matured areas for the decade and failed areas as percentages of the actual sown areas for each harvest.

The inauspicious circumstances under the decade opened will be strikingly apparent when these figures are compared with similar figures for the year 1920—1921, the last year of the previous decade, which was an exceptionally bad one. For the kharif crop of that year, the area sown amounted to only 87 per cent. of the average sown area for the decade 1921—1931 ; of this area sown as much as 34 per cent. failed. The area sown for the Rabi crop amounted to only 71 per cent. of the average sown area for the decade 1921—1931 and of this sown area as much as 49 per cent. failed. Finally the total matured area for both crops of the agricultural year 1920—21 was only 53 per cent. of the average matured area for the decade 1921—31. These disastrous conditions which have been described more fully in paragraph 16 above, were due to the fact that, from the spring of 1902, the Province was in the grip of a severe drought which lasted long enough to cause a very heavy failure in the autumn crop of 1921.

But a rapid improvement in the weather permitted extensive sowings for the spring crop of 1922, and the continuance of favourable conditions resulted in bumper spring harvest, which, more than counteracting the failure of the Kharif crop, produced a total of the matured crop for the year 8 per cent. above average. **1921-22.**

Conditions during the next year were still better. The rainfall was well distributed and favourable both for the autumn harvest of 1922 and for the spring harvest of 1923, with the result that both crops were exceptionally good, and the total matured crop was by far the best in the whole decade. **1922-23.**

But these abnormal conditions could not be expected to last. The autumn harvest of 1923 suffered from a lack of rain in September, and for the same reason there was a considerable drop in the area sown with wheat and barley for the spring crop in 1924. The yield of these crops was consequently a poor one. **1923-24.**

Sowing operations for the autumn crop of 1924 were adversely affected by a lack of rain, but owing to good rain in September the area that failed to yield crops was less than that of the previous Kharif. Poor rain and abnormal cold weather were responsible for a large failure in the spring crop of 1925, and the total cropped area of both harvests was five per cent. below the normal for the decade. **1924-25.**

In 1925-26, conditions began to improve agian. Good rains in May and June led to extensive sowings for the autumn crop of 1925, but owing to scanty rain in September a large proportion of the sown area failed to yield crops. Favourable conditions again during the winter led to an excellent spring harvest in 1926, and the total matured crop for the year was 6 per cent. above the average. **1925-26.**

Conditions were unfavourable to sowings for the autumn crop of 1926, with the result that the sown area was exceptionally small ; but well distributed rains in September improved the situation everywhere, except in the Peshawar District where the valuable maize crop was wrecked by wind and rain in August. Very scanty rain fell during the winter ; sowings for the spring crop were consequently much restricted, and the continued lack of rain, together with an unfortunate plague of locusts were responsible for a large amount of failure, especially in the Peshawar and Hazara Districts. The outturn for the year was 10 per cent. below the normal for the decade, though the wheat crop was a good one. **1926-27.**

1927-28 saw a slight improvement. Conditions were favourable autumn sowings and the sown area was almost normal for the decade. In spite of **1927-28.**

inadequate rain in August and September the outturn was generally satisfactory. The season was favourable for the Rabi sowings, and the spring crop would have been a good one, but for a serious failure of the wheat crop, due to acute atrophic shrivelling.

1928-29. The summer of 1928 was unfavourable for autumn sowings, and inadequate rain in August and September caused a certain amount of failure. Climatic conditions during the winter were generally favourable for Rabi sowings, but the area failing to yield crops was large, owing to a scanty rainfall in March. The total outturn was 5 per cent. below the average for the decade.

1929-30. Copious and well distributed rains in July 1929 led to extensive sowings for the autumn crop, which, in spite of heavy rains and serious floods in August, yielded a good harvest, particularly in the Peshawar District. Late winter rains produced a fair Rabi harvest and the total of the matured crop for the year was 5 per cent. above the normal for the decade.

1930-31. But this improvement was destined to be shortlived. As the world trade depression deepened, the outlook for the farmer became more and more unfavourable. The autumn harvest of 1930 was only a little below the average, but the spring harvest of 1931 was an exceedingly poor one. Rabi sowings were restricted both by insufficient rain and by a catastrophic fall in prices, and inadequate spring rains caused a large amount of failure. The matured area for the whole year was as much as 12 per cent. below the average for the decade, which thus closed amid a general gloom.

With the object of supplementing the above short description of the seasons, diagrams are given below illustrating the sown areas and produce of the principal crops in the five districts of the North-West Frontier Province during the decade.

No. 6.

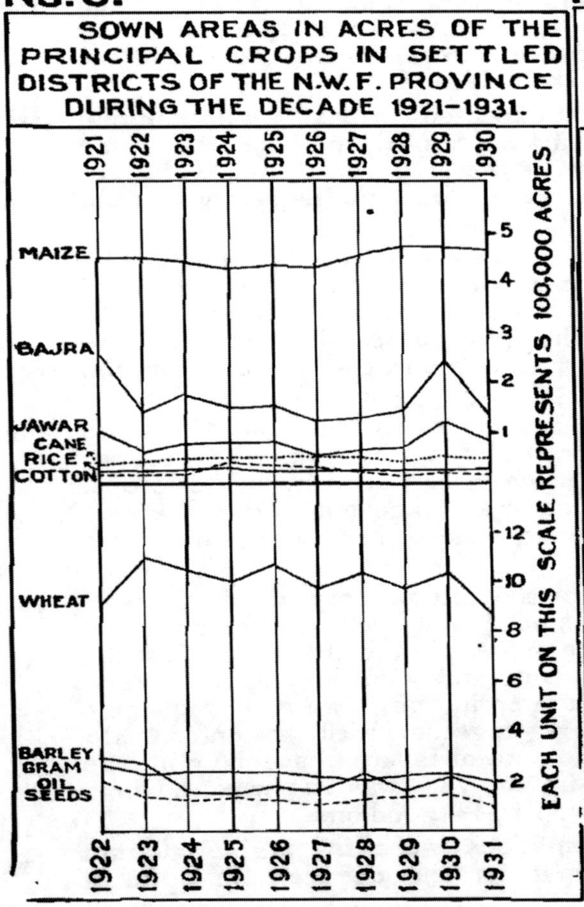

No. 7.

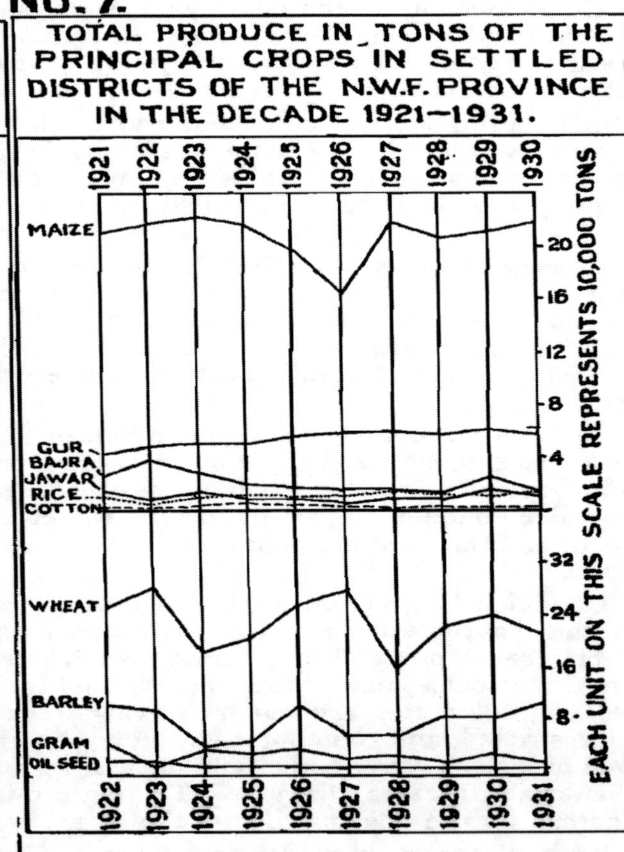

The relative importance of the crops shown in these diagrams can be readily understood from a glance at the marginal table which gives the average sown area, and produce in tons of each crop during the decade. The third column of figures is inserted merely as a guide to the comparative value of the total produce of each crop, the values being calculated from the average of the annual harvest prices at Peshawar and Dera Ismail Khan during the decade 1921—1931. The 10 crops shown represent 90 per cent. of the total average area sown during the decade, and it is upon them that the agricultural welfare of the Province principally depends. The autumn crop is a particularly important one in the Peshawar District, but taking all districts together both harvests are almost equally valuable. The value of the combined produce of the wheat and maize crops is equal to about two-thirds of the value of the total produce of all crops.

Crop	Average area sown (in thousands of acres)	Average produce (in thousands of tons)	Value (in lakhs of rupees)	District where principally grown
Autumn crops.				
(1) Maize ...	456	208	216	Hazara and Peshawar.
(2) Sugarcane ...	45	56	114	Peshawar and Bannu.
(3) Bajra ...	168	21	25	Kohat and Dera Ismail Khan.
(4) Jowar ...	69	11	11	Dera Ismail Khan and Peshawar.
(5) Rice ...	25	11	10	Hazara and Peshawar.
(6) Cotton ...	21	3	7	Peshawar.
Spring crops.				
(1) Wheat ...	1,001	229	273	All districts.
(2) Barley ...	196	75	58	Hazara, Peshawar and Bannu.
(3) Gram ...	223	28	28	Bannu, Dera Ismail Khan and Kohat.
(4) Oil-seeds ...	129	11	18	Dera Ismail Khan.

28. The heights to which prices soared towards the end of the decade 1911—1921 led to the conviction in some quarters that much of the phenomenal rise would be permanent and that there was very little likelihood of an early return to pre-war levels. But that theory has been belied by an equally phenomenal fall during the last decade, as illustrated in the diagram below. **Prices and wages.**

No. 8.

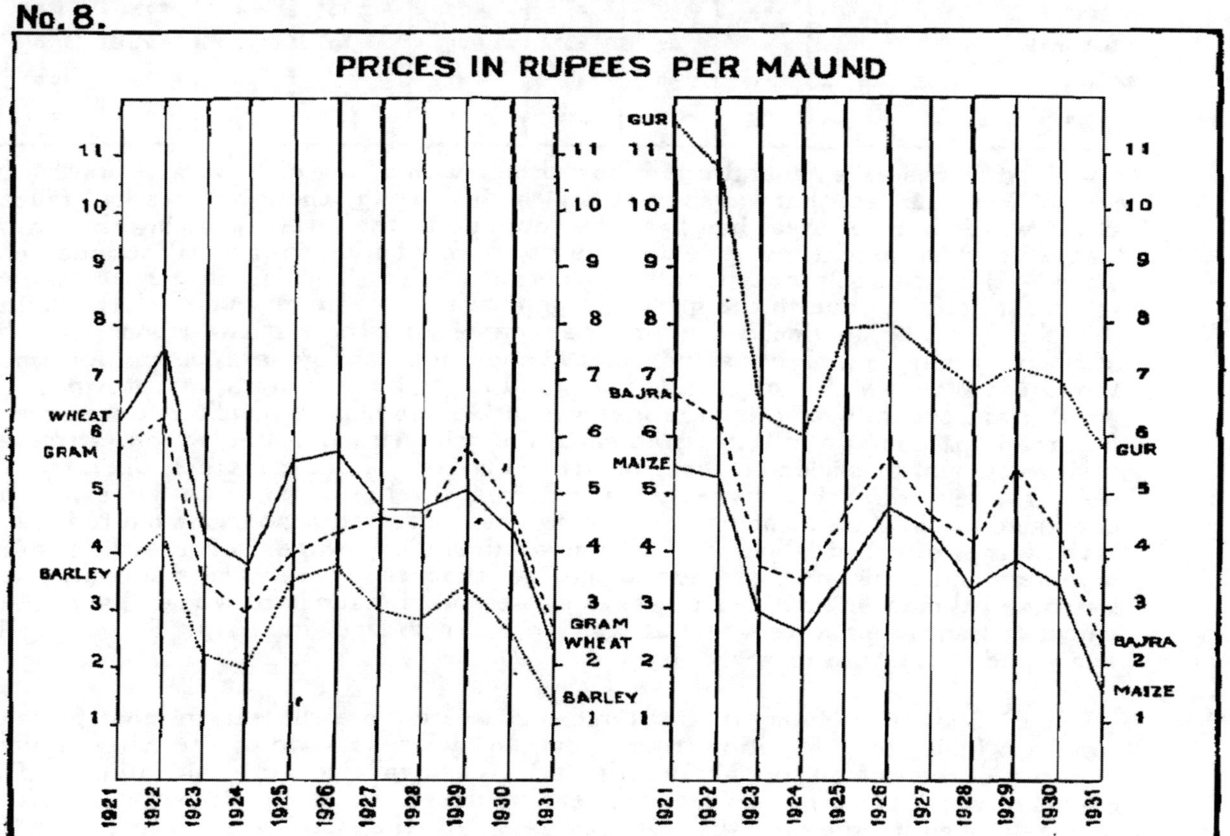

The prices shown in this diagram are those obtaining in Peshawar, the principal market of the Province, and are quite distinct from the prices realised by the agriculturist at harvest time, which are generally lower than market prices. Prices remained high in 1922 in spite of the bumper spring harvest of that year, as the Province had not yet recovered from the severe and prolonged drought of 1920-21. But more bumper harvests in 1923 combined with the general re-action after the Afghan War, brought prices down with a run. The two subsequent rises in 1926 and 1929 were due to poor harvests in 1926-27 and the failure of the Rabi crop in 1928. The final and unprecedented fall in 1931 reflects the world trade depression.

A regular wage Census is held in the five settled districts of the North-West Frontier Province every five years. The figures in the statement below have been taken from the last three censuses.

Class of labour	Daily wages in annas			Increase or decrease per cent		Wages expressed in maunds of wheat per month		
	1917	1923	1928	1917—1923	1923—1928	1917	1923	1928
Urban.								
Iron and lead ware ...	22	32	35	+ 45	+ 13	9·9	14·2	14·5
Brass and copper ...	17	22	28	+ 29	+ 27	7·6	9·8	11·3
Carpenters ...	17	27	34	+ 59	+ 26	7·6	12·0	13·6
Cotton weavers ...	15	24	16	+ 60	− 33	6·7	10·7	6·4
Masons and builders ...	18	27	34	+ 50	+ 26	8·1	12·0	13·6
General unskilled ...	10	12	15	+ 20	+ 35	4·5	5·3	6·0
Rural								
General unskilled ...	9	9	9	...	...	4·0	4·0	3·6
Carpenters ...	21	28	21	+ 33	− 33	9·4	12·5	8·4
Blacksmiths ...	21	27	22	+ 29	− 19	9·4	12·0	10·0
Masons ...	21	30	25	+ 41	− 17	9·4	13·4	10·0
Ploughmen ...	5·3	6·9	5·3	+ 30	− 30	2·4	3·1	2·1

That wages as a general rule follow prices with a lag of several months is evident from the fact that wages were still high in 1923, though prices had fallen. While wages in rural areas had by 1928 returned to the level obtaining in 1917, wages in urban areas show a continuous rise during both quinquennial periods from 1917—1928, the only exception being cotton weavers, the fall in whose wages is almost certainly due to the growing popularity of foreign-made cloth during this period. The continued rise in the wages of other urban labour can be attributed firstly to a higher standard of living among the general population since the Great War, which increased the demand for town comforts and town-made goods; and secondly to the large increase in Government expenditure on buildings and roads particularly in Waziristan since the 3rd Afghan War, which attracted a large amount of skilled labour from the Punjab. These factors operated to delay the return of urban wages to their normal level in relation to prices. The continued fall in prices since 1928, has no doubt effected a considerable reduction in the wages of urban labour. The comparatively low wages of unskilled rural labourers and ploughmen are due to the fact that they are usually accompanied by some payment in kind. The wages expressed in maunds of wheat have been calculated on the price of wheat at Rs. 4-3-0 per maund in 1917, Rs. 4-3-5 in 1923, and Rs. 4-10-9 in 1928.

Extension of cultivation.

29. Statistics relating to areas under cultivation are subject, in most parts of Northern India, to fluctuation from year to year, according to the varying capacity of the rainfall to make unirrigated areas available for cultivation. The extent to which the North-West Frontier Province is liable to these fluctuations may be judged by the fact that 65 per cent. of the total area sown during the last decade was unirrigated and only 35 per cent. irrigated.

Year	Area in acres						
	Irrigated from state canals	Irrigated from private canals	Irrigated from wells	Irrigated from other sources	Total area irrigated	Double cropped area	Gross cultivated area (sown area)
1901 ...	...	...	...	...	809 736	...	2,738,480
1911 ...	225,890	412,792	94,270	45,209	778,161	...	2,714,110
1921 ...	333,809	375,998	69,161	49,821	828,789	...	1,973,691
1921-22 ...	355,968	407,599	68,176	69,658	901,401	4,012	2,816,172
1922-23 ...	381,176	387,537	131,692	44,984	945,389	3,610	2,702,783
1923-24 ...	359,419	385,472	81,445	39,112	865,448	4,398	2,575,656
1924-25 ...	359,020	377,700	79,713	39,072	855,505	3,449	2,497,357
1925-26 ...	368,058	387,375	85,381	39,980	880,794	4,750	2,644,195
1926-27 ...	358,052	387,782	82,817	41,938	870,589	1,278	2,359,165
1927-28 ...	375,716	383,436	83 072	43,077	885,301	1,222	2,504,041
1928-29 ...	382,427	390,102	83,314	44,284	900,127	1,183	2,537,820
1929-30 ...	388,064	393,120	81,078	44,544	906,806	1,954	2,817,650
1930-31 ...	392,055	393,833	81,318	40,215	907,421	1,909	2,355,565
Average 1921—31	371,996	389,396	85,801	44,686	891,878	2,776	2,581,040
Area per 1000 irrigated acres	417	437	96	50	1000*	...	...

The actual fluctuations during the last decade, as contrasted with the single years 1901, 1911 and 1921 are shown in the margin.

An examination of these figures shows firstly that, as long ago as 1901, when the North-West Frontier Province was separated from the Punjab, cultivation had already been extended almost to its limit, and that no further material extension is discernible among the fluctuations since that year; secondly that there is a fairly progressive increase in the area irrigated from all sources at the expense of the unirrigated area; and thirdly that while the area irrigated by state canals rapidly increased, the area irrigated by other means has, except for seasonal variations, remained almost stationary since 1901. Thus progress during the last thirty years is to be measured not by an extension of the area under cultivation, but by an extension of the area under an *assured* cultivation. The two-fold object of canal irrigation is to carry available water to available wastes and to render cultivable land independent of the vagaries of the rainfall. Our figures show that, if no further progress towards attainment of the first object has been possible, much has been done during the last decade towards fulfilment of the second. The area irrigated by state canals has increased by 17 per cent. since 1921 and by 74 per cent. since 1911. From the marginal statement it will be observed that, out of the four state canals in the Province, two, the Lower Swat Canal and the Kabul River Canals, have reached the limit of the cultivable area commanded by them, but that there is still room for extension of the area irrigated by the remaining two, the Upper Swat and Paharpur Canals. No new irrigation schemes of any importance have been undertaken during the last decade, though some have been under consideration affecting the Dera Ismail Khan District. From Subsidiary Table I at the end of this chapter it will be observed that a considerable culturable area has not yet been brought under cultivation, and that a large portion of the total cultivated area is still unirrigated. From this it would seem that there is still room for further development of irrigation facilities; but the physical obstacles to be overcome are immense, and with prices of agricultural produce at their present level, it is unlikely that any scheme can be devised in the near future capable of benefiting a substantial area of culturable land, and of bringing in a return sufficient to cover the interest on the capital outlay. For these reasons, we cannot look with confidence to agriculture to provide any economic justification for a further increase of population in the North-West Frontier Province.

Name of canal	Length of main lines in miles		Culturable area commanded by each in acres	Average area irrigated annually in acres	Date of first irrigation
	Main canals and branches	Distributories			
Lower Swat Canal	22	173	150,406	159,744	1887-88
Kabul River Canal	65	13	34,913	47,708	1903-04
Upper Swat Canal	138	403	309,899	155,689	1914-15
Paharpur Canal ...	42	15	63,450	21,163	1907-08

Note.—The above canals are designed to discharge the following number of cubic feet per second:—

Lower Swat Canal 700; Kabul River Canal 417; Upper Swat Canal 2,178; Paharpur Canal 1,100.

The economic position of the agriculturist.

30. If the decade has been an anxious and uncertain one from the point of view of agriculture, it would be wrong to dismiss it as possessing no redeeming features. Apart from a disastrous opening, the first five years saw an average of fair harvests together with the return of settled conditions on the Frontier, which should, in spite of the fall in prices, have enabled the agricultural community to consolidate the advantages accruing from abnormally high price levels during the Great War. The unfavourable conditions in the second half of the decade and the catastrophic fall in prices at the end cannot, we consider, altogether account for the steady deterioration since the beginning of the decade in the economic position of the farmer apparent from the figures in the margin. Extravagance and improvidence, two weak points in the Pathan character, are accentuated in times of ease and affluence, and it is to unwise expenditure during the first half of the decade, as well as to natural causes and world depression in the second half, that we must attribute the apparent decline in the agricultural prosperity of the North-West Frontier Province during the last 10 years. As the statement in this paragraph shows, the proportion of cultivated land under mortgage has steadily increased year by year, and, but for the first year, more land has been mortgaged than redeemed in every year of the decade. The abnormal increase in sales in the year 1924 is largely due to many hitherto unrecorded transactions having been brought to light during settlement operations in the Peshawar District It is interesting to note that the general decline in economic prosperity is reflected in a corresponding fall in the price of land.

Cultivated areas under mortgage, redeemed and sold

Year		Percentage of cultivated area under mortgage	Area out of every 10,000 acres of cultivated land which was			Average price of cultivated land per acre
			Mortgaged	Redeemed	Sold	
						Rs.
1921	...	17·4	150	150	103	297
1922	...	17·7	134	110	85	271
1923	...	17·9	143	127	95	276
1924	...	18·8	183	160	138	244
1925	...	19·0	142	125	99	254
1926	...	19·0	150	127	106	245
1927	...	19·3	132	130	91	238
1928	...	19·4	140	123	107	233
1929	...	19·9	138	113	104	257
1930	...	20·0	115	105	96	181

Co-operative Credit Societies.

31. The decade has seen the foundations of the co-operative credit movement in the North-West Frontier Province well and truly laid. After a false start in the year 1922, further efforts were postponed until 1925, when the Registrar of the Punjab (also Registrar for the North-West Frontier Province) deputed an inspector to commence work in the Haripur Tahsil of the Hazara District. Activities were confined almost entirely to this district until 1929, when the scope of the movement was extended to the trans-Indus Districts. These apparently slow beginnings were inspired by a wise restraint. Experience had shown the difficulties that had to be overcome in instilling into the Pathan mind the true spirit of co-operation, without which the movement could not hope for success. Again, early efforts to reform useless and extravagant customs retarding the economic progress of the people met with a stubborn resistance, which gave warning of the danger of a too hurried advance. But as the success achieved by the movement in the Punjab became generally known in the North-West Frontier Province, public interest both in Hazara and in the trans-Indus districts gradually increased until the only obstacle to rapid progress at the end of the decade was the lack of a trained staff to start educative propaganda in the more backward rural areas and to ensure that new societies were opened on sound lines and their working properly inspected.

The statement below illustrates in a striking manner the progress made by the movement during the first five years of its life in the North-West Frontier Province.

	Societies					Members					Working capital				
	1926	1927	1928	1929	1930	1926	1927	1928	1929	1930	1926	1927	1928	1929	1930
											Rs.	Rs.	Lakhs	Lakhs	Lakhs
Central Bank ...	1	1	1	1	1	27	46	68	123	150	26,150	66,600	1·25	2·36	3·42
Agricultural Credit.	9	27	50	89	152	212	681	1,400	2,500	4,122	9,278	50,099	1·10	2·13	3·41
Non-Agricultural Credit.	1	1	3	3	3	46	77	643	677	714	2,662	13,554	1·18	1·29	1·44
Non-Agricultural Non-Credit.	5	5	6	8	10	80	80	125	638	839	1,227	2,519	·04	·40	·65
Total ...	16	34	60	101	106	365	884	2,235	3,938	5,825	39,317	132,772	3·57	6·18	8.92

In April 1925 the only society in the Province was that of a cavalry regiment in Risalpur, which was transferred soon afterwards to Baluchistan. A thrift society was registered in August and the first credit society in December 1925. The Hazara Central Bank, still the only Central Bank in the Province, was registered in March 1926. Up to the end of the decade, local bodies remained the chief source of deposits and the Bank had not been successful in attracting money from the general public, among whom many important depositors are found in the Punjab. Though, for this reason, deposits were not what they should be, recoveries were good in comparison with the Punjab. At the end of 1928 there were 60 societies and 2,236 members in the Province, mostly in the Hazara District, where the movement was still centralised. But the next year witnessed an all-round expansion. In the spring of 1929, a whole-time Assistant Registrar was appointed for the North-West Frontier Province, and the movement was definitely extended to the Peshawar and Dera Ismall Khan Districts, 41 new societies sprang up in this year, and the membership was increased to 3,938. In the following year 1930, progress continued in spite of the prevailing political unrest and the decade closed with 166 societies, 5,825 members and a working capital of nearly 9 lakhs.

Joint Stock Companies.

32. The North-West Frontier Province suffers from an almost complete lack of joint stock enterprise. Of the five joint stock companies in existence in 1931, 3 are public and 2 private; 2 are registered in Bannu and the remaining three in Dera Ismail Khan District. The marginal statement gives the situation during the last ten years in summary form.

Joint Stock Companies

Nature of company		No.	Capital		
			Authorised	Subscribed	Paid-up
			Rs.	Rs.	Rs.
Banking and Loan ...	1921	1	2,50,000	2,50,000	1,40,509
	1931	1	10,00,000	2,50,000	1,25,000
Trading and Manufacturing ...	1921	..	...	...	...
	1931	3	15,20,000	9,66,400	9,49,515
Mills and Presses ...	1921	...	...	...	...
	1931	1	2,00,000	45,100	40,537
Total ...	1921	1	2,50,000	2,50,000	1,40,509
	1931	5	27,20,000	12,61,500	11,15,052

Trade.

33. Statistics showing the trans-frontier trade of the North-West Frontier Province during the decade 1921—1931 do not unfortunately, exist. The two statements below, obtained from the Department of Commercial Intelligence and Statistics, India, give some admittedly incomplete statistics up to the year 1925. Similar statistics for subsequent years are not available owing to the discontinuance of the old system of land frontier trade registration, and the introduction, with effect from the 1st April 1925, of a new system, under which registration is limited to selected commodities only at selected railway stations, adjacent to land frontier routes. Under the new system these railway stations are divided into groups, each group comprising the trade with two or more trans-frontier countries, and the result is that statistics for the trans-frontier trade of the North-West Frontier Province are now merged inextricably in those for the land frontier trade of the whole of India.

North-West Frontier Province

Year	Total	
	Imports	Exports
	Rs.	Rs.
1921-22	1,16,44,717	1,31,25,382
1922-23	94,10,825	1,45,21,024
1923-24	*24,46,646	*97,93,671
1924-25	1,14,25,963	2,22,31,054

* Exclusive of the figures for the months July 1923 to February 1924 for which the returns were not received.

Statement showing main directions of trade of the North-West Frontier Province during each of the years 1921-22 to 1924-25

Countries whence imported / whither exported	Imports				Exports			
	1921-22	1922-23	*1923-24	1924-25	1921-22	1922-23	*1923 24	1924-25
	Rs.	Rs.	Rs.	Rs.	Rs.	Rs.	Rs.	Rs.
Afghanistan ...	19,50,498	45,17,693	7,92,669	51,58,913	17,97,806	50,71,611	70,68,922	1,35,91,323
Tirah ...	5,12,103	6,50,152	2,41,027	10,46,560	10,09,565	10,24,035	4,84,885	13,36,837
Dir, Swat and Bajaur	31,51,038	30,75.788	10,6[illegible],391	35,03,285	65.35,054	65 99,352	14,32,175	51,56,000
Buner ...	1,84,402	1,49,242	48,788	1,32,624	2,82,719	3,27,534	82,455	1,26,066
Waziristan ...	57,80,013	9 67,146	2,87,528	14,82.254	31,44,285	7,48,509	4,56,146	6,43,371
Kurram	66,663	50.804	16,243	1,02,327	3.55,953	7.49.983	2,69,088	13,77,457

* Exclusive of the figures for the months July 1923 to February 1924 for which returns were not received.

Industrial development.

34. A regular survey of the industrial and economic rescources of the North-West Frontier Province was for the first time carried out in 1928, and an interesting report by the Industrial Investigator, Mr. M. A. Rafee, B Sc., was published in 1929. This report not only describes the industries in actual working, but also contains an investigation of the economic resources of the Province with a view to discovering how they can best be exploited. The following quotation from the opening paragraph of Mr. Rafee's introduction to his report well describes the position which industry occupies in the life of the North-West Frontier Province under present conditions :—

> " To bring about a complete transformation in the North-West Frontier "Province—to change its traditions, to alter its atmosphere and to guide a new "the ambitions of its people—would be no light task for any administration to "undertake. This Province has always hitherto been regarded more as a military "than a settled area. Its name has generally been associated with constant unrest "and with the spirit of turbulence. And indeed the past outlook of the people, their "lack of productive pursuits, their constant temptations to engage in deeds of "daring which appeal so strongly to their virile instincts—all these have prevent-"ed a settled economic outlook. The people are poor; as they need must be in "a territory whose soil is apparently unproductive (*sic*). The ignorance in which "they have long remained as to the manner in which the resources which they "possess can profitably be utilised, has prevented them from attaining the same "progress as has occurred in other parts of British India."

That little progress has in fact been made during the last 10 years towards a " settled economic outlook " is well illustrated by the figures in the margin. These figures, however, do not permit an exact comparison to be drawn between the two censuses, as the system adopted at the present Census for classifying earners and dependents according to the various occupations is different from that adopted at previous censuses. It is clear, however, that industry and trade still occupy a comparatively small place in the working life of the Province.

General distribution of the total population of the North-West Frontier Province (districts) by occupation

Occupation	Percentage of actual workers in 1921	Percentage of workers and working dependents in 1931
Agriculture ...	61	62
Industry ...	14	13
Trade ...	7	7
Public Force and Public Administration.	7	6
Miscellaneous ...	11	12

Communications.

35. Considerable attention has been devoted to the extension and improvement of communications during the decade. The statement in the margin shows the progress which has been made in the construction of new metalled and unmetalled

Mileages of metalled and unmetalled roads

Districts	1921			1931		
	Metalled	Unmetalled	Total	Metalled	Unmetalled	Total
Hazara , and Peshawar.	440·03	304·16	744·19	440·03	340·16	744·19
Kohat ...	*111·59	*88·75	*200·34	196·67	181·44	378·11
Bannu ...	56·58	27·12	83·70	82·74	25·62	108·36
Dera Ismail Khan...	194·62	217·38	412·00	237·10	176·25	413·35
Total (districts) ...	802·82	637·41	1,440·23	956·54	687·47	1,644·01
Agencies and Tribal Areas.	126·01	585·28	711·29	332·42	634·63	967·05
Total (North-West Frontier Province).	928·83	1,222·69	2,151·52	1,288·96	1,322·10	2,611·06

* Figures relate to year 1925, those for 1921 not being available.

roads both in the settled districts and in the trans-frontier area since 1921. The progress is most marked in the Kohat, Bannu and Dera Ismail Khan Districts and in trans-frontier areas where it has been mainly confined to Waziristan. In the Peshawar District an important improvement in communications was effected by the replacement of all the boat bridges over the rivers on the Peshawar Shabkadar and Peshawar-Charsadda roads by vibro-concrete pile bridges at a cost of about 8½ lakhs.

Railway construction during the decade comprised the conversion of 40 miles of narrow gauge railway from Nowshera to Durgai into broad gauge in 1921 and the construction of the Khyber Railway (broad gauge) from Jamrud to Landi Khana, a distance of 26 miles, which was opened in 1926.

Buildings and communications in the North-West Frontier Province suffered severely from two unprecedented floods in the River Indus in quick succession on the 18th and 28th August 1929. The first flood was due to the bursting of the famous Shyok Dam, and the second to one week's continuous heavy rain extending over the whole of Kashmir The gauge at Attock Bridge recorded the peak of the first flood at 92-·75 feet, and that of the second at 933·78 feet, the normal monsoon level being 895 feet. Abbottabad and Nathia Gali were completely cut off from Peshawar by the loss of bridges and the breaching of roads and walls, and the raised road from Darya Khan to Dera Ismail Khan with all the bridges was completely washed away. The cost of repairing the damage done, and of re-opening communications permanently has been estimated at Rs. 14,12,558.

In the North-West Frontier Province there is no regular traffic on rivers which are used mainly for floating down timber from the hill forests beyond the Frontier.

Among a large variety of works unconnected with communications may be mentioned the construction of the following public buildings :—The Civil Provincial Lady Reading Hospital, the Provincial Normal Training College, the Government High School, and the Normal School for Women, all at Peshawar, and the large new Central Jail at Haripur which was not quite completed by the end of the decade. The expenditure incurred throughout the Province on roads, buildings and communications, other than irrigation and railways, for each year of the decade is given in the margin.

Year		Expenditure
		Rs.
1920-21	...	29,21,048
1921-22	...	23,12,485
1922-23	...	24,02,862
1923-24	...	39,17,258
1924-25	...	50,98,041
1925-26	...	52,88,791
1926-27	...	50,65,908
1927-28	...	76,21,414
1928-29	...	70,98,692
1929-30	...	88,17,918
Total	...	5,05,44,417

SECTION VI—MOVEMENT OF POPULATION 1921—1931

36. According to the Census of 1931, the population of the five districts of the North-West Frontier Province has increased by 173,736 persons (86,502 males and 87,234 females) during the last 10 years, that is an increment of 7·7 per cent. on the population in 1921. **Variation 1921—1931.**

The figures in the margin show how the percentage of increase is distributed between the sexes and between urban and rural areas. The urban population, though only a small portion of the total population, is yet increasing at a much greater rate than the rural population. The number of urban to 1,000 of the rural population has increased from 175 in 1921 to 189 in 1931. Part of this increase is due to the addition of Mansehra with a population of 5,780 to the list of towns at the present Census, and to the corresponding decrease in the rural population.

		Percentage of increase		
		Persons	Males	Females
N.-W. F. P. districts.	...	7·7	7·0	8·5
Urban areas	...	15·0	9·4	25·0
Rural areas	...	6·4	6·5	6·3

The higher rate of increase among females generally may be largely accounted for by the fact that the Census of 1921 followed closely on the influenza epidemic of 1918, which was considerably more fatal to females then males. This loss in females has still not been fully made up. The proportion of females to 1,000 males has risen from 831 in 1921 to 843 in 1931, but is still less than the figure for 1911, which was 858. In urban areas females have increased very much faster than males; but the change in the sex proportions in towns is largely due to the decrease of military forces, followers, labour corps, etc., stationed in cantonments since 1921.

Increase per cent. different age-groups	Per cent. increase or decrease
All ages ...	+ 7·7
(N.-W. F. P. Districts)	
Under 10 ...	+ 8·2
10 – 15 ..	+ 18·7
15—40 ...	+ 14·9
40 - 60 ...	– 4 3
60 and over ...	– 31·0

The influenza epidemic of 1918 is distinctly reflected in the changes in the age-distribution. The largest increase occurs in those age groups which, 13 years ago, were least affected by the epidemic while there has been a considerable decline in the higher age-groups in which the disease was most fatal. The low birth-rate consequent on the epidemic has produced a correspondingly low increase among children under 10 years of age. The figures in the margin may be compared with those relating to deaths from influenza given in paragraph 20 above.

Variation in population of District.

37. Variations in the population of districts since 1921 are illustrated in diagram No. 9 below. The percentage of variation during each intercensal period since 1881 are shown in Subsidiary Table III. From this table it will be observed that the two districts Kohat and Bannu, which possess the highest percentage increases (10·3 and 9·6 respectively) since 1921, were the only two districts to show a decline in population from 1911—1921. The causes of this decline have been fully set out in paragraphs 57 and 58 of the North-West Frontier Province Census Report for 1921, and have been briefly referred to in paragraph 18 above. It is sufficient to recall here that the Census of 1921 was taken under circumstances which were exceptional as regards the three southern districts in two ways: firstly owing to Frontier disturbances and secondly owing to the prevalence of a severe drought. While disturbances on the Frontier interfered with the usual immigration of Powindah tribesmen from Afghanistan, the drought drove large sections of the resident population of unirrigated tracts either across the border or into other districts in search of food and employment for themselves and fodder for their cattle. The Dera Ismail Khan district was affected by these abnormal conditions no less than Bannu and Kohat, but in Dera Ismail Khan the loss in the resident population was largely made up by the presence of an unusual number of troops in connection with the military operations in Waziristan, and no actual decline in the total population was recorded. These peculiar conditions no longer existed in 1931 when the present Census was taken, as peace had by then been restored on the Frontier, and the Province was not suffering from any seasonal calamity. Among other important changes during the last decade affecting the population returns in the three southern

No.9

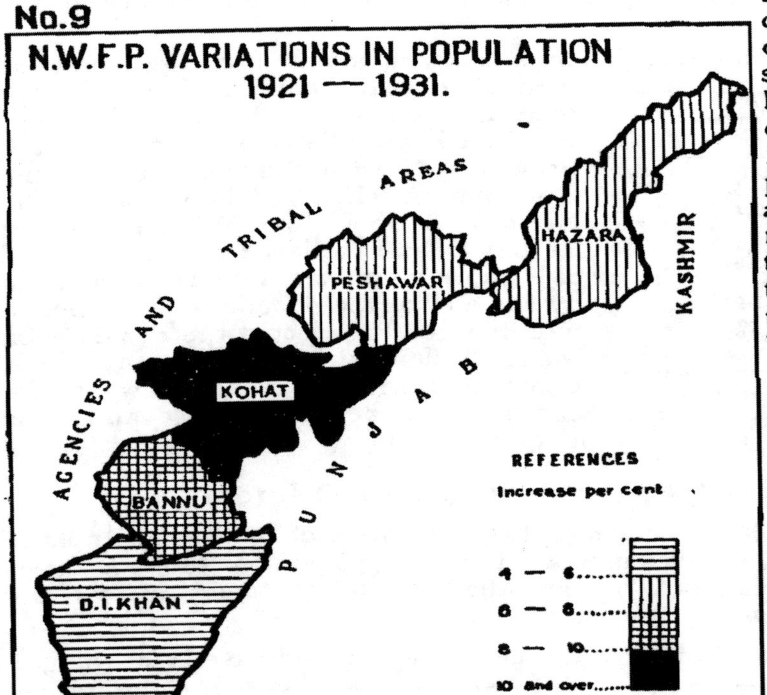

districts must be mentioned the abolition of the military cantonment at Tank, the reduction of almost the whole of the military garrison of Dera Ismail Khan Cantonment, and the large expansion of the Royal Air Force Station at Kohat. The changes in Dera Ismail Khan have seriously undermined the commercial prosperity of this important municipal town, which has also been threatened with complete inundation by the Indus River, and has only been saved by the construction at great expense of a large protecting embankment and wall. But the abnormal conditions prevailing in the south of the Province at the time of the Census of 1921 did not apply in the name degree to the Peshawar and Hazara Districts, which were further removed from the centre of disturbance, and were not appreciably affected by any temporary migration due to the drought. The increase in the Hazara District possesses no abnormal features beyond an unexpectedly large increase in Feudal Tanawal, due probably to more accurate enumeration; and the only exceptional circumstances affecting the increase in the Peshawar District are (1) the transfer from Swat Territory in 1928 of a population of 1,020 persons (534 males and 486 females) belonging to the Malandri tract, not previously censused, and (2) the maintenance of the blockade of the Afridi Tribe throughout the winter of 1930-31, which prevented the usual number of Afridi immigrants from entering the district. The extent to which the Peshawar District population suffered in the latter respect may be judged from the statement in the margin comparing the number of trans-frontier immigrants enumerated in that district in 1921 and 1931.

	Immigration from agencies and tribal areas.	
	1921	1931
Peshawar District ...	25,378	17939

No. 10.

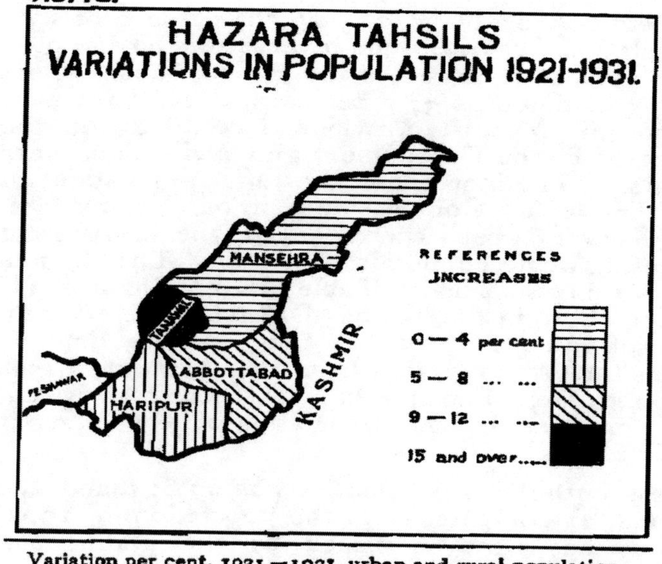

HAZARA TAHSILS
VARIATIONS IN POPULATION 1921-1931.

No. 11.

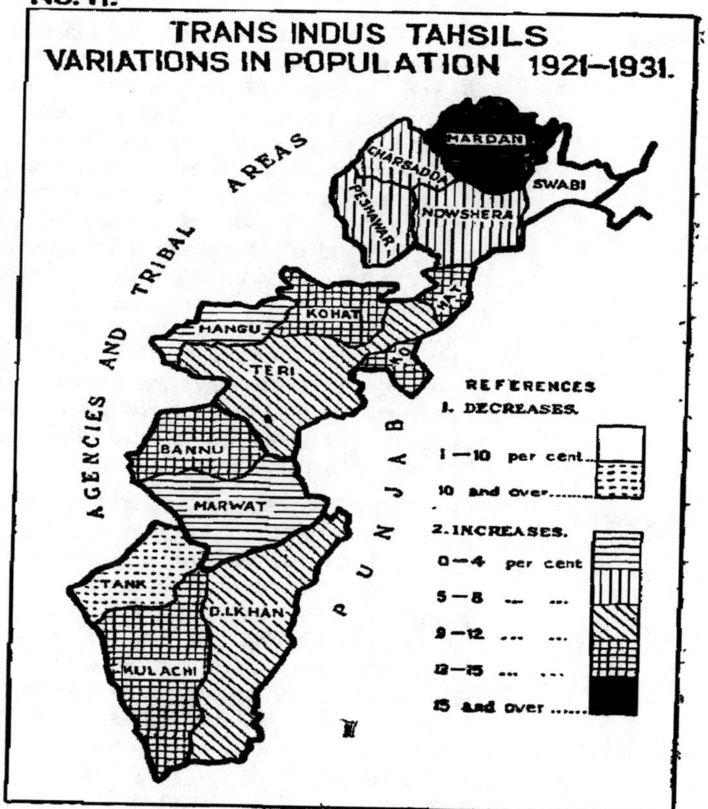

TRANS INDUS TAHSILS
VARIATIONS IN POPULATION 1921—1931.

Variation per cent. 1921—1931, urban and rural population by tahsils

Name of tahsil	Variation in per cent. 1921—1931		
	Total	Urban	Rural
Mansehra ...	+ 3·8	71·5	1·2
Abbottabad ...	+ 9·4	13·8	8·9
Haripur ...	+ 4·8	30·0	3·8
Amb ...	+ 43·9	...	43·9
Phulra ...	+ 16·5	...	16·5
Peshawar ...	+ 5·9	10·2	2·9
Mardan ...	+ 15·7	140·4	7·2
Swabi ...	— 0·5	...	0·5
Nowshera ...	+ 7·9	3·6	9·3
Charsadda ...	+ 8·2	1·6	9·6
Kohat ...	+ 14·4	23·3	9·4
Teri ...	+ 11·7	...	11·7
Hangu ...	+ 0·5	...	0·5
Kulachi ...	+ 14·9	7·0	16·7
Dera Ismail Khan ...	+ 9·6	2·5	22·3
Tank ...	— 14·2	40·8	8·2
Bannu ...	+ 13 6	37·2	9·2
Marwat ...	+ 4·1	3·0	4·1

Variation in Tahsils.

38. We will now deal with the variation in more detail, noting how the population of each tahsil has fared during the last 10 years. Diagrams Nos. 10 and 11 illustrate the variations in cis-Indus and trans-Indus tahsils respectively, and the accompanying statement gives the actual percentage increase and decrease distributed between urban and rural areas. Further

statistics relating to tahsils will be found in Provincial Tables I, II and III at the end of this volume.

Only two tahsils, Swabi and Tank, show a decrease in population since 1921; all the rest show percentage increases varying from 43·9 in Amb State (which is not actually, of course, a tahsil) to 0·5 in Hangu. We will now discuss the tahsil variations, district by district.

Kohat.

Taking that district first which shows the largest increase in population since 1921, we find that the excess of births over deaths in the Kohat District amounted to 16,183. The actual increase was 22,150. It will be recalled that Kohat was the district which showed the greatest decline in population at the Census of 1921, and that this decline was attributed mainly to the temporary emigration of a large section of the population owing to the severe drought then prevailing. It must be assumed therefore that a large proportion of the increase recorded at the present Census is due to the return of these temporary emigrants, as soon as climatic conditions improved. This is specially true of the Teri Tahsil where the increase of 11·7 per cent. exactly sets off the decrease of 11·7 per cent. recorded in 1921. In the Kohat Tahsil, however, the urban population has contributed proportionately more than the rural population to the total increase of 14·4 per cent. This is due to the large expansion of the Royal Air Force Station in Kohat Cantonment during the last 10 years. In the Hangu Tahsil the population has remained almost stationary during the last 20 years. In this connection the Deputy Commissioner has stressed the unhealthiness of the Miranzai Valley, but it may be recalled from paragraph 15 above that the density of the rural population per square mile of cultivated area in this tahsil is almost the largest in the whole Province. From this it would appear that the population of this tahsil has actually reached the limit of its expansion.

Bannu.

The population of the Bannu District has advanced by 23,567 persons or 13·6 per cent as compared with the population in 1921, the excess of births over deaths being 13,639 persons. The increase is largest in the Bannu Tahsil, where the urban population has increased by as much as 37·2 per cent. This increase must be mainly due to the occupation of Waziristan, which has advanced the strategic and commercial importance of Bannu Cantonment and civil town very considerably during the last ten years. The increase in the rural population of the Bannu Tahsil is attributed by the Deputy Commissioner, in part at any rate, to a temporary migration from the Marwat Tahsil, where, as at the Census of 1921, the lack of rain was again causing acute economic distress. The figures for migration between districts shown in Subsidiary Table III of Chapter III indicate that as many as 5,000 persons born in the Bannu District were enumerated in the Dera Ismail Khan District and it is probable that, at the time of the present Census, there was a simultaneous migration from the Marwat Tahsil both into the Bannu Tahsil and also into Dera Ismail Khan District. It is not surprising therefore to find that the increase in the population of the Marwat Tahsil is comparatively small.

Hazara.

The excess of births over deaths in the Hazara District was 29,674 and the actual increase 47,768 or 7·7 per cent. as compared with the population in 1921. The urban population of the district has been increased by the addition of Mansehra (formerly a rural area) to the list of towns, the result being a corresponding loss to the rural population of the Mansehra Tahsil. The urban populations of Abbottabad and Haripur show substantial increases, that in Haripur being to some extent due to the construction of a large new Central Jail, which was nearing completion at the time of the present Census. The large increases in Amb and Phulra States (Eeudal Tanawal, which, in accordance with past practice, we have anomalously treated as a tahsil in the Hazara District) are explained by the Deputy Commissioner as due to better enumeration, and no alternative explanation is forthcoming. The rural population is advancing more rapidly in the Abbottabad Tahsil than in either of the other two tahsils, Mansehra and Haripur, probably owing to the large and flourishing cantonments at Abbottabad and Kakul, which encourage the intensive cultivation of the land in its vicinity and the growth of a population in the neighbouring villages almost entirely dependent on domestic service.

Peshawar.

The percentage increase in population in the Peshawar District since 1921 is 7·4, the actual number of persons having advanced by 66,954. The total number of births registered exceeded the total number of deaths registered by 19,748, of which only 482 were females. As we have already remarked in paragraph 23 above, these figures throw some considerable doubt on the accuracy of the registration of births and deaths in the Peshawar District. Of the five tahsils in this district, Mardan, with a percentage increase of 15·7 is growing the most rapidly, and indeed more rapidly than any other tahsil in the Province. Its growth may be attributed entirely to trade, the large majority of which is in foreign cloth. Mardan Municipality is an important trade centre for the Dir, Swat and Chitral Agency across the border, and for the thickly populated rural areas in the Charsadda, Nowshera and Swabi Tahsils The town was raised to the status of a municipality just before the Census was taken, and the increase of 140·4 per cent. in its population is mainly due to the extension of the urban area and to the inclusion of the large village of Hoti within municipal limits. The population of the Mardan Cantonment shows a slight decrease, due to the temporary absence of troops in Charsadda at the time of the Census. The increase in the rural population apart from natural growth is attributed by the Deputy Commissioner to the opening of minor trade centres at Takht Bhai, Hathian and Parkho, and to the extension of the area under irrigation from the Upper Swat Canal, on which large numbers of trans-border Mohmand tribesmen have recently settled as tenants.

In the Peshawar Tahsil most of the increase relates to the urban population of Peshawar Municipality and Cantonment where there would have been a still larger increase, but for the military blockade of the Afridi Tribe which prevented the usual number of immigrants from entering the district. In the Nowshera and Charsadda Tahsils the main increase is among the rural population, there being a slight decrease in the cantonment populations of Nowshera and Risalpur. The urban population of the Charsadda Tahsil has made very small progress probably owing to the fact that it is strictly rural in character, this tahsil possessing no town in the true sense of the word. The decrease in the population of Tangi, for instance, is due to the fact that a large number of the residents have in recent years left their original homes and settled on the lands newly irrigated by the Upper Swat Canal. There was a fall of 0·5 per cent. in the population of the Swabi Tahsil, which is entirely rural. The decrease being a small one, it is difficult to attribute it to any particular cause. It may be remarked, however, that this tahsil is situated in the easternmost corner of the Peshawar District, sandwiched between the River Indus and the Gadun hills, without railway communication, and with very poor facilities for marketing its agricultural produce. These conditions are obviously not conducive to a healthy growth of population.

Dera Ismail Khan. The district which shows the smallest percentage increase since 1921 (5·1) is Dera Ismail Khan. During the decade, 14,365 more births were registered than deaths, but the actual population advanced by only 13,297 persons, all of which were females. Males actually decreased by 544. This curious result is due to the presence of an abnormally large number of troops at the time of the Census of 1921, when the Dera Ismail Khan District formed the base of the military operations against the Mahsuds in Waziristan; it is due also to the removal of the military garrisons from the Tank and the Dera Ismail Khan Cantonments during the decade. The abnormal conditions in 1921 are also reflected in the increases of 22·3 and 16·7 per cent. in the rural population of the Dera Ismail Khan and Kulachi Tahsils respectively. In the Census of that year, the absence of the Powindah tribesmen from their allotted grazing grounds in these tahsils caused a marked decline in the rural population, which the increases recorded at the present Census have hardly made up, although in February 1931, the Powindah immigrants were present again in their customary strength. The truth is that there is nothing in the broad arid plains of these tahsils, dependent for cultivation on the vagaries of an uncertain rainfall, to encourage any substantial increase in population. The existing resources are indeed barely sufficient to maintain the present population. We have already indicated most of the factors which accounted for the large decline of 14·2 per cent. in the population of the Tank Tahsil. The rapid rise of 25·6 per cent. recorded in 1921 was occasioned by the presence of a large number of troops, stationed in Tank Cantonment in connection with the Waziristan operations. The subsequent withdrawal of these troops and the abolition of Tank Cantonment are the natural causes of the decrease at the present Census.

Variations in density.

39. Variations in relation to density since 1881 will be found in Subsidiary Table III. The variations in individual districts during the last decade are also illustrated in the diagram No. 12, the most striking feature of which is the large increase in the density of the Peshawar and Hazara Districts. In the Peshawar District, the increase, amounting to 21 persons per square mile, is mainly due to urban growth. The same may be said of the increase of 15 persons per square mile in the Hazara District, where the urban areas in Haripur and Abbottabad show a substantial increase in population. In the Bannu and Kohat Districts where the density has increased by 12 and 8 persons per square mile respectively, urban areas are again largely responsible, but in Dera Ismail Khan, the small increase of 4 persons per square mile must be attributed entirely to the rural population, as urban areas in Dera Ismail Khan and Tank showed considerable decreases in population during the last decade.

No. 12

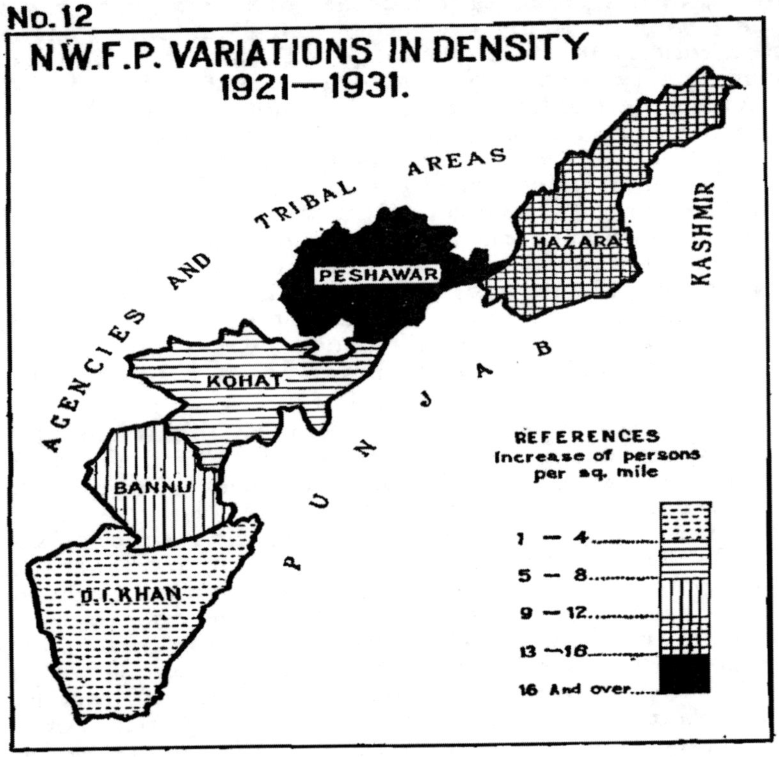

Effect of health on variation in population of districts.

40. The statement in the margin compares the Vital Statistics recorded in each district with the actual percentage increase in population during the decade. The districts are arranged in order according to the average birth-rate per *mille* which it will be seen varies inversely with the average death-rate. If Peshawar is the healthiest district in the Province it also has the lowest birth-rate, and if Kohat is the unhealthiest district, it enjoys the advantage of the highest birth rate. The figures will raise doubts as to the accuracy of the registration of births and deaths, at any rate in the Peshawar District, which we have previously mentioned in connection with inaccurate registration in paragraph 23 above. Further research into the exact relation between health and variations in population is beyond the scope of a Census, but the above figures might well repay a deeper study.

District	Average birth-rate	Average death-rate	Increase per cent
Kohat	34·5	27·0	10·3
Dera Ismail Khan ...	30·5	25·0	5·1
Bannu ...	29·3	23·0	9·6
Hazara ...	27·1	22·7	7·7
Peshawar ...	23·1	20·9	7·4

Effect of migration.

41. From Subsidiary Table IV it will be observed that the percentage increase in the natural population of the five districts (that is, the population which would exist if there had been no migration at all) is 9·5 as compared with the actual percentage increase of 7·7. That the balance of migration has become less and less in favour of the five settled districts during the last 20 years will be evident from the figures in the margin. The decrease in the number of immigrants is not so marked as the increase in the number of emigrants, which is an indication that the population of these districts is feeling the pressure on resources. Though the proportion of

North-West Frontier Province Districts

	1911	1921	1931
Immigrants ...	184,504	163,502	155,191
Emigrants ...	64,591	75,618	99,896
Balance ...	119,913	87,884	55,295

immigrants to the total population is only 6·4 per cent., these immigrants are an important factor in the life of the Province, and will receive more detailed attention in Chapter III of this report. Migration between districts is limited to small scale movements of a purely temporary nature, the largest being the temporary migration (on account of lack of rain) of about 5,000 persons from unirrigated tracts in the Marwat Tahsil of the Bannu District into the Dera Ismail Khan District in search of employment and fodder for their cattle.

Pressure on resources.

42. A slight acquaintance with Census statistics reveals the fact that many temporary variations are apt to occur in the course of a single intercensal period, which conceal the true growth of population. That the last decade suffers peculiarly from this defect will be evident from a comparison of the population figures of the present Census with those of the Census of 1921, which was taken under particularly abnormal conditions. To measure the true growth of population, therefore, we must widen our survey so as to cover several intercensal periods, as this will tend to eliminate variations which are of a temporary nature only. In the statement in the margin the percentage increases shown against each district since 1891 (the first really accurate Census) give some idea of the true growth of population during the last forty years.

Percentage increase in population by districts from 1891—1931

District	Percentage increase 1891—1931
N.-W. F. P. (Districts)	30·6
Hazara ...	29·8
Peshawar ...	36·9
Kohat ...	21·1
Bannu ...	32·2
D. I. Khan ...	19·3

The question now arises as to how far this growth has been impeded by what is known as "a pressure on resources". To examine this problem in detail is beyond the scope of a Census Report and we can here only point to indications (where they exist) that the growth of population is exceeding the local means of production. It should be noted first of all that the North-West Frontier Province is in a peculiar position in this respect compared to the rest of India. The importance of the "North-West Frontier" as an Imperial as well as an "All-India" responsibility has always been recognised as a justification for its dependence on more than purely local resources, for the administration of the five Frontier districts, for the control of the border tribes, and for the promotion of those civilising influences, such as roads and canals, which make an important contribution towards the establishment of permanently peaceful conditions. Thus the growth of population in the five border districts during the last forty years, as illustrated above, has not been achieved with the help of local resources alone. The wealth expended in this small corner of India has in fact been out of all proportion to the local means of production. It would be unwise, however, to assume that outside resources will always be available to provide the means of subsistence for an unlimited increase in population. The present world-wide financial stringency is a reminder of the perils of uneconomic administration, and, furthermore, the permanent dependence of one community on another for its means of subsistence must have a degrading effect on the moral of the former. We may expect therefore that, as the peace of the border becomes more firmly established, the sphere of Imperial responsibility will be narrowed down and the people of the North-West Frontier Province will be called upon to rely more and more on their own resources for the conduct of their affairs. The development of these resources to their utmost limit is thus likely to engage the earnest attention of future Governments of the Province.

In the earlier paragraphs of this chapter, we have endeavoured to show that agriculture, the main existing source of wealth, has almost reached the limit of its expansion and that the last ten years have indeed placed an increasing strain on the agriculturist, which will only be intensified by any further world depreciation of agricultural products. On the other hand, during the last decade, new and expensive needs have arisen owing to the spread of education and the awakening of a new political consciousness. The prospect of meeting these needs from local resources under existing conditions is gloomy enough, but when it is realised that the North-West Frontier Province (like other parts of India where birth control is unknown or unpractised) is faced with the certainty, apart from unforeseen calamity, of an increase in population during the coming decade either equivalent to, or only slightly less than, that which has occurred during the last decade, the prospect becomes gloomier still. The people of the five border districts have so much social and political headway to make up that an increase in population, unless accompanied by a simultaneous increase in wealth and productive efficiency, must be regarded as a positive danger. If there is one sure means of avoiding a future of poverty, discontent and destructive agitation, it is the development of that settled economic outlook, which is at present so foreign to the Pathan temperament, but which is yet so essential to all human progress under modern conditions.

SECTION VII—HOUSES AND FAMILIES.

Definition of house.

43. Two definitions of house have in the past been in use for Census purposes one based on the "structural" house, and the other on the "social" household. The former, which defined the house as the residence of one or more families with a separate independent entrance leading out of the common way, was abandoned in 9 as being capable of too wide an interpretation. The latter based on the social household or commensal family, is the one used at the last three censuses. According to this definition, "house" means the dwelling-place of one commensal family with its resident dependents, such as widows and servants. At the present Census, the principle contained in this definition was applied as far as possible to hotels and *serais* in towns, where each room or suite of rooms allotted to a different traveller or family was treated as a separate house; so also in the case of large bungalows, each tenement in a row of servants' quarters was treated as a separate house. Thus the Census definition of house adopted since 1911 affords an important clue to the average size of the family in the North-West Frontier Province.

The number of houses and size of families.

44. In view of the change in the definition of house, the figures in the margin (taken from Subsidiary Table VII (showing the number of persons per house and the number of houses per square mile will only bear comparison with one another from 1911 onwards. The actual numbers of occupied houses in districts and tahsils will be found in Imperial Table I and Provincial Table I. The average number of houses to the square mile is about the same as for the rest of India, but would have been very much lower but for the Peshawar and Hazara Districts where there are 72·1 and 47·9 houses respectively to the square mile. There is no reason to believe that, in a predominantly Muslim community, there has been any variation of importance in the average size of the family for many years; but it is of interest to note that urban families are slightly larger than rural families on the whole as the marginal statement shows. This may be due to the difficulty of allotting house numbers correctly to hotels and *serais* in towns containing travellers, and also possibly to the presence of a larger proportion of Hindus and Sikhs in towns than in rural areas.

Census		Persons per house	Houses per square mile
1881	...	6·0	15·0
1891	...	6·1	17·9
1901	...	6·0	21·3
1911	...	5·0	32·4
1921	...	5·2	32·6
1931	...	5·0	36·0

Districts, etc.		Average number of persons per house	
		In towns	In villages
N.-W. F. P. (districts)	...	5·2	4·9
Hazara	...	5·0	4·6
Trans-Indus districts	...	5·3	5·1
Peshawar	...	5·3	5·1
Kohat	...	6·5	5·2
Bannu	...	5·2	5·5
Dera Ismail Khan	...	4·7	4·7

SUBSIDIARY TABLE I—*Density, water-supply and crops*

District and natural division	Mean density per square mile in 1931	Percentage of total area		Percentage of cultivated area which is irrigated	Normal rainfall	Percentage of cultivated area under			
		Culturable	Cultivated			Wheat	Barley	Maize	Jowar, bajra and other cereals
1	2	3	4	5	6	7	8	9	10
N.-W. F. P. (total districts) ...	179	58	34	26·9	18·6	36·6	7·7	15·9	21·3
Hazara	223	52	27	9·2	43·8	30·8	9·1	42·7	13·5
Total Districts, Trans-Indus ...	167	60	35	30·2	12·1	37·6	7·5	10·8	22·7
Peshawar	369	72	51	56·6	12·2	39·7	17·0	23·2	7·4
Kohat	88	30	19	11·2	16·2	41·6	2·7	5·9	29·8
Bannu	159	70	50	22·6	10·8	40·5	2·9	7·4	2·3
Dera Ismail Khan ...	79	69	30	12·1	9·8	30·7	1·4	0·1	55·4
Trans-frontier area ...	99	...	...	...	...	...	...	...	...

Note.—Figures in column 2 have been calculated from survey area figures given in Imperial Table I. Figures in columns 3 to 5 and 7 to 10 have been calculated from area given in agricultural reports for 1929-30. The figures for rainfall in column 6 represent the average annual rainfall recorded at district headquarters during the decade 1921—1930.

SUBSIDIARY TABLE I-A—*Statistics of density and rainfall, irrigated and cultivated area for tahsils*

Tahsil and district	Area in square miles	Percentage of total area		Rainfall in inches	Number of persons per square mile of cultivated area	Rural population	Rural population per square mile	Rural population per square mile of cultivated area
		Cultivated	Irrigated					
1	2	3	4	5	6	7	8	9
N.-W. F. P. (districts) ...	13,518	34	9	...	552	2,038,899	151	464
Hazara District ...	3,009	27	3	43·81	910	628,132	209	409
Mansehra	1,449	20	2	35·61	799	195,623	131	730
Abbottabad	699	33	2	43·81	1,250	232,484	340	1,171
Haripur	651	38	5	27·21	735	162,082	249	702
Tanawal	210	...	...	...	...	37,943	181	...
Peshawar District ...	2,637	51	29	12·25	739	757,898	287	575
Peshawar	455	47	33	12·25	1,322	157,081	345	744
Charsadda	383	69	56	13·40	674	147,407	385	558
Swabi	471	60	19	27·59	560	158,411	336	560
Mardan	623	63	39	21·55	523	172,282	277	453
Nowshera	705	26	8	16·60	892	122,717	174	682
Kohat District	2,703	19	2	16·27	463	201,923	75	396
Kohat	745	17	5	16·27	674	53,960	72	412
Teri	1,533	22	0	19·09	307	103,011	67	307
Hangu	425	10	3	24·63	1,045	44,952	106	1,045
Bannu District	1,698	50	21	10·80	323	232,059	137	277
Bannu	462	51	26	10·80	683	131,343	284	554
Marwat	1,236	50	6	11·18	181	100,716	81	168
Dera Ismail Khan District ...	3,471	30	4	9·80	267	218,887	63	212
Dera Ismail Khan ...	1,736	34	2	9·80	287	130,688	75	220
Tank	646	30	12	12·51	271	44,773	69	237
Kulachi	1,089	23	2	8·68	210	43,426	40	176

SUBSIDIARY TABLE II—*Distribution of the population classified according to density*

Districts, etc.	Tahsil with a population per square mile of															
	under 100		100—150		150—200		200—300		300—350		350—450		450—600		600—650	
	Area	Population (000's omitted).	Area	Population (000's omitted).	Area	Population (000's omitted).	Area	Population (000's omitted).	Area	Population (000's omitted).	Area	Population (000's omitted).	Area	Population (000's omitted).	Area	Population (000's omitted).
1	2	3	4	5	6	7	8	9	10	11	12	13	14	15	16	17
N.-W. F. P. (Districts)	6,240 *15·9*	486 *10·4*	2,619 *6·0*	342 *7·3*	210 *0·5*	38 *0·8*	1,356 *3·5*	329 *7·0*	1,556 *4·0*	519 *11·1*	699 *1·8*	254 *5·4*	383 *0·9*	178 *3·8*	455 *1·2*	279 *5·9*
Hazara ...	... ...	... ...	1,449 *3·7*	209 *4·5*	210 *0·5*	38 *0·8*	651 *1·7*	169 *3·6*	... ...	... ...	699 *1·8*	254 *5·4*	... ...	... ...	... ...	... ...
Trans-Indus Districts.	6,240 *15·9*	486 *10·4*	1,170 *2·9*	133 *2·8*	... ...	... ...	705 *1·8*	160 *3·4*	1,556 *4·0*	519 *11·1*	... ...	... ...	383 *0·9*	178 *3·8*	455 *1·2*	279 *5·9*
Peshawar ...	... ...	... ...	... ...	... ...	... ...	... ...	705 *1·8*	160 *3·4*	1,094 *2·8*	357 *7·6*	... ...	... ...	383 *0·9*	178 *3·8*	455 *1·2*	279 *5·9*
Kohat ...	1,533 *3·9*	103 *2·2*	1,170 *2·9*	133 *2·8*	... ...	... ...	... ...	... ...	... ...	... ...	... ...	... ...	... ...	... ...	... ...	... ...
Bannu ...	1,236 *3·1*	109 *2·3*	... ...	... ...	... ...	... ...	... ...	... ...	462 *1·2*	162 *3·5*	... ...	... ...	... ...	... ...	... ...	... ...
Dera Ismail Khan	3,471 *8·9*	274 *5·9*	... ...	... ...	... ...	... ...	... ...	... ...	... ...	... ...	... ...	... ...	... ...	... ...	... ...	... ...

SUBSIDIARY TABLE III—*Variation in relation to density since 1881*

District and Natural Division.	Percentage of variation. Increase (+) decrease (−)					Percentage of nett variation	Mean density per square mile					
	1921—1931	1911—1921	1901—1911	1891—1901	1881—1891	1881—1931	1931	1921	1911	1901	1891	1881
1	2	3	4	5	6	7	8	9	10	11	12	13
N.-W. F. P. (Districts)	+7·7	+2·5	+7·6	+9·9	+17·9	+53·9	179	168	164	152	138	117
Hazara ...	+7·7	+3·2	+7·6	+8·5	+26·8	+64·6	223	208	207	188	173	136
Trans-Indus Districts.	+7·7	+2·2	+7·6	+10·4	+14·7	+50·1	167	156	152	142	129	112
Peshawar ...	+7·4	+4·9	+9·6	+10·8	+17·1	+60·3	369	348	332	303	273	233
Kohat ...	+10·3	−3·8	+2·2	+11·6	+11·6	+35·2	87	79	82	81	72	65
Bannu ...	+9·6	−1·3	+10·3	+10·9	+11·8	+47·9	159	147	149	135	122	109
Dera Ismail Khan ...	+5·1	+1·8	+3·3	+7·8	+12·8	+34·5	79	75	74	72	66	59

SUBSIDIARY TABLE IV—*Variation in natural population*

District and natural division	Population in 1931				Population in 1921				Variation per cent (1921–1931) in natural population increase (+) decrease (—)
	Actual population	Immi-grants	Emi-grants	Natural population	Actual population	Immi-grants	Emi-grants	Natural population	
1	2	3	4	5	6	7	8	9	10
N.-W. F. P. (districts) ...	2,425,076	155,191	99,896	2,369,781	2,251,340	163,540	75,618	2,163,456	9·5
Hazara	670,117	15,869	...	...	622,349	18,232	31,154	635,271	..
Peshawar ...	974,321	84,850	...	...	907,367	90,783	34,371	850,955	...
Kohat	236,273	23,185	...	...	214,123	24,240	16,483	206,366	...
Bannu	270,301	17,368	...	...	246,734	17,557	8,109	237,286	...
Dera Ismail Khan ...	274,064	38,584	...	...	260,767	44,684	11,686	227,769	...

Note.—(1) Excludes emigrants enumerated in Madras Presidency and States who were not separately sorted. For last Census figures see Subsidiary Table IV, Chapter III, 1921 Census Report.

(2) The term "actual population" means the population actually present at the time of the Census irrespective of birth-place "Natural population" means the population born in the districts irrespective of the place of enumeration.

SUBSIDIARY TABLE V—*Comparison with vital statistics*

District and natural division	In 1921—1930 total number of		Number per cent. of population of 1921		Excess (+ or deficiency (—) of births over deaths	Increase (+) or decrease (—) of population of 1931 compared with 1921	
	Births	Deaths	Births	Deaths		Natural population	Actual population
1	2	3	4	5	6	7	8
N.-W. F. P. (districts) ...	603,870	508,261	26·8	26·6	+95,609	+206,325	+173,736
Hazara	168,850	139,176	27.1	22·4	+29,674	Not available.	+47,768
Trans-Indus Districts ...	435,020	369,085	26·7	22·7	+65,935		+125,968
Peshawar	209,276	189,517	23·1	20·9	+19,759		+66,954
Kohat	73,908	57,733	34·5	27·0	+16,175		+22,150
Bannu	72,408	56,770	29·3	23·0	+15,638		+23,567
Dera Ismail Khan ...	79,428	65,065	30·5	25·0	+14,363		+13,297

Note.—(1) No vital statistics being available for Feudal Tanawal (Amb and Phulra States) and Kaghan Valley, the population of these tracts has been omitted in calculating columns 4 and 5.

(2) This table includes births and deaths registered in cantonments.

SUBSIDIARY TABLE VI—*Variation by tahsils classified according to density*

(*a*) ACTUAL VARIATION

Natural division	Decade	Variation in tahsils with a population per square mile at beginning of decade of				
		Under 150	150—300	300—450	450—600	600—750
1	2	3	4	5	6	7
N.-W. F. P. (districts)	1881—1891	+146,445	+95,121	+48,183	...	...
	1891—1901	+70,042	+82,187	+31,786	...	...
	1901—1911	+38,831	+77,428	+25,559	+13,581	...
	1911—1921	−3,433	+34,196	+22,058	+1,586	...
	1921—1931	+47,448	+29,967	+67,180	+13,422	+15,719
Hazara	1881—1891	+50,640	+58,573	...	...	...
	1891—1901	+17,084	+26,916	...	...	...
	1901—1911	+14,316	+28,424	...	...	...
	1911—1921	+4,063	+4,276	+10,982	...	...
	1921—1931	+7,781	+18,242	+21,745	...	...
Trans-Indus districts	1881—1891	+95,805	+36,548	+48,183	...	...
	1891—1901	+52,958	+55,271	+31,786	...	...
	1901—1911	+24,515	+49004	+25,559	+13,581	...
	1911—1921	−7,496	+29,920	+11,076	+1,586	...
	1921—1931	+39,667	+11,725	+45,435	+13,422	+15,719

(*b*) PROPORTIONATE VARIATION

Natural division	Decade	Variation per cent. in tahsils with a population per square mile at beginning of decade of				
		Under 150	150—300	300—450	450—600	600—750
1	2	3	4	5	6	7
N.-W. F. P. (districts)	1881—1891	+18·7	+20·1	+15·6	...	...
	1891—1901	+10·4	+9·9	+8·9	...	...
	1901—1911	+5·2	+10·2	+8·9	+5·5	...
	1911—1921	−·4	+7·1	+3·2	+0·6	...
	1921—1931	+6·1	+8·8	+9·5	+8·2	+5·9
Hazara	1881—1891	+34·6	+22·5	...	...	...
	1891—1901	+10·3	+7·7	...	...	...
	1901—1911	+7·8	+7·5	...	...	...
	1911—1921	+1·8	+2·6	+4·7	...	...
	1921—1931	+3·3	+9·7	+9·4	...	...
Trans-Indus districts	1881—1891	+15·1	+17·1	+15·6	...	...
	1891—1901	+10·1	+11·7	+8·9	...	...
	1901—1911	+4·4	+12·8	+8·9	+5·5	...
	1911—1921	−1·3	+9·3	+2·4	+0·6	...
	1921—1931	+6·8	+7·9	+8·8	+8·2	+5·9

SUBSIDIARY TABLE VII—*Persons per house and houses per square mile*

District and natural division	Average number of persons per house						Average number of houses per square mile					
	1931	1921	1911	1901	1891	1881	1931	1921	1911	1901	1891	1881
1	2	3	4	5	6	7	8	9	10	11	12	13
N.-W. F. P. (districts)...	5·0	5·2	5·0	6·0	6·1	6·0	36·0	32·6	32·4	21·3	17·9	15·0
Hazara ...	4·6	5·0	4·7	5·5	6·3	6·0	47·9	42·2	42·0	33	27	25
Trans-Indus Districts...	5·1	5·2	5·1	6·2	6·0	6·1	32·6	29·9	29·0	22·0	16·0	18·0
Peshawar ...	5·1	5·2	5·2	6·4	6·6	6·7	72·1	66·5	63	46	44	42
Kohat ...	5·4	5·3	5·2	7·3	8·9	8·2	16·3	14·9	15	10	8	9
Bannu ...	5·4	5·2	5·5	6·2	5·6	5·8	29·3	28·2	27	22	18	18
Dera Ismail Khan ...	4·8	5·1	4·7	5·1	4·9	4·9	16·9	14·7	16	14	10	12

CHAPTER II

THE POPULATION OF CITIES, TOWNS AND VILLAGES

SECTION I—GENERAL

Reference to Imperial and Subsidiary Tables.

45. Statistics illustrating the distribution of the population in urban and rural areas by categories of those who live in cities, towns and villages are exhibited in Imperial Tables I, III, IV and V, and in the four Subsidiary Tables at the end of this chapter.

Definition of village.

46. As on previous occasions, the Census definition of "village" was identical with that of estate (*mauza*) given in Section 3 of the Punjab Land Revenue Act, *viz.* :—

"Estate" means any area—

(*a*) for which a separate record-of-rights has been made ; or

(*b*) which has been separately assessed to Land Revenue or would have been assessed, if the Land Revenue had not been released, compounded for or redeemed ; or

(*c*) which the Local Government may, by general rule, or special order, declare to be an estate.

The Census village is therefore not a unit of residence but a unit of area, inhabited or not, into which the country has been divided for the administration of Land Revenue. As a rule each Census village in the plains contains one main residential site, sometimes fortified by an outer wall and towers for protection against raiders. But these single fortified village sites represent a phase of Frontier life which is gradually disappearing. The complete restoration of peace after the disturbances which accompanied the 3rd Afghan War, has enabled the agriculturist of the plain districts to take less thought for his own protection and to devote more to the interests of his land. Thus, in the Peshawar and Bannu Districts where facilities for irrigation encourage intensive cultivation, a larger proportion of the agricultural population will now be found living in hamlets (*bandas*) or isolated groups of homesteads built apart from the main residential site for the protection and better cultivation of outlying fields. In the hilly tracts of the Hazara District there are no large residential sites, the houses generally lie scattered over the hill sides, each in the centre of a small patch of cultivation, and there is nothing which corresponds to a village in the ordinary sense of the word.

Definition of town.

47. For Census purposes a town has been defined as follows :—

Town includes—

(1) every municipality ;

(2) all Civil Lines not included within municipal limits ;

(3) every cantonment ;

(4) every other continuous collection of houses inhabited by not less than 5,000 persons which the Provincial Superintendent may decide to treat as a town for Census purposes.

While the first 3 categories of the above definition cover places with more or less urban characteristics, the fourth category introduces places in which the urban element is not so clearly distinguishable.

In dealing with questions arising under category (4), therefore, the Provincial Superintendent was required to take into consideration the character of the population, the relative density of the dwellings, the importance of the place as a centre of trade, and its historic associations, and to bear in mind that it was undesirable to treat as towns overgrown villages which had no urban characteristics.

The only places which fall under the fourth category in the North-West Frontier Province are Charsadda, Prang and Tangi in the Peshawar District, and Mansehra in the Hazara District. Of these, Prang and Tangi have been classed as towns since the Census of 1881 (Imperial Table IV) mainly on account of their size and importance as centres for the distribution of the produce of the neighbourhood. Contrary to expectation, however, they have since made little or no progress towards the development of urban characteristics, and are still, in reality, nothing more than overgrown villages. The population of Tangi has actually decreased during the last decade, and there has been no particularly encouraging increase in the population of Prang. It must be admitted, therefore, that there is little justification for the continued classification of these two places as towns. Charsadda and Mansehra on the other hand derive a definite urban character from the fact that they are headquarters of sub divisions.

Definition of city.

48. A city has been defined as meaning—

(1) every town containing not less than 100,000 inhabitants ;

(2) any other town which the Provincial Superintendent with the sanction of the Local Government may decide to treat as a city for Census purposes.

As before there is only one city in the North-West Frontier Province, namely Peshawar, but it should be noted that, while at the last Census, Peshawar "City" included both the cantonment and the municipality, at the present Census it comprises the municipality only, Peshawar Cantonment forming a separate town. The reason for this change will be found explained in paragraph 60 below.

Comparison of urban and rural population.

49. Of the 2,856 inhabited urban and rural "places" into which the Province is divided, the population of the 26 towns (including municipal and non-municipal towns, and treating cantonments as separate towns) amounted to 386,177 persons, while the population of the villages (numbering 2,830) was 2,038,899. Thus the proportion now living under urban and rural conditions may broadly be regarded as 16 and 84 per cent. respectively. The marginal table, giving similar statistics of earlier Censuses, shows that the large predominance of the rural as compared with the urban population has always existed, and that though there has been a slight increase in the proportion of the urban population since 1911, there is yet no marked tendency for the population to congregate in towns.

		1881	1891	1901	1911	1921	1931
Number of places	Urban...	15	17	18	19	19	26
	Rural ...	Not available		3,150	3,033	3,356	2,830
Percentage of total population.	Urban...	12	13	13	13	15	16
	Rural ..	88	87	78	87	85	84

The figures in the margin enable a comparison to be made with the proportions of the urban and rural population in other provinces and States, adjacent to the North-West Frontier Province.

Name of Province or State	Proportion per cent. of the total population	
	Urban	Rural
Baluchistan (districts) ...	19·9	80·1
N.-W. F. P. (districts) ...	15·9	84·1
Punjab (British territory)	12·4	87·6
Kashmir State ...	9·4	90·5

The number of towns and villages.

50. There are 26 towns and 2,830 villages in the 5 settled districts of the North-West Frontier Province as compared with 19 towns and 3,356 villages in 1921. The reasons for these variations must be given in some detail. As explained in the fly leaf to Imperial Table III, the figures quoted in this report for the number of villages indicate the number of *inhabited* villages only. The boundaries of these villages are often altered in the course of a district "settlement", and variations both in the total number of village estates, and in the number inhabited or uninhabited occur in consequence. The settlement which took place in the Peshawar District during the last decade is mainly

responsible for an increase of 59 inhabited villages in that district since the Census of 1921; but the decrease of as many as 526 in the total number of inhabited villages in the Province since 1921 is due to a decrease of 587 villages in Feudal Tanawal, for which a short explanation is necessary. The population of the tract known as Feudal Tanawal, though included in the Census population of the Hazara District since 1881, is strictly separate. The political status of the Amb and Phulra States, which comprise Feudal Tanawal, is a curious one, and will be found described fully in Chapter VII of the *Hazara District Gazetteer* of 1907. It is sufficient to state here that, with the exception of certain criminal offences, the internal administration of the two States, including the collection of revenue, is vested in their chiefs and that the Punjab Land Revenue Act, and consequently the Census definition of a "village", do not apply. In Feudal Tanawal, therefore, there are no clearly defined village estates and the formation of villages for Census purposes was left, as in previous censuses, to the discretion of the Census staff. At the last Census each hamlet was treated as a separate village, but, at the present Census, it was found more convenient to group a number of hamlets together and to treat them as one village. The large decrease thus occasioned in the number of villages in Feudal Tanawal is due merely to a change in the organisation of the Census. Detailed statistics regarding this tract will be found in Provincial Tables I and II.

The increase from 26 to 19 in the number of towns since the last Census is due to the fact that 7 cantonments in the Province (Abbottabad, Peshawar, Mardan, Nowshera, Kohat, Bannu and Dera Ismāil Khan) have been treated on this occasion as separate towns, instead of being subordinated to the municipalities and civil lines adjacent to them, as in previous censuses. Besides these 7 cantonments, there are others, namely Tank (subordinated to Tank Notified Area at the last Census and Jamrud, which, though appearing in the statistics of former censuses, have been omitted at the present Census from the list of towns. Of these, the former was abolished entirely during the last decade and the latter, which is not (and probably never was, a regular cantonment, has been held to be situated in the Khyber Agency, outside the boundaries of the Peshawar District, and has accordingly been classed as a "trans-frontier post". A glance at the statement in Note 4 on the fly leaf of Imperial Table IV will show that the omission of Tank and Jamrud Cantonments this Census has occasioned a loss of 10,611 persons to the urban population. This loss has been partly recouped by the addition of Mansehra, the headquarters of a sub division in the Hazara District, with a population of 5,780. The net result is a decrease of 4,831 persons in the urban population, due solely to changes in the list of towns. The mere treatment of cantonments as separate towns has, of course, had no effect on the figures for the total urban population.

SECTION II—URBAN AREAS.

General distribution of urban population.

51. Detailed statistics for towns arranged *(a)* by certain population classes and *(b)* by territorial units will be found in Imperial Tables IV and V. The separation of cantonments from the towns adjacent to them, explained in the preceding paragraph, has occasioned certain changes in these tables, which must be taken into account when comparisons are drawn with previous censuses. Such changes are noticeable in the distribution of towns and villages by population classes in Imperial Tables III and IV, where the splitting up of single towns into two separate units has in most cases relegated both to a lower class of town. Peshawar City, for instance, at the last Census included both Peshawar Cantonment and Peshawar Municipality and ranked in the population class "100,000 and over", but is now reduced, owing to the treatment of Peshawar Cantonment as a separate town, to Peshawar Municipality only, with a population of 87,440, and ranks in the class 50,000 to 100,000, while Peshawar Cantonment falls into a lower class still. In Imperial Table IV, however, it has still been possible to give variations in the populations of towns since 1881, as the separate figures shown for municipalities and cantonments in previous census tables, are available for purposes of comparison. The distribution of towns and the urban population by territorial units in Imperial Table V has not been affected by the change, except that the number of towns situated in each district has automatically increased. The treatment of cantonments as separate towns has the advantage of accentuating an important aspect of urban life in the North-West Frontier Province. Cantonments with their strong military garrisons are more urbanised and less rural than municipalities and other places treated as towns, which invariably contain a considerable population which is agricultural in character.

Apart from cantonments, there is a definite distinction between those towns whose main urban characteristic is that they have attained local self-government in the form of a Municipal or Notified Area Committee, and those which, not possessing that characteristic, are not easily distinguishable from an overgrown village. The statement in the margin shows how the urban population is distributed among these various classes of towns, the classification following generally the four clauses of the Census definition of a town given in paragraph 47 above.

	Number	Population	Percentage of total urban population
Total towns ...	26	386,177	100
Municipalities, Notified Areas and Civil Lines.	13	263,380	68·2
Cantonments ...	9	86,564	22·4
Other towns ...	4	36,233	9·4

Growth of urban population.

52. In Imperial Table IV will be found statistics exhibiting the growth of towns since 1881.

As the North-West Frontier Province is lacking in those factors which elsewhere in India make for rapid urban development, namely the expansion of trade and the development of organized industries, it is not surprising to find that the progress of urbanisation has been generally slow. While the figures in the margin (which take no account of the increase in the number of towns) indicate that the growth of the urban population since 1881 has been twice as rapid as that of the rural population, it must be remembered that the large preponderance of the latter over the former has undergone little change during the last 50 years. The exact extent of the change in the ratio between the urban and rural population in each district as recorded by each successive census since 1881 is illustrated in the accompanying statement.

	Percentage variations in urban and rural population since 1881					
	1881—1891	1891—1901	1901—1911	1911—1921	1921—1931	1881—1931
N.-W. F. P. (Districts)	17·9	9·9	7·6	2·5	7·7	53·9
Urban population ...	19·5	10·9	12·7	15·1	15·0	98·6
Rural population ...	17·6	9·8	6·9	·5	6·4	47·7

District	Number of urban to 1,000 of the rural population					
	1881	1891	1901	1911	1921	1931
N.-W. F. P. (Districts) ...	141	144	145	153	175	189
Hazara ...	48	58	46	52	55	67
Peshawar ...	232	220	214	240	261	286
Kohat ...	116	160	164	113	149	121
Bannu ...	77	70	94	95	137	165
Dera Ismail Khan ...	173	188	224	245	287	252

It will be seen from this statement that the progress of urbanisation has been remarkably slow in every district except Bannu, which, 50 years ago, was almost the least urbanised district in the Province.

The urban population of a country is said to expand in three ways :— (*a*) by natural growth ; (*b*) by migration from rural to urban areas ; and (*c*) by the gradual extension of urban at the expense of rural areas due to the addition of places and their populations which were previously classed as rural. In the North-West Frontier Province, however, many towns owe their existence, and a great deal of their growth as well, to immigration, not from neighbouring towns and villages, but from outside the Province altogether This is, of course, true of the many cantonments in the Province, which, owing to their strategical situation as military bases for border defence, form some of the largest and most important centres of urban life. It is true, also, of some municipal towns where the population is largely composed of Hindu and Sikh traders from the Punjab. To the vast majority of the inhabitants of the North-West Frontier Province, town life presents few attractions. The link with the agricultural and rural element in tribal life is a strong one, and no general inclination towards the settled conditions of town life has yet begun to develop. Nevertheless, in view of the progress of education and the growing popularity of clerical as opposed to agricultural occupations among educated youth, it must be assumed that some tendency to move from villages to towns exists, which, though still small, is likely to increase as town life becomes more attractive; but this movement from country to town must be distinguished from any temporary influx such as that mentioned in the North-West Frontier Province Census Report for 1921, which was due to the disturbed condition of the border at the time the Census was taken It is customary at such times of disturbance and insecurity for some of the inhabitants of exposed border villages (especially Hindus) to take refuge in the nearest towns from the depredations of trans border raiders; but these persons invariably return to their villages as soon as normal conditions are restored.

Special information on the subject of migration from country to town, collected during the census operations in Peshawar City, will be found discussed in paragraph 62 below.

Growth of towns classed as such since 1881.

53. Further light on the growth of the urban population can be obtained by excluding altogether transfers from the rural to the urban category and by noting the variations in the population of the towns, given in the margin, which have existed as such since 1881. In column 10 of Subsidiary Table III, an increase of 68·9 per cent. is shown in the total population of these towns, among whom the most important are the 5 municipal towns, forming the headquarters of the 5 districts, which are shown in the next marginal statement with decennial percentage variations since 1881.

	Towns classed as such since 1881	Percentage increase 1881—1931
1.	Abbottabad Municipality	322·5
2.	Abbottabad Cantonment	258·1
3.	Nawan Shehr	19·1
4.	Baffa	34·1
5.	Peshawar Municipality	47·5
6.	Peshawar Cantonment	66·4
7.	Nowshera Cantonment	194·8
8.	Mardan Cantonment	—12·1
9.	Tangi	— 3·9
10.	Charsadda	38·0
11.	Prang	15·2
12.	Kohat Municipality	86·1
13.	Kohat Cantonment	97·3
14.	Bannu Municipality	374·9
15.	Bannu Cantonment	50·2
16.	Lakki	89·4
17.	Dera Ismail Khan Municipality	105·2
18.	Dera Ismail Khan Cantonment	—56·7
	Total population of above towns	68·9

Name of municipal town	Percentage increases in population					
	1881—1891	1891—1901	1901—1911	1911—1921	1921—1931	1881—1931
Abbottabad Municipality	33·5	40·7	17·9	33·9	42·5	322·5
Peshawar "	6·4	16·3	1·0	7·2	10·1	47·5
Kohat "	6·4	26·1	7·7	11·1	35·3	86·1
Bannu "	24·5	53·7	16·7	39·2	52·7	374·9
Dera Ismail Khan "	22·4	21·7	3·9	15·3	15·0	105·2

The comparatively large increases in the Abbottabad and Bannu Municipalities, particularly during the last decade, are due in the main to military and administrative causes. The occupation of Waziristan, which has enhanced the importance of Bannu as a strategic and commercial centre, and the move of the Judicial Commissioner's Court to Abbottabad in summer, together with the growing popularity of that place as a summer health resort are the main factors responsible for these increases. The increase in Kohat Municipality is also mainly due to military causes, namely the large expansion of the Royal Air Force Station there during the last decade. The growth of population in Peshawar City will be dealt with separately in a later paragraph, but it is of interest to note in passing that the rate of growth in Peshawar has been considerably slower than that in any of the other four municipalities. Dera Ismail Khan has been expanding steadily during the last 50 years, but its recent abolition as a military centre is bound to have a restricting effect on its future growth.

Of the 18 towns (mentioned above) which have been in existence as such since 1881, only 3, Tangi, Mardan Cantonment and Dera Ismail Khan Cantonment, have declined in population during the last 50 years, the last decade being responsible for the decline in each case. In Tangi, which has no real urban characteristics, the decline is accounted for by the emigration of a number of the original residents who have recently settled on neighbouring land newly irrigated by the Upper Swat Canal. The fall in the population of Mardan Cantonment is due solely to the temporary absence of troops in Charsadda in view of the political disturbances there at the time of the Census. In Dera Ismail Khan Cantonment, as we have already noted, the decrease in population naturally follows the large reduction of the military garrison during the last decade.

Accretions to the urban area since 1881.

54. The extent to which the growth of the urban population during the last 50 years can be attributed to accretions to the urban area is illustrated in the marginal statement which shows new additions to the list of towns since 1881 with their present populations. Of these, Mardan Municipality, which owes its rapid growth to its position as a centre of trade in foreign goods for the trans-border states of Dir, Swat and Chitral, as well as for the local agricultural population of the Peshawar District, is by far the most important. In the year 1881, Mardan Cantonment and Civil Lines only were classed as a town, and it was not until 1911 that the new Notified Area of Becket Ganj Khwaja Ganj was added to the cantonment as part of the town of Mardan. Subsequently in 1931, just before the present Census was taken, the notified area was extended and raised to a municipality which, at the present Census, has been classed apart from the cantonment as a separate town. To the fact that the municipal boundaries now include the large and populous village of Hoti, which was previously part of the rural area, the remarkable increase of 140 per cent. in the Mardan Urban Area since 1921 is mainly due.

Places aded to list of towns since 1881

Town	Year in which classed as town	Population, 1931 Census
Haripur Municipality ...	1891	7,653
Cherat Cantonment ...	1891	843
Kulachi Notified Area ...	1891	8,425
Tank Notified Area ...	1901	6,421
Mardan Municipality ...	1911	23 848
Nowshera Notified Area ...	1911	12 829
Risalpur Cantonment ...	1911	8,016
Mansehra ...	1931	5,780

From the above list, it will be observed that the only addition to the list of towns since 1911 is Mansehra, which, with its population of 5,780, was classed as a town for the first time at the present Census.

Natural growth of towns.

55. We have already remarked that the system adopted by the Public Health Department in publishing vital statistics for urban and rural areas is not in conformity with the Census definition of those areas. Although, for this reason, no exact comparison is possible between the natural growth in towns and that in rural areas as understood by the Census, some interesting light is thrown on the subject by the statement in the margin, in which the "urban population" is that of municipalities and notified areas only. The figures indicate that both the proportionate number of births and deaths registered and the rate of natural growth during the last decade are higher in these towns than in rural areas. In the towns, however, the natural increase accounted for only one-quarter of the actual increase which was 23·8 per cent. The urban population seems to have suffered more than the rural population in the two unhealthy years of the decade, 1921 and 1924, particularly the latter. On the whole, however, the statement gives the impression that the registration of births is less accurate in rural than in urban areas.

Year	Rural		Urban	
	Ratio per *mille*		Ratio per *mille*	
	Births	Deaths	Births	Deaths
1921 ...	26·6	31·56	33·02	31·78
1924 ...	26·64	30·73	30·61	33·45
1921—1930 ...	27·6	23·3	32·6	26·5

Sex Proportions in towns.

56. The number of females to every 1,000 males residing in towns, as compared with those residing in rural areas, is shown in the marginal statement, which gives also the corresponding figures for 1921 It will be observed that cantonments are solely responsible for the large increase in the proportionate number of females in urban areas. The reason for this, as explained further in the next paragraph, is that the proportion of females in cantonments in 1921 was abnormally low, owing to the presence in connetion with Frontier disturbances of an unusually large number of troops. While the sex proportions in rural areas have hardly changed since 1921, they still present a striking contrast to those in urban areas. In explaining this phenomenon, which is common almost to the whole of India, we may distinguish two main factors which contribute to a lower proportion of females in towns as compared with rural areas: (*a*) the foreign factor which operates particularly in cantonments and civil lines to cause a distinct preponderance of males, and (*b*) the factor of occupations which, especially in larger municipal towns, causes an increase in the proportion of males, as the male population in these towns is largely composed of immigrants, traders, labourers, etc., who have no womenfolk with them.

	Number of females per 1,000 males	
	1921	1931
N.-W. F. P. (districts) ...	831	843
Rural area	889	886
Urban area	562	642
(*a*) Cantonments ...	199	322
(*b*) Outside cantonments ...	768	766

Population of Cantonments.

57. The military and civil populations of the 9 cantonments in the North-West Frontier Province were enumerated separately at the present Census, the military population being defined as those persons (almost all males) who are subject to military law. Details of the enumeration will be found on the fly leaf to Imperial Table V. The military and civil populations form 28·6 and 71·4 per cent. respectively of the tota cantonment population. In the marginal statement, the progress of the cantonment population is compared with that of the urban population outside cantonments since 1881. These figures show a remarkably small difference in the rates of increase of the two kinds of urban population, which now contribute to the total urban population in almost exactly the same proportions as they did in 1881. The high proportion of the cantonment population in 1921 reflects the disturbed state of the border at that time and the presence of unusually large military garrisons in the Bannu and Dera Ismail Khan Districts.

Year	Urban population, North-West Frontier Province (districts)			
	Actual proportion residing		Proportion per cent. residing	
	In cantonments	Outside cantonments	In cantonments	Outside Cantonments
1881 ...	42,875	151,615	22·04	77·96
1891 ...	58,906	174,579	25·2	74·8
1901 ...	61,828	197,102	23·9	76·1
1911 ...	70,254	221,460	24·8	75·2
1921 ...	93,450	242,399	27·8	72·2
1931 ...	86,564	299,613	22·4	77·6
Total increase, 1881—1931.	+ 102 per cent.	+ 98 per cent.	...	...

Religion in towns.

58. The proportion of each main religion who live in towns is given in Subsidiary Table II for this Census, and in the margin for the last 3 censuses. This statement, in which the Muslim community appears at a disadvantage in comparison with other communities, should be studied in conjunction with the figures for the actual distribution of the urban population by religion given in the next paragraph. The proportion of each community living in towns is determined mainly by occupation, *e.g.* service of the state (military and civil) in the case of Christians, and trade

Religion	Number per *mille* who live in towns		
	1911	1921	1931
All religions ...	133	149	159
Muslims ...	100	103	115
Hindus ...	540	631	651
Sikhs ...	550	668	597
Christians ...	980	935	934

and industry in the case of Hindus and Sikhs. Muslims, being mainly agriculturists, live for the most part in the country villages. The fall in the proportion of Sikhs living in towns at the present Census is due to a decrease in the military garrisons of cantonments and to changes in Indian regiments during the last decade. It is due also to the return of a large number of Sikhs to their villages from towns in the trans-Indus districts, where at the time of the Census of 1921 they had temporarily taken refuge owing to the disturbed condition of the border.

Distribution of urban population by religion.

59. When it is remembered that Muslims form 95 per cent. of the total population of the 5 districts, it is natural, in spite of the figures given in the last paragraph, to find that they predominate over all other religions in the towns as well as in the villages, as the marginal statement shows. The only individual towns in which Muslims are not in a majority are Abbottabad Cantonment and Bannu Municipality, where Hindus are in the majority. This is due in the case of Abbottabad Cantonment to the fact that it is a permanent Gurkha station, and in the case of Bannu Municipality to the preponderance of Hindu traders, which has for many years been a distinctive feature of that town.

Religion	Proportion of urban population	
	Actual	Per cent.
All religions ...	386,177	100
Muslims ...	256,189	66·3
Hindus ...	93,127	24·1
Sikhs ...	25,377	6·6
Christians ...	11,411	3·0
Others ...	73	...

Peshawar City.

60. Peshawar, the only city in the North-West Frontier Province, was raised to that dignity in 1921. The city then included the cantonment as well as the municipality; but at the present census, as already explained, with the separation of cantonments from the towns adjacent to them, the boundaries of Peshawar City have been reduced to those of the municipality only, the cantonment being now shown in all census statistics as a separate town. Nevertheless, for the the sake of comparison, we have included figures for Peshawar Cantonment with those of the municipality in the marginal statement, which shows the progress of the population of both since 1881.

Population of Peshawar

Census	Municipality	Cantonment	Total
1881 ...	59,293	20,690	79,982
1891 ...	63,079	21,112	84,191
1901 ...	73,343	21,804	95,147
1911 ...	74,062	23,873	97,935
1921 ...	79,427	25,025	104,452
1931 ...	8 7 0	34,426	121,866

The percentage increases in the population of Peshawar City at each Census since 1881 are given in Subsidiary Table IV. The increase of 10·1 per cent. during the recent decade in the Peshawar Municipality is mainly confined to Muslims, as the marginal statement shows. A still larger increase might have been expected but for the "blockade" of the Afridi tribe, which was in force at the time of the Census. This blockade not only prevented the access of the usual number of Afridi immigrants into British Territory, but also caused the temporary emigration of Afridi residents of Peshawar City, who, on the outbreak of hostilities, left the city to protect their lands in Tirah.

Peshawar Municipality

Religion	Percentage increase 1921—1931
All religions	+10·1
Muslims	+8·4
Hindus	—0·5
Sikhs	+1·7
Christians	+0·8
Others	—0·3

Density and overcrowding in Peshawar City.

61. The number of persons per square mile in Peshawar Municipality and cantonment combined has fallen from 34,817 in 1921 to 13,801 in 1931 in spite of an increase of 16·7 per cent. in population. As the areas of the municipality (3·83 square miles) and of the cantonment (5 square miles) are the same as in 1921, the figure for the last Census is clearly wrong. In Peshawar City (Municipality), where the density is highest, the number of persons per square mile is 22,830. The result of an enquiry into the question of overcrowding in Peshawar City (Municipality) made in the course of the census operations will be found in an appendix at the end of this volume.

Immigration from Peshawar rural area to Peshawar City.

62. In the marginal table will be found the result of a special enquiry into the volume of migration from Peshawar rural area to Peshawar City (Municipality). In this table the three categories of those born (*a*) in Peshawar City, (*b*) eleswhere in the Peshawar District, and (*c*) outside the Peshawar District represent 72, 6, and 22 per cent.

Religion	Peshawar City (Municipality)							
	Population		Born in Peshawar City		Born elseswhere in Peshawar District		Born outside Peshawar District	
	Males	Females	Males	Females	Males	Females	Males	Females
Muslims ...	39,915	29,078	27,683	23,996	3,282	1,380	8,950	4,602
Hindus ...	6,781	4,813	3,929	3,427	167	178	2,685	1,208
Sikhs ...	2,992	2,158	1,761	1,505	72	70	1,159	583
Christians	452	340	151	136	...	1	301	203
Others ...	11	...	...	...	...	...	11	...
Total ...	50,151	37,289	33,524	29,064	3,521	1,629	13,106	6,596

of the total population, respectively. As regards the female population, the accuracy of these figures is doubtful, owing to the customary reluctance to give any detailed information about the womenfolk of a household; but, as the proportion of those returned as born in Peshawar rural area is as low as 6 per cent., there has probably been very little immigration from neighbouring villages into Peshawar City during recent years. What immigration there has been was naturally confined almost entirely to Muslims.

SECTION III—RURAL AREAS.

Distribution of rural population.

63. The distribution of the urban and rural population among places of different sizes is given in Imperial Table III, while columns 10 to 13 of Subsidiary Table I at the end of this chapter show the distribution of the rural population only by means of proportionate figures for each territorial unit. As the Census village is not a unit of residence but an irregular unit of area (often containing more than one separate residential site) into which the country has been divided for the administration of land revenue, no discussion of the manner in which the rural population is distributed among these villages would seem to lead to any profitable result We have already shown that considerable variations occur in the number and size of these villages from census to census, due both to the modification of village boundaries in the course of a revenue settlement, and to changes in the organisation of the Census as in Feudal Tanawal. We are thus precluded from drawing any comparison between the distribution of the rural population among these villages at different censuses. So far as the present Census is concerned, therefore, all that we can say is that the largest proportion of the rural population of each district is living in the smaller villages with populations ranging from 500 to 2,000, this being particularly the case in the hilly tracts of the Hazara District.

SUBSIDIARY TABLE I—*Distribution of the population between Towns and Villages*

District	Average population per		Number per *mille* residing in		Number per *mille* of urban population residing in towns with a population of				Number per *mille* of rural population residing in villages with a population of			
	Town	Village	Towns	Villages	20,000 and over	10,000 to 20,000	5,000 to 10,000	Under 5,000	5,000 and over	2,000 to 5,000	500 to 2,000	Under 500
1	2	3	4	5	6	7	8	9	10	11	12	13
N.-W. F. P. (districts) ...	14,853	720	159	841	608	131	249	12	49	292	479	180
Hazara	6,997	678	63	937	...	...	1,000	...	18	2-9	504	·99
Peshawar	19,675	896	222	778	673	235	77	15	39	359	478	123
Kohat	17,175	719	145	855	731	...	269	...	153	232	430	185
Bannu	12,747	611	141	859	653	...	347	...	28	212	520	240
Dera Ismail Khan ...	13,794	553	201	799	706	...	269	25	102	233	411	254

SUBSIDIARY TABLE I-A—*Distribution of population in groups of places according to size and rural territory, 1891—1931*

Class of places	1931		1921		1911		1901		1891		Percentage of total population				
	Number of places	Population	Number of places	Population	Number of places	Population	Number of places	Population	Number of places	Population	1931	1921	1911	1901	1891
1	2	3	4	5	6	7	8	9	10	11	12	13	14	15	16
N.-W. F. P. (districts) ...	2,856	2,425,076	3,375	2,251,340	3,052	2,196,933	3,168	2,041,534	Not available	1,857,519	100	100	100	100	100
Urban Territory ...	26	386,177	19	335,849	19	291,714	18	258,930	17	233,485	16	15	13	13	13
(I) Towns of 100,000 and over.	...	...	1	104,452	...	...	...	...	...	...	...	...	...	...	...
(II) Towns of 50,000 to 100,000.	1	87,440	...	...	1	97,935	1	95,147	1	84,191	4	5	4	5	5
(III) Towns of 20,000 to 50,000.	5	147,310	4	117,197	3	83,283	2	62,499	2	53,887	6	5	4	3	3
(IV) Towns of 10,000 to 20,000.	4	50,730	4	45,628	4	49,532	2	24,526	3	33,109	2	2	2	1	2
(V) Towns of 5,000 to, 10,000.	13	5604	9	68,311	6	46,641	8	62,446	7	53,212	4	3	2	3	3
(VI) Towns of under 5,000	3	4,649	1	261	5	14,323	5	14,312	4	9,086	...	...	1	1	...
Rural Territory ...	2'300	2,038,899	3,356	1,915,491	3,033	1,905,219	3,150	1,782,604	Not available	1,624,034	84	85	87	87	87

Note.—The figures in this statement are those of the various classes as recorded at each Census without adjustment of any kind.

SUBSIDIARY TABLE I-B—*Population of urban classes and of rural territory as constituted in 1931 with increase*

Class of places	Number of places in 1931	Population		Variation 1921—1931	
		1931	1921	Number	Per cent.
1	2	3	4	5	6
North-West Frontier Province (districts) ...	2,856	2,425,076	2,251,340	+ 173,736	+ 7·8
Territory urban in 1931	26	386,177	335,849	+ 50,328	+ 14·9
Towns having in 1931—					
(I)—100,000 and over	...	...	104,452	− 104,452	...
(II)—50,000 to 100,000	1	87 440	...	+ 87,440	...
(III)—20,000 to 50,000	5	147,310	117,197	+ 30,113	+ 25·7
(IV)- 10,000 to 20,000	4	50,730	45,628	+ 5,102	+ 11·2
(V)—5,000 to 10,000	13	96,048	68,311	+ 27,737	+ 40·6
(VI)—Under 5,000	3	4,649	261	+ 4,388	+ 16·81
Territory rural in 1931	2,830	2,038,899	1,915,491	+ 123,408	+ 6·4

SUBSIDIARY TABLE II—*Number per* mille *of the total population and of each main religion who live in towns*

District	Number per *mille* who live in towns				
	Total population	Muslims	Hindus	Sikhs	Christians
1	2	3	4	5	6
North-West Frontier Province (districts) ...	159	115	651	597	934
Hazara	63	40	522	348	833
Peshawar	222	176	808	630	942
Kohat	145	112	501	662	928
Bannu	141	64	681	769	984
Dera Ismail Khan	201	137	591	573	836

SUBSIDIARY TABLE III—*Towns classified by population*

Class of town	Number of towns of each class in 1931	Proportion to total urban population	Number of females per 1,000 males	Variation per cent. in towns as classed at previous censuses: 1921—1931	1911—1921	1901—1911	1891—1901	1881—1891	Variation per cent. in urban population of each class from 1881—1931: (a) In towns as classed in 1881	(b) In the total of each class in 1931 as compared with the corresponding total in 1881
1	2	3	4	5	6	7	8	9	10	11
N.-W. F. P. (districts) ...	26	100	642	+17·0	+11·6	+4·8	+9·0	+19·5	+68·9	+98·6
(i)—100,000 and over ...	...	...	...	+16·7	...	...	...	...	+52·4	+52·4
(ii)—50,000 to 100,000 ...	1	23	744	...	...	+2·9	+1·3	+5·2		
(iii)—20,000 to 50,000 ...	5	38	628	+14·3	+14·0	—7·5	+16·0	+21·3	+82·0	+564·6
(iv)—10,000 to 20,000 ...	4	13	621	+32·4	+18·4	+13·5	—18·1	+48·5	+89·0	+310·21
(v)—5,000 to 10,000 ...	13	25	604	+1·5	—0·6	+18·2	+10·4	+21·3	+50·3	+78·0
(vi)—Under 5,000 ...	3	1	399	+222·9	+117·5	—1·6	+21·2	+42·9	+93·3	—77·0

NOTE—The percentage in column 5 represents the variation shown by the Census of 1931 in the population of the towns included in each class in the Census of 1921. The figures in columns 6, 7, 8, 9 and 10 similarly represent the variation in the periods 1911—1921, 1901—1911, 1891—1901, 1881—1891, and 1881—1931. In none of these columns are the variations due to the classing of additional areas as urban taken into account. Column 11 shows the increase in the population of towns as classed in 1931 over the population of towns as classed in 1881, *i.e.* it shows the gross increase including new areas classed as urban and including the population of towns which have come up from a lower class during the period under comparison.

SUBSIDIARY TABLE IV—*Cities*

Cities	Population in 1931	Number of persons per square mile	Number of females to 1,000 males	Proportion of foreign born per *mille*	Percentage of variation: 1921—1931	1911—1921	1901—1911	1891—1901	1881—1891	Total 1881—1931
1	2	3	4	5	6	7	8	9	10	11
Peshawar	1 21,866	13,801	607	287	+16·7	+6·7	+2·9	+13·0	+5·3	+30·6
Peshawar City (Municipality) ...	87,440	22,830	744	154	+10·1	+7·2	+1·0	+16·3	+6·4	+47·5
Peshawar Cantonment ...	34,426	6,885	115	626	+37·6	+4·8	+9·5	+3·3	+2·0	+66·4

CHAPTER III

BIRTH-PLACE AND MIGRATION

Reference to statistics.

64. Birth-place statistics are given in Imperial Table VI and in the subsidiary tables at the end of this chapter. Imperial Table VI by giving the birth-place of persons enumerated in the Province, supplies data towards the determination of the increase or decrease of the natural population of the Province, the movements of people within the Province, and the contribution made to the population of the Province by persons born outside its boundaries.

Subsidiary Table I shows the immigration into each of the districts and natural divisions with the place of birth classified under six main headings; No. II shows the number of emigrants from the Province found in certain natural divisions of the rest of India; No. III compares migration from district to district within the Province, and from tribal areas to districts, with the figures recorded in 1921; Nos. IV—IV-A deal with the currents of migration between the Province and other parts of India both in 1921 and in the present Census year.

Discussion confined to administered districts.

65. So far as this Province is concerned the discussion of migration is of necessity confined to the statistics furnished by the administered districts. No reliable figures are available for trans border territory, where only the occupants of British posts, or of inconsiderable areas immediately adjoining such posts, were enumerated on the regular schedule. The troops and followers so enumerated do not in any way represent the composition of the inhabitants of the surrounding country. A certain amount of migration, mostly periodic, takes place between the trans-border tribes of this Province and Afghanistan, but the number of migrants from the administered districts to tribal territory, other than those found in the posts, is negligible.

General accuracy of indications.

66. It is probable that the records of birth-place are on the whole accurate. The extent to which they illustrate the actual facts of migration must vary from case to case, but in a Province so stay-at-home by habit that 92·6 per cent. were found in the district of birth, the general indications may also be accepted as accurate.

Different types of migration distinguished.

67. It is customary in Indian Census Reports to distinguish 5 different types of migration, as follows :—

(*i*) Casual migration, or the minor movements between adjacent villages. This is a distinction of space not of kind, for such migration is as likely to be permanent as any other form of migration. It occurs most frequently when a wife leaves her parents' village to reside with her husband, or when a child who was born in his grand-parents' home has returned to live with his father. This type of migration does not affect the census returns unless the two villages are on opposite sides of a district boundary; owing to natural features and to ethnographical boundaries such inter-district marriages are less common in this Province than elsewhere in India.

(*ii*) Temporary migration, due to journeys on business or pleasure, visits to places of pilgrimage, and temporary demands for labour. This of course is not really migration at all, but little more than travel which accidentally disturbs the statistics of migration

(*iii*) Periodic migration, due to the movements of people who change their quarters at certain seasons. The great bulk of winter migration from the hills into the settled districts of the Province is of this nature.

(*iv*) Semi-permanent migration, where the natives of one place spend their working lives in another, but retain their connection with their homes, returning there at intervals and ultimately retiring there. Instances are persons in the public services and a large number of the Hindu and Sikh traders of the Province.

(*v*) Permanent migration, when overcrowding drives people away, or the superior attractions of a locality induce people to settle there.

Distinction is of duration.

68. As indicated above, there are really only three types of migration—periodic, semi-permanent and permanent. The so-called casual type has no content : and the so-called temporary type is not migration at all, but needs to be eliminated from the statistics before the true extent of migration can be gauged. Semi-permanent migration in the Province is exceedingly common, and unless recognised as such is likely to lead to many wrong conclusions with regard to the Hindu, Sikh and Christian populations.

Impossibility of distinguishing by census figures alone.

69. The Census figures do not distinguish between the various forms of migration. This can only be done by local inquiry. As a general rule the proportion between the sexes provides a useful guide, the semi-permanent and periodic immigrants showing a high proportion of males, and the permanent migrants showing more nearly equal proportions. This is however an unreliable rule in the North-West Frontier Province, for the majority of Afghan immigrants found in Dera Ismail Khan bring their wives and families with them, while those who come to Peshawar come unaccompanied ; yet both are periodic.

General figures for the Province.

3

Corrigendum to para. 70.

Line 7 *for* ·6 *read* 1·6.

Figures for emigration from the Province to other parts of India have been obtained from other Census Superintendents, and show a total of 90,618 emigrants, including persons born in tribal territory. This represents less than 2 per cent. of the total enumerated and estimated population. Figures for emigration to other parts of the world are not available, nor, if they were available, is it likely that they would be sufficiently large to be of statistical value.

Types of migration compared in regard to numbers.

71. The figures in the margin show that district to district migration, which forms the bulk of that classified as casual, is practically the same as in the previous Census year. Out of every 1,000 persons who were enumerated in the Province and recorded as having been born in the Province, 989 were found in the district of their birth, while in 1921 the proportion was 985. The actual figures for this year give a total of 24,465 persons born in districts of the Province other than that in which they were enumerated, of whom 18,493 were born in an adjacent district.

Distribution per *mille* of persons who were both born in the Province and enumerated in the Province

Where enumerated	Enumerated in	
	1921	1931
All districts ...	1,000	1,000
District of birth ...	985	989
District adjoining district of birth.	10	8
Other districts of the Province.	5	3

Semi-permanent, periodic and permanent migration may similarly be considered in relation to the areas from which the immigrants come. Proportions for certain arbitrary divisions are given in the margin. The largest figure, as is usual in India, is for persons enumerated in the district in which they were born.

Distribution by birth-place per 1,000 persons enumerated in the N.-W. F. P. (districts)

Born in district in which enumerated ...	926
Born in some contiguous district of the Province ...	8
Born in other districts of N.-W. F. P.	3
Born in tribal area contiguous to N.-W. F. P.	11
Born elsewhere in India—	
(i) In areas contiguous to N.-W. F. P.	14
(ii) In more distant areas	22
Born outside India	16

Natural population generally stay-at-home.

72. The general conclusion to be drawn from these figures is that the people of the Province are not inclined to migrate, but that a considerable number of immigrants are attracted from outside. The natural population is mainly agricultural and illiterate. Such a population is invariably found to be extremely conservative. It will not leave its holdings except in the face of some catastrophe in the nature of a severe drought or a general failure of the crops

and then only to return at the earliest opportunity. The Province is moreover a "deficit" Province in the sense that it forms a heavy charge on Central Revenues. Enormous sums of money, out of all proportion to the natural resources of the Province, are spent annually within its limits by Government, and it is only to be expected that a large proportion of this money should find its way directly or indirectly into the pockets of the inhabitants and so contribute to keeping them at home. Peshawar District alone, it may be remembered, contains four cantonments. The heavy expenditure from Central Revenues which helps to keep the natural population at home, is also the cause of the greater part of the immigration from other parts of India and from countries outside India, excepting Afghanistan.

INTRA-PROVINCIAL MIGRATION.

District to district migration.

73. It has not been possible this year to obtain figures to show the emigration by districts to other parts in India. The figures in the margin show the migration within the Province between one district and another and between districts and agencies and tribal areas. Modified in the light of certain temporary conditions it may be taken that the proportions are probably similar to those which would be found to exist among emigrants to other parts of India. The large figure of 6,672 from Bannu may be discounted as it is composed mainly of temporary migrants driven by drought to Dera Ismail Khan. The low figure of emigrants from Dera Ismail Khan is typical of the district, the people of which move very little beyond their own boundaries. The people of Hazara are very enterprising and move all over the world in search of service, both public and private. The nature of the migration from Kohat, which heads the list in spite of the fact that its total population is smaller than that of any of the other districts, is reflected in the large number found in trans-frontier posts. Residents of Kohat, and particularly Khattaks, are very heavily recruited into the Army, the Police, the Frontier Constabulary and all forms of military or semi-military service. The figures for emigration from Peshawar to trans-frontier posts are similarly swollen by the number of persons enlisted from the Yusafzai tribe. The largest groups among the remainder of the emigrants from Peshawar District would be (*i*) labourers and (*ii*) clerks; owing to the educational facilities of the district, clerks from Peshawar are to be found in all parts of the Province.

Statement showing migration between districts within the Province and agencies and tribal areas

District	Immigration			Emigration		
	From other districts in the Province	From agencies and tribal areas	Total	To other districts in the Province	To trans-frontier posts	Total
Hazara ...	1,032	2,243	3.275	5,368	1,423	6,791
Peshawar ...	7,158	17,939	25,097	4,909	2,961	7,870
Kohat ...	2,979	5,604	8,583	5,798	3,686	9,484
Bannu ...	5,047	331	5,378	6,672	764	7,436
Dera Ismail Khan	8,449	1,735	10, 84	1,918	579	2,497
Total ...	24,665	27,852	52,517	24,665	9,413	34,078

The table also illustrates the extent to which each district gains or loses by intra-provincial migration. Hazara draws little on other districts at the time of year when the Census was taken, although in the summer it attracts considerable numbers by its cool hill climate. Kohat with its military and quasi-military garrisons attracts almost as many migrants as it loses. Dera Ismail Khan shows a large number of temporary immigrants from Bannu. Only in Peshawar is the gain considerable. This is inevitable in a district which contains four cantonments, and is the headquarters of the trade, Government and education of the Province.

EXTRA-PROVINCIAL MIGRATION.

(Including migration between the districts and tribal areas.)

Comparison of immigration with emigration with reasons for excess of former over later.

74. The two tables in the margin provide a comparison between the general figures for immigration and emigration in 1931 with those recorded in the previous Census. Figures for emigration to countries outside India are not available, but it may be assumed that, although emigration is increasing the excess of immigration over emigration is hardly less than the total figure for immigration. Among reasons for this general excess may be considered the following :—

I—Migration between the N.-W. F. P. and other parts of India

	1931	1921	Variation
Immigrants to N.-W. F. P.	111,868	118,395	−6,527
Emigrants from N.-W. F. P. ...	90,618	67,970	+22,648
Excess of immigrants over emigrants ...	21,250	50,425	−29,175

II—Immigration to the N.-W. F. P. (districts) from certain other areas

—	1931	1921
Immigrants from countries outside Asia	10,686	9,744
Immigrants from Afghanistan	27,855	22,098
Immigrants from tribal areas	27,852	38,599

(*i*) the stationing of large bodies of troops in the Province for the defence of India :

(*ii*) the presence of the headquarters of a Provincial Government :

(*iii*) the large clerical establishment necessitated by both the above in an area in which the population is largely illiterate :

(*iv*) the existence of grazing grounds superior to those in adjoining areas :

(*v*) the demand for labour created by the continued undertaking of extensive public works.

It will be noticed that the excess of immigration over emigration has fallen to less than half the excess noted in 1921. A modification in most of the above inducements has contributed to this. The number of troops stationed in the Province is less than the number present 10 years ago when the border was in a particularly disturbed state ; the establishment of a Provincial Government is leading to the replacement of outsiders by persons recruited from the Province ; more and more residents of the Province are becoming qualified by education for the clerical establishment. At the same time a number of the immigrants previously recorded have been supplemented or replaced by their own families born in the Province. Special reasons affecting the decrease in Afghan and other trans-border immigrants are discussed in the relevant paragraphs.

Direction of main currents of immigration.

75. An idea of the direction and nature of the main currents of immigration can be obtained from the figures shown in the margin. Immigration from the West is almost entirely of the periodic type, while the remainder is largely semi-permanent. The figures from which these totals are obtained are to be found in Subsidiary Tables IV and IV-A at the end of this chapter. In studying these, care must be taken to distinguish figures for the Province as a whole from those given for the districts only.

Actual figures of immigration

Total immigrants from outside the Province (districts) ...		155,191
Immigrants from the West—		
(*i*) from Afghanistan ...	27,855	
(*ii*) from agencies ...	27,852	
	55,707	55,707
Immigrants from the Punjab		66,890
Immigrants from the rest of India		20,901
Immigrants from outside India, excluding those from Afghanistan		11,693

Historical importance of immigration from the West.

76. The most important, though no longer the largest, stream of migration is that from the West. The nature of the inhabitants, the constitution of the immigrant population, the whole history of the Province, in fact its very existence as a Province, all depend on the frequency with which in the past the inhabitants of the hills on its western border have thought fit to descend as conquerors or as raiders into the plains. The policy now adopted on the Frontier has to a great extent ensured that the tribesmen shall no longer come down as enemies, but the economic necessity which drove their ancestors to conquest and pillage, still sends them annually into British territory to graze, to trade or to labour.

Connection between immigrants from Afghanistan and from tribal areas.

77. The number of immigrants from the West enumerated during the present Census is made up almost equally of persons from Afghanistan and persons from the tribal areas of the North-West Frontier Province. From certain points of view it is convenient to consider them together, for both are almost entirely migrants of the periodic type, visiting the Province only in the winter and returning to their homes with the approach of the hot weather. Even since the establishment of a settled Government in the Province there have occurred large-scale permanent or semi-permanent immigrations from tribal areas across the border, the largest of which in recent years has been that of Wazirs into Bannu. But as the land available has been taken up, and the population within the Province has increased, this stream of migration has slackened, and has now almost ceased.

Immigration from the West considered in groups.

78. The periodic immigrants from the west may be divided roughly into four groups. The first consists of carriers between Peshawar and Kabul, including those who make up the caravans passing regularly up and down the Khyber Pass These do not pass the winter in British territory, but spend it in journeys to and fro, and therefore have little effect on the population of the Province. The second group consists mainly of labourers, including Hazara coolies from the mountainous country west of Kabul, and Mohmands from the hills immediately adjoining the Peshawar District. These are to be found all along the Frontier but are recorded in the greatest number in Peshawar. The third group comprises the Powindahs, who are found for the most part in Dera Ismail Khan They are almost wholly engaged in the carrying trade between India and Afghanistan and the Northern States of Central Asia. They assemble every autumn in the plains east of Ghazni, with their families, flocks, herds and long strings of camels laden with goods of Bokhara and Kandahar, and forming caravans numbering many thousands, march in military order to the Gomal and Zhob Passes through the Sulaiman hills. Entering the Dera Ismail Khan District they leave their families and flocks and a considerable proportion of their fighting men in the grazing grounds on either side of the Indus, and while some wander off in search of employment, others pass on either with their merchandise by rail to all the centres of trade of Northern India, or with their camels to act as carriers wherever opportunity offers. Even Australia is not beyond the limit of their enterprise. In the spring they return by the same route to Afghanistan, where the summer sees them adventuring westwards with the Indian and European merchandise which they have brought from Hindustan. The fourth group of immigrants from the West includes graziers who pass the summer in the hills, and come in the cold weather to the plains in search of pasture. A number of Powindahs, who are graziers as well as warrior-traders, are to be found among this group, but it consists mostly of those from the neighbouring hills who occupy the grazing grounds of Kohat and Peshawar every winter.

Decrease in immigration from the West.

79. The general tendency of immigration from the West, as from Hindustan, is to become less every year. The enumerated totals for the last 5 Census years are shown in the margin. The figures for Peshawar and for "all districts" for 1931 might show a slight increase over the figures for 1921 but for the Afridi

Statement showing immigrants from Afghanistan and the tribal areas of the Province enumerated at each Census since 1881

District	1881	1891	1901	1911	1921	1931
N.-W. F. P. (Districts)	101,898	123,625	115,905	96,597	60,697	55,707
Hazara ...	7,231	7,259	6,087	4,418	3,354	2,328
Peshawar ...	35,892	56,089	55,537	45,366	30,886	25,577
Kohat ...	18,405	19,653	20,827	14,025	6,579	7,280
Bannu ...	11,416	11,781	7,578	7,436	3,308	3,361
Dera Ismail Khan ...	28,954	28,843	* 25,876	25,352	16,570	17,161

* Includes persons shown in Punjab Census Report, 1901, as born in Persia.
Note.—Figures for 1881 were mainly based on estimates.

blockade, which seems to have reduced the immigration from agencies into Peshawar District by some 10,000 persons. This slight increase would not affect the general tendency to decrease, as the figures for 1921 were considered to be exceptionally low on account of the disturbed state of the border. Among the more important reasons for the decrease are the following :—

(*i*) The figures for 1901 were somewhat swollen by an exceptionally bad harvest year in Afghanistan.

(*ii*) Economic prosperity is increasing in Afghanistan with the emergence of a settled government. Not only is an income from land more secure, but there is greater scope both for casual employment on public and private works and for permanent employment in the State services. Emigration is moreover discouraged by the authorities, and passports have to be taken out by all but the nomadic classes.

(*iii*) Increased railway facilities have resulted in both traders and labourers travelling far afield instead of being content to try their fortune in the districts of the Province. It is interesting to note that although the number of immigrants shows a steady decline, the volume of trade, revealed by the Khyber tolls, continues to increase.

(*iv*) The extension of the area under cultivation in the districts, as a result of the extension of irrigation and of the growth in population, has led to a decrease in the area available for grazing.

(*v*) Grazing fees have been increased both in Dera Ismail Khan and in Kohat Districts, and are collected more rigorously than formerly

(*vi*) More settled conditions in tribal areas are making the migrations less and less popular every year with the tribes through whose areas they take place. Not only do the tribesmen require the grazing grounds for themselves, but with the modern improvement in their armament they are becoming increasingly able to make their objections felt.

Figures for last two Census years considered together.

80. In addition to the general tendency of immigration from the West to decrease, there are certain specific variations between the Census figures of the last two enumerations to be considered. The statement for immigration from Afghanistan shows an increase. This is almost entirely divided between the districts of Kohat and Bannu.

Statement showing the number of Afghan immigrants enumerated in the last two Census years

District where enumerated	1931			1921		
	Persons	Males	Females	Persons	Males	Females
N.-W. F. P. (districts)	27,855	16,221	11,634	22,098	13,052	9,046
Hazara ...	85	73	12	5	5	...
Peshawar ...	7,638	4,670	2,968	5,508	3,081	2,427
Kohat ...	1,676	1,068	608	15	13	2
Bannu ...	3,030	1,951	1,079	...	...	...
Dera Ismail Khan ...	15,426	8,459	6,967	16,570	9,953	6,617

The increase in Kohat is due to the fact that in 1921 a severe drought occurred in that district, rendering all the usual grazing grounds worthless. In Bannu in the same year the usual stream of immigration was checked by the activities of the Mahsuds and Wazirs against whom military operations were in progress. The well-organized and well-armed Powindahs who visit Dera Ismail Khan, ran the gauntlet of these tribes and migrated as usual. Peshawar and Hazara show little variation.

Striking variations between figures of immigration from tribal areas are large decreases in the figures for Peshawar and Bannu and an increase in the figures for Dera Ismail Khan. The decrease in Peshawar is due to the Afridi blockade, and that in Bannu to drought. The increase in Dera Ismail Khan is due to the fact that the tribes who usually migrate to that district were in 1921 at war with Government.

Immigration from agencies and tribal areas to districts within the Province

Districts	Immigration from agencies and tribal areas	
	1921	1931
Hazara	3,349	2,243
Peshawar	25,378	17,939
Kohat	6,564	5,604
Bannu	3,308	331
Dera Ismail Khan ...	...	1,735
Total ...	38,599	27,852

Other extra-provincial migration considered.

81. We have now considered migration within the settled districts, between the districts and tribal areas, and between the Province and Afghanistan. It remains to consider migration between the Province and—

(*i*) the rest of India,

(*ii*) other Asiatic countries,

(*iii*) countries beyond the limits of Asia.

Migration between the Province and other parts of India.

82. Migration between the Province as a whole and the rest of India is compared for the years 1931 and 1921 in Subsidiary Table IV at the end of this chapter, and summarised in the marginal figures. As previously remarked the excess of immigration over emigration is being decreased both by growing figures for emigration and by a fall in immigration. The principal variations are in the figures for the Punjab, the United Provinces and Kashmir State.

Migration between N.-W. F. P. (districts and trans-frontier posts) and the rest of India (excluding tribal areas of the N.-W. F. P.)

	1931	1921	
Immigrants	111,868	118,395	...
Decrease in immigration ...	...	...	6,527
Emigrants	90,618	67,970	...
Increase in emigration ...	...	...	22,648
Excess of immigration over emigration ...	21,250	50,425	...
Decrease in excess of immigration over emigration.	...	...	29,175

(i) Punjab.

The Punjab shows a decrease in immigration and an increase in emigration. The Punjab is a large contributor to the Indian Army, and the decrease from 97,624 to 83,118 in figures for immigration may be attributed to a reduction in the number of Indian troops serving in the Province, which in 1921 was exceptionally large. The increase from 33,838 to 50,046 in the number of emigrants in also due partly to changes in the military Stations of Pathan troops, and partly to an increase in temporary and casual migration resulting from an increased familiarity with the facilities of rail and road transport. The fact that the excess of immigrants over emigrants remains as high as it does, is due to the presence of large number of Sikh and Hindu traders, the majority of whom, though they spend their working lives in the Province, are born and die in the Punjab.

Migration between N.-W. F. P. and Punjab

	1921	1931
Immigrants	97,624	83,118
Emigrants...	33,838	50,046
Excess of immigrants	63,786	33,072

(ii) United Provinces.

The figures of immigrants from the United Provinces are made up mainly of various classes of servants including bearers, table-servants, syces, *dhobis* and others. An increasing number of these servants who are usually brought by officers who have been transferred from stations in the United Provinces to the stations on the Frontier, are settling down in the Frontier and becoming permanent or semi-permanent migrants. The total also includes Jats, Garwhalis and other serving soldiers who have been recruited from the United Provinces.

Migration between N.-W. F. P. and United Provinces

	1921	1931
Immigrants ...	7,684	11,177
Emigrants ...	1,872	3,536
Excess of immigrants ...	5,812	7,641

(iii) Other groups of immigrants.

Immigrants from Kashmir have increased from 3,006 in 1921 to 8,263 in 1931. The increase is principally due to the demand for labour on public works, and the majority of the immigrants are coolies. Increases in the figures for Punjab States (from 1,208 to 2,028) and Rajputana (from 743 to 1,545) are due to the movements of troops recruited from these areas. A similar decrease (from 2,489 to 723) in immigrants from Bombay is due to the same cause.

(iv) Other groups of emigrants.

In addition to the Punjab (50,046) and the United Provinces (3,536), which have already been considered, Baluchistan (6,183) and Bombay (11,393) in British India, and Kashmir (6,480) receive considerable numbers of emigrants from the Province. Emigrants to Baluchistan are mostly soldiers serving in the Army. The Pathans found in Bombay are employed either as dock-labourers or as chaukidars, for which service they are much in demand.

Migration between the Province and Asiatic countries outside India.

Number of immigrants recorded in districts and trans-frontier posts in 1931	
Immigrants from Afghanistan ...	28,324
Immigrants from Nepal ...	8,051
Immigrants from elsewhere in Asia, outside India ...	237

83. Migration between the Province and countries outside India can only be considered with relation to the figures for immigration. Immigration from other countries in Asia totals 36,612, but this figure includes 28,324 immigrants from Afghanistan, the. nature of whose migration has already been discussed. The only other important contributor is Nepal, from whence the Gurkha regiments stationed on the Frontier are recruited. About half the number of Nepal-born persons enumerated were found in Abbottabad, which is a permanent Gurkha station. Out of the total of 4,183 enumerated 822 were females. A few of these, both male and female, are settling down in the district.

Migration between the Province and countries outside Asia.

Statement showing the number of immigrants from countries beyond India

Countries outside India	N.-W. F. P. (districts and trans-frontier posts) 1931	1921
Other Asiatic countries ...	36,612	29,423
European countries ...	10,558	9,703
American countries ...	46	16
Australian countries ...	38	20
Total ...	47,298	39,167

84. A summary of the figures for immigration from countries outside Asia is given in the margin, with figures for Asiatic countries added for purposes of comparison. Out of the total of 10,558 persons born in European countries 10,336 were born in the United Kingdom of Great Britain and Ireland. These consist almost entirely of serving soldiers and other Government servants, with their wives, families and friends. Such persons are also to be found in the list of those born in Africa, Australia and America. The remainder include a certain number of tourists and a few persons present on business.

SUBSIDIARY TABLE I—*Immigration.* (*Actual figures*)

District and natural division where enumerated	Number (00's omitted) born in																	
	District or natural division			Other districts of the Province			Agencies and tribal areas of the Province			Contiguous parts of other provinces, etc.			Non-contiguous parts of other provinces, etc.			Outside India		
	Persons	Males	Females	Persons	Males	Females	Persons	Males	Females	Persons	Males	Females	Persons	Males	Females	Persons	Males	Females
	2	3	4	5	6	7	8	9	10	11	12	13	14	15	16	17	18	19
N.-W. F. P. (districts)	22,699	12,089	1 0610	...	...	...	278	172	106	336	235	101	542	403	139	396	259	137
Hazara ...	6,543	3,468	3,075	10	7	3	22	15	7	42	27	15	40	30	10	44	35	9
Trans-Indus districts ...	16,092	8,571	7,521	54	43	11	256	157	99	180	121	59	616	460	156	351	224	127
Peshawar ...	8,895	4 778	4,117	72	58	14	179	112	67	63	44	19	40.	294	107	133	95	38
Kohat ...	2,131	1,101	1,030	30	21	9	56	28	28	20	14	6	101	81	20	25	17	8
Bannu ...	2,529	1,322	1,207	50	36	14	4	3	1	17	13	4	67	54	13	36	24	12
Dera Ismail Khan ...	2,355	1,233	1,122	85	66	19	17	14	3	64	37	27	63	45	18	157	86	71

Note.—The figures in columns 2 to 7 and 11 to 16 for total districts North-West Frontier Province, and for trans-Indus districts are not the totals of the figures for the districts contained in these two areas. Those in columns 2 to 4, for instances include not only the persons enumerated in each of said districts who were born there, but also those who were born in any other district in the group concerned. The area referred to as contiguous parts of other provinces is different in the case of each district or group of districts dealt with and, as a natural consequence, the figures in columns 14 to 16 refer to different areas in the case of different entries in column 1. In the case of the North-West Frontier Province (total districts) the contiguous districts of other provinces, etc., are the Rawalpindi, Attock, Mianwali and Dera Ghazi Khan Districts of the Punjab, and Kashmir State. In the case of Hazara the Rawalpindi and Attock Districts, and Kashmir, in the case of Trans-Indus districts the Attock, Mianwali and Dera Ghazi Khan Districts, in the case of Peshawar the Attock District, in the case of Kohat the Attock and Mianwali, Districts, in the case of the Bannu the *Mianwali District and in the case of Dera Ismail Khan the Mianwali and Dera Ghazi Khan* Districts.

SUBSIDIARY TABLE II—*Emigration* (*Actual figures*)

District and natural division where born	Number (00's omitted) enumerated in														
	District or natural division			*Other districts* of the Province			Trans-frontier posts, N.-W. F. P.			Contiguous parts of other provinces, etc.			Non-contiguous parts of other provinces, etc.		
	Persons	Males	Females	Persons	Males	Femals	Persons	Males	Famles	Persons	Males	Females	Persons	Males	Females
1	2	3	4	5	6	7	9	9	10	11	12	13	14	15	16
N.-W. F. P. (districts) ...	22,699	12,089	10,610	...	...	...	94	90	4	291	176	115	614	451	163
N.-W. F. P. agencies and tribal areas ...	...	...	...	278	172	106	52	43	9	...	...	...	2	1	1

Note.—Figures for individual districts and natural divisions are not available as sorting operations were restricted for the sake of economy.

SUBSIDIARY TABLE III—*Migration between districts, etc. (actual figures) compared with 1921*

District of birth		Number enumerated in districts				
		Hazara	Peshawar	Kohat	Bannu	Dera Ismail Khan
1		2	3	4	5	6
Hazara	1931	654,248	3,954	697	277	440
	1921	604,117	3,819	2,231	864	692
Peshawar	1931	747	889,471	1,767	723	1,672
	1921	3,139	816,584	2,373	1,094	2,165
Kohat	1931	140	1,974	213,088	2,995	689
	1921	26	2,568	189,883	4,630	1,036
Bannu	1931	63	605	356	252,933	5,648
	1921	32	631	1,985	229,177	1,735
Dera Ismail Khan	1931	82	625	159	1,052	235,480
	1921	22	1,001		1,344	216,083
Agencies and tribal areas, North-West Frontier Province.	1931	2,243	17,939	5,604	331	1,735
	1921	3,349	25,378	6,564	3,308	...

SUBSIDIARY TABLE IV—*Migration between the North-West Frontier Province and other parts of India*

Province or State	Immigrants to North-West Frontier Province			Emigrants from North-West Frontier Province			Excess (+) or deficiency (—) of immigration over emigration	
	1931	1921	Variation	1931	1921	Variation	1931	1921
1	2	3	4	5	6	7	8	9
I—Total ...	111,868	118,395	—6,527	90,618	67,970	+ 22,648	+ 21,250	+ 50,425
II—Total Provinces ...	98,310	111,497	—13,187	79,491	57,621	+ 21,870	+ 18,819	+ 53,876
1. Ajmer-Merwara ...	88	24	+ 64	289	641	—352	—201	—617
2. Andamans and Nicobars ...	2	...	+ 2	398	477	—79	—396	—477
3. Assam	48	505	—457	593	318	+ 275	—545	+ 187
4. Baluchistan	444	11	+ 433	6,183	4,953	+ 1,230	—5,739	—4,942
5. Bengal	795	917	—122	1,964	1,015	+ 949	—1,169	—98
6. Bihar and Orissa ...	152	129	+ 23	1,257	389	+ 868	—1,105	—260
7. Bombay	723	2,489	—1,766	11,393	11,693	—300	—10,670	—9,204
8. Burma	76	95	—19	907	1,057	—150	—831	—962
9. Central Provinces and Berar ...	280	60	+ 220	1,167	606	+ 561	—887	—546
10. Delhi	631	...	+ 631	1,758	616	+ 1,142	—1,127	—616
11. Madras	776	1,959	—1,183	...	146	—146	+ 776	+ 1,813
12. Punjab	83,118	97,624	—14,506	50,046	33,838	+ 16,208	+ 33,072	+ 63,786
13. United Provinces of Agra and Oudh	11,177	7,684	+ 3,493	3,536	1,872	+ 1,664	+ 7,641	+ 5,812
III—Total States ...	12,736	5,902	+ 6,834	11,127	10,349	+ 778	+ 1,609	—4,447
1. Assam States	32	...	+ 32	...	...	...	+ 32	...
2. Baluchistan States ...	...	...	...	...	63	—63	...	—63
3. Baroda State	8	228	— 220	341	65	+ 276	—333	+ 163
4. Bengal States	...	...	...	...	11	—11	...	—11
5. Bihar and Orissa States ...	7	...	+ 7	42	40	+ 2	—35	—40
6. Bombay States ...	29	...	+ 29	269	358	—89	— 240	—358
7. Central India Agency ...	280	...	+ 280	533	367	+ 166	—253	—367
8. Central Provinces States ...	58	32	+ 26	...	44	—44	+ 58	—12
9. Gwalior State ...	156	...	+ 156	144	307	— 163	+ 12	—307
10. Hyderabad State ...	182	329	—147	184	218	—34	—2	+ 111
11. Kashmir State ...	8,263	3,006	+ 5,257	6,489	7,738	—1,258	+ 1,783	—4,732
12. Madras States... ...	...	25	— 25	9	2	+ 7	—9	+ 23
Cochin State ...	...	17	—17	2	...	+ 2	—2	+ 17
Travancore State ...	...	8	— 8	7	2	+ 5	—7	+ 6
13. Mysore State	148	331	— 183	93	44	+ 49	+ 55	+ 287
14. Punjab States Agency ...	2,028	1,208	+ 820	2,727	414	+ 2,313	—699	+ 794
15. Rajputana Agency ...	1,545	743	+ 802	279	656	—377	+ 1,266	+ 87
16. United Provinces States ...	...	...	...	26	22	+ 4	—26	—22
IV—India unspecified ...	755	996	—241	...	...	...	+ 755	+ 996
V – French and Portuguese Settlements	67	...	+ 67	...	...	...	+ 67	...

Note.—(1) In addition to the emigrants from the Province shown in this table 15 persons (15 males) were enumerated in Ceylon.

(2) This table unlike Subsidiary Tables I, II and III appended to Chapter III include migrants to and from trans-frontier posts as well as British territory.

SUBSIDIARY TABLE IV-A—*Migration between the North-West Frontier Province (Districts) and other parts of India*

Province or State	1931		
	Immigrants to North-West Frontier Province (Districts)	Emigrants from North-West Frontier Province (Districts)	Excess (+) or deficiency (—) of immigration over emigration
1	2	3	4
I—Total ...	115,643	99,881	+15,762
II—Total Provinces ...	78,408	79,443	—1,035
1. Ajmer-Merwara	68	289	—221
2. Andamans and Nicobars	2	398	—395
3. Assam	36	593	—557
4. Bengal	704	1,962	—1,258
5. Bihar and Orissa	129	1,257	—1,128
6. Bombay	655	11,393	—10,738
7. Burma	76	907	—831
8. Baluchistan	426	6,148	—5,722
9. Central Provinces and Berar	248	1,158	— 910
10. Delhi	515	1,758	—1,243
11. Madras	461	...	+461
12. Punjab	66,890	50,046	+16,844
13. United Provinces of Agra and Oudh	8,198	3,534	+4,664
III—Total States ...	36,597	20,438	+16,159
1. North-West Frontier Province agencies and tribal areas ...	27,852	9,413	+18,439
2. Kashmir State	5,849	6,392	—543
3. Punjab States Agency	1,121	2,727	—1,606
4. Assam States	...	...	...
5. Baluchistan States	...	...	...
6. Baroda State	8	338	—330
7. Bengal States	...	...	...
8. Bihar and Orissa States	7	42	—35
9. Bombay States	29	269	—240
10. Central India Agency	280	524	—244
11. Central Provinces States	27	...	+27
12. Gwalior State	74	144	—70
13. Hyderabad State	171	184	—13
14. Madras States	...	9	—9
Cochin State	...	2	—2
Travancore State	...	7	—7
15. Mysore State	83	93	—10
16. Rajputana State	1,096	277	+819
17. United Provinces States	...	26	— 25
IV—India unspecified ...	604	...	+604
V—French and Portuguese Settlements ...	34	...	+34

Note.—In addition to the emigrants from the Province shown in this table 15 persons (15 males) were enumerated in Ceylon.

CHAPTER IV

AGE

AGE-STATISTICS

Reference to statistics.

85. Age-statistics by sex and civil condition for the Province as a whole (excluding tribal territory), for the districts, for Transfrontier posts, and for Peshawar Municipality are given in Imperial Table VII. Ten subsidiary tables printed at the end of this chapter give the same information in other forms. No. I gives the age-distribution per 10,000 of each sex throughout the Province as recorded in each Census since 1881; No. II gives similar statistics for each of the main religions; No. III is for certain castes only, and for the present Census alone; the proportion of children under 14 and of persons over 43, to the total number of persons and to the number of married females between these two ages, are shown in Table IV; Nos. V and VI gives similar statistics by religion and for slightly different age-periods, and compare the figures recorded since 1891; No. VI shows variations in the distribution by age-periods since the last Census; No. VII exhibits the birth-rate and No. VIII the death-rate per 1,000 during the last decade; No. IX distributes the death-rate in certain years through different age-periods; and No. X gives the incidence of the death-rate from certain diseases during the last ten years.

Unreliability of returns.

86. The instructions given to enumerators were to enter the age to the nearest birthday; in the case of children under 6 months of age the entry was to be 0; where the age given was obviously absurd, the enumerator was to use his own discretion. In previous enumerations instructions have sometimes been given to enter "age next birthday", and sometimes "age last birthday". In practice the ignorance of the mass of the population of anything approaching their correct age is so complete that the instructions given can make little difference. Mis-statements of age occur both deliberately and from ignorance. Deliberate under-statements are made by the fathers of unmarried girls with regard to their daughters, by middle-aged widowers who intend to re-marry, and by middle-aged women who wish to appear younger than they are, while those over 60 years of age are inclined to over-state for the sake of the prestige which longevity confers. The fact that the Census returns are confidential, impresses no one. In addition to deliberate mis-statement, mis-statement from ignorance is almost universal. This is hardly to be wondered at when only 26 per 1,000 of the Muslim population, which forms ·92 per cent. of the total population, have any claims to literacy. Enumeration of ages by actual years would be hopelessly inaccurate, the tendency of both subjects and enumerators to plump for years which are multiples of 10, and for certain other favourites, being ineradicable. A smoothing-out process has been adopted for the quinary groups given in Imperial Table VII, and figures for certain of the broader groupings, such as under 15, under 10, over 53, between 14 and 43, which refer to periods of life not too difficult to estimate, may be taken as sufficiently accurate to warrant the drawing of conclusions. Further, since the reasons for mis-statement persist from Census to Census, the present figures are of some value for showing the variations from decade to decade.

Distribution of population by age-groups.

87. It is difficult to say what is a normal population, but figures taken over sufficiently large populations throughout the world show that it is normal to find the largest numbers of both males and females in the lowest age-groups, with the numbers in each group decreasing successively as the age-period increases. The figures in the margin show that this is the case with the total population of the five districts. The statement gives figures per 10,000 of each sex, and it will be noticed that the proportionate number of females in each group approaches

Distribution of 10,000 of each sex by decennial periods in the Province (Districts)

Age-period	Males	Females
0—10	2,883	3,083
10—20	2,134	2,011
20—30	1,797	1,905
30—40	1,394	1,359
40—50	861	825
50—60	516	474
60—70	258	221
70 and over ...	157	122

Distribution of 10,000 of each sex by 20-year periods in the Province (Districts)

Age-period	Males	Females
0—20	5,017	5,094
20—40	3,191	3,264
40—60	1,377	1,299
60 and over ...	415	343

or exceeds the proportionate number of males up to the age of 30, and thereafter falls below it. This is partly explained by the greater mortality of females during the early child-bearing periods. It becomes even more noticeable if the division is made by periods of 20 years. Out of every 10,000 males 1,792 have passed the age of 40, while the proportionate number of females is less by 150.

Distribution by years not available.

88. At the last Census a subsidiary table was prepared to show the proportional distribution per 100,000 for each year of enumerated age up to 25. For reasons of economy it has not been possible to prepare this table this year.

Reference to Sundbarge's theory.

89. A theory bearing the name of Sundbarge, a Swedish statistician, is to the effect that the number of persons between the ages of 15 and 50 may normally be expected to be half the total population, the variations being confined to the other two main age-periods, from 0—15 and 50 and upwards. This theory is based on observations of all Western countries. In a virile and growing community the numerical strength of the children will be greater than that of the aged, and if the population is stationary the two groups will remain about equal; the incidence of the death-rate will be high on those at the extremes of life, and less heavy on those in the prime of life, except when affected by some calamity such as war, pestilence, or famine. The theory provides a convenient criterion by which to judge the statistics presented by the present Census.

Population considered with reference to Sundbarge's theory.

90. The figures in the margin show the proportion of persons per *mille* for the total population and for each of the main religions, as analysed for Sundbarge's theory. Almost exactly half the total population are to be found in the middle age-group, while of the remainder by far the greater number are to be found in the younger group. This preponderance in the younger group agrees with the recorded tendency of the population towards steady increase. It is higher than it was in 1921 when the influenza epidemic of 1918 had but recently wrought its worst havoc among those in the procreative period of life. Divergence from the normal, to accept Sundbarge's theory, is to be found in the figures for Hindus, Sikhs and Christians, but as the majority of the followers of these religions are soldiers, Government servants and other immigrants into the Province, who have neither been born there nor expect to die there, the divergence is easily explained. If any conclusion is to be drawn from the figures for non-Muslims it is that the proportionate increase in the lowest age-group indicates a more settled state of affairs in the Province; it is brought about partly by the withdrawal of many of the troops whose presence was necessary in 1921, and partly as a result of the remaining male immigrants bringing their families with them in response to an increased feeling of security.

The proportion of persons per *mille* in each of the three age-groups for the principal religions returned at the two last censuses of the Province (Districts)

Age.		All religions	Muslims	Hindus	Sikhs	Christians
0–15	1921 ...	404	415	296	284	129
	1931 ...	416	422	367	358	206
15–50	1921 ...	479	465	615	631	846
	1931 ...	496	489	559	569	760
50 and over	1921 ...	117	120	89	85	25
	1931 ...	88	89	74	73	34

Muslim population considered by districts with reference to Sundbarge's theory.

91. When it is remembered that Muslims constitute 92 per cent. of the total population under discussion, it will be realised that the figures for the age-distribution of Muslims alone are those which will reflect the true state of affairs in the Province. They may more profitably be examined district by district

Age-distribution per *mille* of the Muslim population in the North-West Frontier Province (Districts)

Districts		0—15	15—50	50 and over
N.-W. F. P. ...	...	422	489	89
Hazara ...	...	433	469	98
Peshawar ...	...	409	501	90
Kohat ...	...	443	473	84
Bannu ...	...	431	494	75
Dera Ismail Khan	...	414	503	83

according to the figures in the margin. It will be found that the divergence from 500 per *mille* in the figures for the age-group 15—50, small though it is, varies directly with the nature of the migration which takes place to and from the districts under consideration. The reason for this, as has been previously indicated, is that the majority of semi-permanent and periodic migration, which is the most considerable in the Province, is on the part of those in the middle period of life. Hazara and Kohat provide the two populations most inclined to emigrate, and as a consequence have the lowest proportion of persons between the ages of 15 and 50. Bannu shows a deficiency as a result of the temporary migration of large numbers to Dera Ismail Khan on account of drought. Peshawar, though its young men are not averse to moving abroad, gains an excess of persons in the prime of life by its opportunities for education and Government service. Dera Ismail Khan is the most stay-at-home district, and shows the highest proportion in this age-group, 503 per *mille* compared with the average of 489 for the Province.

Increase in proportion of children to those of other ages.

92. The proportions in the lowest age-group are in every case higher than they were in 1921. The reasons for this among Hindus, Sikhs and Christians have already been noted. The increase among Muslims is small, but is entirely at the expense of those in the highest age-group. This may be attributed to the influenza epidemic of 1918, which was heaviest in its incidence on those in the prime of life and carried off many who might now have been over 50 years of age. Figures showing the proportion of children under 10 years old to married females of child-bearing age are useful as an indication, though not a certain indication, of the fertility of the population. The figures in the margin compare the proportions recorded in each of the last two enumerations. The highest proportion of children is among Muslims but the figure still falls below that recorded 20 years ago. The influenza epidemic is probably still to blame, as the birth-rate remained low for some years after this affliction. It is dangerous to draw conclusions from the limited numbers on which the figures for other religions are based, but it is interesting to note how the excess of the Muslim figures over those for Sikhs and Hindus has shrunk since 1921 as a result of increased security.

Proportion of children under 10 years of age per 100 married females aged 15—40

Religion			1921	1931
All religions	...	...	206	195
Muslims...	...	...	209	196
Hindus ...	...	...	164	184
Sikhs ...	...	...	162	187
Christians	...	...	142	146

Distribution by age-groups compared with figures for 1921.

93. The age-distribution of the total population in 1921 and in 1931 is shown in the margin. The most striking variations are an increase of 25 per cent. in the number of children under 5, a decrease in those from 5—10, an increase in all groups between 10 and 40, and a fall in all groups over 40. The numbers of those between 10 and 40 were depleted in 1921 both by the incidence

Statement showing the age-distribution of the total population of the Province (Districts) at the two last censuses

Age-group (all religions)		Population		Variation	
		1921	1931	Actual	Percentage
All ages	...	2,251,340	2,425,076	+173,736	+8
0—5	...	308,858	386,719	+77,861	+25
5—10	...	357,630	334,706	—22,924	—6
10—15	...	242,958	288,425	+45,467	+19
15—20	...	169,947	215,504	+45,557	+27
20—30	...	384,625	447,754	+63,129	+16
30—40	...	313,466	334,228	+20,762	+7
40—50	...	210,930	204,738	—6,192	3
50—60	...	128,771	120,475	—8,296	—6
60 and over	...	134,155	92,527	—41,628	—31

Increase in number of children under the age of 5 compared with increase in number of married women between 15 and 40	1921	1931
Children under age of 5 ...	308,858	386,719
Married women aged 15—40 ...	323,641	370,604

of the influenza epidemic and by the absence on military service of many males of that age-period. The increase of children under 5 corresponds with an increase in the number of married females of child-bearing age. The decrease among persons of advanced age, as well as the increase noted in the number of married females, is traceable directly to the influenza epidemic. Variations in the distribution *between the age-groups in each district* are almost identical with those for the Province as a whole. Only Dera Ismail Khan shows a fall in the numbers over 20 years of age as a result of the removal of the garrisons of Dera Ismail Khan and Tank Cantonments.

Mean age of the population.

94. The mean age of the population worked out for each Census since 1881 is shown in the margin. Mean age means the average age of all the persons who were enumerated in the Province on the night of the Census, and is calculated in the manner described on page 390 of the India Administration Volume of the Census Report for 1901. Mean age is of course affected by the birth-rate, by the immigration or emigration of persons in the prime of life, by the longevity and general health of the population, and by many other factors, but the factor which affects it most is the birth-rate. As already stated, it is a sign of a growing and healthy population to have a preponderance of persons in the lower age-groups. It follows that as a general rule a low mean age is an encouraging sign. The lowest mean age hitherto recorded in the Province was 21·7 years for males and 21·1 for females. The fall from 1881—1891 was due to the enhanced birth-rate resulting from general prosperity and security, and was reflected in an increase of 18 per cent. in the population during the same 10 years. The highest mean age was that recorded in 1921, 24·7 among males and 24·1 among females. This was due to the heavy mortality from malaria and influenza during the last half of the preceding decade, which had reduced the average birth-rate from 34·5 to 31·0 per *mille*, and raised the *corresponding average death-rate from 24 per mille to 36. The mean age* of Muslims is practically the same as for the whole population. For Hindus and Sikhs it is slightly higher owing to the number of temporary and semi-permanent immigrants of the later age-periods.

Mean age of the total population for the last six censuses

Year	Male	Female
1931 ...	23·3	22·4
1921 ...	24·7	24·1
1911 ...	24·2	23·5
1901 ...	23·8	23·0
1891 ...	21·7	21·1
1881 ...	23·9	23·6

Mean age of the sexes compared.

95. It is noticeable that the mean age of males is always slightly in excess of that of females. A clue to this is found in the subjoined graph which shows the higher proportion of females in the earlier age-groups.

The figures selected for the graph are those for the Muslim population alone.

No. 13

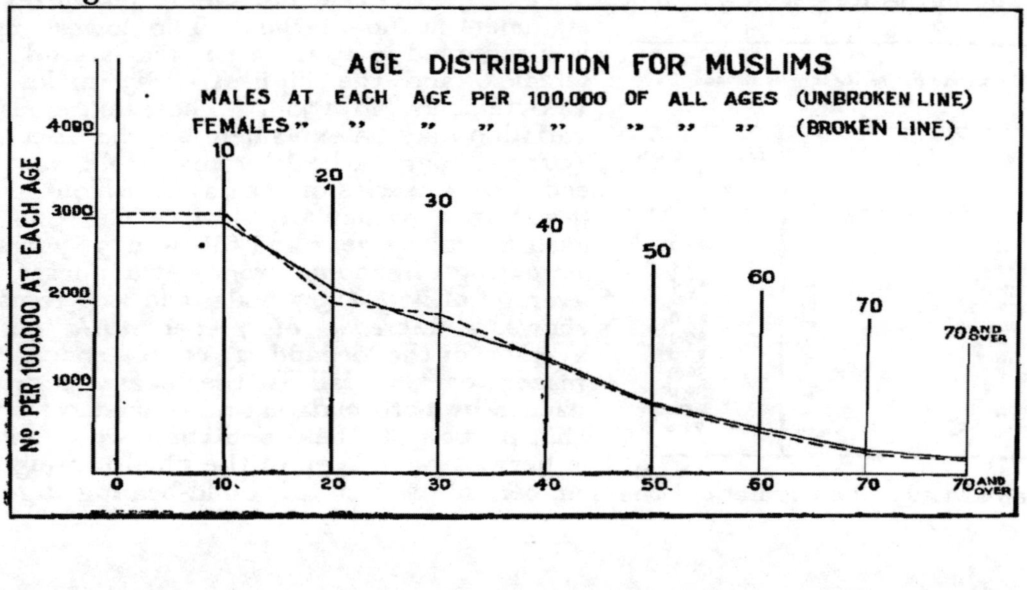

Figures for "all religions" give practically the same line. The figures for Hindus alone, which are not reproduced, show a very much sharper drop in the female line between the ages of 10 and 20. Mortality among Hindu females in this age-period is heavier than among Muslim females as a result of earlier marriage and earlier child-bearing.

Proportions in certain age groups for certain castes.

96. A brief reference may here be made to Subsidiary Tables III and IV at the end of this chapter. Certain results of Table III are summarised in the margin. It will be observed that Sayads, Swatis and Tanaolis, all tribes found in the largest numbers in Hazara, have the largest proportion of children. Hazara is a district from which large numbers of men in the prime of life travel abroad in search of employment. The castes with the lowest proportion of children under the age of 13 are Brahmans and Chuhras, both tribes which are mainly found in the Province as immigrants. The figures for the various castes are much nearer to one another in Subsidiary Table IV where the proportion of children to married females of child-bearing age is considered.

Statement showing the age-distribution of 1,000 persons in selected castes

Caste or tribe	0—16	17—43	44 and over	Children under 13 years of age
Arora ...	439	420	141	377
Awan ...	445	400	155	374
Brahman ...	359	476	165	279
Chamar ...	441	439	120	336
Chuhra ...	353	500	147	270
Gujar ...	467	378	155	392
Jat ...	404	451	145	321
Khatri ...	394	439	167	319
Pathan ...	447	402	151	382
Sayad ...	459	393	148	389
Swathi ...	487	303	120	387
Tanaoli ...	471	394	135	405

VITAL STATISTICS.

General.

97. The vital statistics of the Province vary considerably in accuracy from one area to another, and must be accepted with caution. It has already been shown in Chapter I, paragraph 22, of this report how prevalent is failure to register either births or deaths of females. The system of registration is discussed in the same chapter, where the conclusion is reached that the registration in urban areas is fairly reliable, but in rural areas leaves much to be desired.

Of the many factors which affect the birth-rate, the principal is the variation in the numbers of married females of the child-bearing age. The death-rate falls heaviest on the groups of persons at each of the extremes of life, and may normally be expected to fluctuate with the birth-rate.

Birth-rate per *mille* considered for the decade.

98. The area under registration of births and deaths is now the whole of the 5 settled districts with the exception of Feudal Tanawal and the Kagan Valley in Hazara District. The population of the two areas excluded was enumerated as 31,381 males and 26,404 females.

The birth-rate per *mille* for each year of the last decade is shown in the statement in the margin. The lowest figure was recorded in 1922, 13·1 males and 10·3 females, and the highest, 18·3 males and 14·0 females, in 1908. These extremes of variation may be explained by the fact that 1922, although a healthy year itself, was preceded by a series of years in which public health was particularly low, while 1928 was itself a healthy year and followed 3 years of increasing freedom from epidemics. The average of 27·8 (15·7 males and 12·1 females) shows a decrease of 7 per *mille* on the average of the decade 1911 to 1920. The reason for this fall is the heavy mortality caused by both malaria and influenza among that portion of the population which would otherwise have been of the child-bearing age.

Birth-rate per *mille* for the decade 1921—1930

Year	Birth-rate per *mille*
1921	27·0
1922	23·4
1923	27·4
1924	26·8
1925	26·6
1926	29·9
1927	29·0
1928	32·3
1929	30·6
1930	25·4
Average ...	27·8

As has already been remarked the number of wo.. en of child-bearing age has-increased from 323,641 in 1921 to 370,604 in the present enumeration. This increase is reflected in the increase of the birth-rate during the latter half of the decade, the average from 1921 to 1925 being 26·2 per *mille* and that from 1926 to 1930 being 29·4.

Variation by districts.

99. The statement in the margin shows the variation between the total number of births recorded in each district in the last two decades. All districts except Kohat show a decrease, the decrease being greatest in Peshawar. The variation can only be attributed to the low birth-rate at the beginning of the decade, reasons for which have already been discussed.

Number of births in past 2 decades registered in each district of the Province

Districts		1911—1920	1921—1930	Actual variation	Variation per *mille*
Total Districts	...	668,880	603,870	−65,010	−97
Hazara ...	...	185,963	168,850	−17,115	−92
Peshawar ...	...	239,115	209,282	−29,833	−125
Kohat ...	...	73,152	73,895	+ 743	+ 10
Bannu ...	...	82,504	72,409	−10,095	−121
Dera Ismail Khan	...	88,144	79,434	−8,710	−99

Death-rate per *mille* through the decade.

100. The death-rate of the decade, as the figures in the margin show, has varied considerably more than the birth-rate. Both sets of figures are calculated on the population enumerated in 1921. It will be seen that there is a rough correspondence in that the years which show a rise in the birth-rate generally show a rise in the death-rate also. The average death-rate compares favourably with that of the previous decade when the figure was 23·4 per *mille*. The highest figure, 31·0 per *mille*, marks a period when the general vitality was low as a result of a third unhealthy year in succession; as remarked above, the same cause produced a low birth-rate in the following year The year 1928 shows the highest birth-rate and also the lowest death-rate, and was the healthiest year recorded in either of the last two decades. Not only was the Province entirely free for the first time on record of both cholera and plague, but the light rainfall resulted in an unusually light incidence of malaria.

Death-rate and birth-rate for the Province (districts) during the past decade

Year		Birth-rate per *mille*	Death-rate per *mille*
1921	...	27·0	31·0
1922	...	23·4	21·0
1923	...	27·4	23·6
1924	...	26·8	30·7
1925	...	26·6	19·6
1926	...	29·9	21·6
1927	...	29·0	21·9
1928	...	32·3	19·1
1929	...	30·6	23·9
1930	...	25·4	21·7
Average	...	27·8	23·4

Variation by districts.

101. Figures in the margin show that the fall in the death-rate was shared by all districts. The greatest improvement is shown by Dera Ismail Khan. It was in this district that the mortality from the influenza epidemic was highest.

Statement showing the variation in the number of deaths during the past 2 decades in each district of the Province

District		Deaths		Variation	
		1921	1931	Actual	Per cent.
N.-W F. (districts)	...	618,451	508,261	—110,190	—18
Hazara ...	...	146,800	139,176	—7,624	—5
Peshawar ...	...	226,016	189,534	—36,482	—16
Kohat ...	...	69,934	57,712	—12,222	—17
Bannu ...	...	78,681	56,770	—21,911	—28
Dera Ismail Khan	...	97,020	65,069	—31,951	—33

Incidence of death-rate by age-periods.

102 The incidence of deaths in each age-period is shown in the marginal statement. As is to be expected, the highest figures are for the very young and for those at the other extreme of life. This is made even more obvious in Subsidiary Table IX at the end of this chapter, where it is shown that the annual death-rate per *mille* among males under one year of age has averaged 157·9 throughout the decade, that for those of 60 and over averages 52·4, while that for males of all ages was only 24. The figures for infantile mortality are undoubtedly higher than the records indicate, for it may be taken as certain that babes born in rural areas who die within a few hours or a few days of birth, or even a few weeks in the more remote villages, are never recorded. A high rate of infant mortality is a feature common to the whole of India, as figures in the margin, taken from the India Census Report of 1921, go to show. Although the custom of early marriage and early child-bearing is less common in this Province than elsewhere there remain many of the other causes of high infantile mortality, notably primitive and insanitary methods of midwifery, and it is probable that the true figures for the Province are but little below those for the rest of India. The actual figures recorded for the past decade show the present rate to be 148 per 1,000. Assuming that the proportion of errors and omissions in previous registrations has remained constant, or has shown at the best a slight decrease; the drop from 178 to 148 may, with caution, be taken to represent an improvement.

Incidence by age-periods of the percentage of average annual proportion per *mille* of deaths to population for the decade 1921—1930, calculated on the population recorded in 1921

Age-period		Persons	Males	Females
All ages	...	23	13	10
0—1	...	4	2	2
1—5	...	4	2	2
5—10	...	2	1	1
10—15	...	1	1	...
15—20	...	1	1	...
20—30	...	2	1	1
30—40	...	2	1	1
40—50	...	2	1	1
50—60	...	2	1	1
60 aod over	...	3	2	1

Death-rate of infants per 1,000 births in the year

Chile	...	...	315
Russia	...	...	245
India	...	...	211
Ceylon	...	...	189
North-West Frontier Province	...	...	178
Japan	...	...	156
United Statee	...	...	124
England and Wales	...	...	117
Norway	...	...	70
New Zealand	...	...	70

Incidence of certain epidemics.

103. While considering the death-rate it is convenient to make mention also of the more serious epidemics which occur in the Province. During the last decade fever, usually malaria, has carried off an average of nearly 41,600 persons every year. Cholera carried off 4,285 persons in 1921, but a total of only 700 in the remaining 9 years. Plague was responsible for 15,140 deaths in 1923 and 1924, but has not shown its head since 1928. Small-pox is always present and claims an average of 360 victims a year. The incidence of small-pox, cholera and the fevers is more or less equal on the two sexes; plague has affected females more than males.

SUBSIDIARY TABLE I—*Age-distribution of 10,000 of each sex in the Province and each natural division*

Age	1931 Males	1931 Females	1921 Males	1921 Females	1911 Males	1911 Females	1901 Males	1901 Females	1891 Males	1891 Females	1881 Males	1881 Females
1	2	3	4	5	6	7	8	9	10	11	12	13
N.-W. F. P. total (Districts).												
0—1 ...	291	330	275	327	363	411	335	390	412	478	258	292
1—2 ...	255	304	154	190	133	154	156	183	314	372	187	222
2—3 ...	305	368	236	296	278	335	289	345	354	413	253	316
3—4 ...	317	368	264	335	317	375	303	366	362	400	318	377
4—5 ...	319	352	294	355	329	366	319	369	350	375	347	389
Total 0—5 ...	1,487	1,722	1,223	1,503	1,420	1,641	1,402	1,653	1,792	2,038	1,363	1,596
5—10 ...	1,396	1,361	1,524	1,606	1,564	1,592	1,503	1,548	1,575	1,530	1,584	1,552
10—15 ...	1,243	1,125	1,121	985	1,180	975	1,110	1,002	949	792	1,093	896
15—20 ...	891	886	812	707	774	715	839	770	992	1,082	788	760
20—25 ...	905	966	931	860	755	833	788	831	863	841	839	907
25—30 ...	892	939	914	851	821	858	855	852	1,022	1,051	834	824
30—35 ...	810	793	878	913	875	931	941	968	640	550	991	1,010
35—40 ...	584	566	525	489	522	470	526	471	664	705	442	395
40—45 ...	479	471	581	656	600	644	621	661	299	267	680	749
45—50 ...	382	354	329	296	325	292	296	256	435	436	251	225
50—55 ...	300	284	416	430	437	414	411	403	155	131	462	449
55—60 ...	216	190	147	135	152	126	126	106	331	324	116	100
60—65 ...	176	155	303	296	301	276	522	479	283	253	557	537
65—70 ...	82	66	66	65	68	59	...	...	...	...	...	...
70 and over ...	157	122	230	208	206	174	...	...	...	...	...	...
Mean age ...	23·3	22·4	24·7	24·1	24·2	23·5	23·6	23·0	21·7	21·1	23·9	23·6
Hazara.												
0—5 ...	1,563	1,767	1,384	1,496	1,463	1,664	1,428	1,622	1,963	2,249	1,367	1,585
5—10 ...	1,452	1,382	1,669	1,654	1,560	1,606	1,630	1,667	1,619	1,598	1,693	1,654
10—15 ...	1,291	1,117	1,231	1,026	1,275	1,062	1,361	1,147	966	791	1,260	1,010
15—20 ...	825	844	724	739	795	792	834	809	1,017	1,147	848	875
20—40 ...	2,929	3,264	2,683	3,091	2,759	3,051	2,737	2,984	3,063	3,016	2,976	3,184
40—60 ...	1,397	1,231	1,503	1,365	1,469	1,293	1,418	1,284	1,058	943	1,308	1,218
60 and over ...	543	395	806	629	679	532	592	487	314	256	548	474
Mean age ...	23·6	22·4	24·8	24·1	24·2	22·9	23·4	22·3	21·0	19·9	22·9	21·2
Trans-Indus Districts.												
0—5 ...	1,459	1,705	1,219	1,506	1,403	1,633	1,396	1,666	1,743	1,977	1,361	[illegible]
5—10 ...	1,375	1,354	1,539	1,588	1,566	1,587	1,456	1,502	1,562	1,510	1,566	1,524
10—15 ...	1,226	1,128	1,130	969	1,145	942	1,100	944	944	792	1,051	866
15—20 ...	916	902	821	693	767	686	840	756	986	1,063	773	729
20—40 ...	3,289	3,264	3,240	3,121	3,052	3,107	3,248	3,176	3,225	3,185	3,140	3,124
40—60 ...	1,368	1,326	1,501	1,579	1,531	1,546	1,467	1,479	1,267	1,221	1,560	1,605
60 and over ...	367	321	550	544	536	499	497	477	273	252	559	553
Mean age ...	23·1	22·4	24·8	24·5	24·3	23·7	23·9	23·3	21·9	21·4	24·2	23·9

SUBSIDIARY TABLE II—*Distribution of 10,000 of each sex in each main religion (districts only)*

Age	1931		1921		1911		1901		1891		1881	
	Male	Female	Male	Female	Male	Female	Male	Female	Male	Female	Male	Female
1	2	3	4	5	6	7	8	9	10	11	12	13
MUSLIMS												
0—5 ...	1,517	1,719	1,298	1,508	1,462	1,653	1,455	1,661	1,850	2,053	1,409	1,607
5—10 ...	1,436	1,363	1,635	1,626	1,616	1,603	1,563	1,560	1,629	1,541	1,646	15,63
10—15 ...	1,277	1,124	1,183	983	1,203	973	1,203	1,003	966	790	1,118	895
15—20 ...	865	877	789	695	759	708	829	763	983	1,080	783	760
20—40 ...	3,089	3,264	2,929	3,093	2,847	3,075	2,951	3,110	3,065	3,136	2,978	3,125
40—60 ...	1,388	1,308	1,526	1,511	1,523	1,477	1 461	1,423	1,217	1,148	1,495	1,515
60 and over ...	428	345	640	574	590	511	538	480	290	252	571	535
Mean age ...	23·2	22·5	24·7	24·4	24·1	23·5	23·5	23.0	21·5	21·0	23·7	23·4
HINDUS												
0—5 ...	1,249	1,763	706	1,426	1,013	1,457	979	1,517	1,386	1,840	1,015	1,457
5—10 ...	1,055	1,342	733	1,323	1,079	1,437	1,027	1,394	1,188	1,403	1,096	1,400
10—15 ...	970	1,128	703	1,025	1,002	1026	950	980	867	818	923	927
15—20 ...	1,104	1,008	990	890	974	834	932	896	1,107	1,106	848	762
20—40 ...	4,027	3,233	5,432	3 364	3,934	3,308	4,214	3,289	3,860	3,272	3,965	3,257
40—60 ...	1,311	1,222	1,119	1,494	1,514	1,481	1,496	1,454	1,357	1,297	1,707	1,643
60 and over ...	284	304	317	478	424	457	402	470	235	264	446	554
Mean age ...	24·0	21·9	27.1	24·6	25·5	23·8	25·7	23·6	23·4	22·0	26·1	24·5
SIKHS												
0—5 ...	1,175	1,793	604	1,451	814	1,443	531	1,501	716	1,891	429	1,358
5—10 ...	993	1,413	660	1,380	896	1,405	563	1,187	587	1,291	469	1,402
10—15 ...	902	1,212	646	1,077	890	995	606	980	500	808	488	833
15—20 ..	1,217	1,029	1,045	855	1,035	855	1,101	935	1,116	1,325	967	878
20—40 ...	4,146	3,183	5,604	3,375	4,698	3,381	5,735	3,370	6,030	3,275	6,050	3,485
40—60 ...	1,246	1,078	1,123	1,360	1,261	1,361	1,164	1,514	880	1,164	1,314	1,466
60 and over ...	321	292	318	502	406	560	300	513	171	246	283	578
Mean age ...	24·2	21.0	27.6	24·2	25.8	24·0	26·8	24·1	25.1	21·4	27·5	24·3

SUBSIDIARY TABLE III—*Age distribution of 1,000 of each sex in certain castes*

Caste	Males—number per *mille* aged						Females—number per *mille* aged					
	0—6	7—13	14—16	17—23	24—43	44 and over	0—6	7—13	14—16	17—23	24—43	44 and over
1	2	3	4	5	6	7	8	9	10	11	12	13
Awan ...	186	175	71	113	283	172	224	165	72	123	282	134
Arora ...	197	170	62	124	294	153	223	168	59	134	290	126
Brahman ...	123	122	73	175	339	168	194	141	95	149	262	159
Chamar ...	187	150	108	148	281	126	210	125	101	164	289	111
Chuhra ...	122	116	81	197	333	151	181	159	89	134	300	137
Gujar ...	197	195	83	108	257	160	236	155	67	99	295	148
Jat ...	143	142	97	169	305	144	226	146	63	128	291	146
Khatri ...	154	134	74	102	296	180	200	160	77	151	262	150
Pathan ...	196	182	68	115	280	159	218	167	62	119	291	143
Sayad ...	207	185	73	115	269	151	220	164	66	120	285	145
Swathi ...	195	193	130	128	251	103	206	170	72	99	312	141
Tanaoli ...	213	204	78	97	267	141	228	165	52	111	316	128

SUBSIDIARY TABLE IV—*Proportion of children under 14 and of persons over 43 to those aged 14—43 in certain castes, also of married females aged 14—43 per 100 females*

Castes	Proportion of children, both sexes, per 100		Proportion of persons over 43 per 100 aged 14—43		Number of married females aged 14—43 per 100 females of all ages
	Persons aged 14—43	Married females aged 14—43	Male	Female	
1	2	3	4	5	6
Awan	79	230	37	28	36
Arora	78	235	32	26	37
Brahman	50	192	29	31	38
Chamar	62	234	24	20	36
Chuhra	46	210	25	26	41
Gujar	86	228	36	32	38
Jat	60	218	25	30	35
Khatri	62	194	34	31	38
Pathan	82	239	34	30	34
Sayad	84	239	33	31	34
Swathi	77	222	20	29	38
Tanaoli	88	224	32	27	33

SUBSIDIARY TABLE V—*Proportion of children under 10 and of persons over 60 to those aged 15—40, also of married females aged 15—40 per 100 females*

District and natural division	Proportion of children (both sexes) per 100										Proportion of persons over 60 per 100 aged 15—40										Number of married females aged 15 - 40 per 100 females of all ages				
	Persons aged 15—40					Married females aged 15—40					1931		1921		1911		1901		1891						
	1931	1921	1911	1901	1891	1931	1921	1911	1901	1891	Male	Female	Male	Female	Male	Female	Male	Female	Male	Female	1931	1921	1911	1901	1891
1	2	3	4	5	6	7	8	9	10	11	12	13	14	15	16	17	18	19	20	21	22	23	24	25	26
N.-W. F. P. (Districts).	72	74	82	77	82	195	206	212	205	213	10	8	16	15	16	13	13	12	7	6	33	32	32	32	35
Hazara	79	86	85	86	90	192	199	203	206	220	14	10	24	16	19	14	17	13	8	6	34	33	33	33	36
Trans-Indus Districts.	70	74	81	74	80	196	209	215	205	210	9	8	14	14	14	13	12	12	6	6	33	31	31	32	35
Peshawar ...	66	72	78	74	75	192	203	208	201	203	9	8	16	16	16	14	14	13	7	5	33	31	31	32	36
Kohat ...	78	83	92	75	81	208	228	243	224	238	9	8	12	14	13	13	10	12	5	6	33	30	30	32	33
Bannu ...	77	83	88	78	89	207	227	234	216	223	7	6	11	12	10	10	9	10	7	6	33	30	31	32	34
Dera Ismail Khan ...	71	65	76	72	81	187	197	198	190	201	8	8	10	13	12	13	10	11	7	7	34	33	33	34	36

SUBSIDIARY TABLE-V-A.—*Proportion of children under 10 and of persons over 60 to those aged 15—40 in certain religions; also of married females aged 15-40 per 100 females*

Religion and natural division	Proportion of children both sexes per 100: Persons aged 15—40: 1931	1921	1911	1901	1891	Married females aged 15—40: 1931	1921	1911	1901	1891	Proportion of persons over 60 per 100 aged 15 40: 1931 Male	1931 Female	1921 Male	1921 Female	1911 Male	1911 Female	1901 Male	1901 Female	1891 Male	1891 Female	Number of married females aged 15—40 per 100 females of all ages: 1931	1921	1911	1901	1891
1	2	3	4	5	6	7	8	9	10	11	12	13	14	15	16	17	18	19	20	21	22	23	24	25	26
N.-W. F. P. districts all religions Hazara.	72	74	82	77	82	195	206	212	205	213	10	8	16	15	15	13	13	12	7	6	33	32	32	32	31
All religions ...	79	86	85	86	90	192	199	203	206	220	14	10	24	16	19	14	17	13	8	6	34	33	33	33	36
Muslim ...	80	89	88	88	93	193	202	205	209	222	15	10	25	17	20	14	17	13	8	6	34	33	33	33	36
Hindu ...	48	45	46	54	48	166	145	157	162	172	6	8	10	13	9	11	11	11	4	7	38	38	37	36	38
Sikh ...	68	56	58	Not available	31	191	160	176	Not available	190	11	10	15	14	13	14	Not available	Not available	3	9	35	36	36	Not available	39
Christian ...	48	25	16	Not available	22	159	133	79	Not available	223	1	2	1	8	2	8	Not available	Not available	1	...	39	17	41	Not available	35
Trans-Indus Districts all religions.	70	74	81	74	80	196	209	215	205	210	9	8	14	14	14	13	12	12	6	6	33	31	31	32	35
Muslim ...	72	80	85	79	83	197	212	219	208	212	9	8	15	15	15	13	13	12	7	6	33	31	31	32	35
Hindu ...	57	38	54	48	63	187	170	176	170	191	5	7	6	11	8	11	7	11	5	6	34	34	34	36	35
Sikh ...	49	32	37	Not available	27	185	163	169	Not available	206	5	6	5	11	6	13	Not available	Not available	2	5	36	37	36	Not available	33
Christian ...	21	12	13	Not available	8	146	142	141	Not available	166	1	3	1	7	...	4	Not available	Not available	...	2	40	8	42	Not available	40

SUBSIDIARY TABLE VI—*Variation in population of certain age-periods*

Natural division	Period	Various per cent. in population increas (+) and decrease (—): All ages	0—10	10—15	15—40	40—60	60 and over
	2	3	4	5	6	7	8
North-West Frontier Province Districts	1921-1931	+8	+8	+19	+15	−4	−31
	1911-1921	+4	−2	+2	+8	+4	+12
	1901-1911	+7	+9	+6	+3	+11	+16
	1891-1901	+10	−3	+88	+3	+33	+106
Hazara	1921-1931	+8	+7	+15	+17	−1	−29
	1911-1921	+3	+2	...	+1	+7	+22
	1901-1911	+8	+7	+2	+8	+10	+21
	1891-1901	+9	−7	+55	−3	+46	+105
Trans-Indus Districts	1921-1931	+8	+9	+20	+.4	−5	−32
	1911-1921	+2	−4	+3	+6	+2	+8
	1901-1911	+7	+10	+9	+1	+12	+14
	1891-1901	+11	−2	+31	+6	+31	+106

SUBSIDIARY TABLE VII—*Reported birth-rate by sex and natural division*

Year	Number of births per 1,000 of total population (Census of 1921)					
	Province (all districts)		Hazara		Trans-Indus districts	
	Male	Female	Male	Female	Male	Female
	2	3	4	5	6	7
1921	15·1	11·9	14·9	12·7	15·1	11·6
1922	13·1	10·3	10·5	9·2	14·1	10·7
1923	15·3	12·1	15·8	14·0	15·1	11·4
1924	15·1	11·7	16·6	14·4	14·6	10·6
1925	15·0	11·6	16·2	14·1	14·6	10·7
1926	16·9	13·0	16·8	14·9	17·0	12·3
1927	16·4	12·6	15·8	13·5	16·6	12·3
1928	18·3	14·0	17·0	14·6	18·8	13·7
1929	17·3	13·3	15·8	13·8	17·8	13·1
1930	14·4	11·0	14·5	12·4	14·4	10·6

SUBSIDIARY TABLE VIII—*Reported death-rate by sex and natural division*

Year	Number of deaths per 1,000 of each sex (Census 1921)					
	Province (total districts)		Hazara		Trans-Indus districts	
	Male	Female	Male	Female	Male	Female
1	2	3	4	5	6	7
1921	30·3	29·8	47·3	40·1	26·5	25·7
1922	20·8	20·6	25·1	25·5	19·2	18·6
1923	22·5	23·0	25·2	24·7	21·5	22·3
1924	27·9	31·6	24·9	25·8	29·0	34·0
1925	19·0	18·8	16·8	16·8	19·8	19·6
1926	20·6	21·0	18·4	18·5	21·3	22·1
1927	21·4	20·6	17·8	17·9	22·8	21·7
1928	18·3	18·6	17·3	17·8	18·7	18·9
1929	22·1	23·2	18·7	19·5	23·4	24·7
1930	21·2	20·5	17·9	17·9	22·4	21·6

SUBSIDIARY TABLE IX—*Reported death-rate by sex and age in decade and in selected years per* mille *living at same age according to the Census of 1921*

Age	Average of decade		1921		1924		1925		1928	
	Male	Female	Male	Female	Male	Female	Male	Female	Male	Female
1	2	3	4	5	6	7	8	9	10	11
All ages ...	24·0	23·3	32·5	30·5	29·8	32·3	20·4	19·2	19·6	19·0
0 and under 1 ...	157·9	123·4	189·2	155·8	159·0	124·1	136·3	106·2	153·9	125·1
1 " 5 ...	39·7	34·4	54·1	49·0	46·8	39·5	31·3	25·8	33·4	29·5
5 " 10 ...	10·3	10·2	16·4	15·6	14·5	15·7	8·2	8·1	7·2	7·2
10 " 15 ...	9·5	11·5	14·8	15·1	16·1	23·0	8·5	9·4	6·1	7·9
15 " 20 ...	12·1	14·8	19·9	20·2	16·7	22·9	10·0	11·4	7·4	13·7
20 " 30 ...	12·0	13·9	16·6	16·8	17·1	22·9	10·3	11·5	8·8	10·8
30 " 40 ...	17·0	18·0	22·4	22·6	24·6	29·7	14·7	15·2	12·2	13·6
40 " 50 ...	23·4	21·7	31·0	25·6	30·5	35·2	20·4	18·3	17·6	15·8
50 " 60 ...	34·5	31·2	45·5	38·5	40·5	43·1	28·9	25·7	28·0	25·1
60 and over ...	52·4	47·1	70·4	64·3	59·6	59·3	47·2	41·6	42·9	37·3

SUBSIDIARY TABLE X—*Reported deaths from certain diseases per mille of each sex*

Year	Fever					Cholera					Plague					Small-pox				
	Actual number of deaths			Ratio per *mille* of each sex		Actual number of deaths			Ratio per *mille* of each sex		Actual number of deaths			Ratio per *mille* of each sex		Actual number of deaths			Ratio per *mille* of each sex	
	Total	Male	Female	Male	Female	Total	Male	Female	Male	Female	Total	Male	Female	Male	Female	Total	Male	Female	Male	Female
1	2	3	4	5	6	7	8	9	10	11	12	13	14	15	16	17	18	19	20	21
1921	53,833	29,340	24,493	25·72	24·62	4,285	2,439	1,846	2·14	1·86	138	48	90	0·04	0·09	576	314	262	0·28	0·27
1922	39,984	21,777	18,207	19·09	18·31	92	60	32	0·05	0·03	124	80	44	0·07	0·04	104	52	52	0·04	0·05
1923	39,881	21,438	18,443	18·79	18·54	2	1	1	0·001	0·001	3,743	1,926	1,817	1·69	1·83	94	50	44	0·04	0·04
1924	45,699	24,291	21,408	21·29	21·52	9	6	3	0·01	0·003	11,397	4,713	6,684	4·13	6·72	212	128	84	0·11	0·08
1925	35,258	19,176	16,082	16·81	16·17	116	76	40	0·07	0·04	217	116	101	0·10	0·11	586	328	258	0·29	0·26
1926	38,221	20,609	17,612	18·05	17·71	...	...	...	...	...	638	249	389	0·22	0·39	777	391	386	0·34	0·39
1927	38,673	21,378	17,295	18·74	17·39	2	1	1	0·001	0·001	232	92	140	0·08	0·14	165	81	84	0·07	0·08
1928	33,159	17,688	15,471	15·50	15·55	..	...	...	...	...	...	...	...	...	...	572	288	284	0·25	0·29
1929	42,415	22,387	20,028	19·62	20·13	30	17	13	0·01	0·01	...	...	...	...	...	586	295	291	0·26	0·29
1930	38,884	21,396	17,488	18·76	17·58	449	263	186	0·23	0·15	...	...	...	...	...	73	45	28	0·04	0·03

CHAPTER V

SEX

INTRODUCTORY.

104. The proportion of females to males in the Province is of particular interest from the marked contrast which it bears to the proportion found in the countries of Western Europe. The proportion recorded in the present census (districts only) is 843 females to 1,000 males, while the figures for England and Wales in the census of 1921 were 1,096 females per 1,000 males. Owing to the greater accuracy of census proceedings in Europe, and the known disinclination among Indians to disclose details of the female members of their families, it was for a long time doubted if the figures showing an excess of males were correct. It was however shown in the India Census Report of 1911 that the Western Europe proportions should not necessarily be taken as the standard, that all external evidence was against the theory of wholesale omissions, that in any case there could not possibly have been enough omissions to turn the balance between defect and excess of females, and that excessive defect of females does not occur in the localities, communities and age-periods in which it would be expected under the theory of omission. The theory was finally refuted by the fact that the census of 1911, admittedly much more accurate than any of its predecessors, disclosed a decrease in the proportion of females compared to previous censuses.

Excess of males in India compared with excess of females in Europe.

105. Special reasons for the general excess of males over females in India as a whole are usually given as follows :—

Some reasons for excess of males in India.

(*i*) The prevalence of female infanticide, though this is now comparatively rare.

(*ii*) A neglect of female infants, found most commonly in those communities which pay for bridegrooms, and which are therefore involved in considerable expense in possessing daughters, who sooner or later have to be married.

(*iii*) Infant marriage, with premature sexual intercourse and child-bearing.

(*iv*) A very high birth-rate, which is inevitably accompanied by a high female death-rate.

(*v*) Unskilful and insanitary methods of midwifery.

(*vi*) The hard life of widows.

(*vii*) The severe labour which women of the lower class are called upon to perform.

106. The conditions summarised above do not for the most part obtain in the Frontier Province. This is a Province in which a bride-price, not a bridegroom price, has to be paid. The custom of the payment of a bride-price is in itself a proof of the deficiency of women, and it also removes the financial and economic inducement to parents to rid themselves of daughters. Infant marriage, as shown in paragraph 105 of the following chapter, is practically unknown in the Province. Unskilful and insanitary methods of midwifery undoubtedly contribute heavily to the mortality of women, and so does the severe labour which women of the lower classes are required to undertake ; in certain parts of the Province the main consideration in selecting a wife is stated to be the amount of physical labour, both in the fields and at home, which she is likely to be able to endure. It seems possible, however, that the principal cause of the excess of females over males is one of those factors in sex-determination which scientists have not yet been able to define. In all countries of the world more males are born than females, but in addition to this it is a well-established fact that when a nation particularly needs males, as when a war or other catastrophe has fallen more heavily on males than on females, nature provides an even greater excess of male births to make good the deficiency. The reason for this is unknown ; the fact remains. Two reasons were traced by Mr Latimer in his Census Report of 1911 to show why nature might be expected to restrict the proportionate increase of females. In the first place, the more females are born the more rapidly is the population likely to increase, and the tribal area, which forms more than half the area of the whole Province, is wild and rugged country, hardly able to support the existing number of its inhabitants. In the second place the inhabitants of the settled districts are only now emerging, and those of the trans-border tract have not yet emerged,

Special reasons for excess of in N.-W. F. P.

from a condition of society not far removed from perpetual warfare. In such a society the birth of sons is ardently to be desired. If women were lacking they could always be seized or bought from others ; but if men were wanting, the tribe went to the wall. "*The result of such an environment for many generations*", writes Mr. Latimer, " might well be to turn out a race in which males predominate; and once the type were fixed, it would take more than a few generations of altered circumstances to change it ".

DETAILS OF THE CURRENT CENSUS.

Reference to statistics.

107. The statistics of sex for the Province are combined with those for age, religion and civil condition in Imperial Table VII, and with those for caste tribe or race in Imperial Table VIII. The sexes will also be found distinguished in most of the other tables. Certain proportional figures are worked out in the subsidiary tables at the end of this chapter, as follows :—

No. I Number of females per 1,000 males in districts and natural divisions for each census since 1881.

No. II Number of females per 1,000 males by different periods and religious in each census since 1911.

No. III Number of females per 1,000 males at different age periods by religious and natural divisions in the present census.

No. IV Number of females per 1,000 males in certain selected castes.

No. V Actual number of births and deaths of each sex reported in each of the last thirty years.

No. VI Number of reported deaths in each sex at different ages in the most unhealthy years of the past decade.

Reasons for variations in excess of males to be considered.

108. As already indicated, the number of females in the Province exceeds the number of males. The actual figures for those enumerated in the Districts are 1,315,818 males and 1 109,258 females, giving a proportion of 843 females to every 1,000 males. The proportionate figure is compared in the margin with figures for other parts of India. More males than females are born, infant mortality is higher among male babies than females, mortality in the early reproductive age is more common among females, more immigrants and emigrants are males, and the proportion who survive to old age is greater among males than females.

Proportion of females per 1,000 males		
Madras	...	1,025
Behar and Orissa	...	1,008
Central Province and Berar	...	1,000
Burma	...	958
Bengal	...	924
Bombay	...	918
Assam	...	909
Ajmer Merwara	...	908
United Provinces of Agra and Oudh		904
N.-W. F. P.	...	843
Punjab	...	831
Coorg	...	803
Baluchistan	...	778
Delhi	...	722

The result produced by these variations is illustrated in the graph, below which shows the rise and fall in the proportion of females to males in the various periods of life.

No: 14.

DIAGRAM ILLUSTRATING VARIATIONS IN PROPORTION OF FEMALES TO 1,000 MALES IN VARIOUS AGE-GROUPS

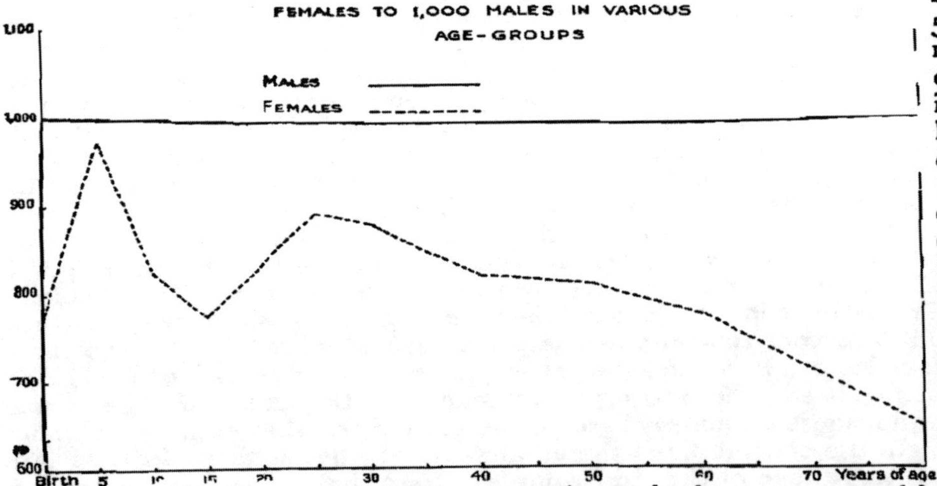

The rise between 0 and 5 years of ages represents the excess of male infant mortality ; the steep drop between 10 and 20 the early deaths in child-birth ; the rise to 25 the period of emigration of males, and the final steady decline the greater mortality among females. The steepness of the curves is no doubt exaggerated by mis-statement of age, but the general indication is accurate.

It will be convenient to consider this variation in relation to the four causes which affect the proportions most, namely birth-rate, mortality in infancy and at other ages, migration, and death-rate. In doing so it is necessary to remember that the statistics of age are probably the least accurate of all those that have been collected, and that the registration of births and deaths is far from complete.

Excess of male births.

109. The number of male births recorded in the decade 1921—1930 is 340,379 and the number of female births 263,491. This gives a proportion of 774 female to 1,000 male births. The proportion in each year of the decade is shown in the figures in the margin. It is probable that the proportion of female births which were not registered is very much higher than the proportion of male births, since the birth of a son to a Pathan is an occasion of general rejoicing and festivity, while the birth of a daughter is as nearly as possible ignored. Indeed the figure obtained by adding the excess of reported births over deaths to the female population of 1921 is only 1,053,714; add to this again 20,040, the excess of recorded immigrants, over recorded emigrants and the total is still less by 24,504 than the female population enumerated in 1931. This number must consist principally of those whose birth was not registered but who have survived up to the time of the enumeration. In spite of this, however there is no doubt of the excess of male over female births.

Proportion of male births to 100 female births.

Year		Proportion of male births to 100 female births
1921	...	125·9
1922	...	127·3
1923	...	126·5
1924	...	129·7
1925	...	129·9
1926	...	130·7
1927	...	130·1
1928	...	130·9
1929	..	130·0
1930	...	130·1

The proportion of females to males is higher in Hazara than in any other district. This will be discussed again later, but it is convenient to note here that the number of female births recorded per 1,000 male births in this district is 866, while in the rest of the Province it is only 739. A theory has been advanced elsewhere that the cold and damp climate of the Punjab hills has some effect on the number of females born. These figures seem to bear out the theory.

Infant mortality higher among males.

110. The proportion of females to males is more nearly equal in the age-group from 0 to 5 years than at any other period of life. Since more males than females are born it is obvious that infantile mortality must be higher among boys than among girls.

That this is so is shown by the figures in the margin which show the average death rate and the death rate in certain years of the past decade among children of under one year of age. The figures are extracted from Subsidiary Table IX of Chapter IV, and are calculated on the number of children under one year of age recorded in the 1921 enumeration. The death-rate is in every case higher among boys. The figures of actual numbers, not resolved into proportions, are to be found in Subsidiary Table No. VI at the end of this chapter.

Reported death-rate per *mille* among infants under one year of age

		Male	Female
Average of decade	...	157·9	123·4
1921	...	189·2	155·8
1924	...	159·0	124·1
1925	...	136·3	105·2
1928	...	163·9	125·1

Mortality at later ages higher among females.

111. Between the ages of one and five the death-rate is only slightly higher among boys than among girls, from 5 to 10 years of age it is about equal, and in every age-group from 10 to 40 years it is higher among females. The causes for the higher death-rate among females in the middle age-periods

have already been discussed, and though many of them can be, and are being, eradicated they are at present so prevalent that they can be regarded as natural causes. Were they the only factors to be considered after the proportions in the birth-rate and infant mortality, the number of females in the population would still fall below the number of males, though the proportion would be 850 to 1,000 instead of 843. The method by which this figure is obtained is shown in the margin. There remains the important question of migration to consider.

Proportion of females to males in actual population compared to that in natural population

	Males	Females	Total	Proportion of females to 1,000 males
Actual enumerated population ...	1,315,818	1,109,258	2,425,076	843
Deduct immigrants ...	106,961	48,230	155,191	451
Add emigrants ...	71,706	28,190	99,896	393
Natural population ...	1,280,563	1,089,218	2,369,781	850

Effect of migration on proportion between sexes.

112. The effect of migration on the proportion between the sexes is most easily seen in the figures for districts and natural divisions, for castes, and for the different religions. The greater number of migrants are males in the prime of life. It follows that immigration will decrease and emigration increase, the proportion of females in a given area. Similarly the Muslims, who are for the most part permanent residents of the Province, may be expected to show a higher proportion of females to males than the Hindus, Sikhs and Christians, who are principally temporary or semi-permanent immigrants.

Effect of migration illustrated by figures for districts.

113. The figures showing the sex proportions in the district and natural divisions are given in the margin. The proportion of females is highest in Kohat and Hazara. These are the two districts whose young men travel most freely abroad in search of employment. Dera Ismail Khan, the stay-at-home district, is low in the scale. Peshawar, the centre of Government, trade and education in the Province and the location of four military cantonments, attracts the largest number of immigrants and has the highest proportion of males to females. The figures for Agencies and tribal areas are only a guess, based on the assumption that the proportion will be the same as among the Muslims of the settled districts.

District and Natural Division	Proportion of females per 1,000 males
Districts ...	843
Hazara ...	871
Trans-Indus districts ...	833
Peshawar ...	811
Kohat ...	872
Bannu ...	862
Dera Ismail Khan ...	850
Agencies and tribal areas ...	864

Effect of migration illustrated by figures for religions.

114. The proportion by religions is shown in the margin. In order to bring out the effect even more clearly the proportions recorded in each of the last three censuses are given. The Muslims, the most settled part of the population, show the highest proportion of females in each of the three years. Among Sikhs, the least settled of the three main religions, the proportion is in each year the lowest. Hindus, who are not yet properly settled, but among whom the proportion of permanent settlers is higher than among Sikhs, show figures intermediate between the other two. The variations from census to census in the figures for these two religions is also instructive. The rise from 1911 to 1931 shows that the two communities are gradually becoming more settled; the exceptionally low figures in 1921 indicate a period of disturbed conditions, when not only had women and children been sent away, but large numbers of Hindu and Sikh troops were present in the Province for special military reasons.

Proportion of females to every 1,000 males in the three principal religions

Religions	Proportion of females to every 1,000 males		
	1911	1921	1931
Muslims ...	880	866	862
Hindus ...	680	559	695
Sikhs ...	520	484	617
All religions ...	858	831	843

The same facts are illustrated in a different way by the marginal statement showing the proportion of females to males in the different religions at each age period up to the age of fifteen, the proportions in each of the religions are very similar. After this age, when young men may be expected to go out in search of their own livelihood, the proportion of females is far higher among Muslims than in either of the other religions. A curious feature, however, for which no explanation is forthcoming, is that for the age-group 60 and over the proportion of females is highest among Hindus.

same facts considered in relation to age periods.

Proportion of females to every 1,000 males at different age periods

Age period	All religions	Muslim	Hindu	Sikh
All Ages ...	843	862	695	617
0—5 ...	976	977	981	942
5—10 ...	822	818	884	878
10-15 ...	763	759	808	830
15—20 ...	838	874	635	522
20—25 ...	900	963	601	480
25—30 ...	887	945	530	470
30 40 ...	821	858	544	471
40—50 ...	808	827	633	533
50 60 ...	776	787	675	536
60 and over ...	695	695	745	562

116. The proportion of females to males in each of twelve selected castes, is given in the margin. The castes which are typical of the Province are Pathan, Awan, Sayed, Gujar, Swathi and Tanaoli. Of these the Pathans and Awans, who are widely distributed in all the Trans-Indus districts, show figures not far distant from the proportion of 843 recorded for the Province. Pathans migrate a little more than Awans, and the figure is correspondingly higher. The Gujars are mainly nomads who take their families with them. Sayads, Swathis and Tanaolis are all more common in Hazara than in any other district, Swathis and Tanaolis being almost entirely confined to this district. The reasons which govern the proportion of females in Hazara as a whole, are also those which account for the high proportion in each of these tribes. Aroras, Brahmans, Chamars and Khatris are all castes which are gradually becoming more settled. Chuhras, who show the lowest proportion in the table are mainly temporary immigrants who do not bring their families with them. The figure for Jats is curiously low seeing that the Jat caste is the only caste in which females out-number males under the age of five years.

Proportion of females in certain castes.

Statement showing the proportion of females to 1,000 males in selected castes

Caste	Proportion of females to 1,000 males
1. Arora ...	776
2. Awan ...	828
3. Brahman ...	604
4. Chamar ...	668
5. Chuhra ...	455
6. Gujar ...	835
7. Jat ...	720
8. Khatri ...	757
9. Pathan ...	865
10. Sayad ...	922
11. Swathi ...	832
12. Tanaoli ...	895

117. One more illustration of the effect of the migration on the proportion between the sexes is provided by the figures in the margin which campare the natural population, the stay-at-home population, and the actual population. The actual population means the actual number of persons found and enumerated in the Province on the night of the census; by deducting from this total the number of immigrants found in the Province, the total of those both born and enumerated in the Province, *i. e.*, the stay-at-home population, is

Natural, stay-at-home, and actual proportions compared.

Figures for North-West Frontier Province (Districts)

Classification	Total	Males	Females	Number of females to 1,000 males
Enumerated in the Province wherever born (actual population).	2,425,076	1,315,818	1,109,258	843
Born in the Province and enumerated either in the Province or elsewhere in India (natural population).	2,369,781	1,280,563	1,089,218	850
Born in the Province and enumerated in the Province (stay-at-home population)	2,259,885	1,208,857	1,061,028	878

obtained ; while the natural population is this latter figure with the addition of emigrants from the Province found elsewhere in India. As is to be expected, the proportion of females is higher among the stay-at-home population than in the natural population, but is lowest of all after the inclusion of the immigrants.

VARIATIONS FROM PREVIOUS CENSUS.

Variation in proportions since 1921.

118. The proportion of females in the population, and the majority of the causes affecting it, have now been considered for the census of 1931. It remains to consider the variation from the figures recorded ten years before. The figures reproduced in the margin show the variations by religion to which reference has already been made in paragraph 114 above. The increase in the proportion among Hindus and Sikhs does not warrant the drawing of any conclusions about the habits of the two communities, but is only an indication of more settled conditions in the Province. There is however a slight fall in the figure for Muslims. Although the vital statistics can not be accepted as entirely accurate, they undoubtedly provide some clue to the decrease in the proportion of females. The figures in the margin show how the population would compare with the present population of 1921 if (*i*) the vital statistics were correct, and (*ii*) there had been no migration. The proportion of female deaths recorded exceeds, and the proportion of female births is less than, the original proportion of females to males. The figures refer to the whole population, but since Muslims form 92 per cent. of the population they may be accepted as applying in the main to Muslims. They offer a decrease of 18 per *mille*. The actual decrease to be accounted for is only 4 per *mille*. The difference may be explained,

Proportion of females to every 1,000 males in the actual population, by religions

Religion		Proportion of females per 1,000 males	
		1921	1931
All religions	...	831	843
Muslims	...	866	862
Hindus	...	559	695
Sikhs	...	484	617

Effect of vital statistics on the proporation of females in the Province in the absence of migration

		Males	Females	Proportion of females per 1,000 males
Population in 1921	...	1,229,316	1,022,024	831
Add birth in 1921—1930	...	340,379	263,491	774
Deduct deaths in 1921—1930	...	275,460	232,801	845
Total	...	1,294,235	1,052,714	813

(*i*) by failure to register female births,

(*ii*) by the increase of emigration, and

(*iii*) by the decrease of immigration, which has occurred during the last ten years.

Variation over last fifty years considered by districts.

119. The figures may be examined again district by district for each successive census since 1881. The proportion of females in Hazara shows a steady rise from 1881 to 1921. This is explained by the fact that both the total birth-rate and the proportion of females born are higher in Hazara than in the Trans-Indus districts, while in addition the men of the district are more prepared than most to emigrate. The fall in 1931 may be attributed to the fact that the number of females born per 1,000 of the population had actually exceeded the number of males born in the decade 1911 to 1920, but fell slightly below it in the succeeding decade. Kohat also shows a steady increase owing to the number of its young men who move abroad in service or in search of employment. Bannu does not send out many emigrants

Proportion of females to every 1,000 males at different censuses

		Proportion of females to 1,000 males					
		1881	1891	1901	1911	1921	1931
Districts	...	819	843	846	858	831	843
Hazara	...	862	855	869	881	894	871
Peshawar	...	781	838	840	838	805	811
Kohat	...	788	796	783	870	851	872
Bannu	...	838	859	859	870	847	862
Dera Ismail Khan	...	862	860	860	850	754	850

and the proportion of females in the population shows a slight tendency to increase as conditions become more settled. Dera Ismail Khan is the most conservative district, and the figures hardly vary save in 1921 when there were large bodies of troops in the district. The proportion in Peshawar, omitting the figures for 1881 for which no explanation is available, decreases as Peshawar attracts more immigrants. The nett result is a slight rise in the figure for all districts, attributable to more settled conditions, more emigration, and less immigration.

SUBSIDIARY TABLE I—*General proportions of the sexes by natural divisions and districts*

District and natural division	Number of females per 1,000 males											
	1931		1921		1911		1901		1891		1881	
	Actual population	Natural population	Actual population	Natural population	Actual population	Natural population	Actual population	Natural population	Actual population	Natural population	Actual population	Natural population
1	2	3	4	5	6	7	8	9	10	11	12	13
N.-W. F. P. Districts ...	843	850	831	848	858	887	846	885	843	892	819	879
Hazara ...	871	Not available	894	878	881	878	869	866	855	878	862	869
Trans-Indus Districts ...	833		809	838	849	892	837	894	838	897	814	882
Peshawar ...	811		805	831	838	878	840	893	838	897	781	880
Kohat ...	872		851	835	870	906	783	915	796	910	788	900
Bannu ...	862		847	860	870	915	859	863	859	908	838	9[illegible]8
Dera Ismail Khan ...	850		754	840	850	904	860	911	860	883	862	860

Note.— The figures in column 13 are based on the population of the Districts of Peshawar, Kohat, Bannu and Dera Ismail Khan as constituted in 1881, when the two latter districts comprised a large area now forming the Mianwali District of Punjab and when the Kohat District contained 24 villages now forming part of the Peshawar District. See pages 85 and 86 of Volume I, Punjab Census Report, 1881.

The figures in column 11 do not take into account emigrants to places beyond the Punjab and the North-West Frontier Province.

SUBSIDIARY TABLE II—(*Districts only*)

Number of females per 1,000 males at different age-periods by religions at each of the last three Censuses

Age	All religions			Muslim			Hindu			Sikh		
	1911	1921	1931	1911	1921	1931	1911	1921	1931	1911	1921	1931
1	2	3	4	5	6	7	8	9	10	11	12	13
0—1 ...	972	954	957	975	956	953	940	929	964	872	957	953
1—2 ...	995	992	1,005	1,003	994	1,008	857	966	983	1,069	1,021	956
2—3 ...	1,036	1,010	1,016	1,037	1,016	1,018	1,044	968	1,005	936	834	943
3—4 ...	1,018	1,023	979	1,020	1,024	982	972	1,028	1,000	945	976	929
4—5 ...	955	974	930	953	977	929	1,036	921	954	892	1,022	930
Total 0—5 ...	993	989	976	995	992	977	978	959	981	921	956	942
5—10 ...	874	849	822	873	849	818	905	859	884	815	831	878
10—15 ...	709	708	763	712	710	759	697	698	808	581	667	830
15—20 ...	793	738	838	821	779	874	583	491	635	429	436	522
20—25 ...	947	837	900	1;047	1,023	963	561	312	601	323	261	480
25—30 ...	898	829	887	963	935	945	537	364	530	385	285	470
Total 0—30 ...	872	833	866	894	874	884	703	541	738	525	480	668
30—40 ...	861	842	821	894	889	858	584	504	544	417	403	471
40—50 ...	868	856	808	887	877	827	670	661	633	579	560	533
50—60 ...	788	814	776	801	825	787	657	691	675	527	596	536
60 and over ...	759	765	695	760	768	695	732	725	745	716	642	562
Total 30 and over...	833	828	794	854	853	816	637	597	604	507	493	506
Total all ages (actual population)	858	831	843	880	866	862	680	559	695	520	484	617
Total all ages (natural population)	887	848	851	891	Not available		834	Not available		801	Not available	

SUBSIDIARY TABLE III—*Number of females per 1,000 males at different age-periods by religions and Natural Divisions (Census 1931)*

Age	Hazara				Trans-Indus Districts			
	All religions	Muslim	Hindu	Sikh	All religions	Muslim	Hindu	Sikh
1	2	3	4	5	6	7	8	9
0—1 ...	991	991	995	942	942	937	958	955
1—2 ...	996	999	924	990	1,009	1,012	995	948
2—3 ...	1,002	1,007	879	923	1,022	1,023	1,032	948
3—4 ...	982	985	911	942	985	980	1,018	926
4—5 ...	956	957	918	952	920	917	961	924
Total 0—5 ...	985	987	927	947	973	972	992	941
5—10 ...	829	829	827	850	820	814	895	885
10—15 ...	754	754	743	791	766	761	821	840
15—20 ...	890	920	539	691	820	858	661	495
20—25 ...	1,048	1,100	537	733	855	918	618	445
25—30 ...	1,041	1,081	512	724	838	898	533	432
Total 0—30 ...	909	922	666	801	850	869	754	642
30—40 ...	884	907	508	635	799	839	552	442
40—50 ...	784	794	616	560	817	840	637	527
50—60 ...	739	747	584	594	790	803	697	521
60 and over ...	633	633	661	630	729	730	767	540
Total 30 and over ...	793	865	562	607	794	820	613	484
Total all ages (actual population) ...	871	884	634	737	833	850	709	593
Total all ages (natural population)	Not available							

SUBSIDIARY TABLE IV—*Number of females per 1,000 males for certain selected castes*

Castes	Number of females per 1,000 males						
	All ages	0—6	7—13	14—16	17—23	24—43	44 and over
1	2	3	4	5	6	7	8
Arora	776	877	767	739	839	764	643
Awan	828	993	783	845	898	824	645
Brahman	604	956	699	788	517	466	569
Chamar	668	749	557	628	741	687	588
Chuhra	455	676	622	503	309	410	413
Gujar	835	997	665	670	771	958	772
Jat	720	1,143	742	464	545	687	731
Khatri	757	982	904	788	709	669	630
Pathan	865	963	792	787	897	899	776
Sayad	922	979	816	836	963	976	886
Swathi	832	879	733	460	642	1,036	1,141
Tanaol	895	957	728	594	1,022	1,061	809

SUBSIDIARY TABLE V—*Actual number of births and deaths reported for each sex during the decades 1901—1910, 1911—1920 and 1921—1930*

Year	Number of births			Number of deaths			Difference between columns 2 and 3. Excess of latter over former (+), defect (−)	Difference between columns 5 and 6. Excess of latter over former (+), defect (−)	Difference between columns 4 and 7. Excess of former over latter (+), defect (−)	Number of female births per 1,000 male-births	Number of female-deaths per 1,000 male-deaths
	Males	Females	Total	Males	Females	Total					
1	2	3	4	5	6	7	8	9	10	11	12
1901—1910	373,219	305,850	679,069	292,358	266,658	559,016	—67,369	—25,700	+ 125,053	819·49	912·09
1901 ...	33,345	27,068	60,413	20,826	18,382	39,208	—6,277	—2,444	+21,205	811·76	882·65
1902 ...	36,751	30,153	66,904	25,574	23,050	48,624	—6,598	— 2,524	+ 18,280	820·47	901·31
1903 ...	34,655	28,211	62,866	29,393	27,146	56,539	—6,444	— 2,247	+6,327	814·05	923·55
1904 ...	38,140	31,404	69,544	29,480	27,379	56,859	—6,736	— 2,101	+ 12,685	823·39	928·72
1905 ...	38,761	31,608	70,369	27,941	25,386	53,327	—7,153	—2,555	+ 17,042	815·46	908·56
1906 ...	41,722	35,112	76,834	33,834	33,315	67,149	—6,610	—519	+ 9,685	841·57	984·66
1907 ...	33,899	28,163	62,062	35,031	31,986	67,017	—5,736	—3,045	—4,955	830·79	913·07
1908 ...	39,344	31,837	71,181	35,888	32,473	68,361	—7,507	—3,415	+ 2,820	809·20	904·08
1909 ...	36,247	29,864	66,111	26,979	23,712	50,691	— 6,383	—3,267	+ 15,420	823·90	878·91
1910 ...	40,355	32,430	72,785	27,412	23,829	51,241	—7,925	—3,583	+21,544	803·62	869·29
1911 - 1920	370,516	298,364	668,880	326,928	291,523	618,451	—72,152	—35,405	+ 50,429	805·27	891·70
1911 ...	39,430	32,176	71,606	25,477	22,081	47,558	—7,254	—3,396	+ 24048	816·03	866·70
1912 ...	41,734	33,919	75,653	25,416	22,333	47,749	—7,815	—3,083	+ 27,904	812·74	878·70
1913 .	41,230	32,603	73,833	26,361	23,942	50,303	—8,627	—2,419	+ 23,530	790·76	908·24
1914 ...	36,546	30,155	66,701	27,768	24 792	52,560	— 6,391	—2,976	+ 14,141	825·12	892·83
1915 ...	36,039	28,725	64,764	25,707	22,487	48,194	— 7,314	—3,220	+ 16,570	797·05	874·74
1916 ...	38,151	30,923	69,074	32,461	28,961	61,422	—7,228	— 3,500	+ 7,652	810·54	892·13
1917 ...	36,216	29,333	65,549	32,590	28,572	61,162	—6,883	—4,018	+ 4,387	809·95	876·71
1918 ...	34,328	28,093	62,421	73,314	70,192	143,506	— 6,235	— 3,122	—81,085	818·37	957·42
1919 ...	32,592	25,819	58,411	31,203	27,099	58,302	—6,773	—4,104	+ 109	792·19	868·47
1920 ...	34,250	26,618	60,868	26,631	21,064	47,695	—7,632	—5,567	+ 13,173	777·17	790·96
1921 1930	340,379	263,491	603,870	275,460	232,801	508,261	— 76,888	— 42,659	+ 95,609	774·12	845·14
1921 ...	32,612	25,900	58,512	37,235	30,519	67,754	— 6,712	—6,716	—9,242	794·19	819·63
1922 ...	28,472	22,360	50,832	25,545	21,024	46,569	—6,112	— 4,521	+ 4,263	785·33	823·02
1923 ...	33,146	26,205	59,351	27,644	23,465	51,109	—6,941	—4,179	+ 8,242	790·59	848·83
1924 ...	32,775	25,272	58,047	34,270	32,328	66,598	—7,503	— 1,942	—8,551	771·08	943·33
1925 ...	32,644	25,128	57,772	23,354	19,194	42,548	—7,516	—4,160	+ 15,224	769·76	821·87
1926 ...	36,764	28,133	64,897	25,264	21,502	46,766	—8,631	—3,762	+ 18,131	765·23	851·09
1927 ...	35,603	27,365	62,968	26,361	21,070	47,431	—8,238	—5,291	+ 15,537	768·62	799·29
1928 ...	39,648	30,295	69,943	22,494	19,033	41,527	— 9,353	—3,461	+ 28,416	764·10	846·14
1929 ...	37,516	28,850	66,366	27,179	23,695	50,874	—8,666	—3,484	+ 15,492	769·01	871·81
1930 ...	31,199	23,983	55,182	26,114	20,971	47,085	—7,216	— 5,143	+ 8,097	768·71	803·06

SUBSIDIARY TABLE V—*Actual number of births and deaths reported for each sex during the decades 1901—1910, 1911—1920 and 1921—1930—concluded*

Year	Number of births: Males	Number of births: Females	Number of births: Total	Number of deaths: Males	Number of deaths: Females	Number of deaths: Total	Difference between columns 2 and 3. Excess of latter over former (+), defect (—)	Difference between columns 5 and 6. Excess of latter over former (+), defect (—)	Difference between columns 4 and 7. Excess of former over latter (+), defect (—)	Number of female-births per 1,000 male-births	Number of female-deaths per 1,000 male-deaths
1	2	3	4	5	6	7	8	9	10	11	12
						Hazara					
1921—1930	90,341	78,509	168 850	73,233	65,943	139,176	—11,832	—7,290	+29,674	869·03	900·45
1921 ...	8,727	7,481	16,208	13,385	11,779	25,164	—1,246	—1,606	—8,956	857·22	880·02
1922 ...	6,169	5,413	11,582	8,260	7,499	15,759	—756	—761	—4,177	877·45	907·87
1923 ...	9,270	8,235	17,505	8,285	7,261	15,546	—1,035	—1,024	+1,959	888·35	876·40
1924 ...	9,740	8,442	18,182	8,167	7,571	15,738	—1,298	—596	+2,444	866·74	927·02
1925 ...	9,486	8,285	17,771	5,520	4,948	10,468	—1,201	—572	+7,303	873·39	896·38
1926 ...	9,889	8,733	18,622	6,062	5,425	11,487	—1,156	—637	+7,135	883·10	894·92
1927 ...	9,293	7,932	17,225	5,836	5,263	11,089	—1,361	—583	+6,136	853·55	900·10
1928 ...	9,955	8,601	18,556	5,691	5,236	10,927	—1,354	—455	+7,629	863·99	920·05
1929 ...	9,312	8,088	17,400	6,130	5,724	11,854	—1,224	—406	+5,546	868·56	933·77
1930 ...	8,500	7,299	15,799	5,897	5,247	11,144	—1,201	—650	+4,655	858·71	889·77
						Trans-Indus Districts					
1921—1930	250,038	184,982	435,020	202,227	166,858	369,085	—65,056	—35,369	+65,935	739·82	825·10
1921 ...	23,885	18,419	42,304	23,850	18,740	42,590	—5,466	—5,110	—286	771·15	785·74
1922 ...	22,303	16,947	39,250	17,285	13,525	30,810	—5,356	—3,760	+8,440	759·85	782·47
1923 ...	23,876	17,970	41,846	19,359	16,204	35,563	—5,906	—3,155	+6,283	752·64	837·03
1924 ...	23,035	16,830	39,865	26,103	24,757	50,860	—6,205	—1,346	—10,995	730·63	948·44
1925 ...	23,158	16,843	40,001	17,834	14,246	32,080	—6,315	—3,588	+7,921	727·31	798·81
1926 ...	26,875	19,400	46,275	19,202	16,077	35,279	—7,475	—3,125	+10,996	721·86	837·26
1927 ...	26,310	19,433	45,743	20,525	15,817	36,342	—6,877	—4,708	+9,401	738·62	770·62
1928 ...	29,693	21,694	51,387	16,803	13,797	30,600	—7,999	—3,006	+20,787	730·61	821·10
1929 ...	28,204	20,762	48,966	21,049	17,971	39,020	—7,442	—3,078	+9,946	736·14	853·77
1930 ...	22,699	16,684	39,383	20,217	15,724	35,941	—6,015	—4,493	+3,442	735·01	777·76

SUBSIDIARY TABLE VI—*Number of deaths of each sex at different ages*

Age	1921 Males	1921 Females	1923 Males	1923 Females	1924 Males	1924 Females	1927 Males	1927 Females	1929 Males	1929 Females	Total Males	Total Females	Average number of female deaths per 1,000 males deaths
1	2	3	4	5	6	7	8	9	10	11	12	13	14
0—1 ...	6,296	5,055	5,058	3,761	5,292	4,025	5,445	3,982	6,228	4,807	28,319	21,630	763·80
1—5 ...	6,220	5,785	3,657	3,295	5,383	4,667	4,698	3,938	5,153	4,803	25,111	22,488	895·54
5—10 ...	3,057	2,511	2,026	1,721	2,715	2,539	1,622	1,284	1,794	1,640	11,214	9,695	864·54
10—15 ...	2,042	1,483	1,551	1,502	2,215	2,270	986	760	1,001	926	7,795	6,941	890·44
15—20 ...	1,833	1,417	1,417	1,377	1,537	1,606	857	813	992	909	6,636	6,122	921·04
20—30 ...	3,079	2,837	2,455	2,583	3,177	3,898	2,034	2,136	1,866	2,066	12,611	13,520	1072·08
30—40 ...	3,368	3,135	2,933	2,785	3,698	4,113	2,286	2,191	2,085	2,021	14,370	14,245	991·30
40—50 ...	3,227	2,424	2,566	2,200	3,172	3,323	2,417	1,909	2,127	1,937	13,509	11,793	872·97
50—60 ...	3,004	2,147	2,312	1,709	2,671	2,406	2,270	1,613	2,149	1,725	12,406	9,600	773·82
60 and over ...	4,951	3,587	3,441	2,364	4,196	3,309	3,538	2,302	3,604	2,715	19,730	14,277	723·62
Total ...	37,077	30,381	27,416	23,297	34,056	32,156	26,153	20,928	26,999	23,549	151,701	130,311	859·00

CHAPTER VI
CIVIL CONDITION

Reference to statistics.

120. The figures for civil condition are given according to age, sex and religion in Imperial Table VII, and for selected castes in Imperial Table VIII. Proportional figures based on these tables are given in five subsidiary tables at the end of this chapter. Subsidiary Table I compares the distribution by civil condition for each sex, religion and main age-period in each of the last 5 Census ; No. II and No. III give distribution by age-periods and regilions and by natural divisions ; No. IV shows the proportion between the sexes of the married, unmarried and widowed by religions, age-periods and natural divisions, and No. V similar figures for selected castes.

Meanings and value of the statistics.

121. The instructions given to enumerators were that every person, male or female, infant, child or adult, was to be entered as either married, unmarried or widowed. The instructions were further elaborated as follows :—" A woman who has neverbeen married must be shown in column 6 as unmarried even though she be a prostitute or a concubine. Persons who are recognized by custom as married are to be entered as such even though they have not gone through the full ceremony, *e. g.* widows who have taken a second husband by the rite known as karewa or *chadar-andazi*. Divorced persons will be entered as widowed ." These instructions are perfectly clean to any one who knows the customs of the country, and since this description may be said to apply to all the enumerators, there is no reason to suppose they were misunderstood. The statistics on the whole may therefore be taken as fairly accurate. The only confusion which might arise in comparing the statistics with those of Western countries, would be owing to the existence of a ceremony of betrothal, which is usually spoken of as marriage In European countries the marriage cremony is normally followed by the parties living together ; in this Province a ceremony which has many of the same rites and much of the same finality as marrige, is frequently nothing more than a formal and inviolable betrothal, and it is not until some time afterwards that another ceremony takes place and the bride goes permanently to her husbands house to reside. When the parties are of marriageable age before marriage, the second ceremony, the ceremony which precedes consummation, usually takes place along with the first, but where the parties are not of mature age, and sometimes even when they are so, there is an interval between the two which may extend to several year nevertheless the first ceremony is spoken of as a wedding and the parties are known as husband and wife. The effect of this custom on the statistics is that a certain number of persons among the lower age-groups have been entered as married, who although technically and legally married, would not appear so in European statistics. The principal object of recording the number of married children is to determine the physical effect on the race of premature co-habitation. Since the figures for this Province are negligible even when increased by the number of the " inviolably betrothed ", the possible effect of the difference in notation is not worth considering.

DISTRIBUTION BY CIVIL CONDITION

Distribution of total population.

122. The figures in the margin show the distribution of both males and females in the 5 settled districts according to civil condition. These general figures are worth consideration for they offer a very fair indication of all that is to be found in subsequent paragraphs of this chapter. It will be seen that the number of married males, including widowers, is a little over 42 per cent. and the number of females a litttle over 54 per cent. When it is remembered that the average age of all the males enumerated in the Census is 23·3 years and that of females 22·4 years, and that approximately 40 per cent. of the total population is under 15 years of age, it will be realised that the proportion of marriage among those of marriageable age is high. It will be noticed further that the proportion of married per 1,000 among females is higher than among males, and that the proportion of widowed among males is less than half the proportion among females. The actual

Per 1,000 of each sex		
Civil condition	Males	Females
Unmarried ...	574	458
Married ...	379	433
Widowed	47	109

figures, which are to be found in Imperial Table VII, show 761,520 unmarried males to 508,291 unmarried females, 491,044 married males to 479,733 married females, and an excess of females over males among the widowed where the totals are 121,234 and 62,954 respectively. The points which emerge from these figures for special enquiry are (*i*) the high general proportion of marriages, (*ii*) the higher proportion of married among the females enumerated, although marriage is almost universal among both, and (*iii*) the excess of females among the widowed. These points are to be considered not only for the Province as a whole, but for each of the main religions and by natural divisions.

High populations of marriage.

123. The three religions which are numerically the most important in the Province, are Muslim, Hindu and Sikh. All three religions treat marriage as a religious obligation, rather than as a social function or as a matter of convenience. Among Hindus in particular, marriage is a sacrament which must be performed regardless of the fitness of the parties for married life. Every Hindu must marry and beget himself at least one son to save his spirit from wandering hopelessly in the nether regions. The very word for son, *putra*, means one who saves his father's soul from hell. Similarly, in parts of India where Hindu sentiment is strong, " if a Hindu maiden is unmarried at puberty, her condition brings social obloquy on her family, and on a strict reading of certain texts entails retrospective damnation on three generations of ancestors "*. Sikhs are not influenced by quite the same considerations as a Hindus, but still regard marriage as a religious duty. Among Muslims there are not the same religious penalties attached to failure to marry, but marriage is nevertheless almost equally common, as the figures in the margin show. Owing to the small proportion of Hindus and Sikhs among the total population of the Province, and the fact that a large number of these are immigrants, it would not be safe to draw conclusions from the difference between the respective figures for the religions. Reasons for the lowness of the figure among Muslims are many. Among others may be noted the fact that the population is only now emerging from a state of society when marriage and the begetting of sons were a duty to the tribe, and that wives are still required by the majority of the population for the sake of their labour both in the fields and at home. The prevalence of marriage among Muslims is also to some extent affected by Hindu customs, and in this connection it will be interesting to note that the marriage statistics of Hazara and Dera Ismail Khan, the two districts most affected by the proximity of the Punjab, differ slightly from those of other parts of the Province. In particular, marriage takes place at a later age among the Pathans of the hills which border the Province on the west, than among the plainsmen of the Punjab on the east. Marriage among the former is made to depend very much more on economic conditions than is the case among the latter. The customs of the inhabitants of the settled districts derive principally from the customs of the hills, but are now gradually being modified by influences from the east.

Number of persons per 10,000 of each sex remaining unmarried after the age of 40

	Males	Females
All religions ...	88	46
Muslims ...	85	46
Hindus ...	121	28
Sikhs ...	116	31

Proportion of marriages compared with records of other proportions.

124. The figures giving the proportion per 1,000 of the sex concerned who are or have been married are compared in the margin with those recorded in India as a whole and in other countries in the Census of 1921. It will be seen that the figures for both males and females fall considerably below those for the rest of India. This discrepancy is however to a large extent illusory, since, as will be shown later, the average age at which marriage takes place is higher in this Province than elsewhere in India. The discrepancy is greater in the case of females than in the case of males, and an explanation for this may be found in the fact that there is a custom among agriculturists by which a female is, in the absence of male issue, allowed to inherit and enjoy patrimony, so long as she does not marry.

Number per *mille* who are or have been married

Country	Males	Females
India ...	502	642
England ...	408	429
Italy ...	402	455
N.-W. F. Province ...	426	542

* *Vide* India Census Report, 1901, paragraph 693.

Figures of marriage to be considered in regard to age.

125. The figures which have so far been considered have been for the most part those for the population as a whole. Since infant marriage is unknown in the Province, and child-marriage practically negligible, a fairer indication of the prevalence of marriage is obtained by considering the population by age-groups. The diagram below shows what proportion of each sex in each age-group throughout life are married, unmarried or widowed. It will be convenient to examine certain of the groups separately.

No 15

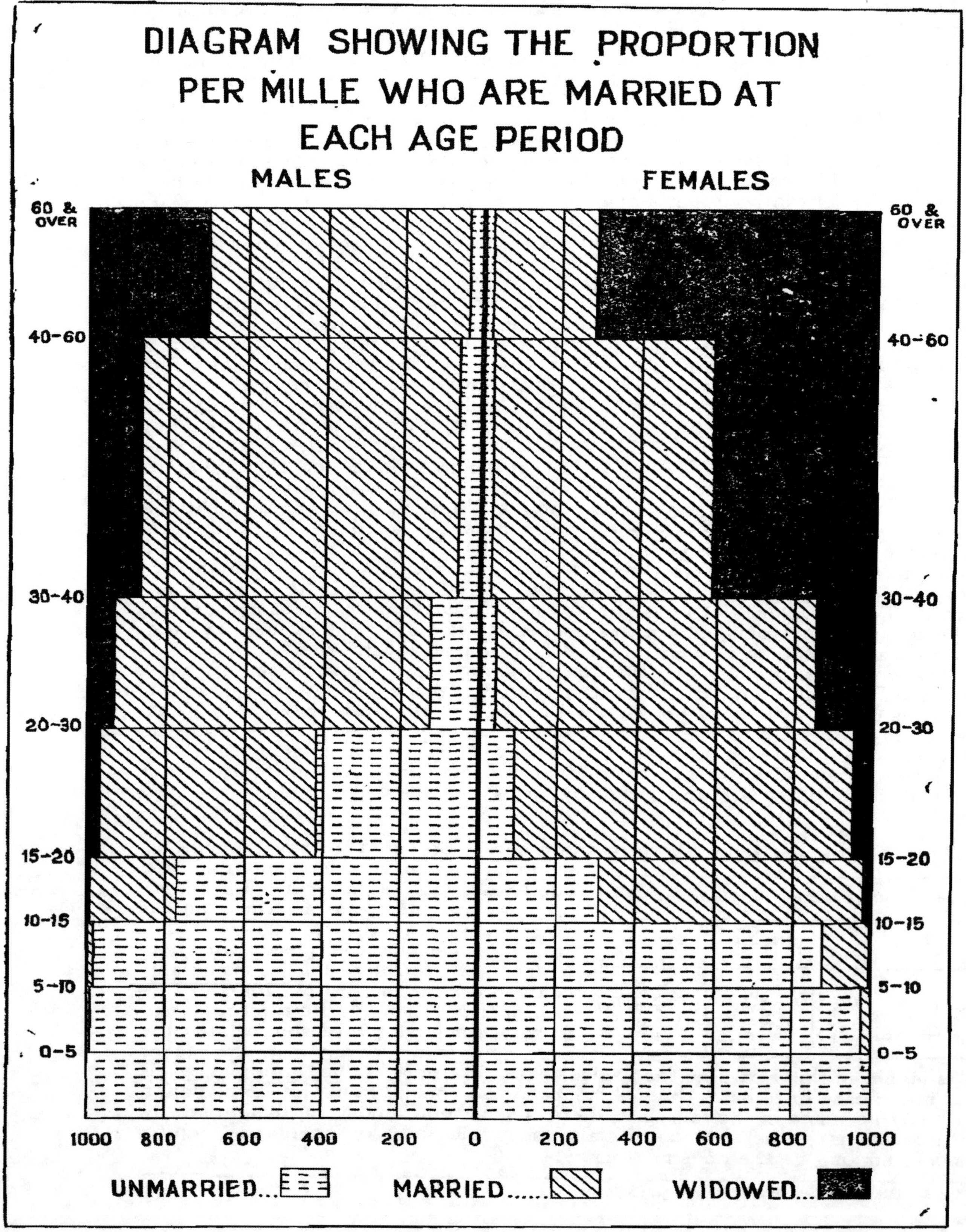

126. The first point to notice is that no persons under the age of 5 have been returned as married. The figures for India as a whole in the Census of 1921 showed 6 per *mille* among males and 11 per *mille* among females. In addition to this, 1 per *mille* among females were shown as widowed. Between the ages of 5 and 10 the proportion of married in both sexes is still extremely low, being 5 per *mille* among males and 18 per *mille* among females. Corresponding figures for all India in 1921 were 32 and 88 respectively. The next age-group, from 10 to 15 years showed a considerable rise in the all-India figures to 116 for males and 382 for females, but the figures for this Province are still low, being 23 and 151, or 25 and 154 if the widowed are included. The age-group from 15 to 20 years is the first which shows a really substantial increase in the proportion for this Province. The proportion of married females in this group is 674 per *mille*, or more than two-thirds. The reason for this sudden rise is that between 15 and 20 years is the common age for the marriage of females in the Province. The corresponding rise in the proportion among males does not occur until the 20 to 30 years' group, when the proportion of married per *mille* rises from 221 to 657; the reason for the rise is the same. After these two age-groups the proportion of those remaining unmarried in each sex becomes negligible, falling finally as low as 88 among males and 46 among females, and it becomes more convenient to consider the relative proportions of the married and the widowed. In this connection the first point which strikes the eye is that the proportion of widowed among males is always, as it were, one age-group behind that for females, and that it never reaches so large a figure as among females. The reason for this is, of course, the later marrying age among males. A secondary reason is that males re-marry to a greater extent than females. The figures for the age-gronps at the extremes of life may also be compared with the all-India figures of 1921. Among males of the age of 60 and over the proportion of widowed per *mille* in this Province is 298; among females it exceeds this figure in the previous age-group, and reaches 720 per *mille* in the age-group under consideration. The figures for all-India were 394 and 859 respectively. In this Province there are no widows under the age of 10, 3 per *mille* between the ages of 10 and 15, and 19 between 15 and 20; the corresponding all India figures showed 1 per *mille* widows under the age of 5, 5 per *mille* between 5 and 10, 17 between 10 and 15, and 41 in the age-group 15 to 20.

Proportion of married persons found in each of various age-groups.

127. The figures may now be considered in regard to each of the three main religions. The figures in the margin show the proportion of married, including widowed, in the enumerated population of all ages. Since, as has been already remarked, a large proportion of the population is too young to marry, little is to be gained by consideration of these figures until they are re-divided into age-groups.

Proportion of married persons considered by religions.

Proportion of married (including widowed) per 1,000 of sex concerned, by religion and sex

	Male	Female
All religions ...	421	541
Muslims ...	418	540
Hindus ...	471	458
Sikhs ...	565	558

128. The first age-groups to consider are those containing the children and young adults. As already stated, no persons have been returned as married under the age of 5 years. The figures for the age-groups 5 to 10, 10 to 15 and 15 to 20 are given in the margin, being those among which married persons would be considered by western standards to be young. All three religions show a very low proportion of married males between the ages of 5 and 10 years. The highet proportion is among Hindus, and is only 9 per *mille*. Among females the proportion, though still low, is noticeably higher. The earlier age of marriage among females shows itself even at this age, and becomes more and more marked in each of the succeeding periods. The proportion among Hindus and Sikhs is more than twice as high as among Muslims, since not only

Low proportions in the younger age-groups.

Proportion of married females and males per *mille* at different age-periods

Age-period	Males			Females		
	Muslims	Hindus	Sikhs	Muslims	Hindus	Sikhs
0—5 ...	...	...	...	...	...	...
5—10 ..	4	9	6	16	35	39
10—15 ...	23	30	27	116	179	212
15—20 ...	207	286	279	664	788	816

are the Muslims of this Province reluctant on humane grounds to allow their daughters to marry until they consider them old enough, but they see no religious or social objection to allowing them to reach puberty unmarried.

In the age-group 10 to 15, the highest proportion of married males is again to be found among Hindus, but the figure is still only 30 per *mille*. The number of married females, on the other hand, shows a considerable advance, being as high as 212 per *mille* among Sikh.

The next age-group, that from 15 to 20, shows a large increase in the proportions for each sex and for all three religions. As in the age-groups already considered, the highest proportion among females is in the Sikhs, and among males in the Hindus. From the sudden rise in the figures for females in this age-group, it may be inferred that 15 to 20 years is the common age of marriage in the Province, and this is indeed the case. The earlier relative age of marriage among Sikhs and Hindus in comparison with Muslims will have to borne in mind when the figures for districts and natural divisions are considered.

Proportion in younger age-groups lower than elsewhere in India.

129. The interest of the figures in the preceding paragraph is increased by consideration of the marginal table, which shows corresponding figures for India as a whole. Even among Muslims the figures for India as a whole show 3 per *mille* married among males of under 5 years of age, and 6 among females, while for Hindus the figures are 7 and 14 respectively. Among Sikhs no infant males and only one infant female per *mille* are married. In the next 3 age-groups again the proportion of each sex married both among Muslims and among Hindus is very considerably lower in this Province than in the rest of India. Among Sikhs the proportion for the Province is lower in the case of each sex in the age-group 10 to 15, but in the case of each of the other age-groups it is higher than in the rest of India. These comparisons establish even more firmly the conclusion that the marrying-age in the North-West Frontier Province is comparatively late.

Number of married persons per *mille* in 1921 in India as a whole

Age-period		Males			Females		
		Muslims	Hindus	Sikhs	Muslims	Hindus	Sikhs
India							
0—5	...	3	7	...	6	14	1
5—10	...	14	41	6	50	111	25
10—15	...	66	144	63	344	437	224
15—20	...	241	339	258	815	814	785

Decrease of proportion in last 40 years.

130. The proportion of early marriages in each sex is also of sufficient interest to trace through the last 40 years. Up to 1921 the figures have shown a steady decline. Under the age of 5 one male child and one female per 1,000 were shown as married in 1891, and one female in 1901, since when no person of either sex has been shown as married under this age. Between the ages of 5 and 10 the figures from 1891 to 1921 run 4—2—2—1 for males, and 11—6—6—2 for females. The figures of the present year still show no persons married under the age of 5, but in the next period they show a rise to 5 per *mille* in the case of males and 18 per *mille* in the case of females. This unfortunate set-back may be attributed to false propaganda against the Sarda Act, and does not represent the true state of feeling in the Province.

130-A.—Since the writing of the preceding paragraphs a note has been received from the Census Commissioner for India to the effect that for presentation of the figures of marital condition in quinary groups, the conversion of alternate ternary and septenary groups by the same formula as yield increased accuracy in the case of the total population of all marital canditions is unsatisfactory, because within the ternary and septenary groups of persons of different marital conditions the distribution by single year or smaller age-periods is proportionately the same. The septenary and ternary groups from 4 to 23 for civil condition have accordingly been extracted mathematically and are shown in Subsidiary Table I-A at the end of this chapter, where they may be compared with the figures for the quinary groups. The figures for married persons are however so low even in the possibly inaccurate quinary groups that the comparison does not render necessary any change in the remarks already recorded.

Proportion of married population in younger age-groups, by religions.

131. Figures for the population as a whole must always include a certain number of persons who for one reason or another cannot marry. It is therefore advisable, in considering the prevalence of early marriage, to examine the proportion of those in the younger age-groups to the total married population. The figures for the Province for each of the 3 main religions are given in the margin. The proportions in the age-groups 15 to 20 are similar to those found in India as a whole, but the divergence in the earlier age-groups is striking. In the age-group 0 to 10 years, where the figure for the Province is 3·6 per *mille*, the all-India figure in 1921 was 21·8; in the age-group 10 to 15 years, the figures for comparison are 19·5 and 60·8. The all-India figures for different religions are not reproduced, but it may be noted that the excess of the all-India over the Provincial figures is common to both Hindus and Muslims, though among Sikhs the reverse is found.

Proportion in certain age-groups per 1,000 of the married population

Religion		Age-group		
		0—10	10—15	15—20
All religions	...	3·6	19·5	94·1
Muslim	...	3·4	19·1	91·7
Hindu	...	5·9	23·6	121·1
Sikh	...	5·8	26·7	125·6

Early marriage considered by caste.

132. A Table, reproduced in the margin, has also been extracted from Subsidiary Table V to show the proportion in selected castes of married males and females between the ages of 7 and 13 years, the youngest period in which marriage is at all common in the Province. The castes selected are those which are numerically the most important, or depressed. It is not possible to draw any conclusion from the order in which the proportions run. The highest proportion is found among Chuhras, a low caste, but the next highest is among Brahmans, a high caste. Pathans and Sayads consider themselves of higher caste than Tanaolis, Swathis and Awans, and are lower on the list than these three, but on the other hand Gujars and Jats are lower still. The 2 highest proportions are in castes which are included among Hindus, but on the other hand other Hindu castes are found low down on the list.

Proportion of married per *mille* in the age-periods 7 to 13 in certain castes

Caste		Married persons per *mille* in age-periods 7 to 13	
		Males	Females
Chuhra	...	182	148
Brahman	...	90	69
Tanaoli	...	32	31
Swathi	...	26	24
Chamar	...	23	55
Arora	...	19	34
Awan	...	16	42
Khatri	...	14	94
Sayad	...	11	27
Pathan	...	9	34
Gujar	...	8	32
Jat	...	8	27

Proportion remaining unmarried in the later age-groups.

133. After the age of 20 it becomes unusual for a female to remain unmarried. The proportions so remaining unmarried in the various religions are shown in the statement in the margin. Although they are small in each case, they are sufficient to provide a comparison. The relative proportions between the religions remain as they have been in previous groups, Sikhs and Hindus being the most-married and Muslims the least-married. The majority of those who remain unmarried to the end probably do so for some physical or similar reason, though among Muslims the number is swollen by the practice, already mentioned, of allowing females to inherit and retain property so long as they remain unmarried.

Proportion of unmarried females per 1,000 at certain age-periods

Religion		Age-periods		
		20 to 40	40 to 60	60 and over
All religions	...	67	29	21
Muslim	...	69	29	22
Hindu	...	46	19	17
Sikh	...	39	24	15

Proportion of widowed in various age-groups.

134. The proportion of widows may be expected to be highest in the religion in which the females marry at the earliest age. The figures in the margin show the proportions among children, among those

Proportion of widowers and widows in 1,000 of each sex at certain ages

Religion	All ages		10 to 15		15 to 40		40 and over	
	Males	Females	Males	Females	Males	Females	Males	Females
Muslim ...	47	108	2	3	41	75	171	467
Hindu ...	54	129	2	4	45	95	212	577
Sikh ...	48	128	1	5	37	75	207	549

from 15 to 40 years of age, and among those of 40 years of age and over. The Muslims show the lowest proportion of widows in each of the three groups, since their women folk marry at a later age than those of either of the other two religions. Between the ages of 10 and 15 there is a greater proportion of Sikh widows than of Hindus, but in each of the other groups the reverse is the case. Among widowers the proportion is highest among the Hindus ; the lowest proportion of "all-ages" is found among Muslims, although Sikhs show a slightly lower proportion in the earlier age-groups. The low proportion among Muslims is again due to a later age of marriage.

Comparison with Punjab.

135. The proportion of widows and widowers may also be compared with the proportions in the same age-groups recorded in the Punjab Census of 1921. Except in the case of females of the age of 40 and over, the proportion of the widowed is higher in the Punjab than in this Province.

Proportion of widowers and widows in 1,000 of each sex in Punjab in 1921

Religion	All ages		10 to 15		15 to 40		40 and over	
	Males	Females	Males	Females	Males	Females	Males	Females
Punjab								
Muslim ...	78	119	2	4	59	62	250	448
Hindu ...	99	158	7	8	77	99	293	540
Sikh ...	95	136	3	3	61	62	289	464

This may be taken as an indication that widow remarriage is more commonly practised in this Province. Among Muslims there is no religious objection to the practice in either province, and its greater frequency in this Province may be attributed partly to the relatively greater scarcity of females and partly to the custom among Pathans of a widow re-marrying with a brother of her deceased husband. The lower proportion of widowers is probably due to the later age of marriage in this Province, which makes it less likely that a husband will survive his wife. Among Hindus the lower proportion of widows is to be attributed to the work of certain religious societies which are aiming to this end. These societies are also at work in the Punjab, but are meeting with greater proportionate success here, partly on account of the scarcity of females, partly as a result of the influence of the Pathan customs of the country, and partly because there is a higher literate, and so presumably teachable, proportion among the Hindus of this Province than among the very much larger Hindu population of the Punjab. The effect of the work of these societies is also reflected in the fall in the proportion of Hindu widows in the Province, to which a further reference will be made later

Summary of conclusions hitherto reached.

136. The figures that have so far been considered are for the population as a whole and for each of the three main religions. The facts which these figures have illustrated may be briefly summarised as follows :—

(*i*) Marriage is almost universal among both sexes and in all three religions.

(*ii*) It is more nearly universal among females than among males, and among Hindus and Sikhs than among Muslims.

(*iii*) Infant marriage is unknown in the Province, and child marriage very uncommon.

(*iv*) The average age at which marriage takes place is higher than elsewhere in India ; within the Province it is higher among males than among females, and higher among Muslims than in the followers of other religions.

The varations between districts and natural div'sions of the Province, and between the present results and those tabulated in 1921, remain for consideration.

VARIATIONS

Variation in proportion of married persons by districts.

137. The table in the margin shows the proportion of married persons in 1,000 of the population of each sex in each of the 5 administered districts. For the purposes of this table, widowed are included as married. The two highest figures for each sex are provided by Hazara and Dera Ismail Khan, and these are the only districts for which the figures are above the Provincial average. They are the two districts which are most affected by the influence of the Punjab. Hazara is a cis-Indus district, and Dera Ismail Khan is the district with the lowest proportion of Muslims and the highest proportion of Hindus and Sikhs. The particularly low proportion of married males in Peshawar is explained by the presence in the district of large numbers of unmarried immigrants, including serving soldiers and students.

Proportion of married and widowed per 1,000 of each sex

		Males	Females
All districts	...	421	541
Hazara	...	429	553
Peshawar	...	413	536
Kohat	...	420	531
Bannu	...	420	527
Dera Ismail Khan	...	432	557

Districts considered by age-groups. The younger age-groups.

138. The proportion of the married population of each district found in the early age-groups is also lowest in Peshawar, as may be seen from the figures in the margin. The proportions in Hazara, Bannu and Dera Ismail Khan vary little from the Provincial figure. The highest proportion in each of the three groups is found in Kohat District. This however does not indicate a prevalence of early marriage in Kohat. It is explained by the absence on military and quasi-military service of large numbers of persons in the prime of life. The majority of these persons are married, and their exclusion from the married population of the district reduces the natural proportion of married persons in the later age-groups and so increases the proportion in the earlier groups

Propoition of married persons per 1,000 of total married population

District		Age-group		
		0 to 10	10 to 15	15 to 20
Districts	...	3·6	19·5	94·1
Hazara	...	4·0	24·1	94·2
Peshawar	...	2·5	16·3	90·8
Kohat	...	6·7	24·4	101·5
Bannu	...	4·2	16·6	94·3
Dera Ismail Khan	...	3·4	17·7	98·6
Peshawar City (Municipality)		2·5	15·4	90·0

Actually the lowest of all the proportions are those found in Peshawar Municipality, but they vary so little from the figures for the district and are so much affected by immigration, that it would be unsafe to draw from them any conclusions with regard to the effect of urban life.

The figures of each district for the lower age-groups have also been considered by religions, but do not show sufficient variation to be worth reproducing. The figures for Muslims, as is to be expected, follow those for "all religions" which have been already considered Among Hindus the proportions are highest in Hazara and lowest in Dera Ismail Khan and Bannu, and among Sikhs they are highest in Kohat and lowest in Hazara. The total numbers present in each of these districts are too small to allow of the drawing of any conclusions from these variations.

The middle and older age-groups.

139. The marginal statement shows the proportion by districts of married persons in the middle and advanced periods of life, per 1,000 of the total married population. The figure for those in the age-group 20 to 40 years is highest in Bannu and almost the same in Dera Ismail Khan. These are the two districts in which the inhabitants are least inclined to migrate. In Hazara, the most enterprising district, the proportion in this group is the lowest. The figures for Peshawar and Kohat are also low. Kohat sends out a high proportion of emigrants, and the proportion in Peshawar is reduced by the presence of students, young soldiers and others who are just inside this age-group

Proportion of married persons in middle and advanced ages per 1,000 of married population

District		Age-periods	
		20 to 40	40 and over
Districts	...	600	283
Hazara	...	583	294
Peshawar	...	599	291
Kohat	...	604	264
Bannu	...	624	261
Dera Ismail Khan	...	617	264

but are not yet married. In the age group for those of 40 years of age and over the highest figure is that for Hazara. Hazara is the district with the highest proportion of females to males, and the highest total proportion of married persons ; its young men who emigrate in early life in search of employment, return to their homes in old age ; it is therefore to be expected that it should show a higher proportion than any other district. Peshawar of necessity shows a high figure, since for reasons already discussed its figures are low in the young and middle groups. Bannu, Dera Ismail Khan and Kohat are low for similar reasons.

Variation in distribution since previous Census.

140. The total population of the Province has undergone an increase of approximately 7 per cent. since the last Census. The figures in the margin show how this increase is distributed between the married, unmarried and widowed. The only decrease is in the number of widowed males. A decrease in the number of widowed persons is to be expected in a growing population at the end of a prosperous and healthy period such as the last has been. The fact that the decrease is not larger among males, and that there is an actual increase among females, who are less inclined to re-marry, is explained by the number of persons who were widowed in the influenza epidemic of 1918. The increase in the number of married females is lower than might have been expected, and the increase in unmarried females considerably higher. The proportion of married females to the total female population is in fact lower at the present Census than in any previous Census since 1881. * It was 444 per *mille* in 1921 and is now 433. This again is a result of the influenza epidemic as may be judged from the division into age-groups shown in the margin. The figures for those under 20 years of age, who were little affected by the epidemic, have risen slightly, but those in the higher age-groups have been reduced by the high mortality of the epidemic affecting them both directly through death and indirectly through widowhood. The proportion of married males per 1,000 of the male population was 380 in 1921 and is now 379. It shows on the whole a steady increase since 1881, due to increasing economic prosperity.

Distribution by civil condition of the total population compared with last Census

Year	Total		Unmarried		Married		Widowed	
	Males	Females	Males	Females	Males	Females	Males	Females
1931 ...	1,315,818	1,109,258	761,820	508 291	491,044	479.733	62,954	121,234
1921 ...	1,229,316	1,029,024	703,827	449,361	461 390	454,001	64,099	118,662
Variation ...	+86,502	+87,234	+57,993	+58,930	+29,654	+25,732	−1,145	+2,572
Variation per cent	+7	+9	+8	+13	+6	+6	−2	+2

Proportion of married females per 1,000 females (districts)

Age-period	Proportion of married females per 1,000 females	
	1931	1921
10—15 ...	121	122
15—20 ...	674	642
20—40 ...	841	872
40—60 ...	566	640
60—and over ...	258	316

Variation among widowed by religions.

141. Variations in the proportion of the widowed in each sex provide a clue to the attitude of the communities towards widow re-marriage. The figures for the last two enumerations are therefore given in the margin for each of the three main religio[ns]. The figures for Hindus and for Muslims both show a decrease in the total proportions The figures for Sikhs are unchanged. The decrease among Muslims is too small to require comment, but since widow re-marriage is already favourably regarded by Muslims change was hardly to be expected. The decrease among Hindus is small for males but considerable for females. The reduction in the proportion among females

Proportion of widowers and widows per 1,000 of each sex in each religion

Religion		Males	Females
All religions	1931 ...	47	109
	1921 ...	52	116
Mulims	1931 ...	47	108
	1921 ...	51	114
Hindu	1931 ...	54	129
	1921 ...	60	149
Sikh	1931 ...	48	128
	1921 ...	48	128

* Vide Subsidiary Table No. I, at end of chapter.

from 149 to 129 per *mille* may be attributed to the efforts of certain societies which are working for this end.

Limited extent of polygamy in the Province.

142. Polygamy is very little practised in the North-West Frontier Province, although it is not generally regarded as prohibited by religion. When a man does take a second wife during the life-time of the first, it is usually due either to the failure of the first marriage to produce male issue, or to the custom of a Pathan marrying the widow of a brother who has died without sons. No figures for polygamy are available, but the figures in Subsidiary Table IV, which show the proportion of married females to married males, indicate how little it is practised. These figures show 1,005 married wives to 1,000 husbands among Muslims, 733 among Hindus and 685 among Sikhs. The figures for Hindus and Sikhs certainly carry no suggestion of polygamy. Those for Muslims are deceptive owing to the effect of emigration, but it is probable that they are to some extent swollen by the practice. They are higher in Hazara than in the trans-Indus districts. In Hazara there are 1,051 wives to 1,000 husbands among Muslims, 741 among Hindus and 880 among Sikhs. The figure among Muslims is certainly raised by emigration, but since the proportion of females born in Hazara is also higher than that in other districts, it is probable that polygamy is also more practised there than elsewhere.

SUBSIDIARY TABLE I—*(For North-West Frontier Province including Trans-Frontier Posts)*
Distribution by civil condition of 1,000 of each Sex, religion and main age-period at each of the last five Censuses

Religion, Sex and Age	Unmarried					Married					Widowed				
	1931	1921	1911	1901	1891	1931	1921	1911	1901	1891	1931	1921	1911	1901	1891
1	2	3	4	5	6	7	8	9	10	11	12	13	14	15	16
ALL RELIGIONS MALES															
All ages ...	574	568	581	580	581	379	380	373	375	372	47	52	46	45	47
0—5 ...	1,000	1,000	1,000	1,000	999	...	...	...	...	1	...	...	...	...	...
5—10 ...	995	999	998	998	996	5	1	2	2	4	...	...	...	...	...
10—15 ...	975	977	973	978	958	23	22	26	21	40	2	1	1	1	2
15—20 ...	767	840	848	843	737	221	153	146	150	251	12	7	6	7	12
20—40 ...	296	321	315	311	234	657	630	640	647	712	47	49	45	42	54
40-60 ...	54	62	59	53	44	811	8.1	827	833	800	135	127	114	114	156
60 and over ...	33	37	34	30	31	669	689	701	694	648	298	274	265	276	321
ALL RELIGIONS FEMALES															
All ages ...	458	440	454	451	447	433	444	434	436	435	109	116	112	113	118
0—5 ...	1,000	1,000	1,000	999	999	...	...	...	1	1	...	...	...	...	...
5—10 ...	982	998	994	994	989	18	2	6	6	11	...	...	...	...	...
10—15 ...	876	874	883	881	778	121	122	114	116	218	3	4	3	3	4
15—20 ...	307	340	352	362	201	674	642	635	625	776	19	18	13	13	23
20—40 ...	67	47	50	42	24	841	872	878	884	858	92	81	72	74	118
40-60 ...	29	22	27	13	10	566	640	624	614	492	405	338	349	373	498
60 and over ...	22	17	16	12	11	258	317	261	244	207	720	666	723	744	782
MUSLIM MALES															
All ages ...	579	574	584	588	586	374	375	371	369	369	47	51	45	43	45
0—5 ...	1,000	1,000	1,000	1,000	1,000	...	...	...	...	...	...	...	...	...	...
5—10 ...	995	999	998	998	997	5	1	2	2	3	...	...	...	...	...
10—15 ...	975	977	974	979	962	23	22	25	19	36	2	1	1	2	2
15—20 ...	777	851	855	854	745	212	142	139	139	243	11	7	6	7	12
20—40 ...	284	297	302	303	219	668	653	655	656	727	48	50	43	41	54
40—60 ...	51	58	55	49	38	816	818	835	841	810	133	124	110	110	152
60 and over ...	32	34	31	27	26	675	697	710	703	660	293	269	259	270	314
MUSLIM FEMALES															
All ages ...	460	443	458	456	452	432	443	433	434	434	108	114	109	110	114
0—5 ...	1,000	1,000	1,000	999	999	...	...	...	1	1	...	...	...	...	...
5—10 ...	983	998	995	989	16	2	5	5	11	1	...	...	...	...	...
10—15 ...	881	879	888	891	790	116	117	109	106	206	3	4	3	3	4
15—20 ...	317	353	365	379	210	664	630	623	609	768	19	17	12	12	22
20—40 ...	69	47	51	43	25	840	874	881	887	861	91	79	68	70	114
40—60 ...	29	22	28	14	10	572	647	634	623	501	399	331	338	363	489
60 and over ...	22	18	17	13	12	264	322	266	249	214	714	660	717	738	774

SUBSIDIARY TABLE I—(*For North-West Frontier Province including Trans-Frontier posts*) *Distribution by civil condition of 1,000 of each sex, religion and main age-period at each of the last five Censuses*

Religion, Sex and Age	Unmarried 1931	Unmarried 1921	Unmarried 1911	Unmarried 1901	Unmarried 1891	Married 1931	Married 1921	Married 1911	Married 1901	Married 1891	Widowed 1931	Widowed 1921	Widowed 1911	Widowed 1901	Widowed 1891
1	2	3	4	5	6	7	8	9	10	11	12	13	14	15	16
HINDU MALES															
All ages ...	506	500	523	499	525	440	440	403	437	410	54	60	69	64	65
0—5 ...	1,000	1,000	1,000	999	998	...	...	...	1	2	...	...	...	...	...
5—10 ...	990	996	9[illegible]6	996	992	9	3	4	4	7	1	1	...	...	1
10—15 ...	968	967	964	953	918	30	32	33	46	79	2	1	3	1	3
15—20 ...	676	755	7[illegible]9	748	654	311	236	210	242	329	13	9	11	10	17
20—40 ...	291	369	330	302	263	659	580	606	643	673	50	51	64	55	64
40—60 ...	81	97	104	93	97	746	732	716	744	697	173	171	180	163	206
60 and over ...	58	71	82	71	95	569	554	563	559	501	373	375	355	370	404
HINDU FEMALES															
All ages ...	435	390	395	379	385	436	461	443	461	447	129	149	162	160	168
0—5 ...	1,000	1,000	1,000	998	997	...	...	...	2	3	...	...	..	...	...
5—10 ..	963	989	988	985	976	35	10	11	14	22	2	1	1	1	2
10—15 ...	817	810	809	728	629	179	183	188	266	361	4	7	3	6	10
15—20 ...	191	205	170	151	86	788	770	806	822	873	21	25	24	27	41
20—40 ...	46	40	24	12	9	836	842	847	864	10	118	118	129	124	181
40—60 ...	19	10	11	6	4	468	534	451	464	382	513	456	438	530	614
60 and over ...	17	10	8	6	4	153	198	166	163	118	830	792	826	831	878
SIKH MALES															
All ages ...	525	528	539	457	464	427	424	395	497	488	48	48	66	46	48
0—5 ...	1,000	1,000	1,000	1,000	1,000	...	...	...	...	...	...	...	...	...	...
5—10 ...	992	995	996	995	990	6	5	3	4	8	2	...	1	1	2
10—15 ...	971	976	967	931	918	28	23	32	68	79	1	1	1	1	3
15-20 ...	684	801	792	734	671	303	196	104	257	317	13	3	14	9	12
20-40 ...	350	426	405	358	340	610	531	531	607	620	40	43	64	35	40
40-60 ...	76	128	95	98	87	766	750	756	764	738	158	122	149	138	175
60 and over ...	61	76	78	82	62	568	624	524	609	534	371	300	398	309	403
SIKH FEMALES															
All ages ...	443	376	385	336	350	450	496	467	507	507	107	128	148	157	143
0—5 ...	1,000	1,000	1,000	998	995	...	...	...	2	5	...	...	...	...	...
5—10 ...	960	983	986	982	956	38	16	14	17	41	2	1	...	1	3
10—15 ...	786	694	764	626	474	209	301	228	366	575	5	5	8	8	21
15—20 ...	164	113	177	66	33	817	874	796	905	915	19	13	27	29	52
20—40 ...	39	24	22	6	4	869	878	866	879	847	92	98	112	115	149
40—60 ...	24	13	9	1	1	490	552	528	512	436	486	435	463	487	563
60 and over ...	15	15	26	..	...	208	305	170	183	180	777	680	804	817	820

SUBSIDIARY TABLE I-A.—*Proportion per* mille *of each sex by septenary and ternary age-groups (4-23) for civil condition North-West Frontier Province (Districts)*

Groups	Males Unmarried	Males Married	Males Widowed	Females Unmarried	Females Married	Females Widowed
4—6 ...	1,000	...	...	1,000	...	...
7—13 ...	992	7	1	970	29	1
14—16 ...	927	69	4	606	386	8
17—23 ...	686	298	16	160	816	24
Total ...	902	93	5	692	300	8

SUBSIDIARY TABLE II—*Distribution by civil condition of 1,000 of each sex at certain ages in each religion and Natural Division*

Religion and Natural Division	Males																	
	All ages			0—5			5—10			10—15			15—40			40 and over		
	Unmarried	Married	Widowed	Unmarried	Married	Widowed	Unmarried	Married	Widowed	Unmarried	Married	Widowed	Unmarried	Married	Widowed	Unmarried	Married	Widowed
1	2	3	4	5	6	7	8	9	10	11	12	13	14	15	16	17	18	19
N.-W. F. P. (DISTRICTS.)																		
All religions ...	579	373	48	1,000	...	...	995	5	...	975	23	2	363	598	39	49	777	174
Muslims ...	582	371	47	1,000	...	...	995	5	...	975	23	2	391	569	40	47	783	170
Hindus ...	529	414	57	1,000	...	...	990	9	1	968	30	2	377	578	45	76	712	212
Sikhs ...	542	406	52	1,000	...	...	993	6	1	973	27	...	423	540	37	74	719	207
Christians ...	728	245	27	1,000	...	...	993	5	2	980	17	3	749	232	19	123	743	134
HAZARA.																		
All religions ...	571	380	49	1,000	...	...	996	4	...	968	31	1	363	598	39	47	778	175
Muslims ...	572	379	49	1,000	...	...	996	4	...	968	31	1	358	604	40	44	783	173
Hindus ...	549	399	52	1,000	...	...	990	9	1	968	30	2	434	538	28	108	659	233
Sikhs ...	550	392	58	1,000	...	...	986	14	...	963	37	...	392	468	40	62	728	210
Christians ...	621	363	16	1,000	...	...	1,000	...	...	1,000	...	...	514	464	22	143	829	28
TRANS-INDUS DISTRICTS																		
All religions ...	582	371	47	1,000	...	...	995	5	...	978	20	2	406	553	41	50	777	173
Muslims ...	586	367	47	1,000	...	...	995	5	...	979	19	2	402	557	41	48	783	169
Hindus ...	525	417	58	1,000	...	...	990	9	1	968	30	2	364	587	49	69	723	208
Sikhs ...	541	408	51	1,000	...	...	995	3	2	976	24	...	428	536	36	77	717	206
Christians ...	732	241	27	1,000	...	...	992	5	3	979	18	3	753	228	19	122	739	139

Distribution by civil condition of 1,000 of each sex at certain ages in each Religion and Natural Division

Religion and Natural Division	Females																	
	All ages			0—5			5—10			10—15			15—40			40 and over		
	Unmarried	Married	Widowed	Unmarried	Married	Widowed	Unmarried	Married	Widowed	Unmarried	Married	Widowed	Unmarried	Married	Widowed	Unmarried	Married	Widowed
1	2	3	4	5	6	7	8	9	10	11	12	13	14	15	16	17	18	19
N.-W. F. P. (DISTRICTS)																		
All religions ...	459	432	109	1,000	...	...	982	18	...	876	121	3	119	805	76	28	502	470
Muslims ...	460	432	108	1,000	...	...	983	16	1	881	116	3	121	803	76	28	508	464
Hindus ...	435	436	129	1,000	...	...	963	35	2	817	179	4	80	825	95	18	405	577
Sikhs ...	442	450	108	1,000	...	...	959	39	2	784	212	4	70	855	75	22	429	549
Christians ...	460	490	50	1,000	...	...	991	9	...	887	106	7	177	794	29	128	607	265
HAZARA.																		
All religions ...	447	451	102	1,000	...	...	978	21	1	847	150	3	90	837	73	21	541	438
Muslims ...	449	451	100	1,000	...	...	980	20	...	851	146	3	90	838	72	21	547	432
Hindus ...	395	406	139	1,000	..	...	951	47	2	742	251	7	58	842	100	17	371	612
Sikhs ...	424	468	108	1,000	...	...	923	77	...	738	262	...	61	868	71	8	472	520
Christians ...	443	483	74	1,000	...	...	1,000	...	...	1,000	...	...	183	742	75	214	572	214
TRANS-INDUS DISTRICTS																		
All religions ...	463	425	112	1,000	...	...	983	16	1	887	110	3	130	792	78	30	487	483
Muslims ...	464	424	112	1,000	...	...	985	15	...	893	104	3	133	790	77	31	492	477
Hindus ...	443	430	127	1,000	...	...	965	33	2	831	166	3	85	821	94	19	411	570
Sikhs ...	446	446	108	1,000	...	...	968	29	3	795	199	6	72	852	76	26	417	557
Christians ...	461	491	48	1,060	...	...	991	9	...	884	109	7	177	797	26	121	610	269

SUBSIDIARY TABLE III—*Districts only*

Distribution by main age-periods and civil condition of 10,000 of each sex and religion

Religion or Sex	Number per 10,000 of sex concerned											
	0—10			10—15			15—40			40 and over		
	Unmarried	Married	Widowed	Unmarried	Married	Widowed	Unmarried	Married	Widowed	Unmarried	Married	Widowed
1	2	3	4	5	6	7	8	9	10	11	12	13
ALL RELIGIONS												
Males ...	2,876	6	...	1,213	29	2	1,613	2304	165	88	1 393	311
Females ...	3,059	24	1	986	136	3	492	3,341	317	46	823	772
MUSLIM												
Males ...	2,946	6	1	1,246	29	2	1,545	2,248	160	85	1,422	310
Females ...	3,059	22	1	991	131	3	502	3,326	3·2	46	839	768
HINDU												
Males ...	2,294	10	1	939	29	2	1,937	2,964	229	121	1,135	339
Females ...	3,056	47	2	922	202	4	341	3,496	404	28	618	880
SIKH												
Males ...	2,161	6	2	877	24	...	2,269	2,898	196	116	1,127	324
Females ...	3,147	55	3	950	256	5	294	3,602	317	31	588	752

SUBSIDIARY TABLE IV—*Proportion of the sexes by civil condition at certain ages for religions and natural divsions*

Natural Division and Religion	Number of females per 1,000 males														
	All ages			0—10			0·15			15—40			40 and over		
	Unmarried	Married	Widowed	Unmarried	Married	Widowed	Unmarried	Married	Widowed	Unmarried	Married	Widowed	Unmarried	Married	Widowed
1	2	3	4	5	6	7	8	9	10	11	12	13	14	15	16
N.-W. F. P. (DISTRICTS)															
All religions ...	667	977	1,926	897	3,105	1,162	685	3,962	1,402	257	1,223	1,1[illegible]	437	499	2,095
Muslim ...	681	1005	1977	895	3 021	1,115	686	3,853	1,335	280	1,275	1,681	470	509	2,135
Hindu ...	571	733	1 574	926	3,355	1,625	682	4,833	1,857	122	819	1,227	162	378	1,807
Sikh ...	503	685	1,276	899	6,000	1,250	668	6,500	9,000	80	767	998	164	322	1,434
Christian ...	224	711	660	902	1,500	...	695	4,833	2,000	56	807	362	530	417	1,009
HAZARA															
All religions ...	681	1,035	1,811	903	4,585	2,500	660	3,640	2,000	236	1,334	1,783	328	508	1,822
Muslim ...	693	1,051	1,824	904	4,603	2,55 6	664	3,538	1,979	252	1,370	1,789	351	514	1,837
Hindu ...	456	741	1,688	858	4,385	2,000	570	6,143	2,333	71	820	1,848	96	346	1,617
Sikh ...	568	880	1,379	876	4,500	...	606	5,611	...	108	1,055	1,208	77	380	1,455
Christ'an ...	491	914	3,250	746	...	...	400	...	...	239	1,078	2,333	1,200	552	6,000
TRANS-INDUS DISTRICTS															
All religions ...	662	955	1,970	894	2,654	953	695	41,56	12,50	263	1,182	1,564	479	495	2210
Muslim ...	676	986	2,040	895	2,533	865	695	4,057	1,170	289	1,239	1,644	521	506	226
Hindu ...	598	731	1,551	937	3,206	2,571	704	4,562	1,727	137	819	1,140	185	385	1,854
Sikh ...	490	6. 8	1,252	905	7,714	1,250	684	6,848	9,000	76	719	561	182	307	1428
Christian ...	218	702	616	912	1,500	...	713	4,833	2,000	53	795	315	495	410	963

SUBSIDIARY TABLE V—(*For North-West Frontier Province including trans-frontier posts*)

Distribution by civil condition of 1,000 of each sex at certain ages for selected castes

Caste	Distribution of 1,000 males of each age by civil condition																				
	All ages			0—6			7—13			14—16			17—23			24—43			44 and over		
	Unmarried	Married	Widowed	Unmarried	Married	Widowed	Unmarried	Married	Widowed	Unmarried	Married	Widowed	Unmarried	Married	Widowed	Unmarried	Married	Widowed	Unmarried	Married	Widowed
1	2	3	4	5	6	7	8	9	10	11	12	13	14	15	16	17	18	19	20	21	22
Arora ...	558	376	66	1,000	...	...	980	19	1	921	68	11	628	347	25	165	749	86	70	689	241
Awan ...	560	354	86	1,000	...	...	984	16	...	868	112	20	670	283	47	180	734	86	79	603	318
Brahman ...	490	428	82	1,000	...	...	909	90	1	716	272	12	554	409	37	251	655	94	135	612	253
Chammar ...	527	407	66	1,000	...	...	966	23	11	729	218	53	409	545	45	146	758	96	122	683	195
Chuhra ...	471	444	85	1,000	...	..	817	182	1	726	249	25	531	443	26	250	627	123	53	703	244
Gujar ...	590	362	48	1,000	...	...	992	8	...	886	109	5	628	346	26	170	769	61	93	726	181
Jat ...	537	403	60	1,000	...	...	992	8	...	875	119	6	605	376	19	204	710	86	29	763	208
Khatri ...	516	413	71	1,000	...	...	981	14	5	786	182	32	571	389	40	217	704	79	86	705	209
Pathan ...	579	366	55	1,000	...	...	987	9	4	897	85	18	678	294	28	191	736	73	63	749	188
Sayad ...	583	366	51	1,000	...	...	988	11	1	899	91	10	634	336	30	171	759	70	55	758	187
Swathi ...	519	349	32	1,000	...	...	974	26	...	787	207	6	463	520	17	224	723	53	172	669	159
Tanaoli ...	585	374	41	1,000	...	...	968	32	...	819	179	2	505	373	22	163	786	51	60	764	176

Distribution of 1,000 females of each age by civil condition

Caste	Distribution of 1,000 females of each age by civil condition																				
	All ages			0—6			7—13			14—16			17—23			24—43			44 and over		
	Unmarried	Married	Widowed	Unmarried	Married	Widowed	Unmarried	Married	Widowed	Unmarried	Married	Widowed	Unmarried	Married	Widowed	Unmarried	Married	Widowed	Unmarried	Married	Widowed
1	2	3	4	5	6	7	8	9	10	11	12	13	14	15	16	17	18	19	20	21	22
Arora ...	444	418	138	1,000	...	...	965	34	1	559	433	8	108	861	31	32	785	183	16	349	635
Awan ...	459	430	111	1,000	...	...	957	42	1	472	467	61	173	781	46	60	812	128	38	483	479
Brahman ...	397	460	143	1,000	...	...	922	69	9	380	618	2	175	805	20	31	785	184	15	414	571
Chamar ...	509	412	79	1,000	...	..	945	55	...	466	534	...	323	646	31	225	683	92	146	431	423
Chuhra ...	376	496	128	1,000	..	...	848	148	4	421	575	4	77	910	13	29	790	181	33	452	515
Gujar ...	4 3	462	100	1,000	...	...	967	32	1	409	580	11	110	865	25	38	856	106	20	542	438
Jat ...	454	424	122	1,000	...	...	972	27	1	636	352	12	225	726	49	46	815	139	25	464	511
Khatri ...	411	464	125	1,000	...	...	904	94	2	390	600	10	169	796	35	31	818	151	17	456	527
Pathan ...	472	415	113	1,000	.	...	965	34	1	634	348	18	230	732	38	64	810	126	51	457	492
Sayad ...	443	453	104	1,000	..	...	972	27	1	618	370	12	219	743	38	68	792	140	44	474	482
Swathi ...	443	453	104	1,000	..	...	976	24	...	664	330	6	129	846	25	29	872	99	7	491	502
Tanaoli ...	450	447	103	1,000	...	...	969	31	...	503	489	8	130	847	23	58	834	108	28	459	513

CHAPTER VII

INFIRMITIES.

Intention of the records.

143. In accordance with past practice the infirmities for which information was asked at the present census were four in number, insanity, deaf-mutism, leprosy and total blindness. The instructions given to enumerators were that if any person were found blind of both eyes, insane, suffering from corrosive leprosy, or deaf and dumb, the name of the infirmity was to be entered in the relevant column of the schedule, persons were not to be entered as blind who were blind of one eye only, nor as lepers if suffering from leucoderma. These instructions were the same as those given in 1921, before which date attempts had been made to distinguish those who were deaf and dumb from birth from those who had become so in later life.

Inaccuracy of the returns.

144. The returns under the heads for infirmities are probably the least accurate of all returns in the Census. This is believed to be the case not only in India but in all countries in which census proceedings are conducted. Mistakes and inaccuracies occur not only through accidental omissions and intentional suppressions on the part of the defectives or their friends, but from wrong diagnosis of diseases which require an expert to distinguish. Blindness is one out of the four infirmities which there is least reason to suppose might be deliberately concealed, but even in the case of blindness there can be no doubt that the enumerators were bothered by different degrees of imperfect vision. The other three infirmities are all regarded as some kind of reproach either by the afflicted person or by the relatives, and are consequently concealed if concealment is in any way possible. Even when concealment is not deliberate, it frequently occurs that parents will not admit to themselves the existence of deaf-mutism or insanity in a child until it becomes impossible to do otherwise. Some degree of accuracy was claimed for the statistics of this Province in 1921 on the ground that the enumerators and supervisors were all local men from whom the existence of infirmities could not be concealed. This would not get over the difficulties of either unintentional concealment on the part of the family afflicted or imperfect diagnosis on their own part, nor is it likely that many cases would occur in which they would venture to enter an infirmity in the schedule against the wishes of the head of a household. The best that can be said for the statistics is that errors and omissions are probably no more frequent than elsewhere in India, or than in previous enumerations in this Province, and that there is therefore some use in them for purposes of comparison.

Reference to statistics.

145. The recorded figures for the four specified infirmities are shown in Imperial Table No. IX. The table is divided into two parts, one showing distribution by age and the other distribution by districts. The classification by age is of interest to determine both the age at which the infirmities make themselves known, and the manner in which they affect length of life. Classification by districts is adopted as a result of past experience which has shown the general incidence of these infirmities to be much more affected by locality than by religion or social custom. Three subsidary tables at the end of this chapter show the figures reduced proportionately for 100,000 of the population in order to provide a flat rate of comparison with the rest of India and elsewhere. Before considering the figures further, it is necessary to remember that the total number of persons recorded as afflicted is under 5,000 and that it is extremely dangerous to draw conclusions from such small data as this number can furnish.

Difficulty of comparisons.

146. The proportion of persons afflicted with any of the four infirmities is compared in the margin with similar figures recorded since 1881. It will be observed that the figures show a steady decrease with the exception of the year 1911 which showed a sudden rise. It is pleasant to suppose that the steady decline is due partly to greater accuracy in enumeration resulting in fewer wrong diagnoses, and partly to the progressive improvement in sanitation and material condition

Proportion of persons afflicted with each infirmity to every 100,000 of the population.

Infirmity	1931	1921	1911	1901	1891	1881
Total ...	206	261	303	261	356	472
Insane ...	31	36	40	29	33	54
Deaf-mute ...	66	84	95	88	89	83
Blind ...	102	132	156	130	222	318
Lepers ...	10	9	12	14	12	17

and in the accessibility of medical relief. On the other hand it is certain that if the figures had shown a rise instead of a decline, the rise would just as comfortingly have been ascribed to greater accuracy in enumeration resulting in fewer errors and omissions, and to the increased accessibility of medical relief resulting in persons having less hesitation in declaring themselves. In any case no reason has been ascribed to the sudden rise in 1911. The sudden fall from the 1911 figures to those of 1921 was ascribed to the excessive vulnerability of the infirm in the influenza epidemic of 1918. On the other hand the Census Superintendents of Bihar and Orissa, and of the Central Provinces stated as an axiom that the epidemic was particularly adverse to strong and healthy adults in the prime of life; the Census Superintendent of Bihar and Orissa found that this reacted adversely on the infirm in that it took away their support and tightened the purse-strings of charity, while the Census Superintendent of the latter province found that it increased their numbers in that it threw them on to the support of Government and so brought them to the notice of enumerators and supervisors. In such circumstances it is almost impossible to draw conclusions from the figures. There has certainly been no improvement in the sanitation and material condition of the Gujars of Hazara, although statistics for Hazara have become less. On the other hand there has been a steady advance in medical methods of curing and preventing blindness, and the credit for the reduction in the prevalence of this affliction must without doubt be given to the doctors.

General tendency to decline.

147. The general tendency to decline, and the relative vulnerability of the two sexes, may be more easily judged from the diagram below. It will be noticed that blindness is the disease in which the proportions between the sexes remain most nearly equal, although the curves for each of the other three infirmities run more or less parallel. The diagram may be taken to illustrate what has already been remarked, namely that the figures for blindness are the most reliable, and that the other figures, being affected by more or less constant errors, have some value for purposes of comparison.

No. 16

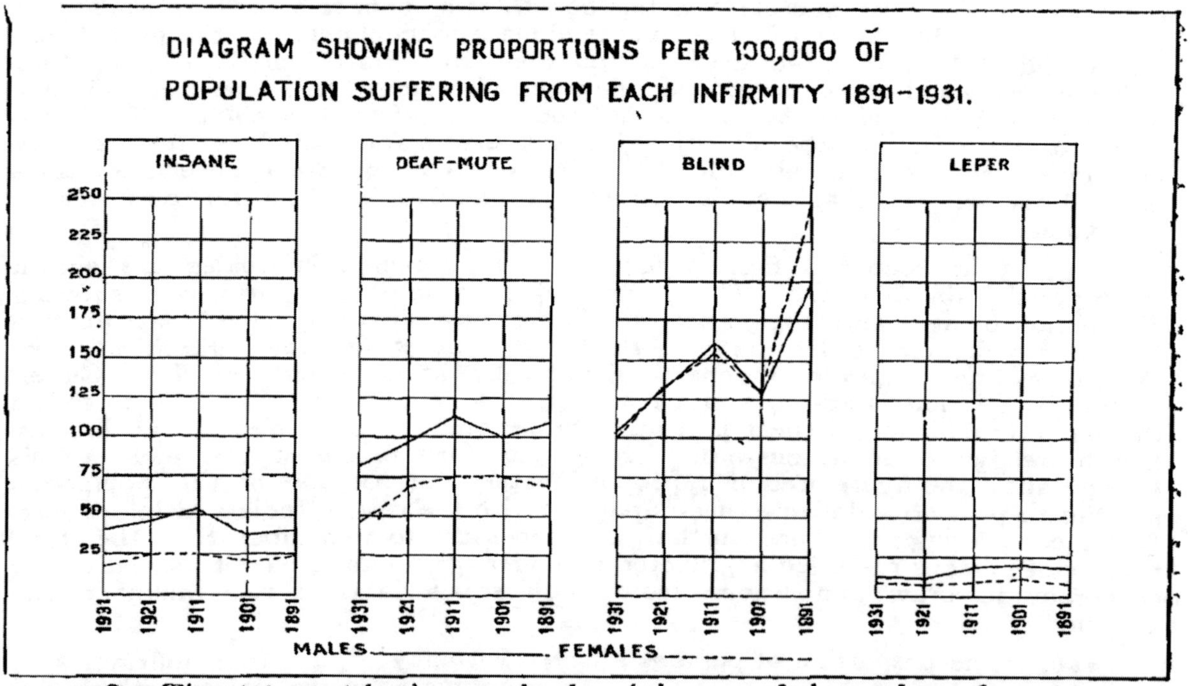

Comparison with census figures from 1901.

148. The statement in the margin shows the recorded number of persons suffering from each infirmity at each of the last four census enumerations The total showed an advance of 25 per-cent. between 1901 and 1911 and a decline of 12 per cent. between 1911

Number of persons suffering from each infirmity at each of the last four censuses

Infirmity	1901	1911	1921	1931
Insane ...	606	884	833	741
Deaf-mute ...	1,807	2,100	1,897	1,597
Blind ...	2,668	3,440	2,980	2,463
Leper ...	294	282	211	249
Total ...	5,375	6,706	5,921	4,984

and 1921. Between 1921 and 1931 there has occurred a further decline of 9 per cent. The actual figures of insane persons are still higher than in 1901, but the population has increased and so the proportion has fallen.

Relative prevalence of selected infirmities.

149. The relative prevalence of the four selected infirmities among 100 afflicted persons is shown in the margin. It will be seen that the proportions have varied little in the last twenty years. Blindness always accounts for about half the total number, and leprosy for only a very small proportion. Since, however, blindness is usually admitted while leprosy is concealed, these figures are not of great value.

Percentage relative prevalence of each infirmity at the last three censuses

Infirmity	1911	1921	1931
Insane	13	14	15
Deaf-mute	32	32	31
Blind	51	50	49
Leper	4	4	5

INSANITY.

Impossibility of distinguishing between different kinds of mental abnormality.

150. The figures for the insane are meant to include only those persons who are afflicted with the more active forms of mental derangement, and not the merely half-witted or weak-minded. In practice however it is quite impossible to distinguish between the two. In neither of the two common vernaculars of the Province are there separate words for lunacy and idiocy : "Jewanai" in Pashto and "pagal" in Lahnda and Hindustani, may both mean anything from a raving lunatic to one whose development is hardly more than retarded. Even experts in charge of lunatic asylums like to keep their patients under observation for some time before they will certify whether they are insane or not. It is therefore hardly to be expected that the statistics will be of any value save for comparison with others equally unreliable.

Comparison with other parts of India.

151. In point of comparison with the rest of India the position of the Province appears to be improving. In the census of 1911 only Baluchistan and Burma returned a higher proportion of insane than the Frontier. In 1921 the proportion on the Frontier, although still above the general average for India, was lower than that found in Baroda, Bengal, Bombay, Kashmir or Cochin as well as in both the two provinces previously mentioned The situation has improved again in the present Census, although the proportion is still slightly higher than that found in the neighbouring province of the Punjab.

Variation by districts from Census to Census.

152. The figures in the margin give by districts the number of insane per 100,000 of the population as recorded in each Census since 1901. Insanity appears always to have affected males more than females. This is presumably due to the comparatively quieter and less exciting lives led by the women of the Province than by the men. The women take less part than the men in such excitements as dancing, religious celebrations, riots, sudden deaths and the like, and are also less addicted to the use of drugs or intoxicating liquors. It is probable also that the percentage of cases of concealment of insanity is greater among women than among men ; certainly there is less opportunity for the enumerator to enter the infirmity from his own knowledge.

Number of insane per 100,000 of the population at each of the last five censuses

District and Natural division	Males					Females					Total				
	1931	1921	1911	1901	1891	1931	1921	1911	1901	1891	1931	1921	1911	1901	1891
N.-W. F. P. (Districts).	41	47	54	37	41	18	25	25	21	24	31	36	40	29	33
Hazara ...	27	54	50	37	23	14	30	23	22	21	21	42	38	30	22
Trans-Indus Districts.	47	44	55	37	46	19	23	25	20	25	34	34	40	29	36
Peshawar ...	47	48	52	38	45	18	23	20	18	18	34	36	36	28	32
Kohat ...	46	45	45	31	28	18	14	27	25	18	33	30	36	28	23
Bannu ...	48	51	74	31	45	18	31	37	19	35	34	41	56	25	40
Dera Ismail Khan...	44	26	54	32	55	25	23	28	18	28	35	25	41	25	42

Hazara.

153. Hazara has always hitherto been the worst district for insanity and showed a continuous increase in the number of insane from 1891 to 1921. It is believed that there is some connection between insanity and the cold climate of the hills, but this has yet to be definitely established. The climatic conditions of Hazara approximate to those of Kashmir and the Punjab hills, in both of which the proportion of insanity runs high. On the other hand it was found in the course of the Assam Census of 1921 that the proportion of insane in that Province was nowhere lower than in the Kashi and Jaintia hills, where the altitude at which the people were accustomed to live was exceptionally high. Hazara is the district in which there is the highest proportion of Muslims, and if there is anything in the theory of consanguineous marriages as a cause of insanity, the proportion of insanity might naturally be expected to be high in the district where consanguineous marriages are also high. No explanation is forthcoming for the sudden drop in the proportion of insane in Hazara at the present Census and it is impossible to believe that it represents the true state of affairs.

Peshawar.

154. Peshawar District shows a total number of insane only one higher than in the previous Census, but there is an increase of 14 in the number of males and a decrease of 13 among females. It is impossible to ascribe any reason to this peculiar variation, unless it be that a slightly hostile feeling to the Census in Peshawar City has led to less perfect enumeration among females.

The Southern districts.

155. The variations in the figures returned from the three Southern districts of the Province are shown in the margin. The total figures are too small and the variations too erratic to justify the drawing of any conclusions. It may be noted however that a large number of the persons returned as insane in each Census are religious mendicants of one sort or another, most of whom wander into British Territory from across the border. The entry of such persons into the Southern Districts was restricted in 1921 by the existence of a state of war in Waziristan.

Variation in insanity figures in the three Southern Districts of the Province

District	1911	1921	1931	Variation 1911—1921	Variation 1921—1931
Kohat ...	82	66	78	−16 (20 P. C.)	+12 (18 P. C.)
Bannu ...	142	103	92	−39 (27 P. C.)	−11 (11 P. C.)
Dera Ismail Khan...	108	64	97	−44 (41 P. C.)	+33 (52 P. C.)

Early mortality among the insane.

156. Congenital idiots of varying degrees are usually treated with a certain amount of kindness, but those who become insane in later life are made the subject of all kinds of violent and dangerous treatment. Since the latter kind escape omission from the records less frequently than do the former, while both have a short expectation of life, it is to be expected that the proportion of recorded insane will be low at each of the extremes of life and comparatively high in the middle age periods. The figures in the margin show that this is the case. The particularly low proportion of each sex under 10 years of age reflects the reluctance of parents to recognize insanity in their children until they are compelled to do so. Among males the proportion falls steadily from the moment insanity begins to make itself unmistakable. Among females there are more found insane in the age-group 20—30 than in any of the other periods. This may mean that those who were previously only bordering on the insane, have been rendered unmistakably insane by the effort of child-bearing.

Distribution of insanity by sex and by decennial age-periods (actual figures)

Age-period	Males	Females
0—10	63	29
10—20	134	45
20—30	128	49
30—40	97	30
40—50	67	24
50—60	38	17
60 and over	16	4
All ages	543	198

No. 17.

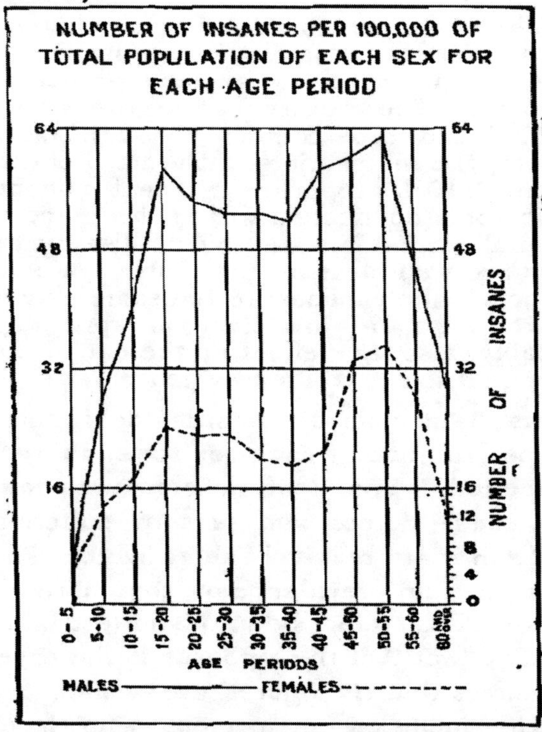

Proportion of the sexes.

157. Out of every 100 insane persons the proportion is 73 males and 27 females. Reasons for the excess of males have already been discussed. The expectation of life among both is short. The marginal diagram shows the distribution per 100,000 of each sex through the different age-periods of life.

Classification by castes not made.

158. For reasons of economy it has not been possible to prepare statistics showing the prevalence of insanity by castes. It may be noted that in the Census of 1911 the Gujars of Hazara District were found to be the most affected caste. They live in a cold and hilly tract of country, and under extremely insanitary conditions of life.

DEAF MUTISM.

Deaf mutism.

159. The figures for deaf-mutism are intended to include all persons who were found both deaf and dumb, whether they were congenitally so or had acquired the defect in later life. Persons who were deaf only or dumb only were not to be included. At all Censuses previous to 1921 it was laid down that only those who were deaf and dumb from birth were to be shown. It was expected that the removal of this restriction in 1921 would lead to a sudden rise in the number of deaf-mutes. That this was not the case showed that the instructions were never observed and that the change in the instructions need not be considered to vitiate comparison with previous Census figures. The proportion of 97 males and 69 females per 100,000 of the population recorded in 1921 was considerably lower than that of any previous Census in the case of males, and was the lowest recorded in the case of females since 1891. The figures of the present Census are lower again, being 82 males and 47 females per 100,000 of the population. Corresponding figures for the whole of India in 1921 were 70 and 49. The figures for the Province are mainly affected by a sudden fall in the returns from Hazara, and little value must therefore be attached to them except in the examination of the distribution by districts and by age-groups.

Decline in returns from each district.

160. The total number of recorded deaf-mutes has declined from 1897 in the last Census to 1,597 in the year under consideration. The proportion per 100,000 of the population was 84 in 1921 and is now 66. The figures in the margin give the proportion per 100,000 by

Number of deaf-mutes per 100,000 at each of the last five Censuses

District and Natural division	Males					Females					Total				
	1931	1921	1911	1901	1891	1931	1921	1911	1901	1891	1931	1921	1911	1901	1891
N.-W. F. P. (Districts).	82	97	113	100	109	47	69	75	75	69	66	84	95	88	89
Hazara ...	90	155	166	111	125	55	89	120	92	81	74	122	143	102	103
Trans-Indus Districts.	78	75	93	95	103	44	61	58	68	66	64	68	76	82	85
Peshawar ...	83	77	80	88	107	42	62	48	56	65	65	70	64	72	86
Kohat ...	76	97	117	111	87	42	64	73	91	61	60	81	95	101	74
Bannu ...	56	91	84	72	111	30	56	58	61	78	44	74	71	67	95
Dera Ismail Khan...	85	40	129	104	99	68	62	79	71	58	77	51	104	88	79

dristricts for the last five enumerations. The only constant factor is the higher proportion of deaf-mutes in Hazara than in the Trans-Indus districts. In spite of the sudden fall in the figures for the present year, for which no explanation can be given, Hazara remains a district highly affected. The greater part of the district is a hilly Himalayan tract, and the infirmity is found to be common to such tracts throughout India. Sikkim, Kashmir, Mysore, the hill districts of Burma, Bengal, the Punjab and the United Provinces all show a high proportion of deaf-mutism. In the United Provinces it appears to have some connection with goitre, and is thought to depend in some way on some mineral carried in water, which disappears from the water in the rivers soon after they are well clear of the hills. In cold climates, too, people do not attend to their personal cleanliness to the same extent as they might in warmer climates, and dirt, want and low living are probably predisposing causes of the infirmity. Probably, also, the effect on the ear of the cold and rare ed atmosphere of the heights contributes to its prevalence.

Variation by age.

161. The diagram in the margin shows the number of recorded deaf mutes per 100,000 of each sex for each age-period. True deaf-mutism is a congenital defect and persons suffering from it are relatively short-lived. The maximum prevalence of the infirmity should therefore be in the lowest age. The fact that the opposite is the case, shows that the figures are swollen by the inclusion of persons who have lost their speech and hearing with the approach of old age, and are therefore of little value for the purpose for which they are usually studied. As in the case of insanity the proportion returned is higher among males than among females. This is probably largely due to more successful concealment among females. The actual proportion at the present census is 487 deaf mute females to 1,000 deaf-mute males, as against 575 ten years ago.

No. 18

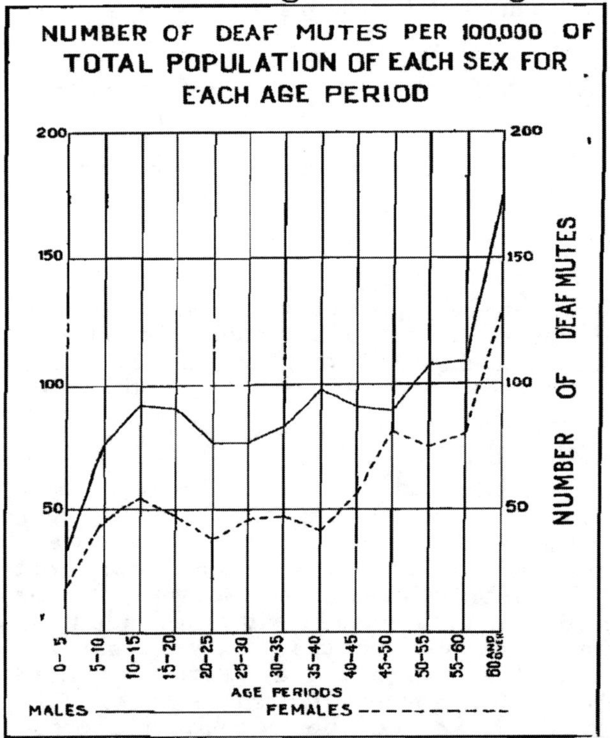

Comparison with other Provinces.

162. The position of the North-West Frontier Province compared with other provinces in respect of deaf-mutism shows a slight improvement since the last census, but the figures are too much affected by the sudden drop in Hazara to be regarded with much confidence. The figure of 66 per 100,000 for the Province occupies a position midway between the figures of 159 returned from Kashmir and 23 from Delhi. However, even the figure of 70 per 100,000 returned from Hazara in 1921 compares favourably with the present figures for Kashmir, where the climate and manner of life of the inhabitants are not too different from those of Hazara.

BLINDNESS.

Statistics reasonably accurate

163. The figures for blindness can be approached with more confidence than those for any of the other three infirmities, since blindness is not only comparatively easy to diagnose, but does not carry with it any feeling of shame or disgrace such as to render its concealment probable. It is possible that a certain number of persons who are not totally blind of both eyes have been included, but enumerators were particularly warned against their inclusion and it is hoped that the returns represent the facts with a fair amount of accuracy.

Causes affecting blindness.

164. Blindness, although decreasing, is still regrettably prevalent. The total number of persons afflicted in the province was 2,980 in 1921 and is now 2,463. The proportion per 100,000 of the population is 103 males and 100 females; the corresponding all-India proportion in 1921 was 145 males and 160 females. The infirmity is found to be commonest in India in tracts with a dry

hot climate and a dusty soil. The glaring sunshine and dust-laden winds of the hot weather cause inflammation of the eyes, which frequently results in ulceration and permanent injury. The infirmity is least prevalent in those parts of India where the climate is damp and the country green. On the other hand a smoky atmosphere inside dark ill-ventilated houses and huts is also a frequent cause of affections of the eyes, resulting in blindness, and the prevalence of the disease in hilly tracts may often be due to the fact that the people are driven by the cold to live in dark ill ventilated huts.

Comparison with other parts of India.

165. Figures showing the prevalence of blindness for seventeen other provinces and States of India have been received.

The North-West Frontier Province shows a lower proportion than any of these save Bengal and Hyderabad. Figures for Madras, which were low in 1921, have not been received.

Variation by districts from census to census.

166. The number of blind persons recorded in the present census (1,351 males and 1,112 females) compares favourably with the figures of 1,620 males and 1 360 females recorded in 1921. The table in the margin shows also a satisfactory general tendency to decrease through the last half-century. No doubt the decrease is partly due to increased care in enumeration, but it must in addition be very largely due to the advance in medical science and the increased accessibility of facilities. Small-pox, a common cause of blindness, has been almost eliminated by vaccination, while cataract, and especially double cataract, is now being removed by operation with increasing certainty of success. More important still, not only is the skill of surgeons increasing, but the knowledge of their skill is becoming widely spread among even the poorest and most backward people, till there are few left who do not offer themselves for treatment with an almost pathetic confidence in the success of the operation.

Distribution of blind persons at each census since 1881, per 100,000 of population.

District or Natural division	Males 1931	1921	1911	1901	1891	1881	Females 1931	1921	1911	1901	1891	1881
N.-W F. P. (Districts) ...	103	132	161	124	198	295	100	133	151	132	245	341
Hazara ...	58	73	120	73	114	161	52	86	112	71	114	186
Trans-Indus Districts ...	119	153	176	148	223	324	119	152	166	156	284	383
Peshawar ..	111	166	182	153	200	267	102	148	154	141	246	304
Kohat ...	78	103	122	92	150	276	72	108	111	119	175	339
Bannu ...	70	109	113	116	196	259	54	108	99	120	258	296
Dera Ismail Khan ...	232	186	263	199	308	470	286	252	325	248	402	569

Distribution by district for each sex.

167. The distribution by districts per 100 blind persons, and the proportion of blind persons per 100,000 of each sex within the districts, are shown in the margin. The figures for Peshawar must to some extent be disregarded, since they are swollen by the large number of persons who are present in the district either as blind beggars or in search of medical treatment. Next to Peshawar the highest proportion per 100 blind persons is found in Dera Ismail Khan, where the glare and heat in the summer months are worse than anywhere else in the Province. The next highest figure is in Hazara, due to the insanitary conditions of life of the Gujars. The proportions per 100,000 of each sex are higher in Kohat and Bannu, where the conditions of heat and glare are more universal than are the conditions of insanitary living in Hazara.

Distribution of blind persons of the five settled districts.

District	Proportion per 100 blind persons	Proportion of blind persons per 100,000 of population: Males	Females
Hazara ...	15	58	52
Peshawar ...	42	111	102
Kohat ...	7	78	72
Bannu ...	7	70	54
Dera Ismail Khan ...	29	232	286

Proportion between the sexes.

168. Blindness is usually the only one of the four recorded infirmities which is proportionately more common among females than among males. This is due partly to the fact that women are confined more than men to the smoky atmosphere of ill-ventilated houses, and partly to their not yet entrusting them-

selves with the same freedom as men to surgical and medical relief. In the present census the proportion among females is lower than among males. The explanation may perhaps again be found in the slight feeling of hostility to the census in Peshawar City, which resulted in greater difficulty in the enumeration of females.

Blindness a disease of advancing age.

169. Blindness is to a great extent a disease of increasing age. It is therefore to be expected that increasing numbers will be found in each successive age-group. The figures in the margin show that this is the case in the present census, as it has always been before. More than half the total number of blind persons in each sex are over 40 years of age. The great majority of the cases of blindness in advanced age are caused by cataract.

Age period		Males	Females
0—10	...	125	82
10—20	...	144	100
20—30	...	150	107
30—40	...	148	121
40—50	...	182	165
50—60	...	206	207
60 and over	...	496	330

Distribution by age-groups.

No. 19

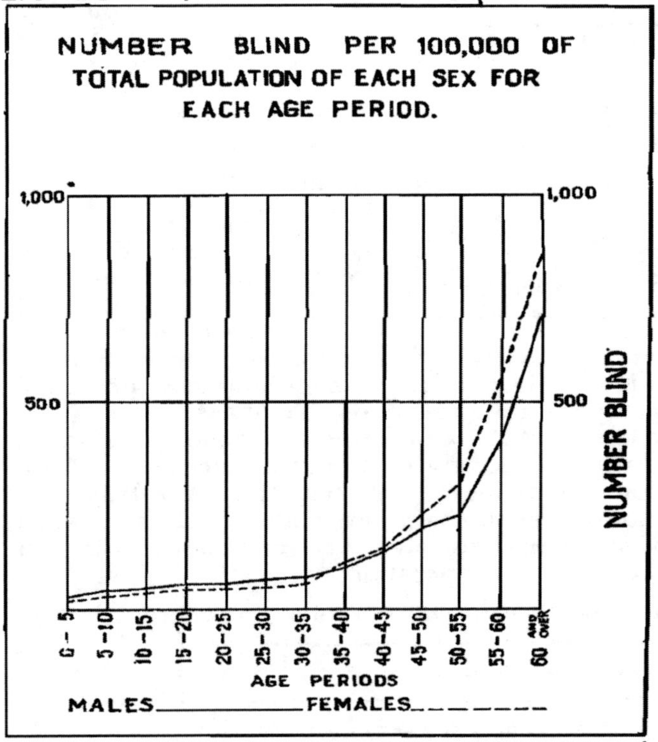

170. A diagram illustrating the above figures but calculated on the proportion of blind persons per 100,000 of each sex is placed in the margin. The curves follow the course which is to be expected in such a diagram, and may be taken as a further indication of the comparatively high reliability of the blindness-statistics.

LEPROSY.

Recorded figures only a fraction of actual.

171. The returns of lepers are probably vitiated more than those of any of the other infirmities both by wilful concealment and by wrong diagnosis. The disease is felt to carry with it not only a social stigma, but many actual social disabilities, and is therefore concealed till as late a stage as possible. In diagnosis it is confused with leucoderma, or discolouration of the skin. Although both the common vernaculars of the Province have separate words for the two diseases, it is often by no means easy for the non-expert to distinguish between them, particularly in the early stages. Reasons for regarding the actual figures of the returns as representing hardly a tenth of the total number of sufferers throughout India, are to be found on page 213 of the India Volume of the Census Report for 1921. Since however it is probable that concealment is attempted with equal vigour in every census and in every part of India, the figures obtained have their uses for purposes of comparison.

In comparison with the rest of India the proportion of lepers in the Province is low. As many as 76 per 100,000 of the population have been found afflicted in Burma, 70 in the Central Provinces and Berar, 60 in Assam, 56 in Kashmir and 54 in Behar and Orissa, while in this Province the recorded proportion is only 10 per 100,000.

Variation from census to census.

172. As may be seen from the table in the margin the number of lepers decreased from 1901 to 1921 but has increased again slightly during the last decade. It would be unwise to attach much importance to these fluctuations since those lepers who are at all likely to get recorded as such are to a large extent migratory mendicants, and are as likely to be found in one Province as in another on the actual night of the census. Beyond the fact that personal uncleanliness is conducive to leprosy, neither climate, altitude nor race appear to offer any explanation of its distribution. The castes most afflicted in the Province are the lowest and most backward among those in Hazara. These have certainly not increased in cleanliness. It is therefore probable that the apparent decrease in the prevalence of the disease since 1901 is due more to the establishment of asylums in the Punjab than to any natural cause. The low proportion of females to males is almost certainly due to more successful concealment.

Proportion of females to 1,000 male lepers.

Year		Number of lepers	Proportion of female lepers to 1,000 male lepers
1901	...	294	480
1911	...	282	382
1921	...	211	563
1931	...	249	518

Variation by districts in last decade.

173. The variation by districts during the last 10 years is shown in the margin. The figures are no doubt largely affected by migration, and if there is anything of interest to note from them it is that lepers only visit the three Southern districts of the Province in very small numbers.

Variation among lepers by districts since 1921

District		1921			1931		
		Males	Females	Total	Males	Females	Total
Hazara	...	87	28	115	63	21	84
Peshawar	...	31	32	63	90	46	136
Kohat	...	4	4	8	3	9	12
Bannu	...	6	5	11	5	6	11
Dera Ismail Khan		7	7	14	3	83	6
Total	...	135	76	211	164	5	249

The variations in incidence in the different age-periods, if the figures are to be believed, indicate that congenital leprosy is rare. On the other hand the high proportion found among persons of 60 years of age and over must be regarded with suspicion, since leprosy is known to produce early mortality. In particular there ought to be few lepers alive after the age of 60, but the figures for females in both years and for males in 1921 are higher in the age-group 60 and over than in any other age-group.

Statement showing the number of lepers per 100,000 of each sex at the last two censuses by decennial age-periods

Age-period		1921		1931	
		Males	Females	Males	Females
0—10	...	4	4	5	6
10—20	...	5	9	13	8
20—30	...	10	3	12	8
30—40	...	11	7	14	8
40—50	...	21	17	18	9
50—60	...	24	5	27	11
60 and over	...	39	21	26	13

Distribution by age.

No. 20

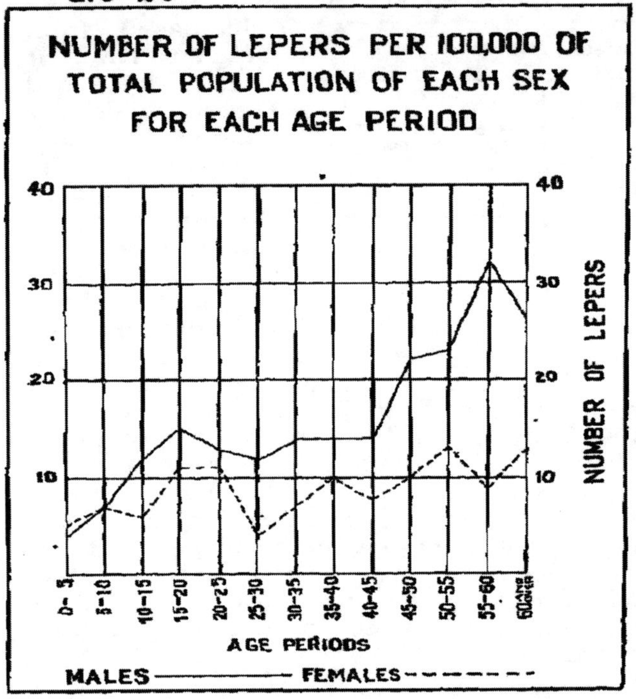

174. The marginal diagram shows the proportion of lepers per 100,000 of each sex by quinquennial age-periods. In the light of the above remarks it is unsafe to regard it as anything more than a further proof of the inaccuracy of both the diagnosis of leprosy and the records of age.

Prevalence among lower castes.

175. As in the case of the other three infirmities, motives of economy have prevented the study of the prevalence of leprosy by caste or by religion. All-India figures for 1921 indicate that higher castes are less afflicted than lower, and this is believed to be due to greater personal cleanliness and better habits of life. Of the tribes of the Frontier, Gujars, who live with their animals in the same rooms, in houses which are ill-ventilated and insanitary beyond belief, were found to be the most affected.

SUBSIDIARY TABLE I—*Number of infirm per 100,000 of the total population at each of the last five censuses*

District and Natural Division	Insane										Deaf-mutes										Blind										Lepers									
	Males					Females					Males					Females					Males					Females					Males					Females				
	1931	1921	1911	1901	1891	1931	1921	1911	1901	1891	1931	1921	1911	1901	1891	1931	1921	1911	1901	1891	1931	1921	1911	1901	1891	1931	1921	1911	1901	1891	1931	1921	1911	1901	1891	1931	1921	1911	1901	1891
1	2	3	4	5	6	7	8	9	10	11	12	13	14	15	16	17	18	19	20	21	22	23	24	25	26	27	28	29	30	31	32	33	34	35	36	37	38	39	40	41
N.-W. F. P. (Districts).	41	47	54	37	41	18	25	25	21	24	82	97	113	100	109	47	69	75	75	69	103	132	161	128	198	100	133	151	132	245	12	11	17	18	16	8	7	8	10	7
Hazara ...	27	54	50	37	23	14	30	23	22	21	90	155	166	111	125	55	89	120	92	81	58	73	120	73	114	52	86	112	71	114	18	26	33	44	44	7	10	11	18	14
Trans-Indus Districts.	47	44	55	37	46	19	23	25	20	25	78	75	93	95	103	44	61	58	68	66	119	153	176	148	223	119	152	166	156	284	11	5	11	8	8	8	7	6	7	5
Peshawar ...	47	48	52	38	45	18	23	20	18	18	83	77	80	88	107	42	62	48	56	65	111	166	182	153	200	102	148	154	141	246	17	6	9	11	17	11	8	5	7	6
Kohat ...	46	45	45	31	28	18	14	27	25	18	76	97	117	111	87	42	64	73	91	61	78	103	121	92	150	72	108	111	119	175	2	3	18	2	6	8	4	9	5	7
Bannu ...	48	51	74	31	45	18	31	37	19	35	56	91	84	72	111	30	56	58	61	78	70	109	113	116	19	54	108	99	120	258	3	4	7	8	12	5	4	5	7	5
Dera Isma'l Khan	44	26	54	32	55	25	23	28	18	28	85	40	129	104	99	68	62	79	71	58	232	186	263	199	308	286	252	325	248	402	2	5	19	4	2	2	6	12	6	5

SUBSIDIARY TABLE II—*Age distribution of 10,000 infirm (Five Censuses)*

Age	Insane										Deaf-mutes									
	Males					Females					Males					Females				
	1931	1921	1911	1901	1891	1931	1921	1911	1901	1891	1931	1921	1911	1901	1891	1931	1921	1911	1901	1891
1	2	3	4	5	6	7	8	9	10	11	12	13	14	15	16	17	18	19	20	21
0—5	221	139	237		319	505	...	320		438	577	286	554		900	650	480	759		895
5—10	939	799	883		1,397	960	856	1,280		1,476	1,294	1,960	1,782		1,808	1,319	1,187	1,584		2,011
10—15	1,197	1,718	1,104		1,457	1,061	856	1,320		1,235	1,397	1,657	1,355		1,365	1,281	2,260	1,610		1,267
15—20	1,271	868	931		1,457	1 212	973	1.440		1,832	987	1,194	1,220		1,073	879	1,398	942		1,281
20—25	1,215	1,528	1,246		1,496	1,263	583	1160		1,076	857	597	816		915	784	565	681		689
25—30	1,142	1,024	1,167		1,496	1,212	1,556	600		1,076	838	740	621		900	918	890	956		909
30—35	1,050	1,285	1,230	Not available	679	909	1,401	1,280	Not available	676	819	815	943	Not available	638	784	946	982	Not available	523
35—40	737	1,233	725		660	606	2,257	280		756	698	362	599		518	497	367	484		620
40—45	681	538	726		200	555	467	600		320	540	622	576		360	574	579	72[illegible]		220
45—50	553	191	584		479	657	195	440		556	419	219	307		465	612	297	340		455
50—55	460	208	489		60	555	428	440		279	391	412	471		165	440	254	367		179
55—60	239	87	189		140	303.	...	320		240	289	160	157		450	325	141	78		441
60 and over.	295	382	489		160	202	428	520		40	894	976	599		443	937	636	497		510

Age	Blind										Lepers									
	Males					Females					Males					Females				
	1931	1921	1911	1901	1891	1931	1921	1911	1901	1891	1931	1921	1911	1901	1891	1931	1921	1911	1901	1891
1	22	23	24	25	26	27	28	29	30	31	32	33	34	35	36	37	38	39	40	41
0—5	370	173	284		491	333	257	247		346	427	148	196		303	1,176	132	385		513
5—10	555	327	625		844	405	588	508		610	793	815	686		455	1,176	1,710	1,282		641
10—15	570	673	593		667	441	346	514		524	1,158	519	539		555	823	1,316	1,410		1,283
15—20	496	562	478		753	459	610	508		695	1,097	370	882		858	1,294	658	769		1 154
20—25	541	574	562		545	485	331	507		419	915	593	981		859	1,412	526	897		766
25—30	570	586	551		655	477	669	547		734	854	889	686		909	471	132	385		1,026
30—35	555	691	772	Not available	479	477	787	697	Not available	373	914	1,111	1,979	Not available	606	706	789	1,282	Not available	641
35—40	540	302	594		762	611	213	430		796	671	296	981		1,566	706	526	385		1,026
40—45	629	1,043	767		377	665	1,147	801		443	549	1,037	784		657	471	1,711	769		641
45—50	718	556	499		852	818	537	573		1,099	670	740	490		1,061	471	526	385		1,154
50—55	659	1,124	877		368	872	1,397	1,016		342	549	667	784		505	471	263	641		257
55—60	866	216	320		1,200	989	243	397		1 503	549	593	343		555	235	132	256		385
60 and over.	2,931	3,173	3,078		2,007	2,968	2,875	3,255		2,116	854	2,222	1,569		1,111	588	1,579	1,154		513

SUBSIDIARY TABLE III—(*a*) *Infirm per 100,000 and* (*b*) *female infirm per 1,000 males* } *at certain age-periods*

Age	Number afflicted per 100,000								Number of females afflicted per 1,000 males			
	Insane		Deaf-mutes		Blind		Lepers					
	Males	Females	Males	Females	Males	Females	Males	Females	Insane	Deaf-mutes	Blind	Lepers
1	2	3	4	5	6	7	8	9	10	11	12	13
0—5	6	5	32	18	26	19	4	5	833	548	740	1,429
5—10	28	13	76	46	41	30	7	7	373	496	600	769
10—15	40	17	92	54	47	39	12	6	323	447	636	368
15—20	59	24	90	47	57	52	15	11	348	434	761	611
20—25	55	23	77	38	61	50	13	11	379	446	740	800
25—30	53	23	77	46	66	51	12	4	387	533	688	286
30—35	53	20	83	47	70	60	14	7	316	466	707	400
35—40	52	19	58	41	95	108	14	10	300	347	932	545
40—45	59	21	92	57	135	142	14	8	297	517	871	444
45—50	60	33	90	81	193	232	22	10	433	711	938	364
50—55	63	25	107	73	226	308	23	13	440	548	1,090	444
55—60	46	28	109	81	412	521	32	9	462	940	548	222
60 and over ...	29	11	176	129	725	870	26	13	250	510	833	357
All ages ...	41	18	82	47	103	100	12	8	365	487	823	518

CHAPTER VIII

OCCUPATIONS

INTRODUCTORY

The scheme of classification.

176. The classification scheme for occupations is that prescribed by the Census Commissioner for India, and includes four main classes, with 55 orders and 195 groups. The principal change from previous census tables is that in the present census no attempt has been made to distribute dependence among occupations ; totals are, however, given for dependents who work at some occupation, thus helping to maintain the household in which they are dependent, additional figures are given for subsidiary occupations, and the sex figures are distributed to occupational groups instead of merely to classes and orders.

Reference to statistics.

177. The results obtained are shown in Imperial Tables Nos. X and XI. Imperial Table X shows the total number of recorded earners and working dependents in each of the classes, orders and groups, both for the Province as a whole and for districts, trans-frontier posts and Peshawar Municipality. No. XI is divided into two parts, one of which deals with the distribution by occupation among 12 selected castes, and the other with occupations of Europeans and Anglo-Indians. Table XII is a new table, introduced for the first time in the present census, and is intended to show the extent of unemployment among educated persons. The subsidiary tables placed at the end of this chapter are arranged as follows :—

(*i*) General distribution of occupation per 10,000 of the population, (*a*) for earners (principal occupation) and working dependents, and (*b*) for subsidiary occupations.

(*ii*) Distribution of important sub-classes of occupation in each district, sub-divided as above.

(*iii*) Proportion of females to males in certain occupations, with actual numbers of each sex.

(*iv*) Comparison of figures for 1921 with those of 1931 in regard to selected occupations.

(*v*) Occupations of selected castes.

(*vi*) Number of persons employed on railway communications, irrigation posts and telegraphs on the 26th February 1931.

Other subsidiary tables prescribed for India as a whole have not been prepared for this Province, as the figures would have been too small to be of any practical interest.

Certain tables which were prepared at the last census, or which were proposed for this census, have been abandoned, both for reasons of economy and for other reasons. In particular no table showing occupation by religion has been prepared, and no table showing the extent to which agriculture is combined with other occupations.

Principles of classification.

178. The chief difficulty in preparing the chapter on Occupations is always in deciding the group in which any individual is to be classified. On this occasion an alphabetical list of occupations showing the groups in which they were to be entered was received from the Census Commissioner for India, and utilised both in compilation and in the issuing of instructions to enumerators and others. In spite of the care thus exercised the number of persons entered as "shopkeepers" without any further description, and the number whose returns were so indefinite as not to indicate any specific occupation, have risen since the last census from 19,306 to 30,916 and from 23,461 to 42,620, respectively. It is open to question whether the larger figures do not more accurately describe the true state of affairs in the Province.

The main principle on which the Census Commissioner's list was prepared were as follows :—

(1) Where a person both makes and sells, he is classed as a "maker". On the same principle, when a person extracts some substance, such as

saltpetre, sulphur, carbonate of soda, etc., from the ground and also refines it, he is shown in Sub-Class II—Exploitation of Minerals, and not in Sub-Class III—Industry.

(2) Industrial and trading occupations are divided into two main categories :—

(*a*) those where the occupation is classified according to the material worked in, and

(*b*) those where it is classified according to the use which it serves.

As a general rule the first category is reserved for the manufacture or sale of articles the use of which is not finally determined, but it also includes specified articles for which there is no appropriate head in the second category. For example, while shoemakers are included in the second category (Order 12, Group 82), the makers of waterbags, saddlery, leather portmanteaus and the like are included in the first category (Order 6, Group 51).

In a few cases occupations have been classed according to the material worked in, even though certain articles made of it are specified, because the material used is more characteristic of the occupation than the article made. Thus makers of palm-leaf fans have been shown in Group 56 rather than Group 99. Makers of bamboo screens, leaf plates, etc., have also been shown in Group 56.

(3) Persons employed in Railway Carriage factories have been shown in Group 112 instead of under Order 15, because these factories in India are always worked direct by the railways. The manufacture and repair of railway trucks and carriages is an integral part of the operations of the railway authorities. The principle on which the classification is made is analogous to that followed in the case of makers and sellers or diggers and refiners.

(4) On the other hand, railway police and railway doctors are classified in Groups 157 and 169, respectively, because the primary duty of persons thus employed is, in the one case the prevention and detection of crime, and in the other the healing of disease. The fact that their pay is derived from the railway is merely an incident, and does not affect the character of the occupation.

As a general rule it may be said that wherever a man's personal occupation is one which involves special training *e.g.*, that of a doctor, engineer, surveyor, etc., he is classed under the head reserved for that occupation. Exceptions have been made, however, in cases where the work in which he is employed involves further specialization. For this reason a marine engineer is classed in Group 102 and a river surveyor in Group 103. Officers of Government whose occupation is covered by some other group (*e.g.*, doctors, clergymen, professors, postal, forest, settlement and railway officers and other establishment, etc.,) will be included in that group and not under Group 159. Government peons and chaprasis other than those in the above-mentioned establishments will be included under this group and not in Group III.

179. The instructions given to enumerators and printed on the schedule were :— **Instructions to enumerators.**

"Column 9 (Worker or Dependent) :—Enter "earner" or "dependent". A woman who does house work is a dependent, so is a son who works in the fields but does not earn separate wages. A cultivator cultivating as a principal occupation is an earner.

"Column 10 (principal occupation of actual workers) :—Enter the principal means of livelihood of all persons who actually do work or carry on business, whether personally or by means of servants or who live on house-rent, pension, etc. Enter the exact occupation and avoid vague terms such as "service" or "writing" or "labour". Replies such as are given to a Magistrate in court are not enough. For example, in the case of labour, say whether in the fields, or in a coal mine, or jute factory, or cotton mill or lac factory, or earth-work, etc. In the case of agriculture distinguish between persons who do not cultivate personally, who cultivate their own land, who cultivate rented land and who are hired labourers. If a person makes the articles he sells he should be entered as "maker and seller" of them. Women and children who work at any occupation which helps to augment the family income must be entered in column 9, and in column 11. For dependents make a × only in column 10.

"Column 11 (Subsidiary occupation of actual workers):—Enter here any occupation which actual workers pursue at any time of the year in addition to their principal occupations. Thus if a person lives principally by his earnings as a boatman, but partly also by fishing, the word "boatman" will be entered in column 10 and "fisherman" in column 11 If an actual worker has no additional occupation a cross (×) will be put. Dependents who help to support the family by subsidiary work, *e.g.*, a woman who helps in the fields as well as doing house work will be shown in this column.

Column 12 (Industry in which employed):—For managers, clerks, operatives or workmen employed in a factory or by any person employing industry fill up the name of the industry, *i.e.*, biscuit making, coal mining. For individual workers not employed by others put a ×."

Instructions to supervisors and others.

180. These instructions were further elaborated for supervisors as follows:—

"Column 9 to 11.—The entry of occupation in column 9 to 11 is also a matter requiring special care. The first thing is to distinguish between an earner and a dependent. Only those women and children will be entered as earners who help to augment the family income by permanent and regular work for which a return is obtained in cash or kind Thus a woman, whose sole business is to look after her husband's house and prepare his meal, is a dependent and not an earner, but a woman who habitually collects and sells firewood or cowdung, thereby adds to the family income and should be shown as an earner. A boy, who sometimes looks after his father's cattle, is a dependent, but one who is a regular cowherd and earns a wage in cash or kind should be recorded as an earner in column 9 and a cowherd in column 10. As a rough and ready rule it may be assumed that boys and girls over the age of 10, who actually do field labour or tend cattle are adding to the family income and should therefore be entered in column 10 or 11 according to whether they earn pay or not. Boys at school and college should be shown as dependents. Dependents who assist in the work of the family and contribute to its support without actually earning wages should be shown as dependents in column 9 and under subsidiary occupation in column 11. Thus a woman who regularly works in the fields for her husband is a dependent and should be entered as such in column 9, but has the subsidiary occupation of cultivation which will be recorded in column 11. Household work, done by a woman in her house, will not count as a subsidiary occupation. Women and children, who are doing no manual work should be entered as "dependents" in column 9, but not at all in either column 10 or 11.

Domestic servants must be entered in column 9 as earners, not dependents, and in column 10 as cook, bahishti, etc.

Persons temporarily out of employ should be shown in column 9 as earners and in column 10 as following their previous occupation.

When a man has two occupations, the principal one is that on which he relies mainly for his support and from which he gets the major part of his income. A subsidiary occupation should be entered if followed at any time of the year (whether followed throughout the year or during a part of it).

Only one subsidiary occupation (the most important one) should be entered in column 11).

Persons living on agriculture must be distinguished as rent-receivers (*i.e.* non-cultivating owners, and lessees and tenants who have sub-let their land), cultivating owners, cultivating tenants or agricultural labourers. Where a person cultivates part of his land and sub-lets part, he should be shown in column 10 as cultivator and in column 11 as rent-receiver, if he gets the greater part of his income from the self cultivated land, and *vice versa*. Gardeners or growers of special products, such as vegetables, mangoes, etc., must be shown separately. Persons whose income is derived from the rent of houses or land in towns should be distinguished from those who derive it from agricultural land, their occupation being noted as house-rent (*kiraya makan*), etc.

Stress must be laid on the importance of avoiding vague words like "labour" or "service" or "shopkeeping". The enumerator must enter the exact kind of labour or service and the nature of the goods sold. In the case of service, it is necessary not merely to distinguish Government service, railway service, Municipal service, village service, service in a shop or office, and domestic service, etc., but also to show the exact occupation followed, *e.g.* in the case of Government service, whether Collector, or Army Officer, or Civil Court Clerk, or Police Inspector, Patwari, Constable, etc. In the case of clerks, the occupation of their employer must also be shown *e.g.* lawyer's clerk, bank clerk.

Whenever large gangs of coolies are employed on earthwork of any kind, special instructions should be given to the enumerators to enter not only the words "earthwork" but also the nature of the undertaking (railway, road, canal, etc), in connection with which it is being done. Pensioners should be shown Civil, Military or Political, as the case may be.

For shopkeepers and traders the nature of the articles sold should be stated, *e.g.*, "General Merchant", "cloth merchant", "Seller of food-stuffs" (*dukan nuntal*). In the case of industries the precise nature of the industries should be given as "cotton weaver", "carpet-maker," "silk weaver", "maker of glass bangles".

Column 12.—Only those persons will be entered in this column who are working in organised industries. Thus a carpenter employed by a furniture-manufactory will be entered "carpenter" in column 10 and "furniture-making" in column 12. A village carpenter working at home or a jobbing carpenter working for his own hand must not appear in column 12 at all. Agricultural labourers should only be entered in this column when they are employed in some special branch of agriculture or other industry involving agriculture incidentally, or when they are employed by some person or company practising agriculture on an extensive scale. In the former case the name of the particular industry will be entered, *e.g.* "dairy-farming," "horse-breeding," in the latter the entry will be agriculture."

Difficulties in the way of correct enumeration.

181. The difficulties in the way of accurate enumeration and compilation, are noticed in para 413 to 425 of the North-West Frontier Province, Volume of the Census Report of 1911. However carefully the instructions may have been framed, they have certainly not decreased since that date. It is not necessary here to recapitulate them in detail, but it may be said in brief that the chief difficulty lies in overlapping To the non statistical mind the population might be divided into four classes, traders, those who make their money from land, hired workers, and Government servants ; the latter are recruited from any of the other three classes into which they may have been born. Every one in the country who can possibly manage to do so likes to own some land, and is prepared to fall back on this for support if his other enterprise fails, be it lorry-driving, military employment, private service, crime or what-not. Workers for hire are prepared to work at almost anything that offers, and a man who is regarded as a shepherd by caste may be an agricultural labourer one day, a builder the next and a porter the third. Similarly a trader will sell almost anything in which he sees a profit, and one who has failed as a photographer one month will be trying his luck as a general store-keeper the next.

The intention of the instructions was understood by enumerators and supervisors, and there is no doubt that they have filled up the schedules to the best of their ability. Compilation and tabulation were carried out with particular care by a selected staff. That there still remain so many persons inexactly classified is not due to negligence on the part of the staff, but truly reflects the haphazard and ill-defined means of support of numbers of the population.

GENERAL STATISTICS.

Distinction between earners and others.

182 In this fluctuating condition of affairs, the figures returned at the Census can only be accepted as giving a very broad general indication of the real circumstances. Their accuracy will decrease as their sub-division increases. The first classification which calls for consideration is that of workers and non-workers. Even this cannot be accurate since there is no word in the English language which accurately describes the class to which reference is to be made. The description "worker" is inaccurate, since not only do a number of those who are intended to work manage to avoid doing so, but the class is required to include those who derive an income from land or other forms of investment without any effort on their own part ; on the other hand the classification does not include house-wives and others who work hard all their lives but receive no

wages. The expression "earner" is equally inaccurate, since the classification includes both persons who get their money without ever earning it and persons who may work very hard and never win the reward of their labour. "Earner" is however the expression which has been officially adopted for the purpose of this census, and may be understood to mean all those who derive money, or seek to derive money, from the occupation under consideration.

Proportion of workers to total population.

183. The enumeration of the five settled districts shows a total of 857,968 persons returned as workers This figure gives a proportion of 354 workers and 646 non-working dependents per 1,000 of the population of the districts. Whether or not the phrase "non-workirg dependent" will be allowed to stand when women attain to equality of status with men, remains to be seen, but for the present its meaning is well enough understood.

This distribution is compared in the margin, with figures for other parts of India recorded in the same year. It will be seen that the proportion of male earners is comparatively high in the North-West Frontier Province but that the proportion of female earners is lower than any where else except Baluchistan.

Proportion of "Earners," "Working Dependents" and "Non-Working Dependents" per *mille* of the total population

Province or state	Earners		Working Dependents		Non-Working Dependents	
	Males	Females	Males	Females	Males	Females
N W. F. P. (Districts) ...	304	10	30	10	209	437
United Provinces ...	331	87	11	58	183	330
Punjab	280	19	36	33	230	402
Delhi	348	30	16	28	217	361
Travancore State ...	219	71	32	151	252	275
Central Provinces and Berar...	284	135	29	80	187	285
Baluchistan ...	336	6	13	13	213	419
Rajputana Agency ...	308	67	35	118	181	291
Ajmer Merwara ...	314	56	29	125	185	291
Bihar and Orissa ...	282	118	7	9	209	375
Assam	274	61	46	71	203	345
Mysore State ...	295	63	19	78	197	348
Central India Agency ...	315	151	18	27	180	309
Bombay	265	65	24	38	235	373
Burma	258	97	32	37	220	356
Bengal	244	31	6	7	270	442
Cochin State ...	259	129	6	116	224	266
Hyderabad State ...	225	108	68	69	217	313
Kashmir State ...	206	15	61	245	265	208

Distribution of workers by four main classes.

184. The next classification is into four main classes, and since the sub-division is into only four units, the figures may still be taken as fairly satisfactory. Class A, which accounts for 62 per cent. of the workers, includes the exploitation of animals, vegetation and minerals. Its numbers are principally made up of those engaged in agricultural or pastoral pursuits. Class B includes industry, transport and trade and is concerned mostly with the distribution of the products of the workers in class A. Class C includes those serving in the public forces and in the public administration, and those engaged in the practice of law, education, religion, medicine, and other arts and ciences. Class D will be discussed with regard to its sub-classes.

Class	Actual Numbers	Percentage of total workers
		Per cent.
A—(Production of raw materials) ...	528,843	62
B—(Preparation and supply of material substances).	188,803	22
C—(Public administration and Liberal arts) ..	70,735	8
D—(Miscellaneous)	69,587	8

Proportion of population workers in twelve sub-classes.

Earners Principal occupation and working dependents per *mille* of the total population

Class and sub-class	Earners (Principal occupation) and Working Dependents
A—Production of raw materials ...	218
(1) Exploitation of animals and vegetation	218
(2) Exploitation of minerals ...	·1
B—Preparation and supply of material substances	78
(3) Industry	45
(4) Transport	8
(5) Trade	25
C—Public adminstration and liberal arts ...	29
(6) Public Force	16
(7) Public administration ...	4
(8) Professions and liberal arts ...	9
D—Miscellaneous	29
(9) Persons living principally on their income.	1
(10) Domestic service ...	
(11) Insufficiently described occupations ...	
(12) Unproductive	

185. In the system of classification prescribed these four main classes are divided again into 12 sub-classes. The statement in the margin shows the proportion per *mille* of the total population of the districts who were recorded as workers in each of these sub-classes. The proportion of those who depend on each of these classes would probably be about the same. It will be seen that more than one-fifth of the total population is engaged in agriculture and allied occupations. The actual figure of those so recorded in the districts is 528,725, the next highest total is for industry and is only 108,742.

Distribution of workers by sub-classes.

186. The diagram below shows the proportionate distribution of all the workers among the 12 sub-classes. It shows even more clearly the preponderating importance of agriculture in the life of the Province. The blocks represent the percentage of followers of each class to the total money-drawing population. By considering each of them separately it will be possible to gain an idea of the attractions to wage-earners which each type of occupation offers. In examining the variations which the figures show from those of the previous census, it must be remembered that the total population has increased by 7·7 per cent. in the last 10 years, and the number of recorded workers by 6 per cent.

No. 21.

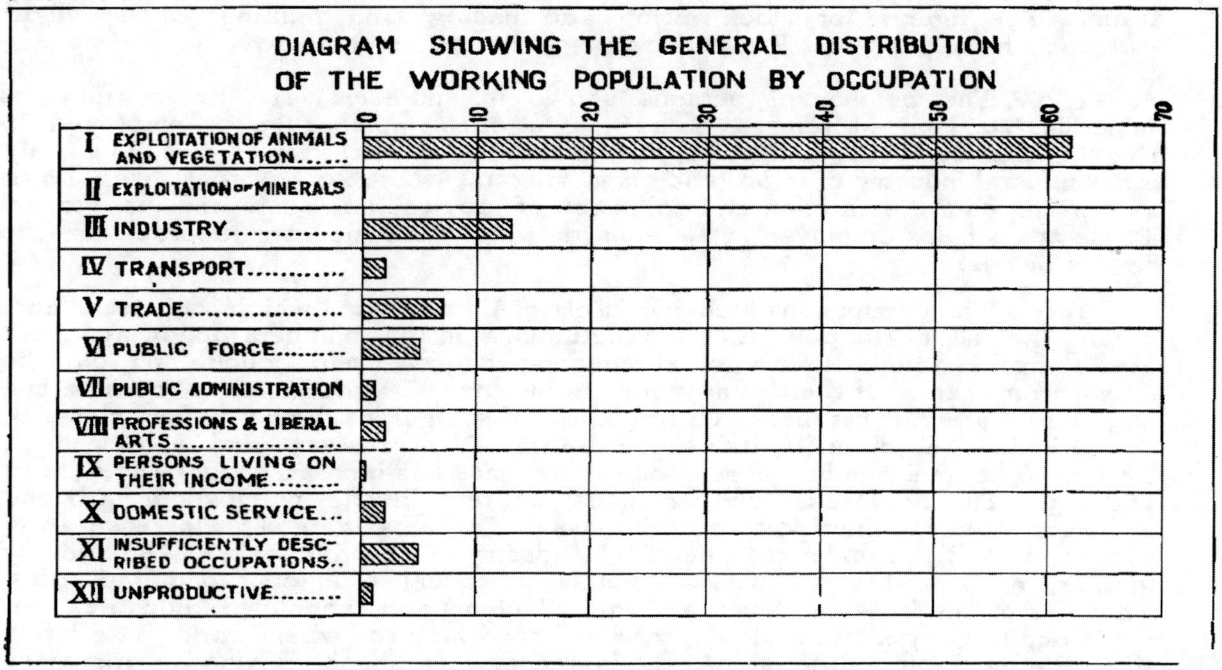

Distribution not affected by any abnormal circumstances.

187. It might be expected that the classification thus shown would be affected by the season of the year at which the census was taken or by any abnormal conditions prevailing at the time. This however is not the case, since there is no seasonal alternative employment to draw workers away from agriculture. In the slack season of agriculture the workers also slack, and a census taken at any other time of year would produce very much the same result. The only big difference might be made by the absence in the hot weather of Powindah and other immigrant graziers from Afghanistan and Tribal Territory; but since seasonal immigration introduces considerable numbers of traders and

soldiers into the Province, as well as graziers and agriculturists, it is probable that the totals rather than the proportions would be effected.

Similarly changes in economic conditions may affect changes in occupation, but in the present case they can only have done so to a limited extent. The economic conditions of the decade 1921 to 1931 are described in paragraphs 21 to 35 of this report. There have been no big catastrophes such as to cause a swing over from agriculture to industry, or *vice versâ*, and there is nothing more remarkable to note than a general rise in the standard of living, to which passing references are made in subsequent paragraphs.

Agriculture and allied occupations.

188. Class A. Production of raw materials, includes sub-class I, Exploitation of animals and vegetation, and sub-class II, Exploitation of minerals. The largest numbers in sub-class I are those engaged in agricultural and pastoral pursuits. Agriculture alone accounts for 616 per 1,000 of the total workers. The percentage distribution of those classed under the heading cultivation is shown in the margin. The method of classification which it was sought to observe is that shown in paragraph 180 above, but there can be no doubt that there was a great deal of inaccuracy due to overlapping. The small percentage of agricultural labourers shows how few are the persons in the rural areas who do not own some share in the crops which they produce. The figure is in a way deceptive, since it does not include the women and children of the household, although the women are frequently given the hardest labour. Owing to different methods of classification it is not possible to compare these figures with those of the last census. Other occupations included in sub-class I are forestry, stock-raising, fishing and hunting. The number of persons returned as engaged in forestry shows a decrease in the last 10 years from 1,018 to 267 actual workers. This is explained partly by the Afridi blockades which kept a large number of such persons out of British Territory, and partly by the slump in the timber-trade. The figures for stock-raising and fishing and hunting show slight increases, from 4,563 to 4,815 and from 259 to 272 respectively.

Percentage distribution of agriculturists	
Non-cultivating proprietors ...	8
Cultivating proprietors ...	43
Tenant cultivators ...	38
Agricultural labourers ...	11

Extraction of mineral wealth.

189. The number of persons shown in sub-class II, Exploitation of minerals, has declined from 183 to 118. Out of this number 83 are employed in the salt-quarries of Kohat District, but the number in 1921 was 178. The only other mineral industry of importance is in Hazara, where 49 persons are shown as working on the extraction and collection of precious and semi-precious stones. These are persons employed in lime-quarries, and were not so recorded in the census of 1921.

Decline in Industry.

190. The occupations included in class A are those which are traditional among the bulk of the population. Fluctuations in the numbers following them are so small in comparison to actual numbers, that few useful conclusions can be drawn from them. If there is any change over from agriculture to commercial life, or *vice versâ*, it can better be traced in the figures shown under class B. These include sub-class III, Industry, sub-class IV, Transport, and sub-class V, Trade. The total number of persons in the class has increased from 182,248 to 188,803. The increase is however almost entirely in the occupations grouped under sub-class IV Transport and sub-class V Trade. There is a decrease from 113,919 to 108.742 under the heading Industry. This decrease is shared by textiles, hides and skins, woods, metals, chemical products, food industries, industries of the dress and toilet, and miscellaneous and undefined industries It is not due to the general trade depression from which the whole world is suffering since the figures for trade show an increase. Rather it is due to increased activity in trade, for import of factory-made articles from Hindustan and other parts of the world are destroying the markets which local products used to enjoy. The heaviest fall is under the heading Textiles, where cotton-spinning, sizing and weaving shows a fall in the number of workers from 13.446 to 9.753; the number of female workers in this group has gone down from 2,387 in 1921 to 996 in the present census. Order 9, Ceramics, and order 14, building industries, both show an increase, from 7,412 to 9,948 (34 per cent.) in the case of the former and from 3,454 to 6,435 (86 per cent.) in the case of the latter. These may both be attributed to a rise in the standard of living. Ceramics, being

concerned with brittle articles, has not suffered from the increase of import in the same way as other industries, and the building industry has profited both by private enterprise and by the large building-schemes undertaken by Government and by municipalities.

Increase in transport.

191. The rise from 14,656 to 18,403 (26 per cent.) in the figures for transport workers is a natural result of the world-wide improvement and cheapening of mechanical transport; it has been assisted even more in this Province by the improvement of old roads and construction of new roads which have been carried out in the last 10 years. It is reflected in an increase from 181 to 370 in the number of persons engaged in the construction of means of transport, who are included in the previous sub-class, Industry. The advance in mechanical knowledge which has contributed to it is also echoed in another group included under industry, namely persons engaged in the production and transmission of mechanical force. The number in this group has risen from 7 to 147.

Increase in trade.

192. The figures for Trade, sub-class V, show a larger rise even than those for Transport. The total figure in 1921 was 54,652 and is now 61,658, an increase of 15 per cent. As reference to the diagram in paragraph 1.6 will show, Trade has the next largest number of workers after Industry, and is only exceeded by Industry and the Exploitation of Anima's and Vegetation. It is unfortunately difficult to say in what trades the increase has particularly occurred, since the increase is to be found almost entirely in order 39, trade of other sorts. In this group there has been an increase from 19,306 to 30,916 due to the use by enumerators of the vague word "shopkeeper" instead of some more detailed description. This must also affect the reliability of the figures for other orders in this sub-class. There is recorded for example, a decline from 879 to 706 in order 36, trade in means of transport although there can be no doubt that the actual numbers have increased There are recorded increases in order 31, Hotels, Cafes and Restaurants, order 33 Clothing and toilet articles, and order 38, Trade in articles of luxury and those pertaining to letters and the arts and sciences All these suggest an improved standard of living and are probably significant.

Public Force.

193. Sub Class VI, Public Force, includes the Army, the Royal Air Force and the Police. The group for the Royal Navy was excluded in 1921 and should have been excluded again in the present census, but was in fact included and has by some unexplained means acquired a total of 7 males and 1 female. The head "Army" includes all persons governed by military law, whether serving soldiers or followers. The total is now 39,973 and was 47,618 ten years ago. The decrease may be taken to indicate more settled conditions across the border. The numbers in the army enumerated in trans-frontier posts shows a smaller decrease from 36,247 to 33,836 The numbers recorded in the Royal Air Force are not correct, and it seems probable that members of the Royal Air Force have been included both in Kohat and in trans-frontier posts in the returns for the Army. The figures for the Police are practically the same as they were 10 years ago.

Persons serving in the two bodies known as Frontier Constabulary and Frontier Corps have been entered as being in the Army.

Public Administration.

194. The figures of those employed in the Public Administration are also practically the same as those recorded in 1921. It may be noted that a certain number of professional men, including doctors, lawyers, teachers and others, who are Government servants, have been included under the heading of their respective professions rather than under the head "Public Administration".

Assuming that the general proportion of dependents to workers holds good for "Public Force" and "Public Administration" as it does for the populatian as a whole, about 60 per thousand of the population may be said to be supported under these two heads. The corresponding figure for All-India was 15·3 per *mille* in the enumeration of 1921.

Professions and Liberal Arts.

195. There is a considerable decline in the number of workers shown in Sub Class VIII, Professions and liberal arts. The main decrease is under the head Religion, where the figures have gone down from 17,848 to 12,849. This is mainly due to a difference in classification, "Mullahs" having been mostly included as mendicants instead of as priests. There is also a decrease in order 49, Letters, arts and sciences, from 5,784 to 2,202. It is difficult to

believe that there has in actual fact been a decrease, and this difference is also probably due to unintentional differences in enumeration. The number of lawyers (Group 167) has increased from 107 to 246. This is due not so much to any increase in the demand for lawyers, as to the general spread of education. Had there been such an increase in litigation as to demand a doubling of the number of lawyers, there might have been expected a similar increase in the number of lawyers' clerks, the contrary has been the case, the numbers having declined from 561 to 310. Order 47, Medicine, and order 48, Instruction, both show a slight increase.

Persons living on their income.

196. The number of persons recorded as living on their income has decreased from 3,184 to 2,229. This may be due to the death in the interval of a number of war-pensioners who were returned in this group in 1921, but is more probably due to pensioners having described themselves as land-holders

Domestic service.

197. The figures for Sub Class X, Domestic service, show an increase of 22 per cent. from 10,467 to 12,803. These figures vary from census to census, as the meaning of the entry is differently understood by the subjects and by the enumerators, and no conclusions can be drawn from the variations.

Undefined occupations.

198. Sub-Class XI includes persons whose return is too general to indicate any definite occupation. The number under this head has increased from 23,461 to 42,620, an increase of 82 per cent. The increase is mainly found among labourers and workmen otherwise unspecified. It would be dangerous to attribute this to slovenly enumeration, since it is probable that it more accurately describes the true state of affairs than do the figures of 1921 It is certainly no exaggeration to say that there are 42,620 persons in the Province who are labourers pure and simple, ready to turn their hands to any employment that offers

Unproductive.

199. Sub-Class XII includes a number of occupations grouped together as "unproductive". It covers the inmates of jails, asylums and alms houses, beggars, vagrants, prostitutes and others unclassified, few of whom can be described as having any occupation and fewer still as being earners. There are no asylums or Government alms-houses in the Province, but the number of inmates of jails has increased from 2,636 to 6,051. Crime in the Province is generally found to go in waves and the period of the census happened to co-incide with a serious increase of crime. This is reflected by the figures for Army and Police, already considered; although an improvement in conditions across the border has resulted in a reduction in the number of troops found in the Province, no corresponding reduction in Police has been possible. The increase is also partly due to the building of a Central Jail at Haripur where sufficient accommodation has been provided for the prisoners of the Province, who for want of accommodation were sent to the Punjab prior to the opening of this Jail.

The numbers shown under order 54, beggars, vagrants and prostitutes, show a decrease of 35 per cent. from 8,916 to 5,797. Too much significance must not, however, be attached to this decline, as the figures for prostitutes have obviously been incorrectly recorded. It is unfortunately impossible to believe that there are only 3 prostitutes in Hazara, 5 procurers and 1 prostitute in Bannu, and none of either sex in Kohat.

LOCAL DISTRIBUTION.

Main occupations by districts and natural divisions.

200. The distribution of earners and working dependents by the 12 sub-classes in each district and natural division is shown in Subsidiary Table II-A at end of this chapter. The proportions per 1,000 of the population occupied in agriculture, industry, and trade are extracted and displayed in the margin. Hazara being a mountainous tract in which communication is difficult and which is not on any important line of trade,

Number per mille of total earning population (principal occupation and working dependents) found in

District or natural divisions	Sub-Class I Exploitation of animals and vegetation	Sub-Class III Industry	Sub-Class V Trade
N.-W. F. P. (Districts) ...	616	127	72
Hazara ...	784	93	31
Trans-Indus Districts ...	558	138	86
Peshawar ...	573	130	79
Kohat ...	532	153	66
Bannu ...	557	149	114
Dera Ismail Khan ...	529	146	100

shows naturally the lowest figures for industry and trade and the highest figure for agricultural pursuits. As regards the figures for agriculture the other four districts forming for this purpose a homogeneous natural division, are all more or less equal. Peshawar, in spite of being the centre of trade, education and Government, shows the highest figure of the four, the reason being that it is better irrigated and offers more assured cultivation and more certain grazing-lands. In the figures for Industry Kohat is the highest and Dera Ismail Khan the lowest of the Trans Indus districts. In actual figures the numbers are—Peshawar 47,166, Dera Ismail Khan 15,090 and Kohat 11,970. In Trade the highest proportion is shown by Bannu and the lowest by Kohat, but in actual figures Peshawar is highest with 28,659 and Kohat lowest with 5,136. Peshawar owes its importance as a trading-centre to its position between the mouth of the Khyber Pass from Afghanistan and the Indus crossing at Attock.

Local distribution of subsidiary occupations.

201. The distribution of earners who have recorded themselves as having a subsidiary occupation is similarly shown by sub-classes and districts in Subsidiary Table II-B at the end of the chapter. The figures for Sub-Class I, exploitation of animals and vegetation, are reproduced in the margin. It is surprising that the figures are even as high as they are, since most persons who have any connection with land record land as their principal means of subsistence. The majority of those who are shown are serving soldiers and other Government servants with a hereditary interest in land. All the other entries in Subsidiary Table II-B are below 10 per *mille*, with the exception of Sub-Class VI, Public Force, in Kohat where the figure is 19. This high figure is complementary to the high figure shown by Kohat in Sub-Class I, already quoted in the margin, and both are due to the high percentage of recruitment into the army and *quasi*-military services from the agricultural classes of Kohat District.

District or natural divisions	Number per *mille* of earners who have a subsidiary occupation in Sub-Class I
N.-W. F. P ...	38
Hazara ...	22
Trans-Indus Districts ...	42
Peshawar ...	37
Kohat ...	63
Bannu ..	45
Dera Ismail Khan ...	42

Distribution by castes.

202. The details of occupation among 12 selected castes are given in Subsidiary Table No. V. The table in the margin has been prepared to show the proportion in these castes who are following what is regarded as their traditional occupation. The intention of the table is to show the extent to which classes or castes are abandoning their hereditary occupations to strike out on new lines, and with this in view the corresponding figures for 1921 have been inserted for purposes of comparison. With very few exceptions, such as Nai (barber) and Mirasi (singing and dancing entertainer), the hereditary following of occupations is not rigidly observed in this Province. Opportunity, initiative and inclination are the factors which govern occupation, and heredity hardly counts save in so far as it affects one or other of these.

Statement showing the castes which adhere to their traditional occupation, with the proportion of actual workers (Earners as principal occupation and working dependents)

Caste	Traditional Occupation	Workers per *mille* following traditional occupation	
		1921	1931
Arora ...	Trade ...	704	631
Awan ...	Agriculture ...	894	709
Brahman ...	Priests ...	500	124
Chamar ...	Working in leather ...	941	583
Chuhra ...	Scavenging ...	751	557
Gujar ..	Herdsmen ...	882	192
Jat ...	Agriculture ...	707	644
Khatri ...	Trade ...	679	487
Pathan ...	Agriculture and military service ...	873	793
Sayad ...	Priests and agriculture ...	840	783
Swathi ...	Agriculture ...	910	621
Tanaoli ...	Agriculture ...	865	874

A comparison of the actual figures for this year with those for 1921 in the case of one or two of the castes selected at random will show how dangerous it would be to draw conclusions. The actual figures for Brahmans and Gujars are placed below :—

Sub-class	Actual number recorded as earners			
	Brahmans		Gujars	
	1921	1931	1921	1931
III. Industry ...	340	60	126	269
IV. Transport ...	...	117	141	213
V. Trade ...	1,282	950	265	132
VI. Public Force ...	1,871	1,236	676	597
VII. Public Administration ...	185	642	140	68
X. Domestic Service ...	19	1,279	192	688
XI. Labourers ...	162	173	463	555

Among these figures the most striking changes among Brahmans are in Industry from 340 to 60, Trade 1,282 to 950, Public Force 1,871 to 1,236, Public Administration 185 to 642, and Domestic Service 19 to 1,279 : among Gujars the greatest variation is from 192 to 688 in Domestic Service. Now although priesthood may be the hereditary occupation of Brahmans in the sense that they above all others of their religion are entitled to undertake it, yet it is since long before the present series of census operations began, that they have been equally ready to take part in most of the other occupations under consideration. The fact that the numbers following Industry and Trade have decreased, while those engaged in Transport have increased, and that the numbers have decreased in the Public Force and increased in the Public Administration, are purely fortuitous and contribute nothing to the discussion. The enormous increase in Sub-Class X, Domestic Service, is probably due in each case to differences in enumeration. If any figures might be expected to be of value it would be those for Pathans, but even these can not be trusted since confusion has been caused by allowing them two distinct hereditary occupations. The figures for Chuhras, who correspond to the depressed classes in other parts of India, would be of particular interest were they accurate, but they also, when analysed, mean nothing ; rises from 114 to 765 under the head Domestic Service, from 0 to 661 under Industry, from 145 to 370 under Public Administration, and a fall from 795 to 121 among Labourers, can only indicate differences of enumeration.

Europeans and Anglo-Indians.

203. The distribution by occupation of Europeans and Anglo-Indians is to be found in Part B of Imperial Table XI. Both these races are confined almost entirely to Government service. Among 9,724 Europeans in the whole Province, including trans frontier posts, 9,618 are employed in the Army, 19 in the Police, and 47 in other State services. Out of 57 Anglo-Indians 14 are in the Army and 17 in other branches of State service.

OCCUPATION OF FEMALES.

Low proportion of female to male earners.

204. The figures for occupation of females, as already indicated, are vitiated by the exclusion of female workers who do not work for a wage. Were it possible to include all females who do in fact have to work, and to work very hard, for their living, the figures would show almost every married female in the Province as a domestic worker and probably far more women than men under the head Agricultural Labourers.

The statement in the margin gives the proportion of recorded female to male earners in those occupations in which the amount of female labour recorded is appreciable. Apart from Group 194, in which the figures are certainly inaccurate, the only occupation in which there is a recorded excess of female workers are group 45, Rope, twine, string, etc. and Group 56, Basket makers etc. The general proportion of females recorded as earners to the total female population of the districts is only 1 per cent. and is the lowest recorded anywhere in India. The lowness of the figure is explained by the strict manner in which "purdah" is observed throughout the Province. The figures for the twelve selected castes are not without interest in this connection and are to be found in Subsidiary Table No. V at the end of this chapter. A summary of these figures is reproduced in the margin to show the percentage of female earners to male earners. The actual figures are too small to justify the making of any comparisons.

Statement showing the number of females per 1,000 males working in occupations in which female work is in an appreciable degree in the Province (districts)

.oup	Occupation	Number of females per 1,000 male workers
1	Non-cultivating proprietors taking rent in money or kind	122
5	Cultivating owners	894
6	Tenant cultivators	105
7	Agricultural labourers	105
42	Cotton ginning, cleaning and pressing ...	146
43	Cotton spinning sizing and weaving ...	114
45	Rope twine, string and other fibres ..	1,154
56	Basket makers and other industries of woody materials, including leaves, and thatchers and builders working with bamboo reeds or similar materials ...	1,544
71	Rice pounders, huskers and flour grinders ..	276
72	Grain parchers, etc.	89
83	Tailors, milliners, dress makers and darners ...	115
84	Embroiderers, hat makers and makers of other articles of wear	126
111	Porters and messengers	112
145	Dealers in fire-wood, charcoal, coal, cowdung, etc. ...	173
172	Midwives, vaccinators, compounders, nurses, masseurs, etc.	292
174	Professors and teachers of all kinds ...	136
175	Clerks and servants connected with education ...	244
182	Musicians (composers and performers other than military) actors, dancers, etc.	135
184	Conjurors, acrobats, reciters, exhibiters of curiosities and wild animals, etc. ...	85
185	Proprietors (other than of agricultural land), fund, scholarship holders and pensioners ...	95
187	Other domestic service	200
191	Labourers and workmen otherwise unspecified ...	116
193	Beggars and vagrants	176
194	Procurers and prostitutes	2,787

Caste	Proportion of female earners per 100 male earners
Arora	3
Awan	12
Brahman	6
Chuhra	11
Pathan	9
Sayad	11

Variation since 1921 and by districts.

205. Low though it still remains, the proportion of female earners among the population has increased considerably since the last census. The total number of recorded workers has increased by 6 per cent. but the number among females has increased by as much as 91 per cent. from 25,497 in 1921 to 49,887 in the present enumeration. The increase is almost entirely due to an increase under Sub-Class I among the females of Hazara District. It is impossible to resist the conclusion that the size of this increase is due to a difference in enumeration, for the figures have grown from 1,737 to 23,300. Hazara, with the aid of these figures, shows by far the highest proportion of female to male workers. In Hazara the proportion is 137 females to 1,000 males, while in the Trans-Indus districts it varies from 54 in Kohat to 33 in Peshawar. These figures are not sufficiently explained by the high proportion of young males who emigrate from the district. The extent to which local industry has been killed by the import of factory-made articles may be judged from the figures for cotton-spinning, sizing and weaving. In 1921 there were 2,387 females shown as earners under this head, but the present figure is only 996. The industrial development of the Province is at present so inconsiderable that no industrial

census has been carried out on the present occasion. An industrial census was conducted by Mr. A. Rafee in his Industries and Economic Resources of the North-West Frontier Province, the results of which are published by the Government Press, Peshawar.

EDUCATED UNEMPLOYMENT.

Educated unemployment.

206. Educated unemployment has been tabulated by class and according to degree in Imperial Table XII. The standard has perhaps been set too high for satisfactory results, since a total of only 150 persons has been recorded. The lowest degree considered was School Leaving Certificate or Matriculation. It is probable that a considerably higher proportion of unemployment, and considerably more consequent discontent, would be found among persons who have not reached this standard of education but have nevertheless been educated far enough to refuse the occupations of their forefathers. It is significant that almost two-thirds of those recorded as educated unemployed are persons whose fathers were cultivators.

SUBSIDIARY TABLE I (*a*)—*Earners (principal occupation) and working dependents*

Class, sub-class and order	Number per 10,000 of total population	Percentage recorded: In cities and urban industrial areas (Peshawar City)	Percentage recorded: In rural areas (exclusive)
NON-WORKING DEPENDENTS	6,462	4	96
ALL OCCUPATIONS			
Earners (principal occupation) and working dependents	3,538	4	96
A.—Production of Raw Materials	2,181	1	99
I.—EXPLOITATION OF ANIMALS AND VEGETATION... ...	2,180	1	99
1. Pasture and agriculture...	2,179	1	99
(*a*) Cultivation	2,156	1	99
(*b*) Special crops	2	6	94
(*c*) Forestry	1	...	100
(*d*) Stock raising	20	1	99
(*e*) Raising of insects, etc.	...	...	...
2. Fishing and hunting, etc.	1	1	99
II.—EXPLOITATION OF MINERALS	1	...	100
3. Metallic minerals	...	...	...
4. Non-metallic minerals	1	...	100
B.—Preparation and Supply of Material Substances	778	1	99
III.—INDUSTRY	448	8	92
5. Textiles	67	4	96
6. Hides, skins and hard materials from the animal kingdom ...	3	11	89
7. Wood	55	5	95
8. Metals	41	4	96
9. Ceramics	41	2	98
10. Chemical products properly so called and analogous	12	25	75
11. Food industries	42	8	92
12. Industries of dress and the toilet	124	12	88
13. Furniture industries	1	13	87
14. Building industries	27	5	95
15. Construction of mean of transport	1	12	88
16. Production and transmission of physical force	1	15	85
17. Miscellaneous and undefined industries	33	12	88
IV.—TRANSPORT	76	4	96
18. Transport by air	...	...	...
19. Transport by water	4	...	100
20. Transport by road	58	4	96
21. Transport by rail	10	5	95
22. Post office, telegraph and telephone services	4	9	91

SUBSIDIARY TABLE I (*a*)—*Earners (principal occupation) and working dependents*—contd.

Class, sub-class and order	Number per 10,000 of total population	Percentage recorded	
		In cities and urban industrial areas (Peshawar City)	In areas rural (exclusive)
V—TRADE	254	9	91
23. Banks, establishments of credit, exchange and insurance ...	5	13	87
24. Brokerage commission and export...	4	37	63
25. Trade in textiles	16	16	84
26. Trade in skins, leather and furs	1	17	83
27. Trade in wood	5	15	85
28. Trade in metals	1	11	89
29. Trade in pottery, bricks and tiles	2	15	85
30. Trade in chemical products	...	11	89
31. Hotels, cafés, restaurants, etc.	13	10	90
32. Other trade in food-stuffs	59	11	89
33. Trade in clothing and toilet articles	7	17	83
34. Trade in furniture	3	9	91
35. Trade in building materials	2	11	89
36. Trade in means of transport	3	11	89
37. Trade in fuel	2	33	67
38. Trade in articles of luxury and those pertaining to letters and the arts and sciences	4	31	69
39. Trade of other sorts	127	4	96
C.—Public Administration and Liberal Arts	292	5	95
VI.—PUBLIC FORCE	165	1	99
40. Army	129	...	100
41. Navy	...	...	100
42. Air Force	2	...	100
43. Police	34	7	93
VII.—PUBLIC ADMINISTRATION	41	15	85
44. Public Administration	41	15	85
VIII.—PROFESSIONS AND LIBERAL ARTS	86	7	93
45. Religion	53	3	97
46. Law	2	30	70
47. Medicine	13	11	89
48. Instruction	9	14	86
49. Letters, arts and sciences (other than 44)	9	11	89
D.—Miscellaneous	287	7	93
IX.—PERSONS LIVING ON THEIR INCOME	9	9	91
50. Persons living principally on their income	9	9	91
X.—DOMESTIC SERVICE	53	19	81
51. Domestic service	53	19	81

SUBSIDIARY TABLE I (*a*)—*Earners* (*principal occupation*) *and working dependents*—concld.

Class, sub-class and order	Number per 10,000 of total population	Percentage recorded	
		In cities and urban industrial areas (Peshawar City)	In rural areas (exclusive)
XI.—INSUFFICIENTLY DESCRIBED OCCUPATIONS	176	5	95
52. General terms which do not indicate definite occupation ...	176	5	95
XII.—UNPRODUCTIVE	49	4	96
53. Inmates of jails, asylums and alms houses	25	...	100
54. Beggars, vagrants, prostitutes	24	7	93
55. Other unclassified non-productive industries	...	24	76

SUBSIDIARY TABLE I (*b*)—*Earners (subsidiary occupation)*

Class, sub-class and order	Number per 10,000 of total population	Percentage recorded: In cities and urban industrial areas (Peshawar City)	Percentage recorded: In rural areas (exclusive)
ALL OCCUPATIONS ...			
Earners (with subsidiary occupations)	227	1	99
A.—Production of Raw Materials	118	...	100
I.—EXPLOITATION OF ANIMALS AND VEGETATION... ...	118	...	100
1. Pasture and agriculture	118	...	100
(*a*) Cultivation	116	...	100
(*b*) Special crops	...	...	100
(*c*) Forestry	...	...	100
(*d*) Stock raising	2	...	100
(*e*) Raising of insects, etc.	...	...	...
2. Fishing and hunting, etc.	...	...	100
II.—EXPLOITATION OF MINERALS	...	...	100
3. Metallic minerals	...	...	...
4. Non-metallic minerals	...	...	100
B.—Preparation and Supply of Material Substances	48	...	100
III.—INDUSTRY	20	...	100
5. Textiles	2	1	99
6. Hides, skins and hard materials from the animal kingdom ...	...	...	100
7. Wood	5	...	100
8. Metals	2	...	100
9. Ceramics	1	1	99
10. Chemical products properly so called and analogous	1	...	100
11. Food industries	2	...	100
12. Industries of dress and the toilet	6	...	100
13. Furniture industries	...	...	100
14. Building industries	...	3	97
15. Construction of means of transport	...	...	100
16. Production and transmission of physical force	...	...	100
17. Miscellaneous and undefined industries	1	2	98
IV.—TRANSPORT	14	...	100
18. Transport by air	...	...	...
19. Transport by water	...	...	100
20. Transport by road	13	...	100
21. Transport by rail	1	...	100
22. Post Office, telegraph and telephone services	...	...	100

SUBSIDIARY TABLE I.(b)—*Earners (subsidiary occupations)*—contd.

Class, sub-class and order	Number per 10,000 of total population	Percentage recorded: In cities and urban industrial areas (Peshawar City)	Percentage recorded: In rural areas (exclusive)
V.—TRADE	14	1	99
23. Banks, establishments of credit, exchange and insurance ...	1	1	99
24. Brokerage commission and export	...	1	99
25. Trade in textiles	...	1	99
26. Trade in skins, leather and furs	...	...	100
27. Trade in wood	1	1	99
28. Trade in metals	...	...	100
29. Trade in pottery, bricks and tiles	...	...	100
30. Trade in chemical products	...	..	100
31. Hotels, cafes, restaurants, etc.	...	...	100
32. Other trade in food-stuffs	5	...	100
33. Trade in clothing and toilet articles	...	...	100
34. Trade in furniture	...	...	100
35. Trade in building materials	...	...	...
36. Trade in means of transport	1	10	90
37. Trade in fuel	1	...	100
38. Trade in articles of luxury and those pertaining to letters and the arts and sciences.	...	...	100
39. Trade of other sorts	5	...	100
C.—Public Administration and Liberal Arts	31	3	97
VI.—PUBLIC FORCE	16	4	96
40. Army	11	...	100
41. Navy	..	...	100
42. Air Force	...	...	100
43. Police	5	13	87
VII.—PUBLIC ADMINISTRATION	7	2	98
44. Public Administration	7	2	98
VIII.—PROFESSIONS AND LIBERAL ARTS	8	1	99
45. Religion	6	1	99
46. Law	...	...	100
47. Medicine	1	...	100
48. Instruction	1	2	98
49. Letters, arts and sciences (other than 44)	...	6	94
D.—Miscellaneous	30	3	97
IX.—PERSONS LIVING ON THEIR INCOME	8	3	97
50. Persons living principally on their income	8	3	97

SUBSIDIARY TABLE I (*b*)—*Earners* (*subsidiary occupations*)—concld.

Class, sub-class and order	Number per 10,000 of total population	Percentage recorded	
		In cities and urban industrial areas (Peshawar City)	In rural areas (exclusive)
X.—DOMESTIC SERVICE	10	6	94
51. Domestic service	10	6	94
XI.—INSUFFICIENTLY DESCRIBED OCCUPATIONS	11	1	99
52. General terms which do not indicate definite occupation ...	11	1	99
XII.—UNPRODUCTIVE	1	1	99
53. Inmates of jails, asylums and alms houses	...	...	100
54. Beggars, vagrants, prostitutes	1	1	99
55. Other unclassified non-productive industries	..	...	100

SUBSIDIARY TABLE II (*a*)—*Distribution by sub-classes in natural divisions and districts of earners and working dependents*

District and Natural Division	Total per 1,000			Number per *mille* of the total population occupied as earners (principal occupation) and working dependents in											
	Non-working dependents	Working dependents	Earners (principal occupation)	Sub-class I—Exploitation of animals and vegetation	Sub-class II—Exploitation of minerals	Sub-class III—Industry	Sub-class IV—Transport	Sub-class V—Trade	Sub-class VI—Public Force	Sub-class VII—Public Administration	Sub-class VIII—Professions and liberal arts	Sub-class IX—Persons living on their income	Sub-class X—Domestic service	Sub-class XI—Insufficiently described occupation	Sub-class XII—Unproductive
	2	3	4	5	6	7	8	9	10	11	12	13	14	15	16
N.-W. F. P. (Districts)	646	40	314	616	...	127	21	72	46	12	24	3	15	50	14
Hazara ...	672	58	270	784	...	93	8	31	24	4	14	3	10	16	13
Trans-Indus Districts	636	34	330	558	...	138	26	86	54	14	29	3	17	61	14
Peshawar ...	628	41	331	573	...	130	26	79	49	17	25	2	23	64	12
Kohat ...	669	22	309	532	1	153	28	66	111	8	31	3	7	54	6
Bannu ...	653	23	324	557	...	149	19	114	48	13	35	2	3	47	13
Dera Ismail Khan ...	622	28	350	529	...	146	31	100	36	12	26	4	16	69	31

SUBSIDIARY TABLE II (*b*)—*Distribution by sub-classes in natural divisions and districts of earners (subsidiary occupation)*

District and Natural Division	Number per *mille* of total population of earners having a subsidiary occupation in											
	Sub-class I	Sub-class II	Sub-class III	Sub-class IV	Sub-class V	Sub-class VI	Sub-class VII	Sub-class VIII	Sub-class IX	Sub-class X	Sub-class XI	Sub-class XII
1	2	3	4	5	6	7	8	9	10	11	12	13
N.-W. F. P. (Districts) ...	38	...	6	4	5	5	2	3	3	3	4	...
Hazara	22	...	9	2	4	3	2	3	4	5	3	1
Trans-Indus Districts	42	...	5	5	5	6	2	2	2	2	4	...
Peshawar	37	...	6	6	4	4	1	2	1	2	4	...
Kohat	63	...	8	6	4	19	7	4	9	3	3	1
Bannu	45	...	4	3	7	3	3	4		1	2	...
Dera Ismail Khan	42	...	4	5	6	4	3	3		3	5	1

SUBSIDIARY TABLE III—*Occupations of females by sub-classes and selected orders and groups*

Group No.	Occupation sub-class and order)	Number of actual workers		Number of females per 1,000 males
		Males	Females	
1	2	3	4	5
	ALL OCCUPATIONS	808,081	49,887	62
	Sub-class I—Exploitation of animals and vegetation	493,998	34,727	70
	ORDER 1—PASTURE AND AGRICULTURE	493,727	34,726	70
	ORDER I—(a) CULTIVATION	488,182	34,658	71
1	Non-cultivating proprietors taking rent in money or kind	36,966	4,508	122
5	Cultivating owners	6,994	6,254	894
6	Tenant cultivators	178,690	18,711	105
7	Agricultural labourers	49,418	5,185	105
	ORDER I—(b) CULTIVATION OF SPECIAL CROPS, FRUITS, ETC. (PLANTERS, MANAGERS, CLERKS AND LABOURERS).	517	14	27
16	Market gardeners, flower and fruit growers	517	14	27
	ORDER I—(c) FORESTY	254	13	51
18	Wood-cutters and charcoal burners	175	8	46
	ORDER I—(d) STOCK RAISING	4,774	41	9
21	Cattle and buffalo breeders and keepers	4,560	31	7
23	Herdsmen, shepherds and breeders of other animals	213	9	42
	ORDER 2—FISHING AND HUNTING	271	1	4
27	Fishing and pearling	264	1	4
	Sub-class II—Exploitation of minerals	118	...	...
	ORDER 4—NON-METALLIC MINERALS	118	...	...
40	Salt, saltpetre and other saline substances	82	...	...
	Sub-class III—Industry	102,693	6,049	59
	ORDER 5—TEXTILES	14,718	1,636	111
42	Cotton ginning, cleaning and pressing...	2,091	305	146
43	Cotton spinning, sizing and weaving	8,757	996	114
44	Jute pressing, spinning and weaving	...	...	...
45	Rope, twine, string and other fibres	214	247	1,154
46	Wool carding, spinning and weaving	605	4	7
47	Silk spinning and weaving	267	...	...
49	Dyeing bleaching printing, preparation and sponging of textiles ...	2,597	58	22
50	Lace, crepe, embroideries, fringes, etc., and insufficiently described textile industries	156	6	38
	ORDER 6—HIDES, SKINS AND HARD MATERIALS FROM THE ANIMAL KINGDOM	613	8	13
51	Working in leather	613	8	13
	ORDER 7—WOOD	12,083	1,357	112

SUBSIDIARY TABLE III—*Occupations of females by sub-classes and selected orders and groups*—continued

Group No.	Occupation (sub-class and order)	Number of actual workers: Males	Number of actual workers: Females	Number of females per 1,000 males
1	2	3	4	5
54	Sawyers	189	...	...
55	Carpenters, turners and joiners, etc.	11,379	562	49
56	Basket makers and other industries of woody materials, including leaves and thatchers and builders working with bamboo, reeds or similar materials ...	515	795	1,544
	ORDER 8—METALS	9,959	67	7
59	Blacksmiths, other workers in iron, makers of implements	9,420	65	7
60	Workers in brass, copper and bell metal	161	...	...
61	Workers in other metals (except precious metals)	378	2	5
	ORDER 9—CERAMICS	9,849	199	20
63	Potters and makers of earthenware	4,343	149	34
64	Brick and tile makers	5,503	50	9
	ORDER 10—CHEMICAL PRODUCTS PROPERLY SO CALLED AND ANALOGOUS	2,788	42	15
66	Manufacture of matches, fire works and other explosives	107	4	37
67	Manufacture of ærated and mineral waters and ice	234	...	...
68	Manufacture and refining of vegetable oils	288	30	14
70	Others	259	8	31
	ORDER 11—FOOD INDUSTRIES	9,293	919	99
71	Rice pounders and huskers and flour grinders	2,523	696	276
72	Grain parchers, etc.	1,340	119	89
73	Butchers	3,383	61	18
74	Makers of sugar, molasses and gur	120	...	...
75	Sweetmeat, Bakhar preparer and condiment makers	507	...	...
78	Manufacturers of tobacco	213	1	5
81	Others	1,171	42	36
	ORDER No. 12—INDUSTRIES OF DRESS AND THE TOILET ...	28,949	1,075	37
82	Boot, shoe, sandal and clog makers	11,150	216	19
83	Tailors, milliners, dress-makers and darners	5,024	577	115
84	Embroiderers, hat-makers and makers of other articles of wear ...	597	75	126
85	Washing and cleaning	4,669	169	36
86	Barbers, hair dressers and wig makers	7,455	38	5
	ORDER 13—FURNITURE INDUSTRIES	252	1	4
88	Cabinet-makers, carriage painters, etc.	202	...	...
	ORDER 14—BUILDING INDUSTRIES	6,398	37	6
90	Lime-burners, cement workers, excavators and well sinkers; stone cutters and dressers; brick layers and masons; builders (other than buildings made of bamboo or similar materials), painters, decorators of houses, tilers, plumbers, etc.	6,398	37	6
	ORDER 15—CONSTRUCTION OF MEANS OF TRANSPORT ...	370	...	...
	Persons engaged in making, assembling or repairing motor vehicles or cycles ...	248	...	...

SUBSIDIARY TABLE III—*Occupations of females by sub-classes and selected orders and groups*—continued

Group No.	Occupation (sub-class and orders)	Number of actual workers: Males	Number of actual workers: Females	Number of females per 1,000 males
1	2	3	4	5
92	Carriage, cart, palki, etc. makers and wheel wrights	102	...	...
	ORDER 16—PRODUCTION AND TRANSMISSION OF PHYSICAL FORCE ...	147	...	...
94	Heat, light, electricity, motive power, etc., gasworks and electric light and power	147	...	...
	ORDER 17—MISCELLANEOUS AND UNDEFINED INDUSTRIES ...	7,274	708	97
95	Printers, engravers, book binders, etc....	364	...	...
97	Makers of clock and surgical or scientific instruments, etc.... ...	143	1	7
98	Makers of jewellery and ornaments	3,095	53	17
	Sub-class IV—Transport	18,306	97	5
	ORDER 19—TRANSPORT BY WATER	929	2	2
102	Ship owners, boat owners and their employees, officers, marines, etc., ships brokers, boatmen and tow-men	647	2	
104	Labourers employed on harbours, docks, rivers and canals	202	...	...
	ORDER 20—TRANSPORT BY ROAD	14,124	82	6
105	Persons (other than labourers) employed on the construction and maintenance of roads and bridges	553	1	2
106	Labourers employed on roads and bridges	1,119	32	29
107	Owners, managers and employees (including personal servants) connected with mechanically driven vehicles (excluding trams)	1,644	...	...
108	Owners, managers and employees (excluding personal servants) connected with other vehicles...	5,152	12	2
109	Palki, etc., bearers and owners	133	...	...
110	Pack elephant, camel, mule, ass and bullock, owners and drivers ...	5,416	25	5
111	Porters and messengers	107	12	112
	ORDER 21—TRANSPORT BY RAIL	2,314	10	4
112	Railway employees of all kinds other than coolies	1,945	9	5
113	Labourers employed on railway construction and maintenance and coolies and porters employed on railway premises	369	1	3
	ORDER 22.—POST OFFICE, TELEGRAPH AND TELEPHONE SERVICES ...	939	3	3
114	Telegraph and Telephone services	939	3	3
	Sub-class V—Trade	60,907	751	12
	ORDER 23—BANKS, ESTABLISHMENTS OF CREDIT, EXCHANGE AND INSURANCE	1,135	13	11
115	Bank managers, money lenders, exchange and insurance agents, money changers and brokers and their employees	1,135	13	11
	ORDER 24—BROKERAGE COMMISSION AND EXPORT ...	911	3	3
116	Brokers, commission agents, commercial travellers, warehouse owners and employees	911	3	3
	ORDER 25—TRADE IN TEXTILES	3,854	45	12
117	Trade in piece goods, wool, cotton, silk, hair and other textiles ...	3,854	45	12

SUBSIDIARY TABLE III—*Occupations of females by sub-classes and selected orders and groups*—continued

Group No.	Occupation (sub-class and orders)	Number of actual workers		Number of females per 1,000 males
		Males	Females	
1	2	3	4	5
	ORDER 26—TRADE IN SKINS, LEATHER AND FURS	250	7	28
118	Trade in skins, leather, furs, feathers, horn, etc.. and the articles made from these	250	7	28
	ORDER 27—TRADE IN WOOD	1,276	11	9
119	Trade in wood (not firewood)	1,065	19	9
120	Trade in barks	160	...	...
	ORDER 28—TRADE IN METALS	252	1	4
123	Trade in metals, machinery, knives, tools, etc.	262	1	4
	ORDER 29—TRADE IN POTTERY, BRICKS AND TILES	408	...	...
124	Trade in pottery, bricks and tiles	408	...	...
	ORDER 30 TRADE IN CHEMICAL PRODUCTS	130	1	8
125	Drugs, dyes, paints, petroleum, explosives, etc.	130	1	8
	ORDER 31—HOTELS, CAFES, RESTAURANTS, ETC.	3,113	6	2
126	Vendors of vine, liquors, acrated waters and ice	742	1	1
127	Owners and managers of hotels, cook-shops, sarais, etc.	2,085	4	2
128	Hawkers of drink and food stuffs	286	1	3
	ORDER 32—OTHER TRADE IN FOOD STUFFS	14,098	216	15
129	Grain and pulse dealers	6,596	89	13
130	Dealers in sweetmeats, sugar and spices	2,002	23	11
131	Dealers in dairy product, eggs and poultry	1,490	52	35
132	Dealers in animals for food	215	...	...
133	Dealers in fodder for animals	2,145	35	16
134	Dealers in other food stuffs	862	17	20
135	Dealers in tobacco	178	...	...
136	Dealers in opium	309	...	...
137	Dealers in Ganja	301	...	...
	ORDER 33—TRADE IN CLOTHING AND TOILET ARTICLES ...	1,751	14	8
138	Trade in ready-made clothing and other articles of dress and the toilet (hats, umbrellas, socks, ready-made shoes, perfumes, etc.)	1,751	14	8
	ORDER 34—TRADE IN FURNITURE	686	1	1
139	Trade in furniture, carpets, curtains and bedding	334	1	3
140	Hardware, cooking utensils, porcelain, crockery, glassware, bottles, articles for gardening, etc.	352	...	...
	ORDER 35—TRADE IN BUILDING MATERIALS	404	...	...
141	Trade in building materials (other than bricks, tiles and woody materials) ...	404	...	...
	ORDER 36—TRADE IN MEANS OF TRANSPORT	689	17	25
142	Dealers and hirers in mechanical transport, motors, cycles, etc. ...	210	..	...
143	Dealers and hirers in other carriages, carts, boats, etc.	115	...	...
144	Dealers and hirers of elephants, camels, horses, cattle, asses, mules, etc. ...	364	17	47

SUBSIDIARY TABLE III—*Occupations of females by sub-classes and selected orders and groups*—continued

Group No.	Occupation (sub-class and order)	Number of actual workers		Number of females per 1,000 males
		Males	Females	
1	2	3	4	5
	ORDER 37—TRADE IN FUEL	323	56	173
145	Dealers in firewood, charcoal, coal, cowdung, etc.	323	56	173
	ORDER 38—TRADE IN ARTICLES OF LUXURY AND THOSE PERTAINING TO LETTERS AND THE ARTS AND SCIENCES	1,051	...	...
146	Dealers in precious stones, jewellery (real and imitation), clocks, optical instruments, etc.	301	...	...
147	Dealers in common bangles, bead-necklaces, fans, small articles, toys, hunting and fishing tackle, flowers, etc.	213	...	...
148	Publishers, booksellers, stationers, dealers in music, pictures, musical instruments and curiosities	547	...	...
	ORDER 38—TRADE OF OTHER SORTS	30,556	360	12
149	Dealers in rags, stable refuse, etc.	246	...	...
150	General store-keepers and shop-keepers otherwise unspecified ...	29,889	360	12
151	Itinerant traders, pedlars and hawkers (of other than food, etc.) ...	302	...	...
152	Other trades (including farmers of pounds, tools and markets) ...	119	...	...
	Sub-class VI—Public Force	39,944	29	1
	ORDER 40—ARMY	31,164	28	1
153	Army (Imperial)	31,016	28	1
154	Army (Indian States)	148	...	...
	ORDER 42—AIR FORCE	435	...	...
156	Air Force	435	...	...
	ORDER 43—POLICE	8,338	...	...
157	Police	5,937	..	...
158	Village watchmen	2,401	...	...
	Sub-class VII—Public Administration	9,864	148	15
	ORDER 44—PUBLIC ADMINISTRATION	9,854	148	15
159	Service of the State	8,053	114	14
161	Municipal and other local (not village) service	663	32	48
162	Village officials and servants other than watchmen	1,136	2	18
	Sub-class VIII—Professions and liberal arts...	19,870	880	44
	ORDER 45—RELIGION	12,693	156	12
163	Priests, ministers etc	212	...	...
164	Monks, nuns, religious mendicants	11,730	145	12
165	Other religious workers	309	5	16
166	Servants in religious edifices, burial and burning grounds, pilgrim conductors circumcisers, etc.	442	6	14
	ORDER 46—LAW	521	35	67
167	Lawyers of all kinds, including Qazis, law agents and Mukhtiars ...	220	26	118
168	Lawyers' clerks, petition writers, etc.	301	9	30

SUBSIDIARY TABLE III—*Occupations of females by sub-classes and selected orders and groups*—concluded

Group No.	Occupation (sub-class and order)	Number of actual workers: Males	Number of actual workers: Females	Number of females per 1,000 males
1	2	3	4	5
	ORDER 47—MEDICINE	2,780	310	112
169	Registered medical practitioners including occulists	1,361	11	8
170	Other persons practising the healing arts without being registered ...	321	5	16
172	Midwives, vaccinators, compounders, nurses, masseurs, etc. ...	1,008	294	292
	ORDER 48—INSTRUCTIONS	1,799	254	141
174	Professors and teachers of all kind	1,717	234	136
175	Clerks and servants connected with education	82	20	244
	ORDER 49—LETTERS, ARTS AND SCIENCES (OTHER THAN 44) ..	2,077	125	60
176	Public scribes, stenographers, etc.	176	...	...
177	Architects (not being State servants)	223	...	...
178	Authors, editors, journalists and photographers	149	...	...
179	Artists, sculptors and image-makers	101	...	...
182	Musicians, composers and performers (other than military) actors, dancers, etc.	318	43	135
184	Conjurors, acrobats, reciters, exhibitors of curiosities and wild animals, etc. ...	969	82	85
	Sub-class IX—Persons living on their income	2,099	200	95
	ORDER 50—PERSONS LIVING PRINCIPALLY ON THEIR INCOME ...	2,099	200	95
185	Proprietors (other than of agricultural land fund and scholarship holders and pensioners)	2,099	200	95
	Sub-class X—Domestic service	10,737	2,066	192
	ORDER 51—DOMESTIC SERVICE	10,737	2,066	192
186	Private motor drivers and cleaners	439	3	7
187	Other domestic service	10,298	2,063	200
	Sub-class XI—Insufficiently described occupations	38,705	3,915	101
	ORDER 52—GENERAL TERMS WHICH DO NOT INDICATE A DEFINITE OCCUPATION	38,705	3,915	101
188	Manufacturers, business men and contractors otherwise unspecified ..	4,567	62	14
189	Cashiers, accountants, book-keepers, clerks and other employees in unspecified offices and warehouses and shops	816	...	...
191	Labourers and workmen otherwise unspecified	33,296	3,853	116
	Sub-class XII—Unproductive	10,840	1,025	95
	ORDER 53—INMATES OF JAILS, ASYLUMS AND ALMS HOUSES ...	5,996	55	9
192	Inmates of jails, asylums and alms houses	5,996	55	9
	ORDER 54—BEGGARS, VAGRANTS, PROSTITUTES	4,827	970	201
193	Beggars and vagrants	4,780	839	176
194	Procurers and prostitutes	47	131	2,787
	ORDER 55—OTHER UNCLASSIFIED NON-PRODUCTIVE INDUSTRIES ...	17	...	...
195	Other unclassified non-productive industries	17	...	...

SUBSIDIARY TABLE IV—*Variations in selected occupations, 1921—1931*

Group No.	Occupation (sub-class and order)	1931 Earners (principal occupations) and working dependents	1931 Earners (subsidiary occupations)	1921 Actual workers
1	2	3	4	5
	ALL OCCUPATIONS	857,968	55,132	809,177
	Class A—Production of Raw Materials	528,843	28,640	491,384
	Sub-Class I—Exploitation of Animals and Vegetation	528,725	28,626	491,201
	ORDER I—PASTURE AND AGRICULTURE	528,453	28,567	490,942
	ORDER 1 (*a*) CULTIVATION	522,840	28,065	485,072
1	Non-cultivating proprietors taking rent in money or kind ...	41,474	12,475	241,231
2	Estate agents and managers of owners	...	..	
3	Estate agents and managers of Government	6	3	105 (groups 2–4)
4	Rent collectors, clerks, etc.	80	...	
5	Cultivating owners	227,276	4,995	239,526 (groups 5–6)
6	Tenants cultivators	197,401	7,826	
7	Agricultural labourers	56,603	2,766	4,210
8	Cultivators of Jhum, taungya and shifting areas	...	...	...
	ORDER 1 (*b*)—CULTIVATION OF SPECIAL CROPS, FRUITS, ETC. (PLANTERS, MANAGERS, CLERKS AND LABOURERS)	531	60	276
16	Market gardeners, flowers and fruit growers	531	60	276
	ORDER 1 (*c*)—FORESTRY	267	60	1,018
17	Forest Officers, rangers, guards, etc.	42	15	164
18	Wood cutters and charcoal burners	183	45	
19	Collectors of forest produce	42	...	854 (groups 18–20)
20	Collectors of lac	...	...	
	ORDER 1 (*d*)—STOCK RAISING	4,815	382	4,563
21	Cattle and buffalo breeders and keepers	4,591	360	457
22	Breeders of transport animals	2	...	16
23	Herdsmen, shepherds and breeders of other animals	222	22	4,090
	ORDER 1 (*e*)—RAISING OF SMALL ANIMALS AND INSECTS ...	...	...	13
24	Birds, bees, etc.	...	...	13
	ORDER 2—FISHING AND HUNTING	272	59	259
27	Fishing and pearling	265	56	232
28	Hunting	7	3	47
	Sub-Class II—Exploitation of Minerals	118	14	183
	ORDER 4—NON-METALLIC MINERALS	118	14	183
39	Precious and semi-precious stones	36	13	...
40	Salt, saltpetre and other saline substances	82	1	183

SUBSIDIARY TABLE IV—*Variations in selected occupations, 1921—1931*—continued

Group No.	Occupation (sub-class and order)	1931 Earners (principal occupations) and working dependents	1931 Earners (subsidiary occupations)	1921 Actual workers
1	2	3	4	
	Class B—Preparation and supply of material substances	188,803	11,644	
	Sub-Class III—Industry	108,742	4,831	113,919
	ORDER 5—TEXTILES	16,354	456	19,640
42	Cotton ginning cleaning and pressing	2,396	45	2,465
43	Cotton spinning, sizing and weaving	9,753	389	13,446
44	Jute pressing, spinning and weaving	51	2	269
45	Rope, twine, string and other fibres...	461	...	
46	Wool carding, spinning and weaving	699	...	622
47	Silk spinning and weaving	267	...	219
49	Dyeing, bleaching, printing, preparation and sponging of textiles ...	2,655	20	2,448
50	Lace, crepe, embroideries, fringes, etc., and insufficiently described textile industries	162	...	171
	ORDER 6—HIDES, SKINS AND HARD MATERIALS FROM THE ANIMAL KINGDOM	621	5	1,307
51	Working in leather	614	4	1,252
53	Bone, ivory, horn, shell, etc., workers (except buttons)	7	1	55
	ORDER 7—WOOD	13,440	1,328	14,049
54	Sawyers	189	369	1,258
55	Carpenters, turners and joiners, etc.	11,941	890	8,628
56	Basket makers and other industries of woody materials, including leaves and thatchers and builders working with bamboo, reeds or similar materials ...	1,310	69	4,163
	ORDER 8—METALS	10,026	371	10,443
58	Makers of arms, guns, etc.	...	...	55
59	Blacksmiths, other workers in iron, makers of implements ...	9,485	354	9,831
60	Workers in brass, copper and bell metal	161	...	130
61	Workers in other metals (except precious metals)	380	17	427
	ORDER 9—Ceramics	10,048	183	7,412
63	Potters and makers of earthen ware	4,492	136	6,161
64	Brick and tile makers	5,553	47	1,232
65	Other workers in ceramics	3	...	19
	ORDER 10—CHEMICAL PRODUCTS PROPERLY SO CALLED AND ANALOGOUS	2,830	256	3,190
66	Manufacture of matches, fire works and other explosives... ...	111	...	48
67	Manufacture of aerated and mineral waters and ice	234	...	110
68	Manufacture and refining of vegetable oils	2,218	233	2,932
70	Others	267	23	100
	ORDER 11—FOOD INDUSTRIES	10,212	495	11,007
71	Rice pounders and huskers and flour grinders	3,219	102	3,779
72	Grain parchers, etc.	1,459	50	2,702
73	Butchers	3,444	268	3,003
74	Makers of sugar, molasses and *gur*	120	1	102

SUBSIDIARY TABLE IV—*Variations in selected occupations, 1921—1931*—contd.

Group No.	Occupation (sub-class and order)	1931 Earners (principal occupation) and working dependents	1931 Earners (subsidiary occupations)	1921 Actual workers
1	2	3	4	5
75	Sweetmeat, bakhar preparer and condiment makers	507	...	1,223
77	Brewers and distillers	19	...	...
78	Manufacturers of tobacco	214	...	153
79	Manufacturers of opium	...	...	
80	Manufacturers of *ganja*	17	...	
81	Others	1,213	74	45
	ORDER 12—INDUSTRIES OF DRESS AND THE TOILET ...	30,024	1,457	31,305
82	Boot, shoe, sandal and clog makers	11,366	459	11,218
83	Tailors, milliners, dress-makers and darners	5,601	430	5,134
84	Embroiderers, hat-makers and makers of other articles of wear ...	672	3	784
85	Washing and cleaning	4,838	160	5,398
86	Barbers, hair dressers and wig-makers.	7,493	405	8,663
87	Other industries connected with the toilet	54	...	108
	ORDER 13—FURNITURE INDUSTRIES	253	5	387
88	Cabinet-makers, carriage painters, etc.	202	3	338
89	Upholsterers, tent-makers, etc.	51	2	49
	ORDER 14—BUILDING INDUSTRIES	6,435	87	3,454
90	Lime burners, cement workers ; excavaters and well sinkers ; stone cutters and dressers ; brick layers and masons ; builders (other than buildings made of bamboo or similar materials), painters, decorators of houses, tilers, plumbers, etc.	6,435	87	3,454
	ORDER 15—CONSTRUCTION OF MEANS OF TRANSPORT ...	370	15	181
91	Persons engaged in making, assembling or repairing motor vehicles or cycle	248	12	35
92	Carriage, cart, palki, etc., makers and wheel wrights ...	102	3	48
93	Ship, boat, aeroplane builders	20	...	98
	ORDER 16—PRODUCTION AND TRANSMISSION OF PHYSICAL FORCE	147	7	7
94	Heat, light, electricity, motive power, etc., gas works and electric light and power	147	7	7
	ORDER 17—MISCELLANEOUS AND UNDEFINED INDUSTRIES ...	7,982	166	11,537
95	Printers, engravers, book binders etc.	364	7	168
96	Makers of musical instruments	28	...	34
97	Makers of clocks and surgical or scientific instruments, etc ...	144	6	187
98	Makers of jewellery and ornaments	3,148	115	5,882
99	Other miscellaneous and undefined industries (toy-making, taxidermy, etc.) ... ... – ...	17	6	108
100	Scavenging	4,281	32	5,158
	Sub-Class IV—Transport	18,403	3,300	14,656
	ORDER 19—TRANSPORT BY WATER	931	21	1,171
102	Ship owners, boat owners and their employees, officers, mariners, etc., ships brokers, boatmen and tow-men	649	20	33

SUBSIDIARY TABLE IV—*Variations in selected occupations, 1921—1931*—contd.

Group No.	Occupation (sub-class and order)	1931 Earners (principal occupation) and working dependents	1931 Earners subsidiary occupation	1921 Actual workers
1		3	4	5
103	Persons (other than labourers) employed in harbours, docks, rivers and canals including pilots	80	1	529
104	Labourers employed on harbours, docks, rivers and canals ...	202	...	609
	ORDER 20—TRANSPORT BY ROAD	14,206	2,992	10,273
105	Persons (other than labourers) employed on the construction and maintenance of roads and bridges	624	77	1,470
106	Labourers employed on roads and bridges	1,151	244	...
107	Owners, managers and employees (excluding personal servants) connected with mechanically driven vehicles (including trams) ...	1,644	96	413
108	Owners, managers, and employees (excluding personal servants) connected with other vehicles	5,164	994	2,566
109	Palki, etc., bearers and owners	133	2	104
110	Pack elephant, camel, mule, ass and bullock owners and drivers ...	5,441	1,564	3,623
111	Porters and messengers	119	15	2,097
	ORDER 21—TRANSPORT BY RAIL	2,324	233	2,273
112	Railway employees of all kind other than coolies	1,954	194	1,966
113	Labourers employed on railway construction and maintenance and coolies and porters employed on railway premises	370	39	307
	ORDER 22—POST OFFICE, TELEGRAPH AND TELEPHONE SERVICES ..	942	54	939
114	Post Office, Telegraph and Telephone services	942	54	939
	Sub-Class V—Trade	61,658	3,513	53,673
	ORDER 23—BANKS, ESTABLISHMENTS OF CREDIT EXCHANGE AND INSURANCE	1,148	248	1,702
115	Bank managers, money-lenders, exchange and insurance agents, money changers and brokers and their employees	1,148	248	1,702
	ORDER 24—BROKERAGE COMMISSION AND EXPORT ...	914	81	1,768
116	Brokers, commission agents, commercial travellers warehouse owners and employees	914	81	1,768
	ORDER 25—TRADE IN TEXTILES	3,899	114	4,159
117	Trade in piece goods, wool, cotton, silk, hair and other textiles ...	3,899	114	4,159
	ORDER 26—TRADE IN SKINS, LEATHER AND FURS ...	257	44	602
118	Trade in skins, leather, furs, feathers, horn, etc., and the articles made from these	257	44	602
	ORDER 27—TRADE IN WOOD	1,287	182	1,724
119	Trade in wood (not firewood)	1,075	157	1,724 (groups 119–121)
120	Trade in barks	160	24	
121	Trade in bamboos and canes	52	1	
122	Trade in thatches and other forest produce	...	...	Included in groups 119 to 121.
	ORDER 28 TRADE IN METALS	263	1	115
123	Trade in metals, machinery, knives, tools etc.	263	1	115

SUBSIDIARY TABLE IV—*Variations in selected occupations, 1921—1931*—contd.

Group No.	Occupation (sub-class and order)	1931 Earners (principal occupation) and working dependents	1931 Earners subsidiary occupation	1921 Actual workers
1	2	3	4	5
	ORDER 29—TRADE IN POTTERY, BRICKS AND TILES ...	408	1	166
124	Trade in pottery, bricks and tiles	408	1	166
	ORDER 30—TRADE IN CHEMICAL PRODUCTS	131	3	85
125	Drugs, dyes, paints, petroleum, explosives, etc.	131	3	85
	ORDER 31—HOTELS, CAFES, RESTAURANTS, ETC. ...	3,119	16	2,241
126	Vendors of wine, liquors, ærated waters and ice	743	4	402
127	Owners and managers of hotels, cook-shops, sarais	2,089	10	1,839
128	Hawkers of drink and food stuffs	287	2	...
	ORDER 32—OTHER TRADE IN FOOD STUFFS	14,314	1,188	18,120
129	Grain and pulse dealers	6,685	595	2,906
130	Dealers in sweetmeats, sugar and spices	2,025	115	570
131	Dealers in dairy product, eggs and poultry	1,542	402	1,568
132	Dealers in animals for food	215	12	195
133	Dealers in fodder for animals	2,180	19	2,052
134	Dealers in other food stuffs	879	34	10,499
135	Dealers in tobacco	178	7	330
136	Dealers in opium	309	4	
137	Dealers in Ganja	301	...	
	ORDER 33—TRADE IN CLOTHING AND TOILET ARTICLES ...	1,765	36	1,327
138	Trade in ready-made clothing and other articles of dress and the toilet hats, umbrellas, socks, ready-made shoes perfumes etc.)	1,765	36	1,327
	ORDER 34—TRADE IN FURNITURE	687	1	282
139	Trade in furniture, carpets, curtains and bedding	335	...	151
140	Hardware, cooking utensils, porcelain, crockery, glassware, bottles, articles for gardening, etc.	352	1	131
	ORDER 35—TRADE IN BUILDING MATERIALS	404	...	97
141	Trade in building materials (other than bricks, tiles and woody materials) ...	404	...	97
	ORDER 36—TRADE IN MEANS OF TRANSPORT	706	158	879
142	Dealers and hirers in mechanical transport, motors, cycles etc. ...	210	1	19
143	Dealers and hirers in other carriages, carts, boats, etc.	115	...	93
144	Dealers and hirers of elephants, camels, horses, cattle, asses, mules, etc. ...	381	157	767
	ORDER 37—TRADE IN FUEL	379	116	740
145	Dealers in firewood charcoal, coal, cowdung, etc.	379	116	740
	ORDER 38—TRADE IN ARTICLES OF LUXURY AND THOSE PERTAINING TO LETTERS AND THE ARTS AND SCIENCES ...	1,061	3	360
146	Dealers in precious stones, jewellery (real and imitation), clocks, optical instruments, etc.	301	...	199
147	Dealers in common bangles, bead-necklaces, fans, small articles, toys, hunting and fishing tackle, flowers, etc.	213	1	23
148	Publishers, book-sellers, stationers, dealers in music, pictures, musical instruments and curiosities	547	2	138

SUBSIDIARY TABLE IV—*Variations in selected occupations, 1921—1931*—contd.

Group No.	Occupation (sub-class and order)	1931 Earners (principal occupation) and working dependents	1931 Earners subsidiary occupation	1921 Actual workers
1	2	3	4	5
	ORDER 39—TRADE OF OTHER SORTS	30,916	1,321	19,306
149	Dealers in rags, stable refuse, etc.	246	1	68
150	General store-keepers and shop-keepers otherwise unspecified ...	30,249	1,306	18,184
151	Itinerant traders, pedlars and hawkers (of other than food, etc.) ...	302	...	983
152	Other trades (including farmers of pounds, tools and markets) ...	119	14	41
	Class C—Public administration and liberal arts	**70,735**	**7,445**	**86,881**
	Sub-class VI—Public force	**39,973**	**3,729**	**47,618**
	ORDER 40—ARMY	31,192	2,602	39,032
153	Army (Imperial)	31,044	2,592	39,032
154	Army (Indian States)	148	10	...
	ORDER 41—Navy	8	1	...
155	Navy	8	1	...
	ORDER 42—AIR FORCE	435	...	258
156	Air Force	435	...	258
	ORDER 43—POLICE	8,338	1,126	8,328
157	Police	5,937	772	5,479
158	Village watchmen	2,401	354	2,849
	Sub-class VII—Public administration	**10,012**	**1,765**	**10,299**
	ORDER 44—PUBLIC ADMINISTRATION	10,012	1,765	10,299
159	Service of State	8,167	983	8,411
160	Service of Indian and Foreign States	12	...	12
161	Municipal and other local (not village) service	695	40	717
162	Village officials and servants other than watchmen	1,138	742	1,159
	Sub class VIII—Professions and liberal arts	**20,750**	**1,951**	**28,964**
	ORDER 45—RELIGION	12,849	1,480	17,848
163	Priests, ministers, etc., etc.	212	...	7,850
164	Monks, nuns, religious medicants	11,875	1,429	9,440
165	Other religious workers	314	49	59
166	Servants in religious edifices, burial and burning grounds, pilgrim conductors, circumcisers, etc.	448	2	499
	ORDER 46—LAW	556	35	668
167	Lawyers of all kinds, including Qazis, law agents and Mukhtiars ...	246	24	107
168	Lawyers' clerks, petition-writers, etc.	310	11	561
	ORDER 47—MEDICINE	3,090	126	2,857
169	Registered medical practitioners including occulists	1,372	41	} 1,691
170	Other persons practising the healing arts without being registered ...	326	55	
171	Dentists	38	...	

SUBSIDIARY TABLE IV—*Variations in selected occupations, 1921—1931*—contd.

Group No.	Occupation (sub-class and order)	1931 Earners (principal occupation) and working dependents	1931 Earners subsidiary occupation	1921 Actual workers
1	2	3	4	5
172	Midwives, vaccinators, compounders, nurses, masseurs, etc. ...	1,302	30	1,166
173	Veterinary surgeons	52	...	Included in groups 169, 171.
	ORDER 48—INSTRUCTION	2,053	224	1,807
174	Professors and teachers of all kind	1,951	216	1,734
175	Clerks and servants connected with education	102	8	73
	ORDER 49—LETTERS, ARTS AND SCIENCES (OTHER THAN 44) ...	2,202	86	5,784
176	Public scribes, stenographers, etc.	176	21	34
177	Architects (not being state servants)	223	...	649
178	Authors, editors, journalists and photographers	149	4	117 (groups 178–181)
179	Artists, sculptors and image-makers	101	...	
180	Scientists (astronomers, botanists, etc.)	60	6	
181	Horoscope casters, astrologers, fortune-tellers, wizards, witches and mediums...	30	...	
182	Musicians composers and performers (other than military) actors, dancers, etc.	361	19	4,644
183	Managers and employees of places of public entertainments, race courses societies, clubs, etc.	51	...	...
184	Conjurors, acrobats, reciters, exhibitors of curosities and wild animals, etc. ...	1,051	36	340
	Class D—Miscellaneous	69,587	7,403	48,664
	Sub-class IX—Persons living on their income	2,299	2,039	3,184
	ORDER 50—PERSONS LIVING PRINCIPALLY ON THEIR INCOME ...	2,299	2,039	3,184
185	Proprietors (other than of agricultural land fund and scholarships holders and pensioners)	2,299	2,039	3,184
	Sub-class X—Domestic service	12,803	2,340	10,467
	ORDER 51—DOMESTIC SERVICE...	12,803	2,340	10,467
186	Private motor drivers and cleaners	442	15	212
187	Other domestic service	12,361	2,325	10,255
	Sub-class XI—Insufficiently described occupations	42,620	2,674	23,461
	ORDER 52—GENERAL TERMS WHICH DO NOT INDICATE DEFINITE OCCUPATIONS	42,620	2,674	23,461
188	Manufacturers, business men and contractors otherwise unspecified ...	4,629	536	1,305
189	Cashiers, accountants' book-keepers, clerks and other employees in unspecified offices and warehouses and shops	816	4	...
190	Mechanics otherwise unspecified	26	3	...
191	Labourers and workmen otherwise unspecified	37,149	2,131	22 156
	Sub-class XII—Unproductive	11,865	350	11,552
	ORDER 53—INMATES OF JAILS, ASYLUMS AND ALMS HOUSES ...	6,051	18	2 636
192	Inmates of jails, asylums and alms houses	6,051	18	2,636

SUBSIDIARY TABLE IV—*Variations in selected occupations, 1921—1931*—concld.

Group No.	Occupation (sub-class and order)	1931 Earners (principal occupation) and working dependent	1931 Earners (subsidiary occupation)	1921. Actual workers
1	2	3	4	5
	ORDER 54—BEGGARS, VAGRANTS, PROSTITUTES ...	5,797	302	8,916
193	Beggars and vagrants	5,619	294	8,628
194	Procurers and prostitutes	178	8	288
	ORDER 55—OTHER UNCLASSIFIED NON-PRODUCTIVE INDUSTRIES	17	30	...
195	Other unclassified non-productive industries	17	30	...

SUBSIDIARY TABLE V—*Occupations of selected castes*

Caste and occupation	Number per 1,000 workers engaged on each occupation	Number of female workers per 100 males
1	2	3
ARORA		
Exploitation of animals and vegetation ...	107	6
Industries	20	7
Transport	10	...
Trade	631	1
Public administration	58	...
Professions and liberal arts ...	28	10
Persons living on their income ...	14	8
Domestic service	43	6
Others	89	11
AWAN		
Exploitation of animals and vegetation ...	711	14
Ordinary cultivation	709	14
Others	2	2
Public force	39	...
Industries	47	18
Others	203	7
BRAHMAN		
Trade	139	...
Public force	180	...
Public administration	94	...
Professions and liberal arts ...	140	8
Religions	124	8
Others	16	10
Domestic service	186	1
Others	261	18
CHAMAR		
Exploitation of animals and vegetation ...	181	1
Industries	583	8
Others	236	8
CHUHRA		
Exploitation of animals and vegetations ...	25	3
Industries	702	13
Domestic service	168	1
Others	105	23

Caste and occupation	Number per 1,000 workers engaged on each occupation	Number of female workers per 100 males
1	2	3
GUJAR		
Exploitation of animals and vegetation ...	754	9
Cultivation	529	2
Raisers of live-stock, milkmen and herdsmen ...	192	33
Others	33	20
Public force	17	...
Domestic service	20	3
Labourers unspecified	16	20
Others	193	107
JAT		
Exploitation of animals and vegetation ...	672	1
Cultivation	644	1
Others	28	...
Industries	27	2
Public force	143	...
Others	158	12
KHATRI		
Transport	25	...
Trade	487	2
Public force	133	...
Public administration	63	1
Professions and liberal arts ...	32	8
Domestic service	93	4
Others	167	13
PATHAN		
Exploitation of animals and vegetation, and public force	805	5
Cultivation and military service ...	800	5
Others	5	...
Industries	17	12
Labourers unspecified	56	13
Others	122	4
SAYAD		
Exploitation of animals and vegetation, and religions	787	12
Cultivation and priests	783	12
Others	4	...

SUBSIDIARY TABLE V—*Occupations of selected castes—concld.*

Caste and occupation	Number per 1,000 workers engaged on each occupation	Number of female workers per 100 males
1	2	3
SAYAD—*concluded*		
Others	213	11
SWATHI		
Exploitation of animals and vegetation ...	629	13
Cultivation	621	13
Others	8	1
Domestic service	38	8
Others	333	57
TANAOLI		
Exploitation of animals and vegetation ...	876	6
Cultivation	874	6
TANAOLI—*concluded*		
Others	2	...
Domestic service	16	14
Others	108	11
EUROPEANS		
Public force	979	...
Others	21	96
ANGLO-INDIANS		
Transport	159	...
Public force	238	7
Public administration	397	19
Domestic service	95	...
Others	111	17

SUBSIDIARY TABLE VI—PART I—*Number of persons employed on the 26th February 1931 and 18th March 1921 on Railways and in the Irrigation Department*

Class of persons employed	Europeans and Anglo-Indians		Indians		Remarks
	1931	1921	1931	1921	
1	2	3	4	5	6
RAILWAYS.					
Total persons employed	20	36	4,110	14,136	
Persons directly employed	20	36	3,827	7,181	
Officers	1	14	2	7	
Subordinates drawing more than Rs. 75 per mensem ...	19	22	138	249	
Subordinates drawing from Rs. 20 to Rs. 75 per mensem ...	...	...	2,399	3,700	
Subordinates drawing under Rs. 20 per mensem ...	...	...	1,288	3,225	
Persons indirectly emyloyed	...	...	283	6,955	
Contractors	...	...	9	117	
Contractors regular employees	...	...	54	208	
Coolies	...	...	220	6,630	
IRRIGATION DEPARTMENT.					
Total persons employed	8	6	2,783	2,918	
Persons directly employed	8	6	1,655	1,340	
Officers	8	5	14	13	
Upper subordinates	...	...	27	24	
Lower subordinates	...	1	14	98	
Clerks	...	...	1,069	75	
Peons and other servants	...	...	507	1,002	
Coolies	...	...	24	128	
Persons indirectly employed	...	...	*1,128	1,578	
Contractors	...	...	*82	101	*23 Civil canals Division, Dera Ismail Khan, are
Contractors regular employees	...	...	60	91	*23 not knwon.
Coolies	...	...	986	1,386	

SUBSIDIARY TABLE VI—PART II.—*Number of persons employed in the Post Office, Telegraph Department and Engineer Branch (including Wireless at Peshawar Station) on the 26th February 1931 and 18th March 1921*

Class of persons employed	Post Office				Telegraph Department				Engineer Branch				Remarks
	Europeans and Anglo-Indians		Indians		Europeans and Anglo-Indians		Indians		Europeans and Anglo-Indians		Indians		
	1931	1921	1931	1921	1931	1921	1931	1921	1931	1921	1931	1921	
1	2	3	4	5	6	7	8	9	10	11	12	13	14
Total persons employed ...	2	8	1,748	1,124	22	36	69	166	11	...	295	...	
(1) Post and Telegraphs ...	2	8	1,614	1,060	22	36	69	128	11	...	295	...	
Supervising officers (including Probationary Superintendents and Inspectors of Post Offices and Assistant and Deputy Superintendents of Telegraphs and all officers of higher ranks than these)	...	4	11	15	1	2	...	...	3	...	4	...	
Postmasters, including Deputy Assistant, Sub and Branch Postmasters ...	2	4	168	119	...	..	...	...	...	...	...	...	
Signalling establishment, including warrant officers, non-commissioned officers, military telegraphists and other employees ...	...	...	...	...	21	34	13	8	8	...	...	...	
Miscellaneous agents, school masters, station master, etc. ...	...	...	298	137	...	...	...	...	...	...	...	...	
Clerks of all kinds ...	...	...	303	284	...	...	4	29	...	...	76	...	
Postmen	...	...	481	352	...	...	...	...	...	...	...	...	
Skilled and labour establishment, including foremen, instrument makers, carpenters blacksmiths, mechanics, sub-inspectors, line-men and line-riders and other employees ...	...	...	...	...	...	...	5	89	...	...	173	...	
Unskilled labour establishment, including line-coolies, cable guards, battery men, telegraph messengers, peons and other employees ...	...	...	185	...	...	...	47	2	...	...	42	...	
Road establishment consisting of overseers, runners, clerks and booking agents, boatmen, syces, coachmen, bearers and others ...	...	...	168	153	...	...	...	...	...	...	...	...	
(2) Railway Mail Service ...	...	...	56	6	...	...	...	...	...	...	...	...	
Supervising officers (including superintendents and inspectors of sorting) ...	...	...	...	...	...	...	...	...	...	...	...	...	
Clerks of all kinds ...	...	...	4	...	...	...	...	...	...	...	...	...	
Sorters	...	...	23	5	...	...	...	...	...	...	...	...	
Mail guards, mail agents, van-peons, porters, etc.	...	...	29	1	...	...	...	...	...	...	...	...	
(3) Combined Offices ...	...	..	78	58	...	...	...	38	...	...	...	...	
Signallers	...	...	44	8	..	...	...	...	...	...	...	...	
Messengers and other servants ...	...	...	34	50	...	...	...	38	...	...	...	...	

CHAPTER IX

LITERACY

GENERAL.

Reference to statistics.

207. The statistics of literacy by religion and age are to be found in Imperial Table No. XIII, and those for selected castes, tribes, or races in Imperial Table No. XIV. Imperial Table No. XII deals with the amount of unemployment found among the educated. Subsidiary Tables at the end of this chapter are arranged as follows :—

I. Proportion of literacy by sex and religion in different age-groups.
II. Proportion of literacy by sex and religion in different localities.
III. Improvement in literacy in English through the last forty years, by sex and locality.
IV. Improvement in literacy among selected castes during the last decade.
V. Variation in extent of literacy by districts since 1881.
VI. Improvement in literacy by religions since 1901.
VII. Proportion of literacy by sexes at certain ages at the present Census.
VIII. Number of institutions and pupils by districts according to the returns of the Department of Education.

Method of classification.

208. Some difficulty has been experienced in the past in determining the classification according to which returns dealing with education were to be considered. At one time there were three alternative classifications — learning, literate and illiterate. "Learning" was intended to include all persons who were undergoing instruction, at whatever stage. In practice, however, it was found that these classifications overlapped to an undesirable extent ; advanced pupils preferred to see themselves entered as literate, while beginners were arbitrarily entered by *enumerators as "learning" or as "illiterate" according to the* individual enumerator's idea of a suitable standard. At the present Census, and ever since 1911, only two classifications have been adopted, literate and illiterate. Only those persons are supposed to have been entered as literate who can write a letter to a friend and read the answer to it. In so un-learned an area as the North-West Frontier Province this standard is a comparatively high one.

An additional entry to show literacy in English is also made in the schedule. The definition of literacy for this entry too was the ability to read and write a letter.

It was intended at one time to show how many of those returned as literate had passed the primary course, but the necessary instructions reached outlying areas too late, and no tabulation of the results was found possible.

Literacy in tribal areas not estimated.

209. No attempt has been made to estimate the extent of literacy among residents of the trans-border tracts. There are however an increasing number of literate persons in these areas. There are schools in the protected areas of Malakand, Kurram and North Waziristan Agencies, and even here and there in strictly Tribal Territory. Residents of Tribal Territory are sending their sons not only to the primary schools in their own villages but further afield to Mission Schools and High Schools in the Districts. Even Waziristan now boasts a Bachelor of Arts. Swat State in Malakand Agency is spending large sums annually on education, and is about to open a High School of its own. In addition the number of literates in Tribal Territory is increased annually by the return of pensioned and other time-expired soldiers, who have learned in their regimental schools to read and write Roman Urdu. Nevertheless, as has been stated above, the number of literates in Tribal Territory has not been recorded, and the discussion in the remainder of the present chapter must be confined to the districts and trans-frontier posts.

Proportion of literates in total population.

210. Out of a total population of 2,471,527 enumerated in the districts and trans-frontier posts, only 106,026 males and 11,412 females were returned as literate. These figures give a proportion of 56 literates per 1,000 of the total population. The proportion among females is considerably lower than this, bieng only 12 per *mille* while the corresponding figure for males is 91. Figures received from other parts of India show the North-West Frontier Province to be well down the list. The proportion of male literates in Burma is 562 per thousand, in Baroda State it is 331, in Bombay Presidency 176, in Bengal 182, the Punjab (British Territory) 100, and Baluchistan 76. The all-India figure in

1921 was 139 per 1,000 In this Province the figure for the districts both for this year and for 1921 is only 80 per 1,000. Literacy in English is also low in comparison with total literacy. The total number of persons returned as literate in English is 11,264, of whom 9,922 are males and 1,342 females. This gives a proportion of 21 per 1,000. The highest proportion in other Provinces of India, excluding Delhi where the circumstances are exceptional, is 43 per 1,000 in Bengal.

DISTRIBUTION BY LOCALITY.

Trans-frontier posts.

211. Of the three natural divisions into which the Province is divided, the largest is the trans-border tract. As has been already mentioned, no figures of literacy are available for the permanent inhabitants of this area, while the age and sex distribution of those who were enumerated therein in trans-frontier posts is so abnormal that the figures are of no value for the present discussion. The figures actually recorded are to be found in Part II (*b*) of Imperial Table No. XIII. They show a population of 44,635 males and 1,816 females, of whom 16,968 males and 104 females are literate; one in three of the literate males and 1 in 12 of the literate females are literate in English. These figures will be excluded from the greater part of the discussion in the remainder of this chapter.

Hazara and Trans-Indus districts.

212. The other two Natural Divisions are Hazara and the trans-Indus districts. Hazara is a mountainous district of small scattered hamlets and no large towns; the plains of the trans-Indus districts are densely populated and contain many centres of education and commerce. It is therefore to be expected that the proportion of literacy will be higher in the latter than in the former. The proportions are calculated on the number of persons of 5 years of age and over, since it is not to be expected that persons under this age can honestly be recorded as literate. For this reason, as may be seen from the headings and footnotes of the subsidiary tables concerned, persons under the age of 5 have been excluded from most of the proportionate calculations which are discussed in this chapter, and unless otherwise stated the expression "the population" means the population of persons of the age of 5 years and over.

Natural Division	Proportion per *mille* who are					
	Literate			Literate in English		
	Persons	Males	Females	Persons	Males	Females
Districts ...	49	80	12	13	21	2
Hazara ...	32	55	5	4	6	0·5
Trans-Indus Districts ...	56	89	15	16	27	2

Proportion of literacy by districts.

213. The diagram reproduced in the margin illustrates the prevalence of literacy per 1,000 of each sex in each of the five districts. The total population for which the figures are prepared was 2,038,257 persons aged 5 and over, of whom only 89,058 males and 11,308 females were returned as literate. The proportion of literacy in the districts thus becomes 80 per *mille* among males and 12 per *mille* among females. The figures for literacy in English are so small that they have to be considered in relation to ten times as large a group; 214 males and

No. 22

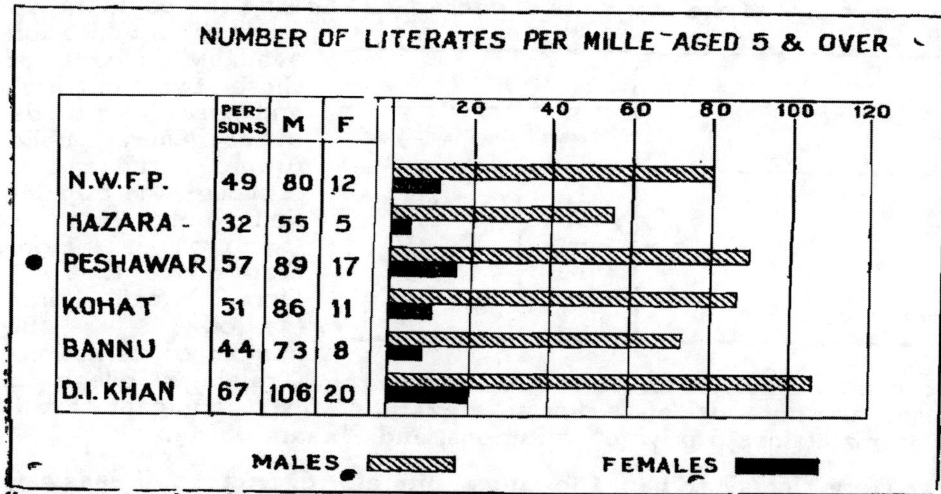

20 females per 10,000 of the same sex of the age of 5 and over can read and write English.

The distribution of the 1,109 institutions and 84,490 scholars in the Province, according to returns received from the Department of Public Instruction, may be found in Subsidary Table VII at the end of this chapter.

Effect of religion on distribution by districts.

214. Before considering the relative proportion of literacy as between one district and another, it is as well to consider the proportions of literacy in the three principal religions, since the extent of literacy in each district will be found to vary with the numbers of followers of each religion found in that district. The table in the margin shows the proportion of literacy by religion for the combined figures of districts and trans-frontier posts. The figures will be discussed again later in more detail, but for the present it is important to notice that the proportion of general literacy is very high among Christians, approximates to one in three among Hindus and Sikhs, and is very low among Muslims.

Religion	Number per *mille* of the age of 5 and over who are					
	Literate			Literate in English		
	Persons	Males	Females	Persons	Males	Females
All religions ...	56	91	12	15	23	2
Muslim ...	26	44	3	5	10	...
Hindu ...	304	418	101	55	83	4
Sikh ..	375	462	193	61	88	4
Christians—						
Total ...	785	839	534	734	786	492
Indians ...	370	472	184	80	94	55
Europeans ...	990	994	962	954	957	932

Hazara and Dera Ismail Khan contrasted.

215. Bearing these facts in mind it is not surprising that the diagram shows the lowest proportion of literacy in Hazara and the highest in Dera Ismail Khan. In Hazara 95 per cent. of the population is Muslim and not quite 4 per cent. Hindu, while in Dera Ismail Khan 13 per cent. of the population is Hindu and 86 per cent. Muslim. Moreover the Hindus of Dera Ismail Khan are mostly persons who would not be there at all if they were not literate; they are either in some form of employment for which education is a *sine qua non*, or else they are shopkeepers and traders to whom literacy is an essential item in their stock in trade. It may be noticed also that even among Muslims the percentage of literates is higher in Dera Ismail Khan than in Hazara. The Muslims of Dera Ismail Khan consist for the most part of Jats, Baluchis and other non-Pathan tribes, who are by nature as peaceful and law-abiding as the Hindus and as anxious to avail themselves of the advantages offered by education. In Hazara on the other hand distances are great, communications are difficult, and the population consists for the most part of agriculturists and graziers who have no literary leanings.

Facilities in each.

216. The statement in the margin is of interest as showing the comparative facilities for education available in each of these two districts, and also the attitude of the general public towards education. Although the population of Hazara (670,177) is more than twice that of Dera Ismail Khan (274,064), the number of institutions in each is about equal. There is an Arts College and a Training College in Dera Ismail Khan, and not one of either in Hazara. Most significant of all, Dera Ismail Khan maintains 46 private institutions, and Hazara only 9.

Nature of Institution	Number in	
	Hazara	Dera Ismail Khan
Total Institutions	221	217
Total Public Institutions	212	171
Arts Colleges	...	1
Secondary Schools	60	46
Primary Schools	152	123
Training Schools	...	1
Total Private Institutions	9	46

Peshawar.

217 After Dera Ismail Khan the most literate district is Peshawar. Peshawar contains several large military garrisons, and its population includes 8,974 out of the 12,213 Christians found in the five districts. It is the centre

of commerce of the Province, and the seat of learning, of the headquarters of the Local Government and of the highest law courts. It is probable that in addition to providing the largest total number of literate persons, it could also boast the highest average standard of education among those who are educated at all.

The public educational institutions in Peshawar include 2 Arts Colleges, 3 Training Schools, 82 Secondary Schools, and 214 Primary Schools, while there are in addition 72 private institutions.

Literacy in English by districts.

218. Figures to illustrate the proportion of literacy in English by districts are given in the margin. Since higher education is at present conducted almost entirely in English, and the business of Government and the law is mainly carried on in the same tongue, while literacy in English is almost universal among the large Christian population of the district, it is to be expected that the highest figure will be shown by Peshawar. It is odd to find an equally high figure in Kohat. It will in fact be noted later that the proportion of persons literate in English among the non-Christian population is higher in Kohat than in Peshawar, but the difference between the actual figures is so great that comparison is hardly fair. There are 15,402 persons literate in English in Peshawar District, and 3.391 in Kohat.

District	Proportion per 10,000 of each sex of the age of 5 and over who are literate in English	
	Males	Females
All districts	214	20
Hazara	60	5
Peshawar	306	32
Kohat	306	17
Bannu	129	14
Dera Ismail Khan	,243	:8

Literacy higher in urban than in rural area.

219. The proportion of literacy in urban areas is naturally higher than in the surrounding country, for literacy is in its greatest demand in the public offices, in the law courts, in the courts of commerce, and in schools, all of which are to be found concentrated in towns rather than villages. The proportion of literacy in Peshawar municipality is compared in the margin with the two highest figures found elsewhere in the Province.

Locality	Number per *mille* who are					
	Literate			Literate in English		
	Persons	Males	Females	Persons	Males	Females
Peshawar City ...	187	265	79	45	74	5
Kohat District ...	51	86	11	17	31	2
Dera Ismail Khan District.	67	106	20	14	24	2
Districts ...	49	80	12	13	21	2

Literacy by age periods.

220. The figures in the margin show the number per 1,000 of each sex at certain age periods who are literate. The figures are interesting in comparison with the corresponding figures for the last Census. The figures for those of twenty years of age and over, who are sometimes described as "effective literates", show a rise from 91 per *mille* to 98 per *mille* in the case of males and from 11 to 12 in the case of females. Free education was introduced into the Province in 1912, and it is not to be expected that the figures in the highest age group will exceed those in the younger age-groups, until the generation of those who were young before this date has begun to pass way.

Age period	Number per *mille* who are literate	
	Males	Females
All ages (5 & over)	80	12
5—10	22	8
10—15	44	13
15—20	114	20
20 and over	98	12

DISTRIBUTION BY RELIGION.

Literacy by religion.

221. In considering literacy by religion the figures for Trans-Frontier Posts are taken into consideration as well as those for the Districts. The relative proportion of literate persons in each of the main religions has already been noted in paragraph 214 and is shown again in the margin. Before considering the religions separately it is as well to remember the incentives to literacy felt by each.

Religion		Proportion per *mille* of the age of 5 and over who are literate		
		Persons	Males	Females
All Religions		56	91	12
Christian	Total	785	839	534
	Indian	370	472	184
	European	990	994	962
Sikh		375	462	193
Hindu		304	418	101
Muslim		26	44	3

What determines literacy in any community, as was noted in the India Census Report of 1921, is in the first instance the nature of the occupations it usually follows, that is, whether they are such as require a knowledge of reading and writing, and in the second instance whether there are any special facilities within reach which attract the members of the community to learn, though there be no great need for the learning. The pursuit of letters purely as a means for intellectual growth, or "learning for learning's sake", is a figment of theorists.

Christians.

222. It follows that in the present constitution of the Province European Christians must be the best educated community. The vast majority of male European adults found in the Province are in some form of Government service which they could neither have obtained in the first place, nor subsequently retained, without the qualification of literacy. A number more who are present may never have had to work for their living, but have acquired literacy because their manner of life in the country of their birth requires it. The actual figures in the present enumeration give a return of 994 males and 962 females literate in every thousand, and 957 males and 932 females per 1,000 literate in English.

Somewhat below European Christians, but still high, come Indian Christians. The reason for this is that the methods of work of the missionary societies at present active in the Province are such that conversion is almost always either accompanied by, or preceded by, education. There are 4,266 Indian Christians, among whom 1,350 can read and write.

Sikhs and Hindus.

223. After Christians the next highest proportion is found among Sikhs. The proportion of literates per 1,000 of the total population is 462 for Sikh males and 193 for Sikh females, the corresponding figures for Hindu males and females being 418 and 101. The comparatively high proportion among the two communities is due to the fact that the majority of those found in the Province are either traders or government servants, including many soldiers serving in the army. Traders and most government servants require literacy in their ordinary round of life, while serving soldiers receive education in their regimental schools. The higher proportion among Sikhs than among Hindus, and especially among Sikh females, is due to the fact that Sikh males generally and Sikh females invariably correspond in their mother-tongue Punjabi written in the Gurmukhi script, which takes a much shorter time to master than either Urdu or Hindi.

Muslims.

224. As is to be expected in the community which forms the bulk of the agricultural population of the Province, the Muslims are a very long way behind the others in respect of literacy. Out of the total number of 117,438 literate persons enumerated in the present Census only 48,395 were Muslims, although the Muslims represent nearly 92 per cent. of the total population. In respect of female education the discrepancy in even more striking, for the Muslims, who constitute 98 per cent. of the total female population, have only 2,414 out of the 11, 412 recorded literate females. The reason for the low proportion among females will be discussed later. The explanation of the low total proportion may be summed up in one phrase—there is no incentive. The majority of the Muslim population see no other task in life in front of them than the physical tasks of agriculture, and in these tasks they expect to get no help from the art of reading and writing. Nor is there any advantage to them in being able to read or write in their leisure hours, for they have nothing to read and no one

to whom to write. Literacy is advancing decade by decade, but before it can advance much further it will be necessary to create both an incentive and an interest.

Literacy in English by religion.

225. The proportion of persons literate in English in the total enumerated population is 26 per *mille* in the case of males and 2 per *mille* in the case of females. English literacy among Christians depends so much on artificial circumstances that it is of no interest in studying the general spread of education in the Province. Next to Christians, Sikhs and Hindus show the highest proportions of literacy in English. Among Sikhs 88 per *mille* among males and 4 per *mille* among females are returned as knowing English, and among Hindus 83 males and 4 females.* The proportion among Muslims is 26 per *mille* males and only 2 per 10,000 females. The proportion of English knowing persons to literate persons is not far from one in eight in each of the three religions. It follows that Muslims who have once taken to education, are no more averse than the followers of other religions to continuing their studies into the higher classes.

Effect of exclusion of figures for trans-Frontier Posts.

226. The figures considered in the preceding paragraphs are for districts and trans-frontier posts. Since the distribution of the communities in these posts varies from year to year, and since the proportion of literate persons within them is swollen by special considerations, a fairer idea of the spread of education among the general population may be obtained by considering the figures for the districts alone. The effect of the exclusion of the trans-frontier posts on the figures for communities is shown in the margin. The decrease affects all communities more or less equally, and their relative order of literacy remains unchanged.

Community	Proportion per *mille* of both sexes literate in	
	Districts and trans-frontier posts	Districts only
All communities	56	41
Muslims	26	19
Hindus	304	249
Sikhs	375	289

Literacy by religions considered by locality.

227. The proportion of literacy by sexes and communities for each district and for Peshawar city is shown in Subsidiary Tables No. III at the end of this chapter. It will be noticed that the proportion of Muslims literate in Peshawar City is nearly five times as high as the general proportion of Muslims for the Province, while in the case of Hindus and Sikhs the difference is not great. The reason for this is that the difference in the conditions and manner of life is very much greater in the case of Muslims than in the case of either of the other two communities, who are mostly town-dwellers by instinct even when found in villages.

Muslims.

228. So far as districts are concerned the proportion of literate Muslims is highest in Peshawar in the case both of males (51 per *mille*) and of females (4 per *mille*). These figures are no doubt swollen by the number under instruction. The second highest figure for males is provided by Dera Ismail Khan (45 per *mille*), with Kohat (44 per *mille*) almost equal. Hazara (31 per *mille*) and Bannu (27 per *mille*) are a long way below the Provincial average. The figure for Dera Ismail Khan has always been comparatively high since the Muslim population of that district is more law-abiding and peaceable by nature than that of the Northern districts. The figure for Kohat might be lower but for the number of soldiers and others recruited from the district who become literate in the course of their employment. The figures for Hazara and Bannu are low owing to the difficulty of communications; in Hazara the difficulty is caused by mountains and rivers, and in Bannu by scorching desert.

Hindus.

229. The proportion of literacy among Hindus is highest (478 per *mille*) in Hazara, and lowest (335 per *mille* in Bannu). It is raised as high as it is in Hazara by the inclusion of literate Gurkha troops stationed in Abbottabad. But for these, Dera Ismail Khan, where private effort on behalf of the Hindu community is particularly strong, would no doubt head the list with its figure of 470 per *mille*.

* See Subsidiary Table I at the end of chapter.

Sikhs.

230. In Hazara the proportion of male literates among Sikhs is slightly lower than among Hindus owing to the presence of a certain number of the more backward classes in the hills, but with this exception Sikhs have a higher proportion of both males and females who are literate than either of the two communities hitherto considered. Next to Peshawar city (574 per *mille*) the proportion among Sikh males is highest (520 per *mille*) in Dera Ismail Khan, and lowest (284 per *mille*) in Hazara. The figures for district variations are to some extent misleading since the total number of Sikh males in the districts is only 26,284, and out of the 9,549 who are literate only 492 live in Dera Ismail Khan. Peshawar on the other hand contains 5,625 literate Sikh males.

Christians.

231. Reasons for the high proportion of literate persons among Christians have already been discussed, and since the conditions which govern the variation from district to district are purely artificial, nothing is to be gained by inquiring into them further.

Corresponding figures for females.

232. The figures in the margin show the corresponding variations by communities and localities in the extent of female education. The spread of literacy among females of the Muslim faith is so small that the figures are hardly worth considering, but it is worth noting that Peshawar, where the proportion is highest, also has the highest total number of Muslim females who can read and write. In all three communities the proportion is highest in Peshawar City, where female education receives a fair measure of attention. In the districts the figure for Hindus is comparatively high in Peshawar, Kohat and Dera Ismail Khan, in all of which the Hindus are to a large extent concentrated in towns, and low in Bannu and Hazara where they are scattered through the villages.

Locality.	Number of females per *mille* who are literate.		
	Muslim.	Hindu.	Sikh
Hazara	2	71	78
Peshawar	4	163	200
Kohat	2	103	302
Bannu	1	19	262
Dera Ismail Khan	3	116	198
Peshawar City	28	266	387

LITERACY BY CASTE.

Literacy by caste Males.

233. It is an almost universal rule that males show a higher proportion of literacy than females. The figures for male literacy in twelve selected castes of the Province are shown in the margin and illustrated in diagrammatic form on the following page. Points to be noticed from these figures are that the Hindu and Sikh castes show a considerably higher proportion of literacy than the Muslims, that in each case the highest proportion is shown by the priestly caste; that the proportion in the trading-classes is also high, and that the proportion in the agricultural-classes is low. These figures again illustrate how the presence or absence of incentive affects literacy.

Traditional occupation	Number of male literates per *mille*			
	Hindu and Sikh castes.		Muslims.	
Priesthood	Brahman ...	518	Sayad ...	119
Trade	Khatri ...	515		
Agriculture	Arora ...	392	Jat ...	106
			Awan ...	67
			Pathan ...	48
			Swathi ...	47
			Tanaoli ...	22
			Gujar ...	16
Scavenging	Chuhra ...	68		
Leather-work	Chamar ...	29		

LITERACY AMONGST MALES IN SELECTED CASTES

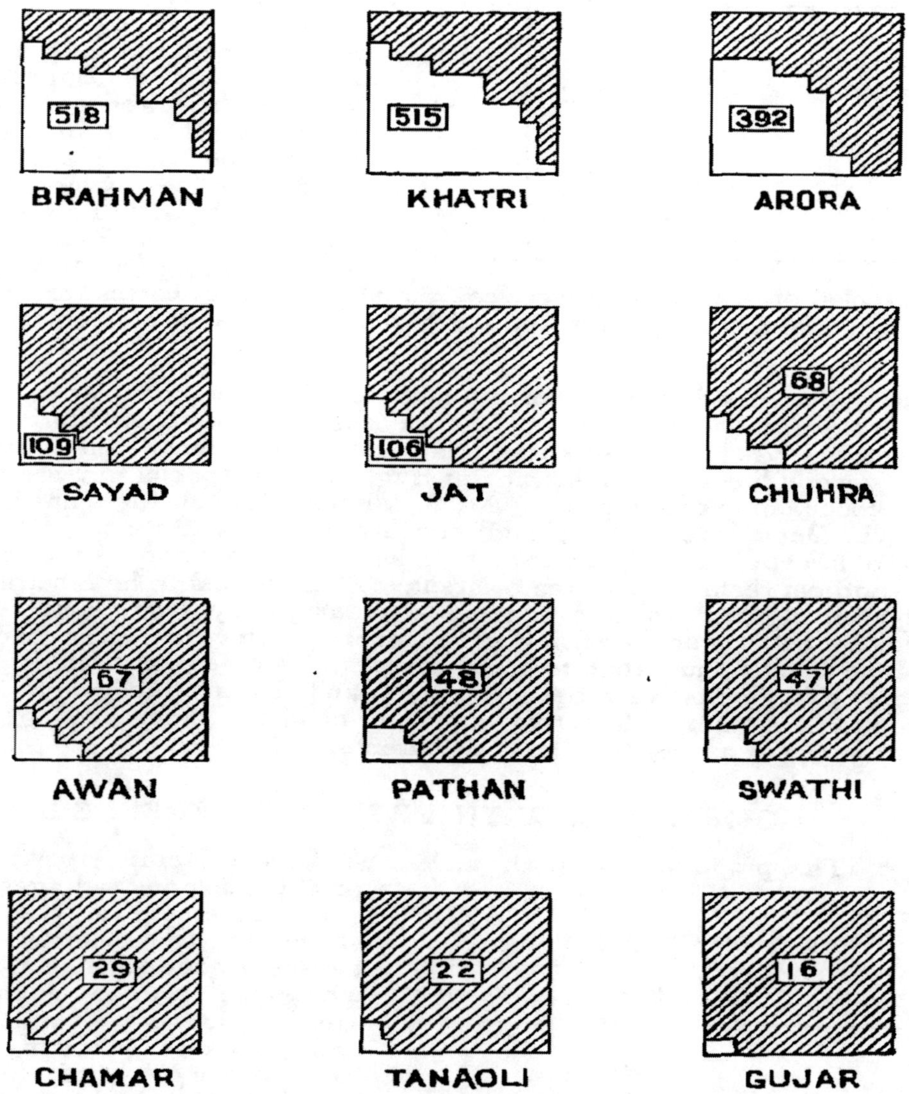

NOTE 1. LARGE SQUARE = 1000 MALES.

2. NUMBER LITERATE PER 1000 MALES SHOWN IN CENTRE

Females.

234. The figures for female literacy by caste show a fair proportion of literacy only among Khatris, Brahmans and Aroras. Since these are the castes with the highest proportion of literate males, it is only natural that they should take the lead. The total actual figures are too small to justify any comparison

Number of female literates per *mille*			
Hindu and Sikhs castes.		Muslims.	
Brahman ...	242	Sayad ...	10
Khatri ...	218	Jat ...	10
Arora ...	103	Awan ...	6
Chuhra ...	11	Pathan ...	4
Chamar ...	...	Swathi ...	3
		Tanaoli ...	2
		Gujar ...	1

among the three. The figures for Muslims are still almost negligible, though it may be observed that the same rule appears to hold true.

Literacy in English by caste.

235. The table in the margin shows the proportion of literacy in English by sexes for the same twelve castes. The figures are for persons of 7 years of age and over. There is little variation from the figures of general literacy. It is noticeable however that the priestly caste among Hindus no longer heads the list. The reason for this is obvious. A knowledge of English is of no value in the practice of the priestly profession, but is of value in the professions of trade and Government service which Brahmans share with Khatris and Aroras. Among Muslims Sayads are found in a much higher proportion in the higher ranks of Government service than the other castes or tribes under consideration, and consequently show a higher proportion of persons literate in English.

Caste or Tribe.	Number per 10,000 literate in English	
	Males	Females
Khatri ...	1,175	323
Brahman ...	1,030	115
Arora ...	806	82
Sayad ...	299	29
Awan ...	167	29
Jat ...	135	...
Pathan ...	120	14
Chuhra ...	39	17
Swathi ...	38	1
Gujar ...	24	5
Chamar ...	21	...
Tanaoli ...	19	...

Literacy among Chuhras.

236. The caste which corresponds to the Untouchables or Depressed classes in the rest of India is the Chuhra caste, whose hereditary occupation is scavenging. As the figures show, this caste is by no means the most backward either in general literacy or in literacy in English. No special provision is made for their education except for a C. M. S. Mission School for Punjabi Christian sweepers in Dera Ismail Khan, and one Arya Hindu School. Otherwise the children of sweepers are eligible for admission to the ordinary schools, although they do not join them to any great extent. There is said to be a certain amount of prejudice against them in schools maintained by the Hindu and Sikh communities, but it is not so strong as in other provinces. Their backwardness is due more to economic than to social causes. Women as well as men work, hence boys and girls between the ages of 5 and 10 are obliged to look after the younger children. After that age the children themselves go to work, either for wages or as assistants to their parents.

COMPARISON WITH PREVIOUS CENSUSES.

Proportion of literacy rising.

237. The proportion of both male and female literates per 1,000 of the total population (all ages of each sex enumerated in the districts, is shown in the margin for each census since 1881. Comparisons with years up to and including 1901 are fallacious; no classification by age-groups was made in 1881, and for the purposes of this table all persons then shown as under instruction have been included as literate; in the 1891 totals the figures for persons "learning" have been excluded; in 1901 the enumerators were instructed to record as literate all persons who could read or write, but no standard of proficiency in either was laid down; in 1911 the criterion of ability to read and write a letter was first applied, but it was not properly understood and was in many cases applied too severely; the standards in 1921 and in 1931, it is believed, were the same, and comparisons between these two years rest on firmer ground. Withal the figures for male literacy show a slight but steady increase through the half-century under consideration, while the proportion of females who are literate has increased ten-fold.

Number of literate persons per *mille*		
Year	Male	Female
1881 ...	58	1
1891 ...	61	2
1901 ...	62	5
1911 ...	57	6
1921 ...	64	9
1931 ...	68	10

Increase during last decade.

238. The actual total of literate persons in the districts increased from 75,434 in 1911 to 87,053 in 1921, and has now increased again to 100,366.

The increase during the last decade is therefore approximately 15 per cent. and has more than kept pace with the increase of the population which amounts to 7·7 per cent. The figures are even more encouraging when considered by religions. Christians have decreased by 173, and Hindus by 210, while Sikhs have increased by 849. Since the figures for these three religions are very argely affected by migration, and, as will be seen later, the variation in the proportion of literacy within each is explained by changes in the population, it is necessary to look to the figures for Muslims to see the true progress of education. The number of literates among Muslims has increased from 31,672 in 1921 to 44,496 in the present year. This represents an increase of approximately 40 per cent. among those who form the bulk of the permanent population.

Variation in proportion of literate persons between ages of 15 and 20.

239. The majority of those who leave school before they have attained the standard of being able to read and write do so at or before the age of 10; the majority of those who continue their studies long enough to reach this standard, leave school at or about the age of 15. For these reasons the progress of the general spread of a comparatively satisfactory education may to some extent be judged by looking to the number of persons in the next age-group, *viz* between 15 and 20 years of age, who are returned as literate. The figures for the last four censuses are given in the margin. It will be noticed that there is a large increase between 1911 and 1921 in the proportion of each sex returned as literate. This is no doubt explained by the introduction from the 1st April 1912 of free primary education in all schools under public management throughout the Province. The figures for the last decade on the other hand, are stationary for females and show an increase of less than 4 per cent. among males. This is in spite of the fact that the total number of public institutions in the Province has increased from 779 to 968 and the total number of scholars on the rolls of such institutions from 45,770 to 81,093. There is no doubt that a very large number of both boys and girls who are sent to primary schools, never attain the standard of being able to read and write a letter, and were never either expected or intended by their parents to do so; a number more, who do acquire the art, lose it again almost as soon as they leave school. There is, as has been mentioned above, no incentive for the bulk of the population to learn to read and write; whatever the advantages of literacy may be, they are not recognized, and until they are recognized, and until the practical application of reading and writing in every day life is understood, there is no likelihood that the population as a whole will profit by the opportunities that are spread so lavishly before it.

Number of literate persons per thousand of each sex between the ages of 15 and 20

Year	Males	Females
1901	76	10
1911	82	12
1921	110	20
1931	114	20

Variation by castes.

240. The variations in literacy by caste are shown in the figures in the margin for the 12 selected castes to which reference has already been made. The figures for the two trading castes, Arora and Khatri, show a decline, but as the figures for these castes are largely affected by migration, with the presence or absence of women and young children, too much attention need not be paid to them. It is remarkable, however, that among the agricultural tribes, who do not take to education except in response to the presence of Government or private enterprise, the proportions show a considerable increase in almost every case. It must be noted that the comparison is not exact, as the figures for 1921 were calculated on the population aged 5 years and over, while the figures of the present year are for those of 7 and over.

Caste	Proportion per *mille* literate in	
	1921	1931
I—Agriculture ...		
Awan ...	17	42
Gujar ...	11	10
Jat ...	59	66
Pathan ...	15	29
Swathi ...	16	27
Tanaoli ...	6	12
II—Priests—		
Brahman ...	205	411
Sayad ...	32	62
III—Traders—		
Arora ...	326	268
Khatri ...	311	401
IV—Others		
Chamar ...	9	17
Chuhra ...	19	51

Variation by districts among non-Christian population.

241. The variation by districts of total literacy and of literacy in English are considerably affected by the movements of the European population, the majority of whom do not receive any part of their education in the Province. The figures in the margin, which show variation from 1921 to 1931, have accordingly been prepared for the non-Christian population. Taking first the figures for general literacy among males, the three Northern districts show an increase, while Bannu and Dera Ismail Khan show a decline. The reason for the decline in the two southern districts is the withdrawal or reduction of the large garrisons which happened to be in each of these districts in 1921. The figures for literacy in English, on the other hand, show a higher proportion in all 5 districts, due to the increase in educational facilities. General literacy among females shows an advance in Peshawar, Bannu and Dera Ismail Khan, and a decline in each of the other 2 districts. Literacy in English among females is so small that the variations by districts are hardly worth considering. The total number of females literate in English in the districts, excluding Christians, is now 457, and in 1921 was 211.

Proportion per thousand of the non-Christian population (5 and over)

District		Literate		Literate in English	
		Males	Females	Males	Females
Districts	1931	74	11	16	0·5
	1921	67	9	8	0·2
Hazara	1931	55	5	6	0·2
	1921	45	6	3	0·02
Peshawar	1931	79	14	20	0·8
	1921	60	10	9	0·1
Kohat	1931	80	9	24	0·3
	1921	77	0	10	0·6
Bannu	1931	70	7	12	0·5
	1921	72	8	9	0·02
Dera Ismail Khan	1931	105	19	23	0·4
	1921	120	14	20	0·6

Variation by religion.

242. The variation in the returns of literacy by religion for the 5 districts as a whole is shown in the margin. The first table shows general literacy, and the second literacy in English. The figures for Muslims show an increase in both sexes both in general literacy and in literacy in English. The figures for females are still very small, but show an increase in proportion of 50 per cent. in one case and 900 per cent. in the other. The actual figures are 2,386 females literate and 213 literate in English as contrasted with 1,545 and 13 in 1921. The figures for Hindus also show a slight rise in every case, the largest proportionate rise being among Hindus literate in English. The figures for Sikhs show a decline in both sexes in the proportion for general literacy. The decline among males is due to the departure of a number of Sikh troops who were in the Province in 1921; among females it is probably to be attributed to similar changes caused by migration. Even among Sikhs, however, the proportion of persons literate in English has increased as a result of increased facilities for education.

Community		Proportion per 1,000 returned as literate		
		Persons	Males	Females
Muslim	1921	18	31	2
	1931	24	42	3
Hindu	1921	269	355	99
	1931	292	416	101
Sikh	1921	446	546	222
	1931	333	412	195

Community		Proportion per 1,000 literate in English		
		Persons	Males	Females
Muslim	1921	2	4	0·02
	1931	5	9	0·22
Hindu	1921	35	51	3·0
	1931	57	92	4·0
Sikh	1921	37	52	5·0
	1931	62	94	4·0

243. The increase in literacy among Muslims by districts is shown in the marginal statement. Hazara shows an increase among each sex. Peshawar, which was low on the list in 1921, now heads the list of general literacy both among males and among females and is second only to Kohat in literacy in English. Kohat is stationary as regards general male literacy but has reached the head of the list as regards literacy of males in English, and shows a decline by half in the proportion of literate females. Bannu shows a decline among each sex in general literacy and an increase in literacy in English. Dera Ismail Khan shows an increase in all details except general literacy among males. Considering the number of troops which have been withdrawn from this district since 1921, and the number of trans-border immigrants present in the district in 1931 who were not found in 1921, it may be taken that these stationary figures conceal an actual increase of literacy among the permanent population. **Muslim by districts.**

District		Proportion of Muslim population per 1,000 of each sex returned as					
		Literate			Literate in English		
		Persons	Males	Females	Persons	Males	Females
Districts	1931 ...	24	42	3	5	9	·2
	1921 ...	18	31	2	2	4	·02
Hazara	1931 ...	17	31	2	2	3	·08
	1921 ...	11	20	1	1	1	·02
Peshawar	1931 ...	30	51	4	7	12	·4
	1921 ...	19	33	2	2	4	·02
Kohat	1931 ...	24	44	2	8	15	·2
	1921 ...	25	44	4	2	4	...
Bannu	1931 ...	15	27	1	3	5	·2
	1921 ...	17	30	2	2	5	...
Dera Ismail Khan.	1931 ..	26	45	3	6	10	·1
	1921 ...	20	45	2	4	6	·04

244. Statements showing the variation by districts among Hindus and Sikhs have also been prepared, but since the figures are seen to depend almost entirely on the movements of garrisons, to which reference has already been made, they have not been included. **Hindus and Sikhs.**

EDUCATIONAL STATISTICS.

245. The amount of Government and other effort directed towards education has increased very considerably during the last 10 years. The expenditure as the statement in the margin shows has increased from Rs. 14,60,370 in 1920-21 to Rs. 28,27,631 in 1930-31, an increase to very nearly double. As may be seen from Subsidiary Table No. VIII at the end of this chapter, the increase is due to a steady increase in the number of institutions and a corresponding increase in the number of scholars. The average cost of educating one pupil for one year is Rs. 26-5-0; the average cost per annum of a pupil at a Training College is Rs. 610-2-0, at an Arts College Rs. 412·9-0, at a Training School Rs. 319, at a Secondary School Rs. 29·15-0, and at a primary school Rs. 14-6-0. **Expenditure on education.**

Source of expenditure	Expenditure in rupees		Increase
	920-21	1930-31	
	Rs.	Rs.	Rs.
Provincial revenue ...	9,44,735	19,99,468	+ 10,54,733
District funds ...	83,718	1,23,489	+ 39,771
Municipal funds ..	1,34 356	1,84,027	+ 49,671
Fees, tution and other ...	1,09,490	2,32,988	+ 1,23,498
Other sources ...	1,88,071	2,87,659	+ 99,588
Total ..	14,60,370	28,27,631	+ 13,67,261

246. The total number of institutions for male education has increased from 859 in 1920-21 to 964 in 1930-31, and the number of male pupils on the registers from 44,255 to 73,583. The latter figure represents about 21 per cent. of the male population of school-going age (5—15 years). The increase is to be found principally in Anglo-Vernacular and Vernacular middle schools, which have increased from 58 to 213. This increase has been effected largely by the conversion of primary schools to middle schools, which has proceeded faster than the creation of new primary schools, and is therefore accompanied by a fall in the total number of the latter. High schools also show a large **Statistics of primary and secondary education.**

proportionate increase, the number having risen from 18 to 29. In 1921 the upper and lower primary examinations were taken by 6,432 male pupils of whom 4,735 were successful; in 1931, 11,495 were successful out of 14,115 who offered the examination. At the other end of the school scale 137 out of 243 examinees passed the Matriculation in 1921, and 574 out of 936 in 1931.

There are 677 male teachers employed in Anglo-Vernacular Secondary schools, of whom 600 possess professional certificates; in Vernacular Secondary schools there are 850, of whom 667 are certificated.

Higher education.

247. The number of male students taking and passing the more advanced examinations in 1920-21 and 1930-31 is shown in the margin; of the students who were successful in the M.A. Examination two were from the Islamia College, Peshawar, and one was private. The two arts Colleges, the Edwardes Church Mission College, Peshawar, and the Islamia College, Peshawar, which were noticed in the Census Report of 1921 are still in existence and a third, the Vedic Bharatri, Intermediate College at Dera Ismail Khan, has been opened.

Examination	Number of examinees		Number successful	
	1921	1931	1921	1931
M.A ...	1	3	1	3
B.A. and B.Sc. ...	36	120	20	51
B.T ...	...	1	...	1
M.B., B.S. ...	...	8	...	6
Intermediate ...	27	212	17	73

Education among females.

248. The number of institutions devoted to female education has increased from 106 to 145. There are no arts colleges for females, but in the year 1930-31 one female from the Province passed the B.A. Examination, and two more offered but failed in the Intermediate Examination. The numbers who passed primary and secondary examinations are shown in the margin. The increase among girls' schools is to be found in all grades; primary schools have increased from 24 to 45; middle schools from 4 to 23, and high schools from 0 to 2. In addition there is a very little co-education in outlying rural areas. The number of female pupils has increased from 49,717 to 84,940, a larger increase than that recorded among males. A little over 4 per cent. of the girls of school-going age are now on the registers of Schools. There are 415 female teachers of whom 154 are certificated.

Examination	Number of examinees		Number successful	
	1921	1931	1921	1931
Matriculation ...	2	16	...	9
School final ...	...	...	...	...
Anglo-Vernacular Middle ...	19	24	5	14
Vernacular Middle ...	...	82	...	66
Upper and lower primary ...	693	1,934	485	1,595

Obstacles to further expansion.

249. Although education is expanding rapidly, as the above figures show, it is still not expanding as rapidly as some people would wish. The following factors difficult to overcome were brought to notice by witnesses before the Education Committee which toured the Province in 1929, namely (*a*) the poverty of the people, who look upon their children as economic assets in earning a small daily wage, or in performing tasks for which a hired worker would otherwise have to be employed, (*b*) the illiteracy of the masses, with consequent apathy towards education, particularly towards the education of girls; (*c*) the prevalence of factions and parties, so common in rural areas, preventing any co-operation in the establishment of a school; (*d*) the inutilitarian nature of the course and resultant disinclination of parents to risk alienating their children from agricultural pursuits by sending them to school: (*e*) the secular nature of the school course which does not make religious instruction compulsory; (*f*) the absence of propaganda advocating the education of children. The majority of these objections may again be summed up in the phrase which has already been introduced — the people do not see any incentive to learning to read and write. As soon as they see any incentive they will gladly send their children to school. For example in areas in which military recruitment is heavy, the people have realised that an educated recruit has the advantage in chances of promotion, and are clamouring for more schools to be opened. But they can see no advantage to an agriculturist in education, and until they do they will remain apathetic.

SUBSIDIARY TABLE I—(*Total North-West Frontier Province including trans-frontier posts*) *Literacy by age, sex and religion*

Religion	Number per *mille* who are literate											Number per *mille* who are literate in English		
	All ages 5 and over			5—10		10—15		15—20		20 and over				
	Persons	Males	Females	Males	Females	Males	Females	Males	Females	Males	Females	Persons	Males	Females
1	2	3	4	5	6	7	8	9	10	11	12	13	14	15
All religions ...	56	91	12	23	8	45	13	131	20	113	12	15	26	2
Muslims ...	26	44	3	14	2	28	3	68	5	53	3	5	10	...
Hindus ...	304	418	101	136	72	273	126	470	167	473	89	55	83	4
Sikhs ...	375	462	193	148	95	285	158	499	267	521	217	61	88	4
Christians ... Total ...	785	839	534	271	337	334	390	707	415	914	612	734	786	492
Christians ... Indians ...	370	472	184	156	98	116	22	208	137	228	125	80	94	55
Christians ... Europeans ...	990	994	962	314	477	709	1,000	772	988	997	970	954	957	932

SUBSIDIARY TABLE II—*Literacy by age, sex and locality*

District and Natural Division	Number per *mille* who are literate										
	All ages 5 and over			5—10		10—15		15—20		20 and over	
	Persons	Males	Females	Males	Females	Males	Females	Males	Females	Males	Females
1	2	3	4	5	6	7	8	9	10	11	12
N.-W. F. P. (Districts) ...	49	80	12	22	8	44	13	114	20	98	12
Hazara	32	55	5	14	3	31	5	91	8	67	5
Trans-Indus Districts ...	56	89	15	26	10	49	16	122	25	109	15
Peshawar ...	57	89	17	28	11	48	18	117	27	109	16
Kohat	51	86	11	17	7	40	12	125	18	111	10
Bannu	44	73	8	20	2	45	3	107	10	89	11
Dera Ismail Khan ...	67	106	20	0	15	68	28	151	35	128	17
Peshawar City ...	187	265	79	106	56	186	93	323	151	299	67

SUBSIDIARY TABLE III—*Literacy by religion, sex and locality*

District and Natural Division	Number per *mille* who are literate							
	Muslim		Hindu		Sikh		Christian	
	Males	Females	Males	Females	Males	Females	Males	Females
1	2	3	4	5	6	7	8	9
N.-W. F. P. (Districts) ...	42	3	416	101	412	195	786	544
Hazara ...	31	2	478	71	284	78	679	748
Trans Indus (Districts) ...	46	3	402	107	437	224	789	532
Peshawar ...	51	4	383	163	416	209	808	512
Kohat	44	2	424	103	463	302	797	165
Bannu	27	1	335	19	487	262	739	455
Dera Ismail Khan	45	3	470	116	520	198	519	696
Peshawar City	200	28	530	266	574	387	113	91

Note.—The figures in this table are for persons of five years of age and over only

SUBSIDIARY TABLE IV—*English literacy by age, sex and locality—Four decades*

Literate in English per 10,000

District and natural division	1931										1921										1911										1901		1891	
	5 to 10		10 to 15		15 to 20		20 and over		All ages 5 and over		5 to 10		10 to 15		15 to 20		20 and over		All ages 5 and over		5 to 10		10 to 15		15 to 20		20 and over		All ages 5 and over		All ages		All ages	
	Males	Females	Males	Females	Males	Females	Males	Females	Males	Females	Males	Females	Males	Females	Males	Females	Males	Females	Males	Females	Males	Females	Males	Females	Males	Females	Males	Females	Males	Females	Males	Females	Males	Females
1	2	3	4	5	6	7	8	9	10	11	12	13	14	15	16	17	18	19	20	21	22	23	24	25	26	27	28	29	30	31	32	33	34	35
N.-W. F. P. (Districts)	30	10	83	14	329	21	277	23	214	20	20	6	50	19	261	14	191	17	148	15	6	4	32	2	130	6	134	12	96	9	72	6	46	3
Hazara ...	11	3	33	3	105	5	75	7	60	5	3	...	14	3	54	6	46	5	33	4	...	...	16	...	64	2	35	4	29	2	13	1	14	1
Trans-Indus Districts	38	14	102	18	405	26	350	29	270	25	27	8	64	26	328	17	241	22	189	19	8	5	39	3	156	7	169	15	121	11	93	8	55	4
Peshawar ...	42	21	99	27	413	33	407	36	306	32	43	14	66	43	279	19	280	28	212	27	14	10	35	5	130	9	231	21	158	16	115	11	115	7
Kohat ...	35	5	104	6	498	18	403	24	306	17	26	8	45	5	249	17	143	19	116	15	1	...	23	2	123	7	107	11	76	7	75	4	31	4
Bannu ...	22	5	67	7	253	16	133	19	129	14	2	...	38	...	328	6	103	3	95	2	1	...	41	1	202	4	69	5	63	3	55	2	10	...
Dera Ismail Khan ...	39	6	146	9	437	17	288	24	243	18	...	...	100	11	557	16	292	20	247	15	3	3	65	1	231	4	105	9	93	6	75	5	12	2

SUBSIDIARY TABLE V—*Literacy by caste, 1931 and 1921*

Caste	1931									1921								
	Number per 1,000						Number per 10,000 literate in English			Number per 1,000						Number per 10,000 literate in English		
	Literate			Illiterate						Literate			Illiterate					
	Persons	Males	Females	Persons	Males	Females	Persons	Males	Females	Persons	Males	Females	Persons	Males	Females	Persons	Males	Females
1	2	3	4	5	6	7	8	9	10	11	12	13	14	15	16	17	18	19
Arora	268	392	103	732	608	897	495	800	82	326	447	103	674	553	897	347	521	26
Awan	42	67	10	958	933	990	106	167	29	17	33	2	983	967	998	25	50	...
Brahman	411	518	218	589	482	782	703	1,030	115	205	261	93	795	739	907	332	477	42
Chamar	17	29	...	983	971	1,000	13	21	...	9	15	...	991	985	1,000	...	...	...
Chuhra	51	68	11	949	932	989	33	29	17	19	26	6	981	974	994	39	53	12
Gujar	10	16	2	990	981	998	15	24	5	11	18	1	989	982	999	8	14	...
Jat	66	106	4	934	894	996	82	135	...	59	99	1	941	901	999	42	71	...
Khatri	401	515	242	599	485	758	819	1,175	323	311	400	116	689	600	884	354	492	52
Pathan	29	48	6	971	952	994	72	120	14	15	27	1	985	973	999	19	35	...
Sayad	62	109	10	938	891	990	171	299	29	32	54	7	968	945	993	48	90	1
Swathi	27	47	3	973	953	997	21	38	1	16	26	4	984	974	996	7	14	...
Tanaoli	12	22	1	988	978	999	10	19	...	6	12	...	994	988	1,000	4	7	...

Note.—The figures in this table are for persons of seven years of age and over only

SUBSIDIARY TABLE VI—*Progress of literacy since 1881—Six decades*

District and Natural Division	Number literate per *mille*																																			
	All ages												All ages 10 and over								15—20								20 and over							
	Males						Females						Males				Females				Males				Females				Males				Females			
	1931	1921	1911	1901	1891	1881	1931	1921	1911	1901	1891	1881	1931	1921	1911	1901	1931	1921	1911	1901	1931	1921	1911	1901	1931	1921	1911	1901	1931	1921	1911	1901	1931	1921	1911	1901
1	2	3	4	5	6	7	8	9	10	11	12	13	14	15	16	17	18	19	20	21	22	23	24	25	26	27	28	29	30	31	32	33	34	35	36	37
N.-W. F. P. (Districts)	68	64	57	62	61	58	10	9	8	5	2	1	91	86	80	86	13	12	8	7	114	110	82	76	20	20	12	10	98	91	89	98	12	11	7	7
Hazara ...	46	40	37	35	43	31	4	5	3	1	1	...	63	56	53	50	5	7	4	2	91	61	56	49	8	18	7	3	67	64	60	57	5	5	4	2
Trans-Indus Districts	76	72	64	72	66	65	13	10	7	7	3	2	101	97	89	99	16	14	10	9	122	126	93	87	25	21	18	12	109	101	99	112	15	14	9	8
Peshawar ...	76	64	61	65	71	80	14	11	9	10	5	4	100	83	83	89	18	14	12	13	117	96	91	74	27	16	17	17	109	89	93	102	16	15	12	12
Kohat ...	72	69	56	72	51	48	9	9	2	3	2	...	100	96	82	99	12	13	4	4	125	87	62	78	18	32	7	6	111	110	96	114	10	12	3	4
Bannu ...	61	64	61	73	52	50	7	7	3	2	1	...	84	91	89	102	10	10	4	3	107	175	88	94	10	26	5	4	89	78	99	114	11	6	3	3
Dera Ismail Khan ...	90	112	84	93	74	64	17	13	7	5	1	1	121	149	117	128	21	19	10	7	151	217	129	126	35	26	19	11	128	149	124	141	17	19	8	5

Note.—The figures for distribution by age being not available in 1881, all persons returned as "under instruction" are treated as "literate". In the year 1891 all persons aged 15 and over who were recorded as "learning" have been treated as "literate".

SUBSIDIARY TABLE VI-A—*Progress of literacy since 1901 by religion*

Number of literates per *mille*

District and Natural Division	Muslims								Hindus								Sikhs							
	Males				Females				Males				Females				Males				Females			
	1931	1921	1911	1901	1931	1921	1911	1901	1931	1921	1911	1901	1931	1921	1911	1901	1931	1921	1911	1901	1931	1921	1911	1901
1	2	3	4	5	6	7	8	9	10	11	12	13	14	15	16	17	18	19	20	21	22	23	24	25
N. W. F. P. (Districts)	42	31	28	29	3	2	1	3	416	355	416	431	101	99	66	46	412	546	498	534	195	222	154	148
Hazara ...	31	20	19	18	2	1	1	...	478	440	435	432	71	130	48	21	284	478	357		78	32	69	...
Trans-Indus Districts.	46	36	32	33	3	2	1	4	402	339	410	431	107	91	71	51	437	558	525	Not obtainable	224	276	176	...
Peshawar ...	51	33	32	33	4	2	2	4	383	272	371	Not obtainable	163	123	144	Not obtainable	416	525	491		209	267	210	...
Kohat ...	44	44	33	34	2	4	1	1	424	304	363		103	119	24		463	617	610		302	237	77	...
Bannu ...	27	30	26	32	1	2	...	1	335	317	399		19	18	15		487	777	623		262	374	107	...
Dera Ismail Khan.	45	45	37	30	3	2	2	2	470	451	500		116	95	51		520	430	494		198	116	127	...

Note.—The figures in this table are for persons of five years of age and over only.

SUBSIDIARY TABLE VII—*Proportion of literacy at certain ages (absolute figures)*

Age group	Total population			Total literate			Total literate in English		
	Persons	Males	Females	Persons	Males	Females	Persons	Males	Females
1	2	3	4	5	6	7	8	9	10
7 to 13 years ...	426,513	241 04	185,009	9,649	7,510	2,139	1,272	1,025	247
14 to 16 years ...	150,438	85,739	64,699	8,119	6,947	1,172	1,789	1,682	107
17 to 23 years ...	280,702	148,775	131,927	22,576	19,773	2,803	6,315	6,025	290
24 years and over ...	1,059,372	581,217	478,155	59,590	54,471	5,119	16,285	15,161	1,124

SUBSIDIARY TABLE VII—*Proportion of literacy at certain ages (percentage)*

Age groups	Total population			Total literate			Total literate in English		
	Persons	Males	Females	Persons	Males	Females	Persons	Males	Females
1	2	3	4	5	6	7	8	9	10
7 to 13 years ...	426,513	241,504	185,009	2	3	1	...	...	...
14 to 16 years ...	150,438	85,739	64,699	5	8	2	1	2	...
17 to 23 years ...	280,702	148,775	131,927	8	13	2	2	4	...
24 years and over ...	1,059,372	581,217	478,155	6	9	1	2	3	...

SUBSIDIARY TABLE VIII—*Number of institutions and pupils according to the returns of the Education Department—Four censuses*

Class of institution.	1931		1921		1911		1901	
	Number of		Number of		Number of		Number of	
	Institutions	Scholars	Institutions	Scholars	Institutions	Scholars	Institutions	Scholars
1	2	3	4	5	6	7	8	9
Total Institutions, N.-W. F. Province ...	1,109	84,949	965	49,717	976	31,891	1,199	27,184
Total Public Institutions ...	968	81,093	779	45,770	323	23,012	222	13,921
Total Private Institutions ...	141	3,847	186	3,947	653	8,879	977	13,263
Hazara District Total Institutions ...	221	20,116	195	11,962	217	7,075	195	4,260
Total Public Institutions ...	212	19,894	171	11,502	70	4,926	38	2,505
Secondary Schools ...	60	9,780	17	3,228	7	1,442	5	751
Primary Schools ...	152	10,114	153	8,250	63	3,484	33	1,754
Training Schools ...	...	—	1	24	...	...	...	...
Total Private Institutions ...	9	222	24	460	147	2,149	157	1,755
Advanced ...	...	...	5	80	14	295	Not available	
Elementary ...	...	...	2	60	11	199		
Teaching Qoran and other religious books ...	9	222	17	320	121	1,647		
Other Private Schools ...	...	...	...	...	1	8		
Peshawar District Total Institutions ...	373	30,024	334	18,568	231	9,817	377	9,244
Total Public Institutions ...	301	27,785	233	16,130	108	7,795	81	4,774
Arts Colleges ...	2	413	2	132	1	22	1	6
Secondary Schools ...	82	14,663	29	6,391	10	2,881	13	1,935
Primary Schools ...	214	12,558	199	9,524	96	4,839	67	2,833
Training Schools ...	3	151	3	83	1	53	...	...
Total Private Institutions ...	72	2,239	101	2,438	123	2,022	296	4,479
Advanced ...	28	586	1	360	8	87	36	549
Elementary ...	...	...	15	522	20	462	6	6
Teaching Qoran and other religious books ...	40	1,219	85	1,556	95	1,473	...	...
Other Private Schools ...	4	434	...	...	...	...	254	254
Kohat District Total Institutions ...	143	9,355	134	4,796	89	2,655	72	1,691
Total Public Institutions ...	143	9,355	119	4,41[illegible]	49	2,175	14	1,038
Secondary Schools ...	41	5,7[illegible]	11	1,732	3	707	1	392
Primary Schools ...	102	3,614	108	2,679	46	1,468	13	646
Total Private Institutions ...	...	...	15	385	40	480	58	653
Advanced ...	...	...	...	...	11	90	12	165
Elementary ...	...	...	...	...	2	50	3	28
Teaching Qoran and other religious books ...	...	...	15	385	27	349	43	460
Bannu District Total Institutions ...	155	11,121	164	6,764	215	5,985	258	5,347
Total Public Institutions ...	141	10,566	118	6,100	50	3,896	32	2,073
Secondary Schools ...	39	5,766	9	1,846	4	991	3	585
Primary Schools ...	102	4,800	109	4,254	46	2,815	29	1,488

SUBSIDIARY TABLE VIII (continued)—*Number of institutions and pupils according to the returns of the Education Department—Four censuses*

Class of Institution	1931		1921		1911		1901	
	Number of		Number of		Number of		Number of	
	Institutions	Scholars	Institutions	Scholars	Institutions	Scholars	Institutions	Scholars
1	2	3	4	5	6	7	8	9
Total Private Institutions ...	14	555	46	664	165	2,179	226	3,274
Advanced	...	...	10	129	36	574	Not available.	
Teaching Qoran and other religious books ...	12	335	36	535	129	1,604		
Other Private Schools	2	220	...	...	...	1		
Dera Ismail Khan District Total Institutions ..	217	14,324	138	7,627	224	6,359	297	6,642
Total Public Institutions	171	13,493	138	7,627	46	4,310	57	3,531
Arts Colleges	1	60	..	...	...	...	...	...
Secondary Schools	46	7,766	14	3,458	6	2,107	8	1,194
Primary Schools	123	5,628	123	4,145	40	2,203	49	2,337
Training Schools	1	39	1	24	...	...	...	...
Total Private Institutions ..	46	831	...	..	178	2,049	240	3,111
Advanced	3	64	...	...	4	62	Not available	
Elementary	6	162	...	...	6	227		
Teaching Qoran and other religious books ...	37	605	...	...	168	1,760		

CHAPTER X

LANGUAGE.

GENERAL.

Reference to statistics.

250. Statistics relating to language are to be found in Imperial Table XV and in the two Subsidiary Tables at the end of this chapter. Part I of Table XV deals with the mother-tongue of the persons enumerated, and part II with bilingualism. The Subsidiary Tables give the same information in a more compendious form. Subsidiary Table No. I compares the distribution of the population by language for each census since 1901, No. II gives the distribution for mother-tongue and subsidiary languages by districts and natural divisions.

In the present Census, a column (No. 15) has been provided for the first time in the General Schedule for subsidiary languages. It is the results of this column that are shown in the part II of Imperial Table XV. Those who previously had any hesitation which of two languages they should record, were on this occasion able to record one language as their mother-tongue and one as their subsidiary language.

The system of classification.

251. The system of classification adopted in Imperial Table XV differs from that adopted in the two Subsidiary Tables, while neither would be understood by the persons enumerated. The non-scientific mind would divide the languages spoken into three groups, Pashto, Hindko, and languages named after the locality of birth. Pashto is the language of the Pathans, Hindko is the language spoken by non-Pathan residents of the Province and by immigrants from the Punjab, while the remaining group would include English spoken by Europeans, Baluchi by persons born in Baluchistan, Kohistani by immigrants from Kohistan, Nepali by Gurkhas from Nepal, and so on. Regarded in this way, Pashto and Hindko would be the only two indigenous languages of the districts, and the classifications adopted in the tables would be useful rather to indicate the distribution of persons speaking certain languages than as a guide to the languages of the Province.

Pashto.

252. The classification adopted in the Subsidiary Tables, and the nomenclature adopted in Imperial Table XV and in the the present chapter, are based on Sir George Grierson's Linguistic Survey. This Survey shows Pashto, which is spoken by over 52 per cent. of the enumerated population, to be a language of the Eastern Group of the Eranian Branch in the Aryan Sub-Family and the Indo-European Family. There should have been no difficulty in its recognition by enumerators, since it is quite distinct from any other language which subjects may have wished to return. It has two principal dialects, hard in the North of the Province and soft in the South. The northern dialect, more properly known as Pakhto, is spoken in Bajaur, Swat and Buner, and by the Yusarfzais, Bangash, Orakzais, Afridis, Mohmands and tribes of Peshawar District, while Khattaks, Wazirs, Marwats and other tribes towards the South speak the softer dialect. The speech of the Yusafzais is regarded as the classical dialect, and it is in this that most of the Pashto literature is written. The roots of words differ little from dialect to dialect, but the pronunciation of many of both the vowels and the consonants differs from tribe to tribe.

Lahnda.

253. The next most important language in point of numbers is that which is entered as Lahnda both in the Imperial Table and in the Subsidiary Tables. Lahnda is thus described by Sir John Grierson in the India Census Report of 1901 :—

"Lahnda is a language the existence of which has long been recognised, but under many names. In the last Census Report it was called Jatki, but this, like Multani, Punjabi, and other titles given to it has the disadvantage of not being sufficiently comprehensive. It is not spoken only by Jats ; it is not peculiar to Multan ; and it is not a Western dialect of the Punjabi of Moujh. I therefore think it best to give it the name which is indicated by the natives of the Punjab themselves *i. e.* Lahnda or the

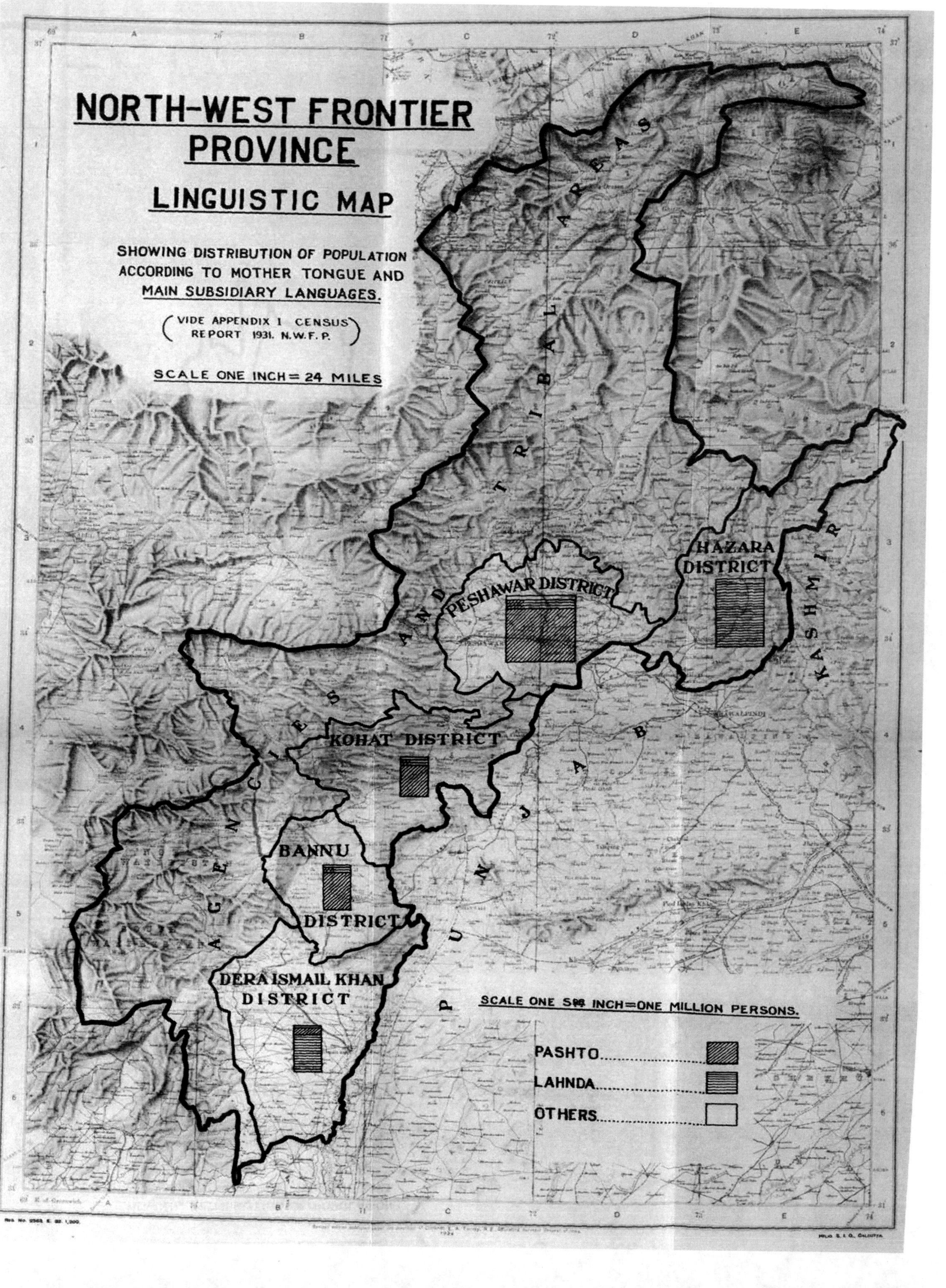

NORTH-WEST FRONTIER PROVINCE
LINGUISTIC MAP
SHOWING DISTRIBUTION OF POPULATION ACCORDING TO MOTHER TONGUE AND MAIN SUBSIDIARY LANGUAGES.
(VIDE APPENDIX 1 CENSUS REPORT 1931. N.W.F.P.)
SCALE ONE INCH = 24 MILES
TRIBAL AREAS
AND
AGENCIES
PESHAWAR DISTRICT
HAZARA DISTRICT
KASHMIR
KOHAT DISTRICT
BANNU DISTRICT
DERA ISMAIL KHAN DISTRICT
PUNJAB
SCALE ONE SQ INCH=ONE MILLION PERSONS.
PASHTO
LAHNDA
OTHERS

language of the West (Punjabi *Lahnde di Boli*). It has no literature, and has no standard form, so that it is rather a group of connected dialects than a language with a definite standard. The eastern boundary of Lahnda may be taken as the river Chanab from the Kashmir Frontier down to the town of Ramnagar in the district of Gujranwala. Thence it runs in a straight line to the northwest corner of Montgomery and across that district to the south-west corner. Its northern boundary may be taken as coinciding on the east with the range of mountains forming the southern limit of the Kashmir Valley, while to the west it skirts that valley and reaches as far north as the watershed dividing the Indus from the Jhelum Valley. Here it is bounded on the west by the Kohistani of the Indus Valley, till we reach the Hazara District. Thence the western boundary may be roughly taken as the Indus itself. These eastern and western boundaries are, however, very indefinite. Pashto is spoken in several places close to the Indus, and from the Indus westwards up to Afghan mountain country we find Lahnda also spoken, but principally by Hindus, the Mussalman language being Pashto. As we get further south into the Derajat, Lahnda more than holds its own, and is the principal language of the plains west of the Indus."

254. The name Lahnda is practically unknown to subjects, enumerators and supervisors. In order to reduce as far as possible the difficulties of enumeration, the following instructions were issued to supervisors :— **Method of enumeration and tabulation.**

Column 14—A person's mother-tongue should be entered exactly as he describes it. In the case of both Hindi and Urdu speakers "Hindustani" is the proper entry for this column, but if literate this should be followed in column 16 by the entry "Hindi" or "Urdu" according as the person enumerated writes in the one or in the other scrip.

Enumerators, when making entries in columns 14 and 15, should try to distinguish between those persons who speak true Punjabi or true Hindi, and those who speak Western Punjabi (or Lahnda).

In this Province the latter language is believed to be synonymous with the dialects variously known as Hindi, Hindko, Jatki, Peshawari, Derawali and Kohati. Such dialects should be entered in column 14 and 15 as they are decribed, and not as Punjabi or Hindi. Punjabi and Hindi should only be entered for those who speak pure Punjabi and pure Hindi, so far as this can be ascertained.

When the time for sorting and compilation arrived, it was assumed that these instructions had been correctly understood and carried out. On this assumption entries of Hindi, Urdu and Hindustani were classified as they appeared on the schedule, while entries of Hindko, Peshawari, Derawali, Tanaoli and similar entries were classified under the head Lahnda

The extent to which the speakers of Pashto and Hindko dominate the five settled districts can be judged from the linguistic map placed at the beginning of this chapter. There are no other languages which show a proportion higher than 35·1 per thousand of the population. The languages returned will now be considered in the groupings adopted by Sir George Grierson.

ERANIAN BRANCH.

255. All the important languages enumerated in the Province belong to the Indo-European family. Of these the only two belonging to the Eranian Branch are Pashto and Persian. The general characteristics of Pashto have already been mentioned; it is the language of Pathans, and should have presented no difficulty in enumeration. It is almost universally spoken in the tribal territory of the Province, but since no enumeration was carried out in this area, the figure must be disregarded. With them must be disregarded also the figures for certain ancient languages such as Ormuri in Waziristan, the Kafir language of Chitral, Dehgani and others which are known to be still spoken but of which no statistics are available. **Distribution of Pashto.**

256. The figure for Pusto-speakers given in the Linguistic Survey is 3,905,725. If the figure for enumerated Pashto-speakers at the present Census (1,290,484) is added to the estimated population of the tribal area the total obtained is 3.503.321. This falls short of the Sir George Grierson's figures **Comparison with figures of Linguistic Survey.**

in as much as the estimates of the population of the tribal area have decreased from decade to decade.

Pashto in the districts.

257. The geographical distribution of Pashto-speakers in the districts is shown in the map at the beginning of this chapter. In Hazara it is habitually spoken by the Mishwanis, by the residents of the Agror and Konsh Valleys, and in villages on the Western fringe of the Pakhli plain. It is also spoken by the Utmanzais of Tarbala and Khalsa, the Torkhelis, and in many villages in Pakhli outside the fringe already mentioned. Very few of those who speak it in Hazara cannot also converse with equal fluency in Hindko.

In Peshawar, Bannu and Kohat Pashto is the language of the agricultural population, and Hindko the language of the trading and town-dwelling populations. In the villages the trading-classes are for the most part Hindus whose mother-tongue is Lahnda, but who are equally fluent in Pashto for the sake of their business. In towns the Hindus are less bilingual, but the Muslims, who have left their homes in the country to dwell in towns, are gradually acquiring Lahnda either in addition to Pashto or to its exclusion.

In Dera Ismail Khan, Pashto is the language of frontier Pathans along the whole length of the district border, with the exception of the town of Tank and the district around it, where the population is mainly Jat and speaks Lahnda. This Jat tract is usually known as Jatatar, and is surrounded by tribes speaking Pashto on all-sides With this exception, the Pashto speaking tribes form an unbroken line, beginning with the Khaisors and Bilots at Paniala and in the Largi Valley, the Marwats along the Bannu boundary from Paniala to Mullazai, the Bhittanni and Kundi and Tator tribes in Tank, and Gandapurs, Mian Khel, Usterana and Babar in Kulachi with some minor tribes. The large migratory Powinda population of the district universally speak Pashto.

Variation by districts.

258. Although Pashto is the mother-tongue of practically the whole of the estimated population (2,212,837) of the trans-border territory of the Province, the proportion of Pashto-speakers in the settled districts is only 53 per cent. It is recorded as their mother-tongue by 1,290,484 persons among the enumerated population of the districts and trans-frontier posts. Its distribution in the trans-frontier posts is largely a matter of chance and need not be discussed. In the districts, as the map shows, it is the dominant language in Peshawar, Kohat and Bannu, where it is habitually spoken by some four-fifths of the total number of persons enumerated. In Dera Ismail Khan and Hazara Lahnda predominates, and Pashto is only spoken by the minority. In Hazara the proportion of persons speaking Pashto is as low as 438 per 10,000 of the population. It is highest (8,449 per 10,000) in Bannu, but the greatest actual number (781,773 or 80 per cent. of Pashto speakers) is found in Peshawar.

Comparison with 1921.

259. The figures in the margin show the number of Pashto speakers in each district in each of the last two census years. During this period the total population of the five districts has increased by 7·7 per cent. and the number of Pashto-speakers by 6·4 per cent. There is a slight decrease in Hazara and a larger decrease in Dera Ismail Khan. In both these districts the decrease may be attributed to the spread of education. Both are districts in which Pashto is already in a minority; no education and no business is conducted in Pashto, and any spread of literacy must inevitably increase the number of Lahnda-speakers at the expense of the speakers of Pashto. In this connection it may be recalled that Dera Ismail Khan is the district with the highest proportion of literate persons, and Hazara the district in which literacy is advancing at the greatest speed.

Number of persons returning Pashto as their mother-tongue

District	1921	1931
Hazara ...	31,975	29,735
Peshawar ...	738,325	781,773
Kohat ...	171,223	186,299
Bannu ...	201,592	228,381
Dera Ismail Khan ...	59,211	53,643

General decline in proportion of Pashto speakers.

260. In spite of the fact that the actual number of persons returning Pashto as their mother-tongue has increased, the proportion to the total population is gradually declining. The figures in the margin show the proportion by districts since 1901. The general proportion for the five districts is now lower than in any previous census. Bannu is the only district which shows an increase in proportion during the last decade, and even there the figure is lower than in 1901. Peshawar and Kohat show figures actually slightly higher than in 1901, but during the same period the figure for Dera Ismail Khan has declined from 2,893 per 10,000 to 1,957

Proportion of Pashto-speakers per 10,000 of the population

	1901	1911	1921	1931
N.-W. F. P. (Districts) ...	5,408	5,562	5,340	5,276
Hazara	563	483	514	438
Peshawar ...	7,849	8,202	8,137	8,024
Kohat ...	7,799	8,684	7,996	7,885
Bannu ...	8,460	8,751	8,170	8,449
Dera Ismail Khan ...	2,898	2,773	2,271	1,957

Variation in proportion by districts.

Pashto is however not losing ground so rapidly as some writers have anticipated. The figures in the margin show that the percentage increase among Pashto speakers is only 1 per cent. less than the general percentage increase in the population of the districts. The figure is actually higher both in Peshawar and in Kohat, and only 2 lower in Bannu. It is in the Northern and Southern districts of the Province that Pashto is really losing ground. The population has increased by 20 per cent. in Hazara and 11 per cent. in Dera Ismail Khan since 1901, but the number of Pashto-speakers in these districts has decreased by 7 and 27 per cent. respectively. As has been already indicated, the disappearance of Pashto in these two districts is due to the spread of education and improvement of communications in areas where Pashto-speakers are already in a very small minority. Even were Pashto to be made the medium of instruction it is doubtful if this tendency, which will no doubt soon make itself felt in the other districts, could be checked, since Lahnda is already the language of the trading and commercial classes with whom the rural population is increasingly brought into contact.

Variation among Pashto-speakers 1901-1931

District	Variation per cent. in	
	Total population	Pashto speakers
N.-W. F. P. (Districts) ...	+ 19	+ 18
Hazara	+ 20	—7
Peshawar	+ 24	+ 26
Kohat	+ 8	+ 10
Bannu	+ 19	+ 17
Dera Ismail Khan ...	+ 11	—27

Female Pashto speakers.

It is perhaps significant that although the total number of enumerated females has increased in the last twenty years from 1,014831 in 1911 to 1,109,258 in 1931, an increase of 9 per cent., the number of female Pashto speakers has only increased by 5 per cent. in the same period, *viz.* from 573,499 to 602,043. In Kohat, where the female population has increased by 6 per cent. the number of female Pashto-speakers is less by 2 per cent. Only in Peshawar is the increase in female Pashto speakers in this period equal to the increase in the female population. These figures suggest that Pashto is losing ground in the home, and that the proportion of Pashto speakers in the total population will be lower again at the next census.

Persian.

261. Persian, the only other language of the Eranian stock habitually spoken in the Province, is the Court Language of Afghanistan and is the mother-tongue of persons living in and around Kabul. There were at this enumeration 6,380 persons, 3,825 males and 2,555 females, speaking Persian in the districts. The number is made up mostly of immigrants, traders and others, from Kabul. Some are persons who have settled down in Peshawar City and retained their mother-tongue through one or two generations Some again are of the Qazilbash clan and claim to be of Turki origin, being descended from the followers of Nadir Shah.

There is a considerable increase over the figures for 1921, when only 2,469 were enumerated. The principal increases are found in Dera Ismail Khan where the figure has risen from 4 to 1,678, and in Peshawar where it has risen from 1740 to 3952. The increase is to be attributed to more settled conditions on the border and to improvements in communication between the Province and Afghanistan.

Balochi. 262. Balochi, which is also an Eranian language must be mentioned, since 7 persons who speak it happened to be in the Province on the night of the enumeration. It is spoken in Dera Ghazi Khan and in Baluchistan, which adjoin this Province. No such persons were found in 1911 but 124 were found in 1901.

INDIAN BRANCH, NON-SANSCRITIC.

Kashmiri. 263. Kashmiri and Kohistani, which are classified by Sir George Grierson as Dardic languages of the Non-Sanscritic Indian Branch, are both found in the Province. Kashmiri is spoken by persons whose real home is in Kashmir but who happened to be in the Province during the census.

Statistics for 1931.	
Persons returned as Kashmiri by caste ...	21,912
Persons returned as born in Kashmir ...	8,263
Persons returned as speaking Kashmiri ...	2,249

The figures for Kashmiri-speakers do not correspond either with those for persons born in Kashmir or with those who are returned as Kashmiri by caste. The figures for each are given in the margin. The reason for the discrepancy is that persons who habitually visit the Province in the course of business, and persons who have been domiciled in the Province for a generation or more, have abandoned their mother-tongue in favour of one or other of the tongues of the surrounding population with whom they mix in daily intercourse.

Kohistani. 264. Kohistani is the name given to the group of dialects spoken in the Indus Kohistan as well as in the Swat and Panjkora Kohistan, by people who have not yet adopted Pashto as their mother-tongue. It is really a language of the tribal area in which no enumeration was carried out, and variations in the number of its speakers who are found in the districts are not reliable indications of the vitality of the language. The figures actually show an increase from 222 to 388 since the last census. If any reason can be ascribed to this, it must be the improvement in communications between the districts and the area in which the language still persists. In Swat Kohistan, at least, the ruler of the country is of opinion that the language is gradually giving way to Pashto as the country is being opened up.

INDIAN BRANCH, SANSCRITIC.

NORTH-WESTERN GROUP.

Lahnda. 265. The principal language of the Sanscritic group found in the Province is Lahnda. As already indicated, the word Lahnda is unknown to the bulk of the people. The tongue is in fact generally considered to be merely a dialect of Punjabi. The line differentiating Lahnda, as defined by Sir George Grierson, from the standard Punjabi of the Central Punjab runs from the south-eastern boundary of the Jhelum District almost due south, through the middle of the Phalia Tahsil of Gujrat, along the eastern boundary of Hafizabad and through the middle of the Khanqah Dogran Tahsil, touching the north-west corner of Sharakpur (Gujranwala) and Chunian (Lahore) Tahsils, through the Gugera and Dipalpur Tahsils of Montgomery, to the southern boundary of the Pakpattan Tahsil of the same district, where it turns west to the trijunction of the Montgomery and Multan districts with the Bahawalpur State. From this point it comes round to the south, to within 15 miles of the Bikaner border, and then runs almost parallel to the boundary of that state with Bahawalpur. On the west, it is hemmed in by the Bilochi-speaking Biloch trans-frontier tract of Dera Ghazi Khan and on the north-west by the boundary of the North-West Frontier Province. Lahnda is spoken generally in Hazara and Dera Ismail Khan, the two northern and southern districts of the Province, and by the urban population of the other three districts. The indigenous Hindu and Sikh population throughout the Province speak Lahnda, which is also the mother-tongue of immigrants from the Western Punjab. Of 1,036,657 speaker of Lahnda recorded at the recent census, 625,268 were returned from Hazara, 127,189 from Peshawar, 35,755 from Kohat 33,547 from Bannu, 213,115 from Dera Ismail Khan, and 1,783 from the trans-frontier posts. The proportions *which these figures bear to the total population are shown in the margin,* and are illustrated in the map at the beginning of the chapter. The proportion is highest 9,331 per 10,000) in Hazara, and lowest (1,241 per 10,000) in Bannu, and is 4,267 per 10,000 for the whole of the five districts. The proportion of Pashto speakers in the five districts, it may be remembered, is 5,276 per 10,000 of the population. The reason why the proportion is so high in Hazara is that Hazara is the *only* district in which Lahnda is the mother-tongue of the bulk of the indigenous population of all religions. In Peshawar, Kohat and Bannu it is hardly an exaggeration to say that it is the mother-tongue only of immigrants, or of persons whose domicile in the Province is a matter of very recent history. In these three districts it is almost confined to Hindus and Sikhs. In Dera Ismail Khan on the other hand it is the mother- tongue of large numbers of Jats and others among Muslims, whose home was originally in the Punjab.

District or Natural Division		Proportion per 10,000 of the population whose mother-tongue is Lahnda.
N.-W. F. P. (Districts)	...	4,267
Hazara ...	...	9,331
Trans-Indus Districts	...	2,334
Peshawar ...	...	1,305
Kohat ...	...	1,513
Bannu ...	...	1,241
Dera Ismail Khan	...	7,776

Confusion between Lahnda and Punjabi.

266. The confusion in the minds of the public between Lahnda and Punjabi, with a little extra confusion from Urdu, Hindustani and Hindi thrown in, makes it difficult to compare the figures for the present census with any previously recorded. The difficulty is sufficiently illustrated by the fact that in the 1911 census 848,218 persons were recorded as speaking Punjabi and 72,039 as Hindko, while in 1921 the figures were almost reversed, 940,972 giving their mother-tongue as Hindko and only 85,159 as Punjabi. In the present census the figures are 1,036,657 (including trans-frontier posts, for Lahnda, and 86, 26 for Punjabi. It is unlikely that there are many persons speaking pure Punjabi who were not born in the Punjab, and since the figure of 86,726 corresponds closely with the figure of 83,118 persons returned as immigrants from the Punjab, it seems probable that the instructions have on the present occasion proved more easily understood than in the past.

Comparison with previous figures.

267. In 1911 and 1921 certain calculations and estimates were made in the attempt to arrive at true figures for Lahnda-speakers. The results of these calculations are compared in the margin with the enumerated figures of the present census. The figures for all-districts show a steady increase. Since however the figures depend so much on guess-work, it is unsafe to draw conclusions without comparing the figures with those for Pashto already considered. It will be recalled that in Hazara and Dera Ismail Khan, two districts in which education is proceeding apace, the proportion of Pashto-speakers to the general population is showing a decline. *This decline is reflected in the increase among Lahnda-speakers* shown in these two districts, which is due partly to the natural increase of the Lahnda-speaking population and partly to the spread of education. On the other hand the figures for Peshawar and Bannu, where Lahnda is not the language of the resident population, show a decline, and Kohat is practically stationary.

District or Natural Division		Estimated number of Lahnda speakers in		Enumerated number of Lahnda-speakers in
		1911	1921	1931
N.-W. F. P. (Districts)	...	895,521	965,162	1,034,874
Hazara	...	540,671	560,615	625,268
Peshawar	...	122,813	131,875	127,189
Kohat	...	24,255	35,532	35,755
Bannu	...	27,195	40,006	33,547
Dera Ismail Khan	...	180,587	197,134	213,115

Growth of Lahnda and Punjabi considered together.

268. The confusion may also to some extent be resolved by considering the figures for Lahnda and Punjabi together. The proportion per 10,000 of the population speaking one or other of these two languages is shown in the margin for each district for the last thirty years.

Speakers of Lahnda plus Punjabi per 10,000 of the population

	1901	1911	1921	1931
Districts ...	4,292	4,168	4,443	4,548
Hazara ...	8,415	8,990	9,035	9,422
Peshawar ...	1,947	1,560	1,696	1,724
Kohat ...	1,961	1,224	1,833	1,982
Bannu ...	1,453	1,195	1,815	1,473
Dera Ismail Khan ...	6,922	7,111	7,671	7,933

The general tendency is towards increase, and those figures which suggest a decrease can be explained by variations in immigration. It is worthy of note that although the general tendency is for the number of Lahnda-speakers to increase, the number of immigrants from the Punjab, the home of the language is decreasing; there were 97,624 such immigrants recorded in 1921 and only 83.118 in 1931. This shows that the increase among Lahnda-speakers comes from within and not from without.

Tendency of Lahnda and Punjabi to supplant Pashto.

269. These figures taken with those already considered in paragraph 260 seem to indicate that Pashto is being slowly but surely supplanted. Urdu, which is the language of education and of Government Offices, becomes Hindko before it reaches the stage of enumeration in the schedule, and Hindko, which is tabulated as Lahnda, is already the language of commerce. So long as education and commerce are conducted as they are now, for so long will Lahnda continue to drive out Pashto. The process is obscured in Peshawar, Kohat and Bannu by the rapid increase of the uneducated portion of the Pashto speaking population, but can be clearly seen in Dera Ismail Khan and Hazara where it has already gathered momentum.

Figures of Linguistic Survey.

270. The difficulties in identifying the language, which have already been noticed, make any comparison with the figures of the Linguistic Survey of doubtful value. The totals shown in the margin under the heading "Linguistic Survey" are made up in the Linguistic Survey Tables from the figures for Hindko and Tanaoli in Hazara, Hindko and Peshawari in Peshawar, Kohati in Kohat, Hindko and Mulki in Bannu and Hindki and Derawal in Dera Ismail Khan. These languages, wherever returned in the present Census, have been tabulated as Lahnda. It may be noted that the figures of the linguistic survey differ considerably from the estimates of the Census Superintendents of 1911, and 1921 noted in paragraph 267 above.

Comparison with figures of linguistic survey

District	Number of Lahnda-speakers according to	
	Linguistic survey	Census of 1931
All districts ...	729,992	1,034,874
Hazara	363 392	625,268
Peshawar	129,000	127,189
Kohat	34,000	35,755
Bannu	33,700	33,547
Dera Ismail Khan ...	170,000	213,115

CENTRAL GROUP.

Punjabi.

271. The languages included under the Central Group are Urdu, Hindi, Hindustani, Gujuri and Punjabi. Of these Punjabi is numerically the most important. The definition is intended to cover the speakers of the standard Punjabi of the central Punjab. The difficulties of distinguishing it from Lahnda have been already noted, but it is hoped that they have been more successfully overcome on this occasion than in previous years. The figure of 68,031 returned from the districts gives a proportion of 281 per 10,000 of the population. The figure includes 50,226 males and 17,805 females. The high proportion of males to females suggests that the persons recorded are mostly immigrants. This is as it should be, since the language is not indigenous to the Province The figures are confirmed by the figures 47,361 male and 19,529 female immigrants from the Punjab to the five districts. Where they are probably wrong is in the inclusion of too many persons from the Western Punjab whose mother-

tongue is really Lahnda. At least half the persons recorded as born in the Punjab were born in districts in which Lahnda is commonly spoken.

272. Although numerically the least important of the remaining languages of this group, Gujuri is from the philological point of view by far the most interesting. Its peculiar interest lies in the fact that it is a dialect of Rajasthani, its grammar being the same as that of the language of Jaipur in Rajputana. Yet Jaipur is separated by several hundred miles of plain from the mountains of Hazara where Gujuri is spoken. The language is returned in this Province by the Gujars of Mansehra Tahsil in Hazara District, which adjoins Kashmir, and is also spoken in Kashmir. As may be seen from the figures in the margin the numbers returning Gujuri as their mother tongue are rapidly shrinking. Practically all the Gujars of Hazara are bilingual, although they have not recorded themselves as such, and can express themselves equally well in either Lahnda or Gujuri. As communications are improving and their intercourse with the rest of the world is increasing, their old tongue is dying out. The new generation, which learns to read and write in Urdu, will probably be the last which is at all familiar with Gujuri.

Gujuri.

Gujuri speakers in Hazara District

Year	Number	Proportion per 10,000
1901	53,021	948
1911	25,641	425
1921	22,637	364
1931	389	6

Only 291 persons speaking other tongues as their mother tongue have returned Gujuri as their subsidiary tongue. This makes a total of only 680 persons speaking Gujuri altogether. This figure cannot be correct, involving as it does a disappearance of over 20,000 Gujuri speakers in 10 years out of a total of 22,637 recorded in 1921. It does show, however, the unwillingness of the people to acknowledge Gujuri as their tongue any longer.

273. Urdu Hindustani, and Hindi again are easily confused in the popular mind, both one with another and all three with Hindko or Punjabi. In the Linguistic Survey all three are regarded as dialects of Western Hindi, the language spoken in the eastern part of the Indo Gangetic Plain West. In actual practice in this Province Hindustani generally indicates the dialect of Ambala, Delhi and Karnal, or of the United Provinces ; Urdu suggests a more highly educated speaker of Hindustani who is a Muslim, and Hindi one who is a Hindu ; Urdu is Hindustani with an excess of Persian words, and Hindi is Hindustani with an excess of Sanskrit words.

Urdu, Hidustani and Hindi.

The variation by districts among speakers of Urdu and Hindustani since 1911 is shown in the margin. The steep drop from the figures of 1911 to those of 1921 and the even steeper rise from 1921 to 1931 must be to a great extent accounted for by differences in enumeration. It is recorded, for example, in paragraph 277 of the North-West Frontier Province Census Report of 1921 that the tendency among educated Muslims and Hindus of the Punjab, whose mother-tongue was really Lahnda, to return Urdu or Hindi as their language, was much less marked then it had been 10 years previously. In the circumstances it is better not to attempt to draw any conclusions from the variations shown.

District	Urdu and Hindustani speakers		
	1911	1921	1931
All districts ...	16,995	8,814	16,789
Hazara	515	445	4,107
Peshawar ...	11,224	6,041	9,824
Kohat ...	1,521	2,280	1,534
Bannu	1,204	48	907
Dera Ismail Khan ...	2,531	...	417

NORTHERN GROUP.

274. Gorkhali or Nepali, is not indigenous to the Province and is only found in large numbers owing to the presence of Gurkha troops in various frontier stations. The number has increased from 5,892 in 1921 to 9,731 in the present census. More than half this number were enumerated in Abbottabad, Hazara District, which is a permanent Gurkha station, and almost as many in trans-frontier posts.

Gorhkali or Nepali.

OTHERS.

Other Indo-European languages of India.

275. Details of other vernaculars of India found in the enumeration are shown on the fly-leaf of Imperial Table XV under Group A (2) . The totals for those of the Indo-European Group in which a hundred or more persons were enumerated are reproduced in the margin. Purbi means the language of the East and generally indicates an immigrant of the poorer classes from the United Provinces, such as a syce. Bengali and Marathi are spoken mostly by soldiers, and Gujrati by traders. Pahari means the language of the hills, and is applied to the speech of persons from the hills of the North-Eastern Pùnjab and the United Provinces. From the small number of females recorded, it is probable that the language was returned by serving soldiers, presumably of the Royal Garhwal Rifles who were in the Province at the time of the enumeration.

Language	Number of	
	Males	Females
Purbi ...	158	70
Bengali ...	387	48
Marathi ...	341	78
Pahari ...	614	4
Gujrati ...	148	76

EUROPEAN BRANCH.

English.

276. Since a large part of the civil and military business of Government is carried on in English, English is naturally the most important numerically of the European languages spoken in the Province. The number or persons returning English as their mother-tongue increased from 5,839 in 1911 to 11,871 in 1921, but has fallen slightly to 11,665 at the present Census. Out of this number 3,813 were persons serving in trans-frontier posts. The distribution by districts, compared with that for 1921, is shown in the margin. The distribution depends mainly on the composition of the garrisons stationed in the various districts, and can not be utilised for the drawing of any conclusions. The great decrease in Dera Ismail Khan is due to the reduction of the garrison at headquarters, and the complete withdrawal of the garrison previously stationed at Tank.

Number of persons whose mother-tongue was English

District	1921	1931
All districts ...	9,762	7,852
Hazara ...	355	257
Peshawar ...	7,137	5,864
Kohat ...	846	839
Bannu ...	187	556
Dera Ismail Khan ...	1,237	336

The number of persons returning other European languages is shown under Group C on the fly-leaf of Imperial Table XV.

LANGUAGES OF OTHER FAMILIES.

Languages of other families

277. The returns of languages belonging to families other than the Indo-European are reproduced in the margin. Tamil and Telugu, although not of the Indo-European family, are languages of Madras. They are spoken in this Province mostly by serving soldiers or by private servants from Madras. The speakers of the other languages mentioned are all temporary immigrants, mostly traders.

		Males	Females
1.	Tamil ...	349	18
	Telugu ...	250	14
2.	Arabic ...	14	10
3.	Turkish ...	35	27
4.	Chinese ..	...	5
5.	Japanese ...	...	1

BILINGUALISM.

Bilingualism.

278. The total number of persons in the province recorded as speaking subsidiary languages in addition to their mother-tongue is 178,353 Out of this number 26,314 speak two subsidiary languages, 6,726 speak three, 39 speak four, and the remainder speak only one. The power of speaking a subsidiary tongue may come naturally as a result of the associations in which the subject is born or brought up, or may be acquired in the course of, or for the purposes of, the employment by which he gains his livelihood. Of the former description are most of those whose two tongues are Pashto and Lahnda, while traders and most

Government servants fall into the latter category. In Hazara, where the speakers of Pashto are in a small minority surrounded by Lahnda speakers, one in three of those whose mother-tongue is Pashto can also speak Lahnda, while less than one in fifty of Lahnda-speakers can also speak Pashto.

Effect of environment.

279. Since Pashto is the language of the bulk of the uneducated portion of the population and also of those least concerned with commerce, it is to be expected that Pashto-speakers will show the lowest proportion of bilingualism. In every 10,000 persons in the districts whose mother tongue is Pashto, 9,811 speak no other tongue. Corresponding figures for other languages are shown in the margin. The figures for Lahnda, the only other language common among the indigenous population are also high. The number of speakers of Pashto who record Lahnda as a subsidiary language is 3,355 per 10,000 in Hazara, but is nowhere else higher than 816. The bilingualism which they acquire in Hazara is the result of environment rather than of education.

Mother tongue	Proportion per 10,000 who speak no other language
Pashto ...	9,811
Lahnda ...	9,479
Punjabi ...	7,264
Urdu ...	8,047
Other languages ...	7,253

Effect of requirements.

280. The effect of the requirements of business on bilingualism may be seen from the district-to-district variations of those whose mother-tongue is Lahnda but who also speak Pashto. The proportions are comparatively high only in those districts where the bulk of the population (about four-fifths) speak Pashto, and others have to pick up Pashto for the sake of their daily work. In Dera Ismail Khan and Hazara, where the bulk of the population is Lahnda-speaking, the proportion is low.

District	Proportion per 10,000 of the Lahnda-speaking population who can also speak Pashto
Hazara ...	180
Peshawar ...	2,290
Kohat ...	3,341
Bannu ...	3,391
Dera Ismail Khan ...	467

Effect of education.

281. The acquisition of a third or a fourth subsidiary language occurs most often among Government servants, and is a direct result of the spread of education. The average well educated clerk in a Government office has to be able to read and write Urdu, and to understand both Lahnda and Pashto, one or other of which is probably his mother-tongue; the more highly educated must also understand English, and one or two in each office are usually familiar with Persian.

SUBSIDIARY TABLE I—*Distribution of total population by language according to Census*

Language	Total number of speakers (000's omitted)				Number per *mille* of population of the Province	Where chiefly spoken
	1931	1921	1911	1901		
1	2	3	4	5	6	7
N.-W. F. P. Districts and Trans-frontier posts	2,472	2,294	2,210	2,113	1,000	
PART I—INDIAN LANGUAGES						
Indo-European family ... ... / **Aryan sub family**	2,454	2,279	2,200	2,104	992·7	
ERANIAN BRANCH ...	1,290	1,210	1,229	1,142	522·2	
EASTERN GROUP	1,290	1,210	1,229	1,142	522·2	
Pashto	1,290	1,210	1,229	1,142	522·2	Peshawar, Kohat and Bannu.
DARDIC BRANCH... ...	2	1	1		1·1	
DARD GROUP	2	1	1	1	1·1	
Kashmiri	2	1	1	1	1·1	Peshawar.
Indo-Aryan Branch	1,162	1,068	970	961	469·4	
OUTER SUB-BRANCH ...	1,162	068	970	961	469·4	
NORTH-WESTERN GROUP ...	1,037	941	73	583	419·4	
Lahnda	1,037	941	73	583	419·4	Hazara and Dera Ismail Khan.
INNER SUB-BRANCH ...	122	126	896	371	48·9	
CENTRAL GROUP	112	120	891	371	45·0	
Gujuri	1	22	26	53	·3	Hazara.
Hindustani	7				2·8	Peshawar.
Urdu	13	13	17	17	5·1	Hazara and Peshawar
Hindi	4				1·7	Peshawar.
Punjabi	87	85	848	301	35·1	Peshawar.
PAHARI GROUP	10	6	5	...	3·9	
Naipali (Gorkhali) ...	10	6	5		3·9	Hazara.
Others	(*a*) 3	1	1	7	1·1	
PART II—OTHER LANGUAGES						
Indo-Euvopean family ... ... / **Aryan sub-family**	18	15	10	9	7·3	
Eranian Branch and group (Persian) ...	6	2	4	3	2·6	
Tuetonic group (English) ...	12	12	6	5	4·7	
Others	(*b*) and (*c*)	1	...	1	...	

Note.—For details of "others—(*a*), (*b*) and (*c*)", please see fly leaf of Imperial Table XV.

SUBSIDIARY TABLE II (*a*)—*Distribution by language (mother tongue) per 10,000 of the population of each district.*

District and natural division	Number per 10,000 of the population speaking										
	Pashto	Lahnda	Kashmiri	Punjabi	Hindustani	Urdu	Hindi	Naipali (Gorkhali)	Persian	English	Others
1	2	3	4	5	6	7	8	9	10	11	12
N.-W. F. P. (Districts)	5,276	4,267	7	281	24	46	10	21	25	32	11
Hazara	438	9,331	1	81	9	52	...	74	...	4	10
Trans-Indus districts	7,123	2,334	10	357	29	43	14	1	34	43	12
Peshawar	8,024	1,305	16	419	48	53	20	...	41	60	14
Kohat	7,885	1,513	2	469	1	64	7	4	15	36	4
Bannu	8,449	1,241	3	232	16	17	10	3	...	21	8
Dera Ismail Khan	1,957	7,776	1	162	1	15	...	...	61	12	15

SUBSIDIARY TABLE II, PART (*b*—*Distribution by subsidiary languages per 10,000 of the population speaking each language as mother tongue*

Number per 10,000 of the population speaking

District and natural division	Pashto as mother tongue: As mother tongue only	With Lahnda as subsidiary	With Punjabi as subsidiary	With Urdu as subsidiary	With other languages as subsidiary	Total	Lahnda as mother tongue: As mother tongue only	With Pashto as subsidiary	With Punjabi as subsidiary	With Urdu as subsidiary	With other languages as subsidiary	Total	Punjabi as mother tongue: As mother tongue only	With Pashto as subsidiary	With Lahnda as subsidiary	With Urdu as subsidiary	With other languages as subsidiary	Total	Urdu as mother tongue: As mother tongue only	With Pashto as subsidiary	With Lahnda as subsidiary	With Punjabi as subsidiary	With other languages as subsidiary	Total	Other languages as mother tongue: As mother tongue only	With Pashto as subsidiary	With Lahnda as subsidiary	With Punjabi as subsidiary	With Urdu as subsidiary	With other languages as subsidiary	Total
1	2	3	4	5	6	7	8	9	10	11	12	13	14	15	16	17	18	19	20	21	22	23	24	25	26	27	28	29	30	31	32
N.-W.F.P. (Districts)	9,811	267	38	76	35	10,227	9,479	712	83	161	77	10,512	7,264	898	858	1,485	693	11,198	8,047	802	1,273	825	513	11,460	7,253	925	516	511	1,043	83	10,630
Hazara ...	8,771	3,355	12	89	38	12,265	9,754	180	19	90	8	10,051	8,170	149	935	1,727	188	11,169	9,520	184	463	60	63	10,290	9,105	52	657	35	325	34	10,208
Trans-Indus Districts	9,837	194	39	76	35	10,181	9,060	1,523	181	271	1,084	12,119	7,185	963	852	1,463	737	11,200	7,367	1,086	1,647	1,178	721	11,999	6,769	1,153	479	635	1,230	473	10,739
Peshawar ..	9,936	174	18	70	36	10,234	9,801	2,290	280	332	446	13,149	7,851	1,156	567	1,020	86	10,680	7,861	1,015	1,841	1,062	753	12,532	6,478	1,287	543	731	1,084	550	10,673
Kohat ...	9,672	237	58	103	46	10,109	7,242	3,341	422	604	135	11,744	5,486	595	1,694	2,351	606	10,732	6,999	1,064	1,024	1,504	460	11,051	6,757	1,254	642	303	1,723	395	11,074
Bannu ...	9,901	85	4	42	14	1,0046	6,555	3,391	87	239	89	10,361	6,762	455	538	2,492	530	10,777	6,892	1,416	655	930	529	10,422	8,022	361	178	190	1,660	196	10,607
Dera Ismail Khan ...	8,695	816	458	209	75	10,253	9,317	467	97	184	50	10,115	5,909	819	1,808	1,869	270	10,675	2,940	1,709	2,688	1,734	1,533	10,604	8,241	556	69	386	1,767	93	11,112

Note.—The excess over 10,000 in columns 7, 13, 19, 25 and 32 shows the number of persons speaking more than one subsidiary language.

CHAPTER XI

RELIGION.

GENERAL.

Reference to statistics.

282. The numerical strength of each religion returned is given in Imperial Table XVI. The figures are given separately for each district and for the trans-frontier posts in each political grouping. Subsidiary tables at the end of this chapter are arranged as follows :—

(*i*) General distribution of the population of the districts by religion, showing variations since 1881.
(*ii*) Distribution of the main religions by districts, with variations since 1881.
(*iii*) Number and variation of Christians by districts.
(*iv*) Comparison between distribution in urban and rural areas.
(*v*) Distribution by sects.

The religions which are of sufficient numerical importance to be considered in detail are Muslim, Hindu, Sikh and Christian. Buddhist, Parsis, Jews and others, reference to whom is made in a foot-note to Imperial Table XVI have been grouped together under the heading "Others."

Meaning and value of statistics.

283. The instructions given to enumerators were to enter in the appropriate column the religion which each person returns. The conditions in this Province are such that there should have been little difficulty in making the entries. Certainly there should have been no mistake in the classification of Muslims and Christians. A number of persons, 1,249 in all, returned religions which were not recognized as such and have been classified in the manner shown in Note 2 on the fly-leaf of Imperial Table XVI. Apart from this, complaints were received by the Census Superintendent that Sikh enumerators were wrongly recording Hindus as Sikhs, that Hindu enumerators were recording Sikhs as Hindus, that Shia Muslims were afraid to declare themselves, and so on. Wherever such complaints were received the persons concerned were given the opportunity to declare themselves on oath before a magistrate in case any correction was necessary. Complaints did not appear to be particularly well-founded, and both the complaints and the justification for them, if any, were occasioned by the impending distribution of seats in the Legislative Council on a basis of population. Another difficulty, which arises at every census, is the classification of the classes of indigenous population who either profess no religion or who have not yet given any definite name to the religious beliefs and practices prevalent among them. The most important of these are the Chuhras, also called Mehtars and Bhangis, the hereditary scavengers of the country. These number some 9,000 in all. Some of them have returned their religion as Hindu, and these, in addition to those mentioned at the beginning of the paragraph, have swollen the numbers beyond the figure which many high-class Hindus would admit. On the whole, however, the division of the population into Muslim, Hindu, Sikh and Christian is well enough understood for the purpose for which it is intended and the figures may be accepted as reasonably accurate.

Apart from the intrinsic interest of the figures for the different religions religion is used as a basis of classification for most of the statistics presented in the Imperial Tables. The value of this basis of classification has been impugned on the grounds that whatever homogeneity of race, tradition and custom may have been connoted by the terms Hindu, Muslim, Christian etc., in the past has ceased to exist to a sufficient degree to influence the statistics. It is argued that so far as customs of demological importance are concerned e.g. early marriage, seclusion of women, treatment of children, etc., the divisions, of real significance are not vertical sections of society by differences of religion, but horizontal divisions into strata differentiated from one another by social and economic conditions. This criticism is not justified in the North-West Frontier Province, at any rate so far as the indigenous population is concerned. Of the total enumerated population, 94 per cent. were born in the districts of the Province, and among these the classifications Muslim, Hindu, and Sikh refer to three homogeneous wholes. The interests and customs of the Muslims are the same through practically all the strata of society, the poorer folk living as dependents of the more fortunately placed, and imitating them as closely as they may. The Hindus and Sikhs are the money-lending, trading and clerkly classes. They bind themselves together by the artificial ties which they feel

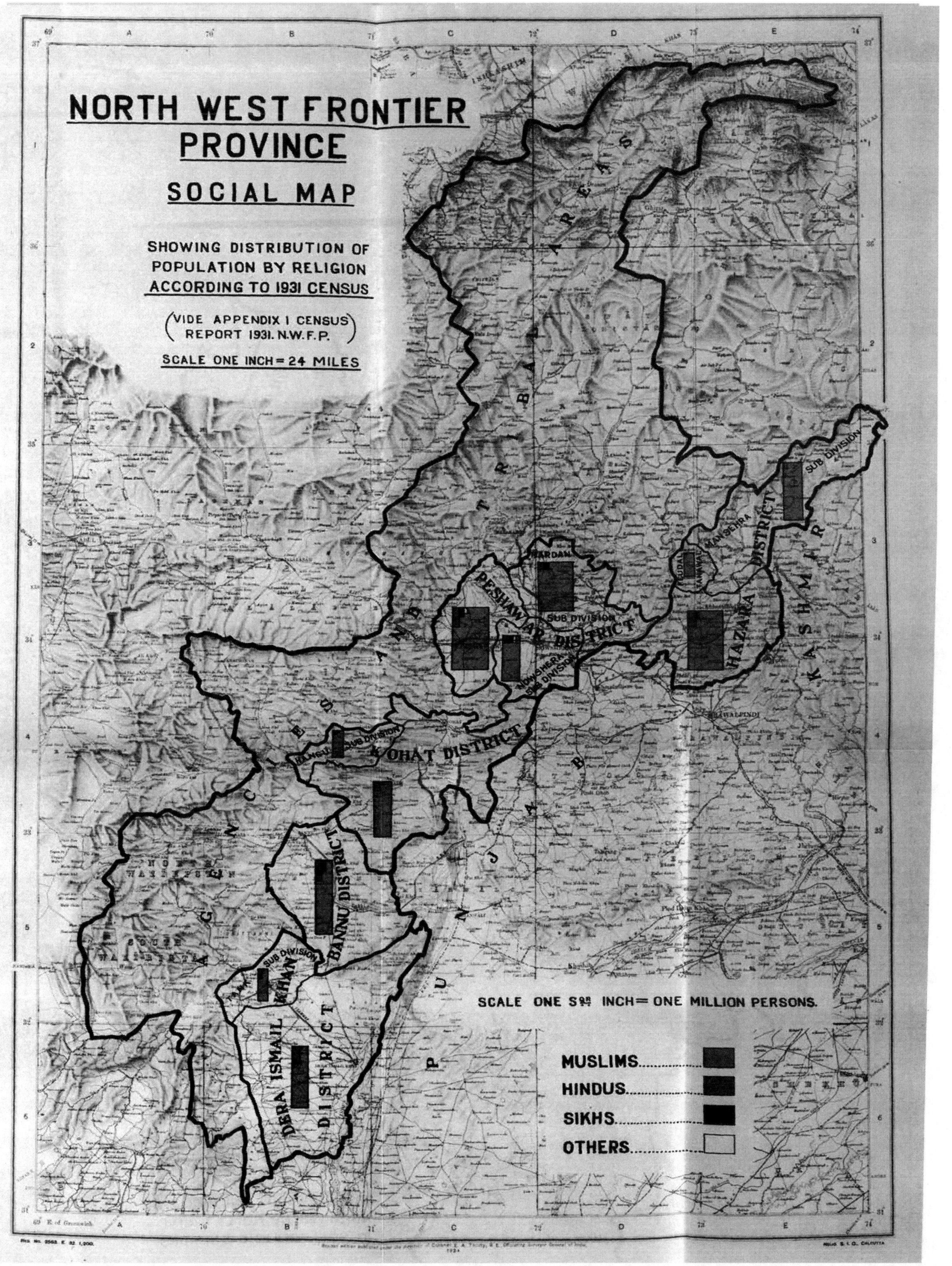

NORTH WEST FRONTIER PROVINCE
SOCIAL MAP
SHOWING DISTRIBUTION OF POPULATION BY RELIGION ACCORDING TO 1931 CENSUS
(VIDE APPENDIX I CENSUS REPORT 1931. N.W.F.P.)
SCALE ONE INCH = 24 MILES
TRIBAL AREAS
AGENCIES AND TRIBAL AREAS
PESHAWAR DISTRICT
MARDAN SUB DIVISION
NOWSHERA SUB DIVISION
HAZARA DISTRICT
MANSEHRA
SUB DIVISION
KOHAT DISTRICT
HANGU SUB DIVISION
BANNU DISTRICT
DERA ISMAIL KHAN DISTRICT
SUB DIVISION
KASHMIR
PUNJAB
RAWALPINDI
NORTH WAZIRISTAN
SOUTH WAZIRISTAN
SCALE ONE SQ. INCH = ONE MILLION PERSONS.
MUSLIMS
HINDUS
SIKHS
OTHERS

they require as a minority, and which are of even more force in their own minds than the ties of religion by which they are bound together in the minds of outsiders.

Numbers under discussion.

284. The number of the population enumerated in the districts and the trans-frontier posts was 2,471,527 persons, of whom 2,250,389 were Muslims, 156,628 were Hindus, 47,935 were Sikhs, and 16,499 were Christians. There were recorded in addition 62 Parsis, 11 Jews, and three Buddhists. The distribution of the population in trans-frontier posts is artificial, and the discussion for the remainder of the chapter will be confined to the figures for the districts.

Comparative strengths.

285. The table in the margin shows the general actual and comparative strengths of the different religions which make up the population of the districts. The proportion of the Muslims is overwhelming, while that of Hindus is greater than the combined total of Sikhs, Christians, Parsis, Jews and Buddhists. The proportions would be very little affected by any change in the classification of persons over whom there may at present be some doubt.

Religion	Actual number	Number per *mille* of the population
Muslim ...	2,227,303	918
Hindu ...	142,977	59
Sikh ...	42,510	17
Christian ...	12,213	5
Parsi ...	60	1 (Parsi, Jew, Buddhist together)
Jew ...	11	
Buddhist ...	3	

External characteristics.

286. The external characteristics of the various religions, other than Christianity, are discussed in paragraph 110 of the North-West Frontier Province Census Report of 1921. For further consideration of the tenets and characteristics both of religions and of sects, reference may be made to the relevant chapter of the Punjab Census Report of 1891, and the North-West Frontier Province Census Report of 1911. In the present census no reference will be made to these matters except in so far as they may have influenced the figures.

Distribution by districts (i) Muslims.

287. The distribution by districts is shown in the margin, and in graphic form in the map placed at the beginning of this chapter. Muslims form an overwhelming majority in every district in the Province. The reason for this of course, is that Islam is practically universal among the indigenous population. The proportion of Muslims is highest (95 per cent.) in Hazara, a mountainous and generally unproductive district into which outsiders are little attracted, and lowest in Dera Ismail Khan (86 per cent.) and Bannu (88 per cent.), where the numbers of Hindu traders are high. The number of Hindu immigrants is high in Peshawar district also, but the proportion of Muslims in the population is kept high by immigration from Afghanistan and neighbouring tribal territory and by the number of Muslim troops stationed in the district.

District	Muslim	Hindu	Sikh	Christian
Hazara ...	636,794	25,260	7,630	432
Peshawar ...	898,683	42,321	24,271	8,974
Kohat ...	218,445	13,393	3,249	1,186
Bannu ...	237,674	26,181	5,482	964
Dera Ismail Khan ...	235,707	35,822	1,878	657

(ii) Others.

288. The proportion of Hindus varies from 13 per cent in Dera Ismail Khan to a little under four per cent. in Hazara. The reasons are the opposite of those affecting the high proportion of Muslims. Sikhs contribute a little over two per cent. to the population in Peshawar and Bannu, and less than one per cent in Dera Ismail Khan. They are mostly immigrants, save in certain parts of Hazara where the proportion between the sexes is more or less equal. Christians are in their largest numbers in Peshawar, where they number 8,974, but this is chiefly due to the presence of large numbers of European troops in the district.

Historical reasons governing local distribution.

289. In considering the local distribution of the population by religion, it is as well to remember certain facts in the history of the Province which have affected it. These are summarised by Mr. Latimer in the Census Report of 1911 as follows :—The high-road along which the Muhammadan conquerors and rulers of India passed and repassed, lay through the north (the Khyber, Kurram and other routes) ; and it is probable that Islam never took so firm a

hold of the inhabitants of the southern districts as of the people to the north of them. In this connection it is interesting to note that the Muslims of the Derajat are less strict in their observance of the duties of religion, such as fasts, prayers and the like, than their northern neighbours. Through Hazara lay the road by which the emperors of Delhi went to and fro between their capital and their summer residence in Kashmir, and it was natural that Islam should thoroughly permeate the district. Similarly Kohat, from its situation with regard to the Kurram Valley, has been more influenced in the past by its Muhammadan neighbours to the west than have the districts to the south of it. There is no need to consider here the probable date at which the bulk of the Pathans living in the Province, or rather their ancestors, were converted to Islam. It is enough to notice that they had long been Muhammadan when they settled in their present homes, and that their fanaticism and intolerance, especially in the districts where they are strongest, rendered the Province no very inviting place for settlers of a different creed. If no fanaticism in its inhabitants acted as a bar to the settlement of Hindus in Hazara, the absence of any large trade centres was equally efficacious. The only other district in which the non-Pathan element in the population is in any way commensurate with that of Hazara is Dera Ismail Khan. The population here is mainly composed of tribes of Indian origin. Its conversion to Islam is of much later date ; fanaticism does not exist, and no particular dislike of the Hindu seems ever to have been found. The history of the district at the beginning of the nineteenth century also throws some light on the comparatively high proportion of non-Muslims found there. The Saddozai Nawabs, who ruled it, as well as part of Bannu, until overthrown by the Sikhs, commonly employed Hindus as generals and governors, and it was in the hands of a Hindu, Diwan Daulat Rai, that it was left by the Sikhs. This is in strong contrast with their action, for instance, in Kohat, where the Khattak chiefship of Teri, we are told, "was but little affected by the Sikh conquest," and the Teri chief "at annexation was continued in the management of the whole Teri Tahsil" The Sikhs at present form but a trifling element in the population any-where in the Province, and their comparatively high numbers in Peshawar are no doubt to be explained by the fact that the attractions of the district are greater than those of others from the greater importance of the markets contained in it.

MUSLIMS.

Muslims.

290. Certain points with regard to Muslims which have already been noticed may be summarised as follows :—

(*i*) Muslims constitute almost the whole of the indigenous population, and are mostly agriculturist by occupation.

(*ii*) Marriage is almost universal among them, but takes place both among males and among females at a later age than in the Hindu or Sikh communities. Remarriage of widows is quite common, and polygamy is practiced, but not to any great extent.

(*iii*) The Muslim community is the least advanced in literacy, (26 per *mille*) has the highest proportion of children to women of child-bearing age (209 : 100), and is the least migratory part of the population.

Variations.

291. The actual distribution of Muslims by districts has already been noticed in paragraph 287 above and is illustrated in the map placed at the beginning of the chapter. The statement in the margin shows the growth of the Muslim population in the districts during the last 50 years It will be noticed that there has been a steady increase, though in varying proportions, and that for every 100 Muslims in 1881 there are now 153. The increase is to be attributed to natural growth and to immigration rather than to conversion from other religions. The progressive decline in the rate of growth, setting aside the decade 1911-1921 which was affected by the influenza epidemic, may be easily explained. The high rate of increase

Census year		Number of Muslims per 10,000 of the population	Percentage increase since previous census
1881	...	9,212	...
1891	...	9,230	18
1901	...	9,221	10
1911	...	9,286	8
1921	...	9,162	1
1931	...	9,182	8
Variation 1881-1931	...	...	53

during the first decade was due to the influx of a large number of persons both from the east and from the west to settle in a fertile province where the resources were for the first time being developed, and where the establishment of a settled Government was beginning to offer peace and prosperity. As the amount of new land available for development decreased, and as Government service began to expand towards its fullest extent, the stream of immigration began to slacken and the increase became confined to the natural increase of a virile population.

Variations in proportion.

292. The table in the margin of the preceding paragraph shows also the proportion of Muslims to the total population at each census. The preponderance of Muslims was lowest at the census of 1921, and although it is now slightly above that figure it is still lower than at any other census. The sudden drop from 92·8 per cent. in 1911 to 91·6 in 1921 was due to an equal rise in the proportion of Hindus. The reason was, however, not to be found in the relative fecundity of the two communities, but in a great increase in the number of Hindu immigrants. Most of these were soldiers or followers who came to the Province in connection with the military concentration that was in process at the time of the census. The Muslim population had moreover suffered from the influenza epidemic of 1918 in a way that the immigrants had not. The recovery from 91·6 per cent. in 1921 to 91·8 per cent. in the present year has not been so great as the Census Superintendent of 1921 anticipated.

Rate of growth by districts.

293. The figures in the margin show the rate of increase or decrease among the Muslim population of each district since 1881. The total population of the districts has increased since that date by 54 per cent. and the Muslim population by 53 per cent. The Muslim population comprises the bulk of the population of the Province and is mainly dependent on agriculture. The conditions affecting its growth in each district are therefore for the most part the agricultural and climatic conditions of the district under consideration. The growth has been greatest in Hazara (65 per cent.), which in point of health conditions and rainfall is the most favoured district in the Province. Next to Hazara is Peshawar, where there are now 161 Muslims for every 100 present in 1881. Peshawar has not only the largest proportion of cultivated area, but is by far the best irrigated part of the Province. Bannu comes next, a long way below Peshawar. A large portion of the Bannu Tahsil is extremely fertile with abundant canal water, but a portion is unirrigated and dependent on rainfall, as is the case with practically the whole of the Marwat tahsil. The agricultural and climatic conditions of Dera Ismail Khan are the worst in the Province, and the growth of the Muslim population there is consequently the slowest. Kohat has not too bad a climate, but agricultural conditions in the district are poor The percentage of cultivated and culturable area to total area is the smallest in the Province, and the irrigated area is extremely small. The district is also liable to periodical droughts.

Rate of growth among Muslims by districts

District	Variation per cent.					
	1881-91	1891-01	1901-11	1911-21	1921-31	1881-31
N.-W. F. P. (Districts) ...	+18	+10	+8	+1	+8	+53
Hazara ...	+27	+9	+7	+3	+8	+65
Trans-Indus Districts	+15	+10	+9	...	+8	+49
Peshawar ...	+18	+11	+10	+4	+7	+61
Kohat ...	+11	+11	+5	−5	+11	+34
Bannu ...	+12	+9	+11	−3	+8	+44
Dera Ismail Khan ...	+12	+8	+5	−3	+8	+33

Sects.

294. The sects for which statistics have been collected among Muslims are Sunni, Shia, Ahmadi, Ahl-i-Hadis and Ismaili. The figures for each are shown in the margin. The origin of sects in the Islamic Religion is related as follows in the Punjab Census Report of 1921. " The birth of sects in Islam dates back to the death of the holy Prophet, when the dispute on the question of his successorship gave rise to strong difference of opinion among the followers of Islam. Abu Bakar was

Sect	Males	Females
Sunni ...	1,193,757	1,014,660
Shiah ...	20,326	15,135
Ahmadi ...	2,468	1,256
Ahl-i-Hadis ...	1,543	1,013
Ismaili ...	123	79

the first Caliph, then Umar, then Usman, and Ali was the fourth. But there was a section of Musalmans who opined that Ali was the only rightful successor to the Prophet. Thus two divisions sprang up among Musalmans holding divergent views on this point. Those who sided with Ali were styled Shias and the rest Sunnis. There have been four great Jurists in Islam on the Sunni side—Abu Hanifah, Shafi, Malak, and Ahmad Hanbal. Every Muslim has a perfect right to follow any one of them or to make his own judgement on the things concerned in the light of the traditions of the Prophet. Those who are guided by the traditions of the Prophet are called Traditionalists or Ahl-i-Hadis, and the schools of those which accept the teaching of praticular Jurists are named after them. Again every century in Islam saw men of great piety and learning, who gathered roun· themselves groups of pupils and admirers. These admirers were sometimes named after these Muslim Saints, such as Qadris, Chishtis, Naqshbandis, Soharwardis, and Ahmadis. These great divines enriched Islamic literature with their learned expositions of Islam, but never preached anything inconsistent with the fundamental tenets of Islam It follows that the so-called sect of Islam are not sects in the received sense of the word, and the basic structure of the Faith, notwithstanding all minor divergences, remains unshaken."

The vast majority of Muslims in the Province are Sunnis. If the foregoing explanation is accepted, it is hardly correct to refer to them as a sect. Shias, or the followers of Ali, have the next largest numbers. Among the sects found in smaller numbers the meaning of the names Ahmadis and Ahl-i-Hadis has already been indicated, and Ismailis are persons who accept Ismail and his children as successor to Jafir in the Shiah Imamate. A fuller description of the variation be.ween these sects is to be found in the relevant paragraphs of the Census Report of 1921.

Variation among Shias

295. There is a surprising variation in the number of Shias, who in 1921 were enumerated as 80,200 and in 1931 as only 35,461. Even this variation, however, is not so large as the variation for the previous decade, shown in the margin. The variation is usually explained by the difficulty of obtaining correct returns. On the one hand Mr. Latimer,, Census Superintendent 1911, writes as follows:—

Variations in the number of Shias

Districts	191	1921	1931
Districts ...	2,2825	76,673	33,039
Hazara ...	330	376	827
Peshawar ...	3,577	6,975	5,393
Kohat ...	10,576	40,248	13,556
Bannu ...	415	1,723	196
Dera Ismail Khan	7,927	27,351	13,067

"In view of the fact that Shias are allowed by their religious tenets to deny their sect in order to avoid persecution, it is interesting to notice that I am informed by one of the senior members of the community that the Shias recorded in Peshawar are largely in excess of the actual numbers. It is suggested to me (I give the explanation for what it is worth) that the exaggeration is due to the enmity of Sunni enumerators, who, if they had a grudge against any one residing in the block with which they had to deal would be likely to record him as a Shia by sect."

On the other hand Rai Bahadur Lehna Singh, Census Superintendent in 1921, writes:—

"These remarks were intended to suggest an explanation of an increase of 39 per cent. in 20 years. How far they apply to the present case which involves an advance of 95 per cent. in ten years, I cannot say. It is suggested to me that the figure for 1911 was not an exaggeration but an under-statement of the Shia population in Peshawar. Almost all the enumerators belonged to the dominant sect and were therefore interested in showing the number of the rival sect as low as possible, but as this tendency has gradually weakened, the number of Shias returned at the present Census is nearer the fact than the figures for the previous Censuses. The Shias are allowed and even encouraged by their religious teachers to conceal their persuasion, when its exposure would be inconvenient, and perhaps a more plausible explanation of the enormous increase in the number of Shias recorded at the last as well as the present census may be found in the abomination in which they are held by the Sunnis. It is said that in old days a man hardly dared admit that he was a Shia, and in order to avoid trouble and even persecution at the hands of the Sunnis, he not unoften concealed his religious convictions. Prejudices, and especially religious prejudices, die hard, but with the advent of British Government, these prejudices have been slowly but surely dying out and the hesitation of the weaker sect in avowing publicly his religious opinions is gradually wearing away"

Whatever the respective value of these two explanations, the figures are now back to something like a normal increase from the figures of 1911. In the face of these enormous variations it is not possible to attach any exact value to the figures whatever.

296. The only districts in which there are a sufficient number of Shias to call for special comment are Peshawar, Kohat and Dera Ismail Khan. The largest contribution to the Shia population is made by Kohat, where large numbers of the Bangash tribe return themselves as Shias. The totals returned in 1881, 1891 and 1911 were almost identical, although the number of Sunnis was steadily increasing. In 1921 the number of Shias suddenly jumped from 10,591 to 40,248, but has now receded to 13,556. The sudden increase in 1921 was partly explained by an influx of Shias from tribal territory, but there was no doubt that for some reason or other large numbers who had been returned as Sunni in previous enumerations, appeared as Shias in that year. The present figure is so consistent with those of 1881, 1891 and 1911 that it seems reasonable to accept it as fairly accurate. **By districts.**

In Peshawar also the figures show no startling variations and are probably correct. In Dera Ismail Khan they have suddenly shrunk to less than half, but the numbers are still almost double those recorded in 1911. Similar variations have however been noticed ever since 1881, the successive totals being 11,273 in 1881, 21,723 in 1891, as low as 2,376 in 1901, and 7,927 in 1911. An officer experienced in the district gave his opinion in 1921, that the figure of 27,351 was probably correct saying that up till that date the Shias of the district had hesitated to avow their sect. If this is so, then the hesitation would appear to have overtaken them again. The tribes which contribute to the total are Jat, Sayad, Baloch Musalli, Mirzai Ghilzai and Rangrez.

297. Of the 35,461 Shias enumerated in the Province, 2,422 were enumerated in trans-frontier posts. The major portion of them belonged to the posts in the Kurram, where the Shias are the dominant sect. The Shia tribes in the Kurram Valley are collectively known as "Turizuna", and they are the Turis, Saids, Shia Bangashes, Shia Chamkanis, Bada Khels, Jalandharis and Sargha Khels. In number the Turizuna tribes hold a strong preponderance of numerical power in the Kurram where they are estimated to exceed 60 per cent. of the population, while in possession they hold over 70 per cent. of the cultivated area. The Saids and Orakzai Pathans of Tirah are for the most part Shias. In other agencies and tribal areas the number of Shias is not appreciable. It is said that the Shias of Kohat, Kurram and Tirah are really followers of a sect known as Roshania, which arose among the Pathans about the middle of the 16th century. The Shias of the Pathan frontier will not kill or eat hares, some say because Ali kept hares, and others because they menstruate monthly, a human characteristic. **Trans-border areas.**

298. The Ahmadi sect, founded in the last century by Mirza Ghulam Ahmad of Qadian in the Punjab, made extremely rapid progress in the Province from 1911 to 1921, but has increased only slowly during the last decade. The total enumerated in the districts was 148 in 1911 and 3,469 in 1921, and is now 3,706. The number has increased from 1,633 to 3,384 in Peshawar during the last decade, but has decreased in all other districts. Wahabis, or Ahl-i-Hadis are found almost exclusively in Hazara, where they number 2,415 out of a total of 2,580. The figures are almost identical with figures of 1901; those for 1911 and 1921, which showed total of 134 and 923 respectively, must be disregarded. There are Wahabi colonies across the border on the Indus and at various places beyond Buner. Ismaili now number only 200. A brief account of each of these sects may be found in paragraphs 124 to 129 of the North-West Frontier Province Census Report of 1921. **Ahmadis and other sects.**

HINDUS.

299. The question 'what is a Hindu?' has never been satisfactorily answered nor it is intended to attempt to find the answer in the present report. For the purposes of this Census, all persons who have returned themselves as Hindus have been so entered, and in addition the numbers have been swollen, as already noted, by the inclusion of certain others whom it has been the custom to include in the past. One difficulty which has been experienced in the past, the difficulty of distinguishing Hindus from Sikhs in the case of those who prefer to regard Sikhism as a sect of Hinduism, has been consider- **Hindus.**

ably reduced on this occasion by the activities of persons interested in showing the Sikh total as high as the facts will possibly permit for political purposes. Whatever may be the true religious criterion of a Hindu, the meaning for census purposes is well enough understood and there need be little hesitation in accepting the statistics.

Distribution by districts.

300. The number of Hindus enumerated in each district is shown in the margin. The total is only 59 per *mille* of the total population of the districts. The importance of the community however, does not depend on its numbers, but on its trade, education and wealth, which are out of all proportion to its numerical strength. Although the total strength of Hindus represents only 5·9 per cent. of the population, yet among the literate population of the districts the proportion of Hindus is as high as 35 per cent. At the census of 1921 there were actually more Hindus than Muslims who were literate, although in total strength the Muslims outnumbered the Hindus by 15 to 1.

Districts	Number of Hindus
All districts ...	142,977
Hazara ...	25,260
Peshawar ...	42,321
Kohat ...	13,393
Bannu ...	26,181
Dera Ismail Khan ...	35,822

Characteristics.

301. The Hindu population, it may be remembered, is largely immigrant or descended from persons who have recently migrated to the Province. The Hindus of the Province are traders or professional men by occupation rather than agriculturists, are concentrated in urban rather in rural areas, and are city-dwellers by habit and inclination. Among the Muslim population of the districts only 11 per cent. are found dwelling in urban areas, while among Hindus 65 per cent. live in towns and cantonments and only 35 per cent. in the country. The Hindus marry at an earlier age than the Muslims, though not at so early an age as elsewhere in India, and are less inclined towards widow re-marriage, though more so than Hindus in other parts of India. Marriage is universal among them as a religious obligation. By virtue of their occupations they show a higher percentage of literacy than Muslims.

Proportion by districts.

302. The proportion of Hindus in each district increases from north to south of the Province. The proportion to 10,000 of the population is 377 in Hazara, 435 in Peshawar, 567 in Kohat, 968 in Bannu, and 1,307 in Dera Ismail Khan. The proportion per 10,000 of the urban population is 2,450 and of the rural population of the districts 244.

Variation.

303. The number of Hindus to every 10,000 of the population is noted in the margin, for the last six censuses, with the rate of variation for each decade. In 1881, the proportion of Hindus to every 10,000 in population was 708 and it fell to 638 by 1891, although their number advanced by six per cent. during the same interval. This was due to the far more rapid growth shown by the other communities of the Province. During the first decade the Muslims increased by 18 per cent., Sikhs by 139 and Christians by 15 per cent., the rate of growth for the total population being the same as for Muslims who constitute the bulk of the people. The Hindus showed an improvement of eight per cent. in numbers in 1901, but the rate of growth among the rival communities was greater, which accounts for a further deterioration in their proportion to the total population. The Muslims advanced by 10 per cent., which was also the rate of growth for the total population, and consequently the proportion of Hindus to every 10,000 of the total population fell from 638 in 1891 to 629 in 1901. The next decade 1901—1911 was an unfortunate one for the Hindus. Although the total population of the Province improved by seven per cent., the Hindus showed a decrease of seven per cent., which reduced their proportion to every 10,000 in population to 546 in 1911. In the last census, the number of the Hindus rose suddenly by 52 per cent. and as Muslims showed an improvement of one and the Sikhs a deterioration of eight per cent., the proportion of the Hindus to the total population rose to the highest figure yet recorded during the last 30 years. In 1911, an extraordinary rise in the number of Sikhs (19 per cent.) was accompanied by a

Censuses	Proportion in 10,000 of total population	Rate of variation per cent. in Hindu population
1881 ...	708	...
1891 ...	638	+6
1901 ...	629	+8
1911 ...	546	−7
1921 ...	666	+25
1931 ...	590	−5
1881—1931 ...	...	+28

marked decrease in the number of Hindus (7 per cent.). At the last census, the reverse was the case. The Hindus advanced by 25 and Sikhs declined by 8 per cent. That the figures for Hindus and Sikhs are closely interconnected, is indicated by a reference to the statistics of these two Indian religions at the censuses of 1901 and 1911. There can be but little doubt that a good many persons recorded as Hindus in 1901, were returned as Sikh in 1911. This was because in Censuses previous to 1911 the term Sikhs was restricted to only a portion of Sikhs. Kesdharies (who wear the Kes and observe certain other rules of conduct) only had been returned as Sikhs and the other section of Sikhs called Sehjdharies (who do not wear Kes and do not observe other rules of conduct enjoined by the last Sikh Guru) had been recorded as Hindus. This arbitrary restriction was removed in 1911 and every person was allowed to call himself the follower of any religion he liked. Religion being a matter of profession, it appeared to be hardly within the competence of enumerators to put down a person as belonging to a religion different to that he alleged to profess. This change in the definition of the term "Sikhs" swelled the number of Sikhs a good deal at the expense of Hindus in 1911, but this was not the only cause of the extraordinary decrease in the number of Hindus in that year. The date of the Hindu festival of Holi coincided with Barawafat, the Muslim day of mourning, in 1910, which led to a very serious riot between the Hindus and Muslims of the Peshawar City resulting in a considerable loss of life. There was a wholesale plunder of Hindu houses and shops. In 1911 the same coincidence, coupled with the memory of the past year, created a panic among the Hindus who left the Province in considerable numbers and had not returned to their homes when the census was taken. This temporary emigration of the Hindus from the Province and the difference in the classification of Sikhs accounted for the decrease of Hindu population in 1911. The figures show a further decrease of five per cent. again in the present decade. This may be attributed partly to propaganda to prevent any persons generally recognized as Sikhs from recording themselves as Hindus, and partly to reductions and changes in the various garrisons

Variation among females.

304. It is difficult to separate the permanent from the shifting population, but some indication at least of the growth of the permanent population may be obtained by considering number of females found at each census. The figures for 1901, 1911 and 1921 are compared in the margin with those of the present year. The total Muslim population increased by eight per cent. in the decade 1901 — 1911, one per cent. between 1911 and 1921, eight per cent. in the last decade, and by 18 per cent. from 1901 to 1931. In the same thirty years the female Muslim population increased by 17 per cent. Unreliable though this comparison undoubtedly is it does at least suggest that the domiciled Hindu population is increasing in much the same way as the Muslims.

Number of Hindu females enumerated in the districts

Year		Number	Variation per cent.
1901	...	50,478	...
1911	...	48,545	−4
1921	...	53,730	+19
1931	...	58,619	+10
Increase 1901 — 1931	...	...	+16

Variation in the Hindu population by districts and tahsils is too much affected by the movements of troops to repay detailed inquiry. It may be noted however that the figures for the past fifty years (1881 — 1931) show an increase of 56 per cent. in the Hindu population of Bannu and five per cent. in that of Peshawar ; Dera Ismail Khan and Kohat show 43 and 42 per cent., respectively, and Hazara 27. The Tahsils which contain large towns show always a comparatively high total of Hindus, while the figures for those which are purely agricultural are low. Dera Ismail Khan Tahsil recorded 39,311 Hindus in 1921 and 35,822 in 1931 ; the figures for Peshawar Tahsil were 25,414 and 23,538 in the same years. At the other end of the scale Phulra, in Hazara District, showed only 64 Hindus in 1921 and 49 in 1931

Sanatan Dharam.

305. As on previous occasions the largest numerical returns of sect are under the heading Sanatan Dharam. The figures for this and the only other sects returned by any considerable number of persons are shown in the margin. Other particulars may be found in Subsidiary Table V at the end of this chapter. "Sanatan Dharam", like the Sunni sect

Sect		Numbers
All sects	...	156,628
Sanatan Dharam	...	134,638
Arya Samaj ...	...	6,682
Vedic Dharam	...	1,144
Sweeper sects	...	3,356
Sect not returned	...	10,596

in the Muslim religion, claims to be the orthodox and true religion, and should therefore perhaps not be described by the word "sect" at all; the same however would apply to Vedic Dharam and to others, and the word "sect" must be retained for the purpose of this chapter.

Others.

306. Sanatan Dharam, as indicated above, is an expression used to cover almost all the orthodox forms of worship and belief. The difficulty of correct classification to sects is illustrated by the variations in the returns both for this sect and for others. In 1911 the Hindus of the Province, except those of the sweeper castes, were classified into 137 different sects; in 1921 the number was reduced to 6, in the present census it is 10. The figures for Sanatan Dharam rose from 52,901 in 1911 to 148,201 in 1921, and have now fallen again to 134,638. Vaishnavas numbered 1,258 in 1911 and 478 in 1921, but only two persons have returned this sect in the present Census. Similarly Nanakpanthis fell from 28,488 in 1911 to 799 in 1921 and again to 123 in 1931. These decreases do not in most cases mean any change in religious conviction but only the preference for a more comprehensive name which the majority of Hindus return.

Arya Samaj.

307. *The most important of the more modern religious movements* among Hindus is the Arya Samaj movement, a description of which may be found in paragraph 151 of the North-West Frontier Province Census Report of 1921. The sect appeared to be making headway at the last census, when the figures had risen from 4,148 in 1911 to 13,984. The present figures show a decline to less than half the figures for 1921.

Shamsi sect.

308. The Shamsis, a sect of Hindus, mostly goldsmiths, who follow the Imam of the Ismaili sect of Shias, have practically disappeared. The figures were 288 in 1911, but are now only 10.

Sweeper sects.

309. An account of the Sweeper sects is given in paragraph 155 of the 1921 Census Report, North-West Frontier Province Volume. The figures for 1921 and 1931 are compared in the margin. Little importance can be attached to them since they vary with the different regiments by whose followers they are mostly returned.

Sect.	1921	1931
Sweeper sects ...	4,878	3,356
Balmiki	1,420	2,584
Lalbegi	586	558
Mehtar	2,872	214

SIKHS.

Sikhs.

310. A considerable proportion of the Sikhs of the Province belong to the army or are in some other form of Government service. Those who are indigenous are for the most part traders following the same occupations as Hindus. The numbers in the Province are too small to justify any remarks on the community as a whole, but it may be remembered that those present show a higher proportion of literate persons than either of the other two main religions, and a higher proportion of males to females.

District	Actual number	Proportion per 10,000 of the population
All Districts ...	42,510	175
Hazara	7,630	114
Peshawar ...	24,271	249
Kohat	2,249	138
Bannu	5,482	203
Dera Ismail Khan ...	1,878	69

Variations.

311. The total number of persons returning themselves as Sikhs in the districts has increased from 28,040 in 1921 to 42,510 in the present enumeration. The explanation of the increase is not to be found in the movement of troops, since the number of Sikh troops in the Province has actually decreased. Rather it is to be found in more correct enumeration. In previous years many Sikhs have shown themselves as Hindus, preferring to regard Sikhism a

Number of Sikhs recorded in the districts		
Year	Males	Females
1921	18,994	9,146
1931	26,284	16,226
Increase... ...	7,390	7,080

a part of Hinduism. However correct this may have been from the religious point of view, it did not fulfil the intentions of the Census record. On the present occasion there has been considerable propaganda to induce all professing Sikhs to record themselves as such, in order that the numbers may appear as large as the facts will permit for the allotment of seats in the Legislative Council and on local bodies. A comparison of the figures by sexes for each of the last two enumerations shows that the increase is almost equally divided between males and females. Since immigrants almost invariably show a great excess of males over females, particularly when the immigrants concerned are for the most part soldiers and other Government servants, it is not unreasonable to suppose that the present increase is mainly due to a different manner of recording themselves on the part of the indigenous population.

The increase is apparent in all districts, but is greatest in Peshawar, where the total has risen from 15,326 (10,540 males and 4,786 females) in 1921 to 24,271 (15,211 males and 9,060 females) in the present year.

Sects.

312. It has been difficult enough in the past to separate Sikhs from Hindus, and still more difficult to separate one sect from another within the Sikh community. The writer of the North-West Frontier Province Volume of the 1921 Report, who is himself a Sikh, shows that the classification of sects in the case of Sikhs is not only uncertain and arbitrary, but practically worthless for census purposes. On the present occasion in particular there has been considerable propaganda to dissuade Sikhs from giving any return of sect. In these circumstances it will be of no value to discuss the distribution or variation among the small total numbers found in the Province. The figures of the present Census, for what they are worth, are to be found in Subsidiary Table V at the end of this chapter. It is sufficient here to note that out of the total of 47,935 Sikhs enumerated in the Province, no less than 32,403 have returned no sect, while 11,859, or more than 75 per cent. of the remainder, have returned themselves as Kes Dhari, a term which was noted in the records of the last census as having disappeared from the Province.

CHRISTIANS.

Christians.

313. The total strength of Christians as recorded at the current Census is 16,499, of whom 4,286 were enumerated in the trans-frontier posts and 12,213 in the districts. They form a very small minority in the Province, their proportion per 10,000 of the population in the districts being 56. They are found chiefly in Peshawar District (8,974), which accounts for nearly three-quarters of the total Christian population of the districts. Their distribution by districts is shown in the margin. Of the Christians enumerated in the districts 7,797 were Europeans, 150 Anglo-Indians, and 4,266 Indians, as against 8,390 Europeans, 200 Anglo-Indians and 2,020 Indian Christians ten years ago.

Distribution of Christians

All Districts	12,213
Hazara	432
Peshawar	8,974
Kohat	1,186
Bannu	964
Dera Ismail Khan	657

Variation and sect.

314. The Christian population of the districts has shown a steady increase since the first regular Census was taken in 1881, except in the decade 1891—1901 when the number declined by 6 per cent. The figure in 1881 was 4,725, and the present figure represents an increase of some 280 per cent. in fifty years. The figures in the margin show the distribution by race for the Province as a whole at the Census of 1921 and in the present Census. By far the largest proportion of the Christians in the Province are Europeans by race 11,737), and Anglican Communion by sect (6,881). Next to Anglican Communion the

Distribution of Christians by race (Districts and Trans-Frontier Posts)

Race	1921	1931	Variation	
			Actual	Per cent
European and allied races ...	10,473	11,737	+ 1264	+ 12
Anglo-Indians ...	200	161	−39	—19
Indians ...	2,353	4,601	+ 2248	+ 96
Total ...	13,026	16,499	+ 3473	+ 27

highest number is among Roman Catholics (1,578). The number of Indian Christians advanced from 877 in 1911 to 2,353 in 1921, and has now advanced again to 4,601. The advance is due almost entirely to the proselytizing activities of missionaries, most of whom belong to the Anglican Communion, and who devote their energies largely to educational and medical work. Their schools and hospitals are among the best in the Province, and one of the three Arts Colleges of the Province is run by them in Peshawar. The value of their humanitarian and educational work is immense, but the actual number of converts to Christianity remains negligible in proportion to the population of the Province.

OTHER RELIGIONS.

Other religion.

315. The figures for other religions are too small to justify separate discussion. The figures returned at the present enumeration are compared in the margin with those for 1911 and 1921. Almost all of those returned are in the Province for purposes of trade, but no conclusion can be drawn from the variations shown.

Religion		1911	1921	1931
Budhists	...	...	116	2
Parsis	...	49	20	62
Jains	...	4	3	...
Jews	...	14	...	11

SUBSIDIARY TABLE I—*General Distribution of the population (N.-W. F. P. Districts) by Religion*

Religion and locality	Actual number in 1931	Proportion per 10,000 of population						Variation per cent. increase (+, decrease (—)					
		1931	1921	1911	1901	1891	1881	1921—1931	1911—1921	1901—1911	1891—1901	1881—1891	1881—1931
1	2	3	4	5	6	7	8	9	10	11	12	13	14
Muslim ...	2,227,303	9,185	9,162	9,286	9,221	9,230	9,212	+8	+1	+8	+10	+18	+53
Hazara ...	636,794	9,503	9,497	9,502	9,515	9,461	9,477	+8	+3	+7	+9	+27	+65
Trans-Indus Districts	1,590,509	9,063	9,035	9,204	9,109	9,141	9,120	+8	...	+9	+10	+15	+49
Hindu ...	142,977	590	666	546	629	638	708	-5	+25	—7	+8	+6	+28
Hazara ...	25,260	377	418	404	411	464	487	—3	+7	+6	—4	+21	+27
Trans-Indus Districts	117,717	671	760	599	711	705	784	-5	+30	—9	+11	+3	+28
Sikh ...	42,510	175	125	138	125	103	50	+52	-8	+19	+34	+139	+439
Hazara ..	7,630	114	78	91	72	70	34	+57	—13	+36	+12	+161	+451
Trans-Indus Districts	34,880	199	142	156	146	116	56	+50	—7	+15	+39	+134	+433
Christian ...	12,213	50	47	33	25	29	30	+15	+61	+29	—5	+15	+158
Hazara ...	432	6	7	3	2	5	2	+7	+126	+76	—57	+162	+433
Trans-Indus Districts	11,781	67	63	41	34	38	39	+15	+59	+28	—3	+12	+158

SUBSIDIARY TABLE II—*Distribution by Districts of the main Religions*

District and natural division	Number per 10,000 of the population who are																	
	Muslim						Hindu						Sikh					
	1931	1921	1911	1901	1891	1881	1931	1921	1911	1901	1891	1881	1931	1921	1911	1901	1891	1881
1	2	3	4	5	6	7	8	9	10	11	12	13	14	15	16	17	18	19
N.-W. F. P. (Districts) ...	9,185	9,162	9,286	9,221	9,230	9,212	590	666	546	629	638	708	175	125	138	125	103	50
Hazara ...	9,503	9,497	9,502	9,515	9,461	9,477	377	418	404	411	464	487	114	78	91	72	70	34
Trans-Indus Districts ...	9,063	9,035	9,204	9,109	9,141	9,120	671	760	599	711	705	784	199	142	156	146	116	56
Peshawar ...	9,224	9,216	9,339	9,292	9,299	9,215	435	531	409	509	503	663	249	169	187	144	129	53
Kohat ..	9,245	9,223	9,379	9,167	9,237	9,321	567	602	487	666	531	541	138	125	123	153	220	124
Bannu ...	8,793	8,904	9,012	8,918	9,060	9,051	968	953	829	958	909	921	203	133	149	115	28	24
Dera Ismail Khan ...	8,600	8,372	8,785	8,651	8,642	8,723	1,307	1,508	1,117	1,166	1,296	1,233	69	73	85	173	58	38

SUBSIDIARY TABLE III—*Christians (number and variations)*

District and natural division	Actual number						Variation per cent.					
	1931	1921	1911	1901	1891	1881	1921—1931	1911—1921	1901—1911	1891—1901	1881—1891	1881—1931
1	2	3	4	5	6	7	8	9	10	11	12	13
N.-W. F. P. (Districts)	12,213	10,610	6,585	5,119	5,437	4,725	+15	+61	+29	—6	+15	+158
Hazara ...	432	403	178	101	236	90	+7	+126	+76	—57	+162	+380
Trans-Indus Districts ...	11,781	10,207	6,407	5,018	5,201	4,635	+15	+59	+28	—4	+12	+154
Peshawar ...	8,974	7,652	5,604	4,288	4,742	4,088	+17	+37	+31	—10	+16	+120
Kohat ...	1,186	1,074	222	317	197	212	+10	+384	-30	+61	—7	+459
Bannu ...	964	244	245	183	58	82	+295	...	+34	+216	—29	+1,076
Dera Ismail Khan ...	657	1,237	336	230	204	253	—47	+268	+46	+13	—19	+160

SUBSIDIARY TABLE IV—*Religions of urban and rural population*

Natural division	Number per 10,000 of urban population who are					Number per 10,000 of rural population who are				
	Muslim	Hindu	Sikh	Christian	Others	Muslim	Hindu	Sikh	Christian	Others
1	2	3	4	5	6	7	8	9	10	11
N.-W. F. P. (Districts) ...	6,634	2,412	657	295	2	9,668	244	84	4	...
Hazara ...	6,142	3,140	632	86	...	9,728	192	79	1	...
Trans-Indus Districts ...	6,694	2,323	660	321	2	9,641	268	86	5	...

SUBSIDIARY TABLE V—SECTS—*N.-W. F. P. (Districts and Trans-Frontier posts)*

Sect	Persons	Males	Females
1	2	3	4
Muslim ...	2,250,389	1,218,234	1,032,155
Ahl-i-Hadis ...	2,556	1,543	1,013
Ahmadi ...	3,724	2,468	1,256
Ismaili ...	202	123	79
Shiah ...	35,461	20,326	15,135
Sunni ...	2,208,417	1,193,757	1,014,660
Sect not returned ...	29	17	12
Hindu ...	156,628	97,552	59,076
Acharji ...	4	4	...
Arya Samaj ...	6,682	2,992	3,690
Jain ...	54	28	26
Nanak Panthi ...	123	109	14
Ram Dassi ...	2	2	...
Sanatan Dharam ...	134,638	84,720	49,918
Saj Dhari ...	17	9	8
Shamsi ...	10	4	6
Vaishnar ...	2	2	...
Vedak Dharam ...	1,144	869	275
Sect not returned ...	10,596	6,804	3,792
Sweeper sects—			
Balmiki ...	2,584	1,576	1,008
Lal Begi ...	558	302	256
Mehtar ...	214	131	83
Sikh ...	47.935	31,409	16,526
Akali ...	679	654	25
Baidi ...	6	5	1
Kes Dhari ...	11,859	8,690	3,169
Nanak Panthi ...	644	477	167
Sanatan Dharam ...	916	561	355
Saj Dhari ...	1,431	908	523
Sect not returned ...	32,400	20,114	12,286
Christian ...	16,499	13,212	3,287
Baptist ...	116	105	11
Church of England ...	6,881	5,722	1,159
Church of Scotland ...	19	10	9
Church of Ireland ...	2	2	...
Congregationalists ...	3	3	...
Lutheran ...	120	110	10
Methodist ...	23	23	...
Presbyterian ...	741	730	11
Protestant ...	416	271	145
Roman Catholic ...	1,578	1,214	364
Wesleyan ...	155	140	15
Sect not returned ...	6,445	4,882	1,563

CHAPTER XII

CASTE, TRIBE, RACE AND NATIONALITY

GENERAL.

316 Imperial Table XVII is devoted to the tabulation of caste, tribe, race or nationality, and gives the distribution by districts and in the trans frontier posts of all persons for whom these particulars were recorded. Reference to caste, etc., is also made in Imperial Tables VIII (Civil Condition), XI (Occupation) and XIV (Literacy). The subsidiary tables at the end of this chapter show (*i*) tribes and castes classified according to their traditional occupation, and (*ii*) variations since 1901. **Reference to statistics.**

317. The necessary particulars were to be entered in column 8 of the General Schedule. The instructions given to enumerators were as follows :— **Instructions to Enumerators.**

For Indians enter caste as ordinarily understood but for wide castes enter sub-caste also. The class titles—Brahman, Kashatriya, Vaisha and Sudra are usually insufficient by themselves. For other subjects of the Empire and for foreigners enter race, as "Anglo-Indian", "Canadian", "Goanese", "Turkish". For Indians such as some Christians who have neither caste nor tribe, enter "Indian".

318. Supervisors were further instructed that great care must be taken to avoid the entry in this column of the name of a sub-caste or of a word indicating locality or occupation; *bania*, for example, it was pointed out, was a functional term, not the name of a caste; words like Punjabi, Hindustani, Madrasi and Nepali were altogether too vague; Sikh is the name of a religion not a caste; any person who described himself as a Sikh and refused to recognize caste distinction was to be recorded as a Sikh in column 4 and a X was to be put in column 8; the same procedure was to be followed in the case of any other communities who objected to the caste system. A caste index was prepared for the guidance of Supervisors and other inspecting officers with the object of securing correct entries. **Instructions to Supervisors.**

319. In spite of these precautions the returns were not too satisfactory, and owing to the necessity for economy, sorting and tabulation were limited to those castes and Pathan tribes, tabulated in 1921, which were distinctly recorded in the schedules. All other and unspecified castes were left unsorted and have been grouped together under the head "Others" at the end of the table. The figure of those who are thus unspecified is 151,063 persons. This is more than six per cent. of the population and represents a considerable set back from the results obtained in 1921, when the total number of persons unclassified was only 13,744. There has also been an increased vagueness in the classification of Pathans by tribes, to which reference will be made later. There was no reluctance on the part of the public to give particulars of caste, except in the case of Sikhs. **Difficulty of tabulation.**

320. The following remarks which still remain true are quoted from the relevant paragraph of the North-West Frontier Province Census Report of 1921 :— **Caste system not rigid in Province.**

Musalmans.

"Caste system, as it is understood in the rest of India, hardly exists in this Province. The bulk of the population are Musalmans who recognise no caste restrictions. They freely interdine with each other. Although they generally marry within their own caste or tribe, but intermarriage between different groups or tribes is not uncommon, at least there is no insuperable social bar to unions between persons of different castes or tribes. So far as social distinctions are concerned, Musalmans may roughly be divided into two classes, the gentlemen and the menials. It will be interesting in this connection to refer to an article in an Urdu magazine, the "Sala-i-Am" for October 1912, from which the following extract, based on an authoritative Persian work on the subject by Mirza Qatil, may be made here with advantage :—

"He divides the Musalmans into Ashraf (the genteel) and Ajlaf (the lower orders) and goes on to say that in India the Ashraf class includes four groups, *viz.* Sheikh, Saiad, Moghal and Pathan, provided that they preserve their purity of blood, *i.e*, if a Moghal adopts the occupation of a Saqqa (water-carrier) for his livelihood, even though it may be out of extreme necessity, he will no longer belong to the Ashraf class and his fraternity with the Moghals will cease. He can thereafter marry only with the water-carrier. Similarly, if a Saiad or Sheikh contracts matrimonial alliance with some artizan group, he will have to assimilate himself with that group and be called by that name. The two essentials of caste, birth and occupation are thus recognised as the condition of preserving the purity of blood and the breach of one of these rules leads to degradation. Of the lower orders, the artizans are distinguished as Bazari which may be taken as an equivalent of business-man. The Attar (distiller, not of liquor) is reckoned the highest. The engravers, trouser-string weavers, book-sellers, cloth-merchants are included amongst the high class artizans. The Halwai (sweatmeat seller), Rangrez, Kanjar, Lohar, Kharadi (carpenter) come next. Khidmatgar (domestic servant), Farrash (servants who look after the carpetting), and Chobdars (baton-bearers) rank next. The barbers and surgeons are considered of equal rank and so are grooms, cooks and confectioners. The water-carrier, syce, Degsho (Mashalchi) and Kahar rank lower. The musicians (the dancing girl class), though not among the Ashraf (genteel) class, claim the rank owing to their association with the higher classes. The Dums (Mirasi) are not Sharif but call themselves Saiads and wish to acquire the title of Mir. Kanjars and Bhatiaras would pass as Pathans. The former are called Nawab Sahib and the latter assume the title of Salim Shahi or Shershahi and consequently suffix the title of Khan to their names. The Kambohs, Parachah Khojas, Boras are separate castes who intermarry within their own circle, and not outside. It is noted that the distinction of Hasb-Nasb (lineage) is more elaborate in the villages than in the cities, the inhabitants of the former thus gaining a superiority The editor notes that the occupations appertaining to the Ashraf class are changing and remarks that while, in the former case service of the State ranks high, commerce is now considered more attractive, because it is the means of accumulating wealth. The marks of equality of status among the castes are :—

"(1) Eating from one Dastar Khan, *i.e.*, table, (2) association on the same level, and (3) intermarriage."

Among the Pathans, especially trans-border Pathans, of the Province the criterion of tribal unity resides not in the law of marriage, but in the obligations of blood revenge. Members of the various divisions intermarry freely, and new divisions are constantly springing up. When applying the term tribe, sub-tribe, etc., to these people, it must be borne in mind that they do not imply any restrictions upon intermarriage.

Hindus and Sikhs.

Surrounded as they are by non-Hindu population, the Hindus and Sikhs in this Province are not a little influenced by the social freedom of their Musalman neighbours. Caste restrictions among them, already lax, have considerably weakened during the last decade. Education is a great disintegrating factor. Political, religious and economic influences have all more or less affected the rigidity of the caste institution. Reform movements like the Arya Samaj and Singh Sabha have done not a little to free the popular mind from caste prejudices. That the restrictions of caste are fast dying out is obvious enough. The present Hindus and Sikhs may be divided into three sections, *viz.* (1) the orthodox who follow the caste system, more or less strictly, (2) those who have ignored the restrictions of interdining, but still adhere rigidly to the limitations prescribed for marriage, and (3) those who have given up both. Although the orthodox portion of both these communities is still in a majority, their numerical strength is being reduced with every year that passes. A considerable proportion observe no restrictions of interdining, and although the number of those, who have freed themselves altogether from caste shackles, is small, the time spirit is with them and they are increasing slowly but surely. A small number of Aryas and as many as 54 per cent. of the total population of Sikhs have refused to name their caste. There is a strong tendency to widen the endogamous groups and narrow down the exogamous circle. Endogamous groups of the same main caste, like Utradhis and Dakhnas among Aroras, are beginning to intermarry. In the matters of breaking down caste shackles Sikhs are far ahead of their Hindu brethren, and the Anand Marriage Act passed for their benefit, has facilitated intermarriage between groups which had hitherto been endogamous."

Certain societies are at work endeavouring to encourage inter-caste marriages, but these have hitherto made little progress.

Division by tribes.

321. In these circumstances it might be doubted whether statistics of caste are worth collecting in this Province. It must be remembered however that column 8 of the general schedule, and the tables compiled therefrom, refer not only to caste but also to tribe, race and nationality. Since the Hindus and Sikhs, to whom the particulars of caste are specially intended to refer, form together only eight per cent. of the population, while the Muslims, among whom tribe and race are matters of pride and importance, form 92 per cent., the table is undoubtedly worth continuing. The importance of the record of the distri-

bution of Pathans is in fact so strongly recognized that a special table has been prepared under the orders of the Local Government to show the division of Pathans by tribes in each tahsil of the Province.

CLASSIFICATION OF CASTES.

Castes classified by hereditary occupation.

Actual figures (000's omitted)

Agriculture—	
Land holders	1,603
Cultivators	42
Cultivators and cattle rearers	122
Fishing and hunting—	
Fishermen and boatmen, etc.	8
Industry—	
Barbers	27
Washermen	12
Weavers and carders	65
Dyers	6
Tailors	2
Carpenters	45
Blacksmiths	29
Potters	23
Goldsmiths and Silversmiths	10
Confectioners, etc.	9
Oil pressers	7
Bucklers	12
Leather workers	30
Scavengers—	
Sweepers	9
Trade—	
Traders and pedlars	130
Professions—	
Priests and devotees	99
Singers and dancers	11

322. Classification by social precedence has been abandoned since the Census of 1911 on account of the bitterness of feeling which it is apt to engender. A classification by traditional occupation has accordingly been made in Subsidiary Table No. I at the end of this chapter. Even this cannot be accepted as authoritative, since the occupation of persons in certain castes is continually changing, and in many cases only one of several professions which have been followed by members of a caste for a considerable time, has had to be taken as the traditional occupation. Certain of the more important totals are reproduced in the margin.

Agricultural castes.

323. The Province being mainly agricultural, the castes connected with land are naturally the most numerous. In the present enumeration they represent 76 per cent. of the total population, an increase of four per cent. over the figures for 1921. The bulk of those thus recorded are land-holders who own as well as cultivate land. The tribes included in this category are Pathan, Awan, Baluch, Dhund, Gakhar, Jat, Karal, Mishwani, Moghal, Qureshi, Rajput, Sarara, Swathi, Tanaoli and Turk. Members of all these tribes regard themselves as land-holders by birth, even though they may be employed in military service or some similar occupation. The majority of them do in actual fact own land, and not only own it but cultivate it with their own hands. In addition to those already mentioned Sayads are for the most part land-holders and were shown as such in the 1911 Report, but they are by tradition a priestly caste and have been shown as such both in the present report and in that of 1921. Similarly Brahmans in Hazara have for generations owned and cultivated land, but they too have been shown as a priestly caste in Subsidiary Table No. I.

Cultivators. Cultivators and cattle rearers.

The castes falling under the head cultivators are Arains, Baghbans and Maliars. Cultivation is the traditional occupation of each of these tribes, they generally grow vegetables and fruits and raise superior crops like sugarcane, cotton, etc. Allied to cultivators is the important tribe of Gujars. Although pastoral by origin, they have for generations also cultivated land, but cattle-rearing forms an important part of their means of livelihood, even now.

Fishermen.

Fishing is the traditional occupation of Jhinwars as well as Mallahs. The later combine fishing with ferrying. Jhinwars are now employed largely in carrying and supplying water and have taken to cooking and various other pursuits, mainly domestic. The total strength of the castes that fall under this head is about 8,000 and they represent three per *mille* of the total population.

Barbers.

The Nais (barbers) are a caste by themselves. They not only do the shaving, but also act as local surgeons, bleed people, treat boils and ulcers, assist at marriages and other festive occasions, and serve as personal attendants. This is in accordance with their traditions, but they have now adopted various other occupations. Their proportion in the total population is 11 per *mille*.

Washermen.

Dhobis (washermen) are a functional caste. In Dera Ismail Khan they are known as Charohas. They number about five per *mille* of the total population and their total strength in the administered districts is about 12,000.

Weavers and carders and dyers. The bulk of the weavers are Jolahas (40,055) who are mostly Muslims, only 69 of them being Hindus. They form a caste by themselves and would seldom marry outside their class. The Penjara caste are carders by tradition. The Rangrez is the traditional dyer. The numerical strength of these two latter castes in the districts is not large, being 2,573 and 5,703 respectively.

Tailors. Darzi (tailor) is a functional caste which, owing to the respectability of the profession, is receiving large accretions, although the tendency of even those persons, who have been assimilated with the caste is to connect themselves with some higher caste.

Carpenters. The Tarkhans (carpenters) are an important caste representing 18 per *mille* of the total population. The bulk of them are Muslims in this Province, the number of Hindu and Sikh Tarkhans being only 50 (43 males and seven females) who are all immigrants. The Tarkhans are allied to Lohars (blacksmiths) and Raj (Masons), and in some places no distinction is made between the Lohar and Tarkhan or Tarkhan and Raj. The division between these functional castes is not therefore always reliable.

Potters. The Kumhars (potters) form an essential adjunct of the agricultural population. They make and supply earthen vessels, which form an important feature of Indian household economy, especially in villages. They are over 23,000 in number, which means a proportion of about nine per *mille* in the total population.

Blacksmiths. Next to Tarkhans, Lohars are numerically the most important functional caste in the Province. They number about 29,000 and there are 12 Lohars in every 1,000 of population.

Gold and silver smiths. The caste of Sonar practically monopolizes the work of gold and silver smiths.

Confectioners and grain-parchers. Bhatiaras and Machhis are the only two castes that fall under this head. Machhis, about 4,130 in number, are 4,124 Muslims and only six Hindus, and the bulk of Bhatiaras (4 998) also profess Islam, a very small proportion of the caste being Hindus and Sikhs. Both the castes are by tradition grain-parchers, but they are also confectioners and sell cooked food.

Oil-pressers. Telis are the traditional oil-pressers in Northern India. They also manufacture country soap, which is also considered to be their hereditary occupation. They are, therefore, sometimes called Sabansaz (soap makers).

Butchers. The Qassab, a Muslim functional caste, is the only one with the traditional occupation of butcher. Among the Hindus and Sikhs, the profession of Jhatkai (butchers) belong to Jhinwars.

Leather workers. The castes connected traditionally with work in leather are Mochis and Chamars, and between themselves they account for 12 per *mille* of the total population. They make shoes and also cure skins. The bulk of these castes in the Province are Muslims, with a sprinkling of Hindus.

Sweepers. The scavenging castes are Chuhras, Musalis and Kotanas. They really form but one caste Chuhra; but when they are converted to Islam they assume the names of Musalis and Kutanas. In Imperial Table XVII and other tables dealing with castes they have been lumped together under ther original name "Chuhra". It is the lowest of Indian castes. The majority of Chuhras in this Province are Hindus, but the proportion of Muslim Chuhras is also considerable. There are only 147 Sikh Chuhras and 723 who profess Christianity.

Traders and pedlars The traditional trading castes are about 130,000 in round numbers, i.e. 53 per *mille* of the population. Arora, Khatri and Bhatia are the principal Hindu trading castes, while Parachas, Sheikhs and Khojas are the traditional traders and pedlars among Muslims. All these castes, both Hindu and Muslim, practically monopolize the trade of the Province.

Priests and devotees. Brahmans among Hindus and Sayads among Muslims are the two priestly classes of the Province. Sayads are very largely agriculturists and so are the Brahmans of Hazara but by tradition they are both ministers of religion. Tradition also connects Qureshis more or less with priestly functions, but not to the same extent as Sayads. Brahmans and Sayads between themselves account or 40 per *mille* of the population.

Mirasis are the traditional musicians. They are also called Dums and those who earn livelihood by singing religious hymns to Sikh congregations are called Rababis. The strength of Mirasis in the administered districts is about 11,000 of whom only four are Hindus and the rest Muslims. Singrers and dancers.

The caste which cannot be classified under any of the above mentioned heads, and races which have no caste distinctions, contribute 69 per *mille* to the total population of the administered districts. Others.

DISTRIBUTION BY CASTE AND TRIBE.

324. The numerically strongest tribes or castes in the Province are Pathans, Awans, Gujars, Tanaolis, Sayads, Jats and Aroras. Of these by far the largest are the Pathans, whose distribution is shown in the statement in the margin. The Pathans are in fact the predominant tribe in the Province, making up almost the whole of the population of the transborder tract and about 37 per cent. of the population of the districts. Their chief occupation is agriculture, but of late their tradition of military and quasi-military service has become so strong that the present records show military service as well as agriculture as their traditional occupation. They are fewest in the Northern and Southern districts of the Province, and in their greatest strength in Peshawar, Kohat and Bannu. More than half their total number are to be found in Peshawar District, while in Bannu and Kohat they form 59 and 63 per cent. respectively of the population. Swathis and Pathans.

Distribution of Pathans in the districts

District	Total population	Pathan population
All districts ..	2,425,076	905,122
Hazara ...	670,117	54,544
Peshawar ...	974,321	473,738
Kohat ...	236 273	148,098
Bannu ...	270,301	159,737
Dera Ismail Khan ...	274,064	69,005

Some account of the numbers, history and characteristics of various of the Pathan tribes is to be found on pages 248 to 253 of the North West Frontier Province Volume of the Census Report of 1921. The strongest in number as in previous years, are the Khattaks (158,253) and the Yusafzais (133,737). The Khattaks are found mostly in Kohat and Peshawar, and the Yusafzais in Peshawar. Third strongest in point of numbers are the Marwats, who number 82,527 and are found almost exclusively in Bannu. Mohmands (63,139) are a transborder tribe settling in increasing numbers in Peshawar district; Muhammadzais are also an important tribe of Peshawar district.

It must be remembered that those figures refer only to persons enumerated in the districts and transfrontier posts. Many of the same tribes reside across the border in tribal territory; their estimated strengths are discussed in publications devoted to the subject, but are outside the scope of the present census. Even the figures obtained by enumeration are not reliable as to detail, since the entries in the schedules for almost a quarter of the Pathans enumerated were such that it was not possible to classify them according to tribe.

325. *As may be seen from the figures* in the margin the Pathan population of the districts, has increased during the last decade by some 2½ per cent. This compares unfavourably with the general increase of 7 7 per cent. in the total population. The variation by districts has little significance since it is largely affected by migration. The largeness of the increase in Dera Ismail Khan, for example, and the smallness of the increase in Bannu, are explained by the temporary migration of large numbers of the Bannu population to Dera Ismail Khan on account of drought; the figures in Dera Ismail Khan are also swollen by the presence of Wazirs and Mahsuds, who in 1921 were at war with Government. Increase in numbers.

Pathan population

District	1921	1931
Total ...	884,269	905,122
Hazara ...	55,802	54,544
Peshawar ...	510,087	473,738
Kohat ...	103,406	148,098
Bannu ...	158,233	159,737
Dera Ismail Khan ...	56,741	69,005

It may be noted also that 5,084 Pathans were enumerated in transfrontier posts in 1921, and 11,508 in 1931.

Awans.

Next to Pathans, the numerically strongest tribe are the Awans, whose distribution by districts is shown in margin, compared with the figures for 1921. The total increase amounts to approximately 12 per cent. and is distributed among all districts except Hazara. Awans are also an agricultural tribe and have many characteristics in common with Pathans. Besides being found in all districts of the Province, they are common also in Campbellpur, Rawalpindi, Multan and other districts of the Punjab.

Awan population			
District		1921	1931
All districts	...	251,135	280,995
Hazara	...	109,580	106,931
Peshawar	...	121,246	134,237
Kohat	...	10,553	19,891
Bannu	...	5,696	13,972
Dera Ismail Khan	...	4,260	5,964

Jats.

326. The distribution of Jats by districts is shown in the margin. Out of the total of 73,919 there are 906 Hindus and 2,226 Sikhs. These are to a large extent immigrants, including serving soldiers. The remainder are Muslims and live for the most part in Dera Ismail Khan District. The figures show a decrease of nearly 20,000 as compared with the figures for 1921. This is partly explained by an increase of 11,000 among Baluchis, since the Jats of the better class prefer to record themselves as Baluch. The decrease is also partly due to the disappearance of Jat troops who were serving in Dera Ismail Khan and Bannu at the time of the previous census.

Jat population				
District		Persons	Males	Females
All districts	...	73,919	41,969	31,950
Hazara	...	353	313	40
Peshawar	...	2,463	2,189	274
Kohat	...	719	638	81
Bannu	...	7,060	3,939	3,121
Dera Ismail Khan	...	63,324	34,890	28,434

Gujars.

327. Most of the Gujars in this Province are Muslim by religion, only 143 having returned their religion as Hindu or Sikh. In Hazara, which is their home in the Province and where they contribute 15 per cent. of the total population, they are all Muslim. They are at present a very backward race, being the least literate of all the important castes and also suffering most from the infirmities of leprosy, blindness and deaf-mutism. As noted in the relevant paragraphs of this report, both their backwardness in education and their liablity to infirmities are largely due to geographical conditions. The large increase in numbers is probably due to more correct enumeration as much as to any other cause; in the localities in which Gujars live they are much mixed up with Swathis, although their social status is much inferior to that of the latter; in 1921 they showed a marked tendency to have themselves recorded as Swathis but this error seems to have been avoided on the present occasion.

Sayads.

328. The Sayads are the priestly class in the Muslim religion, and claim direct descent from the holy Prophet through the female line. Their numbers, as the figures in the margin show, have decreased from 89,730 to 81,972 in the last ten years. Although Sayads are by tradition the priestly caste, the majority of them are occupied as agriculturists. Priesthood among Muslims is not confined to Sayads, and in this their position differs from that of Brahmans in the Hindu religion. The decrease is probably due to more correct enumeration, since many persons like to claim the sanctity of the Sayad caste who have no real right thereto.

Sayad population			
District		1921	1931
All districts	...	89,730	81,972
Hazara	...	42,637	27,629
Peshawar	...	21,939	25,373
Kohat	...	13,768	10,816
Bannu	...	6,533	11,808
Dera Ismail Khan	...	4,853	6,346

If the figures for the present year are compared with those for 1901 (72,000) and 1911 (75,000), a steady and natural increase is apparent.

329. *The most numerous Hindu caste in the Province are the Aroras. Like other leading Hindu castes they make their living mostly from trade, but* are also finding their way to an increasing extent into Government Service. The total number recorded in the Districts is practically the same as it was 10 years ago, a little over sixty thousand. **Aroras.**

330. Swathis and Tanaolis, both Muslims by religion, are practically confined to Hazara, where both are agricultural tribes. The decrease in the number of enumerated Swathis, as has been noticed, is probably due to the more correct enumeration of Gujars. **Tanaolis.**

Population of Swathis and Tanaolis			
Districts		1921	1931
Swathis—			
All districts	...	56,904	46,556
Hazara	...	56,217	44,511
Tanaolis—			
All districts	...	69,502	86,003
Hazara	...	68,440	83,417

331. The variations in number among the tribes, castes and races already :onsidered, as well as in certain others, from 1901 to the present census, are set)ut in Subsidiary Table No. II at the end of this chapter. The largest)roportionate variation is in the number of Europeans and Anglo-Indians, who ıave increased by 72·2 per cent. since 1901. Their distribution depends mainly)n the composition of the garrisons serving in the various districts, and can not)e utilised for the drawing of any conclusions. Other large variations are among Dhunds (+55·7 per cent.), Baluchis (+55·1 per cent), Swathis (+30·3 per :ent.), Tanaolis (+39·1 per cent) and Chuhras (—60·9 per cent.) During his interval the total population of the districts has increased by 7·7 per cent. The increase among Dhunds is probably to be explained by more correct :numeration, Dhunds having previously managed to get themselves recorded in ;ome tribe of higher social status. The large increase among Baluchis may)erhaps be due to confusion between them and Jats. The decrease among Chuhras is almost certainly due to inexact enumeration. It has already been ıoticed (vide paragraph 319) that there has been a very heavy increase among :he number of persons whom it was not possible to classify. Moreover the :ables of 1921, although it is clearly stated in the body of the report that Chuhras ıre mainly Hindus, have shown 16,689 Chuhras as Muslims out of a total of 21,338 enumerated in settled districts. From this it appears probable that other Muslim castes have either been confused with Chuhras or else wrongly added nto the total. **Variations.**

332. The castes and tribes confined to certain localities are shown in the :able below with the locality in which they are mainly found :— **Castes and tribes localised.**

Caste		Locality	Caste		Locality
Arain	...	Dera Ismail Khan ...	Karal	...	Hazara.
Awan	...	Peshawar, Kohat and Hazara...	Kashmiri	...	Hazara and Peshawar.
Baluch	...	Dera Ismail Khan ...	Machhi	...	Dera Ismail Khan.
Bhatia	...	Dera Ismail Khan and Bannu...	Maliar	...	Hazara and Kohat.
Brahman Sikh	...	Hazara and Peshawar ...	Mishwani	...	Hazara
Dhund	...	Hazara	Pathan Afridi	...	Peshawar and Kohat.
Gakkhar	...	Do.	„ Bangash	...	Kohat.
Gujar	...	Hazara and Peshawar ...	„ Bannuchi	...	Bannu.
Gurkha	...	Hazara	„ Bhittani	...	Dera Ismail Khan.
Jat	...	Dera Ismail Khan ...	„ Daudzai	...	Peshawar.

Caste	Locality	Caste	Locality
Pathan Dilazak ...	Hazara and Peshawar ...	Pathan Turi ...	Kohat.
„ Durrani ...	Peshawar ...	„ Ustrana ...	Dera Ismail Khan.
„ Gadun ...	Hazara ...	„ Wazir ...	Kohat, Bannu and Dera Ismail Khan.
„ Gandapur ...	Dera Ismail Khan ...	„ Utman Khel	Peshawar.
„ Ghilzai ...	Peshawar and Dera Ismail Khan ..	„ Yusafzai ...	Do.
„ Gigiani ..	Peshawar ...	„ Zadran ...	Bannu.
„ Khattak ...	Kohat and Peshawar ...	Sarara ...	Hazara.
„ Khalil ...	Peshawar ...	Swathi ...	Do.
„ Marwat ...	Bannu ...	Tanaoli ...	Do.
„ Mohmand ...	Peshawar ...	Turk ...	Do.
„ Mohmandzai	Do. ...		
„ Orakzai ...	Kohat.		
„ Tarin ...	Hazara.		

Reference to ethnographical glossary.

333. An Ethnographical glossary of the 49 castes and tribes considered in Imperial Table XVII is to be found on pages 241 to 255 of the North-West Frontier Province Census Report of 1921.

SUBSIDIARY TABLE I—*Tribes and castes classified according to their traditional occupations*

Group and tribe, caste, etc.	Strength (000's omitted)	Proportion per mille of population of Province
1	2	3
Agricultrists	1,879	760
(a) Land-holders	1,603	649
1. Awan	283	114
2. Baluch	37	15
3. Dhund	39	16
4. Gakhar	7	3
5. Jat	76	31
6. Karal	27	11
7. Mishwani	6	2
8. Moghal	17	7
9. Pathan	917	371
10. Qureshi	27	11
11. Rajput	19	8
12. Sarara	10	4
13. Swathi	47	19
14. Tanaoli	86	35
15. Turk	5	2
(b) Cultivators (including growers of special produce.	42	17
16. Arain	7	3
17. Baghban	28	11
18. Maliar	7	3
(c) Cultivators and cattle rearers.	122	49
19. Gujar	122	49
(d) Fishermen, boatmen and Palki bearers.	8	3
20. Jhinwar	1	...
21. Mallah	7	3
(e) Barbers	27	11
22. Nai	27	11
(f) Washermen	12	5
23. Dhobi	12	5
(g) Weavers and carders	65	26
24. Jolaha	40	16
25. Kashmiri	22	9
26. Penjara	3	1
Dyers	6	2
27. Rangrez	6	2
Tailors	2	1
28. Darzi	2	1
Group and tribe, caste, etc.	Strength (000's omitted)	Proportion per mille of populaton of Province
1	2	3
Carpenters	45	18
29. Tarkhan	45	18
Blacksmiths	29	12
30. Lohar	29	12
Potters	23	9
31. Kumhar	23	9
Gold and silver-smiths	10	4
32. Sonar	10	4
Confectioners and gram parchers.	9	4
33. Bhatiara	5	2
34. Machhi	4	2
Oil pressers	7	3
35. Teli	7	3
Butchers	12	5
36. Qassab	12	5
Leather workers	30	12
37. Chamar	3	1
38. Mochi	27	11
Scavengers	9	4
39. Chuhra	9	4
Traders and pedlars	130	53
40. Arora	61	25
41. Bhatia	7	3
42. Khatri	35	14
43. Khoja	5	2
44. Paracha with Banjara	8	3
45. Sheikh	14	6
Priests and devotees	99	40
46. Brahman	17	7
47. Sayad	82	33
Singers and dancers	11	4
48. Mirasi	11	4
Others	159	64
49. Gurkha	8	3
50. Others	151	61
Europeans and Anglo-Indians.	12	5
51. European British subject	12	5

SUBSIDIARY TABLE II—*Variation in caste and tribe since 1901 (British districts only)*

Caste, tribe or race	Persons (000's omitted)				Percentage of variation increase (+) decrease (—)			Net variation, per cent.
	1931	1921	1911	1901	1921—1931	1911—1921	1901—1911	1901—31
1	2	3	4	5	6	7	8	9
Arora ...	60	60	68	67	+0·3	—12·2	+2·6	—10·0
Awan ..	281	251	276	240	+11·9	—9·0	+14·8	+16·8
Baluch ..	37	26	26	24	+41·4	—0·7	+9·6	+55·1
Brahman ...	16	20	13	16	—17·6	+51·8	—17·3	+5·1
Chamar ..	3	5	5	5	—1·6	—37·0	+2·1	—36·7
Chuhra ...	8	21	19	22	—60·4	+13·6	—13·1	—60·9
Dhund ...	39	27	30	25	+43·1	—9·8	+20·7	+55·7
Gujar ...	121	85	114	108	+41·9	—24·9	+5·3	+2·1
Jat ...	74	94	85	80	—21·0	+9·7	+6·8	—8·0
Jolaha ...	40	35	37	38	+14·3	—6·2	—2·2	+4·5
Khatri ...	34	42	35	32	—20·2	+21·8	+8·4	+4·7
Pathan ...	905	884	838	789	+2·4	+5·5	+6·2	+14·7
Sayad ...	82	90	75	72	—8·6	+19·8	+4·1	+13·8
Swathi ...	47	57	38	33	—18·2	+48·5	+14·6	+39·3
Tanaoli ...	86	70	64	62	+23·7	+8·6	+3·5	+39·1
Tarkhan ...	45	33	43	40	+34·7	—21·4	+6·3	+11·9
Europeans and Anglo-Indians.	8	9	6	5	—7·5	+50·1	+24·0	+72·2
Europeans British subject.	8	8	6	5	—7·3	+50·0	+23·5	+71·8

PART II

CORRIGENDA

PART II—TABLES

No. of page	No. of table	No. of column	Number of line	For	Read
iii	I	10	17	63,652	63,352
xi	IV (Fly-leaf)	...	1	Table I, etc.	Tables I, etc.
"	"	...	3	sa	
"	IV (Statement)	6	...	—1,831	—4,831
xii	IV	3	8	D.	Do.
"	"	5	Lakki	770	7,703
xvii	V	18 and 19	1 and 9	62, 32, 29 and 16 includes two Buddhist males.	...
xxxiv (Parsi)	VI	2	Age-Group 50—55	...	1
"	"	2	55—60	...	2
xxxvi (Muslim)	"	7	c—1	10,980	10,680
xliii (All religions)	"	13	50—60	1,325	1,225
xlvi	VIII	1	Serial No. 5	Chuhr	Chuhra
liii	X	15	Class-A	82,549	28,459
lvii	"	29	Group 63	4	64
lx	"	4	Group 83	508	5,083
lxv	"	25	Order 19	56	656
"	"	24	Group 108	596	4,596
"	"	26	"	...	2
lxvii	"	45	Group 98	706	726
lxxi	"	52	Group 114	2	132
lxxx	"	1	Under order No. 46.	...	167 and 168
"	"	7	Group 169	...	1
lxxxv	"	14	Group 194	...	3
xc	XI	10	Brahman	...	52
cxii (Jews)	XIII	9	Age-group 20 and over	...	5
cxvii	XV	17	Last line	...	1
cxx	XV, Part II	4	Naipali (Hazara District).	200	1,200
cxl	XVII	...	Heading	VII	XVII
cxliv	XIX	3	2	0444	6,444

TABLE I

Area, Houses and Population

1. The areas shown in this table are those recently communicated by the Survey of India. Those relating to the trans-frontier area, and to administrative divisions, adjoining tribal boundaries, are, however, only approximate. The differences between the areas shown in this table and those given in the corresponding table of 1921, are mainly due to the fact that Survey figures were not available at previous Censuses.

2. The following territorial transfers have occurred since the last Census :—

   (1) the transfer of 20 square miles, known as the "Malandri" tract, from Swat territory in the Malakand Agency to the Peshawar District,

   (2) two transfers of small areas of unpopulated hill land on the tribal border of the Kohat District.

3. The areas of Agencies and tribal areas are entered as communicated by the Survey of India, but, in some cases, owing to the fact that exact tribal boundaries are unknown, separate figures cannot be given.

4. The population shown for the five administered districts has been regularly enumerated. In the Agencies and tribal areas, only the population of British posts has been enumerated; but the table includes a rough estimate of the general population of the trans-frontier area, the figures for the estimated and enumerated population being shown separately.

5. The distribution of the population of the administered districts by Tahsils will be found in Provincial Tables I and II at the end of this Volume.

TABLE I

Area, Houses and Population

District, agency, etc.	Area in square miles	Towns	Villages	Occupied houses: Total	Occupied houses: In towns	Occupied houses: In villages
1	2	3	4	5	6	7
North West Frontier Province ...	36,356	26	2,830	486,876	73,790	413,086
Districts	13,518	26	2,830	486,875	73,790	413,086
1. Hazara ...	3,009	6	927	144,233	8,449	135,784
2. Peshawar	2,637	11	846	190,174	41,061	149,113
3. Kohat	2,703	2	281	44,151	5,321	38,830
4. Bannu	1,698	3	380	49,763	7,311	42,452
5. Dera Ismail Khan ...	3,471	4	396	58,555	11,648	46,907
Agencies and Tribal areas ...	22,838	...	...			Total ... Enumerated ... Estimated ...
Agencies.						
1. Malakand (Dir, Swat and Chitral) ...	11,383	...	...			Total ... Enumerated ... Estimated ...
2. Khyber	962	...	...			Total ... Enumerated ... Estimated ...
3. Kurram	739	...	...			Total ... Enumerated ... Estimated ...
4. North Waziristan ...	(a) 5,218 (4 and 5)	...	...			Total ... Enumerated ... Estimated ...
5. South Waziristan ...						Total ... Enumerated ... Estimated ...
Tribal area under the Political control of the Deputy Commissioner of—						
1. Hazara	(b)	...	...			Total ... Enumerated ... Estimated ...
2. Peshawar	(c) 2,299	...	...			Total ... Enumerated ... Estimated ...
3. Kohat	(d) 1,493	...	...			Total ... Enumerated ... Estimated ...
4. Bannu	(e)	...	...			Total ... Enumerated ... Estimated ...
5. Dera Ismail Khan ...	(f) 744	...	...			Total ... Enumerated ... Estimated ...

(a) Includes Bhittanni.

(b) No separate area given.

(c) Includes—

Buner, 1,444 square miles.

Mohmand territory, 855 square miles.

(d) Orakzai tribal area.

(e) Included in Waziristan, *vide* (a) above.

(f) Includes Shirani country, 577 square miles.

TABLE I

Area, Houses and Population

Population									
Persons			Males			Females			Serial No.
Total	Urban	Rural	Total	Urban	Rural	Total	Urban	Rural	
8	9	10	11	12	13	14	15	16	
4,684,364	**386,177**	**4,298,187**	**2,528,165**	**235,126**	**2,293,039**	**2,156,199**	**151,051**	**2,005,148**	
2,425,076	386,177	2,038,899	1,315,818	235,126	1,080,692	1,109,258	151,051	958,207	
670,117	41,985	628,132	358,193	25,520	332,673	311,924	16,465	295,459	1
974,321	216,423	757,898	538,146	133,499	404,647	436,175	82,924	353,251	2
236,273	34,350	201,923	126,210	21,774	104,436	110,063	12,576	97,487	3
270,301	38,242	232,059	145,163	23,420	121,743	125,138	14,822	110,316	4
274,064	55,177	218,887	148,106	30,913	117,193	125,958	24,264	101,694	5
2,259,288	...	2,259,288	1,212,347	...	1,212,347	1,046,941	...	1,046,941	
46,451	...	46,451	44,635	...	44,635	1,816	...	1,816	
2,212,837	...	2,212,837	1,167,712	...	1,167,712	1,045,125	...	1,045,125	
902,075	...	902,075	465,470	...	465,470	436,605	...	436,605	
3,390	...	3,390	2,928	...	2,928	462	...	462	1
898,685	...	898,685	462,542	...	462,542	436,143	...	436,143	
263,566	...	263,566	147,908	...	147,908	115,658	...	115,658	
16,516	...	16,516	16,452	...	16,452	64	...	64	2
247,050	...	247,050	131,456	...	131,456	115,594	...	115,594	
63,352	...	63,652	35,395	...	35,395	27,957	...	27,957	
4,832	...	4,832	3,682	...	3,682	1,150	...	1,150	3
58,520	...	58,520	31,713	...	31,713	26,807	...	26,807	
93,570	...	93,570	56,325	...	56,325	37,245	...	37,245	
13,282	...	13,282	13,154	...	13,154	128	...	128	4
80,288	...	80,288	43,171	...	43,171	37,117	...	37,117	
108,213	...	108,213	61,264	...	61,264	46,949	...	46,949	
6,713	...	6,713	6,711	...	6,711	2	...	2	5
101,500	...	101,500	54,553	...	54,553	46,947	...	46,947	
352,400	...	352,400	190,036	...	190,036	162,364	...	162,364	
...	...	...	...	...	...	...	...	...	1
352,400	...	352,400	190,036	...	190,036	162,364	...	162,364	
305,410	...	305,410	162,510	...	162,510	142,900	...	142,900	
...	...	...	...	...	...	...	...	...	2
305,410	...	305,410	162,510	..	162,510	142,900	...	142,900	
128,900	...	128,900	70,200	...	70,200	58,700	...	58,700	
...	...	...	...	...	...	...	...	...	3
128,900	...	128,900	70,200	...	70,200	58,700	...	58,700	
22,160	...	22,160	11,916	...	11,916	10,244	...	10,244	
...	...	...	...	...	...	...	...	...	4
22,160	...	22,160	11,916	...	11,916	10,244	...	10,244	
19,642	...	19,642	11,323	...	11,323	8,319	...	8,319	
1,718	...	1,718	1,708	...	1,708	10	...	10	5
17,924	...	17,924	9,615	...	9,615	8,309	...	8,309	

TABLE II

Variation in population since 1881

1. A few minor territorial changes have occurred during the last decade affecting the Peshawar and Kohat districts only. The transfer of the "Malandri" tract from Swat Territory to the Peshawar District has added to the latter a population of 1,020 persons, never previously censused. No adjustment on this account has been made in the figures for previous censuses. In the Kohat District two transfers of small areas of unpopulated hill land took place on the tribal border, which have no effect on the figures for population.

2. An estimate of the population of the trans-frontier areas was, for the first time, given in the 1911 Census. The figures given for the Malakand, North Waziristan and South Waziristan agencies in 1901 represent only the population of British posts. The figures for posts in the Khyber in that year are included in the population of Peshawar. The figures for the Kurram in 1901 show the population of the revenue paying portion of the agency only. Previous to 1901 no part of the trans-frontier population was estimated or enumerated with the exception of troops and followers in the Khyber Pass in 1881, who are included (*vide* footnote to table) in the population of the Peshawar District for that year.

3. The agencies, previously termed Tochi and Wano in the Census Reports of 1911 and 1921, are now known as North Waziristan and South Waziristan, respectively.

TABLE II

Variation in population since 1881

Serial No.	District, agency, etc.	Persons 1931	1921	1911	1901	1891	1881	Variation increase (+) Decrease (−) 1921-31	1911-21	1901-11	1891-1901
1	2	3	4	5	6	7	8	9	10	11	12
	N. W. F. Province ...	(a) 4,684,364	5,076,476	3,819,027	2,125,496	1,857,519	1,575,943	−392,112	+1,257,449	+1,693,531	+267,977
	Districts ...	(a) 2,425,076	2,251,340	2,196,933	2,041,534	1,857,519	1,575,943	+173,736	+54,407	+155,399	+184,015
1	Hazara ...	670,117	622,349	603,028	560,288	516,288	407,075	+47,768	+19,321	+42,740	+44,000
2	Peshawar ...	(a) 974,321	907,367	865,009	788,707	711,795	* 607,625	+66,954	+42,358	+76,302	+76,912
3	Kohat ...	236,273	214,123	† 222,690	217,865	195,148	174,762	+22,150	−8,567	+4.825	+22,717
4	Bannu ...	270,301	246,734	250,086	† 226,801	204,469	182,740	+23,567.	−3,352	+23,285	+22,332
5	Dera Ismail Khan ...	274,064	260,767	256,120	‡ 247,873	§ 229,819	203,741	+13,297	+4,647	+8,247	+18,054
	Agencies and Tribal Areas.	2,259,288	2,825,136	1,622,094	83,962	...	...	−565,848	+1,203,042	+1,538,132	...
	Agencies										
1	Malakand (Dir, Swat and Chitral).	902,075	865,860	576,433	8,128	...	...	+36,215	+289,427	+568,305	...
2	Khyber ...	263,566	227,109	181,134	...	...	...	+36,457	+45,975	+181,134	...
3	Kurram ...	63,352	103,142	98,692	54,257	...	...	−39,790	+4,450	+44,435	...
4	North Waziristan ...	93,570	138,859	144,379	4,684	...	...	−45,289	−5,520	+139,695	...
5	South Waziristan ...	108,213	150,612	101,416	4,522	...	...	−42,399	+49,196	+96,894	...
	Tribal area under the political control of the Deputy Commissioner of—										
1	Hazara ...	352,400	146,656	98,302	...	...	...	+205,744	+48,354	+98,302	...
2	Peshawar ...	305,410	1,034,015	240,250	...	...	...	−728,605	+793,765	+240,250	...
3	Kohat ...	128,900	116,600	144,000	...	...	...	+12,300	−27,400	+144,000	...
4	Bannu ...	22,160	11,034	17,884	...	...	...	+11,126	−6,850	+17,884	...
5	Dera Ismail Khan ...	19,642	31,249	19,604	12,371	...	...	−11,607	+11,645	+7,233	...

(a) Peshawar District Census figures of 1931 include the population (1,020 persons—534 males and 486 females) of the Malandri

* Includes 8,173 persons (7,970 males and 203 females) enumerated in the Khyber Pass.

† Excludes a population of 4,684 (4,669 males and 15 females) enumerated in the North Waziristan Agency. It has been shown

‡ Excludes a population of 4,522 (males) enumerated in the South Waziristan Agency and includes 16 persons (11 males

(males) has been shown against the South Waziristan Agency.

§ Includes 15 persons (10 males and 5 females) population of Narangi in 1891. The village was uninhabited in 1881.

TABLE II

Variation in population since 1881

1881-1891	Net variation in period 1881-1931 increase (+) decrease (−)	Males						Females						Serial No.
		1931	1921	1911	1901	1891	1881	1931	1921	1911	1901	1891	1881	
13	14	15	16	17	18	19	20	21	22	23	24	25	26	27
+281,576	+3,108,421	2,528,165	2,747,107	2,046,978	1,159,317	1,007,653	866,333	2,156,199	2,329,369	1,772,049	966,179	849,866	709,610	
+281,576	+849,133	1,315,818	1,229,316	1,182,102	1,105,709	1,007,653	866,333	1,109,258	1,022,024	1,014,831	935,825	849,866	709,610	
+109,213	+263,042	358,193	328,592	320,465	299,708	278,265	218,616	311,924	293,757	282,563	260,580	238,023	188,459	1
+104,170	+366,696	538,146	502,803	470,421	428,582	387,214	341,115	436,175	404,564	394,588	360,125	324,581	266,510	2
+20,386	+61,511	126,210	115,677	119,081	122,174	108,625	97,748	110,063	98,446	103,609	95,691	86,523	77,014	3
+21,729	+87,561	145,163	133,594	133,707	121,991	109,989	99,441	125,138	113,140	116,379	104,810	94,480	83,299	4
+26,078	+70,323	148,106	148,650	138,428	133,254	123,560	109,413	125,958	112,117	117,692	114,619	106,259	94,328	5
...	...	1,212,347	1,517,791	864,876	53,608	...	...	1,046,941	1,307,345	757,218	30,354	...	...	
...	...	465,470	448,254	300,710	8,037	...	...	436,605	417,606	275,723	91	...	...	1
...	...	147,908	125,082	97,077	...	...	...	115,658	102,027	84,057	...	...	...	2
...	...	35,395	57,062	54,271	29,734	...	...	27,957	46,080	44,421	24,523	...	...	3
...	...	56,325	77,678	78,477	4,669	...	...	37,245	61,181	65,902	15	...	...	4
...	...	61,264	91,477	55,350	4,522	...	...	46,949	59,135	46,066	...	...	...	5
...	...	190,036	79,086	52,351	...	...	...	162,364	67,570	45,951	...	...	...	1
...	...	162,510	550,204	127,838	...	...	...	142,900	483,811	112,412	...	...	...	2
...	...	70,200	63,501	78,423	...	...	...	58,700	53,099	65,577	...	...	...	3
...	...	11,916	5,949	9,631	...	...	...	10,244	5,085	8,253	...	...	...	4
...	...	11,323	19,498	10,748	6,646	...	...	8,319	11,751	8,856	5,725	...	...	5

tract added to the Peshawar District during the decade 1921-31 and not previously censused.

against the North Waziristan Agency.

and 5 females) population of 1901 in Narangi village transferred to Dera Ismail Khan from Dera Ghazi Khan, in 1902. The figure 4,522

TABLE III

Cities, Towns and Villages classified by population.

1. No statistics are available of the number of villages situated in the trans-frontier area. This table deals therefore with the five administered districts of the North West Frontier Province only.

2. In this table, as in tables I, IV and V, cantonments have been treated as separate towns. In the case of municipalities with Civil Lines adjoining them, the whole area has been treated as a single town.

3. The revenue Mauza has been taken as a village, except in the case of towns. According to revenue records, the total number of villages in the five administered districts of the North West Frontier Province is 3,006, of which 154 are uninhabited. The total number of inhabited villages and towns according to this table comes to 2,856. The difference of four villages is due to the fact that in some cases revenue estates contain both urban and rural populations, and in other cases more than one revenue estate is included in a single town.

4. Travellers enumerated in encampments, boats and trains, etc., have been shewn separately in this table. No such travellers were enumerated within the limits of any town.

TABLE III

Cities, Towns and Villages classified by population

District	Total number of inhabited towns and villages	Population	Under 500		500—1,000		1,000—2,000		2,000—5,000		5,000—10,000		10,000—20,000		20,000—50,000		50,000—100,000		100,000 and over		Encampments, boat and railway population unclassed
			Number	Population	Number	Population	Number	Population	Number	Population	Number	Population	Number	Population	Number	Population	Number	Population	Number	Population	
1	2	3	4	5	6	7	8	9	10	11	12	13	14	15	16	17	18	19	20	21	22
Hazara	933	670,117	527	125,110	226	157,814	113	158,687	59	175,289	8	53,217	...	...	...	...	...	...	...	...	...
Peshawar	857	974,321	391	93,023	206	148,688	154	213,132	91	275,184	8	46,210	4	50,730	2	58,274	1	87,440	...	...	1,640
Kohat	283	236,273	170	37,276	55	39,371	36	47,531	16	46,766	5	40,229	...	...	1	25,100	...	...	...	...	...
Bannu	383	270,301	235	55,775	79	56,193	46	64,525	19	49,129	3	19,699	...	...	1	24,980	...	...	...	...	...
Dera Ismail Khan	400	274,064	277	55,637	71	50,750	30	40,671	18	50,895	3	21,423	...	...	1	38,956	...	...	...	...	15,732
North West Frontier Province Districts	2,856	2,425,076	1,600	366,821	637	452,816	379	524,546	203	597,263	27	180,778	4	50,730	5	147,310	1	87,440	...	...	17,372

TABLE IV

Towns classified by population with variation since 1881

1. In this table, as in table I, III and V, Cantonments are shown as separate towns. In the case of Municipalities with civil lines adjoining them, the whole area has been treated as sa single town.

2. Since the last census, Jamrud and Tank Cantonments have ceased to exist. The population of these Cantonments is, however, included in the total urban population of the North West Frontier Province at previous censuses.

3. No attempt has been made to adjust the figures affected by changes in the area of towns or by an increase in the number of places treated as towns.

4. The following statement shows the net variation during the decade 1921-31 in the places treated as towns at both censuses :—

Province, State or Agency	Places treated as towns in 1921, but now omitted		Places now treated as towns which were not so treated in 1921		Net variation in decade 1921-31 due to differences in the list of towns	Variation in aggregate population of places which were treated as towns at both censuses
	Number	Aggregate population in 1921	Number	Aggregate population in 1931		
1	2	3	4	5	6	7
North West Frontier Province Districts ...	2	10,611	1	5,780	—4,831	+55,159

TABLE IV

Towns classified by population with variation for fifty years

Serial No.	Town	District	Municipality Suburbs, Cantonment, etc.	Population 1931	1921	1911	1901	1891	1881
1	2	3	4	5	6	7	8	9	10
	Total Urban Population N. W. F. Province ...			386,177	335,849	291,714	258,930	233,485	194,490
	Class I—100,000 and over—Nil.								
	Class II—50,000 to 100,000								
1	Peshawar	Peshawar ...	Municipality ...	87,440	79,427	74,062	73,343	63,079	59,292
	Class III—20,001 to 50,000								
2	Dera Ismail Khan ...	Dera Ismail Khan	Municipality ...	38,956	33,885	29,401	28,287	23,246	18,988
3	Peshawar Cantonment ...	Peshawar ...	Cantonment ...	34,426	25,025	23,873	21,804	21,112	20,690
4	Kohat	Kohat ...	Municipality ...	25,100	18,547	16,697	18,092	14,347	13,490
5	Bannu	Bannu ...	...	24,980	16,361	11,751	10,070	6,550	5,260
	Bannu proper ...	*Do.* ...	*Municipality* ...	*24,768*	*16,361*	*11,751*	*10,070*	*6,550*	*5,260*
	Bannu civil lines ...	*D.* ...	*Civil lines** ...	*212*	...	...	...	...	...
6	Mardan	Peshawar ...	Municipality ...	23,848	7,433	6,134	...	...	...
	Class IV—10,000 to 20,000								
7	Nowshera Cantonment ...	Peshawar ...	Cantonment ...	16,137	16,635	14,543	9,518	6,885	5,473
8	Nowshera	Do. ...	Notified Area ...	12,829	11,107	10,955	...	...	...
9	Charsadda	Do. ...	...	11,537	10,232	9,178	9,119	10,619	8,363
10	Prang	Do. ...	...	10,227	9,886	10,982	10,235	12,327	8,874
	Class V—5,000 to 10,000								
11	Kohat Cantonment ...	Kohat ...	Cantonment ...	9,250	9,306	5,957	12,670	12,656	4,689
12	Tangi	Peshawar ...	...	8,689	9,843	19,907	9,095	9,909	9,037
13	Abbottabad Cantonment ...	Hazara ...	Cantonment ...	8,527	8,260	7,503	4,369	7,750	2,381
14	Kulachi	Dera Ismail Khan	Notified Area ...	8,425	7,895	10,179	9,125	9,447	7,834
15	Risalpur	Peshawar ...	Cantonment ...	8,016	8,499	3,167	...	...	...
16	Lakki	Bannu ...	Notified Area ...	7,70	7,476	4,923	5,218	4,488	4,068
17	Haripur	Hazara ...	Municipality ...	7,653	5,889	6,193	5,578	5,419	4,884
18	Abbottabad... ...	Do ...	Do. ...	7,638	5,360	4,003	3,395	2,413	1,808
19	Baffa	Do. ...	Notified Area ...	7,257	7,603	7,384	7,029	7,437	5,410
20	Tank	Dera Ismail Khan	Do. ...	6,421	6,363	5,050	4,402	...	...
21	Mansehra	Hazara ...	...	5,780	...	...	...	...	...
22	Bannu Cantonment ...	Bannu ...	Cantonment ...	5,559	5,900	5,114	4,221	2,267	3,700
23	Nawan Shehr ...	Hazara ...	Notified Area ...	5,130	5,092	4,661	4,114	5,298	4,307
	Class VI—Under 5,000								
24	Mardan Cantonment ...	Peshawar ...	Cantonment ...	2,431	3,497	2,795	3,572	3,537	2,766
25	Dera Ismail Khan Cantonment ...	Dera Ismail Khan	Do. ...	1,375	5,456	5,730	3,450	3,638	3,176
26	Cherat	Peshawar ...	Do. ...	843	261	120	376	317	...

* Included in Bannu Municipality at previous Censuses.

TABLE IV

Towns classified by population with variation for fifty years

Variation : Increase (+), Decrease (—)					Variation in period 1881—1931 Increase (+) Decrease (—)	Males			Females			Serial No.
1921—1931	1911—1921	1901—1911	1891—1901	1881—1891		1931	1921	1911	1931	1921	1911	
11	12	13	14	15	16	17	18	19	20	21	22	23
+50,328	+44,135	+32,784	+25,445	+38,995	+191,687	235,126	215,041	179,449	151,051	120,808	112,265	
+8,013	+5,365	+719	+10,264	+3,787	+28,148	50,151	45,384	40,993	37,289	34,043	33,069	1
+5,071	+4,484	+1,114	+5,041	+4,258	+19,968	22,141	19,446	16,829	16,815	14,439	12,572	2
+9,401	+1,152	+2,069	+692	+422	+13,736	25,702	19,508	18,03	8,724	5,517	5,186	3
+6,553	+1,850	—1,395	+3,745	+857	+11,610	14,236	10,856	9,295	10,864	7,691	7,402	4
+8,619	+4,610	+1,681	+3,520	+1,290	+19,720	14,771	9,657	6,908	10,209	6,704	4,843	5
+8,407	*+4,610*	*+1,681*	*+3,520*	*+1,290*	*+19,508*	*14,619*	*9,657*	*6,908*	*10,149*	*6,704*	*4,843*	
+212	...	...	...	...	...	*152*	...	...	*60*	...	...	
+16,415	+1,299	+6,134	...	...	...	13,631	4,435	3,835	10,217	2,998	2,299	6
—498	+2,092	+5,025	+2,633	+1,412	+10,664	11,913	13,153	11,068	4,224	3,482	3, 75	7
+1,722	+152	+10,955	...	...	...	7,291	5,953	5,761	5,538	5,154	5,194	8
+1,305	+1,054	+59	—1,500	+2,256	+3,174	6,485	5,538	5,115	5,052	4,694	4,063	9
+341	—1,096	+747	—2,092	+3,453	+1,353	5,609	5,416	5,869	4,618	4,470	5,113	10
—56	+3,349	—6,713	+14	+7,967	+4,561	7,538	8,273	5,134	1,712	1,033	823	11
—1,154	—64	+812	—814	+872	—348	4,619	5,091	5,178	4,070	4,752	4,729	12
+267	+757	+3,134	—3,381	+5,369	+6,146	6,663	6,216	5,871	1,864	2,041	1,632	13
+530	—2,284	+1,054	—322	+1,613	+591	4,008	3,745	5,071	4,417	4,150	5,108	14
—483	+5,332	+3,167	...	...	...	5,685	6,622	2,639	2,331	1,877	528	15
+227	+2,553	—295	+730	+420	+3,635	3,991	4,040	2,565	3,712	3,436	2,358	16
+1,764	—304	+615	+159	+535	+2,769	4,388	3,238	3,477	3,265	2,651	2,716	17
+2,278	+1,357	+608	+982	+605	+5,830	4,717	3,457	2,620	2,921	1,903	1,383	18
—346	+219	+355	—408	+2,027	+1,847	3,893	3,995	3,892	3,364	3,608	3,492	19
+58	+1,313	+648	...	...	...	3,854	4,233	2,980	2,567	2,130	2,070	20
+5,780	...	...	...	...	...	3,298	..	...	2,482	...	...	21
—341	+786	+893	+1,954	—1,433	+1,859	4,658	5,458	4,653	901	442	461	22
+38	+431	+547	—1,184	+991	+823	2,561	2,644	2,453	2,569	2,448	2,208	23
—1,066	+702	—777	+35	+771	—335	1,705	2,904	2,177	726	593	618	24
—4,081	—274	+2,280	—188	+462	—1,801	910	4,994	5,015	465	462	715	25
+582	+141	—256	+59	+317	...	708	235	96	135	26	24	26

TABLE V

Towns arranged territorially with population by religion

1. In this table, as in Tables I, III and IV, Cantonments have been treated as separate towns. In the case of Municipalities with Civil Lines adjoining them, the whole area has been treated as a single town.

2. There are no persons belonging to unspecified religions in any town.

3. The following statement shows the Civil and Military population of Cantonments :—

Serial No.	Name of Cantonment	Population					
		Military			Civil		
		Persons	Males	Females	Persons	Males	Females
1	Abbottabad ...	4,399	4,399	...	4,128	2,264	1,864
2	Peshawar... ...	5,522	5,520	2	28,904	20,182	8,722
3	Mardan	715	715	...	1,716	990	726
4	Nowshera	4,013	4,013	...	12,124	7,900	4,224
5	Risalpur	2,057	2,057	...	5,959	3,628	2,331
6	Cherat	216	216	...	627	492	135
7	Kohat	4,503	4,503	...	4,747	3,035	1,712
8	Bannu	3,036	3,032	4	2,523	1,626	897
9	Dera Ismail Khan ...	336	336	...	1,039	574	465
	Total ...	24,797	24,791	6	61,767	40,691	21,076

TABLE V

Towns arranged territorially with population by religion

District	Town, Municipality, Suburb, Cantonment, etc.	Population			Muslims		
		Persons	Males	Females	Persons	Males	Females
1	2	3	4	5	6	7	8
Total Urban Population N. W. F. Province ...		386,177	235,126	151,051	2[illegible]6,189	153,891	102,298
Hazara ...	1. Abbottabad Cantonment ...	8,527	6,663	1,864	1,712	1,407	305
	2. Abbottabad Municipality ..	7,638	4,717	2,921	5,314	3,260	2,054
	3. Haripur Municipality ...	7,653	4,388	3,265	4,253	2,498	1,755
	4. Baffa Notified Area ...	7,257	3,893	3,364	6,4[illegible]9	3,427	2,[illegible]82
	5. Nawanshehr Notified Area ...	5,130	2,561	2,569	3,8[illegible]4	[illegible]	1,[illegible]77
	6. Mansehra	5,780	3,2[illegible]8	2,482	4,2[illegible]7	2,3[illegible]	1,857
Peshawar ...	7. Peshawar Municipality ...	87,440	50,151	37,289	6[illegible]803	3[illegible]915	29,978
	8. Peshawar Cantonment ...	34,426	25,702	8,724	16,476	13,034	3,442
	9. Mardan Municipality ...	23,848	13,631	10,217	18,588	10,530	8,058
	10. Mardan Cantonment ..	2,431	1,705	726	991	697	294
	11. Nowshera Notified Area ...	12,829	7,291	5,538	12,126	6,886	5,240
	12. Nowshera Cantonment ...	10,137	1[illegible],913	4,[illegible]4	7,5[illegible]6	5[illegible]3	1,873
	13. Charsadda	11,537	6,485	5,052	10,703	5[illegible]5	4,[illegible]8
	14. Parang	10,227	5,609	4,618	10,211	5,[illegible]2	4,6[illegible]
	15. Tangi	8,689	4,619	4,070	8,320	4,420	3,[illegible]0
	16. Risalpur Cantonment ...	8,016	5,685	2,33[illegible]	3,170	2,380	790
	17. Cherat Cantonment ...	843	708	135	396	344	52
Kohat ...	18. Kohat Municipality ...	25,100	14,236	1[illegible],864	2[illegible]	11,647	9,[illegible]8
	19. Kohat Cantonment ...	[illegible]50	7[illegible]8	1,712	3,733	3,136	507
Bannu ...	20. Bannu	24,98[illegible]	14,771	10,209	8,296	5,673	2,623
	Bannu Municipality ..	*24,7[illegible]*	*14,619*	*10,149*	*8,171*	*5,574*	*2,597*
	Bannu Civil Lines ...	*212*	*152*	*6[illegible]*	*125*	*99*	*26*
	21. Bannu Cantonment ...	5,559	4,658	901	2,311	1,965	346
	22. Lakki Notified Area ...	7,703	3,991	3,712	4,630	2,454	2,176
Dera Ismail Khan ...	23. Dera Ismail Khan Municipality ...	38,956	22,141	16,815	21,709	12,959	8,750
	24. Dera Ismail Khan Cantonment ...	1,375	910	465	612	419	193
	25. Kulachi Notified Area ...	8,425	4,008	4,417	6,115	2,924	3,191
	26. Tank Notified Area ...	6,421	3,854	2,567	3,929	2,389	1,540

TABLE V

Towns arranged territorially with population by religion

Hindus			Sikhs			Christians			Parsis			Jews			
Persons	Males	Females	Persons	Males	Females	Persons	Males	Females	Persons	Males	Females	Persons	Males	Females	Serial No.
9	10	11	12	13	14	15	16	17	18	19	20	21	22	23	24
93,127	56,311	36,816	25,377	16,407	8,970	11,411	8,474	2,937	62	32	30	11	11	...	
6,097	4,667	1,430	493	450	43	225	139	86	...	...	...	...	...	...	1
1,656	1,037	619	546	353	193	121	66	55	1	1	...	...	...	...	2
2,693	1,503	1,190	696	382	314	11	5	6	...	...	...	...	...	...	3
762	416	346	86	50	36	...	...	...	...	...	...	...	...	...	4
883	469	414	363	185	178	...	...	...	...	...	...	...	...	...	5
1,091	648	443	469	288	181	3	2	1	...	...	...	...	...	...	6
11,594	6,781	4,813	5,150	2,992	2,158	792	452	340	...	...	...	11	11	...	7
10,379	7,189	3,190	3,480	2,535	945	4,062	2,928	1,134	29	16	13	...	...	...	8
2,720	1,627	1,093	2,521	1,461	1,060	19	13	6	...	...	...	...	...	...	9
885	655	230	406	269	137	149	84	65	...	...	...	...	...	...	10
368	226	142	332	176	156	3	3	...	...	...	...	...	...	...	11
4,307	2,693	1,614	2,710	2,178	532	1,557	1,366	191	27	13	14	...	...	...	12
519	313	206	287	158	129	28	19	9	...	...	...	...	...	...	13
16	7	9	...	...	...	...	...	...	...	...	...	...	...	...	14
362	194	168	7	5	2	...	...	...	...	...	...	...	...	...	15
2,900	1,758	1,142	314	203	111	1,629	1,344	285	3	...	3	...	...	...	16
158	108	50	74	55	19	213	199	14	2	2	...	...	...	...	17
3,249	1,898	1,351	1,110	645	465	86	46	40	...	...	...	...	...	...	18
3,460	2,772	688	1,042	813	229	1,015	817	198	...	...	...	...	...	...	19
13,347	7,272	6,075	3,137	1,714	1,423	200	112	88	...	...	...	...	...	...	20
13,277	*7,230*	*6,047*	*3,136*	*1,713*	*1,423*	*184*	*102*	*82*	...	...	...	...	...	...	
70	*42*	*28*	*1*	*1*	...	*16*	*10*	*6*	...	...	...	...	...	...	
1,689	1,406	283	810	725	85	749	562	187	...	...	...	...	...	...	21
2,805	1,409	1,396	268	128	140	...	...	...	...	...	...	...	...	...	22
16,421	8,703	7,718	638	376	262	188	103	85	...	...	...	...	...	...	23
340	229	111	70	53	17	353	209	144	...	...	...	...	...	...	24
2,182	1,018	1,164	128	66	62	...	...	...	...	...	...	...	...	...	25
2,244	1,313	931	240	147	93	8	5	3	...	...	...	...	...	...	26

TABLE VI

Birth-place.

1. This table is divided into two parts, *viz.* :—

   Part A.—Details for Districts and Trans-Frontier Posts in the North West Frontier Province.

   Part B.—Peshawar City (Municipality).

2. The phrase "within British Dominions" suould be taken to mean "within the British Empire and Mandated Territories".

TABLE VI

Birth Place—Part A—Details for Districts and Trans-Frontier Posts

Serial No.	District, State, Province or Country where born	District, etc., where								
		N. W. F. Province			Hazara			Peshawar		
		Persons	Males	Females	Persons	Males	Females	Persons	Males	Females
	1	2	3	4	5	6	7	8	9	10
	N. W. F. P. Total enumerated population.	2,471,527	1,360,453	1,111,074	670,117	358,193	311,924	974,321	538,146	436,175
	A—Born in India ...	2,424,229	1,326,958	1,097,271	665,665	354,657	311,008	960,977	528,571	432,406
	I—Within the Province ...	2,312,361	1,239,407	1,072,954	657,523	349,034	308,489	914,568	494,788	419,780
	(1) British Territory ...	2,279,298	1,217,878	1,061,420	655,280	347,470	307,810	896,629	483,560	413,069
1	Hazara District ...	661,039	352,420	308,619	654,248	346,774	307,474	3,954	3,127	827
2	Peshawar District ...	897,341	484,382	412,959	747	505	242	889,471	477,795	411,676
3	Kohat District ...	222,572	118,156	104,416	140	103	37	1,974	1,723	251
4	Bannu District ...	260,369	137,787	122,582	63	34	29	605	472	133
5	Dera Ismail Khan District...	237,977	125,133	112,844	82	54	28	625	443	182
	(2) Agencies and Tribal Areas.	33,063	21,529	11,534	2,243	1,564	679	17,939	11,228	6,711
1	Malakand Agency ...	511	381	130	1	...	1	103	69	34
2	Khyber Agency ...	56	56	...	...	...	...	39	39	...
3	Kurram Agency ...	3,771	2,980	791	...	...	...	35	24	11
4	{ North Waziristan Agency... South Waziristan Agency... }	2,172	1,796	376	...	...	...	3	3	...
	II—Provinces and States in India beyond N. W. F. P.	111,868	87,551	24,317	8,142	5,623	2,519	46,409	33,783	12,626
	(a) Provinces and States adjacent to N. W. F. P.	93,853	72,755	21,098	7,312	5,072	2,240	38,329	27,773	10,556
	(1) British Territory ...	83,562	63,506	20,056	5,534	3,687	1,847	34,311	24,259	10,052
1	Baluchistan (Districts and administered territories.).	444	226	218	8	3	5	100	57	43
2	*Punjab* ...	83,118	63,280	19,838	5,526	3,684	1,842	34,211	24,202	10,009
3	Campbellpore District ...	9,703	6,754	2,949	1,058	632	426	6,303	4,424	1,879
4	Rawalpindi District ...	10,770	7,858	2,912	1,491	781	710	4,716	3,059	1,657
5	Mianwali District ...	8,672	5,793	2,879	37	25	12	744	615	129
6	Muzaffargarh District ...	911	688	223	11	6	5	71	45	26
7	Dera Ghazi Khan District	1,314	771	543	2	1	1	64	45	19
8	Jhelum District ...	8,246	6,634	1,612	567	418	149	4,253	3,169	1,084
	(2) Feudatory States ...	10,291	9,249	1,042	1,778	1,385	393	4,018	3,514	504
9	Kashmir State ...	8,263	7,440	823	1,635	1,252	383	3,313	2,960	353
10	Punjab States Agency ...	2,028	1,809	219	143	133	10	705	554	151
	(b) Other Provinces and States in India.	17,193	14,089	3,104	798	527	271	7,681	5,646	2,035
	(1) British Territory ...	14,748	11,984	2,764	634	391	243	6,540	4,677	1,863
11	Ajmer-Merwara ...	88	72	16	...	...	...	44	32	12
12	Andamans and Nicobars...	2	...	2	2	...	2	...	...	...
13	Assam ...	48	33	15	9	3	6	11	6	5
14	Bengal ...	795	604	191	67	56	11	331	215	116
15	Bihar and Orissa ...	152	111	41	5	5	...	72	43	29
16	Bombay ...	723	521	202	38	20	18	410	288	122
17	Burma ...	76	39	37	11	6	5	23	3	20

TABLE VI

Birth Place—Part A—Details for Districts and Trans-Frontier Posts

Enumerated												
Kohat			Bannu			Dera Ismail Khan			Trans-Frontier Posts			Serial No.
Persons	Males	Females	Persons	Males	Females	Persons	Males	Females	Persons	Males	Females	
11	12	13	14	15	16	17	18	19	20	21	22	
236,273	126,210	110,063	270,301	145,163	125,138	274,064	148,106	125,958	46,451	44,635	1,816	
233,817	124,502	109,315	265,717	142,750	123,967	258,352	139,450	118,902	38,701	37,028	1,673	
221,671	115,002	106,669	258,311	135,053	122,258	245,664	131,238	114,426	14,624	13,292	1,332	
216,067	112,220	103,847	257,980	135,785	122,195	243,929	129,822	114,107	9,413	9,021	392	
697	532	165	277	227	50	440	371	69	1,423	1,389	34	1
1,767	1,233	534	723	610	113	1,672	1,475	197	2,961	2,764	197	2
213,088	110,104	102,984	2,995	2,053	942	689	598	91	3,686	3,575	111	3
356	250	106	252,933	132,170	120,763	5,648	4,129	1,519	764	732	32	4
159	101	58	1,052	725	327	235,480	123,249	112,231	579	561	18	5
5,604	2,782	2,822	331	268	63	1,735	1,416	319	5,211	4,271	940	
4	4	...	...	...	...	...	...	...	403	308	95	1
...	...	...	...	...	...	...	...	...	17	17	...	2
68	52	16	1	1	...	...	...	...	3,667	2,903	764	3
6	3	3	278	217	61	1,683	1,373	310	202	200	2	4
12,146	9,500	2,646	8,406	6,697	1,709	12,688	8,212	4,476	24,077	23,736	341	
9,924	7,610	2,314	7,666	6,180	1,486	11,055	6,867	4,188	19,567	19,253	314	
9,488	7,227	2,261	7,112	5,686	1,426	10,871	6,711	4,160	16,246	15,936	310	
30	16	14	4	4	...	284	129	155	18	17	1	1
9,458	7,211	2,247	7,108	5,682	1,426	10,587	6,582	4,005	16,228	15,919	309	2
1,650	1,159	491	315	257	58	377	282	95	...	...	...	3
1,466	1,150	316	598	492	106	327	224	103	2,172	2,152	20	4
350	233	117	1,735	1,308	427	5,283	3,097	2,186	523	515	8	5
30	21	9	43	30	13	674	509	165	82	77	5	6
7	...	7	35	24	11	1,141	636	505	65	65	...	7
798	611	187	549	439	110	221	154	67	1,858	1,843	15	8
435	383	53	554	494	60	184	156	28	3,321	3,317	4	
406	361	45	388	360	28	107	97	10	2,414	2,410	4	9
30	22	8	166	134	32	77	59	18	907	907	...	10
2,179	1,866	313	656	446	210	1,553	1,303	250	4,326	4,301	25	
2,019	1,744	275	559	377	182	1,340	1,163	177	3,656	3,632	24	
5	5	...	7	6	1	12	9	3	20	20	...	11
...	...	...	...	...	...	...	...	...	...	...	...	12
9	8	1	5	3	2	2	1	1	12	12	...	13
193	176	17	50	29	21	63	37	26	91	91	...	14
23	23	...	29	17	12	...	...	...	23	23	...	15
71	52	19	55	33	22	81	62	19	68	66	2	16
19	10	9	10	7	3	13	13	...	...	...	...	17

TABLE VI

Birth Place—Part A—Details for Districts and Trans-Frontier Posts

Serial No.	District, State, Province or Country where born	District, etc., where								
		N. W. F. Province			Hazara			Peshawar		
		Persons	Males	Females	Persons	Males	Females	Persons	Males	Females
	1	2	3	4	5	6	7	8	9	10
18	Central Provinces and Berar.	280	241	39	7	6	1	122	100	22
19	Delhi ...	631	488	143	23	14	9	412	303	109
20	Madras ...	776	627	149	157	91	66	191	123	68
21	*United Provinces of Agra and Oudh.*	11,177	9,248	1,929	315	190	125	4,924	3,564	1,360
	(2) **Feudatory States** ...	**2,445**	**2,105**	**340**	**164**	**136**	**28**	**1,141**	**969**	**172**
22	Assam States (*i.e.* Manipur and Tribal Areas).	32	32	...	...	...	...	...	...	...
23	Baroda State ...	8	5	3	2	1	1	...	...	...
24	*Bihar and Orissa States* ...	7	2	5	...	...	...	7	2	5
25	Bombay States ...	29	19	10	9	5	4	4	2	2
26	Central India Agency ...	280	275	5	2	2	...	203	203	...
27	Central Provinces States	58	31	27	...	...	...	27	...	27
28	Gwalior State ...	156	155	1	...	...	...	56	56	...
29	*Hyderabad State* ...	182	113	69	...	...	...	67	40	27
30	Mysore State ...	148	105	43	2	1	1	28	3	25
31	Rajputana Agency ...	1,545	1,368	177	149	127	22	749	663	86
	(*c*) **French and Portuguese Settlements.**	67	63	4	...	...	...	29	29	...
	(*d*) **India, Unspecified** ...	**755**	**644**	**111**	**32**	**24**	**8**	**370**	**335**	**35**
	B—Born in other Asiatic Countries.	**36,612**	**23,919**	**12,693**	**4,288**	**3,443**	**845**	**8,046**	**5,023**	**3,023**
	(*i*) **Within British Dominions.**	**24**	**20**	**4**	**3**	**3**	...	**2**	**1**	**1**
1	Ceylon ...	5	1	4	...	...	...	1	...	1
2	Straits Settlements and *Malaya.*	1	1	...	...	...	...	...	...	...
3	Elsewhere ...	18	18	...	3	3	...	1	1	...
	(*ii*) **Outside British Dominions.**	**36,559**	**23,877**	**12,682**	**4,283**	**3,440**	**843**	**8,040**	**5,022**	**3,018**
4	Afghanistan ...	28,324	16,558	11,766	85	73	12	7,638	4,670	2,968
5	China ...	23	15	8	14	6	8	7	7	...
6	Nepal ...	8,051	7,197	854	4,183	3,361	822	253	245	8
7	Elsewhere ...	161	107	54	1	...	1	142	100	42
	(*iii*) **Asia, Unspecified** ...	**29**	**22**	**7**	**2**	...	**2**	**4**	...	**4**
	C—Born in Europe ...	**1,0558**	**9,485**	**1,073**	**153**	**89**	**64**	**5,243**	**4,512**	**731**
1	(*i*) United Kingdom and *Ireland.*	10,336	9,401	935	153	89	64	5,160	4,468	692
2	(*ii*) Continental Europe ...	78	28	50	...	..	...	39	7	32
3	(*iii*) Europe, Unspecified ...	144	56	88	...	...	...	44	37	7
	D—Born in Africa ...	46	33	13	4	2	2	32	22	10
	(*i*) **Within British Dominions.**	...	...	...	...	...	...	...	...	...

TABLE VI

Birth Place—Part A—Details for Districts and Trans-Frontier Posts

Enum erated

Kohat			Bannu			Dera Ismail Khan			Trans-Frontier Posts			Serial No.
Persons	Males	Females	Persons	Males	Females	Persons	Males	Females	Persons	Males	Females	
11	12	13	14	15	16	17	18	19	20	21	22	
107	96	11	...	...	...	12	7	5	32	32	...	18
55	38	17	20	17	3	5	...	5	116	116	...	19
18	9	9	55	50	5	40	39	1	315	315	...	20
1,519	1,327	192	328	215	113	1,112	995	117	2,979	2,957	22	21
160	122	38	97	69	28	213	140	73	670	669	1	
...	...	...	...	...	...	...	...	...	32	32	...	22
2	2	...	3	1	2	1	1	...	...	...	...	23
...	...	...	...	...	...	...	...	...	...	...	...	24
1	...	1	6	4	2	9	8	1	...	...	...	25
29	29	...	28	28	...	18	13	5	...	...	...	26
...	...	...	...	...	...	...	...	...	31	31	...	27
14	13	1	3	3	...	1	1	...	82	82	...	28
49	30	19	31	20	11	24	12	12	11	11	...	29
11	3	8	15	13	2	27	20	7	65	65	...	30
54	45	9	11	...	11	133	85	48	449	448	1	31
4	...	4	...	...	...	1	1	...	33	33	...	
39	24	15	84	71	13	79	41	38	151	149	2	
1,717	1,084	633	3,093	2,008	1,085	15,457	8,485	6,972	4,011	3,876	135	
15	12	3	1	1	...	...	...	...	3	3	...	
3	...	3	...	...	...	...	...	...	1	1	...	1
...	...	...	...	...	...	...	...	...	1	1	...	2
12	12	...	1	1	...	...	...	...	1	1	...	3
1,702	1,072	630	3,092	2,007	1,085	15 456	8,485	6,971	3,985	3,851	135	
1,676	1,068	608	3,030	1,951	1,079	15,426	8,459	6,967	469	337	132	4
...	...	...	...	...	...	...	...	...	2	2	...	5
18	1	17	61	55	6	25	24	1	3,511	3,511	...	6
8	3	5	1	1	...	5	2	3	4	1	3	7
...	...	...	...	...	..	1	...	1	22	22	...	
713	603	110	478	398	80	254	170	84	3,717	3,713	4	
604	582	22	471	396	75	240	162	78	3,708	3,704	4	1
17	10	7	7	2	5	8	2	6	7	7	...	2
92	11	81	...	...	...	6	6	...	2	2	...	3
6	6	...	3	2	1	...	...	...	1	1	...	
...	...	...	...	...	...	...	...	...	...	...	...	

TABLE VI

Birth Place—Part A—Details for Districts and Trans-Frontier Posts

Serial No.	District, State, Province or Country where born	District, etc., where								
		N. W. F. Province			Hazara			Peshawar		
		Persons	Males	Females	Persons	Males	Females	Persons	Males	Females
	1	2	3	4	5	6	7	8	9	10
	(*ii*) **Outside British Dominions.**	15	8	7	...	...	...	15	8	7
1	Mozambique ...	...	...	...	...	...	...	...	...	...
2	Elsewhere ...	15	8	7	...	...	...	15	8	7
	(*iii*) **Africa, Unspecified** ...	31	25	6	4	2	2	17	14	3
	E—Born in America ...	44	34	10	5	2	3	12	9	3
	(*i*) **Within British Dominions**	15	12	3	1	...	1	4	4	...
1	Canada ...	11	8	3	1	...	1	4	4	...
2	Elsewhere ...	4	4	...	...	...	...	...	...	...
	(*ii*) **Outside British Dominions**	10	8	2	...	...	...	2	2	...
3	United States ...	8	6	2	...	...	...	...	...	...
4	Elsewhere ...	2	2	...	...	...	...	2	2	...
	(*iii*) **America, Unspecified** ...	19	14	5	4	2	2	6	3	3
	F—Born in Australasia ...	38	24	14	2	...	2	11	9	2
	(*i*) **Within British Dominions**	23	14	9	2	...	2	6	6	...
1	Australia ...	9	4	5	2	...	2	...	...	...
2	New Zealand ...	14	10	4	...	...	...	6	6	...
	(*ii*) **Australasia, Unspecified**	15	10	5	...	...	...	5	3	2

TABLE VI

Birth Place—Part A—Details for Districts and Trans-Frontier Posts

Enumerated												
Kohat			Bannu			Dera Ismail Khan			Trans-Frontier Posts			Serial No.
Persons	Males	Females	Persons	Males	Females	Persons	Males	Females	Persons	Males	Females	
11	12	13	14	15	16	17	18	19	20	21	22	
...	...	...	...	...	...	...	...	...	...	...	...	
...	...	...	...	...	...	...	...	...	...	...	...	1
...	...	...	...	...	...	...	...	...	...	...	...	2
6	6	...	3	2	1	...	...	...	1	1	...	
6	4	2	6	4	2	...	...	...	15	15	...	
3	3	...	3	1	2	...	...	...	4	4	...	
...	...	...	2	...	2	...	...	...	4	4	...	1
3	3	...	1	1	...	...	...	...	...	...	...	2
2	...	2	2	2	...	...	...	...	4	4	...	
2	...	2	2	2	...	...	...	...	4	4	...	3
...	...	...	...	...	...	...	...	...	...	...	...	4
1	1	...	1	1	...	...	...	...	7	7	...	
14	11	3	4	1	3	1	1	...	6	2	4	
4	4	...	4	1	3	1	1	...	6	2	4	
...	...	...	4	1	3	1	1	...	2	2	...	1
4	4	...	...	...	...	...	...	...	4	...	4	2
10	7	3	...	...	...	...	...	...	...	...	...	

TABLE VI

Birth Place—Part B—Peshawar City (Municipality)

Serial No.	District, State, Province or Country where born	Population			Remarks
		Persons	Males	Females	
	1	2	3	4	5
	Peshawar City (Municipality)	87,440	50,151	37,289	
	A—Born in India	82,939	47,367	35,572	
	I—Within the Province	73,999	41,225	32,774	
	(i) British Territory	69,305	38,194	31,111	
1	Hazara District	924	701	223	
2	Peshawar District	67,738	37,045	30,693	
3	Kohat District	328	229	99	
4	Bannu District	156	105	51	
5	Dera Ismail Khan District	159	114	45	
	(ii) Agencies and Tribal Areas	4,694	3,031	1,663	
1	Malakand Agency	34	...	34	
2	Khyber Agency	37	37	...	
3	Kurram Agency	35	24	11	
4	North Waziristan Agency ... ... South Waziristan Agency	2	2	...	
	II—Provinces and States in India beyond N. W. F. P. ...	8,940	6,142	2,798	
	(a) Provinces and States adjacent to N. W. F. P. ...	8,123	5,598	2,525	
	(1) British Territory	6,691	4,307	2,384	
1	Baluchistan	25	12	13	
2	Punjab	6,666	4,295	2,371	
3	Campbellpore District	1,501	1,048	453	
4	Rawalpindi District	687	439	248	
5	Mianwali District	135	110	25	
6	Muzaffargarh District	45	45	...	
7	Dera Ghazi Khan District... ...	2	2	...	
8	Jhelum District	1,377	1,016	361	
	(2) Feudatory States	1,432	1,291	141	
9	Kashmir State	1,384	1,250	134	
10	Punjab States Agency	48	41	7	
	(b) Other Provinces and States in India ...	804	536	268	
	(1) British Territory	683	449	234	
11	Assam	6	1	5	
12	Bengal	24	3	21	
13	Bihar and Orissa	4	3	1	
14	Bombay	49	19	30	
15	Burma	6	...	6	
16	Central Provinces and Berar ...	3	2	1	
17	Delhi	94	57	37	
18	Madras	2	1	1	
19	United Provinces of Agra and Oudh ...	495	363	132	

TABLE VI

Birth Place—Part B—Peshawar City (Municipality)

Serial No.	District, State, Province or Country where born	Population			Remarks
		Persons	Males	Females	
	1	2	3	4	5
	(2) Feudatory States	121	87	34	
20	Central India Agency	1	...	1	
21	Central Provinces States	1	...	1	
22	Gwalior State	2	2	...	
23	Mysore State	2	2	...	
24	Rajputana Agency	115	82	33	
	(c) India, Unspecified	13	8	5	
	B—Born in other Asiatic countries	4,494	2,780	1,714	
1	(i) Within British Dominions	1	1	...	
	(ii) Outside British Dominions	4,493	2,779	1,714	
2	Afghanistan	4,352	2,677	1,675	
3	Nepal	29	25	4	
4	Elsewhere...	112	77	35	
	C—Born in Europe	2	1	1	
1	(i) United Kingdom and Ireland	1	1	...	
2	(ii) Continental Europe	1	...	1	
	D—Born in Africa	5	3	2	
1	(i) Africa, Unspecified	5	3	2	

TABLE VII

Age, Sex and Civil Condition

1. This is divided into three parts. Part I (Provincial Summary) shows for the five Settled Districts and Transfrontier Posts as a whole, the distribution of the total enumerated population (all religions) and of each religion returned dy age, sex and civil condition. Part II shows details (*a*) for Districts and (*b*) for Transfrontier Posts. Part III gives similar details for Peshawar City (Municipality).

2. The age shown in this table represents the age to the nearest birthday.

TABLE VII

Age Sex and Civil Condition Part I—Provincial Summary

Age	Population			Unmarried			Married			Widowed		
	Persons	Males	Females	Persons	Males	Females	Persons	Males	Females	Persons	Males	Females
1	2	3	4	5	6	7	8	9	10	11	12	13
ALL RELIGIONS.	2,471,527	1,360,453	1,111,074	1,290,407	781,235	509,172	995,406	514,871	480,535	185,714	64,347	121,367
0—1	75,033	38,347	36,686	75,033	38,347	36,686	...	...	...	...	...	...
1—2	67,524	33,665	33,859	67,524	33,665	33,859	...	...	...	...	...	...
2—3.	81,103	40,226	40,877	81,103	40,226	40,877	...	...	...	...	...	...
3—4	82,668	41,769	40,899	82,668	41,769	40,899	...	...	...	...	...	...
4—5	81,141	42,042	39,099	81,141	42,042	39,099	...	...	...	...	...	...
Total 0—5	387,469	196,049	191,420	387,469	196,049	191,420	...	...	...	...	...	...
5—10	335,347	184,037	151,310	331,660	183,101	148,559	3,527	862	2,665	160	74	86
10—15	289,203	164,184	125,019	269,591	160,0[illegible]6	109,515	19,007	3,856	15,151	605	252	353
15—20	224,295	125,858	98,437	126,725	96,527	30,198	94,264	27,873	66,391	3,306	1,458	1,848
20—25	239,238	131,826	107,412	88,599	75,365	13,234	143,666	53,535	90,131	6,973	2,926	4,047
25—30	231,534	127,227	104,307	38,706	33,401	5,305	179,662	88,189	91,473	13,166	5,637	7 529
30—35	201,573	113,500	88,073	21,824	18,184	3,640	164,546	88,894	75,652	15,203	6,422	8,781
35—40	142,340	79,481	62,859	9,008	6,761	2,247	113,934	66,300	47,634	19,398	6,420	12,978
40—45	116,656	64,398	52,258	6,243	4,485	1,758	90,140	53,675	36,465	20,273	6,238	14,035
45—50	90,133	50,809	39,324	3,874	2,[illegible]27	1,147	63,315	41,465	21,850	22,944	6,617	16,327
50—55	71,311	39,752	31,559	2,580	1,720	860	47,770	32,024	15,746	20,961	6,008	14,953
55—60	49,678	28,555	21,123	1,463	1,002	461	29,138	21,570	7,568	19,077	5,983	13,094
60—65	40,440	23,273	17,167	1,116	771	345	22,377	17,126	5,251	16,947	5.376	11,571
65—70	18,054	10,765	7,289	480	337	143	9,112	7,231	1,881	8,462	31,97	5,265
70 & over	34,256	20,739	13,517	1,069	729	340	14,948	12,271	2,677	18,239	7,739	10,500
MUSLIM	22,50,389	1,218,234	10,32,155	11,79,935	705,317	474,618	901,427	455,705	445,722	169,027	57,212	111,815
0—1	68,739	35,142	33,597	68,739	35,142	33,597	...	...	...	...	...	...
1—2	62,432	31,090	31,342	62,432	31,090	31,342	...	...	...	...	...	...
2—3	75,346	37,332	38,014	75,346	37,332	38,014	...	...	...	...	...	...
3—4	76,982	38,901	38,081	76,982	38,901	38,081	...	...	..	...	...	...
4—5	75,636	39,214	36,422	75,636	39,214	36,422	...	...	...	...	...	...
Total 0—5	359,135	181,679	177,456	359,135	181,679	177,456	...	...	...	...	...	...
5—10	312,591	171,923	140,668	309,406	171,100	138,306	3,056	762	2,294	129	61	68
10 15	269,119	153,063	116,056	251,533	149,300	102,233	17,034	3.527	13,507	552	236	316
15—20	198,155	107,645	90,510	112,317	8[illegible],635	28,682	82,915	22,778	60 137	2,923	1,232	1,691
20—25	207,420	108,649	98,771	74,338	61,726	12,612	126,871	44,451	82,420	6,[illegible]11	2,472	3,739
25 - 30	204,081	107,689	97,292	32,033	27,019	5,014	161,202	75,860	85,342	11,746	4.810	6 936
30—35	180,232	97.959	82,273	18,377	14,955	3,422	148,320	77,480	70,840	1[illegible],535	5,524	8,011
35—40	129,500	70,911	58,589	7,798	5,688	2,110	104,187	59,564	44,[illegible]23	17,515	5,659	11,856
40—45	106,831	58,064	48,767	5,485	3,828	1,657	83,017	48,[illegible]13	34,304	18,329	5,523	12,806
45—50	83,087	46,315	36,772	3,466	2,380	1,086	58,726	38,069	20,657	20,895	5,866	15,029
50—55	66,027	36,437	29,590	2,309	1,491	818	44,574	29,613	14,[illegible]61	19,144	5,333	13,811
55—60	46,275	26,504	19,771	1,313	878	435	27,412	20,190	7,222	17,550	5,436	12,114
60—65	37,829	21,729	16,100	1,017	689	328	21,146	16 126	5,020	15,666	4,914	10,752
65—70	16,832	10,021	6,811	424	288	136	8,617	6,815	1,802	7,791	2,918	4,873
70 and over	32,375	19,646	12,729	984	661	323	14,350	11,757	2,593	17,041	7,228	9,813
HINDU ...	156,628	97,552	59,076	75,031	49.331	25,700	68,668	42,904	25,764	12,929	5,317	7,612
0—1	4,741	2,412	2,329	4,741	2,412	2,329	...	...	...	...	...	...
1—2	3,754	1,888	1,866	3,754	1,888	1,866	...	...	...	...	...	...
2 3	4,255	2,122	2,133	4,255	2,122	2,133	...	...	...	...	...	...
3 -4	4,229	2,117	2,112	4,229	2,117	2,112	...	...	...	...	...	...
4—5	4,078	2,088	1,990	4,078	2,088	1,990	...	...	...	...	...	...
Total 0—5	21,057	10,627	10,430	21,057	10,627	10,430	...	...	...	...	...	...
5—10	16,930	8,998	7,932	16,552	8,909	7,643	357	81	276	21	8	13
10—15	14,972	8,305	6,667	13,488	8,038	5,450	1,444	253	1,191	40	14	26
15—20	17,809	11,847	5,962	9,146	8,008	11,38	8,382	3,682	4,700	281	157	124
20—25	20,711	14,264	6,447	7,784	7,341	443	12,362	6,598	5,764	565	325	240
25—30	17,681	12,542	5,139	3,164	2,963	201	13,428	8,969	4,459	1,089	610	479
30—35	14,994	10,700	4,294	1,859	1,715	144	11,814	8,300	3,514	1,321	685	636
35—40	9,269	6,072	3,197	723	640	83	7.067	4,855	2,212	1,479	577	902
40—45	7,169	4,534	2,635	496	433	63	5,159	3,563	1,596	1,514	538	976
45—50	5,264	3,284	1,980	301	254	37	3,360	2,447	913	1,603	573	1,030
50 -55	3,956	2,417	1,539	191	166	25	2,348	1,744	604	1,417	507	910
55—60	2,575	1,521	1,054	98	85	12	1,281	1,022	259	1,196	413	783
60—65	1,968	1,139	829	73	61	12	895	728	168	999	350	649
65—70	896	526	370	38	33	5	348	292	56	510	201	309
70 and over	1,377	776	601	61	47	14	422	370	52	894	359	535

TABLE VII

Age, Sex and Civil Condition—Part I—Provincial Summary

Age	Population			Unmarried			Married			Widowed		
	Persons	Males	Females	Persons	Males	Females	Persons	Males	Females	Persons	Males	Females
1	2	3	4	5	6	7	8	9	10	11	12	13
SIKH	**47,935**	**31,409**	**16,526**	**23,807**	**15,481**	**7,326**	**20,836**	**13,408**	**7,428**	**3,292**	**1,520**	**1,772**
0—1	1,300	666	634	1,300	666	634	...	...	...	...	...	...
1—2	1,121	575	546	121	575	546	...	...	...	...	...	...
2—3	1,259	647	612	1,259	647	612	...	...	...	...	...	...
3—4	1,223	630	593	1,223	630	593	...	...	...	...	...	...
4—5	1,210	625	585	1,210	625	585	...	...	...	...	...	...
Total 0—5	**6,113**	**3,143**	**2,970**	**6,113**	**3,143**	**2,970**	...	...	...	...	...	...
5—10	5,008	2,664	2,344	4,892	2,643	2,249	107	17	90	9	4	5
10—15	4,436	2,431	2,005	3,937	2,361	1,576	489	69	420	10	1	9
15—20	5,964	4,273	1,691	3,202	2,924	278	2,673	1,292	1,381	89	57	32
20—25	7,113	5,279	1,834	3,058	2,955	103	3,889	2,218	1,671	166	106	60
25—30	5,601	4,142	1,459	1,254	1,211	43	4,069	2,758	1,311	278	173	105
30—35	4,456	3,325	1,131	718	685	33	3,449	2,473	976	289	167	122
35—40	2,625	1,796	8[illegible]	264	240	24	2,021	1,415	606	340	141	199
40—45	2,010	1,329	681	145	126	19	1,498	1,066	432	367	137	230
45—50	1,455	981	474	70	62	8	988	766	2	397	153	244
50—55	1,094	735	359	55	49	6	684	539	145	355	147	208
55—60	727	45[illegible]	268	40	30	10	385	311	74	302	118	184
60—65	573	358	215	23	19	4	290	238	52	260	101	159
65—70	297	200	[illegible]7	16	15	1	134	114	20	147	71	76
70 and over	463	2[illegible]4	169	20	18	2	160	132	28	283	144	139
CHRISTIAN	**16,499**	**13,212**	**3,287**	**11,599**	**10,086**	**1,513**	**4,438**	**2,830**	**1,608**	**462**	**296**	**166**
0—1	249	124	125	24[illegible]	124	125	...	...	...	...	...	...
1—2	217	112	105	21[illegible]	112	105	...	...	...	...	...	...
2—3	240	124	116	240	124	116	...	...	...	...	...	...
3—4	233	121	112	233	121	112	...	...	...	...	...	...
4—5	216	114	102	216	114	102	...	...	...	...	...	...
Total 0—5	**1,155**	**595**	**560**	**1,155**	**595**	**560**	...	...	...	...	...	...
5—10	812	450	362	804	447	357	7	2	5	1	1	...
10—15	670	383	287	627	375	252	40	7	33	3	1	2
15—20	2,360	2,088	272	2,055	1,956	99	292	120	172	13	12	1
20—25	3,985	3,629	356	3,413	3,339	74	541	267	274	31	23	8
25—30	3,262	2,849	413	2,253	2,206	47	957	599	358	52	44	8
30—35	1,887	1,513	374	870	829	41	959	638	321	58	46	12
35—40	939	698	241	222	192	30	654	463	191	63	43	20
40—45	639	467	172	117	98	19	460	330	130	62	39	23
45—50	320	222	98	37	21	16	235	177	58	48	24	24
50—55	232	161	71	25	14	11	162	126	36	45	21	24
55—60	99	70	29	12	8	4	58	46	12	29	16	13
60—65	69	46	23	3	2	1	44	33	11	22	11	11
65—70	29	18	11	2	1	1	13	10	3	14	7	7
70 and over	41	23	18	4	3	1	16	12	4	21	8	13
PARSI	**62**	**32**	**30**	**32**	**17**	**15**	**26**	**13**	**13**	**4**	**2**	**2**
0—1	4	3	1	4	3	1	...	...	...	...	...	...
1—2	...	...	...	...	...	...	...	...	...	...	...	...
2—3	3	1	2	3	1	2	...	...	...	...	...	...
3—4	1	...	1	1	...	1	...	...	...	...	...	...
4—5	1	1	...	1	1	...	...	...	...	...	...	...
Total 0—5	**9**	**5**	**4**	**9**	**5**	**4**	...	...	...	...	...	...
5—10	6	2	4	6	2	4	...	...	...	...	...	...
10—15	6	2	4	6	2	4	...	...	...	...	...	...
15—20	4	2	2	3	2	1	1	...	1	...	...	...
20—25	8	4	4	5	3	2	3	1	2	...	...	...
25—30	8	4	4	2	2	...	5	2	3	1	...	2
30—35	1	...	1	...	...	...	1	...	1	...	...	...
35—40	5	2	3	1	1	...	3	1	2	1	...	1
40—45	6	3	3	...	...	...	5	2	3	1	1	...
45—50	5	5	...	...	...	...	4	4	...	1	1	...
50—55	1	1	...	...	...	...	1	1	...	...	...	...
55—60	2	1	1	...	...	...	2	1	1	...	...	...
60—65	1	1	...	...	...	...	1	1	...	...	...	...
65—70	...	...	...	...	...	...	...	...	...	...	...	...
70 and over	...	...	...	...	...	...	...	...	...	...	...	...

TABLE VII

Age, Sex and Civil Condition—Part I—Provincial Summary

Age	Population			Unmarried			Married			Widowed		
	Persons	Males	Females	Persons	Males	Females	Persons	Males	Females	Persons	Males	Females
1	2	3	4	5	6	7	8	9	10	11	12	13
JEW	11	11	...	3	3	...	8	8	...	...	...	...
0—1	...	...	...	...	...	...	...	...	...	...	...	...
1—2	...	...	...	...	...	...	...	...	...	...	...	...
2—3	...	...	...	...	...	...	...	...	...	...	...	...
3—4	...	...	...	...	...	...	...	...	...	...	...	...
4—5	...	...	...	...	...	...	...	...	...	...	...	...
Total 0—5	...	...	...	...	...	...	...	...	...	...	...	...
5—10	...	...	...	...	...	...	...	...	...	...	...	...
10—15	...	...	...	...	...	...	...	...	...	...	...	...
15—20	2	2	...	2	2	...	...	...	...	...	...	...
20—25	1	1	...	1	1	...	...	...	...	...	...	...
25—30	1	1	...	...	...	...	1	1	...	...	...	...
30—35	2	2	...	...	...	...	2	2	...	...	...	...
35—40	1	1	...	...	...	...	1	1	...	...	...	...
40—45	1	1	...	...	...	...	1	1	...	...	...	...
45—50	2	2	...	...	...	...	2	2	...	...	...	...
50—55	1	1	...	...	...	...	1	1	...	...	...	...
55—60	...	...	...	...	...	...	...	...	...	...	...	...
60—65	...	...	...	...	...	...	...	...	...	...	...	...
65—70	...	...	...	...	...	...	...	...	...	...	...	...
70 and over	...	...	...	...	...	...	...	...	...	...	...	...
BUDDHIST	3	3	...	...	...	...	3	3	...	...	...	...
0—1	...	...	...	...	...	...	...	...	...	...	...	...
1—2	...	...	...	...	...	...	...	...	...	...	...	...
2—3	...	...	...	...	...	...	...	...	...	...	...	...
3—4	...	...	...	...	...	...	...	...	...	...	...	...
4—5	...	...	...	...	...	...	...	...	...	...	...	...
Total 0—5	...	...	...	...	...	...	...	...	...	...	...	...
5—10	...	...	...	...	...	...	...	...	...	...	...	...
10—15	...	...	...	...	...	...	...	...	...	...	...	...
15—20	1	1	...	...	...	...	1	1	...	...	...	...
20—25	...	...	...	...	...	...	...	...	...	...	...	...
25—30	...	...	...	...	...	...	...	...	...	...	...	...
30—35	1	1	...	...	...	...	1	1	...	...	...	...
35—40	1	1	...	...	...	...	1	1	...	...	...	...
40—45	...	...	...	...	...	...	...	...	...	...	...	...
45—50	...	...	...	...	...	...	...	...	...	...	...	...
50—55	...	...	...	...	...	...	...	...	...	...	...	...
55—60	...	...	...	...	...	...	...	...	...	...	...	...
60—65	...	...	...	...	...	...	...	...	...	...	...	...
65—70	...	...	...	...	...	...	...	...	...	...	...	...
70 and over	...	...	...	...	...	...	...	...	...	...	...	...

TABLE VII

Age, Sex and Civil Condition—Part II (a)—Districts

Age	Population			Unmarried			Married			Widowed		
	Persons	Males	Females	Persons	Males	Females	Persons	Males	Females	Persons	Males	Females
1	2	3	4	5	6	7	8	9	10	11	12	13
ALL RELIGIONS.	**2,425,076**	**1,315,818**	**1,109,258**	**1,270,111**	**761,820**	**508,291**	**970,777**	**491,044**	**479,733**	**184,188**	**62,954**	**121,234**
0—1	74,859	38,257	36,602	74,859	38,257	36,602	...	...	...	...	...	...
1—2	67,391	33,606	33,785	67,391	33,606	33,785	...	...	...	...	...	...
2—3	80,958	40,153	40,805	80,958	40,153	40,805	...	...	...	...	...	...
3—4	82,517	41,690	40,827	82,517	41,690	40,827	...	...	...	...	...	...
4—5	80,994	41,966	39,028	80,994	41,966	39,028	...	...	...	...	...	...
Total 0—5	**386,719**	**195,672**	**191,047**	**386,719**	**195,672**	**191,047**	...	...	...	...	...	...
5—10	334,706	183,669	151,037	331,028	182,738	148,290	3,518	857	2,661	160	74	86
10—15	288,425	163,622	124,803	268,883	159,554	109,329	18,939	3,817	15,122	603	251	352
15—20	215,504	117,251	98,253	120,974	90,806	30,168	91,337	25,096	66,241	3,193	1,349	1,844
20—25	226,255	119,063	107,192	81,107	67,884	13,223	138,399	48,470	89,929	6,749	2,709	4,040
25—30	221,499	117,355	104,144	35,544	30,241	5,303	173,141	81,823	91,318	12,814	5,291	7,523
30—35	194,565	106,608	87,957	20,522	16,885	3,637	159,152	83,608	75,544	14,891	6,115	8,776
35—40	139,663	76,883	62,780	8,714	6,471	2,243	111,708	64,136	47,572	19,241	6,276	12965
40—45	115,205	63,005	52,200	6,109	4,351	1,758	88,940	52,516	36,424	20,156	6,138	14,018
45—50	89,533	50,251	39,282	3,841	2,695	1,146	62,831	41,005	21,826	22,861	6,551	16,310
50—55	70,951	39,420	31,531	2,559	1,699	860	47,490	31,756	15,734	20,902	5,965	14,937
55—60	49,524	28,423	21,101	1,456	995	461	29,027	21,464	7,563	19,041	5,964	13 077
60—65	40,328	23,185	17,143	1,113	769	344	22,301	17,056	5,245	16,914	5,360	11 554
65—70	18,011	10,729	7,282	479	336	143	9,085	7,206	1,879	8,447	3,187	5,260
70 and over	34,188	20,682	13,506	1,063	724	339	14,909	12,234	2,675	18,216	7,724	10,492
MUSLIM	**2,227,303**	**1,196,120**	**1,031,183**	**1,170,488**	**696,336**	**474,152**	**888,526**	**443,251**	**445,275**	**168,289**	**56,533**	**111,756**
0—1	68,647	35,093	33,554	68,647	35,093	33,554	...	...	...	...	...	...
1—2	62,369	31,063	31,306	62,369	31,063	31,306	...	...	...	...	...	...
2—3	75,267	37,293	37,974	75,267	37,293	37,974	...	...	...	...	...	...
3—4	76,896	38,856	38,040	76,896	38,856	38,040	...	...	...	...	...	...
4—5	75,557	39,174	36,383	75,557	39,174	36,383	...	...	...	...	...	...
Total 0—5	**358,736**	**181,479**	**177,257**	**358,736**	**181,479**	**177,257**	...	...	...	...	...	...
5—10	312,253	171,728	140,525	309,072	170,908	138,164	3,052	759	2,293	129	61	68
10—15	268,655	152,709	115,946	251,109	148,971	102,138	16,995	3,502	13,493	551	236	315
15—20	193,848	103,440	90,408	109,470	80,804	28,666	81,499	21,445	60,054	2,879	1,191	1,688
20—25	201,114	102,470	98,644	70,842	58,238	12,604	124,161	41,857	82,304	6,111	2,375	3,736
25—30	200,065	102,868	97,197	30,754	25,741	5,013	157,736	72,486	85,250	11,575	4,641	6,934
30—35	176,766	94,562	82,204	17,889	14,469	3,420	145,496	74,721	70,775	13,381	5,372	8,009
35—40	128,117	69,570	58,547	7,695	5,587	2,108	102,988	58,398	44,590	17,434	5,585	11,849
40—45	106,074	57,333	48,741	5,440	3,783	1,657	82,365	48,079	34,286	18,269	5,471	12,798
45—50	82,753	46,001	36,752	3,450	2,365	1,085	58,453	37,807	20,646	20,850	5,829	15,021
50—55	65,834	36,257	29,577	2,300	1,482	818	44,418	29,463	14,955	19,116	5,312	13,804
55—60	46,187	26,426	19,761	1,311	876	435	27,346	20,127	7,219	17,530	5,423	12,107
60—65	37,760	21,671	16,089	1,015	687	328	21,096	16,080	5,016	15,649	4,904	10,745
65—70	16,803	9,995	6,808	424	288	136	8,596	6,795	1,801	7,783	2,912	4,871
70 and over	32,338	19,611	12,727	981	658	323	14,325	11,732	2,593	17,032	7,221	9,811
HINDU ...	**142,977**	**84,358**	**58,619**	**70,120**	**44,642**	**25,478**	**60,479**	**34,907**	**25,572**	**12,378**	**4,809**	**7 569**
0—1	4,691	2,388	2,303	4,691	2,388	2,303	...	...	...	...	...	...
1—2	3,716	1,874	1,842	3,716	1,874	1,842	...	...	...	...	...	...
2—3	4,221	2,105	2,116	4,221	2,105	2,116	...	...	...	...	...	...
3—4	4,196	2,098	2,098	4,196	2,098	2,098	...	...	...	...	...	...
4—5	4,045	2,070	1,975	4,045	2,070	1,975	...	...	...	...	...	...
Total 0—5	**20,869**	**10,535**	**10,334**	**20,869**	**10,535**	**10,334**	..	...	...	...	...	...
5—10	16,771	8,904	7,867	16,394	8,815	7,579	356	81	275	21	8	13
10—15	14,795	8,183	6,612	13,326	7,924	5,402	1,429	245	1,184	40	14	26
15—20	15,224	9,314	5,910	7,668	6,539	1,129	7,324	2,666	4,658	232	109	123
20—25	17,012	10,623	6,389	5,965	5,524	441	10,568	4,857	5,711	479	242	237
25—30	14,746	9,641	5,105	2,505	2,304	201	11,283	6,854	4,429	958	483	475
30—35	12,746	8,469	4,277	1,551	1,407	144	9,989	6,491	3,498	1,206	571	635
35—40	8,412	5,234	3,178	651	569	82	6,336	4,139	2,197	1,425	526	899
40—45	6,726	4,109	2,617	460	397	63	4,791	3,209	1,582	1,475	503	972
45—50	5,103	3,134	1,969	288	251	37	3,237	2,330	907	1,578	553	1,025
50—55	3,862	2,331	1,531	182	157	25	2,284	1,683	601	1,396	491	905
55—60	2,534	1,487	1,047	94	82	12	1,254	996	258	1,186	409	777
60—65	1,938	1,116	822	72	61	11	876	709	167	990	346	644
65—70	885	518	367	37	32	5	342	287	55	506	199	307
70 and over	1,354	760	594	58	45	13	410	360	50	886	355	531

TABLE VII

Age, Sex and Civil Condition—Part II (a)—Districts

Age	Population			Unmarried			Married			Widowed		
	Persons	Males	Females	Persons	Males	Females	Persons	Males	Females	Persons	Males	Females
1	2	3	4	5	6	7	8	9	10	11	12	13
SIKH	**42,510**	**26,284**	**16,226**	**21,430**	**14,256**	**7,174**	**17,962**	**10,658**	**7,304**	**3,118**	**1,370**	**1,748**
0—1	1,277	654	623	1,277	654	623	...	...	...	...	...	...
1—2	1,099	562	537	1,099	562	537	...	...	...	...	...	...
2—3	1,236	636	600	1,236	636	600	...	...	...	...	...	...
3—4	1,200	622	578	1,200	622	578	...	...	...	...	...	...
4—5	1,185	614	571	1,185	614	571	...	...	...	...	...	...
Total 0—5	5,997	3,088	2,909	5,997	3,088	2,909	...	...	...	...	...	...
5—10	4,903	2,611	2,292	4,789	2,592	2,197	105	15	90	9	4	5
10—15	4,336	2,370	1,966	3,847	2,306	1,541	480	64	416	9	...	9
15—20	4,870	3,200	1,670	2,542	2,267	275	2,256	893	1,363	72	40	32
20—25	5,580	3,770	1,810	2,236	2,133	103	3,209	1,562	1,647	135	75	60
25—30	4,485	3,051	1,434	916	873	43	3,329	2,043	1,286	240	135	105
30—35	3,645	2,537	1,108	531	498	33	2,856	1,902	954	258	137	121
35—40	2,351	1,538	813	217	194	23	1,810	1,216	594	324	128	196
40—45	1,867	1,198	669	133	114	19	1,380	956	424	354	128	226
45—50	1,390	926	464	69	61	8	933	717	216	388	148	240
50—55	1,055	702	353	54	48	6	651	509	142	350	145	205
55—60	714	450	264	40	30	10	375	302	73	299	118	181
60—65	563	353	210	23	19	4	285	234	51	255	100	155
65—70	296	200	96	16	15	1	134	114	20	146	71	75
70 and over	458	290	168	20	18	2	159	131	28	279	141	138
CHRISTIAN	**12,213**	**9,013**	**3,200**	**8,038**	**6,566**	**1,472**	**3,775**	**2,206**	**1,569**	**400**	**241**	**159**
0—1	240	119	121	240	119	121	...	...	...	...	...	...
1—2	207	107	100	207	107	100	...	...	...	...	...	...
2—3	231	118	113	231	118	113	...	...	...	...	...	...
3—4	224	114	110	224	114	110	...	...	...	...	...	...
4—5	206	107	99	206	107	99	...	...	...	...	...	...
Total 0—5	1,108	565	543	1,108	565	543	...	...	...	...	...	...
5—10	773	424	349	767	421	346	5	2	3	1	1	...
10—15	633	358	275	595	351	244	35	6	29	3	1	2
15—20	1,556	1,293	263	1,289	1,192	97	257	92	165	10	9	1
20—25	2,540	2,195	345	2,058	1,985	73	458	193	265	24	17	7
25—30	2,194	1,790	404	1,367	1,321	46	787	437	350	40	32	8
30—35	1,404	1,037	367	551	511	40	807	491	316	46	35	11
35—40	776	537	239	150	120	30	569	380	189	57	37	20
40—45	531	361	170	76	57	19	398	269	129	57	35	22
45—50	282	185	97	34	18	16	203	146	57	45	21	24
50—55	198	128	70	23	12	11	135	99	36	40	17	23
55—60	87	59	28	11	7	4	50	38	12	26	14	12
60—65	66	44	22	3	2	1	43	32	11	20	10	10
65—70	27	16	11	2	1	1	13	10	3	12	5	7
70 and over	38	21	17	4	3	1	15	11	4	19	7	12
PARSI	**60**	**30**	**30**	**32**	**17**	**15**	**25**	**12**	**13**	**3**	**1**	**2**
0—1	4	3	1	4	3	1	...	...	...	...	...	...
1—2	...	...	...	...	...	...	...	...	...	...	...	...
2—3	3	1	2	3	1	2	...	...	...	...	...	...
3—4	1	...	1	1	...	1	...	...	...	...	...	...
4—5	1	1	...	1	1	...	...	...	...	...	...	...
Total 0—5	9	5	4	9	5	4	...	...	...	...	...	...
5—10	6	2	4	6	2	4	...	...	...	...	...	...
10—15	6	2	4	6	2	4	...	...	...	...	...	...
15—20	4	2	2	3	2	1	1	...	1	...	...	...
20—25	8	4	4	5	3	2	3	1	2	...	...	...
25—30	8	4	4	2	2	...	5	2	3	1	...	1
30—35	1	...	1	...	...	...	1	...	1	...	...	...
35—40	5	2	3	1	1	...	3	1	2	1	...	1
40—45	6	3	3	...	...	...	5	2	3	1	1	...
45—50	3	3	...	...	...	...	3	3	...	...	...	...
50—55	1	1	...	...	...	...	1	1	...	...	...	...
55—60	2	1	1	...	...	...	2	1	1	...	...	...
60—65	1	1	...	...	...	...	1	1	...	...	...	...
65—70	...	...	...	...	...	...	...	...	...	...	...	...
70 and over	...	...	...	...	...	...	...	...	...	...	...	...

TABLE VII

Age, Sex and Civil Condition—Part II (a)—Districts

Age	Population			Unmarried			Married			Widowed		
	Persons	Males	Females	Persons	Males	Females	Persons	Males	Females	Persons	Males	Females
1	2	3	4	5	6	7	8	9	10	11	12	13
JEW	11	11	...	3	3	...	8	8	...	...	...	...
0—1	...	...	...	...	...	...	...	...	...	...	...	...
1—2	...	...	...	...	...	...	...	...	...	...	...	...
2—3	...	...	...	...	...	...	...	...	...	...	...	...
3—4	...	...	...	...	...	...	...	...	...	...	...	...
4—5	...	...	...	...	...	...	...	...	...	...	...	...
Total 0—5	...	...	...	...	...	...	...	...	...	...	...	...
5—10	...	...	...	...	...	...	...	...	...	...	...	...
10—15	...	...	...	...	...	...	...	...	...	...	...	...
15—20	2	2	...	2	2	...	...	...	...	...	...	...
20—25	1	1	...	1	1	...	...	...	...	...	...	...
25—30	1	1	...	...	...	...	1	1	...	...	...	...
30—35	2	2	...	...	...	...	2	2	...	...	...	...
35—40	1	1	...	...	...	...	1	1	...	...	...	...
40—45	1	1	...	...	...	...	1	1	...	...	...	...
45—50	2	2	...	...	...	...	2	2	...	...	...	...
50—55	1	1	...	...	...	...	1	1	...	...	...	...
55—60	...	...	...	...	...	...	...	...	...	...	...	...
60—65	...	...	...	...	...	...	...	...	...	...	...	...
65—70	...	...	...	...	...	...	...	...	...	...	...	...
70 and over	...	...	...	...	...	...	...	...	...	...	...	...
BUDDHIST	2	2	...	...	...	...	2	2	...	...	...	...
0—1	...	...	...	...	...	...	...	...	...	...	...	...
1—2	...	...	...	...	...	...	...	...	...	...	...	...
2—3	...	...	...	...	...	...	...	...	...	...	...	...
3—4	...	...	...	...	...	...	...	...	...	...	...	...
4—5	...	...	...	...	...	...	...	...	...	...	...	...
Total 0—5	...	...	...	...	...	...	...	...	...	...	...	...
5—10	...	...	...	...	...	...	...	...	...	...	...	...
10—15	...	...	...	...	...	...	...	...	...	...	...	...
15—20	...	...	...	...	...	...	...	...	...	...	...	...
20—25	...	...	...	...	...	...	...	...	...	...	...	...
25—30	...	...	...	...	...	...	...	...	...	...	...	...
30—35	1	1	...	...	...	...	1	1	...	...	...	...
35—40	1	1	...	...	...	...	1	1	...	...	...	...
40—45	...	...	...	...	...	...	...	...	...	...	...	...
45—50	...	...	...	...	...	...	...	...	...	...	...	...
50—55	...	...	...	...	...	...	...	...	...	...	...	...
55—60	...	...	...	...	...	...	...	...	...	...	...	...
60—65	...	...	...	...	...	...	...	...	...	...	...	...
65—70	...	...	...	...	...	...	...	...	...	...	...	...
70 and over	...	...	...	...	...	...	...	...	...	...	...	...

TABLE VII

Age, Sex and Civil Condition—Part II (*a*)—Districts

Age	Population			Unmarried			Married			Widowed		
	Persons	Males	Females	Persons	Males	Females	Persons	Males	Females	Persons	Males	Females
1	2	3	4	5	6	7	8	9	10	11	12	13
				HAZARA.								
All religions	**670,117**	**358,193**	**311,924**	**344,059**	**204,635**	**139,424**	**276,896**	**136,070**	**140,826**	**49,162**	**17,488**	**31,674**
0—1	22,565	11,334	11,231	22,565	11,334	11,231	...	...	...	...	...	...
1—2	18,911	9,474	9,437	18,911	9,474	9,437	...	...	...	...	...	...
2—3	22,790	11,386	11,404	22,790	11,386	11,404	...	...	...	...	...	...
3—4	23,464	11,836	11,628	23,464	11,836	11,628	...	...	...	...	...	...
4—5	23,366	11,947	11,419	23,366	11,947	11,419	...	...	...	...	...	...
Total 0—5	111,096	55,977	55,119	111,096	55,977	55,119	...	...	...	...	...	...
5—10	95,124	52,003	43,121	93,972	51,793	42,179	1,117	200	917	35	10	25
10—15	81,084	46,227	34,857	74,268	44,740	29,528	6,663	1,436	5,227	153	51	102
15—20	55,876	29,558	26,318	29,051	22,658	6,393	26,078	6,631	19,447	747	269	478
20—30	115,426	56,453	58,973	25,236	21,501	3,735	84,642	33,127	51,515	5,348	1,825	3,723
30—40	91,306	48,476	42,830	6,121	4,716	1,405	76,894	40,613	36,281	8,291	3,147	5,144
40—50	54,932	30,788	24,144	2,542	1,946	596	42,417	25,679	16,738	9,973	3,163	6,810
50—60	33,501	19,260	14,241	948	657	291	22,535	15,419	7,116	10,018	3,184	6,834
60 & over...	31,772	19,451	12,321	825	647	178	16,550	12,965	3 585	14,397	5,839	8,558
Muslim ...	**636,794**	**338,082**	**298,712**	**327,674**	**193,570**	**134,104**	**262,746**	**128,088**	**134,658**	**46,374**	**16,424**	**29,950**
0—1	21,458	10,778	10,680	21,458	10,778	10,980	...	...	...	...	...	...
1—2	18,066	9,039	9,027	18,066	9,039	9,027	...	...	...	...	...	...
2—3	21,856	10,891	10,965	21,856	10,891	10,965	...	...	...	...	...	...
3—4	22,529	11,347	11,182	22.529	11,347	11,182	...	..	...	...	...	...
4—5	22,452	11,472	10,980	22,452	11,472	10,980	...	...	...	...	...	...
Total 0—5	106,361	53,527	52,834	106,361	53,527	52,834	...	...	...	...	...	...
5—10	91,403	49,968	41,435	90,368	49,780	40 588	1,003	179	824	32	9	23
10—15	77,775	44,338	33,437	71,388	42,914	28,474	6,244	1,376	4,868	143	48	95
15—20	51,970	27,062	24,908	27,086	20,875	6,211	24,189	5,936	18,253	695	251	444
20—30	107,810	51,585	56,225	22,989	19,383	3,606	79,549	30,482	49,067	5,272	1,720	3,552
30—40	86,586	45,405	41,181	5,520	4,159	1,361	73,302	38,293	35,009	7,764	2,953	4,811
40—50	52,332	29,166	23,166	2,333	1,760	573	40,663	24,461	16,202	9,336	2,945	6,391
50—60	31,964	18,293	13,671	850	569	281	21,710	14,774	6,936	9,404	2,950	6,454
60 and over	30,593	18,738	11,855	779	603	176	16,086	12,587	3,499	13.728	5,548	8,180
Hindu ...	**25,260**	**15,461**	**9,799**	**12,359**	**8,489**	**3,870**	**10,732**	**6,165**	**4,567**	**2,169**	**807**	**1,362**
0—1	822	412	410	822	412	410	...	...	...	...	...	...
1—2	635	330	305	635	330	305	...	...	...	...	...	...
2—3	697	371	326	697	371	326	...	...	...	...	...	...
3—4	688	360	328	688	360	328	...	...	...	...	...	...
4—5	658	343	315	658	343	315	...	...	...	...	...	...
Total 0—5	3,500	1,816	1,684	3.500	1,816	1,684	...	...	...	...	...	..
5—10	2,656	1,454	1,202	2,583	1,440	1,143	70	13	57	3	1	2
10—15	2,407	1,381	1,026	2,097	1,336	761	300	42	258	10	3	7
15—20	3,148	2,045	1,103	1,586	1,450	136	1,520	583	937	42	12	30
20—30	6,024	3,947	2,077	1,816	1,723	93	3,990	2,146	1,844	218	78	140
30—40	3,603	2,390	1 213	491	463	28	2,697	1,780	917	415	147	268
40—50	1,929	1,194	735	174	155	19	1,244	865	379	511	174	337
50—60	1,161	733	428	75	71	4	604	479	125	482	183	299
60 and over	832	501	331	37	35	2	307	257	50	488	209	279
Sikh ...	**7,630**	**4,393**	**3,237**	**3,789**	**2,417**	**1,372**	**3,239**	**1,723**	**1,516**	**602**	**253**	**349**
0—1	270	139	131	270	139	131	...	...	...	...	...	...
1—2	197	99	98	197	99	98	...	...	...	...	...	...
2—3	225	117	108	225	117	108	...	...	...	...	...	...
3—4	233	120	113	233	120	113	...	...	...	...	...	...
4—5	242	124	118	242	124	118	...	...	...	...	...	...
Total 0—5	1,167	599	568	1,167	599	568	...	...	...	...	...	...
5—10	1,023	553	470	979	545	434	44	8	36	...	...	...
10—15	874	488	386	755	470	285	119	18	101	...	...	...
15—20	729	431	298	355	314	41	364	111	253	10	6	4
20—30	1,487	860	627	388	359	29	1,044	474	570	55	27	28
30—40	1,020	624	396	89	78	11	826	502	324	105	44	61
40—50	621	398	223	28	26	2	471	329	142	122	43	79
50—60	365	229	136	19	17	2	216	161	55	130	51	79
60 and over	344	211	133	9	9	...	155	120	35	180	82	98
Christian...	**432**	**256**	**176**	**237**	**159**	**78**	**178**	**93**	**85**	**17**	**4**	**13**
0—1	15	5	10	15	5	10	...	...	...	...	...	...
1—2	13	6	7	13	6	7	...	...	...	...	...	...
2—3	12	7	5	12	7	5	...	...	...	...	...	...
3—4	14	9	5	14	9	5	...	...	...	...	...	...
4—5	14	8	6	14	8	6	...	...	...	...	...	...
Total 0—5	68	35	33	68	35	33	...	...	...	...	...	...
5—10	42	28	14	42	28	14	...	...	...	...	...	...
10—15	28	20	8	28	20	8	...	...	...	...	...	...
15—20	29	20	9	24	19	5	5	1	4	...	...	...
20—30	105	61	44	43	36	7	59	25	34	3	...	3
30—40	97	57	40	21	16	5	69	38	31	7	3	4
40—50	49	29	20	7	5	2	38	23	15	4	1	3
50—60	11	5	6	4	...	4	5	5	...	2	...	2
60 and over	3	1	2	...	...	..	2	1	1	1	...	1

TABLE VII

Age, Sex and Civil Condition—Part II (*a*)—Districts

Age	Population			Unmarried			Married			Widowed		
	Persons	Males	Females	Persons	Males	Females	Persons	Males	Females	Persons	Males	Females
1	2	3	4	5	6	7	8	9	10	11	12	13
					PESHAWAR.							
All religions	974,321	538,146	436,175	517,968	315,774	202,194	382,777	198,678	184,099	73,576	23,694	49,882
0—1	25,898	13,608	12,290	25,898	13,608	12,290	...	...	...	...	...	...
1—2	26,363	13,297	13,066	26,363	13,297	13,066	...	...	...	...	...	...
2—3	30,594	15,158	15,436	30,594	15,158	15,436	...	...	...	...	...	...
3—4	30,486	15,495	14,991	30,486	15,495	14,991	...	...	...	...	...	...
4—5	30,226	15 945	14,281	30,226	15,945	14,281	...	...	...	...	...	...
Total 0—5	143,567	73,503	70,064	143,567	73,503	70,064	...	...	...	...	...	...
5—10	130,360	72,444	57,916	129,336	72,180	57,156	956	222	734	68	42	26
10—15	117,956	67,193	50,763	111,426	66,062	45,364	6,256	993	5,263	274	138	136
15—20	92,532	51,070	41,462	56,437	41,422	15,015	34,769	9,082	25,687	1,326	566	760
20—30	186,345	102,263	84,082	56,309	47,039	9,270	122,506	52,131	70,375	7,530	3,093	4,437
30—40	134,559	75,760	58,799	13,602	10,837	2,765	106,955	60,303	46,652	14,002	4,620	9,382
40—50	83,428	46,587	36,841	4,308	2,900	1,408	61,532	38,952	22,580	17,588	4,735	12,853
50—60	48,867	27,628	21,239	1,788	1,119	669	31,118	22,082	9,036	15,961	4,427	11,534
60 and over	36 707	21,698	15,009	1,195	712	483	18,685	14,913	3,772	16,827	6,073	10,754
Muslim ...	898,683	489,650	409,033	479,279	288,972	190,307	351,451	179,575	171,876	67,953	21,103	46,850
0—1	23,847	12,564	11,283	23,847	12,564	11,283	...	...	...	...	...	...
1—2	24,495	12,333	12,162	24,495	12,333	12,162	...	...	...	...	...	...
2—3	28,530	14,124	14,406	28,530	14,124	14,406	...	...	...	...	...	...
3 4	28,514	14,501	14,013	28,514	14,501	14,013	...	...	...	...	...	...
4—5	28,349	14,982	13,367	28,349	14,982	13,367	...	...	...	...	...	...
Total 0—5	133,735	68,504	65,231	133,735	68,504	65,231	...	...	...	...	...	...
5—10	122,579	68,300	54,270	121,707	68,079	53,628	816	195	621	56	35	21
10—15	110,965	63,308	47,657	105,178	62,294	42,884	5,531	882	4,649	256	132	124
15—20	83,730	45 103	38 627	51,484	36,957	14,527	31,038	7,649	23,389	1,208	497	711
20—30	166,602	88,082	78 520	48,736	39,787	8,949	111,078	45,664	65,414	6,788	2,631	4,157
30—40	122,967	67,563	55,404	11,875	9,250	2,625	98,293	54,324	43,969	12,799	3,989	8,810
40—50	77,495	42,620	34,875	3,828	2,482	1,346	57,453	35,953	21,500	16,214	4,185	12,029
50—60	45,880	25,690	20,190	1,631	988	643	29 404	20,718	8,686	14,845	3,984	10,861
60 and over	34,730	20,471	14,259	1,105	631	474	17,838	14,190	3,648	15,787	5,650	10,137
Hindu ...	42,321	26,501	15,820	20,229	13,430	6,799	18,530	11,431	7,099	3,562	1,640	1,922
0—1	1,205	610	595	1,205	610	595	...	...	...	...	...	...
1—2	1,096	557	539	1,096	557	539	...	...	...	...	...	...
2—3	1,202	603	599	1,202	603	599	...	...	...	...	...	...
3—4	1,141	576	565	1,141	576	565	...	...	...	...	...	...
4—5	1,076	557	519	1,076	557	519	...	...	...	...	...	...
Total 0—5	5,720	2,903	2,817	5,720	2,903	2,817	...	...	...	...	...	...
5—10	4,505	2,401	2,104	4,407	2,377	2,030	94	21	73	4	3	1
10—15	4,073	2,287	1,786	3,640	2,204	1,436	424	78	346	9	5	4
15—20	4,664	3 002	1,662	2,365	2,106	259	2,231	856	1,375	68	40	28
20—30	10,198	6,996	3,202	2,924	2,773	151	6,808	3,929	2,879	466	294	172
30—40	6,679	4,722	1,957	767	703	64	5,119	3,596	1,523	793	423	370
40—50	3,539	2,365	1,174	273	248	25	2,392	1,771	621	874	346	528
50—60	1,788	1,134	654	82	71	11	996	785	211	710	278	432
60 and over	1,155	691	464	51	45	6	466	395	71	638	251	387
Sikh ...	24,271	15,211	9,060	12,220	8,235	3,985	10,275	6,209	4,066	1,776	767	1,009
0—1	671	345	326	671	345	326	...	...	...	...	...	...
1—2	621	327	294	621	327	294	...	...	...	...	...	...
2—3	695	349	346	695	349	346	...	...	...	...	...	...
3 4	669	339	330	669	339	330	...	...	...	...	...	...
4—5	653	331	322	653	331	322	...	...	...	...	...	...
Total 0—5	3,309	1,691	1,618	3,309	1,691	1,618	...	...	...	...	...	...
5—10	2,698	1,427	1,271	2,646	1,419	1,227	45	5	40	7	3	4
10—15	2,441	1,333	1,108	2,154	1,303	851	280	30	250	7	...	7
15—20	2,891	1,910	981	1,525	1,373	152	1,324	515	809	42	22	20
20—30	5,922	4,083	1,839	1,907	1,824	83	3,788	2,132	1,656	227	127	100
30—40	3,425	2,385	1,040	456	427	29	2,633	1,803	830	336	155	181
40—50	1,856	1,237	619	134	120	14	1,292	954	338	430	163	267
50—60	1,000	671	329	53	45	8	585	483	102	362	143	219
60 and over	729	474	255	36	33	3	328	287	41	365	154	211
Christian...	8,974	6,742	2,232	6,205	5,117	1,088	2,487	1,442	1,045	282	183	99
0—1	171	86	85	171	86	85	...	...	...	...	...	...
1—2	151	80	71	151	80	71	...	...	...	...	...	...
2—3	164	81	83	164	81	83	...	...	...	...	...	...
3—4	161	79	82	161	79	82	...	...	...	...	...	...
4—5	147	74	73	147	74	73	...	...	...	...	...	...
Total 0—5	794	400	394	794	400	394	...	...	...	...	...	...
5—10	572	305	267	570	303	267	1	1	...	1	1	...
10—15	471	263	208	448	259	189	21	3	18	2	1	1
15—20	1,241	1,051	190	1,058	982	76	175	62	113	8	7	1
20—30	3,605	3,092	513	2,734	2,649	85	823	402	421	48	41	7
30—40	1,477	1,083	394	503	456	47	901	574	327	73	53	20
40—50	527	357	170	73	50	23	385	267	118	69	40	29
50—60	195	130	65	22	15	7	129	93	36	44	22	22
60 and over	92	61	31	3	3	...	52	40	12	37	18	19

TABLE VII

Age, Sex and Civil Condition—Part II (a)—Districts

Age	Population			Unmarried			Married			Widowed		
	Persons	Males	Females	Persons	Males	Females	Persons	Males	Females	Persons	Males	Females
1	2	3	4	5	6	7	8	9	10	11	12	13
					KOHAT.							
All religions	236,273	126,210	110,063	124,796	73,124	51,672	93,702	47,311	46,391	17,775	5,775	12,000
0—1	7,560	3,806	3,754	7,560	3,806	3,754	...	...	...	...	...	...
1—2	7,113	3,454	3,659	7,113	3,454	3,659	...	...	...	...	...	...
2—3	8,773	4,321	4,452	8,773	4,321	4,452	...	...	...	...	...	...
3—4	8,864	4,482	4,382	8,864	4,482	4,382	...	...	...	...	...	...
4—5	8,481	4,356	4,125	8,481	4,356	4.125	...	...	...	...	...	...
Total 0—5	40,791	20,419	20,372	40,791	20,419	20,372	...	...	...	...	...	...
5—10	33,763	18,235	15.528	33,118	18,038	15,080	624	186	438	21	11	10
10—15	27,870	15,499	12,371	25,515	14,923	10,592	2,290	553	1,737	65	23	42
15—20	20,541	10,985	9,556	10,691	7,918	2,773	9,512	2,934	6,578	338	133	205
20—30	43,592	23,003	20,589	10,225	8,406	1,819	31,520	13,808	17,712	1,847	789	1,058
30—40	31,378	17,087	14,291	3,040	2,445	595	25,039	13,457	11,582	3,299	1,185	2,114
40—50	18,888	10,173	8,715	878	603	275	13,733	8,379	5,354	4,277	1,191	3,086
50—60	11,399	6,267	5,132	360	251	109	7,055	4,906	2,149	3,984	1,110	2,874
60 and over	8,051	4,542	3,509	178	121	57	3,929	3,088	841	3,944	1,333	2,611
Muslim ...	218,445	114,487	103,958	115,969	67,090	48,879	86,001	42,207	43,794	16,475	5,190	11,285
0—1	7,061	3,550	3,511	7,061	3,550	3.511	...	...	...	..	...	...
1—2	6,716	3,252	3,464	6,716	3,252	3,464	...	...	...	...	...	...
2—3	8,264	4,071	4,193	8,264	4,071	4,193	...	...	...	...	...	...
3—4	8,381	4,242	4,139	8,381	4,242	4,139	...	...	...	...	...	...
4—5	8,039	4,129	3,910	8,039	4,129	3,910	...	...	...	...	...	...
Total 0—5	38,461	19,244	19,217	38,461	19,244	19,217	...	...	...	...	...	...
5—10	31,984	17,287	14,697	31,366	17,093	14,273	599	183	416	19	11	8
10—15	26,318	14,635	11,683	24,109	14,085	10,024	2,150	528	1,622	59	22	37
15—20	18,408	9,505	8,903	9,537	6,901	2,636	8,568	2,495	6,073	303	109	194
20—30	38,696	19,279	19,417	8,515	6,779	1,736	28,535	11,840	16,695	1,646	660	986
30—40	28,526	15,013	13,513	2,663	2,091	572	22,865	11,895	10,970	2,998	1,027	1,971
40—50	17,614	9,343	8,271	813	549	264	12,837	7,717	5.120	3,964	1,077	2,887
50—60	10,750	5,860	4,890	331	229	102	6,681	4,604	2,077	3,738	1,027	2,711
60 and over	7,688	4,321	3,367	174	119	55	3,766	2,945	821	3,748	1,257	2,491
Hindu ...	1,3393	8,504	4,889	6,478	4,215	2,263	5,845	3,830	2,015	1,070	459	611
0—1	397	198	199	397	198	199	...	...	...	...	...	...
1—2	306	156	150	306	156	150	...	...	...	...	...	...
2—3	402	196	206	402	196	206	...	...	...	...	...	...
3—4	389	191	198	389	191	198	...	...	...	...	...	...
4—5	353	180	173	353	180	173	...	...	...	...	...	...
Total 0—5	1,847	921	926	1,847	921	926	...	...	...	...	...	...
5—10	1,455	769	686	1,432	766	666	21	3	18	2	...	2
10—15	1,267	702	565	1,152	682	470	110	19	91	5	1	4
15—20	1,505	998	507	777	668	109	703	313	390	25	17	8
20—30	3,374	2,474	900	978	911	67	2,239	1,468	771	157	95	62
30—40	2,126	1,499	627	220	207	13	1,653	1,165	488	253	127	126
40—50	1,004	644	360	47	42	5	695	505	190	262	97	165
50—60	520	323	197	23	18	5	293	239	54	204	66	138
60 and over	255	174	121	2	...	2	131	118	13	162	56	106
Sikh ...	3,249	2,292	957	1,635	1,204	431	1,403	972	431	211	116	95
0—1	86	50	36	86	50	36	...	...	...	...	...	...
1—2	78	40	38	78	40	38	...	...	...	...	...	...
2—3	87	43	44	87	43	44	...	...	...	...	...	...
3—4	79	41	38	79	41	38	...	...	...	...	...	...
4—5	74	39	35	74	39	35	...	...	...	...	...	...
Total 0—5	404	213	191	404	213	191	...	...	...	...	...	...
5—10	270	149	121	267	149	118	3	...	3	...	...	...
10—15	239	136	103	213	131	82	25	5	20	1	...	1
15—20	491	366	125	271	248	23	210	111	99	10	7	3
20—30	1,017	807	210	385	376	9	591	399	192	41	32	9
30—40	487	390	97	82	77	5	361	286	75	44	27	17
40—50	184	125	39	9	6	3	130	105	25	45	14	31
50—60	99	65	34	3	3	...	57	45	12	39	17	22
60 and over	58	41	17	1	1	...	26	21	5	31	19	12
Christian...	1,186	927	259	714	615	99	453	302	151	19	10	9
0—1	16	8	8	16	8	8	...	...	...	...	...	...
1—2	13	6	7	13	6	7	...	...	...	...	...	...
2—3	20	11	9	20	11	9	...	...	...	...	...	...
3—4	15	8	7	15	8	7	...	...	...	...	...	...
4—5	15	8	7	15	8	7	...	...	...	...	...	...
Total 0—5	79	41	38	79	41	38	...	...	...	...	...	...
5—10	54	30	24	53	30	23	1	...	1	...	...	...
10—15	46	26	20	41	25	16	5	1	4	...	...	...
15—20	137	116	21	106	101	5	31	15	16	...	...	...
20—30	505	443	62	347	340	7	155	101	54	3	2	1
30—40	239	185	54	75	70	5	160	111	49	4	4	...
40—50	86	61	25	9	6	3	71	52	19	6	3	3
50—60	30	19	11	3	1	2	24	18	6	3	...	3
60 and over	10	6	4	1	1	...	6	4	2	3	1	2

TABLE VII

Age, Sex and Civil Condition—Part II (a)—Districts

Age	Population			Unmarried			Married			Widowed		
	Persons	Males	Females	Persons	Males	Females	Persons	Males	Females	Persons	Males	Females
1	2	3	4	5	6	7	8	9	10	11	12	13
					BANNU.							
All religions	270,301	145,163	125,138	143,410	84,167	59,243	106,011	53,231	52,780	20,880	7,765	13,115
0—1	9,223	4,691	4,532	9,223	4,691	4,532	...	...	...	...	...	...
1—2	7,852	3,859	3,993	7,852	3,859	3,993	...	...	...	...	...	...
2—3	10,029	4,873	5,156	10,029	4,873	5,156	...	...	..	...	...	...
3—4	10,492	5,182	5,310	10,492	5,182	5,310	...	...	...	...	...	...
4—5	9,911	5,033	4,878	9,911	5,033	4,878	...	...	...	...	...	...
Total 0—5	47,507	23,638	23,869	47,507	23,638	23,869	...	...	...	...	...	...
5—10	38,027	20,468	17,559	37,561	20,318	17,243	443	144	299	23	6	17
10—15	29,914	16,837	13,077	28,102	16,380	11,722	1,757	437	1,320	55	20	35
15—20	22,328	12,311	10,017	11,966	8,982	2,984	9,998	3,145	6,853	364	184	180
20—30	50,587	27,036	23,551	12,712	10,645	2,067	35,625	15,284	20,341	2,250	1,107	1,143
30—40	38,287	20,941	17,346	3,522	2,819	703	30,544	16,383	14,161	4,221	1,739	2,482
40—50	23,558	12,660	10,898	1,233	842	391	16,800	10,065	6,735	5,525	1,753	3,772
50—60	13,085	7,238	5,847	565	377	188	7,629	5,248	2,381	4,891	1,613	3,278
60 and over	7,008	4,034	2,974	242	166	76	3,215	2,525	690	3,551	1,343	2,208
Muslim ...	237,674	126,671	111,003	126,658	73,816	52,842	92,763	46,068	46,695	18,253	6,787	11,466
0—1	8,025	4,062	3,963	8,025	4,062	3,963	...	...	...	...	...	...
1—2	6,920	3,393	3,527	6,920	3,393	3,527	...	...	...	...	...	...
2—3	8,985	4,359	4,626	8,985	4,359	4,626	...	...	...	...	...	...
3—4	9,433	4,662	4,771	9,433	4,662	4,771	...	...	...	...	...	...
4—5	8,885	4,499	4,386	8,885	4,499	4,386	...	...	...	...	...	...
Total 0—5	42,248	20,975	21,273	42,248	20,975	21,273	...	...	...	...	...	...
5—10	33,867	18,256	15,611	33,484	18,132	15,352	368	120	248	15	4	11
10—15	26,413	14,930	11,483	24,896	14,529	10,367	1,473	384	1,089	44	17	27
15—20	19,164	10,474	8,690	10,348	7,639	2,709	8,494	2,671	5,823	322	164	158
20—30	43,673	22,856	20,817	10,842	8,931	1,911	30,871	12,962	17,909	1,960	963	997
30—40	33,611	18,095	15,516	3,034	2,396	638	26,913	14,172	12,741	3,664	1,527	2,137
40—50	20,857	11,107	9,750	1,101	741	360	14,930	8,842	6,088	4,826	1,524	3,302
50—60	11,669	6,432	5,237	505	334	171	6,835	4,670	2,165	4,329	1,428	2,901
60 and over	6,172	3,546	2,626	200	139	61	2,879	2,247	632	3,093	1,160	1,933
Hindu ...	26,181	14,528	11,653	13,308	8,070	5,238	10,642	5,669	4,973	2,231	789	1,442
0—1	981	526	455	981	526	455	...	...	...	...	...	...
1—2	761	385	376	761	385	376	...	...	...	...	...	...
2—3	854	412	442	854	412	442	...	...	...	...	...	...
3—4	875	422	453	875	422	453	...	...	...	...	...	...
4—5	851	437	414	851	437	414	...	...	...	...	...	...
Total 0—5	4,322	2,182	2,140	4,322	2,182	2,140	...	...	...	...	...	...
5—10	3,428	1,823	1,605	3,358	1,800	1,558	63	21	42	7	2	5
10—15	2,870	1,574	1,296	2,628	1,528	1,100	233	43	190	9	3	6
15—20	2,487	1,397	1,090	1,253	1,026	227	1,199	354	845	35	17	18
20—30	5,309	3,068	2,241	1,260	1,134	126	3,802	1,812	1,990	247	122	125
30—40	3,701	2,199	1,502	322	276	46	2,898	1,746	1,152	481	177	304
40—50	2,188	1,237	951	91	72	19	1,507	980	527	590	185	405
50—60	1,173	650	523	44	33	11	659	478	181	470	139	331
60 and over	703	398	305	30	19	11	281	235	46	392	144	248
Sikh ...	5,482	3,278	2,204	2,851	1,807	1,044	2,271	1,301	970	360	170	190
0—1	193	89	104	193	89	104	...	...	...	...	...	...
1—2	152	70	82	152	70	82	...	...	...	...	...	...
2—3	167	89	78	167	89	78	...	...	...	...	...	...
3—4	162	87	75	162	87	75	...	...	...	...	...	...
4—5	157	87	70	157	87	70	...	...	...	...	...	...
Total 0—5	831	422	409	831	422	409	...	...	...	...	...	...
5—10	670	353	317	658	351	307	11	2	9	1	...	1
10—15	579	305	274	533	296	237	45	9	36	1	...	1
15—20	568	359	209	291	246	45	270	110	160	7	3	4
20—30	1,257	823	434	380	359	21	840	446	394	37	18	19
30—40	795	522	273	104	95	9	621	396	225	70	31	39
40—50	437	268	169	28	20	8	311	209	102	98	39	59
50—60	221	142	79	15	10	5	123	90	33	83	42	41
60 and over	124	84	40	11	8	3	50	39	11	63	37	26
Christian...	964	686	278	593	474	119	335	193	142	36	19	17
0—1	24	14	10	24	14	10	...	...	...	...	...	...
1—2	19	11	8	19	11	8	...	...	...	...	...	...
2—3	23	13	10	23	13	10	...	...	...	...	...	...
3—4	22	11	11	22	11	11	...	...	...	...	...	...
4—5	18	10	8	18	10	8	...	...	...	...	...	...
Total 0—5	106	59	47	106	59	47	...	...	...	...	...	...
5—10	62	36	26	61	35	26	1	1	...	...	...	...
10—15	52	28	24	45	27	18	6	1	5	1	...	1
15—20	109	81	28	74	71	3	35	10	25	...	...	...
20—30	348	289	59	230	221	9	112	64	48	6	4	2
30—40	180	125	55	62	52	10	112	69	43	6	4	2
40—50	76	48	28	13	9	4	52	34	18	11	5	6
50—60	22	14	8	1	...	1	12	10	2	9	4	5
60 and over	9	6	3	1	...	1	5	4	1	3	2	1

TABLE VII

Age, Sex and Civil Condition—Part II (a)— Districts

Age	Population			Unmarried			Married			Widowed		
	Persons	Males	Females	Persons	Males	Females	Persons	Males	Females	Persons	Males	Females
1	2	3	4	5	6	7	8	9	10	11	12	13
				DERA ISMAIL KHAN.								
All religions	274,064	148,106	125,958	139,878	84,120	55,758	111,391	55,754	55,637	22,795	8,232	14,563
0—1	9,613	4,818	4,795	9,613	4,818	4,795	...	...	...	...	...	...
1—2	7,152	3,522	3,630	7,152	3,522	3,630	...	...	...	...	...	...
2—3	8,772	4,415	4,357	8,772	4,415	4,357	...	...	...	...	...	...
3—4	9,211	4,695	4,516	9,211	4,695	4,516	...	...	...	...	...	...
4—5	9,010	4,685	4,325	9,010	4,685	4,325	...	...	...	...	...	...
Total 0—5	43,758	22,135	21,623	43,758	22,135	21,623	...	...	...	...	...	...
5—10	37,432	20,519	16,913	37,041	20,409	16,632	378	105	273	13	5	8
10—15	31,601	17,866	13,735	29,572	17,449	12,123	1,973	398	1,575	56	19	37
15—20	24,227	13,327	10,900	12,829	9,826	3,003	10,980	3,304	7,676	418	197	221
20—30	51,804	27,663	24,141	12,169	10,534	1,635	37,247	15,943	21,304	2,388	1,186	1,202
30—40	38,698	21,227	17,471	2,951	2,539	412	31,428	16,988	14,440	4,319	1,700	2,619
40—50	23,932	13,048	10,884	989	755	234	17,289	10,446	6,843	5,654	1,847	3,807
50—60	13,623	7,450	6,173	354	290	64	8,180	5,565	2,615	5,089	1,505	3,494
60 and over	8,989	4,871	4,118	215	183	32	3,916	3,005	911	4,858	1,683	3,175
Muslim ...	235,707	127,230	108 477	120,908	72,888	48,020	95,565	47,313	48,252	19,234	7,029	12,205
0—1	8,256	4,139	4,117	8,256	4,139	4,117	...	...	...	...	...	...
1—2	6,172	3 046	3,126	6,172	3,046	3,126	...	...	...	...	...	...
2—3	7,632	3,848	3,784	7,632	3,848	3,784	...	...	...	...	...	...
3—4	8.039	4,104	3,935	8,039	4,104	3,935	...	...	...	...	...	...
4—5	7,832	4,092	3,740	7,832	4,092	3,740	...	...	...	...	...	...
Total 0—5	37,931	19,229	18,702	37,931	19,229	18,702	...	...	...	...	...	...
5—10	32,420	17,908	14,512	32,147	17,824	14,323	266	82	184	7	2	5
10—15	27,184	15,498	11,686	25,538	15,149	10,389	1,597	332	1,265	49	17	32
15—20	20,576	11,296	9,280	11,015	8,432	2,583	9,210	2,694	6,516	351	170	181
20—30	44,398	23.536	20,862	10,514	9,099	1,415	31,864	13.395	18,469	2,020	1,042	978
30—40	33,193	18,056	15,137	2,492	2,160	332	27,111	14,435	12,676	3,590	1,461	2,129
40—50	20,529	11,098	9,431	815	616	199	14,935	8,913	6,022	4,779	1,569	3,210
50—60	11,758	6,408	5,350	294	238	56	7,134	4,824	2,310	4,330	1,346	2,984
60 and over	7,718	4,201	3,517	162	141	21	3,448	2,638	810	4,108	1,422	2,686
Hindu ...	35,822	19,364	16,458	17,746	10,438	7,308	14,730	7,812	6,918	3,346	1,114	2,232
0—1	1,286	642	644	1,286	642	644	...	...	...	...	...	...
1—2	918	446	472	918	446	472	...	...	...	...	...	...
2—3	1,066	523	543	1,066	523	543	...	...	...	...	...	...
3—4	1,103	549	554	1,103	549	554	...	...	...	...	...	...
4—5	1,107	553	554	1,107	553	554	...	...	...	...	...	...
Total 0—5	5,480	2,713	2,767	5,480	2,713	2,767	...	...	...	...	...	...
5—10	4,727	2,457	2,270	4,614	2,432	2,182	108	23	85	5	2	3
10—15	4,178	2,239	1,939	3,809	2,174	1,635	362	63	299	7	2	5
15—20	3,420	1,872	1,548	1,687	1,289	398	1,671	560	1,111	62	23	39
20—30	6,853	3,779	3.074	1,492	1,287	205	5,012	2,356	2,656	349	136	213
30—40	5,049	2,893	2,156	402	327	75	3,958	2,343	1,615	689	223	466
40—50	3,169	1,803	1,366	163	131	32	2,190	1,418	772	816	254	562
50—60	1.754	978	776	52	46	6	986	698	288	716	234	482
60 and over	1,192	630	562	47	39	8	443	351	92	702	240	462
Sikh ...	1,878	1,110	768	935	593	342	774	453	321	169	64	105
0—1	57	31	26	57	31	26	...	...	...	...	...	...
1—2	51	26	25	51	26	25	...	...	...	...	...	...
2—3	62	38	24	62	38	24	...	...	...	...	...	...
3—4	57	35	22	57	35	22	...	...	...	...	...	...
4—5	59	33	26	59	33	26	...	...	...	...	...	...
Total 0—5	286	163	123	286	163	123	...	...	...	...	...	...
5—10	242	129	113	239	128	111	2	...	2	1	1	...
10—15	203	108	95	192	106	86	11	2	9	...	...	...
15—20	191	134	57	100	86	14	88	46	42	3	2	1
20—30	382	248	134	92	88	4	275	154	121	15	6	9
30—40	269	154	115	17	15	2	225	131	94	27	8	19
40—50	159	96	63	3	3	...	109	76	33	47	17	30
50—60	84	45	39	4	3	1	45	32	13	35	10	25
60 and over	62	33	29	2	1	1	19	12	7	41	20	21
Christian...	657	402	255	289	201	88	322	176	145	46	25	21
0—1	14	6	8	14	6	8	...	...	...	...	...	...
1—2	11	4	7	11	4	7	...	...	...	...	...	...
2—3	12	6	6	12	6	6	...	...	...	...	...	...
3—4	12	7	5	12	7	5	...	...	...	...	...	...
4—5	12	7	5	12	7	5	...	...	...	...	...	...
Total 0—5	61	30	31	61	30	31	...	...	...	...	...	...
5—10	43	25	18	41	25	16	2	...	2	...	...	...
10—15	36	21	15	33	20	13	3	1	2	...	...	...
15—20	40	25	15	27	19	8	11	4	7	2	2	...
20—30	171	100	71	71	60	11	96	38	58	4	2	2
30—40	187	124	63	40	37	3	134	79	55	13	8	5
40—50	75	51	24	8	5	3	55	39	16	12	7	5
50—60	27	19	8	4	3	1	15	11	4	8	5	3
60 and over	17	7	10	4	2	2	6	4	2	7	1	6

TABLE VII

Age, Sex and Civil Condition, Part II (b)—Trans-Frontier Posts

Age	Population			Unmarried			Married			Widowed		
	Persons	Males	Females	Persons	Males	Females	Persons	Males	Females	Persons	Males	Females
1	2	3	4	5	6	7	8	9	10	11	12	13
All religions	46,451	44,635	1,816	**20,296**	19,415	881	**24,629**	**23,827**	**802**	1,526	1,393	133
0—1	174	90	84	174	90	84	...	...	...	...	...	...
1—2	133	59	74	133	59	74	...	...	...	...	...	...
2—3	145	73	72	145	73	72	..	...	...	...	...	...
3—4	151	79	72	151	79	72	...	...	...	...	...	...
4—5	147	76	71	147	76	71	...	...	...	...	...	...
Total 0—5	**750**	**377**	**373**	**750**	**377**	**373**	...	...	...	...	...	...
5—10	641	368	273	632	363	269	9	5	4	...	...	...
10—15	778	562	216	708	522	186	68	39	29	2	1	1
15—20	8,791	8,607	184	5,751	5,721	30	2,927	2,777	150	113	109	4
20—30	23,018	22,635	383	10,654	10,641	13	11,788	11,431	357	576	563	13
30—40	9,685	9,490	195	1,596	1,589	7	7,620	7,450	170	469	451	18
40—50	2,051	1,951	100	167	166	1	1,684	1,619	65	200	166	34
50—60	514	464	50	28	28	...	391	374	17	95	62	33
60 and over	223	181	42	10	8	2	142	132	10	71	41	30
Muslim	**23,085**	**22,114**	**972**	**9,447**	**8,981**	**466**	**12,901**	**12,454**	**447**	**738**	**679**	**59**
0—1	92	49	43	92	49	43	...	...	...	...	...	...
1—2	63	27	36	63	27	36	...	...	...	...	...	...
2—3	79	39	40	79	39	40	...	...	...	...	...	...
3—4	86	45	41	86	45	41	...	...	...	...	...	...
4—5	79	40	39	79	40	39	...	...	...	...	...	...
Total 0—5	**399**	**200**	**199**	**399**	**200**	**199**	...	...	...	...	...	...
5—10	338	195	143	334	192	142	4	3	1	...	...	...
10—15	464	354	110	424	329	95	39	25	14	1	...	1
15—20	4,307	4,205	102	2,847	2,831	16	1,416	1,333	83	44	41	3
20—30	11;222	11,000	222	4,775	4,766	9	6,176	5,968	208	271	266	5
30—40	4,849	4,738	111	591	587	4	4,023	3,925	98	235	226	9
40—50	1,091	1,045	46	61	60	1	925	896	29	105	89	16
50—60	281	258	23	11	11	...	222	213	9	48	34	14
60 and over	135	119	16	5	5	...	96	91	5	34	23	11
Hindu	**13,651**	**13,194**	**457**	**4,911**	**4,689**	**222**	**8,189**	**7,997**	**192**	**551**	**508**	**43**
0—1	50	24	26	50	24	26	...	...	...	...	...	...
1—2	38	14	24	38	14	24	...	...	...	...	...	...
2—3	34	17	17	34	17	17	...	...	...	...	...	...
3—4	33	19	14	33	19	14	...	...	...	...	...	...
4—5	33	18	15	33	18	15	...	...	...	...	...	...
Total 0—5	**188**	**92**	**96**	**188**	**92**	**96**	...	...	...	...	...	...
5—10	159	94	65	158	94	64	1	...	1	...	...	...
10—15	177	122	55	162	114	48	15	8	7	...	...	...
15—20	2,585	2,533	52	1,478	1,469	9	1,058	1,016	42	49	48	1
20—30	6,634	6,542	92	2,478	2,476	2	3,939	3,856	83	217	210	7
30—40	3.105	3,069	36	380	379	1	2,556	2,525	31	169	165	4
40—50	604	575	29	49	49	...	491	471	20	64	55	9
50—60	135	120	15	13	13	...	91	87	4	31	20	11
60 and over	64	47	17	5	3	2	38	34	4	21	10	11
Sikh	**5,425**	**5,125**	**300**	**2,377**	**2,285**	**152**	**2,874**	**2,750**	**124**	**174**	**150**	**24**
0—1	23	12	11	23	12	11	...	...	...	...	...	...
1—2	22	13	9	22	13	9	...	...	...	...	...	...
2—3	23	11	12	23	11	12	...	...	...	...	...	...
3—4	23	8	15	23	8	15	...	...	...	...	...	...
4—5	25	11	14	25	11	14	...	...	...	...	...	...
Total 0—5	**110**	**55**	**61**	**110**	**55**	**61**	...	...	...	...	...	...
5—10	105	53	52	103	51	52	2	2	...	...	...	...
10—15	100	61	39	90	55	35	9	5	4	1	1	...
15—20	1,094	1,073	21	660	657	3	417	399	18	17	17	..
20—30	2,649	2,600	49	1,160	1,160	...	1,420	1 371	49	69	69	...
30—40	1,085	1,046	39	234	233	1	804	770	34	47	43	4
40—50	208	186	22	13	13	...	173	159	14	22	14	8
50—60	52	42	10	1	1	...	43	39	4	8	2	6
60 and over	16	9	7	...	...	...	6	5	1	10	4	6
Christian	**4,285**	**4,199**	**87**	**3.561**	**3.520**	**41**	**663**	**624**	**39**	**62**	**55**	**7**
0—1	9	5	4	9	5	4	...	...	...	...	...	...
1—2	10	5	5	10	5	5	...	...	...	...	...	...
2—3	9	6	3	9	6	3	...	...	...	...	...	...
3—4	9	7	2	9	7	2	...	...	...	...	...	...
4—5	10	7	3	10	7	3	..	...	...	...	...	...
Total 0—5	**47**	**30**	**17**	**47**	**30**	**17**	...	...	...	...	...	...
5—10	39	26	13	37	26	11	2	...	2	...	...	...
10—15	37	25	12	32	24	8	5	1	4	...	...	...
15—20	804	795	9	766	764	2	35	28	7	3	3	...
20—30	2,513	2,493	20	2,241	2,239	2	253	236	17	19	18	1
30—40	040	637	9	391	390	1	237	230	7	18	17	1
40—50	146	143	3	44	44	...	94	92	2	8	7	1
50—60	46	44	2	3	3	...	35	35	...	8	6	2
60 and over	8	6	2	...	...	...	2	2	...	6	4	2

TABLE VII

Age, Sex and Civil Condition, Part II (b)—Trans-Frontier Posts

Age	Population			Unmarried			Married			Widowed		
	Persons	Males	Females	Persons	Males	Females	Persons	Males	Females	Persons	Males	Females
1	2	3	4	5	6	7	8	9	10	11	12	13
Parsi ...	2	2	...	...	...	...	1	1	...	1	1	...
0—1	...	...	...	...	...	...	...	...	...	...	...	...
1—2	...	...	...	...	...	...	...	...	...	...	...	...
2—3	...	...	...	...	...	...	...	...	...	...	...	...
3—4	...	...	...	...	...	...	...	...	...	...	...	...
4—5	...	...	...	...	...	...	...	...	...	...	...	...
Total 0—5	...	...	...	...	...	...	...	...	...	...	...	...
5—10	...	...	...	...	...	...	...	...	...	...	...	...
10—15	...	...	...	...	...	...	...	...	...	...	...	...
15—20	...	...	...	...	...	...	...	...	...	...	...	...
20—30	...	...	...	...	...	...	...	...	...	...	...	...
30—40	...	...	...	...	...	...	...	...	...	...	...	...
40—50	2	2	...	...	...	...	1	1	...	1	1	...
50—60	...	...	...	...	...	...	...	...	...	...	...	...
60 and over	...	...	...	...	...	...	...	...	...	...	...	...
Buddhist...	1	1	...	...	...	...	1	1	...	...	...	...
0—1	...	...	...	...	...	...	...	...	...	...	...	...
1—2	...	...	...	...	...	...	...	...	...	...	...	...
2—3	...	...	...	...	...	...	...	...	...	...	...	...
3—4	...	...	...	...	...	...	...	...	...	...	...	...
4—5	...	...	...	...	...	...	...	...	...	...	...	...
Total 0—5	...	...	...	...	...	...	...	...	...	...	...	...
5—10	...	...	...	...	...	...	...	...	...	...	...	...
10—15	...	...	...	...	...	...	...	...	...	...	...	...
15—20	1	1	...	...	...	...	1	1	...	...	...	...
20—30	...	...	...	...	...	...	...	...	...	...	...	...
30—40	...	...	...	...	...	...	...	...	...	...	...	...
40—50	...	...	...	...	...	...	...	...	...	...	...	...
50—60	...	...	...	...	...	...	...	...	...	...	...	...
60 and over	...	...	...	...	...	...	...	...	...	...	...	...

TABLE VII

Age, Sex and Civil Condition, Part III—Peshawar Municipality

Age	Population			Unmarried			Married			Widowed		
	Persons	Males	Females	Persons	Males	Females	Persons	Males	Females	Persons	Males	Females
1	2	3	4	5	6	7	8	9	10	11	12	13
All religions	87,440	50,151	37,289	44,401	28,213	16,188	35,070	19,162	15,908	7,969	2,776	5,193
0—1	2,249	1,145	1,104	2,249	1,145	1,104	...	...	...	...	...	...
1—2	2,125	1,068	1,057	2,125	1,068	1,057	...	...	...	...	...	...
2—3	2,373	1,206	1,167	2,373	1,206	1,167	...	...	...	...	...	...
3—4	2,263	1,172	1,091	2,263	1,172	1,091	...	...	...	...	...	...
4—5	2,173	1,116	1,057	2,173	1,116	1,057	...	...	...	...	...	...
Total 0—5	11,183	5,707	5,476	11,183	5,707	5,476	...	...	...	...	...	...
5—10	9,884	5,333	4,551	9,783	5,289	4,494	86	33	53	15	11	4
10—15	9,337	5,203	4,134	8,768	5,099	3,669	541	89	452	28	15	13
15—20	8,790	5,063	3,727	5,518	4,222	1,296	3,156	795	2,361	116	46	70
20—30	18,409	10,894	7,515	6,436	5,572	864	11,169	4,931	6,238	804	391	413
30—40	13,366	8,220	5,146	1,775	1,558	217	10,063	6,021	4,042	1,528	641	887
40—50	8,374	5,072	3,302	590	484	106	5,863	3,978	1,885	1,921	610	1,311
50—60	4,602	2,693	1,909	210	165	45	2,676	2,037	639	1,716	491	1,325
60 and over	3,495	1,966	1,529	138	117	21	1,516	1,278	238	1,841	571	1,270
Muslim ...	69,893	39,915	29,978	35,831	22,681	13,150	27,784	15,025	12,759	6,278	2,209	4,069
0—1	1,734	883	851	1,734	883	851	...	...	...	...	...	...
1—2	1,640	822	818	1,640	822	818	...	...	...	...	...	...
2—3	1,839	935	904	1,839	935	904	...	...	...	...	...	...
3—4	1,767	918	849	1,767	918	849	...	...	...	...	...	...
4—5	1,698	870	828	1,698	870	828	...	...	...	...	...	...
Total 0—5	8,678	4,428	4,250	8678	4,428	4,250	...	...	...	...	...	...
5—10	7,853	4,236	3,617	7,789	4,208	3,581	53	19	34	11	9	2
10—15	7,457	4,152	3,305	7,093	4,080	3,013	339	57	282	25	15	10
15—20	6,913	3,973	2,940	4,556	3,380	1,176	2,270	557	1,713	87	36	51
20—30	14,703	8,635	6,068	5,421	4,630	791	8,667	3,698	4,969	615	307	308
30—40	10,808	6.564	4,244	1,517	1.331	186	8,103	4,720	3,383	1,188	513	675
40—50	6,804	4.087	2,717	493	399	94	4,823	3,208	1,615	1,488	480	1,008
50—60	3,761	2,190	1,571	175	134	41	2,225	1,672	553	1,361	384	977
60 and over	2,916	1,650	1,266	109	91	18	1,304	1,094	210	1,503	465	1,038
Hindu ...	11,594	6,781	4,813	5 665	3,688	1,977	4,769	2,730	2,039	1,160	363	797
0—1	324	161	163	324	161	163	...	...	...	...	...	...
1—2	321	158	163	321	158	163	...	...	...	...	...	...
2—3	345	175	170	345	175	170	...	...	...	...	...	...
3—4	312	163	149	312	163	149	...	...	...	...	...	...
4—5	297	156	141	297	156	141	...	...	...	...	...	...
Total 0—5	1,599	813	786	1,599	813	786	...	...	...	...	...	...
5—10	1,312	709	603	1,288	698	590	22	10	12	2	1	1
10—15	1,236	683	553	1,101	661	440	134	22	112	1	...	1
15—20	1,249	734	515	653	572	81	578	156	422	18	6	12
20—30	2,452	1,532	920	712	669	43	1,609	809	800	131	54	77
30—40	1,730	1,120	610	199	176	23	1,288	854	434	243	90	153
40—50	1,066	661	405	67	58	9	702	522	180	297	81	216
50—60	574	331	243	23	21	2	304	241	63	247	69	178
60 and over	376	198	178	23	20	3	132	116	16	221	62	159
Sikh ...	5,150	2,992	2,158	2,510	1,605	905	2,165	1,213	953	474	174	300
0—1	171	89	82	171	89	82	...	...	...	...	...	...
1—2	140	75	65	140	75	65	...	...	...	...	...	...
2—3	159	82	77	159	82	77	...	...	...	...	...	...
3—4	156	79	77	156	79	77	...	...	...	...	...	...
4—5	153	78	75	153	78	75	...	...	...	...	...	...
Total 0—5	779	403	376	779	403	376	...	...	...	...	...	...
5—10	628	337	291	616	333	283	10	3	7	2	1	1
10—15	560	320	240	497	311	186	61	9	52	2	...	2
15—20	543	314	229	267	241	26	267	70	197	9	3	6
20—30	1,083	634	449	260	236	24	771	373	398	52	25	27
30—40	694	442	252	49	43	6	560	370	190	85	29	56
40—50	439	278	161	27	25	2	289	210	79	123	43	80
50—60	238	154	84	10	8	2	132	113	19	96	33	63
60 and over	186	110	76	5	5	...	76	65	11	105	40	65
Christian...	792	452	340	392	236	155	343	185	157	57	30	27
0—1	20	12	8	20	12	8	...	...	...	...	...	...
1—2	24	13	11	24	13	11	...	...	...	...	...	...
2—3.	30	14	16	30	14	16	...	...	...	...	...	...
3—4	28	12	16	28	12	16	...	...	...	...	...	...
4—5	25	12	13	25	12	13	...	...	...	...	...	...
Total 0—5	127	63	64	127	63	64	...	...	...	...	...	...
5—10	91	51	40	90	50	40	1	1	...	...	...	...
10—15	84	48	36	77	47	30	7	1	6	...	...	...
15—20	83	40	43	40	27	13	41	12	29	2	1	1
20—30	169	91	78	42	36	6	121	50	71	6	5	1
30—40	131	91	40	10	8	2	109	74	35	12	9	3
40—50	62	43	19	3	2	1	46	35	11	13	6	7
50—60	28	17	11	2	2	...	14	10	4	12	5	7
60 and over	17	8	9	1	1	...	4	3	1	12	4	8

TABLE VII

Age, Sex and Civil Condition, Part III—Peshawar Municipality

Age	Population			Unmarried			Married			Widowed		
	Persons	Males	Females	Persons	Males	Females	Persons	Males	Females	Persons	Males	Females
1	2	3	4	5	6	7	8	9	10	11	12	13
Jew ...	11	11	...	3	3	...	8	8	...	...	...	...
0—1	...	...	...	...	...	...	...	...	...	...	...	...
1—2	...	...	...	...	...	...	...	...	...	...	...	...
2—3	...	...	...	...	...	...	...	...	...	...	...	...
3—4	...	...	...	...	...	...	...	...	...	...	...	...
4—5	...	...	...	...	...	...	...	...	...	...	...	...
Total 0—5	...	...	...	...	...	...	...	...	...	...	...	...
5—10	...	...	...	...	...	...	...	...	...	...	...	...
10—15	...	...	...	...	...	...	...	...	...	...	...	...
15—20	2	2	...	2	2	...	...	...	...	...	...	...
20—30	2	2	...	1	1	...	1	1	...	...	...	...
30—40	3	3	...	...	...	...	3	3	...	...	...	...
40—50	3	3	...	...	...	...	3	3	...	...	...	...
50—60	1	1	...	...	...	...	1	1	...	...	...	...
60 and over	...	...	...	...	...	...	...	...	...	...	...	...

TABLE VIII

Civil condition by age for selected castes

1. The twelve castes selected for this table are the same as those selected for tables XI and XIV.

2. The table includes the population of each caste residing in trans-frontier posts.

TABLE VIII

Civil condition by age for selected castes

Serial No.	Caste, tribe or race	Locality	Sex	Population dealt with	Unmarried						
					Total	0 to 6	7 to 13	14 to 16	17 to 23	24 to 43	44 and over
	1	2	3	4	5	6	7	8	9	10	11
1	Awan ...	All districts and trans-frontier posts	Males ...	154,943	86,761	28,883	26,614	9,482	11,749	7,923	2,110
			Females	128,228	58,884	28,690	20,270	4,358	2,735	2,173	657
2	Arora ...		Males ...	34,576	19,297	6,813	5,761	1,984	2,687	1,681	371
			Females	26,826	11,906	5,974	4,349	890	388	250	55
3	Brahman ...		Males ...	10,723	5,258	1,314	1,188	557	1,041	914	244
			Females	6,477	2,569	1,256	843	233	170	52	15
4	Chamar ...		Males ...	1,749	922	327	253	137	106	72	27
			Females	1,169	595	245	138	55	62	76	19
5	Chuhr ...		Males ...	6,380	3,007	777	605	374	668	532	51
			Females	2,905	1,093	525	396	109	90	26	13
6	Gujar ...		Males ...	66,223	39,079	13,061	12,804	4,872	4,471	2,888	983
			Females	55,287	24,220	13,026	8,298	1,508	604	621	163
7	Jat ...		Males ...	44,369	23,832	6,324	6,245	3,784	4,544	2,752	183
			Females	31,958	14,512	7,229	4,538	1,277	922	428	118
8	Khatri ...		Males ...	19,947	10,295	3,072	2,625	1,165	1,839	1,285	309
			Females	15,099	6,207	3,016	2,188	456	387	121	39
9	Pathan ...		Males ...	491,585	284,412	96,448	88,439	29,933	38,410	26,226	4,956
			Females	425,045	200,631	92,847	68,467	16,641	11,697	7,917	3,062
10	Sayad ...		Males ...	42,834	24,970	8,878	7,847	2,811	3,107	1,969	358
			Females	39,478	18,655	8,696	6,294	1,618	1,034	762	251
11	Swathi ...	Hazara and Peshawar districts only	Males ...	25,410	15,727	4,953	4,787	2,606	1,504	1,429	448
			Females	21,150	9,366	4,353	3,517	1,012	269	193	22
12	Tanaoli ...		Males ...	45,414	25,551	9,677	8,946	2,859	2,670	1,975	384
			Females	40,661	18,319	9,263	6,513	1,058	586	753	146

TABLE VIII

Civil condition by age for selected castes

Married							Widowed							
Total	0 to 6	7 to 13	14 to 16	17 to 23	24 to 43	44 and over	Total	0 to 6	7 to 13	14 to 16	17 to 23	24 to 43	44 and over	Serial No.
12	13	14	15	16	17	18	19	20	21	22	23	24	25	
54,889	...	439	1,228	4,955	32,211	16,056	13,293	...	6	216	820	3,777	8,474	1
55,170	...	896	4,307	12,311	29,364	8,292	14,174	...	24	566	724	4,639	8,221	
13,003	...	109	146	1,488	7,623	3,637	2,276	...	7	25	106	869	1,269	2
11,218	...	154	690	3,091	6,098	1,185	3,702	...	5	13	112	1,420	2,152	
4,587	...	118	212	768	2,384	1,105	878	...	1	9	69	341	458	3
2,980	...	63	379	781	1,331	426	928	...	8	1	19	312	588	
712	...	6	41	141	373	151	115	...	3	10	12	47	43	4
482	...	8	63	124	231	56	92	...	...	...	6	31	55	
2,830	...	135	128	557	1,333	677	543	...	1	13	32	262	235	5
1,441	...	68	149	354	690	180	371	...	2	1	5	158	205	
23,962	...	96	599	2,460	13,094	7,713	3,182	...	2	25	187	1,043	1,925	6
25,556	...	279	2,135	4,747	13,962	4,443	5,501	...	7	39	136	1,727	3,592	
17,864	...	48	517	2,827	9,591	4,881	2,673	...	1	25	143	1,174	1,330	7
13,537	...	128	706	2,972	7,560	2,171	3,909	...	2	25	200	1,294	2,388	
8,245	...	36	269	1,255	4,161	2,524	1,407	...	14	48	128	467	750	8
7,010	...	227	701	1,817	3,235	1,030	1,882	...	4	11	79	598	1,190	
179,940	...	838	2,824	16,643	101,056	58,579	27,233	...	314	606	1,572	10,083	14,659	9
176,499	...	2,409	9,130	37,191	100,009	27,760	47,915	...	47	479	1,901	15,606	29,882	
15,670	...	87	285	1,647	8,748	4,903	2,194	...	5	32	144	802	1,211	10
16,263	...	173	969	3,504	8,899	2,718	4,550	...	8	30	180	1,578	2,764	
8,857	...	127	683	1,689	4,613	1,745	826	...	...	21	54	336	415	11
9,577	...	85	503	1,763	5,764	1,462	2,207	...	...	9	52	653	1,493	
17,007	...	291	633	1,646	9,531	4,906	1,856	...	3	8	98	618	1,129	12
18,166	...	207	1,030	3,821	10,726	2,382	4,176	...	4	16	105	1,384	2,667	

TABLE IX

Infirmities

1. This table is divided into two parts. Part I shows the distribution of the persons afflicted according to age, and part II, their distribution according to locality. No afflicted persons were enumerated in Trans-Frontier posts.

2. Combinations of infirmities were recorded. Persons afflicted with two or more infirmities have been shown under each of the infirmaties in question in columns 5 to 16.

The number of persons afflicted includes sixty persons afflicted with two infirmities, and three persons afflicted with three infirmities, as detailed below :—

Combination of infirmities	Persons afflicted	Males	Femaels
Insanity and deaf-muteness	34	22	12
Insanity and blindness	11	6	5
Deaf-muteness and blindness	6	5	1
Deaf-muteness and leprosy	7	3	4
Blindness and leprosy	2	1	1
Insanity, blindness and deaf-muteness	2	2	...
Insanity, blindness and leprosy	1	...	1
Total ...	63	39	24

The total of the infirmaties therefore exceeds the total number of persons afflicted, as given in columns 2 to 4, by 66.

TABLE IX

Infirmities

Part I—Distribution by age

Age	Population afflicted			Insane			Deaf-mutes			Blind			Lepers		
	Persons	Males	Females	Persons	Males	Females	Persons	Males	Females	Persons	Males	Females	Persons	Males	Females
1	2	3	4	5	6	7	8	9	10	11	12	13	14	15	16
0—1 ...	12	5	7	1	...	1	2	1	1	9	4	5	...	...	...
1—2 ...	22	15	7	3	2	1	4	3	1	14	10	4	1	...	1
2—3 ...	43	22	21	3	1	2	15	10	5	23	11	12	2	...	2
3—4 ...	46	29	17	1	1	...	28	19	9	15	9	6	4	1	3
4—5 ...	95	58	37	14	8	6	47	29	18	26	16	10	10	6	4
Total 0—5 ...	218	129	89	22	12	10	96	62	34	87	50	37	17	7	10
5—10 ...	407	269	138	70	51	19	208	139	69	120	75	45	23	13	10
10—15 ...	444	301	143	86	65	21	217	150	67	126	77	49	26	19	7
15—20 ...	383	255	128	93	69	24	152	106	46	118	67	51	29	18	11
20—25 ...	370	241	129	91	66	25	133	92	41	127	73	54	27	15	12
25—30 ...	368	241	127	86	62	24	138	90	48	130	77	53	18	14	4
30—35 ...	352	235	117	75	57	18	129	88	41	128	75	53	21	15	6
35—40 ...	310	199	111	52	40	12	101	75	26	141	73	68	17	11	6
40—45 ...	305	186	119	48	37	11	88	58	30	159	85	74	13	9	4
45—50 ...	322	182	140	43	30	13	77	45	32	188	97	91	15	11	4
50—55 ...	298	165	133	36	25	11	65	42	23	186	89	97	13	9	4
55—60 ...	300	167	133	19	13	6	48	31	17	227	117	110	11	9	2
60—65 ...	267	152	115	10	7	3	44	28	16	206	111	95	8	6	2
65—70 ...	164	93	71	4	4	...	24	18	6	134	70	64	3	2	1
70 and over ...	476	276	200	6	5	1	77	50	27	386	215	171	8	6	2
Total ...	4,984	3,091	1,893	741	543	198	1,597	1,074	523	2,463	1,351	1,112	249	164	85

Part II—Distribution by Districts

District	Population afflicted			Insane			Deaf-mutes			Blind			Lepers		
	Persons	Males	Females	Persons	Males	Females	Persons	Males	Females	Persons	Males	Females	Persons	Males	Females
1	2	3	4	5	6	7	8	9	10	11	12	13	14	15	16
N. W. F. Province ...	4,984	3,091	1,893	741	543	198	1,597	1,074	523	2,463	1,351	1,112	249	164	85
Hazara ...	1,077	685	392	140	97	43	496	324	172	371	209	162	84	63	21
Peshawar ...	2,111	1,374	737	334	254	80	629	447	182	1,044	600	444	136	90	46
Kohat ...	402	249	153	78	58	20	142	96	46	177	98	79	12	3	9
Bannu ...	382	250	132	92	69	[illegible]	118	81	37	168	101	67	11	5	6
Dera Ismail Khan ...	1,012	533	479	97	65	32	212	126	86	703	343	360	6	3	3

TABLE X

Occupation or means of livelihood

GENERAL TABLE

1. All occupations are divided into four main classes and subdivided into twelve sub-classes, fifty-five orders and one hundred and ninety-five groups. This scheme of classification is the same as in 1921, except that there were then fifty-six orders and one hundred and ninety-one groups.

2. The form of the table is different from that used at the last Census in respect of dependents, and additional figures have also been given for subsidiary occupations. Dependents have been split up into working and non-working dependents, and no attempt has been made to distribute the latter among the different occupations.

3. The following groups, indicating occupations which have not been returned in the North-West Frontier Province, have been omitted from the table :—(2) Estate Agents and Managers or owners. (8) Cultivators of jhum, taungya and shifting areas. (9) Cinchona. (10) Cocoanut. (11) Coffee. (12) Ganja. (13) Pan-Vine. (14) Rubber. (15) Tea. (20) Collectors of lac. (24) Birds, bees, etc. (25) Silkworms. (26) Lac cultivation. (29) Gold. (30) Iron. (31) Lead, silver and zinc. (32) Manganese. (33) Tin and wolfram. (34) Other metallic minerals. (35) Coal. (36) Petroleum. (37) Building materials (including stone, materials for cement-manufacture and clays). (38) Mica. (41) Other non-metallic minerals. (48) Hair (horse-hair), etc. (52) Furriers and persons occupied with feathers, and bristles ; brush makers. (57) Smelting, forging and rolling of iron and other metals. (58) Makers of arms, guns, etc. (62) Workers in mints, diesinkers, etc. (69) Manufacture and refining of mineral oils. (76) Toddy drawers. (79) Manufacturers of opium. (101) Persons concerned with aerodromes and aeroplanes. (122) Trade in thatches and other forest produce. The omission of groups 29, 30, 31, 32, 33, 34, and 101 involves the omission of order 3 (Metallic minerals) and order 18 (Transport by air) respectively.

4. For reasons of economy, no figures showing occupations combined with agriculture have been compiled at the present Census.

TABLE X

Occupation or means of livelihood—General Table

Group No.	Occupation	N. W. F. Province — Total earners ... 802,081; Working dependents ... 97,370; Non-working dependents ... 1,572,076; Population ... 2,471,527							N. W F Province — Total earners ...; Working dependents ...; Non-working dependents ...; Population ...		
		Total following occupation	As principal occupation		As working dependents		As subsidiary to other occupations		Total following occupation	As principal occupation	
			Males	Females	Males	Females	Males	Females		Males	Females
1	2	3	4	5	6	7	8	9	10	11	12
	ALL OCCUPATIONS ...	958,381	777,051	25,030	72,493	24,877	58,439	491	913,100	735,649	25,010
	Class A—Production of raw materials.	550,910	439,545	11,727	56,883	23,000	29,575	181	557,483	437,238	11,727
	SUB-CLASS I—EXPLOITATION OF ANIMALS AND VEGETATION.	560,778	439,428	11,727	56,882	23,000	29,560	181	557,351	437,121	11,727
	ORDER I—PASTURE AND AGRICULTURE.	560,444	439,160	11,726	56,879	23,000	29 501	181	557,020	436,853	11,726
	ORDER I (a)—CULTIVATION ...	554,332	434,227	11,678	56,267	22,980	29,003	177	550,905	431,920	11,678
1	Non-cultivating proprietors taking rent in money or kind.	55,802	34,597	3,625	3,970	883	12,604	123	53,949	32,997	3,625
3	Estate agents and managers of Government.	9	6	...	...	...	3	...	9	6	...
4	Rent collectors, clerks, etc. ...	80	80	...	...	...	...	...	80	80	...
5	Cultivating owners ...	233,322	216,475	4,911	4,833	1,343	5,751	9	232,271	216,189	4,911
6	Tenant cultivators ...	205,551	148,137	2,227	30,779	16,484	7,892	32	205,227	147,915	2,227
7	Agricultural labourers ...	59,568	34,932	915	16,685	4,270	2,753	13	59,369	34,733	915
	ORDER I (b)—CULTIVATION OF SPECIAL CROPS, FRUITS, ETC. (PLANTERS, MANAGERS, CLERKS AND LABOURERS).	591	512	8	5	6	60	...	591	512	8
16	Market gardeners, flower and fruit growers.	591	512	8	5	6	60	...	591	512	8
	ORDER I (c)—FORESTRY ...	327	232	11	22	2	59	1	327	232	11
17	Forest officers, rangers, guards, etc.	57	42	...	...	...	15	...	57	42	...
18	Wood cutters and charcoal burners.	228	153	7	22	1	44	1	228	153	7
19	Collectors of forest produce ...	42	37	4	...	1	...	...	42	37	4
	ORDER I (d)—STOCK RAISING ...	5,197	4,189	29	585	12	379	3	5,197	4,189	29
21	Cattle and buffalo breeders and keepers.	4,951	3,981	19	579	12	359	1	4,951	3,981	19
22	Breeders of transport animals ...	2	1	1	...	...	...	...	2	1	1
23	Herdsmen, shepherds and breeders of other animals.	244	207	9	6	...	20	2	244	207	9
	ORDER 2—FISHING AND HUNTING ...	331	268	1	3	...	59	...	331	268	1
27	Fishing and pearling ...	321	261	1	3	...	56	...	321	261	1
28	Hunting	10	7	...	...	...	3	...	10	7	...
	SUB-CLASS II—EXPLOITATION OF MINERALS.	132	117	...	1	...	14	...	132	117	...
	ORDER 4—NON-METALLIC MINERALS	132	117	...	1	...	14	...	132	117	...
39	Precious and semi-precious stones	49	36	...	...	...	13	...	49	36	...
40	Salt, saltpetre and other saline substances.	83	81	...	1	...	1	...	83	81	...

TABLE X

Occupation or means of livelihood—General Table

(Districts)				Hazara							Peshawar						
760,659 97,309 1,567,108 2,425,076				Total earners ... 181,075 Working dependents ... 38,681 Non-working dependents ... 450,361 Population ... 670,117							Total earners ... 322 928 Working dependents ... 39,672 Non-working dependents ... 611,721 Population ... 974,321						
As working dependents		As subsidiary to other occupations		Total following occupation	As principal occupation		As working dependents		As subsidiary to other occupations		Total following occupation	As principal occupation		As working dependents		As subsidiary to other occupations	
Males	Females	Males	Females		Males	Females	Males	Females	Males	Females		Males	Females	Males	Females	Males	Females
13	14	15	16	17	18	19	20	21	22	23	24	25	26	27	28	29	30
72,432	24,877	54,641	491	230,284	173,805	7,270	19,412	19 269	10,382	146	384,052	313,834	9.094	37 295	2,377	21,303	149
56,878	23,000	82,549	181	176,437	131,422	4,943	17,660	18,357	4,000	55	219,754	174,448	3,665	27,700	1,927	11,939	75
56,877	23,000	28,445	181	176,388	131,386	4,943	17,660	18,357	3,987	55	219,754	174,448	3,665	27,700	1,927	11,939	75
56,874	23,000	28,386	181	176,367	131,369	4,943	17,658	18,357	3,985	55	219,480	174,221	3,665	27,699	1,927	11,893	75
56,262	22,980	27, 888	177	174,453	129,781	4,926	17,439	18,349	3,904	54	218,072	172,986	3,657	27,645	1,924	11,786	74
3,969	883	12,352	123	4,687	2,166	733	419	525	802	42	27,898	19,212	1,286	2,200	139	5,012	49
...	...	3	...	6	3	...	...	...	3	...	...	...	...	...	...	...	...
...	...	...	...	23	23	...	...	...	...	...	55	55	...	...	...	...	...
4,833	1,343	4,986	9	64,261	58,632	2,434	1,005	1,144	1,042	4	89,657	84,528	1,412	1,249	151	2,317	...
30,775	16,484	7,794	32	74,237	52,753	1,443	5,711	13,428	899	3	83,826	57,938	572	20,928	1,136	3,230	22
16,685	4,270	2,753	13	31,239	16,204	316	10,304	3,252	1,158	5	16,636	11,253	387	3,268	498	1,227	3
5	6	60	...	49	32	2	1	2	12	...	272	260	2	1	...	9	...
5	6	60	...	49	32	2	1	2	12	...	272	260	2	1	...	9	...
22	2	59	1	250	184	7	22	...	37	...	26	22	...	...	2	1	1
...	...	15	...	50	36	...	...	...	14	...	7	6	...	...	...	1	...
22	1	44	1	196	144	7	22	...	23	...	2	...	...	...	1	...	1
...	1	...	...	4	4	...	...	...	...	...	17	16	...	...	1	...	...
585	12	379	3	1,615	1,372	8	196	6	32	1	1,110	953	6	53	1	97	...
579	12	359	1	1,471	1,244	4	190	6	26	1	1,063	917	6	53	1	86	...
...	...	...	...	1	...	1	...	...	...	...	1	1	...	...	...	...	...
6	...	20	2	143	128	3	6	...	6	...	46	35	...	...	...	11	...
3	...	59	...	21	17	...	2	...	2	...	274	227	...	1	...	46	...
3	...	56	...	20	16	...	2	...	2	...	270	224	...	1	...	45	...
...	...	3	...	1	1	...	...	...	...	...	4	3	...	...	...	1	...
1	...	14	...	49	36	...	...	...	13	...	...	...	...	...	...	...	...
1	...	14	...	49	36	...	...	...	13	...	...	...	...	...	...	...	...
...	...	13	...	49	36	...	...	...	13	...	...	...	...	...	...	...	...
1	...	1	...	...	...	...	...	...	...	...	...	...	...	...	...	...	...

TABLE X

Occupation or means of livelihood—General Table

Kohat

Total earners	...	72,939
Working dependents	...	5,235
Non-working dependents	...	158,099
Population	...	236,273

Bannu

Total earners	...	87,759
Working dependents	...	6,200
Non-working dependents	...	176,342
Population	...	270,301

Group No.	Occupation	Kohat							Bannu							
		Total following occupation	As principal occupation		As working dependents		As subsidiary to other occupations		Total following occupation	As principal occupation		As working dependents		As subsidiary to other occupations	
			Males	Females	Males	Females	Males	Females		Males	Females	Males	Females	Males	Females
1	2	31	32	33	34	35	36	37	38	39	40	41	42	43	44
	ALL OCCUPATIONS ...	87,415	69,599	3,340	4,548	687	9,180	61	100 290	85,476	2,283	4,364	1,836	6,286	45
	CLASS A—PRODUCION OF RAW MATERIALS.	46,215	35,702	1,487	3,912	541	4,558	15	56,279	46,368	1,075	3,197	1,716	3,904	19
	SUB-CLASS I—EXPLOITATION OF ANIMALS AND VEGETATION.	46,132	35,621	1,487	3,911	541	4,557	15	56,279	46,368	1,075	3,197	1,716	3,904	19
	ORDER 1—PASTURE AND AGRICULTURE.	46,127	35,618	1,487	3,911	541	4,555	15	56,275	46,364	1,075	3,197	1,716	3,904	19
	ORDER 1 (*a*)—CULTIVATION...	45,453	35,205	1,475	3,822	536	4,402	13	55,889	46,028	1,072	3,174	1,716	3,880	19
1	Non-cultivating proprietors taking rent in money or kind.	7,174	2,875	583	454	96	3,157	9	7,312	4,555	670	750	78	1,250	9
3	Estate agents and managers of Government.	3	3	...	...	...	...	...	...	...	...	...	...	...	...
4	Rent collectors, clerks, etc.	2	2	...	...	...	...	...	...	...	...	...	...	...	...
5	Cultivating owners ...	28,651	26,985	772	117	26	751	...	26,776	25,512	144	438	21	557	4
6	Tenant cultivators ...	5,422	3,990	63	793	242	332	2	16,736	11,789	95	1,633	1,298	1,918	3
7	Agricultural labourers ...	4,201	1,350	57	2,458	172	162	2	5,065	4,172	63	353	319	155	3
	ORDER 1 (*b*)—CULTIVATION OF SPECIAL CROPS, FRUITS, ETC. (PLANTERS, MANAGERS, CLERKS AND LABOURERS).	23	21	...	1	...	1	...	142	128	1	2	...	11	...
16	Market gardeners, flower and fruit growers.	23	21	...	1	...	1	...	142	128	1	2	...	11	...
	ORDER 1 (*c*)—FORESTRY ...	24	3	...	...	...	21	...	...	...	...	...	...	...	...
17	Forest officers, rangers, guards, etc.	...	...	...	...	...	...	...	...	...	...	...	...	...	...
18	Wood cutters and charcoal burners.	22	1	...	...	...	21	...	...	...	...	...	...	...	...
19	Collectors of forest produce	2	2	...	...	...	...	...	...	...	...	...	...	...	...
	ORDER 1 (*d*)—STOCK RAISING	627	389	12	88	5	131	2	244	208	2	21	...	13	...
21	Cattle and buffalo breeders and keepers.	572	345	6	88	5	128	...	244	108	2	21	...	13	...
22	Breeders of transport animals.	...	...	...	...	...	...	...	...	...	...	...	...	...	...
23	Herdsmen, shepherds and breeders of other animals	55	44	6	...	...	3	2	...	...	...	..	...	...	...
	ORDER 2—FISHING AND HUNTING.	5	3	...	1	...	2	...	4	4	...	...	...	...	...
27	Fishing and pearling ...	4	3	...	...	...	1	...	3	3	...	...	...	...	...
28	Hunting ...	1	...	...	...	...	1	...	1	1	...	...	...	...	...
	SUB-CLASS II—EXPLOITATION OF MINERALS.	83	81	...	1	...	1	...	...	...	..	...	...	...	...
	ORDER 4—NON-METALLIC MINERALS.	83	81	...	1	...	1	...	...	...	...	...	...	...	...
39	Precious and semi-precious stones.	...	...	...	...	...	...	...	...	...	...	...	...	...	...
40	Salt, saltpetre and other saline substances.	83	81	...	1	...	1	...	...	...	...	...	...	...	...

TABLE X

Occupation or means of livelihood—General Table

	Dera Ismail Khan	Trans-Frontier Posts	Peshawar Municipality
Total earners	95,958	41,422	30,514
Working dependents	7,521	61	108
Non-working dependents	170,585	4,968	56,718
Population	274,064	46,451	87,440

Dera Ismail Khan							Trans-Frontier Posts							Peshawar Municipality						
Total following occupation	As principal occupation		As working dependents		As subsidiary to other occupations		Total following occupation	As principal occupation		As working dependents		As subsidiary to other occupations		Total following occupation	As principal occupation		As working dependents		As subsidiary to other occupations	
	Males	Females	Males	Females	Males	Females		Males	Females	Males	Females	Males	Females		Males	Females	Males	Females	Males	Females
45	46	47	48	49	50	51	52	53	54	55	56	57	58	59	60	61	62	63	64	65
111,059	92 935	3,023	6,813	708	7,490	90	45,281	41,402	20	61	...	3,798	...	31,299	28,809	1,805	5	103	573	4
58,798	49,298	557	4,409	459	4,058	17	3,427	2,307	...	5	...	1,115	...	7,331	6,996	235	4	...	96	...
58,798	49,298	557	4,409	459	4,058	17	3,427	2,307	...	5	...	1,115	...	7,331	6,996	235	4	...	96	...
58,771	49,281	556	4,409	459	4,049	17	3,427	2,307	...	5	...	1,115	...	7,329	6,994	235	4	...	96	...
57,038	47 920	548	4,182	455	3,916	17	3,427	2,307	...	5	...	1,115	...	7,259	6,925	234	4	...	96	...
6,878	4,189	353	146	45	2,131	14	1,853	1,600	...	1	...	252	...	552	477	9	...	...	65	...
...	...	...	...	...	...	...	...	...	...	...	...	...	...	...	...	...	...	...	...	...
...	...	...	...	...	...	...	...	...	...	...	...	...	...	...	...	...	...	...	...	...
22,926	20,532	49	2,024	1	319	1	1,051	286	...	...	...	765	...	5,088	4,859	223	3	...	3	...
25,006	21,445	54	1,71	380	1,415	2	324	222	...	4	...	98	...	960	939	..	1	...	26	...
2,228	1,754	92	302	29	51	...	199	199	...	...	...	...	...	653	650	2	...	...	1	...
105	71	3	...	4	27	...	...	...	...	...	...	...	...	32	31	1	...	...	...	...
105	71	3	...	4	27	...	...	...	...	...	...	...	...	32	31	1	...	...	...	...
27	23	4	...	...	...	...	...	...	...	...	...	...	...	...	...	...	...	...	...	...
...	...	...	...	...	...	...	...	...	...	...	...	...	...	...	...	...	...	...	...	...
8	8	...	...	...	...	...	...	...	...	...	...	...	...	...	...	...	...	...	...	...
19	15	4	...	...	...	...	...	...	...	...	...	...	...	...	...	...	...	...	...	...
1,601	1,267	1	227	...	106	...	...	...	...	...	...	...	...	38	38	...	...	...	...	...
1,601	1,267	1	227	...	106	...	...	...	...	...	...	...	...	38	38	...	...	...	...	...
...	...	...	...	...	...	...	...	...	...	...	...	...	...	...	...	...	...	...	...	...
...	...	...	...	...	...	...	...	...	...	...	...	...	...	...	...	...	...	...	...	...
27	17	1	...	...	9	...	...	...	...	...	...	...	...	2	2	...	...	...	...	...
24	15	1	...	...	8	...	...	...	...	...	...	...	...	2	2	...	...	...	...	...
3	2	...	...	...	1	...	...	...	...	...	...	...	...	...	...	...	...	...	...	...
...	...	...	...	...	...	...	...	...	...	...	...	...	...	...	...	...	...	...	...	...
...	...	...	...	...	...	...	...	...	...	...	...	...	...	...	...	...	...	...	...	...
...	...	...	...	...	...	...	...	...	...	...	...	...	...	...	...	...	...	...	...	...
...	...	...	...	...	...	...	...	...	...	...	...	...	...	...	...	...	...	...	...	...

TABLE X

Occupation or means of livelihood—General Table

Group No.	Occupation	N. W. F. Province							N. W. F. Province		
		Total following occupation	As principal occupation		As working dependents		As subsidiary to other occupations		Total following occupation	As principal occupation	
			Males	Females	Males	Females	Males	Females		Males	Females
1	2	3	4	5	6	7	8	9	10	11	12
	CLASS B—PREPARATION AND SUPPLY OF MATERIAL SUBSTANCES.	205,740	180,367	5,942	5,757	975	12,619	80	200,447	176,152	5,922
	SUB-CLASS III—INDUSTRY ...	115,937	101,237	5,320	3,471	749	5,117	43	113,573	99,224	5,300
	ORDER 5—TEXTILES ...	16,954	14,351	1,425	426	212	527	9	16,810	14,292	1,424
42	Cotton ginning, cleaning and pressing.	2,441	2,075	302	16	3	44	1	2,441	2,075	302
43	Cotton spinning, sizing and weaving.	10,286	8,436	830	384	167	462	7	10,142	8,373	829
44	Jute pressing, spinning and weaving.	53	31	20	...	...	2	...	53	31	20
45	Rope, twine, string and other fibres.	461	208	233	6	14	...	...	461	208	233
46	Wool carding, spinning and weaving.	609	605	...	...	4	...	...	609	605	...
47	Silk spinning and weaving ...	267	267	...	...	...	...	...	267	267	...
49	Dyeing, bleaching, printing, preparation and sponging of textiles.	2,675	2,577	35	20	23	19	1	2,675	2,577	35
50	Lace, crepe, embroideries, fringes, etc., and insufficiently described textile industries.	162	156	5	...	1	...	..	162	156	5
	ORDER 6—HIDES, SKINS AND HARD MATERIALS FROM THE ANIMAL KINGDOM.	626	610	8	3	...	5	...	626	610	8
51	Working in leather	618	603	8	3	...	4	...	618	603	8
53	Bone, ivory, horn, shell, etc., workers (except buttons).	8	7	...	...	...	1	...	8	7	...
	ORDER 7—WOOD ...	14,966	11,679	1,296	552	61	1,371	7	14,768	11,531	1,296
54	Sawyers	558	187	...	2	..	369	...	558	187	...
55	Carpenters, turners and joiners, etc.	13,029	10,998	542	529	20	938	2	12,831	10,850	542
56	Basket makers and other industries of woody materials, including leaves, and thatchers and builders working with bamboo, reeds or similar materials.	1,379	494	754	21	41	64	5	1,379	494	754
	ORDER 8—METALS ...	10,580	9,860	50	251	17	402	...	10,397	9,708	50
59	Blacksmiths, other workers in iron, makers of implements.	10,022	9,322	48	250	17	385	...	9,839	9,170	48
60	Workers in brass, copper and bell metal.	161	161	...	...	...	...	...	161	161	...
61	Workers in other metals (except precious metals).	397	377	2	1	...	17	...	397	377	2
	ORDER 9—CERAMICS ...	10,319	9,694	121	158	78	267	1	10,231	9,691	121
63	Potters and makers of earthen ware	4,716	4,194	73	152	76	220	1	4,628	4,191	73
64	Brick and tile makers ...	5,600	5,497	48	6	2	47	...	5,600	5,497	48
65	Other workers in ceramics ...	3	3	...	...	...	...	...	3	3	...

TABLE X

Occupation or means of livelihood—General Table

(Districts)				Hazara							Peshawar						
As working dependents		As subsidiary to other occupations		Total following occupation	As principal occupation		As working dependents		As subsidiary to other occupations		Total following occupation	As principal occupation		As working dependents		As subsidiary to other occupations	
Males	Females	Males	Females		Males	Females	Males	Females	Males	Females		Males	Females	Males	Females	Males	Females
13	14	15	16	17	18	19	20	21	22	23	24	25	26	27	28	29	30
5,754	975	11,564	80	31,642	26,931	647	910	518	2,622	14	90,421	79,011	2,338	3,762	277	4,996	37
3,469	749	4,788	43	22,131	18,880	561	645	395	1,640	9	49,009	42,500	2,103	2,357	206	1,827	16
426	212	447	9	4,718	4,116	208	134	133	125	2	6,682	5,848	379	243	54	152	6
16	3	44	1	929	832	50	10	3	34	...	1,106	897	201	2	...	5	1
384	167	382	7	3,205	2,746	141	117	110	90	1	4,017	3,433	147	238	47	147	5
...	...	2	...	...	...	...	...	...	...	...	47	27	20	...	...	...	...
6	14	...	...	...	...	...	...	...	...	...	34	34	...	...	...	...	...
...	4	...	...	307	303	...	...	4	...	...	104	104	...	...	...	...	...
...	...	...	...	...	...	...	...	...	...	...	253	253	...	...	..	...	...
20	23	19	1	271	229	17	7	16	1	1	971	950	11	3	7	...	...
...	1	...	...	6	6	...	...	...	...	...	150	150	...	...	...	...	...
3	...	5	...	87	83	...	1	...	3	...	378	358	8	2	...	...	...
3	...	4	...	87	83	...	1	...	3	...	378	368	8	2	...	...	...
...	...	1	...	...	...	...	...	...	...	...	...	...	...	...	...	...	...
552	61	1,321	7	2,402	1,707	9	73	10	603	...	5,297	4,378	150	384	36	344	5
2	...	369	...	402	36	...	...	...	365	...	69	69	...	...	...	...	...
529	20	888	2	1,990	1,663	9	73	8	237	...	4,853	4,107	19	374	12	340	1
21	41	64	5	10	8	...	...	2	...	...	375	202	131	10	24	4	4
251	17	371	...	2,320	2,123	8	63	12	114	...	3,662	3,333	33	157	4	135	...
250	17	354	...	2,209	2,013	8	63	12	113	...	3,423	3,095	32	157	4	135	...
...	...	...	...	...	...	...	...	...	...	...	94	94	...	...	...	...	...
1	...	17	...	111	110	...	...	...	1	...	145	144	1	...	...	...	...
158	78	182	1	1,950	1,792	19	37	53	48	1	3,470	3,248	43	98	14	67	...
152	76	135	1	1,113	964	19	37	53	39	1	1,652	1,435	43	98	12	64	...
6	2	47	...	835	826	...	...	...	9	...	1,817	1,812	...	...	2	3	...
...	...	...	...	2	2	...	...	...	...	...	1	1	...	...	...	...	...

TABLE X

Occupation or means of livelihood—General Table

Group No.	Occupation	Kohat: Total following occupation	Kohat: As principal occupation — Males	Kohat: As principal occupation — Females	Kohat: As working dependents — Males	Kohat: As working dependents — Females	Kohat: As subsidiary to other occupations — Males	Kohat: As subsidiary to other occupations — Females	Bannu: Total following occupation	Bannu: As principal occupation — Males	Bannu: As principal occupation — Females	Bannu: As working dependents — Males	Bannu: As working dependents — Females	Bannu: As subsidiary to other occupations — Males	Bannu: As subsidiary to other occupations — Females
1		31	32	33	34	35	36	37	38	39	40	41	42	43	44
	CLASS B—PREPARATION AND SUPPLY OF MATERIAL SUBSTANCES.	20,669	17,798	1,208	265	68	1,316	14	27,672	25,605	332	472	47	1,209	7
	SUB-CLASS III—INDUSTRY ...	12,561	10,690	1,085	143	52	586	5	14,392	13,535	280	186	33	351	7
	ORDER 5· TEXTILES ...	1,354	961	246	29	...	118	...	2,294	2,219	44	12	2	16	1
42	Cotton ginning, cleaning and pressing.	152	134	11	3	...	4	...	1,120	1,098	20	1	...	1	...
43	Cotton spinning, sizing and weaving.	380	242	5	20	...	113	...	247	205	19	7	1	14	1
44	Jute pressing, spinning and weaving.	...	...	...	...	...	...	...	1	1	...	...	...	...	...
45	Rope, twine, string and other fibres.	339	103	230	6	...	...	...	24	24	...	...	...	...	...
46	Wool carding, spinning and weaving.	51	51	...	...	...	...	...	96	96	...	...	...	...	...
47	Silk spinning and weaving ...	...	...	...	...	...	...	...	...	...	...	...	...	...	...
49	Dyeing, bleaching, printing, preparation and sponging of textiles.	432	431	...	...	...	1	...	800	795	...	4	...	1	...
50	Lace, crepe, embroideries, fringes, etc., and insufficiently described textile industries.	...	...	...	...	...	...	...	6	...	5	...	1	...	...
	ORDER 6—HIDES, SKINS AND HARD MATERIALS FROM THE ANIMAL KINGDOM.	95	95	...	...	...	...	...	23	23	...	...	...	...	...
51	Working in leather ...	95	95	...	...	...	...	...	23	23	...	...	...	...	...
53	Bone, ivory, horn, shell, etc., workers (except buttons).	...	...	...	...	...	...	...	...	...	...	...	...	...	...
	ORDER 7—WOOD ...	2 777	1,933	618	40	10	175	1	992	870	7	24	...	90	1
54	Sawyers	42	42	...	...	...	...	...	42	40	...	2	...	...	...
55	Carpenters, turners and joiners, etc.,	1,830	1,663	5	29	...	133	...	946	826	7	22	...	90	1
56	Basket makers and other industries of woody materials, including leaves, and thatchers and builders working with bamboo, reeds or similar materials.	905	228	613	11	10	42	1	4	4	...	...	...	...	...
	ORDER 8—METALS ...	1,131	1,068	...	5	1	57	...	1,693	1,621	9	19	...	44	...
59	Blacksmiths, other workers in iron, makers of implements.	1,098	1,043	...	5	1	49	...	1,653	1,585	8	18	...	42	...
60	Workers in brass, copper and bell metals.	5	5	...	...	...	...	...	2	2	...	...	...	...	...
61	Workers in other metals except p ecious metal.	28	20	...	...	...	8	...	38	34	1	1	...	2	...
	ORDER 9—CERAMICS ...	1,419	1,319	49	6	2	43	...	2,108	2,071	9	8	9	11	...
63	Potters and makers of earthenware	250	225	1	3	2	19	...	1,204	1,178	9	8	9	...	...
64	Brick and tile makers ...	1,169	1,094	48	3	...	24	...	904	893	...	...	...	11	...
65	Other workers in ceramics ...	...	...	...	...	...	...	...	...	...	...	...	...	...	...

TABLE X

Occupation or means of livelihood—General Table

Dera Ismail Khan							Trans-Frontier Posts							Peshawar Municipality						
Total following occupation	As principal occupation		As working dependents		As subsidiary to other occupations		Total following occupation	As principal occupation		As working dependents		As subsidiary to other occupations		Total following occupation	As principal occupation		As working dependents		As subsidiary to other occupations	
	Males	Females	Males	Females	Males	Females		Males	Females	Males	Females	Males	Females		Males	Females	Males	Females	Males	Females
45	46	47	48	49	50	51	52	53	54	55	56	57	58	59	60	61	62	63	64	65
30,043	26,807	1,397	345	65	1,421	8	5,293	4,215	20	3	...	1,055	...	14,988	14,225	696	1	9	55	2
15,480	13,619	1,271	138	62	384	6	2,364	2,013	20	2	...	329	...	8,605	7,960	617	...	8	20	...
1,762	1,148	547	8	23	36	...	144	63	1	...	...	80	...	692	614	71	...	2	5	...
1,134	614	520	...	...	...	...	...	...	...	...	...	...	...	31	30	...	...	...	1	...
293	247	17	2	9	18	...	144	63	1	...	...	80	...	257	239	13	...	1	4	...
5	3	...	...	...	2	...	...	...	...	...	...	...	...	27	27	...	...	...	...	...
64	47	3	...	14	...	...	...	...	...	...	...	...	...	34	34	...	...	...	...	...
51	51	...	...	...	...	...	...	...	...	...	...	...	...	...	...	...	...	...	...	...
14	14	...	...	...	..	...	...	...	...	...	...	...	...	153	153	...	...	...	...	...
201	172	7	6	..	16	...	...	...	...	...	...	...	...	75	66	8	...	1	...	...
...	...	...	...	...	...	...	...	...	...	...	...	...	...	115	65	50	...	...	...	...
43	41	...	...	2	...	...	...	...	...	..	...	...	...	67	67	...	...	...	...	...
35	34	...	...	...	1	...	...	...	..	...	...	...	...	67	67	...	...	...	...	...
8	7	...	...	...	1	...	...	...	...	...	...	...	...	...	...	...	...	...	...	...
3,300	2,643	512	31	5	109	...	198	148	...	...	...	50	...	669	555	112	...	...	2	...
3	...	...	...	...	3	...	...	...	...	...	...	...	...	51	51	...	...	...	...	...
1,712	1,591	2	31	...	88	...	198	148	...	...	...	50	...	407	405	1	...	...	1	...
1,585	1,052	510	...	5	18	...	...	...	...	...	...	...	...	211	99	111	...	...	1	...
1,591	1,563	...	7	...	21	...	183	152	...	...	...	31	...	430	427	2	...	...	1	...
1,456	1,434	...	7	...	15	...	183	152	...	...	...	31	...	256	254	1	...	...	1	...
60	60	...	...	...	...	...	...	...	...	...	...	...	...	89	89	...	...	...	...	...
75	69	...	...	...	6	...	...	...	...	...	...	...	...	85	84	1	...	...	...	...
1,284	1,261	1	9	...	13	...	88	3	...	...	...	85	...	179	177	...	...	...	2	...
409	389	1	6	...	13	...	88	3	...	...	...	85	...	41	41	...	...	...	...	...
875	872	...	3	...	...	...	...	...	...	...	...	...	...	137	135	...	...	...	2	...
...	...	...	...	...	...	...	...	...	...	...	...	...	...	1	1	...	...	...	...	...

TABLE X

Occupation or means of livelihood—General Table

Group No.	Occupation	N.-W. F. Province							N.-W. F. Province		
		Total following occupation	As principal occupation		As working dependents		As subsidiary to other occupations		Total following occupation	As principal occupation	
			Males	Females	Males	Females	Males	Females		Males	Females
1	2	3	4	5	6	7	8	9	10	11	12
	ORDER 10—CHEMICAL PRODUCTS PROPERLY SO CALLED AND ANALOGOUS.	3,086	2,685	31	103	11	256	...	3,086	2,685	31
66	Manufacture of matches, fire works and other explosives.	111	107	4	...	...	...	...	111	107	4
67	Manufacture of aerated and mineral waters and ice.	234	234	...	...	...	...	...	234	234	...
68	Manufacture and refining of vegetable oils.	2,451	2,095	20	93	10	233	...	2,451	2,095	20
70	Others ...	290	249	7	10	1	23	...	290	249	7
	ORDER 11—FOOD INDUSTRIES ...	10,967	9,069	861	404	58	566	9	10,707	8,889	861
71	Rice pounders and huskers and flour grinders.	3,321	2,496	678	27	18	98	4	3,321	2,496	678
72	Grain parchers, etc. ...	1,509	1,301	90	39	29	46	4	1,509	1,301	90
73	Butchers ...	3,833	3,180	55	324	6	267	1	3,712	3,059	55
74	Makers of sugar, molasses and gur.	121	120	...	...	...	1	...	121	120	...
75	Sweetmeat, Bakhar preparers and condiment makers.	507	507	...	...	...	...	...	507	507	...
77	Brewers and distillers ...	19	19	...	...	...	...	...	19	19	...
78	Manufacturers of tobacco ...	214	213	1	...	...	...	...	214	213	1
80	Manufacturers of Ganja ...	17	17	...	...	...	...	...	17	17	...
81	Others ...	1,426	1,216	37	14	5	154	...	1,287	1,157	37
	ORDER 12—INDUSTRIES OF DRESS AND THE TOILET.	32,245	28,343	842	1,368	235	1,447	10	31,481	27,583	840
82	Boot, shoe, sandal and clog makers.	11,919	10,750	113	494	103	458	1	11,825	10,656	113
83	Tailors, milliners, dress makers and darners.	6,271	5,083	491	179	88	422	8	6,031	4,847	489
84	Embroiderers, hat-makers and makers of other articles of wear.	675	597	72	...	3	3	...	675	597	72
85	Washing and cleaning ...	5,267	4,703	137	235	32	160	...	4,998	4,434	137
86	Barbers, hair dressers and wig makers.	8,059	7,156	29	460	9	404	1	7,898	6,995	29
87	Other industries connected with the toilet.	54	54	...	...	...	...	...	54	54	...
	ORDER 13—FURNITURE INDUSTRIES	258	250	...	2	1	4	1	258	250	..
88	Cabinet makers, carriage painters, etc.	205	202	...	...	...	3	...	205	202	...
89	Upholsterers, tent makers, etc. ...	53	48	...	2	1	1	1	53	48	...
	ORDER 14—BUILDING INDUSTRIES.	6,552	6,382	27	44	10	87	2	6,522	6,354	27
90	Lime burners, cement workers; excavators and well sinkers; stone cutters and dressers; brick layers and masons; builders (other than buildings made of bamboo or similar materials), painters, decorators of houses, tilers, plumbers, etc.	6,552	6,382	27	44	10	87	2	6,522	6,354	27

TABLE X

Occupation or means of livelihood—General Table

(Districts)				Hazara							Peshawar						
As working dependents		As subsidiary to other occupations		Total following occupation	As principal occupation		As working dependents		As subsidiary to other occupations		Total following occupation	As principal occupation		As working dependents		As subsidiary to other occupations	
Males	Females	Males	Females		Males	Females	Males	Females	Males	Females		Males	Females	Males	Females	Males	Females
13	14	15	16	17	18	19	20	21	22	23	24	25	26	27	28	29	30
103	11	256	...	996	866	20	31	10	69	...	1,416	1,207	7	62	1	139	...
...	...	...	...	25	21	4	...	...	...	...	42	42	...	...	...	...	...
...	...	...	...	40	40	...	...	...	...	...	86	86	...	...	...	...	...
93	10	233	...	895	789	12	29	9	56	...	1,159	954	5	61	1	138	...
10	1	23	...	36	16	4	2	1	13	...	129	125	2	1	...	1	...
404	58	486	9	1,208	961	46	30	23	147	1	6,547	5,319	621	349	14	240	4
27	18	98	4	383	288	14	10	9	62	...	2,330	1,746	566	3	6	7	2
39	29	46	4	197	121	32	12	11	20	1	570	505	27	24	3	10	1
324	6	267	1	282	231	...	5	2	44	...	2,616	2,077	22	314	3	199	1
...	...	1	...	11	10	...	...	...	1	...	80	80	...	...	...	...	...
...	...	...	...	153	153	...	...	...	...	...	235	235	...	...	...	...	...
...	...	...	...	...	...	...	...	...	...	...	19	19	...	...	...	...	...
...	...	...	...	41	41	...	...	...	...	...	64	63	1	...	...	...	...
...	...	...	...	...	...	...	...	...	...	...	17	17	...	...	...	...	...
14	5	74	...	141	117	...	3	1	20	...	616	577	5	8	2	24	...
1,366	235	1,447	10	6,586	5,531	176	248	136	491	4	13,340	11,175	538	941	56	629	1
494	103	458	1	3,225	2,815	34	136	62	177	1	5,018	4,435	55	310	31	187	...
177	88	422	8	1,088	797	85	24	55	124	3	2,448	1,821	340	103	12	171	1
...	3	3	...	47	47	...	...	...	...	...	515	442	70	...	3	...	...
235	32	160	...	417	320	50	14	12	21	...	2,038	1,636	58	200	9	135	...
460	9	404	1	1,809	1,552	7	74	7	169	...	3,268	2,788	15	328	1	136	...
.	...	...	...	...	...	...	...	...	...	...	53	53	...	...	...	...	...
2	1	4	1	100	94	...	2	1	2	1	122	122	...	...	...	...	...
...	...	3	...	71	70	...	...	...	1	...	98	98	...	...	...	...	...
2	1	1	1	29	24	...	2	1	1	1	24	24	...	...	...	...	...
44	10	85	2	864	845	...	3	...	15	..	3,420	3,348	3	27	...	42	...
44	10	85	2	864	845	...	3	...	16	...	3,420	3,348	3	27	...	42	...

TABLE X

Occupation or means of livelihood—General Table

Group No.	Occupation	Kohat: Total following occupation	Kohat: As principal occupation: Males	Kohat: As principal occupation: Females	Kohat: As working dependents: Males	Kohat: As working dependents: Females	Kohat: As subsidiary to other occupations: Males	Kohat: As subsidiary to other occupations: Females	Bannu: Total following occupation	Bannu: As principal occupation: Males	Bannu: As principal occupation: Females	Bannu: As working dependents: Males	Bannu: As working dependents: Females	Bannu: As subsidiary to other occupations: Males	Bannu: As subsidiary to other occupations: Females
1	2	31	32	33	34	35	36	37	38	39	40	41	42	43	44
	ORDER 10—CHEMICAL PRODUCTS PROPERLY SO CALLED AND ANALOGOUS.	271	249	1	2	...	19	...	204	185	...	7	...	12	..
66	Manufacture of matches, fire works and other explosives.	15	15	...	...	...	...	...	12	12	...	...	...		...
67	Manufacture of ærated and mineral waters and ice.	12	12	...	...	...	...	...	55	55	...	...	...	..	...
68	Manufacture and refining of vegetable oils.	206	189	1	2	...	14	...	73	61	...	...	...	12	...
70	Others ...	38	33	...	...	...	5	..	64	57	...	7	...	...	...
	ORDER 11—FOOD INDUSTRIES ...	684	546	70	14	3	50	1	1,622	1,502	64	7	14	32	3
71	Rice pounders and huskers and flour grinders.	231	145	54	13	2	17	...	303	[illegible]	3	1	...	6	2
72	Grain parchers, etc. ...	75	63	9	...	...	2	1	645	599	20	3	13	9	1
73	Butchers ...	205	181	6	1	1	16	...	447	412	27	2	...	6	...
74	Maker of sugar, molasses and Gur.	5	5	...	...	...	...	...	13	13	...	...	...	...	...
75	Sweetmeat, Bakhar preparers and condiment makers.	42	42	...	...	...	...	...	32	32	...	...	...	...	...
77	Brewers and distillers ...	...	...	...	...	...	...	...	...	...	...	...	...	...	...
78	Manufacturers of tobacco ...	31	31	...	...	...	...	...	41	41	...	...	...	..	...
80	Manufacturers of Ganja ...	...	...	...	...	...	...	...	...	...	...	...	...	...	...
81	Other ...	95	79	1	...	...	15	...	141	114	14	1	1	11	...
	ORDER 12—INDUSTRIES OF DRESS AND THE TOILET.	3,168	2,959	37	41	18	112	1	3,898	3,670	45	81	5	95	2
82	Boot shoe, sandal and clog makers.	686	638	10	8	5	25	...	1,120	1,056	3	23	...	38	...
83	Tailors, milliners, dress makers and darners.	835	759	12	10	2	52	...	942	869	22	24	4	21	2
84	Embroiderers, hat maker and makers of other articles of wear.	61	56	2	...	...	3	...	25	25	...	...	...	...	...
85	Washing and cleaning ...	729	690	12	13	11	3	...	618	599	15	4	...	...	...
86	Barbers, hair dressers and wig makers.	856	815	1	10	...	29	1	1,193	1,121	5	30	1	36	...
87	Other industries connected with the toilet.	1	1	...	...	...	...	...	...	...	...	...	...	...	...
	ORDER 13—FURNITURE INDUSTRIES	9	8	...	...	...	1	...	18	17	...	...	...	1	...
88	Cabinet-makers, carriage painters, etc.	9	8	...	...	...	1	...	18	17	...	...	...	1	...
89	Upholsterers, tent makers, etc....	...	...	...	...	...	...	...	...	...	...	...	...	..	...
	ORDER 14—BUILDING INDUSTRIES	737	730	1	...	...	4	2	537	529	1	1	...	6	...
90	Lime burners, cement worker; excavators and well sinkers; stone cutters and dressers; brick layers and masons; builders (other than buildings made of bamboo or similar materials), painters, decorators of houses, tilers, plumbers, etc.	737	730	1	...	...	4	2	537	529	1	1	...	6	...

TABLE X

Occupation or means of livelihood—General Table

Dera Ismail Khan							Trans-Frontier Posts							Peshawar Municipality						
Total following occupation	As principal occupation		As working dependents		As subsidiary to other occupations		Total following occupation	As principal occupation		As working dependents		As subsidiary to other occupations		Total following occupation	As principal occupation		As working dependents		As subsidiary to other occupations	
	Males	Females	Males	Females	Males	Females		Males	Females	Males	Females	Males	Females		Males	Females	Males	Females	Males	Females
45	46	47	48	49	58	51	52	53	54	55	56	57	58	59	60	61	62	63	64	65
199	178	3	1	...	17	...	..	..	...	...	...	...	...	722	719	2	...	...	1	...
17	17	...	...	...	...	...	...	...	...	...	...	...	...	32	32	...	...	...	...	...
41	41	...	...	...	...	...	...	...	...	...	...	...	...	43	43	...	...	...	...	...
118	102	2	1	...	13	...	...	...	...	...	...	...	...	551	551	...	...	...	...	...
23	18	1	...	...	4	...	...	...	...	...	...	...	...	96	93	2	...	...	1	...
646	561	60	4	4	17	...	260	180	...	...	...	80	...	845	825	16	...	2	2	...
74	26	41	...	1	6	...	...	...	...	...	...	...	...	62	57	5	...	...	...	...
22	13	2	...	2	5	...	...	...	...	...	...	...	...	73	73	...	...	...	...	...
162	158	...	2	...	2	...	121	121	...	...	...	...	...	142	135	5	...	...	2	...
12	12	...	...	...	...	...	...	...	...	...	...	...	...	...	...	...	...	...	...	...
45	45	...	...	...	...	...	...	...	...	...	...	...	...	147	147	...	...	...	...	...
...	...	...	...	...	...	...	...	...	...	...	...	...	...	19	19	...	...	...	...	...
37	37	...	...	...	...	...	.	...	...	...	...	...	...	44	43	1	...	...	...	...
...	...	...	...	...	...	...	...	...	...	...	...	...	...	...	...	...	...	...	...	...
294	270	17	2	1	4	...	139	59	...	...	...	80	...	358	351	5	...	2	...	...
4,489	4,248	44	55	20	120	2	764	760	2	2	...	...	...	3,585	3,336	244	...	4	1	...
1,776	1,712	11	17	5	31	...	94	94	...	...	...	...	...	1,308	1,294	14	...	...	...	...
718	601	30	16	15	54	2	240	236	2	2	...	...	...	875	721	152	...	1	1	...
27	27	...	...	...	...	...	...	...	...	...	...	...	...	338	279	56	...	3	...	...
1,196	1,189	2	4	...	1	...	269	269	...	...	...	...	...	697	677	20	...	...	...	...
772	719	1	18	...	34	...	161	161	...	...	...	...	...	317	315	2	...	...	...	...
...	...	...	...	...	...	...	...	...	...	..	...	...	...	50	50	...	...	...	...	...
9	9	...	...	...	...	...	...	...	...	...	...	...	...	32	32	...	...	...	...	...
9	9	...	...	...	...	...	...	...	...	...	...	...	...	15	15	...	...	...	...	...
...	...	...	...	...	...	...	...	...	...	...	...	...	...	17	17	...	...	...	...	...
964	902	22	13	10	17	...	30	28	...	...	...	2	...	321	315	3	...	...	3	...
964	902	22	13	10	17	...	30	28	...	...	...	2	...	321	315	3	...	...	3	...

TABLE X

Occupation or means of livelihood—General Table

Group No.	Occupation	N. W. F. Province: Total following occupation	As principal occupation: Males	As principal occupation: Females	As working dependents: Males	As working dependents: Females	As subsidiary to other occupations: Males	As subsidiary to other occupations: Females	N. W. F. Province: Total following occupation	As principal occupation: Males	As principal occupation: Females
1	2	3	4	5	6	7	8	9	10	11	12
	ORDER 15—CONSTRUCTION OF MEANS OF TRANSPORT.	385	365	...	5	...	15	...	385	365	...
91	Persons engaged in making, assembling or repairing motor vehicles or cycles.	260	243	...	5	...	12	...	260	243	...
92	Carriage, cart, Palki, etc., makers and wheel wrights.	105	102	...	...	...	3		105	102	..
93	Ship, boat, æroplane builders ...	20	20	...	...	...	..	...	20	20	...
	ORDER 16—PRODUCTION AND TRANSMISSION OF PHYSICAL FORCE	159	151	...	1	...	7	...	154	146	...
94	Heat, light, electricity, motive power, etc., gas works and electric light and power.	159	151	...	1	...	7	...	154	146	...
	ORDER 17—MISCELLANEOUS AND UNDEFINED INDUSTRIES.	8,840	7,794	659	154	66	163	4	8,148	7,120	642
95	Printers, engravers, book binders, etc.	371	364	...	...	...	7	...	371	364	...
96	Makers of musical instruments ...	28	28	...	...	...	...	...	28	28	...
97	Makers of clocks and surgical or scientific instruments, etc.	152	144	1	1	...	6	...	150	142	1
98	Makers of jewellery and ornaments.	3,320	3,058	41	94	12	115	...	3,263	3,001	41
99	Other miscellaneous and undefined industries (toy making, taxidermy, etc.).	23	15	...	2	...	6	...	23	15	...
100	Scavenging ...	4,946	4,185	617	57	54	29	4	4,313	3,570	600
	SUB-CLASS IV—TRANSPORT	22,823	18,827	75	587	22	3,298	14	21,703	17,719	75
	ORDER 19—TRANSPORT BY WATER	952	904	2	25	...	20	1	952	904	2
102	Ship owners, boats owners and their employees, officers, mariners, etc., ship brokers, boatmen and tow men.	669	622	2	25	...	19	1	669	622	2
103	Persons (other than labourers) employed in harbours, docks, rivers and canals, including pilots.	81	80	...	...	...	1	...	81	80	...
104	Labourers employed on harbours, docks, rivers and canals.	202	202	...	...	...	...	...	202	202	...
	ORDER 20—TRANSPORT BY ROAD ...	18,079	14,453	63	540	19	2,992	12	17,198	13,584	63
105	Persons (other than labourers) employed on the construction and maintenance of roads and bridges.	647	561	1	8	...	77	...	[illegible]	[illegible]	1
106	Labourers employed on roads and bridges.	1,544	1,243	20	25	6	243	1	1,395	1,094	26
107	Owners, managers and employees (excluding personal servants) connected with mechanically driven vehicles (including trains).	1,983	1,850	...	25	...	108	...	[illegible]	1,619	...
108	Owners managers and employees (excluding personal servants) connected with other vehicles.	6,158	4,969	7	183	5	990	4	6,158	4,960	7
109	Palki etc., bearers and owners...	135	133	...	...	...	2	...	135	133	..
110	Pack elephant, camel, mule, ass and bullock, owners and drivers.	7,478	5,593	18	296	7	1,557	7	[illegible]	5,120	18
111	Porters and messengers ...	134	104	11	3	1	15	...	134	[illegible]	11

TABLE X

Occupation or means of livelihood—General Table

(Districts)				Hazara							Peshawar						
As working dependents		As subsidiary to other occupations		Total following occupation	As principal occupation		As working defendents		As subsidiary to other occupations		Total following occupation	As principal occupation		As working dependents		As subsidiary to other occupations	
Males	Females	Males	Females		Males	Females	Males	Females	Males	Females		Males	Females	Males	Females	Males	Females
13	14	15	16	17	18	19	20	21	22	23	24	25	26	27	28	29	30
5	...	15	...	31	31	...	...	...	...	...	144	138	...	3	...	3	...
5	...	12	...	9	9	...	...	...	...	...	64	61	...	3	...	...	...
...	...	3	...	22	22	...	...	...	...	...	64	61	...	...	...	3	...
...	...	...	...	...	...	...	...	...	...	...	16	16	...	...	...	...	...
1	...	7	...	...	...	...	...	...	...	...	97	96	...	...	...	1	...
1	...	7	...	...	...	...	...	...	...	...	97	96	...	...	...	1	...
154	66	162	4	869	731	75	23	18	22	..	4,434	3,920	321	91	27	75	...
...	...	7	...	64	63	...	...	...	1	...	239	236	...	...	...	3	...
...	...	...	...	3	3	...	...	...	...	...	24	24	...	...	...	...	...
1	...	6	...	26	23	1	...	...	2	...	73	72	...	...	...	1	...
94	12	115	...	523	477	7	17	4	18	...	1,403	1,285	24	42	5	47	...
2	...	6	...	1	...	...	...	...	1	...	16	14	...	2	...	...	...
57	54	28	4	252	165	67	6	14	...	...	2,679	2,289	297	47	22	24	...
587	22	3,286	14	2,015	1,602	4	61	3	343	2	11,370	9,173	24	358	8	1,797	10
25	...	20	1	82	71	...	11	...	...	...	685	5 6	2	12	...	14	1
25	...	19	1	82	71	...	11	...	...	...	455	426	2	12	...	14	1
...	...	1	...	...	...	...	...	...	...	...	79	79	...	...	...	...	...
...	...	...	...	...	...	...	...	...	...	...	151	151	...	...	...	...	...
540	19	2,980	12	1,643	1,292	2	46	3	298	2	9,090	7,001	16	346	8	1,710	9
8	...	77	...	100	81	...	...	...	19	...	47	35	...	3	...	9	...
25	6	243	1	196	167	...	3	...	26	...	533	458	...	3	1	71	...
25	...	96	...	400	349	...	7	...	44	...	492	476	...	12	...	4	...
183	5	990	4	290	222	1	16	3	46	2	596	3,762		145	...	685	2
...	...	2	...	...	...	...	...	...	...	...	113	113	...	...	...	...	...
296	7	1,557	7	657	473	1	20	...	163	...	3,178	2,054	3	180	6	928	7
3	1	15	...	...	...	...	...	...	...	...	131	103	11	3	1	13	...

TABLE X

Occupation or means of livelihood—General Table

Group No.	Occupation	Kohat: Total following occupation	Kohat: As principal occupation — Males	Kohat: As principal occupation — Females	Kohat: As working dependents — Males	Kohat: As working dependents — Females	Kohat: As subsidiary to other occupations — Males	Kohat: As subsidiary to other occupations — Females	Bannu: Total following occupation	Bannu: As principal occupation — Males	Bannu: As principal occupation — Females	Bannu: As working dependents — Males	Bannu: As working dependents — Females	Bannu: As subsidiary to other occupations — Males	Bannu: As subsidiary to other occupations — Females
1	2	31	32	33	34	35	36	37	38	39	40	41	42	43	44
	ORDER 15—CONSTRUCTION OF MEANS OF TRANSPORT.	40	39	...	1	...	...	...	148	135	...	1	...	12	...
91	Persons engaged in making, assembling or repairing motor vehicles or cycles.	31	30	...	1	...	...	...	141	128	...	1	...	12	...
92	Carriage, cart, *Palki*, *etc.*, makers and wheel wrights.	9	9	...	...	...	...	...	7	7	...	...	...	...	...
93	Ship, boat, æroplane builders ...	...	...	...	...	...	...	...	...	...	...	...	...	...	...
	ORDER 16—PRODUCTION AND TRANSMISSION OF PHYSICAL FORCE.	10	10	...	...	...	...	...	29	22	...	1	...	6	...
94	Heat, light, electricity, motive, power, etc., gas works and electric light and power.	10	10	...	...	...	...	...	29	22	...	1	...	6	...
	ORDER 17—MISCELLANEOUS AND UNDEFINED INDUSTRIES.	866	773	63	5	18	7	...	826	671	101	25	3	26	...
95	Printers, engravers, book binders, etc.	16	16	...	...	...	...	...	25	22	...	...	...	3	...
96	Makers of musical instruments ...	...	...	...	...	...	...	...	1	1	...	...	...	...	...
97	Makers of clocks and surgical or scientific instruments, etc.	15	15	...	...	...	...	...	24	21	...	1	...	2	...
98	Makers of jewellery and ornaments.	308	293	2	3	3	7	...	303	259	7	22	...	15	...
99	Other miscellaneous and undefined industries (toy making, taxidermy, etc.).	...	...	...	...	...	...	...	6	1	...	...	...	5	...
100	Scavenging ...	527	449	61	2	15	...	...	467	367	94	2	3	1	...
	SUB-CLASS IV—TRANSPORT	2,690	2,154	14	55	10	455	2	2,005	1,692	6	52	1	254	...
	ORDER 19—TRANSPORT BY WATER	4	2	...	...	...	2	...	1	...	...	...	...	1	...
102	Ship owners, boat owners and their employees, officers, mariners, etc., ship brokers, boatmen and tow men.	4	2	...	...	...	2	...	...	...	...	...	...	...	...
103	Persons (other than labourers) employed in harbours, docks, rivers and canals, including pilots.	...	...	...	...	...	...	...	1	...	...	...	...	1	...
104	Labourers employed on harbours, docks, rivers and canals.	...	...	...	...	...	...	...	...	...	...	...	...	...	...
	ORDER 20—TRANSPORT BY ROAD ...	1,859	1,459	12	53	7	327	1	1,469	1,203	6	38	1	221	...
105	Persons (other than labourers) employed on the construction and maintenance of roads and bridges.	175	154	...	1	...	20	...	187	162	1	2	...	22	...
106	Labourers employed on roads and bridges.	306	225	7	15	5	53	1	78	59	...	3	...	16	...
107	Owners, managers and employees (excluding personal servants) connected with mechanically driven vehicles (including trams).	345	320	...	3	...	22	...	357	342	...	1	...	14	...
108	Owners, managers and employees (excluding personal servants) connected with other vehicles.	605	455	2	14	2	132	...	438	369	2	6	...	61	...
109	Palki, etc., bearers and owners ...	...	...	...	...	...	...	...	22	20	...	...	...	2	...
110	Pack elephant, camel, mule, ass and bullock, owners and drivers.	428	305	3	20	...	100	...	384	250	3	26	1	104	...
111	Porters and messengers ...	...	...	...	...	...	...	...	3	1	...	...	...	2	...

TABLE X

Occupation or means of livelihood—General Table

Dera Ismail Khan							Trans-Frontier Posts							Peshawar Municipality						
Total following occupation	As principal occupation		As working dependents		As subsidiary to other occupations		Total following occupation	As principal occupation		As working dependents		As subsidiary to other occupations		Total following occupation	As principal occupation		As working dependents		As subsidiary to other occupations	
	Males	Females	Males	Females	Males	Females		Males	Females	Males	Females	Males	Females		Males	Females	Males	Females	Males	Females
45	46	47	48	49	50	51	52	53	54	55	56	57	58	59	60	61	62	63	64	65
22	22	...	...	...	...	...	..	...	...	...	..	...	...	43	43	...	...	...	...	...
15	15	...	...	...	...	...	...	...	...	...	...	...	...	21	21	...	...	...	...	...
3	3	...	...	...	...	...	...	...	...	...	...	...	...	22	22	...	...	...	...	...
4	4	...	...	...	...	...	...	...	...	...	...	...	...	...	...	...	...	...	...	...
18	18	...	...	...	...	...	5	5	..	...	...	...	...	22	22	...	...	...	...	...
18	18	...	...	...	...	...	5	5	...	...	..	...	...	22	22	...	...	...	...	...
1,153	1,025	82	10	...	32	4	692	674	17	...	...	1	...	998	828	167	...	...	3	...
27	27	...	...	...	...	...	...	...	...	...	...	...	...	95	93	....	...	...	2	...
...	...	...	...	...	...	...	...	..	...	...	...	...	...	3	3	...	...	...	...	...
12	11	...	...	...	1	...	2	2	...	...	...	...	...	35	35	...	...	...	...	...
726	687	1	10	...	28	...	57	57	...	...	...	...	...	349	343	6	...	...	...	...
...	...	...	...	...	...	...	...	...	...	...	...	...	...	11	11	...	...	...	...	...
388	300	81	...	...	3	4	633	615	17	...	...	1	...	505	343	161	...	...	1	...
3,623	3.098	27	61	...	437	...	1,120	1,108	...	...	...	12	...	771	761	5	1	...	4	...
180	175	...	2	...	3	...	...	...	...	...	...	...	...	1	1	...	...	...	...	...
128	123	...	2	...	3	...	...	...	...	...	...	...	...	1	1	...	...	...	...	...
1	1	...	...	...	...	...	...	...	...	...	...	...	...	...	...	...	...	...	...	...
51	51	...	...	...	...	...	...	...	...	...	...	...	...	...	...	...	...	...	...	...
3,137	2,629	27	57	...	424	...	881	869	...	...	...	12	...	563	554	4	1	...	4	...
122	113	...	2	...	7	...	16	16	...	...	...	...	...	...	...	...	...	...	...	...
282	185	19	1	...	77	...	149	149	...	...	...	...	...	26	26	...	...	...	...	...
146	132	...	2	...	12	...	243	231	...	...	...	12	...	269	267	...	...	...	2	...
229	161	...	2	...	66	...	...	...	...	...	...	...	...	91	88	2	1	...	...	...
...	...	...	...	...	...	...	...	...	...	...	...	...	...	90	90	...	...	...	...	...
2,358	2,038	8	50	...	262	...	473	473	...	...	...	...	...	67	63	2	...	...	2	...
...	...	...	...	...	...	...	...	...	...	...	...	...	...	20	20	...	...	...	...	...

TABLE X

Occupation or means of livelihood—General Table

Group No.	Occupation	N. W. F. Province							N. W. F. Province		
		Total following occupation	As principal occupation		As working dependents		As subsidiary to other occupations		Total following occupation	As principal occupation	
			Males	Females	Males	Females	Males	Females		Males	Females
1	2	3	4	5	6	7	8	9	10	11	12
	ORDER 21—TRANSPORT BY RAIL ...	2,664	2,403	8	18	2	232	1	2,557	2,295	8
112	Railway employees of all kinds other than coolies.	2,232	2,011	7	18	2	193	1	2,148	1,927	7
113	Labourers employed on railway construction and maintenance and coolies and porters employed on railway premises.	432	392	1	...	...	39	...	409	369	1
	ORDER 22 - POST OFFICE, TELEGRAPH AND TELEPHONE SERVICES.	1,128	1,067	2	4	1	54	...	996	935	2
114	Post Office, Telegraph and Telephone services.	1,128	1,067	2	4	1	54	...	996	935	2
	SUB-CLASS V—TRADE ...	66,980	60,303	547	1,699	204	4,204	23	65,171	59,209	547
	ORDER 23—BANKS, ESTABLISHMENTS OF CREDIT, EXCHANGE AND INSURANCE.	1,396	1,118	12	17	1	248	...	1,396	1,118	12
115	Bank managers, money lenders exchange and insurance agents, money changers and brokers and their employees.	1,396	1,118	12	17	1	248	...	1,396	1,118	12
	ORDER 24—BROKERAGE, COMMISSION AND EXPORT.	1,004	905	3	15	...	81	...	995	895	3
116	Brokers, commission agents, commercial travellers, warehouse owners and employees.	1,004	905	3	15	...	81	...	995	896	3
	ORDER 25—TRADE IN TEXTILES ...	4,067	3,736	29	171	16	115	...	4,013	3,683	29
117	Trade in piece goods, wool, cotton, silk, hair and other textiles.	4,067	3,736	29	171	16	115	...	4,013	3,683	29
	ORDER 26 TRADE IN SKINS, LEATHER AND FURS.	301	242	5	8	2	44	...	301	242	5
118	Trade in skins, leather, furs, feathers, horn, etc., and the articles made from these.	301	242	5	8	2	44	...	301	242	5
	ORDER 27—TRADE IN WOOD ...	1,710	1,243	10	46	1	410	...	1,469	1,230	10
119	Trade in wood (not firewood) ...	1,473	1,047	9	31	1	385	...	1,232	1,034	9
120	Trade in barks ...	184	145	...	15	...	24	...	184	145	...
121	Trade in bamboos and canes ...	53	51	1	...	...	1	...	53	51	1
	ORDER 28—TRADE IN METALS ...	264	262	1	...	...	1	...	264	262	1
123	Trade in metals, machinery, knives, tools, etc.	264	262	1	...	...	1	...	264	262	1
	ORDER 29 TRADE IN POTTERY, BRICKS AND TILES.	409	408	...	...	...	1	...	409	408	...
124	Trade in pottery, bricks and tiles.	409	408	...	...	...	1	...	409	408	...
	ORDER 30—TRADE IN CHEMICAL PRODUCTS.	134	130	1	...	...	3	...	134	130	1
125	Drugs, dyes, paints, petroleum explosives, etc.	134	130	1	...	...	3	...	134	130	1

TABLE X

Occupation or means of livelihood—General Table

(Districts)				Hazara							Peshawar						
As working dependents		As subsidiary to other occupations		Total following occupation	As principal occupation		As working dependents		As subsidiary to other occupations		Total following occupation	As principal occupation		As working dependents		As subsidiary to other occupations	
Males	Females	Males	Females		Males	Females	Males	Females	Males	Females		Males	Females	Males	Females	Males	Females
13	14	15	16	17	18	19	20	21	22	23	24	25	26	27	28	29	30
18	2	232	1	136	101	2	2	...	31	...	1,144	1,069	4	...	...	71	—
18	2	193	1	102	70	2	2	...	28	...	884	834	3	...	...	47	—
...	...	39	...	34	31	...	...	...	3	...	260	235	1	...	...	24	—
4	1	54	...	154	138	...	2	...	14	...	451	447	2	...	...	2	—
4	1	54	...	154	138	...	2	...	14	...	451	447	2	...	...	2	—
1,698	204	3,490	23	7,496	6,449	82	204	119	639	3	30,042	27,338	211	1,047	63	1,372	[illegible]
17	1	248	...	312	211	1	2	...	98	...	448	395	8	...	...	45	—
17	1	248	...	312	211	1	2	...	98	...	448	395	8	...	...	45	—
15	...	81	...	7	6	...	1	...	...	...	533	485	3	7	...	38	—
15	...	81	...	7	6	...	1	...	...	...	533	485	3	7	...	38	—
171	16	114	...	315	262	5	14	13	21	...	1,606	1,393	18	142	1	52	—
171	16	114	...	315	262	5	14	13	21	...	1,606	1,393	18	142	1	52	—
8	2	44	...	63	48	...	3	...	12	...	59	58	...	...	...	1	—
8	2	44	...	63	48	...	3	...	12	...	59	58	...	...	...	1	—
46	1	182	...	123	111	3	3	...	6	...	536	490	3	21	...	22	—
31	1	157	...	111	99	3	3	...	6	...	512	467	2	21	...	22	—
15	...	24	...	...	...	...	...	...	...	...	...	...	...	...	...	...	—
...	...	1	...	12	12	...	...	...	...	...	24	23	1	...	...	...	—
...	...	1	...	34	33	...	...	...	1	...	50	50	...	...	...	...	—
...	...	1	...	34	33	...	...	...	1	...	50	50	...	...	...	...	—
...	...	1	...	103	103	...	...	...	...	...	197	197	...	...	...	...	—
...	...	1	...	103	103	...	...	...	...	...	197	197	...	...	...	...	—
..	...	3	...	43	43	...	...	...	...	...	77	74	1	...	...	2	—
...	...	3	...	43	43	...	...	...	...	...	77	74	1	...	...	2	—

TABLE X

Occupation or means of livelihood—General Table

Group No	Occupation	Kobat: Total following occupation	Kobat: As principal occupation: Males	Kobat: As principal occupation: Females	Kobat: As working dependents: Males	Kobat: As working dependents: Females	Kobat: As subsidiary to other occupations: Males	Kobat: As subsidiary to other occupations: Females	Bannu: Total following occupation	Bannu: As principal occupation: Males	Bannu: As principal occupation: Females	Bannu: As working dependents: Males	Bannu: As working dependents: Females	Bannu: As subsidiary to other occupations: Males	Bannu: As subsidiary to other occupations: Females
1	2	31	32	33	34	35	36	37	38	39	40	41	42	43	44
	ORDER 21—TRANSPORT BY RAIL ...	691	589	2	...	2	97	1	395	350	...	14	...	31	...
112	Railway employees of all kinds other than coolies.	576	486	2	...	2	85	1	395	350	...	14	...	31	...
113	Labourers employed on railway construction and maintenance and coolies and porters employed on railway premises.	115	103	...	...	...	12	...	...	...	...	...	...	...	...
	ORDER 22—POST OFFICE, TELEGRAPH AND TELEPHONE SERVICES.	136	104	...	2	1	29	...	140	139	...	...		1	...
114	Post Office, Telegraph and Telephone services.	136	104	...	2	1	29	...	140	139	...	...	...	1	...
	SUB-CLASS V—TRADE ...	5,418	4,954	109	67	6	275	7	11,275	10 378	46	234	13	604	...
	ORDER 23—BANKS, ESTABLISHMENTS OF CREDIT, EXCHANGE AND INSURANCE.	134	131	...	...	...	3	...	120	118	...	...	...	2	...
115	Bank managers, money lenders exchange and insurance agents, money changers and brokers and their employees.	134	131	...	...	...	3	...	120	118	...	...	...	2	...
	ORDER 24—BROKERAGE, COMMISSION AND EXPORT.	64	57	...	...	...	7	...	83	72	...	2	...	9	...
116	Brokers, commission agents, commercial travellers, warehouse owners and employees.	64	57	...	...	...	7	...	83	72	...	2	...	9	...
	ORDER 25—TRADE IN TEXTILES ...	228	212	2	7	...	7	...	255	237	2	1	1	14	...
117	Trade in piece goods, wool, cotton, silk, hair and other textiles.	228	212	2	7	...	7	...	255	237	2	1	1	14	...
	ORDER 26—TRADE IN SKINS, LEATHER AND FURS.	30	20	...	...	...	10	...	112	86	5	5	2	14	...
118	Trade in skins, leather, furs, feathers, horn, etc., and the articles made from these.	30	20	...	...	...	10	...	112	86	5	5	2	14	...
	ORDER 27—TRADE IN WOOD ...	52	32	4	2	1	13	...	275	166	...	15	...	94	...
119	Trade in wood (not firewood) ...	48	28	4	2	1	13	...	81	12	...	...	...	69	...
120	Trade in barks ...	...	...	...	...	...	...	...	184	145	...	15	...	24	...
121	Trade in bamboos and canes ...	4	4	...	...	...	...	...	10	9	...	...	...	1	...
	ORDER 28—TRADE IN METALS ...	32	32	...	...	...	...	...	44	44	...	...	...	...	...
123	Trade in metals, machinery, knives, tools, etc.	32	32	...	...	...	...	...	44	44	...	...	...	...	...
	ORDER 29—TRADE IN POTTERY, BRICKS AND TILES.	30	30	...	...	...	...	...	40	40	...	...	...	...	...
124	Trade in pottery, bricks and tiles.	30	30	...	...	...	...	...	40	40	...	...	...	...	...
	ORDER 30—TRADE IN CHEMICAL PRODUCTS.	10	10	...	...	...	...	...	...	...	...	...	...	...	...
125	Drugs, dyes, paints, petroleum, explosives, etc.	10	10	...	...	...	...	...	...	...	...	...	...	...	...

TABLE X

Occupation or means of livelihood—General Table

Dera Ismail Khan							Trans-Frontier Posts							Peshawar Municipality						
Total following occupation	As principal occupation		As working dependents		As subsidiary to other occupations		Total following occupation	As principal occupation		As working dependents		As subsidiary to other occupations		Total following occupation	As principal occupation		As working dependents		As subsidiary to other occupations	
	Males	Females	Males	Females	Males	Females		Males	Females	Males	Females	Males	Females		Males	Females	Males	Females	Males	Females
45	46	47	48	49	50	51	52	53	54	55	56	57	58	59	60	61	62	63	64	65
191	187	...	2	...	2	...	107	107	...	...	...	...	...	124	123	1	...	...	...	...
191	187	...	2	...	2	...	84	84	...	...	...	...	...	109	108	1	...	...	...	...
...	...	...	...	...	...	...	23	23	...	...	...	...	...	15	15	...	...	...	...	...
115	107	...	...	...	8	.	132	132	...	...	...	...	...	83	83	...	...	...	...	...
115	107	...	...	...	8	...	132	132	...	...	...	...	...	83	83	...	...	...	...	...
10,940	10,090	99	146	3	600	2	1,809	1,094	...	1	...	714	...	5,612	5,504	74	...	1	31	2
382	263	3	15	1	100	...	...	...	...	...	...	...	...	153	143	7	...	...	3	...
382	263	3	15	1	100	...	...	...	...	...	...	...	...	153	143	7	...	...	3	...
308	276	...	5	...	27	...	9	9	...	...	...	...	...	339	335	3	..	...	1	...
308	276	...	5	...	27	...	9	9	...	...	...	...	...	339	335	3	...	...	1	...
1,609	1,579	2	7	1	20	...	54	53	...	...	...	1	...	640	639	...	...	...	1	...
1,609	1,579	2	7	1	20	...	54	53	...	...	...	1	...	640	639	...	...	...	1	...
37	30	...	...	...	7	...	...	...	...	...	...	...	...	44	44	...	...	...	...	...
37	30	...	...	...	7	...	...	...	...	...	...	...	...	44	44	...	...	...	...	...
483	431	...	5	...	47	...	241	13	...	...	...	228	...	194	191	2	...	...	1	...
480	428	...	5	...	47	...	241	13	...	...	...	228	...	194	191	2	...	...	1	...
...	...	...	...	...	...	...	...	...	...	...	...	...	...	...	...	...	...	...	...	...
3	3	...	...	...	...	...	...	...	...	...	...	...	...	...	...	...	...	...	...	...
104	103	1	...	...	...	...	...	...	...	...	...	...	...	30	30	...	...	...	...	...
104	103	1	...	...	...	...	...	...	...	...	...	...	...	30	30	...	...	...	...	...
39	38	...	...	...	1	...	...	...	...	...	...	...	...	62	62	...	...	...	...	...
39	38	...	...	...	1	...	...	...	...	...	...	...	...	62	62	...	...	...	...	...
4	3	...	...	...	1	...	...	...	...	...	...	...	...	15	14	1	...	...	...	...
4	3	...	...	...	1	...	...	...	...	...	...	...	...	15	14	1	...	...	...	...

TABLE X

Occupation or means of livelihood—General Table

Group No.	Occupation	N.-W. F. Province — Total following occupation	As principal occupation — Males	As principal occupation — Females	As working dependents — Males	As working dependents — Females	As subsidiary to other occupations — Males	As subsidiary to other occupations — Females	N.-W. F. Province — Total following occupation	As principal occupation — Males	As principal occupation — Females
1	2	3	4	5	6	7	8	9	10	11	12
	ORDER 31—HOTELS, CAFES, RESTAURANTS, ETC.	3,135	3,100	6	13	...	16	...	3,135	3,100	6
126	Vendors of wine, liquors, aerated waters and ice.	747	742	1	...	...	4	...	747	742	1
127	Owners and managers of hotels, cook shops, Serais, etc. (and employees).	2,099	2,079	4	6	...	10	...	2,099	2,079	4
128	Hawkers of drink and food stuffs	289	279	1	7	...	2	...	289	279	1
	ORDER 32—OTHER TRADE IN FOOD STUFFS.	15,654	13,783	160	467	56	1,176	12	15,502	13,631	160
129	Grain and pulse dealers ...	7,352	6,343	65	325	24	593	2	7,280	6,271	65
130	Dealers in sweetmeats, sugar and spices.	2,201	2,005	9	58	14	109	6	2,140	1,944	9
131	Dealers in dairy products, eggs and poultry.	1,963	1,436	37	73	15	400	2	1,944	1,417	37
132	Dealers in animals for food ...	227	215	...	...	...	12	...	227	215	...
133	Dealers in fodder for animals ...	2,199	2,144	34	1	1	17	2	2,199	2,144	34
134	Dealers in other food stuffs ...	913	854	15	8	2	34	...	913	854	15
135	Dealers in tobacco ...	185	176	...	2	...	7	...	185	176	...
136	Dealers in opium ...	313	309	...	...	...	4	...	313	309	...
137	Dealers in Ganja ...	301	301	...	...	...	...	...	301	301	...
	ORDER 33—TRADE IN CLOTHING AND TOILET ARTICLES.	2,012	1,762	13	2	1	234	...	1,801	1,749	13
138	Trade in ready made clothing, other articles of dress and the toilet (hats, umbrellas, socks, ready made shoes, perfumes etc.).	2,012	1,762	13	2	1	234	...	1,801	1,749	13
	ORDER 34 TRADE IN FURNITURE	688	686	1	...	...	1	...	688	686	1
139	Trade in furniture, carpets, curtains and bedding.	335	334	1	...	...	...	...	335	334	1
140	Hardware, cooking utensils, porcelain, crockery, glassware, bottles, articles for gardening etc.	353	352	...	...	...	1	...	353	352	...
	ORDER 35—TRADE IN BUILDING MATERIALS.	404	404	...	...	...	...	...	404	404	...
141	Trade in building materials (other than bricks, tiles and woody materials).	404	404	...	...	...	...	...	404	404	...
	ORDER 36—TRADE IN MEANS OF TRANSPORT.	864	680	14	9	3	158	...	864	680	14
142	Dealers and hirers in mechanical transport, motors, cycles, etc.	211	209	...	1	...	1	...	211	209	...
143	Dealers and hirers in other carriages, carts, boats, etc.	115	115	...	...	...	...	...	115	115	...
144	Dealers and hirers of elephants, camels, horses, cattle, asses, mules, etc.	538	356	14	8	3	157	...	538	356	14

TABLE X

Occupation or means of livelihood—General Table

(Districts)				Hazara							Peshawar						
As working dependents		As subsidiary to other occupations		Total following occupation	As principal occupation		As working dependents		As subsidiary to other occupations		Total following occupation	As principal occupation		As working dependents		As subsidiary to other occupations	
Males	Females	Males	Females		Males	Females	Males	Females	Males	Females		Males	Females	Males	Females	Males	Females
13	14	15	16	17	18	19	20	21	22	23	24	25	26	27	28	29	30
13	...	16	...	343	333	1	5	...	4	...	1,402	1,392	1	3	...	6	...
...	...	4	...	108	107	...	...	...	1	...	303	303	...	...	...	...	...
6	...	10	...	229	220	1	5	...	3	...	1,025	1,018	1	...	...	6	...
7	...	2	...	6	6	...	...	...	...	...	74	71	...	3	...	...	...
467	56	1,176	12	2,960	2,632	26	76	37	189	...	6,680	5,920	39	198	10	510	3
325	24	593	2	1,797	1,575	19	67	23	113	...	2,085	1,865	15	78	1	126	...
58	14	109	6	260	215	1	8	8	28	...	1,197	1,093	6	44	...	53	1
73	15	400	2	136	93	5	1	6	31	...	1,448	1,038	14	71	9	314	2
...	...	12	...	58	50	...	...	...	8	...	104	103	...	...	...	1	...
1	1	17	2	515	513	...	...	...	2	...	1,006	1,006	...	...	...	...	...
8	2	34	...	46	42	1	...	...	3	...	464	444	4	4	...	12	...
2	...	7	...	42	40	...	...	...	2	...	73	70	...	1	...	2	...
...	...	4	...	56	54	...	...	...	2	...	153	151	...	...	...	2	...
...	...	...	...	50	50	...	...	...	...	...	150	150	...	...	...	...	...
2	1	36	...	261	256	1	2	...	2	...	1,042	1,026	11	...	1	4	...
2	1	36	...	261	256	1	2	...	2	...	1,042	1,026	11	...	1	4	...
...	...	1	...	119	118	...	...	...	1	...	389	389	...	...	...	...	...
...	...	...	...	50	50	...	...	...	...	...	228	228	...	...	...	...	...
...	...	1	...	69	68	...	...	...	1	...	161	161	...	...	...	...	...
...	...	...	...	84	84	...	...	...	...	...	120	120	...	...	...	...	...
...	...	...	...	84	84	...	...	...	...	...	120	120	...	...	..	...	...
9	3	158	...	110	85	...	1	...	24	...	365	284	...	3	...	78	...
1	...	1	...	42	42	...	...	...	...	...	98	98	...	...	...	...	...
...	...	...	...	...	...	...	...	...	...	...	83	83	...	...	...	...	...
8	3	157	...	68	43	...	1	...	24	...	184	103	...	3	...	78	...

TABLE X

Occupation or means of livelihood—General Table

Group No.	Occupation	Kohat: Total following occupation	Kohat: As principal occupation — Males	Kohat: As principal occupation — Females	Kohat: As working dependents — Males	Kohat: As working dependents — Females	Kohat: As subsidiary to other occupations — Males	Kohat: As subsidiary to other occupations — Females	Bannu: Total following occupation	Bannu: As principal occupation — Males	Bannu: As principal occupation — Females	Bannu: As working dependents — Males	Bannu: As working dependents — Females	Bannu: As subsidiary to other occupations — Males	Bannu: As subsidiary to other occupations — Females
1		31	32	33	34	35	36	37	38	39	40	41	42	43	44
	ORDER 31—HOTELS, CAFES, RESTAURANTS ETC.	386	379	1	1	...	5	...	533	530	1	2	..	...	...
126	Vendors of wine liquors, aerated waters and ice.	119	116	1	...	...	2	...	113	113	...	...	..		...
127	Owners and managers of hotels, cook shops, Serais, etc. (and employees).	237	235	...	1	...	1	...	304	304	...	...	..	...	...
128	Hawkers of drink and food stuffs	30	28	...	...	...	2	..	116	113	1	2	...	..	...
	ORDER 32—OTHER TRADE IN FOOD STUFFS.	1 762	1,580	62	17	3	93	7	1,891	1,560	5	109	5	212	...
129	Grain and pulse dealers ...	747	642	21	11	...	73	...	1,113	849	2	105	..	157	...
130	Dealers in sweetmeats, sugar and spices.	232	216	1	5	1	4	5	229	205	1	...	5	18	...
131	Dealers in dairy products, eggs and poultry.	71	55	8	...	...	8	...	90	78	1	...		11	...
132	Dealers in animals for food ...	26	23	...	...	...	3	...	29	20	...	...	...	...	...
133	Dealers in fodder for animals ...	450	416	25	1	1	5	2	115	105	...	...	...	10	...
134	Dealers in other food stuffs ...	127	119	7	...	1	...	...	226	209	1	3	...	13	...
135	Dealers in tobacco ...	27	27	...	...	...	...	...	30	26	..	1	...	3	...
136	Dealers in opium ...	46	46	...	...	...	...	...	35	35	...	...	...	...	...
137	Dealers in Ganja ...	36	36	...	...	...	...	...	33	33	..	...	...	...	...
	ORDER 33—TRADE IN CLOTHING AND TOILET ARTICLES.	197	194	...	...	...	3	...	179	156	1	...	...	22	...
138	Trade in ready made clothing, other articles of dress and the toilet (hats, umbrellas, socks, ready made shoes, perfumes, etc.).	197	194	...	...	...	3	...	179	156	1	...	...	22	...
	ORDER 34—TRADE IN FURNITURE	93	92	1	...	...	...	...	50	50	...	...	...	...	...
139	Trade in furniture, carpets, curtains and bedding.	16	15	1	...	...	...	...	30	30	...	...	...	...	...
140	Hardware, cooking utensils, porcelain, crockery, glassware, bottles, article for gardening, etc.	77	77	...	...	...	...	...	20	20	...	...	...	...	...
	ORDER 35—TRADE IN BUILDING MATERIALS.	60	60	...	...	...	...	...	70	70	...	...	...	...	...
141	Trade in building materials (other than bricks, tiles and woody materials).	60	60	...	...	...	...	...	70	70	...	...	...	...	...
	ORDER 36—TRADE IN MEANS OF TRANSPORT.	132	119	3	...	...	10	...	201	141	11	4	3	42	...
142	Dealers and hirers in mechanical transport, motors, cycles, etc.	24	24	...	...	...	...	...	22	21	...	...	...	1	...
143	Dealers and hirers in other carriages, carts, boats, etc.	11	11	...	...	...	...	...	21	21	...	...	...	...	...
144	Dealers and hirers of elephants, camels, horses, cattle, asses, mules, etc.	97	84	3	...	...	10	...	158	99	11	4	3	41	...

TABLE X

Occupation or means of livelihood—General Table

Dera Ismail Khan							Trans-Frontier Posts							Peshawar Municipality						
Total following occupation	As principal occupation		As working dependents		As subsidiary to other occupations		Total following occupation	As principal occupation		As working dependents		As subsidiary to other occupations		Total following occupation	As principal occupation		As working dependents		As subsidiary to other occupations	
	Males	Females	Males	Females	Males	Females		Males	Females	Males	Females	Males	Females		Males	Females	Males	Females	Males	Females
45	46	47	48	49	50	51	52	53	54	55	56	57	58	59	60	61	62	63	64	65
471	466	2	2	...	1	...	...	...	...	...	...	...	...	325	324	1	...	...	...	...
104	103	...	...	...	1	...	...	...	...	...	...	...	...	82	82	...	...	...	...	...
304	302	2	...	...	...	...	...	...	...	...	...	...	...	217	216	1	...	...	...	...
63	61	...	2	...	...	...	...	...	...	...	...	...	...	26	26	...	...	...	...	...
2,209	1,939	28	67	1	172	2	152	152	...	...	...	...	...	1,515	1,495	15	...	...	3	2
1,538	1,340	8	64	...	124	2	72	72	...	...	...	...	...	227	226	1	...	...	...	...
222	215	..	1	...	6	...	61	61	...	...	...	...	...	344	340	3	...	...	1	...
199	153	9	1	...	36	...	19	19	...	...	...	...	...	212	203	7	...	...	...	2
19	19	...	...	...	...	...	...	...	...	...	...	...	...	25	25	...	...	...	...	...
113	104	9	...	...	...	...	...	...	...	...	...	...	...	226	226	...	...	...	...	...
50	40	2	1	1	6	...	...	...	...	...	...	...	...	368	362	4	...	...	2	...
13	13	...	...	...	...	...	...	...	...	...	...	...	...	38	38	...	...	...	...	...
23	23	...	...	...	...	...	...	...	...	...	...	...	...	34	34	...	...	...	...	...
32	32	...	...	...	...	...	...	...	...	...	...	...	...	41	41	...	...	...	...	...
122	117	...	...	...	5	...	211	13	...	...	...	198	...	306	295	10	...	1	...	...
122	117	...	...	...	5	...	211	13	...	...	...	198	...	306	295	10	...	1	...	...
37	37	...	..	...	...	...	...	...	...	...	...	...	...	59	59	...	...	...	...	...
11	11	...	...	...	...	...	...	...	...	...	...	...	...	20	20	...	...	...	...	...
26	26	...	...	...	...	...	...	...	...	...	...	...	...	39	39	...	...	...	...	...
70	70	...	...	...	...	...	...	...	...	...	...	...	...	45	45	...	...	...	...	...
70	70	...	...	...	...	...	...	...	...	...	...	...	...	45	45	...	...	...	...	...
56	51	...	1	...	4	...	...	...	...	...	...	...	...	92	76	...	...	...	16	...
25	24	...	1	...	...	...	...	...	...	...	...	...	...	20	20	...	...	...	...	...
...	...	...	...	...	...	...	...	...	...	...	...	...	...	17	17	...	...	...	...	...
31	27	...	...	...	4	...	...	...	...	...	...	...	...	55	39	...	...	...	16	...

TABLE X

Occupation or means of livelihood—General Table

Group No.	Occupation	N. W. F. Province: Total following occupation	N. W. F. Province: As principal occupation: Males	N. W. F. Province: As principal occupation: Females	N. W. F. Province: As working dependents: Males	N. W. F. Province: As working dependents: Females	N. W. F. Province: As subsidiary to other occupations: Males	N. W. F. Province: As subsidiary to other occupations: Females	N. W. F. Province: Total following occupation	N. W. F. Province: As principal occupation: Males	N. W. F. Province: As principal occupation: Females
1	2	3	4	5	6	7	8	9	10	11	12
	ORDER 37—TRADE IN FUEL ...	495	316	49	7	7	114	2	495	316	49
145	Dealers in firewood, charcoal, coal, cowdung, etc.	495	316	49	7	7	114	2	495	316	49
	ORDER 38—TRADE IN ARTICLES OF LUXURY AND THOSE PERTAINING TO LETTERS AND THE ARTS AND SCIENCES.	1,064	1,055	...	6	...	2	1	1,064	1,055	...
146	Dealers in precious stones, jewellery (real and imitation), clocks, optical instruments, etc.	301	301	...	...	...	...	...	301	301	...
147	Dealers in common bangles, bead necklaces, fans, small articles, toys, hunting and fishing tackles, flowers, etc.	214	213	...	...	...	...	1	214	213	...
148	Publishers booksellers, stationers, dealers in music, pictures, musical instruments and curiosities.	549	541	...	6	...	2	...	549	541	...
	ORDER 39—TRADE OF OTHER SORTS	33,379	30,473	243	938	117	1,600	8	32,237	29,619	243
149	Dealers in rags, stable refuse, etc.	247	246	...	...	...	1	...	247	246	...
150	General store keepers and shop keepers otherwise unspecified.	32,697	29,807	243	937	117	1,585	8	31,555	28,953	243
151	Itinerant traders, pedlars and hawkers (of other than food, etc.).	302	302	...	...	...	...	...	302	302	...
152	Other trades (including farmers of pounds, tools and markets).	133	118	...	1	...	14	...	133	118	...
	CLASS C—PUBLIC ADMINISTRATION AND LIBERAL ARTS.	113,181	102,872	988	687	69	8,483	82	78,180	69,041	988
	SUB-CLASS VI—PUBLIC FORCE	77,543	72,628	28	156	1	4,723	7	43,702	39,833	28
	ORDER 40—ARMY ...	67,630	63,893	27	108	1	3,594	7	33,794	31,101	27
153	Army (Imperial) ...	67,472	63,749	27	104	1	3,584	7	33,636	30,957	27
154	Army (Indian States) ...	158	144	...	4	...	10	...	158	144	...
	ORDER 41—NAVY ...	9	7	1	...	...	1	...	9	7	1
155	Navy	9	7	1	...	...	1	...	9	7	1
	ORDER 42—AIR FORCE ...	435	435	...	...	...	...	...	435	435	...
156	Air Force	435	435	...	...	...	...	...	435	435	...
	ORDER 43—POLICE ...	9,469	8,293	...	48	...	1,128	...	9,464	8,290	...
157	Police	6,714	5,911	...	29	...	774	...	6,709	5,908	...
158	Village watchmen ...	2,755	2,382	...	19	...	354	...	2,755	2,382	...
	SUB-CLASS VII—PUBLIC ADMINISTRATION.	12,862	10,687	147	143	1	1,846	38	11,777	9,721	147
	ORDER 44—PUBLIC ADMINISTRATION.	12,862	10,687	147	143	1	1,846	38	11,777	9,721	147
159	Service of the state ...	10,207	8,936	113	55	1	1,070	32	9,150	7,998	113
160	Service of Indian and foreign states.	12	12	...	...	...	...	...	12	12	...
161	Municipal and other local (not service).	758	679	32	7	...	34	6	735	656	32
162	Village officials and servants other than watchmen.	1,885	1,060	2	81	...	742	...	1,880	1,055	2

TABLE X

Occupation or means of livelihood—General Table

(Districts)				Hazara							Peshawar						
As working dependents		As subsidiary to other occupations		Total following occupation	As principal occupation		As working dependents		As subsidiary to other occupations		Total following occupation	As principal occupation		As working dependents		As subsidiary to other occupations	
Males	Females	Males	Females		Males	Females	Males	Females	Males	Females		Males	Females	Males	Females	Males	Females
13	14	15	16	17	18	19	20	21	22	23	24	25	26	27	28	29	30
7	7	114	2	21	16	1	...	4	...	...	286	170	15	5	3	91	2
7	7	114	2	21	16	1	...	4	...	...	286	170	15	5	3	91	2
6	...	2	1	208	206	...	...	...	2	...	629	622	...	6	...	...	1
...	...	...	...	50	50	...	...	...	...	...	201	201	...	...	...	...	...
...	...	...	1	30	30	...	...	...	...	...	104	103	...	...	...	...	1
6	...	2	...	128	126	...	...	...	2	...	324	318	...	6	...	...	...
937	117	1,313	8	2,390	1,902	44	97	65	279	3	15,623	14,273	112	662	48	523	5
...	...	1	...	45	44	...	...	...	1	...	147	147	...	...	...	...	...
936	117	1,298	8	2,294	1,807	44	97	65	278	3	15,237	13,888	112	662	48	522	5
...	...	...	...	30	30	...	...	...	...	...	201	201	...	...	...	...	...
1	...	14	...	21	21	...	...	...	...	...	38	37	...	...	...	1	...
637	69	7,363	82	10,667	8,901	133	147	42	1,403	41	35,191	32,357	423	286	14	2 108	3
111	1	3,722	7	5,743	5,205	4	20	1	508	5	19,083	17,863	6	20	...	1,194	...
63	1	2,595	7	4,479	4,260	4	5	1	204	5	15,109	14,247	6	2	...	854	...
59	1	2,585	7	4,479	4,260	4	5	1	204	5	15,026	14,164	6	2	...	854	...
4	...	10	...	...	...	...	...	...	...	...	83	83	...	...	...	...	...
...	...	1	...	...	...	...	...	...	...	...	...	...	...	...	...	...	...
...	...	1	...	...	...	...	...	...	...	...	...	...	...	...	...	...	...
...	...	...	...	45	45	...	...	...	...	...	335	335	...	...	...	...	...
...	...	...	...	45	45	...	...	...	...	...	335	335	...	...	...	...	...
48	...	1,126	...	1,219	900	...	15	...	304	...	3,639	3,281	...	18	...	340	...
29	...	772	...	959	748	...	9	...	202	...	2,337	2,084	...	13	...	240	...
19	...	354	...	260	152	...	6	...	102	...	1,302	1,197	...	5	...	100	...
143	1	1,727	38	1,172	772	9	63	1	298	29	6,435	5,891	76	53	...	414	1
143	1	1,727	38	1,172	772	9	63	1	298	29	6,435	5,891	76	53	...	414	1
55	1	951	32	855	621	9	29	1	166	29	5,128	4,916	66	7	...	138	1
...	...	...	...	...	...	...	...	...	...	...	10	10	...	...	...	...	...
7	...	34	6	64	55	...	2	...	7	...	270	260	9	1	...	...	...
81	...	742	...	253	96	...	32	...	125	...	1,027	705	1	45	...	276	...

TABLE X

Occupation or means of livelihood—General Table

Group No.	Occupation	Kohat: Total following occupation	Kohat: As principal occupation: Males	Kohat: As principal occupation: Females	Kohat: As working dependents: Males	Kohat: As working dependents: Females	Kohat: As subsidiary to other occupations: Males	Kohat: As subsidiary to other occupations: Females	Bannu: Total following occupation	Bannu: As principal occupation: Males	Bannu: As principal occupation: Females	Bannu: As working dependents: Males	Bannu: As working dependents: Females	Bannu: As subsidiary to other occupations: Males	Bannu: As subsidiary to other occupations: Females
1	2	31	32	33	34	35	36	37	38	39	40	41	42	43	44
	ORDER 37—TRADE IN FUEL ...	27	5	20	...	...	2	...	53	42	...	2	...	9	...
145	Dealers in firewood, charcoal, coal, cowdung, etc.	27	5	20	...	...	2	...	53	42	...	2	...	9	...
	ORDER 38—TRADE IN ARTICLES OF LUXURY AND THOSE PERTAINING TO LETTERS AND THE ARTS AND SCIENCES.	105	105	...	...	...	...	...	64	64	...	...	...	...	...
146	Dealers in precious stones, jewellery (real and imitation), clocks, optical instruments, etc.	20	20	...	...	...	...	...	15	15	...	...	...	...	...
147	Dealers in common bangles, bead necklaces, fans, small articles, toys, hunting and fishing tackle, flowers, etc.	40	40	...	...	...	...	...	21	21	...	...	...	...	...
148	Publishers, booksellers, stationers, dealers in music, pictures, musical instruments and curiosities.	45	45	...	...	...	...	...	28	28	...	...	...	...	...
	ORDER 39—TRADE OF OTHER SORTS	2,076	1,896	16	40	2	122	...	7,305	7,002	21	94	2	186	...
149	Dealers in rags, stable refuse, etc.	29	29	...	...	...	...	...	24	24	...	...	...	...	...
150	General store keepeers and shop keepers otherwise unspecified.	1,970	1,795	16	40	2	117	...	7,238	6,937	21	93	2	185	...
151	Itinerant traders, pedlars and hawkers (of other than food, etc.)	50	50	...	...	...	...	...	20	20	...	...	...	...	...
152	Other trades (including farmers of pounds, tools and markets).	27	22	...	...	...	5	...	23	21	...	1	...	1	...
	CLASS C—PUBLIC ADMINISTRATION AND LIBERAL ARTS.	13,900	11,589	76	37	6	2,184	8	9,860	8,845	88	114	2	810	1
	SUB-CLASS VI—PUBLIC FORCE	10,017	8,586	3	21	...	1,405	2	4,706	4,429	14	42	...	221	...
	ORDER 40—ARMY ...	8,338	7,156	3	14	...	1,163	2	3,622	3,472	14	35	...	101	...
153	Army (Imperial) ...	8,263	7,095	3	10	...	1,153	2	3,622	3,472	14	35	...	101	...
154	Army (Indian States) ...	75	61	...	4	...	10	...	...	...	...	...	...	...	...
	ORDER 41—NAVY ...	...	...	...	...	...	...	...	...	...	...	...	...	...	...
155	Navy ...	...	...	...	...	...	...	...	...	...	...	...	...	...	...
	ORDER 42—AIR FORCE ...	25	25	...	...	...	...	...	15	15	...	...	...	...	...
156	Air force	25	25	...	...	...	...	...	15	15	...	...	...	...	...
	ORDER 43—POLICE ...	1,654	1,405	...	7	...	242	...	1,069	942	...	7	...	120	...
157	Police	1,340	1,180	...	6	...	154	...	826	739	...	1	...	86	...
158	Village watchmen ...	314	225	...	1	...	88	...	243	203	...	6	...	34	...
	SUB-CLASS VII—PUBLIC ADMINISTRATION.	1,169	632	18	12	...	505	2	1,514	1,215	19	5	...	275	...
	ORDER 44 PUBLIC ADMINISTRATION	1,169	632	18	12	...	505	2	1,514	1,215	19	5	...	275	...
159	Service of the State ...	963	506	18	9	...	428	2	1,177	1,030	17	3	...	127	...
160	Service of Indian and Foreign States.	2	2	...	...	...	...	...	...	...	...	...	...	...	...
161	Municipal and other local (not village) service.	68	64	...	1	...	3	...	126	118	1	1	...	6	...
162	Village officials and servants other than watchmen.	136	60	...	2	...	74	...	211	67	1	1	...	142	...

TABLE X

Occupation or means of livelihood—General Table

Dera Ismail Khan							Trans-Frontier Posts							Peshawar Municipality						
Total following occupation	As principal occupation		As working dependents		As subsidiary to other *occupations*		Total following occupation	As principal occupation		As working dependents		As subsidiary to other *occupations*		Total following occupation	As principal occupation		As working dependents		As subsidiary to other *occupations*	
	Males	Females	Males	Females	Males	Females		Males	Females	Males	Females	Males	Females		Males	Females	Males	Females	Males	Females
45	46	47	48	49	50	51	52	53	54	55	56	57	58	59	60	61	62	63	64	65
108	83	13	...	...	12	...	...	...	...	...	...	...	...	124	118	6	...	...	.	...
108	83	13	...	...	12	...	...	...	...	...	...	...	..	124	118	6	...	...	...	...
58	58	...	...	...	...	...	...	...	...	...	...		..	331	331	...	...	...	...	...
15	15	...	...	...	...	...	...	...	...	...	...	...	...	161	161	...	...	...	...	...
19	19	...	...	...	...	...	...	...	...	...	...	...	...	13	13	...	...	...	...	...
24	24	...	...	...	...	...	...	...	...	...	...	...	...	157	157	...	...	...	...	...
4843	4,546	50	44	...	203	...	1,142	854	...	1	...	287	...	1,338	1,303	29	...	...	6	...
2	2	...	...	...	...	...	...	...	...	...	...	...	...	14	14	...	...	...	...	...
4,816	4,526	50	44	...	196	...	1,142	854	...	1	...	287	...	1,246	1,211	29	...	..	6	...
1	1	...	...	...	...	...	...	...	...	...	...	...	...	55	55	..	...	...	...	...
24	17	...	...	...	7	...	...	...	...	...	...	...	...	23	23	...	...	...	...	...
8,562	7,349	268	53	5	858	29	35,001	33,831	...	50	...	1,120	...		3,351	154		1	193	...
4,153	3,750	1	8	...	394	...	33,841	32,795	...	45	...	1,001	...	744	596	1	...	...	147	...
2,246	1,966	...	7	...	273	...	33,836	32,792	...	45	...	999	..	45	43	1	...	...	1	...
2,246	1,966	...	7	...	273	...	33,836	32,792	...	45	...	999	...	44	42	1	...	...	1	...
...	...	...	...	...	...	...	...	...	...	...	...	...	...	1	1	...	...	...	...	...
9	7	1	...	...	1	...	...	...	...	...	...	...	...	...	...	...	...	...	...	...
9	7	1	...	...	1	...	...	...	...	...	...	...	...	...	...	...	...	...	...	...
15	15	...	...	...	...	...	...	...	...	...	...	...	...	...	...	...	...	...	...	...
15	15	...	...	...	...	...	...	...	...	...	...	...	...	...	...	...	...	...	...	...
1,883	1,762	...	1	...	120	...	5	3	...	...	...	2	...	699	553	...	...	...	146	...
1,247	1,157	...	...	...	90	...	5	3	...	...	...	2	...	680	534	...	...	...	146	...
636	605	...	1	...	30	...	...	...	...	...	...	...	...	19	19	...	...	...	...	...
1,487	1,211	25	10	...	235	6	1,085	966	...	...	...	119	...	1,521	1,466	27	...	...	28	...
1,487	1,211	25	10	...	235	6	1,085	966	...	...	...	119	...	1,521	1,466	27	...	...	28	...
1,027	925	3	7	...	92	...	1,057	938	...	...	...	119	...	1,308	1,262	19	...	...	27	...
...	...	...	...	...	...	...	...	...	...	...	...	...	...	10	10	...	...	...	...	...
207	159	22	2	...	18	6	23	23	...	...	...	...	...	185	177	8	...	...	...	...
253	127	...	1	...	125	...	5	5	...	...	...	...	...	18	17	...	...	...	1	...

TABLE X

Occupation or means of livelihood—General Table

Group No.	Occupation	N. W. F. Province: Total following occupation	As principal occupation: Males	As principal occupation: Females	As working dependents: Males	As working dependents: Females	As subsidiary to other occupations: Males	As subsidiary to other occupations: Females	N. W. F. Province: Total following occupation	As principal occupation: Males	As principal occupation: Females
1	2	3	4	5	6	7	8	9	10	11	12
	SUB-CLASS VIII—PROFESSIONS AND LIBERAL ARTS.	22,776	19,557	813	388	67	1,914	37	22,701	19,487	813
	ORDER 45—RELIGION ...	14,394	12,483	114	275	42	1,473	7	14,329	12,418	114
163	Priests ministers, etc. ...	212	212	...	...	...	...	...	212	212	...
164	Monks, nuns, religious mendicants.	13,369	11,523	106	272	39	1,422	/	13,304	11,458	106
165	Other religious workers ...	363	306	3	3	2	49	...	363	306	3
166	Servants in religious edifices, burial and burning grounds, pilgrim conductors; circumcisers, etc.	450	442	5	...	1	2	...	450	442	5
	ORDER 46—LAW ...	591	517	35	4	...	35	...	591	517	35
	Lawyers of all kinds, including Qazis, law agents and Mukhtiars.	270	218	26	2	...	24	...	270	218	26
	Lawyers' clerks, petition-writers, etc.	321	299	9	2	...	11	...	321	299	9
	ORDER 47—MEDICINE ...	3,220	2,774	302	10	8	99	27	3,216	2,770	302
169	Registered medical practitioners including occulists.	1,413	1,301	10	...		40	1	1,413	1,361	10
170	Other persons practising the healing arts without being registered.	381	313	3	8	2	55	...	381	313	3
171	Dentists ...	38	38	...	...	...	...	...	38	38	...
172	Midwives, vaccinators, compounders, nurses, masseurs, etc.	1,336	1,010	289	2	5	4	26	1,332	1,006	289
173	Veterinary surgeons ...	52	52	...	...	...	...	...	52	52	...
	ORDER 48—INSTRUCTION ...	2,277	1,754	249	45	5	221	3	2,277	1,754	249
174	Professors and teachers of all kinds.	2,167	1,6/3	230	44	4	213	3	2,167	1,673	230
175	Clerks and servants connected with education	110	81	19	1	1	8	...	110	81	19
	ORDER 49—LETTERS, ARTS AND SCIENCES (OTHER THAN 44).	2,294	2,029	113	54	12	86	...	2,288	2,028	113
176	Public scribes, stenographers, etc.	197	172	...	4	...	21	...	197	172	...
177	Architects (not being State servants).	223	223	...	...	...	...	...	223	223	...
178	Authors, editors, journalists and photographers.	159	150	...	5	...	4	...	153	149	...
179	Artists, sculptors and image makers.	101	101	...	...	...	...	...	101	101	...
180	Scientists (astronomers, botanists, etc.).	66	60	...	...	...	6	...	66	60	...
181	Horoscope casters, astrologers, fortune tellers, wizards, witches and mediums.	30	30	...	...	...	...	...	30	30	...
182	Musicians (composers and performers other than military), actors, dancers, etc.	380	304	32	14	11	19	...	380	304	32
183	Managers and employees of places of public entertainments, race courses, societies, clubs, etc.	51	51	...	...	...	...	...	51	51	...
184	Conjurors, acrobats, recitors, exhibitors of curiosities and wild animals, etc.	1,087	938	81	31	1	36	...	1,087	938	81

TABLE X

Occupation or means of livelihood—General Table

(Districts)				Hazara							Peshawar						
As working dependents		As subsidiary to other occupations		Total following occupation	As principal occupation		As working dependents		As subsidiary to other occupations		Total following occupation	As principal occupation		As working dependents		As subsidiary to other occupations	
Males	Females	Males	Females		Males	Females	Males	Females	Males	Females		Males	Females	Males	Females	Males	Females
13	14	15	16	17	18	19	20	21	22	23	24	25	26	27	28	29	30
383	67	1,914	37	3,752	2,924	120	64	40	597	7	9,673	8,603	341	213	14	500	2
275	42	1,473	7	2,371	1,793	28	38	27	482	3	6,573	5,865	56	189	11	451	1
...	...	...	...	31	31	...	...	...	...	...	109	109	...	...	...	...	...
272	39	1,422	7	2,233	1,661	28	38	24	479	3	6,247	5,540	55	189	11	451	1
3	2	49	...	8	4	...	...	2	2	...	1	...	1	...	...	...	...
...	1	2	...	99	97	...	...	1	1	...	216	216	...	..	...	...	...
4	...	35	...	75	61	...	1	...	13	...	306	256	35	1	...	4	...
2	...	24	...	42	37	...	...	...	5	...	113	83	26	1	...	3	...
2	...	11	...	33	24	...	1	...	8	...	193	183	9	...	...	1	...
10	8	99	27	291	249	36	2	1	11	1	1,346	1,229	101	3	1	11	1
...	1	40	1	112	111	1	...	...	...	...	599	591	1	...	1	6	...
8	2	55	...	38	25	2	2	...	9	...	140	132	1	2	...	5	...
...	...	...	...	6	6	...	...	...	...	...	11	11	...	...	...	...	...
2	5	4	26	123	86	33	...	1	2	1	576	475	99	1	...	...	1
...	...	...	...	12	12	...	...	...	...	...	20	20	...	...	...	...	...
45	5	221	3	505	372	45	15	1	68	3	633	530	74	2	1	26	...
44	4	213	3	493	368	43	14	1	64	3	565	472	68	2	1	22	...
1	1	8	...	12	4	3	1	...	4	...	68	58	6	...	...	4	...
49	12	86	...	510	458	10	8	11	23	...	815	713	75	18	1	8	...
4	...	21	...	7	3	...	...	...	4	...	102	95	...	4	...	3	...
...	...	...	...	42	42	...	...	...	...	...	85	85	...	...	...	...	...
...	...	4	...	35	34	...	...	...	1	...	49	49	...	...	...	...	...
...	...	...	...	24	24	...	...	...	...	...	26	26	...	...	...	...	...
...	...	6	...	...	...	...	...	...	...	...	24	20	...	...	...	4	...
...	...	...	...	...	...	...	...	...	...	...	22	22	...	...	...	...	...
14	11	19	...	88	64	4	1	11	8	...	125	117	7	...	...	1	...
...	...	...	...	21	21	...	...	...	..	...	30	30	...	...	...	...	...
31	1	36	...	293	270	6	7	...	10	...	352	269	68	14	1	...	...

TABLE X

Occupation or means of livelihood—General Table

Group No.	Occupation	Kohat							Bannu						
		Total following occupation	As principal occupation		As working dependents		As subsidiary to other occupations		Total following occupation	As principal occupation		As working dependents		As subsidiary to other occupations	
			Males	Females	Males	Females	Males	Females		Males	Females	Males	Females	Males	Females
1	2	31	32	33	34	35	36	37	38	39	40	41	42	43	44
	SUB-CLASS VIII—PROFESSIONS AND LIBERAL ARTS.	2,714	2,371	55	4	6	274	4	3,640	3,201	55	67	2	314	1
	ORDER 45—RELIGION ...	1,874	1,654	10	4	4	199	3	2,445	2,206	4	16	...	219	...
163	Priests, ministers, etc. ...	20	20	...	...	...	...	...	16	16	...	...	...	...	...
164	Monks, nuns, religious mendicants.	1,767	1,552	6	4	4	198	3	2,070	1,881	4	13	...	172	...
165	Other religious workers ...	14	13	1	...	...	...	...	339	289	...	3	...	47	...
166	Servants in religious edifices, burial and burning grounds, pilgrim conductors, circumcisers, etc.	73	69	3	...	...	1	...	20	20	...	...	...	...	...
	ORDER 46—LAW ...	47	43	...	...	...	4	...	64	58	..	1	...	5	...
167	Lawyers of all kinds, including Qazis, law agents and Mukhtiars.	21	17	...	...	...	4	...	43	38	...	...	...	5	...
168	Lawyers' clerks, petition writers, etc.	26	26	...	...	...	...	...	21	20	...	1	...	...	...
	ORDER 47—MEDICINE ...	339	299	23	...	1	15	1	452	398	23	4	2	24	1
169	Registered medical practitioners including occulists.	164	152	...	...	...	12	...	229	222	1	...	...	5	1
170	Other persons practising the healing arts without being registered.	28	25	...	...	...	3	...	79	56	...	3	2	18	...
171	Dentists	9	9	...	...	...	...	...	7	7	...	...	...	...	...
172	Midwives, vaccinators, compounders, nurses, masseurs, etc.	133	108	23	...	1	...	1	132	108	22	1	...	1	...
173	Veterinary surgeons ...	5	5	...	...	...	...	...	5	5	...	...	...	...	...
	ORDER 48—INSTRUCTION ...	268	206	21	...	1	40	...	353	258	25	27	...	43	...
174	Professors and teachers of all kinds.	257	198	18	...	1	40	...	353	258	25	27	...	43	...
175	Clerks and servants connected with education.	11	8	3	...	...	...	...	...	...	...	...	...	...	...
	ORDER 49—LETTERS, ARTS AND SCIENCES (OTHER THAN 44).	186	169	1	...	...	16	...	326	281	3	19	...	23	...
176	Public scribes, stenographers, etc.	39	36	...	...	...	3	...	7	5	...	...	...	2	...
177	Architects (not being state servants).	40	40	...	...	...	...	...	30	30	...	...	...	...	...
178	Authors, editors, journalists and photographers.	18	17	...	...	...	1	...	21	19	...	...	...	2	...
179	Artists, sculptors and image makers.	18	18	...	...	...	...	...	18	18	...	...	...	...	...
180	Scientists (astronomers, botanists, etc.).	...	...	...	...	...	...	...	..	...	...	...	...	...	...
181	Horoscope casters, astrologers, fortune tellers, wizards, witches and mediums.	...	...	...	...	...	...	...	3	3	...	...	...	...	...
182	Musicians (composers and performers other than military), actors, dancers, etc.	49	43	1	...	...	5	...	34	20	2	11	...	1	...
183	Managers and employees of places of public entertainments, race courses, societies, clubs, etc.	...	...	...	...	...	...	...	...	...	...	...	...	...	...
184	Conjurors, acrobats, recitors, exhibitors of curiosities and wild animals, etc.	22	15	...	...	...	7	...	213	186	1	8	...	18	...

TABLE X

Occupation or means of livelihood—General Table

Dera Ismail Khan							Trans-Frontier Posts							Peshawar Municipality						
Total following occupation	As principal occupation		As working dependents		As subsidiary to other occupations		Total following occupation	As principal occupation		As working dependents		As subsidiary to other occupations		Total following occupation	As principal occupation		As working dependents		As subsidiary to other occupations	
	Males	Females	Males	Females	Males	Females		Males	Females	Males	Females	Males	Females		Males	Females	Males	Females	Males	Females
45	46	47	48	49	50	51	52	53	54	55	56	57	58	59	60	61	62	63	64	65
2,922	2,388	242	35	5	229	23	75	70	...	5	...	...	...	1,434	1,289	126	...	1	18	...
1,066	900	16	28	...	122	...	65	65	...	...	...	...	...	369	341	19	...	1	8	...
36	36	...	...	...	...	...	...	...	...	...	...	...	...	35	35	...	...	...	...	...
987	824	13	28	...	122	...	65	65	...	...	...	...	...	272	244	19	...	1	8	...
1	...	1	...	...	...	...	...	...	...	...	...	...	...	...	...	...	...	...	...	...
42	40	2	...	...	...	...	...	...	...	...	...	...	...	62	62	...	...	...	...	...
99	89	...	1	...	9	...	...	...	...	...	...	...	...	166	166	...	...	...	...	...
51	43	...	1	...	7	...	...	...	...	...	...	...	...	73	73	...	...	...	...	...
48	46	...	...	...	2	...	...	...	...	...	...	...	...	93	93	...	...	...	...	...
788	604	119	1	3	38	23	4	4	...	...	...	...	...	355	305	50	...	...	...	...
309	285	7	...	...	17	...	...	...	...	...	...	...	...	131	131	...	...	...	...	...
96	75	...	1	...	20	...	...	...	...	...	...	...	...	84	83	1	...	...	...	...
5	5	...	...	...	...	...	...	...	...	...	...	...	...	5	5	...	...	...	...	...
368	229	112	...	3	1	23	4	4	...	...	...	...	...	131	82	49	...	...	...	...
10	10	...	...	...	...	...	...	...	...	...	...	...	...	4	4	...	...	...	...	...
518	388	83	1	2	44	...	...	...	...	...	...	...	...	295	245	45	...	...	5	...
499	377	76	1	1	44	...	...	...	...	...	...	...	...	246	201	44	...	...	1	...
19	11	7	...	1	...	...	...	...	...	...	...	...	...	49	44	1	...	...	4	...
451	407	24	4	...	16	...	6	1	...	5	...	...	...	249	232	12	...	...	5	...
42	33	...	...	...	9	...	...	...	...	...	...	...	...	30	30	...	...	...	...	...
26	26	...	...	...	...	...	...	...	...	...	...	...	...	13	13	...	...	...	...	...
30	30	...	...	...	...	...	6	1	...	5	...	...	...	14	14	...	...	...	...	...
15	15	...	...	...	...	...	...	...	...	...	...	...	...	2	2	...	...	...	...	.
42	40	...	...	...	2	...	...	...	...	...	...	...	...	19	15	...	...	...	4	...
5	5	...	...	...	...	...	...	...	...	...	...	...	...	8	8	...	...	...	...	...
84	60	18	2	...	4	...	...	...	...	...	...	...	...	44	36	7	...	...	1	...
...	...	...	...	...	...	...	...	...	...	...	...	...	...	...	...	...	...	...	...	...
207	198	6	2	...	1	...	...	...	...	...	...	...	...	119	114	5	...	...	...	...

TABLE X

Occupation or means of livelihood—General Table

Group No.	Occupation	N.-W. F. Province: Total following occupation	As principal occupation		As working dependents		As subsidiary to other occupations		N.-W. F. Province: Total following occupation	As principal occupation	
			Males	Females	Males	Females	Males	Females		Males	Females
1	2	3	4	5	6	7	8	9	10	11	12
	CLASS D—MISCELLANEOUS.	78,550	54,267	6,373	9,166	833	7,763	148	76,990	53,218	6,373
	SUB-CLASS IX—PERSONS LIVING ON THEIR INCOME.	4,338	2,053	154	46	46	2,002	37	4,338	2,053	154
	ORDER 50—PERSONS LIVING PRINCIPALLY ON THEIR INCOME.	4,338	2,053	154	46	45	2,002	37	4,338	2,053	154
185	Proprietors (other than of agricultural land), fund and scholarship holders and pensioners.	4,338	2,053	154	46	46	2,002	37	4,338	2,053	154
	SUB-CLASS X—DOMESTIC SERVICE.	15,456	9,931	1,907	927	159	2,495	37	15,143	9,813	1,907
	ORDER 51 DOMESTIC SERVICE.	15,455	9,931	1,907	927	159	2,495	37	15,143	9,813	1,907
186	Private motor drivers and cleaners.	468	442	3	8	...	15	...	457	431	3
187	Other domestic service ...	14,988	9,489	1,904	919	159	2,480	37	14,686	9,382	1,904
	SUB-CLASS XI—INSUFFICIENTLY DESCRIBED OCCUPATIONS.	46,512	37,335	3,485	2,272	430	2,926	64	45,294	36,433	3,485
	ORDER 52—GENERAL TERMS WHICH DO NOT INDICATE A DEFINITE OCCUPATION.	46,512	37,335	3,485	2,272	430	2,926	64	45,294	36,433	3,485
188	Manufacturers, business men and contractors otherwise unspecified.	5,196	4,521	55	77	7	533	3	5,165	4,490	55
189	Cashiers, accountants, book keepers, clerks and other employees in unspecified offices and warehouses and shops.	820	816	...	...	...	4	...	820	816	...
190	Mechanics otherwise unspecified	29	26	...	...	...	3	...	29	26	...
191	Labourers and workmen otherwise unspecified.	40,467	31,972	3,430	2,195	423	2,386	61	39,280	31,101	3,430
	SUB-CLASS XII—UNPRODUCTIVE.	12,244	4,948	827	5,921	198	340	10	12,215	4,919	827
	ORDER 53—INMATES OF JAILS, ASYLUMS AND ALMS HOUSES.	6,069	239	3	5,757	52	18	...	6,069	239	3
192	Inmates of jails, asylums and alms houses.	6,069	239	3	5,757	52	18	...	6,069	239	3
	ORDER 54—BEGGARS, VAGRANTS, PROSTITUTES.	6,128	4,692	824	164	146	292	10	6,099	4,663	824
193	Beggars and vagrants ...	5,942	4,646	696	163	143	284	10	5,913	4,617	696
194	Procurers and prostitutes ...	186	46	128	1	3	8	...	186	46	128
	ORDER 55—OTHER UNCLASSIFIED NON-PRODUCTIVE INDUSTRIES.	47	17	...	...	...	30	...	47	17	...
195	Other unclassified non-productive industries.	47	17	...	...	...	30	...	47	17	...

TABLE X

Occupation or means of livelihood—General Table

(Districts)				Hazara							Peshawar						
As working dependents		As subsidiary to other occupations		Total following occupation	As principal occupation		As working dependents		As subsidiary to other occupations		Total following occupation	As principal occupation		As working dependents		As subsidiary to other occupations	
Males	Females	Males	Females		Males	Females	Males	Females	Males	Females		Males	Females	Males	Females	Males	Females
13	14	15	16	17	18	19	20	21	22	23	24	25	26	27	28	29	30
9,163	833	7,255	148	11,538	6,551	1,547	695	352	2,357	36	38,686	28,018	2,668	5,547	159	2,260	34
46	46	2,002	37	1,430	648	21	16	18	719	8	1,088	754	60	8	5	257	4
46	46	2,002	37	1,430	648	21	16	18	719	8	1,088	754	60	8	5	257	4
46	46	2,002	37	1,430	648	21	16	18	719	8	1,088	754	60	8	5	257	4
924	159	2,303	37	3,098	1,238	634	127	111	974	14	8,958	6,672	774	741	13	755	3
924	159	2,303	37	3,098	1,238	634	127	111	974	14	8,958	6,672	774	741	13	755	3
8	...	15	...	69	67	1	...	...	1	...	152	152	...	...	...	...	...
916	159	2,288	37	3,029	1,171	633	127	111	973	14	8,806	6,520	774	741	13	755	3
2,272	430	2,610	64	4,123	2,747	597	110	121	538	10	24,424	19,552	1,667	1,891	114	1,175	25
2,272	430	2,610	64	4,123	2,747	597	110	121	538	10	24,424	19,552	1,667	1,891	114	11,75	25
77	7	533	3	331	245	1	6	2	77	...	1,228	928	31	33	2	233	1
...	...	4	...	53	51	...	...	...	2	...	405	405	...	...	...	...	...
...	...	3	...	...	...	...	...	...	...	...	17	17	...	...	...	...	...
2,195	423	2,070	61	3,739	2,451	596	104	119	459	10	22,774	18,202	1,636	1,858	112	942	24
5,921	198	340	10	2,887	1,918	295	442	102	126	4	4,216	1,040	167	2,907	27	73	2
5,757	52	18	...	395	6	1	360	15	13	...	2,936	33	2	2,876	24	...	...
5,757	52	18	...	395	6	1	360	15	13	...	2,935	33	2	2,876	24	...	...
164	146	292	10	2,488	1,908	294	82	87	113	4	1,275	1,001	165	31	3	73	2
163	143	284	10	2,485	1,908	291	82	87	113	4	1,130	960	61	31	3	73	2
1		8	...	3	...	3	...	...	...	...	145	41	104	...	...	...	...
...	...	30	...	4	4	...	...	...	...	...	6	6	...	...	...	..	...
...	...	30	...	4	4	...	...	...	...	...	6	6	...	...	...	..	...

TABLE X

Occupation or means of livelihood—General Table

Group No.	Occupation	Kohat: Total following occupation	Kohat: As principal occupation: Males	Kohat: As principal occupation: Females	Kohat: As working dependents: Males	Kohat: As working dependents: Females	Kohat: As subsidiary to other occupations: Males	Kohat: As subsidiary to other occupations: Females	Bannu: Total following occupation	Bannu: As principal occupation: Males	Bannu: As principal occupation: Females	Bannu: As working dependents: Males	Bannu: As working dependents: Females	Bannu: As subsidiary to other occupations: Males	Bannu: As subsidiary to other occupations: Females
1		31	32	33	34	35	36	37	38	39	40	41	42	43	44
	CLASS D—MISCELLANEOUS	6,631	4,510	569	334	72	1,122	24	6,479	4,658	788	581	71	363	18
	SUB-CLASS IX—PERSONS LIVING ON THEIR INCOME.	835	165	23	9	15	619	4	249	113	24	3	4	102	3
	ORDER 50—PERSONS LIVING PRINCIPALLY ON THEIR INCOME.	835	165	23	9	15	619	4	249	113	24	3	4	102	3
185	Proprietors (other than of agricultural land), fund and scholarship holders and pensioners.	835	165	23	9	15	619	4	249	113	24	3	4	102	3
	SUB-CLASS X—DOMESTIC SERVICE.	780	345	175	12	12	233	3	362	149	131	14	5	58	5
	ORDER 51—DOMESTIC SERVICE.	780	345	175	12	12	233	3	362	149	131	14	5	58	5
186	Private motor drivers and cleaners.	35	35	...	...	...	...	...	31	31	...	...	...	...	...
187	Other domestic service ...	745	310	175	12	12	233	3	331	118	131	14	5	58	5
	SUB-CLASS XI—INSUFFICIENTLY DESCRIBED OCCUPATIONS.	4,488	3,815	328	62	38	228	17	4,609	3,780	502	120	29	169	9
	ORDER 52—GENERAL TERMS WHICH DO NOT INDICATE A DEFINITE OCCUPATION.	4,488	3,815	328	62	38	228	17	4,609	3,780	502	120	29	169	9
188	Manufacturers, business men and contractors otherwise unspecified.	154	125	2	6	...	20	1	458	364	10	21	...	63	...
189	Cashiers, accountants, book keepers, clerks and other employees in unspecified offices and warehouses and shops.	204	202	...	...	...	2	...	50	50	...	...	...	...	...
190	Mechanics otherwise unspecified	...	...	...	...	...	...	...	...	...	...	...	...	...	...
191	Labourers and workmen otherwise unspecified.	4,130	3,488	326	56	38	206	16	4,101	3,366	492	99	29	106	9
	SUB-CLASS XII—UNPRODUCTIVE.	528	185	43	251	7	42	...	1,259	616	131	444	33	34	1
	ORDER 53—INMATES OF JAILS, ASYLUMS AND ALMS HOUSES.	246	...	...	244	2	...	...	481	56	...	418	4	3	...
192	Inmates of jails, asylums and alms houses.	246	...	...	244	2	...	...	481	56	...	418	4	3	...
	ORDER 54—BEGGARS, VAGRANTS, PROSTITUTES.	245	178	43	7	5	12	...	778	560	131	26	29	31	1
193	Beggars and vagrants ...	245	178	43	7	5	12	...	760	555	130	25	26	23	1
194	Procurers and prostitutes ...	...	...	...	...	...	...	...	18	5	1	1	3	8	...
	ORDER 55—OTHER UNCLASSIFIED NON-PRODUCTIVE INDUSTRIES.	37	7	...	...	...	30	...	...	...	...	...	...	...	...
195	Other unclassified non-productive industries.	37	7	...	...	...	30	...	...	...	...	...	...	...	...

TABLE X

Occupation or means of livelihood—General Table

Dera Ismail Khan							Trans-Frontier Posts							Peshawar Municipality						
Total following occupation	As principal occupation		As working dependents		As subsidiary to other occupations		Total following occupation	As principal occupation		As working dependents		As subsidiary to other occupations		Total following occupation	As principal occupation		As working dependents		As subsidiary to other occupations	
	Males	Females	Males	Females	Males	Females		Males	Females	Males	Females	Males	Females		Males	Females	Males	Females	Males	F
45	46	47	48	49	50	51	52	53	54	55	56	57	58	59	60	61	62	63	64	65
13,656	9,481	801	2,006	179	1,153	36	1,560	1,049	...	3	...	508	...	5,281	4,237	720	...	93	229	2
736	373	26	10	4	305	18	...	...	...	...	...	...	...	275	171	40	...	1	61	2
736	373	26	10	4	305	18	...	...	...	...	...	...	...	275	171	40	...	1	61	2
736	373	26	10	4	305	18	...	...	...	...	...	...	...	275	171	40	...	1	61	2
1,945	1,409	193	30	18	283	12	313	118	...	3	...	192	...	2,550	2,009	399	...	...	142	...
1,945	1,409	193	30	18	283	12	313	118	..	3	...	192	...	2,550	2,009	399	...	...	142	...
170	146	2	8	...	14	...	11	11	...	...	...	...	...	42	42	...	...	...	...	...
1,775	1,263	191	22	18	269	12	302	107	...	3	...	192	...	2,508	1,967	399	...	...	142	...
7,650	6,539	391	89	128	500	3	1,218	902	...	...	...	316	...	2,015	1,749	243	...	...	23	...
7,650	6,539	391	89	128	500	3	1,218	902	...	...	...	316	...	2,015	1,749	243	...	...	23	...
2,994	2,828	11	11	3	140	1	31	31	...	...	...	...	...	595	563	22	...	...	10	...
108	108	...	...	...	..	...	...	...	...	...	...	...	...	201	201	...	...	...	...	...
12	9	...	...	...	3	...	...	...	...	...	...	...	...	6	6	...	...	...	...	...
4,536	3,594	380	78	125	357	2	1,187	871	...	...	...	316	...	1,213	979	221	...	...	13	...
3,325	1,160	191	1,877	29	65	3	29	29	...	...	...	...	...	441	308	38	...	92	3	...
2,012	144	...	1,859	7	2	...	...	...	...	...	...	...	...	10	10	...	...	...	...	...
2,012	144	...	1,859	7	2	...	...	...	...	...	...	...	...	10	10	...	...	...	...	...
1,313	1,016	191	18	22	63	3	29	29	...	...	...	...	...	427	294	38	...	92	3	...
1,293	1,016	171	18	22	63	3	29	29	...	...	...	...	...	320	279	38	...	...	3	...
20	...	20	...	...	...	...	...	...	...	...	...	...	...	107	15	...	...	92	...	...
...	...	...	...	...	...	...	...	...	...	...	...	...	...	4	4	...	...	...	...	...
...	...	...	...	...	...	...	...	...	...	...	...	...	...	4	4	...	...	...	...	...

TABLE XI

Occupation of selected Castes, Tribes or Races

1. This table is divided into two parts. Part A deals with the occupations of the 12 Castes selected for Tables VIII and XIV. Part B shows the distribution of European and Anglo-Indian earners, working dependents and non-working dependents in certain groups of occupations.

2. In Part A, the sum of columns 4 to 8 represents the total strength of the castes enumerated in Districts and Trans-frontier Posts; the figures in column 17 and onwards are exclusive of those in columns 9 and 10.

TABLE XI

Part A—Occupation of Selected Castes, Tribes or Races

No.	Caste, Tribe or Race	Traditional occupation	Population dealt with: Earners		Population dealt with: Working dependents		Population dealt with: Non-working dependents	Number of earners whose traditional caste occupation was returned as their: Principal means of livelihood		Number of earners whose traditional caste occupation was returned as their: Subsidiary means of livelihood		Number of working dependents following the traditional occupation of their caste	
			Males	Females	Males	Females	Both sexes	Males	Females	Males	Females	Males	Females
1	2	3	4	5	6	7	8	9	10	11	12	13	14
1	Arora ...	Trade ...	17,565	503	755	77	42,502	11,311	128	488	3	456	32
2	Awan ...	Agriculture ...	76,852	3,202	10,937	7,309	184,871	52,130	1,794	1,211	27	9,010	6,753
3	Brahman ...	Priests ...	6,352	146	138	221	10,343	719		19	...	66	15
4	Chamar ...	Working in leather ...	897	52	71	16	1,882	551	33	12	...	6	14
5	Chuhra ...	Scavenging ...	3,953	443	147	20	4,722	2,193	319	5	1	23	6
6	Gujar ...	Herdsmen ...	25,649	1,026	3,604	4,791	86,440	3,681	252	249	2	1,394	1,398
7	Jat ...	Agriculture ...	25,858	523	1,604	232	48,110	17,111	254	2,561	96	810	4
8	Khatri ...	Trade ...	11,365	265	712	200	22,504	5,740	83	151	...	219	65
9	Pathan ...	Agriculture and military service.	232,298	9,185	13,298	4,786	657,063	190,470	6,245	2,668	8	4,997	4,252
10	Sayad ...	Priests and agriculture.	19,613	937	2,481	1,638	57,643	15,449	629	288	51	1,803	1,433
11	Swathi ...	Agriculture ...	11,273	668	2,670	2,759	29,190	9,077	448	43	110	413	842
12	Tanaoli ...	Agriculture ...	19,729	1,194	6,786	577	57,789	17,764	968	141	1	5,534	438

TABLE XI

Part A—Occupation of Selected Castes, Tribes or Races

Number of earners returning their traditional occupation as their principal means of livelihood who had some subsidiary occupation		Recorded principal occupation of earners other than traditional occupation of caste (by sub-classes) — I—Exploitation of animals and vegetation: Income from rent of land		Cultivators of all kinds		Agents and managers of landed estates, planters, forest officers and their clerks rent collectors, etc.		Field labourers, wood-cutters, etc.		Raisers of live-stock, milkmen and herdsmen		Fishing and hunting		No.
Males	Females	Males	Females	Males	Females	Males	Females	Males	Females	Males	Females	Males	Females	
15	16	17	18	19	20	21	22	23	24	25	26	27	28	29
1,022	5	762	38	1,097	68	14	...	6	2	34	...	3	...	1
4,320	24	...	...	...	...	4	...	...	...	161	2	25	1	2
98	1	169	10	650	19	...	...	2	...	1	...	...	...	3
96	...	50	...	132	2	...	...	...	...	3	...	...	...	4
180	6	6	...	90	3	...	...	6	...	12	...	...	...	5
148	2	4,208	84	13,998	254	...	...	880	199	...	...	93	...	6
4,059	4	...	...	...	...	5	...	...	...	778	2	...	..	7
350	2	172	4	271	16	8	...	8	...	26	...	5	...	8
13,104	203	...	...	...	...	35	...	...	...	1,091	2	46	...	9
1,394	19	...	...	...	...	7	...	...	...	91	...	5	...	10
732	30	...	...	...	...	6	...	...	...	136	2	...	...	11
679	29	...	...	..	...	4	...	...	...	47	...	13	...	1

TABLE XI

Part A—Occupation of Selected Castes, Tribes or Races

No.	Caste, Tribe or Race	Traditional occupation	Recorded prinicipal occupation of earners, other than — II—Exploitation of minerals — Owners, managers clerks, etc. — Males	Females	Labourers — Males	Females	III—Industries — Owners, managers, clerks, etc. — Males	Females	Artisans and other workmen — Males	Females	IV— Owners, managers, ship officers, etc. — Males	Females
1	2	3	30	31	32	33	34	35	36	37	38	39
1	Arora ...	Trade ...	5	...	15	...	20	...	329	25	70	...
2	Awan ...	Agriculture ...	10	...	239	4	965	110	2,973	601	261	1
3	Brahman ...	Priests ...	13	...	3	...	3	...	51	6	44	...
4	Chamar ...	Working in leather...	...	...	6	...	6	...	9	3	...	...
5	Chuhra ...	Scavenging ...	...	...	...	...	5	1	614	41	...	...
6	Gujar ...	Herdsmen ...	...	...	1	...	18	1	215	35	20	...
7	Jat ...	Agriculture ...	...	...	5	...	33	...	743	12	8	...
8	Khatri ...	Trade ...	...	...	8	...	60	...	220	30	193	...
9	Pathan ...	Agriculture and military service.	...	1	296	1	770	22	3,265	470	597	3
10	Sayad ...	Priests and agriculture.	8	...	1	...	20	7	367	49	43	1
11	Swathi ...	Agriculture ...	...	...	...	...	2	1	70	3	115	...
12	Tanaoli ...	Agriculture ...	...	...	...	...	3	...	326	25	2	2

TABLE XI

Part A—Occupation of Selected Castes, Tribes or Races

traditional occupation of Caste (by sub-classes)																
Transport		V—Trade		VI—Public force				VII—Public administration				VIII—Profession and liberal arts				No.
labourers, boatmen, carters, palki-bearers, etc.				Commissioned and Gazetted Officers		Others		Gazetted Officers		Others		Religious		Lawyers, doctors and teachers		
Males	Females	Males	Females	Males	Females	Males	Females	Males	Females	Males	Females	Males	Females	Males	Females	
40	41	42	43	44	45	46	47	48	49	50	51	52	53	54	55	56
122	...	...	...	8	...	502	1	245	...	845	5	105	2	297	39	1
2,162	12	2,901	49	121	...	3,674	3	48	...	1,408	5	1,214	10	422	16	2
73	...	948	2	9	...	1,225	2	38	...	604	...	...	...	100	10	3
1	...	15	...	...	...	32	...	...	...	4	...	4	...	1	...	4
1	...	45	...	...	...	49	3	1	...	23	9	1	...	7	...	5
192	1	122	10	19	...	577	1	2	...	65	1	124	8	26	...	6
296	...	388	2	12	...	4,027	...	...	...	370	...	189	...	115	1	7
122	...	...	...	83	...	1,588	...	40	...	742	6	58	4	178	21	8
3,630	10	6,889	112	149	...	1,542	1	42	...	2,624	7	2,410	22	797	31	9
245	...	527	22	1	...	709	...	19	...	328	...	...	...	132	13	10
89	...	147	4	6	...	66	...	6	...	81	...	153	3	18	1	11
140	2	88	5	...	...	215	3	1	...	48	...	194	1	22	3	12

TABLE XI

Part A—Occupation of Selected Castes, Tribes or Races

No.	Caste, Tribe or Race	Traditional occupation	Recorded principal occupation earners, other than traditional occupation of Caste (by sub-classes)											
			VIII—Profession and liberal arts—*concluded*		IX—Persons living on their income		X—Domestic service		XI—Insufficiently described occupations				XII—Unproductive	
			Others						Contractors, clerks, cashiers, etc., otherwise unspecified		Labourers unspecified		Beggars, vagrants and prostitutes	
			Males	Females	Males	Females	Males	Females	Males	Females	Males	Females	Males	Females
1	2	3	57	58	59	60	61	62	63	64	65	66	67	68
1	Arora ...	Trade ...	75	9	243	20	759	47	92	3	555	99	51	17
2	Awan ...	Agriculture ...	316	43	216	10	2,027	52	122	16	5,076	384	377	89
3	Brahman ...	Priests ...	41	...	68	10	1,264	15	19	...	170	3	138	17
4	Chamar ...	Working in leather...	11	...	1	...	37	6	...	...	30	7	4	1
5	Chuhra ...	Scavenging ...	10	26	18	...	760	5	1	1	88	35	23	...
6	Gujar ...	Herdsmen ...	20	6	34	9	665	23	44	16	461	94	184	32
7	Jat ...	Agriculture ...	82	2	50	2	499	76	14	...	912	127	221	45
8	Khatri ...	Trade ...	131	5	161	23	1,126	40	108	4	273	14	44	15
9	Pathan ...	Agriculture and military service	233	63	405	21	2,818	290	272	36	12,932	1,668	985	180
10	Sayad ...	Priests and agriculture.	30	1	76	9	593	38	59	3	447	106	456	59
11	Swathi ...	Agriculture ..	13	2	25	8	621	48	4	4	343	121	295	23
12	Tanaoli ...	Agriculture ...	29	...	27	15	403	58	...	...	246	82	157	30

TABLE XI—PART B

TABLE XI—PART B

Distribution of European and Anglo-Indian Earners,

working dependents and non-working dependents in certain groups of occupations.

Group No.	Occupation	North West Frontier Province									
		Europeans					Anglo-Indians				
		Earners		Working dependents		Non-working dependents	Earners		Working dependents		Non-working dependents
		Males	Females	Males	Females	Both Sexes	Males	Females	Males	Females	Both Sexes
1	2	3	4	5	6	7	8	9	10	11	12
	All Occupations ...	9,724	107	...	2	1,743	57	6	...	...	98
3	Estate Agents and Managers of Government.	...	1	...	...	...	...	...	...	...	...
17	Forest Officers, Rangers, Guards, etc.	2	...	...	...	...	...	...	...	...	...
94	Heat, light, electricity, motive power, etc.	...	...	...	...	...	1	...	...	...	...
103	Persons (other than labourers) employed in harbours, docks, rivers and canals.	2	...	...	...	...	3	...	...	...	...
112	Railway employees of all kinds, other than coolies.	2	...	...	...	...	7	...	...	...	...
114	Post Office, Telegraph and Telephone Services.	...	...	...	...	...	4	...	...	...	...
115	Bank Managers, money-lenders etc.	1	...	...	...	...	...	...	...	...	...
127	Owners and Managers of hotels, etc.	1	...	...	...	...	...	...	...	...	...
150	General Storekeepers, etc. ...	3	2	...	...	...	2	...	...	...	...
153	Army (Imperial) ...	9,618	5	...	...	...	14	1	...	...	...
157	Police	19	...	...	...	...	1	...	...	...	...
159	Service of the State ...	47	14	...	...	...	17	4	...	...	...
165	Other religious workers ...	6	20	...	2	...	...	...	...	...	...
172	Midwives nurses, etc. ...	...	42	...	...	...	...	...	...	...	...
174	Professors and teachers of all kinds.	3	11	...	...	...	2	1	...	...	...
185	Pensioners, etc. ...	3	...	..	...	...	...	...	...	...	...
187	Other domestic service ...	17	12	...	...	...	6	...	...	...	...

TABLE XI—PART B

Distribution of European and Anglo-Indian Earners, Working dependents and non-working dependents in certain groups of occupations.

Districts										Trans-Frontier Posts										
Europeans					Anglo-Indians					Europeans					Anglo-Indians					
Earners		Working dependents		Non-working dependents	Earners		Working dependents		Non-working dependents	Earners		Working dependents		Non-working dependents	Earners		Working dependents		Non-working dependents	
Males	Females	Males	Females	Both Sexes	Males	Females	Males	Females	Both Sexes	Males	Females	Males	Females	Both Sexes	Males	Females	Males	Females	Both Sexes	Group No.
13	14	15	16	17	18	19	20	21	22	23	24	25	26	27	28	29	30	31	32	
5,952	107	...	2	1,736	56	6	...	...	88	3,772	...	...	...	7	1	...	...	...	10	
...	1	...	...	...	...	...	...	...	...	...	...	...	...	...	...	...	...	...	...	3
2	...	...	...	...	...	...	...	...	...	...	...	...	...	...	...	...	...	...	...	17
...	...	...	...	...	1	...	...	...	...	...	...	...	...	...	...	...	...	...	...	94
2	...	...	...	...	3	...	...	...	...	...	...	...	...	...	...	...	...	...	...	103
2	...	...	...	...	7	...	...	...	...	...	...	...	...	...	...	...	...	...	...	112
...	...	...	...	...	4	...	...	...	...	...	...	...	...	...	...	...	...	...	...	114
1	...	...	...	...	...	...	...	...	...	...	...	...	...	...	...	...	...	...	...	115
1	...	...	...	...	...	...	...	...	...	...	...	...	...	...	...	...	...	...	...	127
3	2	...	...	...	2	...	...	...	...	...	...	...	...	...	...	...	...	...	...	150
5,852	5	...	...	...	14	1	...	...	...	3,766	...	...	...	...	...	...	...	...	...	153
18	...	...	...	...	1	...	...	...	...	1	...	...	...	...	...	...	...	...	...	157
43	14	...	...	...	16	4	...	...	...	4	...	...	...	...	1	...	...	...	...	159
5	20	...	2	...	...	...	...	...	...	1	...	...	...	...	...	...	...	...	...	165
...	42	...	...	...	...	...	...	...	...	...	...	...	...	...	...	...	...	...	...	172
3	11	...	...	...	2	1	...	...	...	...	...	...	...	...	...	...	...	...	...	174
3	...	...	...	...	...	...	...	...	...	...	...	...	...	...	...	...	...	...	...	185
17	12	...	...	...	6	...	...	...	...	...	...	...	...	...	...	...	...	...	...	187

TABLE XII

Educated unemployment

1. This table is divided into two parts. Part I shows information regarding educated unemployment by classes, and Part II by degrees.

2. The information contained in this table was obtained on a special schedule, distributed only to those who applied for it of their own accord.

3. The figures in the body of the table refer only to those male persons residing in the five settled districts of the North West Frontier Province, who described themselves as having passed the Matriculation or equivalent examination, or as possessing the School Leaving Certificate, and also as without any paid employment. In addition to these, thirty-eight persons, mentioned in the note to Part I of the table, returned themselves not as totally unemployed, but as having failed to obtain employment with which they are satisfied.

TABLE XII (i)

Educated unemployment (i) by class

Class	Total unemployed	Aged 20—24		Aged 25—29		Aged 30—34		Aged 35—39	
		Unemployed for less than one year	Unemployed for one year or more	Unemployed for less than one year	Unemployed for one year or more	Unemployed for less than one year	Unemployed for one year or more	Unemployed for less than one year	Unemployed for one year or more
1	2	3	4	5	6	7	8	9	10
Brahmans ...	4	...	3	...	1	...	...	...	...
Depressed Hindus ...	...	...	...	...	...	...	...	...	...
Other Hindus ...	59	8	30	2	16	...	2	...	1
Muslims ...	87	10	32	3	28	...	10	...	4
Anglo-Indians ...	...	...	...	...	...	...	...	...	...
All other classes ...	...	...	...	...	...	...	...	...	...
Total ...	150	18	65	5	45	...	12	...	5

Total of English knowing unemployed under twenty years 40
Total of English knowing unemployed forty years of age and over 7
Total number of educated unemployed whose fathers were soldiers ... ...
Total number of educated unemployed whose fathers were cultivators 97
Total number of educated unemployed whose fathers were artizans 6
Total number of educated unemployed whose fathers were menials or servants 54
Total number of educated unemployed passed Matric or S. L. C. who though not totally unemployed failed to obtain employment with which they are satisfied 38

TABLE XII (ii)

Educated unemployment (ii) by degree

Degree	Total unemployed	Aged 20—24		Aged 25—29		Aged 30—34		Aged 35—39	
		Unemployed for less than one year	Unemployed for one year or more	Unemployed for less than one year	Unemployed for one year or more	Unemployed for less than one year	Unemployed for one year or more	Unemployed for less than one year	Unemployed for one year or more
1	2	3	4	5	6	7	8	9	10
British degrees ...	...	...	...	...	...	...	...	...	...
Continental degrees ...	...	...	...	...	...	...	...	...	...
American degrees ...	...	...	...	...	...	...	...	...	...
Other foreign degrees ...	1	...	...	...	1	...	...	...	...
Indian degrees :—	149	18	65	5	44	...	12	...	5
Medical ...	...	...	...	..	...	...	...	...	...
Legal ...	...	...	...	...	...	...	...	...	...
Agricultural ...	...	...	...	...	...	...	...	...	...
Commerce ...	...	...	...	...	...	...	...	...	...
M. A. ...	1	...	...	...	1	...	...	...	...
M. Sc. ...	...	...	...	...	...	...	...	...	...
B. A. ...	7	1	1	1	2	...	2	...	...
B. Sc. ...	7	3	2	...	2	...	...	...	...
B. Eng. or L. C. E....	1	...	...	1	...	...	...	...	...
B. T. or L. T. ...	...	...	...	...	...	...	...	...	...
Sch L. C. or Matric	133	14	62	3	39	...	10	...	5
Total ...	150	18	65	5	45	...	12	...	5

TABLE XIII

Literacy by Religion and Age.

1. This table is divided into three parts. Part I (Provincial Summary) shows the extent of literacy by Religion and Age in the five settled districts and Trans-Frontier Posts as a whole. Part II gives details (*a*) for the five settled districts (for the total population and for each main religion), and (*b*) for Trans-Frontier Posts (for all religions). Part III gives similar details for Peshawar City (excluding Peshawar Cantonment).

2. The figures in the body of the table refer to Christians of all races. The following statement shows the number of Indian Christians, who are literate :—

Age	Total population		Literate		Literate in English		Remarks
	Males	Females	Males	Females	Males	Females	
N. W. F. P. Districts ...	2,569	1,697	1,101	249	214	75	—
0—9	570	505	19	12	8	7	
10—15	227	172	27	4	10	...	
15—20	218	175	49	25	20	12	
20 & over	1,554	845	1,006	208	176	56	
Trans-Frontier Posts ...	422	74	79	2	21	...	
0—9	44	22	...	...	...	...	
10—15	15	7	1	...	...	...	
15—20	22	8	1	...	...	...	
20 & over	341	37	77	2	21	...	

TABLE XIII

Literacy by Religion and Age—Part I—Provincial Summary

Age and Religion	Population									Literate in English		
	Total			Literate			Illiterate					
	Persons	Males	Females	Persons	Males	Females	Persons	Males	Females	Persons	Males	Females
1	2	3	4	5	6	7	8	9	10	11	12	13
NORTH WEST FRONTIER PROVINCE												
All Religions ...	2,471,527	1,360,453	1,111,074	117,438	106,025	11,412	2,354,089	1,254,427	1,099,662	31,515	29,711	1,804
0—5 ...	387,469	196,049	191,420	...	...	...	387,469	196,049	191,420	...	...	...
5—10 ...	335,347	184,037	151,310	5,330	4,155	1,175	330,017	179,882	150,135	711	554	157
10—15 ...	289,203	164,184	125,019	9,020	7,356	1,664	280,183	156,828	123,355	1,543	1,364	179
15—20 ...	224,295	125,858	98,437	18,555	16,538	2,017	205,740	109,320	96,420	5,006	4,803	203
20 & over ...	1,235,213	650,325	544,888	84,533	77,977	6,556	11,50,680	612,348	538,332	24,255	22,990	1,265
Muslims ...	2,250,389	1,218,234	1,032,155	48,395	45,981	2,414	22,01,994	1,172,253	1,029,741	10,280	10,056	214
0—5 ...	359,135	181,679	177,456	...	...	...	359,135	181,679	177 456	...	...	...
5—10 ...	312,591	171,923	140,668	2,665	2,409	256	309,926	169,514	140,412	233	209	24
10—15 ...	269,119	153,063	116,056	4,666	4,270	396	264,453	148,793	115,660	683	644	39
15—20 ...	198,155	107,645	90,510	7,822	7,365	457	190,333	100,280	90,053	1,841	1,796	45
20 & over ...	1,111,389	603,924	507,465	33,242	31,937	1,305	1,078,147	571,987	506,160	7,523	7,417	106
Hindus ...	155,628	97,552	59,075	41,271	36,369	4,902	115,357	61,183	54,174	7,397	7,224	173
0—5 ...	21,057	10,627	10,430	...	...	...	21,057	10,627	10,430	...	...	...
5—10 ...	16,930	8,998	7,932	1,796	1,228	568	15,134	7,770	7,364	198	184	14
10—15 ...	14,972	8,305	6,667	3,101	2,264	837	11,871	6,041	5,830	487	460	27
15—20 ...	17,809	11,847	5,962	6,555	5,562	993	11,254	6,285	4,969	1,180	1,136	44
20 & over ...	85,860	57,775	28,085	29,819	27,315	2,504	56,041	30,460	25,581	5,532	5,444	88
Sikhs ...	47,935	31,409	16,525	15,687	13,064	2,623	32,248	18,345	13,903	2,541	2,481	60
0—5 ...	6,113	3,143	2,970	...	...	...	6,113	3,143	2,970	...	...	...
5—10 ...	5,008	2,664	2,344	617	394	223	4,391	2,270	2,121	69	64	5
10—15 ...	4,436	2,431	2,005	1,010	693	317	3,426	1,738	1,688	166	155	11
15—20 ...	5,964	4,273	1,691	2,583	2,131	452	3,381	2,142	1,239	463	448	15
20 & over ...	26,414	18,898	7,516	11,477	9,846	1,631	14,937	9,052	5,885	1,843	1,814	29

TABLE XIII

Literacy by Religion and Age—Part I—Provincial Summary

Age and Religion	Population									Literate in English		
	Total			Literate			Illiterate					
	Persons	Males	Females	Persons	Males	Females	Persons	Males	Females	Persons	Males	Females
1	2	3	4	5	6	7	8	9	10	11	12	13
NORTH WEST FRONTIER PROVINCE—*concluded*												
Christians ...	16,499	13,212	3,287	12,044	10,587	1,457	4,455	2,625	1,830	11,264	9,922	1,342
0—5 ...	1,155	595	560	...	...	...	1,155	595	560	...	...	...
5—10 ...	812	450	362	248	122	126	564	328	236	208	96	112
10—15 ...	670	383	287	240	128	112	430	255	175	204	104	100
15—20 ...	2,360	2,088	272	1,590	1,477	113	770	611	159	1,518	1,421	97
20 and over ...	11,502	9,696	1,806	9,966	8,860	1,106	1,536	836	700	9,334	8,301	1,033
Parsis ...	62	32	30	35	20	15	26	12	14	33	18	15
0—5 ...	9	5	4	...	...	...	9	5	4	...	...	...
5—10 ...	6	2	4	4	2	2	2	...	2	3	1	2
10—15 ...	6	2	4	3	1	2	3	1	2	3	1	2
15—20 ...	4	2	2	4	2	2	...	...	...	4	2	2
20 and over ...	37	21	16	25	15	10	12	6	6	23	14	9
Jews ...	11	11	...	5	5	...	6	6	...	...	...	...
0—5 ...	...	...	...	...	...	...	...	...	...	...	...	...
5—10 ...	...	...	...	...	...	...	...	...	...	...	...	...
10—15 ...	...	...	...	...	...	...	...	...	...	...	...	...
15—20 ...	2	2	...	1	1	...	1	1	...	...	...	...
20 & over ...	9	9	...	4	4	...	5	5	...	...	...	...
Buddhist ...	3	3	...	...	...	...	3	3	...	...	...	...
0—5 ...	...	...	...	...	...	...	...	...	...	...	...	...
5—10 ...	...	...	...	...	...	...	...	...	...	...	...	...
10—15 ...	...	...	...	...	...	...	...	...	...	...	...	...
15—20 ...	1	1	...	...	...	...	1	1	...	...	...	...
20 & over ...	2	2	...	...	...	...	2	2	...	...	...	...

TABLE XIII

Literacy by Religion and Age—Part II-(a)—Districts

Age and Religion	Population									Literate in English		
	Total			Literate			Illiterate					
	Persons	Males	Females	Persons	Males	Females	Persons	Males	Females	Persons	Males	Females
1	2	3	4	5	6	7	8	9	10	11	12	13
DISTRICTS												
All Religions ...	2,425,076	1,315,818	1,109,258	100,366	89,058	11,308	2,324,710	1,226,760	1,097,953	25,717	23,921	1,796
0—5 ...	386,719	195,672	191,047	...	...	...	386,719	195,672	191,047	...	...	...
5—10 ...	334,706	183,669	151,037	5,267	4,102	1,165	329,439	179,567	149,872	709	552	157
10—15 ...	288,425	163,622	124,803	8,880	7,230	1,650	279,545	156,392	123,153	1,529	1,351	178
15—20 ...	215,504	117,251	98,253	15,365	13,367	1,998	200,139	103,884	96,255	4,063	3,861	202
20 & over ...	1,199,722	655,604	544,118	70,854	64,359	6,495	1,128,868	591,245	537,623	19,416	18,157	1,259
Muslims ...	2,227,303	1,196,120	1,031,183	44,496	42,110	2,386	2,182,807	1,154,010	1,028,797	9,122	8,909	213
0—5 ...	358,736	181,479	177,257	...	...	...	358,736	181,479	177,257	...	...	...
5—10 ...	312,253	171,728	140,525	2,640	2,386	254	309,613	169,342	140,271	231	207	24
10—15 ...	268,655	152,709	115,946	4,598	4,205	393	264,057	148,504	115,553	677	638	39
15—20 ...	193,848	103,440	90,408	7,088	6,636	452	186,760	96,804	89,956	1,766	1,721	45
20 & over ...	1,093,811	586,764	507,047	30,170	28,883	1,287	1,063,641	557,881	505,760	6,448	6,343	105
Hindus ...	142,977	84,358	58,619	35,608	30,739	4,869	107,369	53,619	53,750	6,931	6,759	172
0—5 ...	20,869	10,535	10,334	...	...	...	20,869	10,535	10,334	...	...	...
5—10 ...	16,771	8,904	7,867	1,782	1,216	566	14,989	7,688	7,301	198	184	14
10—15 ...	14,795	8,183	6,612	3,067	2,235	832	11,728	5,948	5,780	485	459	26
15—20 ...	15,224	9,314	5,910	5,555	4,571	984	9,669	4,743	4,926	1,122	1,078	44
20 & over ...	75,318	47,422	27,896	25,204	22,717	2,487	50,114	24,705	25,409	5,126	5,038	88
Sikhs ...	42,510	26,285	16,225	12,141	9,549	2,592	30,369	16,736	13,634	2,245	2,189	57
0—5 ...	5,997	3,088	2,909	...	...	...	5,997	3,088	2,909	...	...	...
5—10 ...	4,903	2,611	2,292	601	383	218	4,302	2,228	2,074	69	64	5
10—15 ...	4,336	2,370	1,966	980	668	312	3,356	1,702	1,654	165	154	11
15—20 ...	4,870	3,200	1,670	1,896	1,448	448	2,974	1,752	1,222	411	396	15
20 & over ...	22,404	15,015	7,389	8,664	7,050	1,614	13,740	7,965	5,775	1,601	1,575	26
Christians ...	12,213	9,013	3,200	8,082	6,637	1,445	4,131	2,376	1,755	7,387	6,048	1,339
0—5 ...	1,108	565	543	...	...	...	1,108	565	543	...	...	...
5—10 ...	773	424	349	240	115	125	533	309	224	208	96	112
10—15 ...	633	358	275	232	121	111	401	237	164	199	99	100
15—20 ...	1,556	1,293	263	821	709	112	735	584	151	760	664	96
20 & over ...	8,143	6,373	1,770	6,789	5,692	1,097	1,354	681	673	6,220	5,189	1,031
Parsis ...	60	30	30	34	18	16	26	12	14	31	16	15
0—5 ...	9	5	4	...	...	...	9	5	4	...	...	...
5—10 ...	6	2	4	4	2	2	2	...	2	3	1	2
10—15 ...	6	2	4	3	1	2	3	1	2	3	1	2
15—20 ...	4	2	2	4	2	2	...	...	...	4	2	2
20 & over ...	35	19	16	23	13	10	12	6	6	21	12	9

TABLE XIII

Literacy by Religion and Age—Part II (a)—Districts

Age and Religion	Population									Literate in English		
	Total			Literate			Illiterate					
	Persons	Males	Females	Persons	Males	Females	Persons	Males	Females	Persons	Males	Females
1	2	3	4	5	6	7	8	9	10	11	12	13
DISTRICTS—*concluded*												
Jews ...	11	11	...	5	5	...	6	6	...	...	...	...
0—5 ...	...	...	...	...	...	...	...	...	...	...	...	...
5—10 ...	...	...	...	...	...	...	...	...	...	...	...	...
10—15 ...	...	...	...	...	...	...	...	...	...	...	...	...
15—20 ...	2	2	...	1	1	...	1	1	...	...	...	...
20 & over ...	9	9	...	4	4	...	5	5	...	...	...	...
Buddhists ...	2	2	...	...	...	...	2	2	...	...	...	...
0—5 ...	...	...	...	...	...	...	...	...	...	...	...	...
5—10 ...	...	...	...	...	...	...	...	...	...	...	...	...
10—15 ...	...	...	...	...	...	...	...	...	...	...	...	...
15—20 ...	...	...	...	...	...	...	...	...	...	...	...	...
20 & over ...	2	2	...	...	...	...	2	2	...	...	...	...
HAZARA DISTRICT												
All Religions ...	670,117	358,193	311,924	17,899	16,611	1,288	652,218	341,532	310,636	1,950	1,819	141
0—5 ...	111,096	55,977	55,119	...	...	...	111,096	55,977	55,119	...	...	...
5—10 ...	95,124	52,003	43,121	855	726	129	94,269	51,277	42,992	68	57	11
10—15 ...	81,084	46,227	34,857	1,619	1,429	190	79,465	44,798	34,667	163	151	12
15—20 ...	55,876	29,558	26,318	2,912	2,694	218	52,964	26,864	26,100	324	310	14
20 & over ...	326,937	174,428	152,509	12,513	11,762	751	314,424	162,666	151,758	1,405	1,301	104
Muslims ...	635,794	338,082	298,712	9,254	8,854	400	627,540	329,228	298,312	976	955	20
0—5 ...	106,361	53,527	52,834	...	...	...	106,361	53,527	52,834	...	...	...
5—10 ...	91,403	49,968	41,435	531	487	44	90,872	49,481	41,391	23	21	2
10—15 ...	77,775	44,338	33,437	1,047	976	71	76,728	43,362	33,366	88	84	4
15—20 ...	51,970	27,062	24,908	1,401	1,320	81	50,569	25,742	24,827	190	186	4
20 & over ...	309,285	163,187	146,098	6,275	6,071	204	303,010	157,116	145,894	675	665	10
Hindus ...	25,250	15,461	9,799	7,102	6,528	574	18,158	8,933	9,225	602	590	12
0—5 ...	3,500	1,816	1,684	...	...	...	3,500	1,816	1,684	...	...	...
5—10 ...	2,656	1,454	1,202	239	181	58	2,417	1,273	1,144	22	21	1
10—15 ...	2,407	1,381	1,026	440	355	85	1,967	1,026	941	50	48	2
15—20 ...	3,148	2,045	1,103	1,292	1,196	96	1,856	849	1,007	99	95	4
20 & over ...	13,549	8,765	4,784	5,131	4,796	335	8,418	3,969	4,449	431	426	5
Sikhs ...	7,630	4,393	3,237	1,286	1,079	207	6,344	3,314	3,030	143	136	7
0—5 ...	1,167	599	568	...	...	...	1,167	599	568	...	...	...
5—10 ...	1,023	553	470	65	45	20	958	508	450	4	3	1
10—15 ...	874	488	386	116	88	28	758	400	358	10	10	...
15—20 ...	729	431	298	202	167	35	527	264	263	23	22	1
20 & over ...	3,837	2,322	1,515	903	779	124	2,934	1,543	1,391	106	101	5

TABLE XIII

Literacy by Religion and Age—Part II (a)—Districts

Age and Religion	Population: Total: Persons	Total: Males	Total: Females	Literate: Persons	Literate: Males	Literate: Females	Illiterate: Persons	Illiterate: Males	Illiterate: Females	Literate in English: Persons	Literate in English: Males	Literate in English: Females
1	2	3	4	5	6	7	8	9	10	11	12	13
HAZARA DISTRICT—*concluded*												
Christians ...	432	256	176	257	150	107	175	106	69	239	137	102
0—5 ...	68	35	33	...	...	...	68	35	33	...	...	...
5—10 ...	42	28	14	20	13	7	22	15	7	19	12	7
10—15 ...	28	20	8	16	10	6	12	10	2	15	9	6
15—20 ...	29	20	9	17	11	6	12	9	3	12	7	5
20 & over ...	265	153	112	204	116	88	61	37	24	193	109	84
PESHAWAR DISTRICT												
All Religions ...	974,321	538,146	435,175	47,256	41,151	6,105	927,065	496,995	430,070	15,402	14,239	1,163
0—5 ...	143,567	73,503	70,064	...	...	...	143,567	73,503	70,064	...	...	...
5—10 ...	130,360	72,444	57,916	2,684	2,038	646	127,676	70,406	57,270	425	305	120
10—15 ...	117,956	67,193	50,763	4,098	3,207	891	113,858	63,986	49,872	803	666	137
15—20 ...	92,532	51,070	41,462	7,090	5,967	1,123	85,442	45,103	40,339	2,246	2,110	136
20 & over ...	489,906	273,936	215,970	33,384	29,939	3,445	456,522	243,997	212,525	11,928	11,158	770
Muslims ...	898,683	489,650	409,033	22,818	21,340	1,478	875,865	468,310	407,555	5,048	4,901	147
0—5 ...	133,735	68,504	65,231	...	...	...	133,735	68,504	65,231	...	...	...
5—10 ...	122,579	68,309	54,270	1,545	1,382	163	121,034	66,927	54,107	147	127	20
10—15 ...	110,965	63,308	47,657	2,364	2,113	251	108,601	61,195	47,406	359	328	31
15—20 ...	83,730	45,103	38,627	3,621	3,352	269	80,109	41,751	38,358	970	940	30
20 & over ...	447,674	244,426	203,248	15,288	14,493	795	432,386	229,933	202,453	3,572	3,506	66
Hindus ...	42,321	26,501	15,820	11,153	9,038	2,115	31,168	17,463	13,705	3,175	3,062	113
0—5 ...	5,720	2,903	2,817	...	...	...	5,720	2,903	2,817	...	...	...
5—10 ...	4,505	2,401	2,104	572	338	234	3,933	2,063	1,870	78	67	11
10—15 ...	4,073	2,287	1,786	949	610	339	3,124	1,677	1,447	182	162	20
15—20 ...	4,664	3,002	1,662	1,677	1,226	451	2,987	1,776	1,211	455	426	29
20 & over ...	23,359	15,908	7,451	7,955	6,864	1,091	15,404	9,044	6,360	2,460	2,407	53
Sikhs ...	24,271	15,211	9,060	7,180	5,625	1,555	17,091	9,586	7,505	1,395	1,363	32
0—5 ...	3,309	1,691	1,618	...	...	...	3,309	1,691	1,618	...	...	...
5—10 ...	2,698	1,427	1,271	390	238	152	2,308	1,189	1,119	51	48	3
10—15 ...	2,441	1,333	1,108	615	401	214	1,826	932	894	119	110	9
15—20 ...	2,891	1,910	981	1,189	864	325	1,702	1,046	656	259	250	9
20 & over ...	12,932	8,850	4,082	4,986	4,122	864	7,946	4,728	3,218	966	955	11
Christians ...	8,974	6,742	2,232	6,066	5,125	941	2,908	1,617	1,291	5,753	4,897	856
0—5 ...	794	400	394	...	...	...	794	400	394	...	...	...
5—10 ...	572	305	267	173	78	95	399	227	172	146	62	84
10—15 ...	471	263	208	167	82	85	304	181	123	140	65	75
15—20 ...	1,241	1,051	190	598	522	76	643	529	114	558	492	66
20 & over ...	5,896	4,723	1,173	5,128	4,443	685	768	280	488	4,909	4,278	631

TABLE XIII

Literacy by Religion and Age—Part II-(a)—Districts

Age and Religion	Population									Literate in English		
	Total			Literate			Illiterate					
	Persons	Males	Females	Persons	Males	Females	Persons	Males	Females	Persons	Males	Females
1	2	3	4	5	6	7	8	9	10	11	12	13
KOHAT DISTRICT												
All Religions ...	235,273	126,210	110,063	10,061	9,099	962	226,212	117,111	109,101	3,391	3,235	156
0—5 ...	40,791	20,419	20,372	...	...	...	40,791	20,419	20,372	...	...	...
5—10 ...	33,763	18,235	15,528	420	319	101	33,343	17,916	15,427	72	64	8
10—15 ...	27,870	15,499	12,371	766	623	143	27,104	14,876	12,228	168	161	7
15—20 ...	20,541	10,985	9,556	1,546	1,376	170	18,995	9,609	9,386	564	547	17
20 & over ...	113,308	61,072	52,236	7,329	6,781	548	105,979	54,291	51,688	2,587	2,463	124
Muslims ...	218,445	114,487	103,958	4,402	4,216	186	214,043	110,271	103,772	1,453	1,435	18
0—5 ...	38,461	19,244	19,217	...	...	...	38,461	19,244	19,217	...	...	...
5—10 ...	31,984	17,287	14,697	236	213	23	31,748	17,074	14,674	41	40	1
10—15 ...	26,318	14,635	11,683	447	413	34	25,871	14,222	11,649	108	106	2
15—20 ...	18,408	9,505	8,903	717	679	38	17,691	8,826	8,865	269	263	6
20 & over ...	103,274	53,816	49,458	3,002	2,911	91	100,272	50,905	49,367	1,035	1,026	9
Hindus ...	13,393	8,504	4,889	3,623	3,214	409	9,770	5,290	4,480	711	707	4
0—5 ...	1,847	921	926	...	...	...	1,847	921	926	...	...	...
5—10 ...	1,455	769	686	124	77	47	1,331	692	639	15	15	...
10-15 ...	1,267	702	565	223	154	69	1,044	548	496	34	34	...
15—20 ...	1,505	998	507	528	452	76	977	546	431	118	117	1
20 & over ...	7,319	5,114	2,205	2,748	2,531	217	4,571	2,583	1,988	544	541	3
Sikhs ...	3,249	2,292	957	1,194	963	231	2,055	1,329	725	411	408	3
0—5 ...	404	213	191	...	...	...	404	213	191	...	...	...
5—10 ...	270	149	121	47	24	23	223	125	98	5	5	...
10—15 ...	239	136	103	82	47	35	157	89	68	14	14	...
15—20 ...	491	366	125	194	149	45	297	217	80	77	76	1
20 & over ...	1,845	1,428	417	871	743	128	974	685	289	315	313	2
Christians ...	1,185	927	259	842	705	135	344	221	123	816	685	131
0—5 ...	79	41	38	...	...	...	79	41	38	...	...	...
5—10 ...	54	30	24	13	5	8	41	25	16	11	4	7
10—15 ...	46	26	20	14	9	5	32	17	15	12	7	5
15—20 ...	137	116	21	107	96	11	30	20	10	100	91	9
20 & over ...	870	714	156	708	596	112	162	118	44	693	583	110
BANNU DISTRICT												
All Religions ...	270,301	145,163	125,138	9,696	8,872	824	250,605	135,291	124,314	1,714	1,568	146
0—5 ...	47,507	23,638	23,869	...	...	...	47,507	23,638	23,869	...	...	...
5—10 ...	38,027	20,468	17,559	441	413	28	37,586	20,055	17,531	54	46	8
10—15 ...	29,914	16,837	13,077	803	764	39	29,111	16,073	13,038	122	113	9
15—20 ...	22,328	12,311	10,017	1,421	1,317	104	20,907	10,994	9,913	328	312	16
20 & over ...	132,525	71,909	60,616	7,031	6,378	653	125,494	65,531	59,963	1,210	1,097	113

TABLE XIII

Literacy by Religion and Age—Part II-(a)—Districts

Age and Religion	Population									Literate in English		
	Total			Literate			Illiterate					
	Persons	Males	Females	Persons	Males	Females	Persons	Males	Females	Persons	Males	Females
	2	3	4	5	6	7	8	9	10	11	12	13
BANNU DISTRICT—*concluded*												
Muslims ...	237,674	126,671	111,003	2,959	2,887	72	234,715	123,784	110,931	549	530	19
0—5 ...	42,248	20,975	21,273	...	...	...	42,248	20,975	21,273	...	...	...
5—10 ...	33,867	18,256	15,611	141	138	3	33,726	18,118	15,608	10	10	...
10—15 ...	26,413	14,930	11,483	270	264	6	26,143	14,666	11,477	34	33	1
15—20 ...	19,164	10,474	8,690	480	464	16	18,684	10,010	8,674	93	90	3
20 & over ...	115,982	62,036	53,946	2,068	2,021	47	113,914	60,015	53,899	412	397	15
Hindus ...	26,181	14,528	11,653	4,308	4,132	176	21,873	10,396	11,477	745	729	16
0—5 ...	4,322	2,182	2,140	...	...	...	4,322	2,182	2,140	...	...	...
5—10 ...	3,428	1,823	1,605	227	215	12	3,201	1,608	1,593	27	26	1
10—15 ...	2,870	1,574	1,296	423	403	20	2,447	1,171	1,276	64	63	1
15—20 ...	2,487	1,397	1,090	694	627	67	1,793	770	1,023	141	138	3
20 & over ...	13,074	7,552	5,522	2,964	2,887	77	10,110	4,665	5,445	513	502	11
Sikhs ...	5,482	3,278	2,204	1,861	1,390	471	3,621	1,888	1,733	175	162	13
0—5 ...	831	422	409	...	...	...	831	422	409	...	...	...
5—10 ...	670	353	317	59	53	6	611	300	311	5	4	1
10—15 ...	579	305	274	95	89	6	484	216	268	2	11	1
15—20 ...	568	359	209	176	162	14	392	197	195	30	26	4
20 & over ...	2,834	1,839	995	1,531	1,086	445	1,303	753	550	128	121	7
Christians ...	964	686	278	568	463	105	396	223	173	245	147	98
0—5 ...	106	59	47	...	...	...	106	59	47	...	...	...
5—10 ...	62	36	26	14	7	7	48	29	19	12	6	6
10—15 ...	52	28	24	15	8	7	37	20	17	12	6	6
15—20 ...	109	81	28	71	64	7	38	17	21	64	58	6
20 & over ...	635	482	153	468	384	84	167	98	69	157	77	80
DERA ISMAIL KHAN DISTRICT												
All Religions ...	274,064	148,106	125,958	15,454	13,325	2,129	258,610	134,781	123,829	3,250	3,060	190
0—5 ...	43,758	22,135	21,623	...	...	...	43,758	22,135	21,623	...	...	...
5—10 ...	37,432	20,519	16,913	867	606	261	36,565	19,913	16,652	90	80	10
10—15 ...	31,601	17,866	13,735	1,594	1,207	387	30,007	16,659	13,348	273	260	13
15—20 ...	24,227	13,327	10,900	2,396	2,013	383	21,831	11,314	10,517	601	582	19
20 & over ...	137,046	74,259	62,787	10,597	9,499	1,098	126,449	64,760	61,689	2,286	2,138	148
Muslims ...	235,707	127,230	108,477	5,063	4,813	250	230,644	122,417	108,227	1,096	1,087	9
0—5 ...	37,931	19,229	18,702	...	...	...	37,931	19,229	18,702	...	...	...
5—10 ...	32,420	17,908	14,512	187	166	21	32,233	17,742	14,491	10	9	1
10—15 ...	27,184	15,498	11,686	470	439	31	26,714	15,059	11,655	88	87	1
15—20 ...	20,576	11,296	9,280	869	821	48	19,707	10,475	9,232	244	242	2
20 & over ...	117,596	63,299	54,297	3,537	3,387	150	114,059	59,912	54,147	754	749	5

TABLE XIII

Literacy by Religion and Age—Part II-(a)—Districts

Age and Religion	Population									Literate in English		
	Total			Literate			Illiterate					
	Persons	Males	Females	Persons	Males	Females	Persons	Males	Females	Persons	Males	Females
1	2	3	4	5	6	7	8	9	10	11	12	13
DERA ISMAIL KHAN DISTRICT—*concluded*												
Hindus ...	**35,822**	**19,364**	**16,458**	**9,422**	**7,827**	**1,595**	**26,400**	**11,537**	**14,863**	**1,698**	**1,671**	**27**
0—5 ...	5,480	2,713	2,767	...	...	...	5,480	2,713	2,767	...	...	...
5—10 ...	4,727	2,457	2,270	620	405	215	4,107	2,052	2,055	56	55	1
10—15 ...	4,178	2,239	1,939	1,032	713	319	3,146	1,526	1,620	155	152	3
15—20 ...	3,420	1,872	1,548	1,364	1,070	294	2,056	802	1,254	309	302	7
20 & over ...	18,017	10,083	7,934	6,406	5,639	767	11,611	4,444	7,167	1,178	1,162	16
Sikhs ...	**1,878**	**1,110**	**768**	**620**	**492**	**128**	**1,258**	**618**	**640**	**122**	**120**	**2**
0—5 ...	286	163	123	...	...	...	286	163	123	...	...	...
5—10 ...	242	129	113	40	23	17	202	106	96	4	4	...
10—15 ...	203	108	95	72	43	29	131	65	66	10	9	1
15—20 ...	191	134	57	135	106	29	56	28	28	22	22	...
20 & over ...	956	576	380	373	320	53	583	256	327	86	85	1
Christians ...	**657**	**402**	**255**	**349**	**193**	**156**	**308**	**209**	**99**	**334**	**182**	**152**
0—5 ...	61	30	31	...	...	...	61	30	31	...	...	...
5—10 ...	43	25	18	20	12	8	23	13	10	20	12	8
10—15 ...	36	21	15	20	12	8	16	9	7	20	12	8
15—20 ...	40	25	15	28	16	12	12	9	3	26	16	10
20 & over ...	477	301	176	281	153	128	196	148	48	268	142	126

TABLE XIII

Literacy by Religion and Age—Part II-(b)—Trans-Frontier Posts

Age and Religion	Population: Total: Persons	Total: Males	Total: Females	Literate: Persons	Literate: Males	Literate: Females	Illiterate: Persons	Illiterate: Males	Illiterate: Females	Literate in English: Persons	Literate in English: Males	Literate in English: Females
1	2	3	4	5	6	7	8	9	10	11	12	13
All Religions ...	46,451	44,635	1,816	17,072	16,968	104	29,379	27,667	1,712	5,798	5,790	8
0—5 ...	750	377	373	...	...	...	750	377	373	...	...	...
5—10 ...	641	368	273	63	53	10	578	315	263	2	2	...
10—15 ...	778	562	216	140	126	14	638	436	202	14	13	1
15—20 ...	8,791	8,607	184	3,190	3,171	19	5,601	5,436	165	943	942	1
20 & over ...	35,491	34,721	770	13,679	13,618	61	21,812	21,103	709	4,839	4,833	6
Muslims ...	23,086	22,114	972	3,899	3,871	28	19,187	18,243	944	1,158	1,157	1
0—5 ...	399	200	199	...	...	...	399	200	199	...	...	...
5—10 ...	338	195	143	25	23	2	313	172	141	2	2	...
10—15 ...	464	354	110	68	65	3	396	289	107	6	6	...
15—20 ...	4,307	4,205	102	734	729	5	3,573	3,476	97	75	75	...
20 & over ...	17,578	17,160	418	3,072	3,054	18	14,506	14,106	400	1,075	1,074	1
Hindus ...	13,651	13,194	457	5,663	5,630	33	7,988	7,564	424	466	465	1
0—5 ...	188	92	96	...	...	...	188	92	96	...	...	...
5—10 ...	159	94	65	14	12	2	145	82	63	...	...	...
10—15 ...	177	122	55	34	29	5	143	93	50	2	1	1
15—20 ...	2,585	2,533	52	1,000	991	9	1,585	1,542	43	58	58	...
20 & over ...	10,542	10,353	189	4,615	4,598	17	5,927	5,755	172	406	406	...
Sikhs ...	5,425	5,125	300	3,546	3,515	31	1,879	1,610	269	295	292	3
0—5 ...	116	55	61	...	...	...	116	55	61	...	...	...
5—10 ...	105	53	52	16	11	5	89	42	47	...	...	...
10—15 ...	100	61	39	30	25	5	70	36	34	1	1	...
15—20 ...	1,094	1,073	21	687	683	4	407	390	17	52	52	...
20 & over ...	40,10	3,883	127	2,813	2,796	17	1,197	1,087	110	242	239	3
Christians ...	4,286	4,199	87	3,962	3,950	12	324	249	75	3,877	3,874	3
0—5 ...	47	30	17	...	...	...	47	30	17	...	...	...
5—10 ...	39	26	13	8	7	1	31	19	12	...	...	...
10—15 ...	37	25	12	8	7	1	29	18	11	5	5	...
15—20 ...	804	795	9	769	768	1	35	27	8	758	757	1
20 & over ...	3,359	3,323	36	3,177	3,168	9	182	155	27	3,114	3,112	2
Parsis ...	2	2	...	2	2	...	...	...	...	2	2	...
0—5 ...	...	...	...	...	...	...	...	...	...	...	...	...
5—10 ...	...	...	...	...	...	...	...	...	...	...	...	...
10—15 ...	...	...	...	...	...	...	...	...	...	...	...	...
15—20 ...	...	...	...	...	...	...	...	...	...	...	...	...
20 & over ...	2	2	...	2	2	...	...	...	...	2	2	...

TABLE XIII

Literacy by Religion and Age—Part II-(b)— Trans-Frontier Posts

Age and Religion	Population									Literate in English		
	Total			Literate			Illiterate					
	Persons	Males	Females	Persons	Males	Females	Persons	Males	Females	Persons	Males	Females
	2	3	4	5	6	7	8	9	10	11	12	13
Buddhists ...	1	1	...	...	...	...	1	1	...	...	...	...
0—5 ...	...	...	...	...	...	...	...	...	...	...	...	...
5—10 ...	...	...	...	...	...	...	...	...	...	...	...	...
10—15 ...	...	...	...	...	...	...	...	...	...	...	...	...
15—20 ...	1	1	...	...	...	...	1	1	...	...	...	...
20 & over ...	...	...	...	...	...	...	...	...	...	...	...	...

TABLE XIII

Literacy by Religion and Age—Part III—Peshawar City (Municipality)

Age and Religion	Population									Literate in English		
	Total			Literate			Illiterate					
	Persons	Males	Females	Persons	Males	Females	Persons	Males	Females	Persons	Males	Females
1	2	3	4	5	6	7	8	9	10	11	12	13
All Religions ...	87,440	50,151	37,289	14,297	11,786	2,511	73,143	38,365	34,778	3,447	3,281	166
0—5 ...	11,183	5,707	5,476	...	...	...	11,183	5,707	5,476	...	...	...
5—10 ...	9,884	5,333	4,551	822	566	256	9,062	4,767	4,295	90	73	17
10—15 ...	9,337	5,203	4,134	1,352	966	386	7,985	4,237	3,748	244	211	33
15—20 ...	8,790	5,063	3,727	2,196	1,633	563	6,594	3,430	3,164	589	547	42
20 & over ...	48,246	28,845	19,401	9,927	8,621	1,306	38,319	20,224	18,095	2,524	2,450	74
Muslims ...	69,893	39,915	29,978	7,814	7,090	724	62,079	32,825	29,254	1,859	1,777	82
0—5 ...	8,678	4,428	42,50	...	...	...	8,678	4,428	4,250	...	...	...
5—10 ...	7,853	4,236	3,617	428	345	83	7,425	3,891	3,534	44	35	9
10—15 ...	7,457	4,152	3,305	695	566	129	6,762	3,586	3,176	114	98	16
15—20 ...	6,913	3,973	2,940	1,145	1,017	128	5,768	2,956	2,812	321	302	19
20 & over ...	38,992	23,126	15,866	5,546	5,162	384	33,446	17,964	15,482	1,380	1,342	38
Hindus ...	11,594	6,781	4,813	4,234	3,161	1,073	7,360	3,620	3,740	1,240	1,175	65
0—5 ...	1,599	813	786	...	...	...	1,599	813	786	...	...	...
5—10 ...	1,312	709	603	257	152	105	1,055	557	498	38	32	6
10—15 ...	1,236	683	553	434	273	161	802	410	392	89	76	13
15—20 ...	1,249	734	515	681	414	267	568	320	248	194	175	19
20 & over ...	6,198	3,842	2,356	2,862	2,322	540	3,336	1,520	1,816	919	892	27
Sikhs ...	5 150	2,992	2,158	2,175	1,486	689	2,975	1,506	1,469	327	319	8
0—5 ...	779	403	376	...	...	...	779	403	376	...	...	...
5—10 ...	628	337	291	130	66	64	498	271	227	7	6	1
10—15 ...	560	320	240	213	122	91	347	198	149	39	36	3
15—20 ...	543	314	229	360	196	164	183	118	65	72	70	2
20 & over ...	2,640	1,618	1,022	1,472	1,102	370	1,168	516	652	209	207	2
Christians ...	792	452	340	69	44	25	723	408	315	21	10	11
0—5 ...	127	63	64	...	...	...	127	63	64	...	...	...
5—10 ...	91	51	40	7	3	4	84	48	36	1	...	1
10—15 ...	84	48	36	10	5	5	74	43	31	2	1	1
15—20 ...	83	40	43	9	5	4	74	35	39	2	...	2
20 & over ...	407	250	157	43	31	12	364	219	145	16	9	7
Jews ...	11	11	...	5	5	...	6	6	...	...	...	...
0—5 ...	...	...	...	...	...	...	...	...	...	...	...	...
5—10 ...	...	...	...	...	...	...	...	...	...	...	...	...
10—15 ...	...	...	...	...	...	...	...	...	...	...	...	...
15—20 ...	2	2	...	1	1	...	1	1	...	...	...	...
20 & over ...	9	9	...	4	4	...	5		...	...	...	...

TABLE XIV

Literacy by selected castes, tribes or races

(1) The twelve castes selected for this table are the same as those selected for tables VIII and XI.

(2) The table includes the population of each caste residing in trans-frontier posts.

TABLE XIV

Literacy by selected Castes, Tribes or Races

Caste, tribe or race	Locality	Population (7 years and over)									Literate in English (7 years and over)		
		Total			Literate			Illiterate					
		Persons	Males	Females	Persons	Males	Females	Persons	Males	Females	Persons	Males	Females
1	2	3	4	5	6	7	8	9	10	11	12	13	14
Awan ...	All districts and trans-frontier posts	225,598	126,060	99,538	9,196	8,467	1,029	216,102	117,593	98,509	2,392	2,107	285
Arora ...	All districts and trans-frontier posts	48,615	27,763	20,852	13,031	10,890	2,141	35,584	16,873	18,711	2,408	2,237	171
Brahman ...	All districts and trans-frontier posts	14,630	9,409	5,221	6,014	4,878	1,136	8,616	4,531	4,085	1,029	969	60
Chamar ...	All districts and trans-frontier posts	2,346	1,422	924	41	41	...	2,305	1,381	924	3	3	...
Chuhra ...	All districts and trans-frontier posts	7,983	5,603	2,380	406	380	26	7,577	5,223	2,354	26	22	4
Gujar ...	All districts and trans-frontier posts	95,423	53,162	42,261	933	855	78	94,490	52,307	42,183	147	125	22
Jat ...	All districts and trans-frontier posts	62,774	38,045	24,729	4,122	4,034	88	58,652	34,011	24,641	514	513	1
Khatri ...	All districts and trans-frontier posts	28,958	16,875	12,083	11,619	8,698	2,921	17,339	8,177	9,162	2,373	1,983	390
Pathan ...	All districts and trans-frontier posts	727,335	395,137	332,198	21,022	19,129	1,893	706,313	376,008	330,305	5,215	4,748	467
Sayad ...	All districts and trans-frontier posts	64,738	33,956	30,782	4,012	3,703	309	60,726	30,253	30,473	1,104	1,016	88
Swathi ...	Hazara and Peshawar Districts only	37,254	20,457	16,797	1,014	962	52	36,240	19,495	16,745	79	78	1
Tanaoli ...	Hazara and Peshawar Districts only	67,135	35,737	31,398	817	801	16	66,318	34,936	31,382	70	69	1

TABLE XV

Language

1. This table is divided into two parts, both of which contain separate statistics for the North-West Frontier Province, Districts and Trans-Frontier Posts. Part I (Mother Tongue) shows the number of persons who speak (A) Vernaculars of India, (B) Vernaculars of other Asiatic countries and Africa, and (C) European languages, as their mother tongue. Part II (Bilingualism) gives figures for subsidiary languages distributed according to Sex and Mother Tongue.

2. Details of the languages, shown as "others" in groups A (2), B and C of column 1 of Part I of this table are given below for the North-West Frontier Province :—

Group	Language	Males	Females	Group	Language	Males	Females
A (2)	Purbi ...	158	70	A (2)	Ladakhi ...	14	...
	Tamil ...	349	18		Chaungtha ...	1	...
	Telugu ...	250	14		Konkani ...	2	...
	Bengali ...	387	48		Kashkari ...	51	32
	Marathi ...	341	78				
	Pahari ...	614	4	B	Arabic ...	14	10
	Balochi ...	7	...		Turkish ...	35	27
	Atsi ...	1	...		Chinese ...	...	5
	Sindhi ...	12	6		Japanese ...	...	1
	Gujrati ...	148	76				
	Khamti ...	34	...	C	Greek ...	1	1
	Mishmi ...	1	...		French ...	2	7
	Goai ...	23	1		Spanish ...	1	...
	Khasi ...	1	...		Portuguese ...	10	3
	Mehar ...	1	...		Welsh ...	17	2
	Sanskrit ...	1	...		Scotch ...	1	...
	Kharia ...	1	...		Irish ...	1	...
	Burmese ...	1	5		Dutch ...	...	1
	Tibetan ...	4	...		German ...	...	3
	Parsi ...	1	12				

3. The language "Lahnda" includes the dialects returned in the Census schedules, as :—

Hindko, Peshawari, Derawali, Tanaoli.

4. The sum of columns 5—36 in Part II of this table exceeds the total number of persons speaking subsidiary languages in addition to their mother tongue, by the number of subsidiary languages in excess of one spoken in addition to the mother tongue. Out of 178,353 persons speaking subsidiary languages in the North-West Frontier Province :—

145,274 speak one subsidiary language,
26,314 speak two subsidiary languages,
6,726 speak three subsidiary languages,
39 speak four subsidiary languages,

in addition to their mother tongue.

TABLE XV

Part I—Language

Languages	N.-W. F. Province			Districts			Hazara			Peshawar	
	Persons	Males	Females	Persons	Males	Females	Persons	Males	Females	Persons	Males
1	2	3	4	5	6	7	8	9	10		12
Population ...	2,471,527	1,360,453	1,111,074	2,425,076	1,315,818	1,109,258	670,117	358,193	311,924	974,32[illegible]	538,146
A—Indian Vernaculars total	2,453,340	1,346,350	1,106,990	2,411,053	1,305,725	1,105,327	669,825	358,025	311,800	964,401	530,674
A (1)—Vernaculars of the N.-W. F. P. total.	2,330,374	1,248,642	1,081,732	2,317,114	1,236,468	1,080,646	655,207	346,842	308,365	911 041	492,552
Pashto	1,290,484	687,488	602,996	1,279,471	6[illegible]7,428	602,043	29,375	17,169	12,206	781 773	414,339
Lahnda	1,036,657	558,899	477,758	1,034,874	557,244	477,630	625,268	329,339	295,[illegible]29	27[illegible]8	[illegible]6,862
Kashmiri ...	2,249	1,819	430	1,79[illegible]	1,371	425	96	75		1,57[illegible]	1,188
Kohistani ...	388	127	261	377	116	261	79	56	23	295	57
Gujuri	596	309	287	596	309	287	389	203	186	[illegible]07	106
A (2)—Other Indian Vernaculars total.	122,96[illegible]	97,708	25,258	93,939	69,258	24,681	14,618	11,183	3,435	53,3[illegible]0	38,122
Panjabi	86,726	68,429	18,297	68,031	50,226	17,805	5,436	3,897	1,53[illegible]	40 80[illegible]	29,408
Hindustani ...	6,918	4,818	2,[illegible]00	5,762	3,686	2,076	627	366	261	4,671	2,966
Urdu	12,651	10,194	2,457	11,027	8,601	2,426	3,480	3,006	[illegible]84	[illegible]	3,776
Hindi	4,173	3,339	834	2,432	1,628	804	6	4	2	[illegible]74	1,380
Naipali (Gorkhali) ...	9,731	8,525	1,206	5,140	3,934	1,206	4,933	3,733	1,200	20	26
Others... ...	2,767	2,403	364	1,547	1,183	364	136	87	49	731	566
B—Vernaculars of other Asiatic countries and Africa total.	6,472	3,874	2,598	6,122	3,664	2,458	34	23	11	4,031	2,538
Persian	6,380	3,825	2,555	6,030	3,615	2,415	24	18	6	[illegible]	2,41[illegible]
Others	92	49	43	92	49	43	10	5	5	7[illegible]	42
C—European languages total.	11,715	10,229	1,486	7,901	6,428	1,473	258	145	113	5,889	4,034
English... ...	11,665	10,196	1,469	7,852	6,396	1,456	257	144	113	5 864	4,916
Others	50	33	17	49	32	17	1	1	...	25	18

TABLE XV

Part I—Language

	Kohat			Bannu			Dera Ismail Khan			Trans-frontier posts		
Females	Persons	Males	Females	Persons	Males	Females	Persons	Males	Females	Persons	Males	Females
13	14	15	16	17	18	19	20	21	22	23	24	25
436,175	236,273	126,210	110,063	270,301	145,163	125,138	274,064	148,106	125,958	46,451	44,635	1,816
433,727	235,054	125,271	109,783	269,731	144,712	125,019	272,042	147,044	124,998	42,287	40,624	1,663
418,489	222,093	115,249	106,844	261,997	138,568	123,429	266,776	143,257	123,519	13,260	12,174	1,086
367,434	186,299	96,344	89,955	228,381	121,438	106,943	53,643	28,138	25,505	11,0[illegible]3	10,0[illegible]	953
50,327	35,755	18,866	16,889	33,547	17,076	16,4[illegible]1	213,[illegible]5	115,101	[illegible]8,014	1,783	1,655	128
389	39	39	...	69	54	15	15	15	...	453	448	5
238	...	...	...	...	...	...	3	3	...	11	11	...
101	...	...	...	...	...	...	...	...	...	...	...	...
15,238	12,961	10,022	2,939	7,734	6,144	1,590	5,266	3,787	1,479	29,027	28,450	577
11,397	11,077	8,594	2,483	6,267	5,077	1,190	4,446	3,250	1,[illegible]6	1[illegible],695	18,[illegible]	492
1,705	11	11	...	434	341	93	19	2	17	1,[illegible]56	1,132	24
1,377	1,523	1,159	364	473	331	142	398	239	15[illegible]	1,624	1,593	31
594	176	91	85	274	152	122	2	1	1	1,741	1,7[illegible]1	30
...	99	99	...	81	75	6	1	1	...	4,591	4,591	...
165	75	68	7	205	168	37	400	294	106	1,220	1,220	...
1,493	363	234	129	13	12	1	1,681	857	824	350	210	140
1,4[illegible]	363	234	129	13	12	1	1,678	855	823	350	210	140
37	...	...	...	...	...	...	3	2	1	...	...	...
955	856	705	151	557	439	118	341	205	136	3,814	3,801	13
948	839	696	143	556	439	117	336	201	135	3,8[illegible]3	3,800	13
7	17	9	8		...	1	5	4	1	1	1	...

TABLE XV

Part II—Bilingualism

Area of Bilingualism	Mother tongue	Number of persons speaking mother tongue		Subsidiary									
				Pashto		Lahnda		Kashmiri		Kohistani		Gujuri	
		Male	Females	Males	Females	Males	Females	Males	Females	Males	Females	Males	Females
1	2	3	4	5	6	7	8	9	10	11	12	13	14
N.-W. F. P.	Total ...	1,360,453	1,111,074	56,667	28,015	34,500	14,591	36	...	191	234	150	141
	A—Indian Vernaculars Total.	1,346,350	1,106,990	55,311	27,492	34,217	14,222	35	...	191	234	150	141
	A (1) Vernaculars of the N.-W. F. P. Total.	1,248,642	1,081,732	48,331	25,825	23,391	12,275	35	...	169	18	150	141
	Pashto ...	687,488	602,996	...	...	22,852	12,038	...	...	30	...	2	137
	Lahnda ...	558,899	477,758	48,213	25,740	...	...	35	...	139	17	148	4
	Kashmiri ...	1,819	430	48	10	328	30	...	...	...	...	...	...
	Kohistani ...	127	261	38	37	38	49	...	...	...	...	..	...
	Gujuri ...	309	287	32	38	173	158	...	...	...	1	...	...
	A (2) Other Indian Vernaculars Total.	97,708	25,258	6,980	1,667	10,826	1,947	...	...	22	216	...	...
	Punjabi ...	68,429	18,297	5,174	1,157	8,844	1,131	...	...	22	215	...	...
	Hindustani ...	4,818	2,100	699	119	232	276	...	...	...	...	...	...
	Urdu ...	10,194	2,457	900	253	1,231	533	...	...	...	...	...	...
	Hindi ...	3,339	834	159	60	...	...	...	...	...	...	...	...
	Naipali (Gorkhali) ...	8,525	1,206	5	...	207	...	...	...	...	...	...	...
	Others ...	2,403	364	43	78	312	7	...	...	...	1	...	...
	B—Vernaculars of other Asiatic Countries and Africa Total.	3,874	2,598	1,056	472	271	363	1	...	...	...	...	...
	Persian ...	3,825	2,555	1,049	471	267	363	1	...	...	...	...	...
	Others ...	49	43	7	1	4	...	...	...	...	...	...	...
	C—European Languages Total.	10,229	1,486	300	51	12	6	...	...	...	...	...	...
	English ...	10,196	1,469	299	50	8	6	...	...	...	...	...	...
	Others ...	33	17	1	1	4	...	...	...	...	...	...	...
Districts ...	Total ...	1,315,818	1,109,258	55,613	27,959	28,585	14,505	36	...	191	234	150	141
	A—Indian Vernaculars Total.	1,305,726	1,105,327	54,414	27,455	28,310	14,153	35	...	191	234	150	141
	A (1) Vernaculars of the N.-W. F. P. Total.	1,236,468	1,080,646	48,064	25,791	22,592	12,247	35	...	169	18	150	141
	Pashto ...	677,428	602,043	...	...	22,147	12,011	...	...	30	...	2	137
	Lahnda ...	557,244	477,630	47,947	25,706	...	...	35	...	139	17	148	4
	Kashmiri ...	1,371	425	47	10	234	29	...	...	...	...	...	...
	Kohistani ...	116	261	38	37	38	49	...	...	...	...	...	...
	Gujuri ...	309	287	32	38	173	158	...	...	...	1	...	...

TABLE XV

Part II—Bilingulism

languages

Punjabi		Hindustani		Urdu		Hindi		Naipali		Bengali		Persian		Arabic		Turkish		English		Others	
Males	Females	Males	Females	Males	Females	Males	Females	Males	Females	Males	Females	Males	Females	Males	Females	Males	Females	Males	Females	Males	Females
15	16	17	18	19	20	21	22	23	24	25	26	27	28	29	30	31	32	33	34	35	36
15,477	2,402	3,772	770	38,979	6,737	176	51	84	...	14	1	4,818	736	727	179	7	...	7,756	917	90	18
15,337	2,362	3,772	770	36,897	5,957	176	51	81	...	14	1	4,814	733	709	177	7	...	7,650	906	82	16
12,726	1,774	2,101	560	23,667	4,876	54	38	47	...	10	1	3,285	669	620	148	6	...	4,499	534	15	3
4,953	308	...	...	9,761	1,292	...	...	...	...	3	...	1,779	234	506	66	6	...	2,029	66	...	...
7,491	1,433	2,101	560	13,459	3,541	54	38	47	...	7	1	1,499	433	114	82	...	...	2,433	467	15	3
282	12	...	...	447	43	...	...	...	...	...	...	6	2	...	...	...	...	37	1	...	...
...	21	...	...	...	...	...	...	...	...	...	...	1	...	...	...	...	...	...	...	...	...
...	...	...	...	...	...	...	...	...	...	...	...	...	...	...	...	...	...	...	...	...	...
2,611	588	1,671	210	13,230	1,081	122	13	34	...	4	...	1,529	64	89	29	1	...	3,151	372	67	13
...	...	1,671	210	11,980	979	92	13	34	...	...	...	869	22	69	24	...	...	2,339	215	44	8
548	296	...	...	...	...	...	...	...	...	...	...	512	6	...	...	...	...	266	63	...	...
885	196	...	...	...	...	...	...	...	...	2	...	118	36	18	5	...	...	387	63	6	...
176	95	...	...	438	7	...	...	...	...	...	...	9	...	...	...	...	...	65	6	...	...
871	1	...	...	262	35	...	...	...	...	...	...	...	...	...	...	...	...	27	...	2	...
131	...	...	...	550	60	30	...	...	...	2	...	21	...	2	...	1	...	67	25	15	5
119	13	...	...	516	331	...	...	...	...	...	...	2	1	18	2	...	...	104	9	...	...
119	13	...	...	510	326	...	...	...	...	...	...	...	...	18	2	...	...	104	9	...	...
...	...	...	...	6	5	...	...	...	...	...	...	2	1	...	...	...	...	...	...	...	...
21	27	...	...	1,556	449	...	...	3	...	...	...	2	2	...	...	...	...	2	2	8	2
21	27	...	...	1,562	448	...	...	3	...	...	...	2	2	...	...	...	...	...	...	8	2
...	...	...	...	4	1	...	...	...	...	...	...	...	...	...	...	...	...	2	2	...	...
13,717	2,334	3,251	770	33,185	6,684	148	51	84	...	14	1	4,605	733	712	179	7	...	6,707	907	84	18
13,596	2,295	3,251	770	31,802	5,911	148	51	81	...	14	1	4,601	730	694	177	7	...	6,605	896	76	16
12,109	1,718	2,101	560	21,959	4,859	54	38	47	...	10	1	3,126	666	613	148	6	...	4,147	531	15	3
4,630	276	...	...	8,478	1,285	...	...	...	...	3	...	1,657	231	499	66	6	...	1,822	64	...	...
7,208	1,411	2,101	560	13,174	3,531	54	38	47	...	7	1	1,464	433	114	82	...	...	2,289	466	15	3
271	10	...	...	307	43	...	...	...	...	...	...	4	2	...	...	...	...	35	1	...	...
...	21	...	...	...	...	...	...	...	...	...	...	1	...	...	...	...	...	...	...	...	...
...	...	...	...	...	...	...	...	...	...	...	...	...	...	...	...	...	...	...	...	...	...

TABLE XV

Part II—Bilingualism

Area of Bilingualism	Mother tongue	Number of persons speaking mother tongue: Males	Number of persons speaking mother tongue: Females	Subsidiary: Pashto: Males	Pashto: Females	Lahnda: Males	Lahnda: Females	Kashmiri: Males	Kashmiri: Females	Kohistani: Males	Kohistani: Females	Gujuri: Males	Gujuri: Females
1	2	3	4	5	6	7	8	9	10	11	12	13	14
Districts—*concld.*	A (2)—Other Indian Vernaculars Total.	69,258	24,681	6,350	1,664	5,718	1,906	...	...	22	216	...	...
	Punjabi ...	50,226	17,805	4,952	1,154	4,750	1,090	...	...	22	215	...	...
	Hindustani ...	3,686	2,076	599	119	31	276	...	...	...	...	...	...
	Urdu ...	8,601	2,426	631	253	871	533	...	...	...	...	...	...
	Hindi ...	1,628	804	159	60	...	...	...	...	...	...	...	...
	Naipali (Gorkhali) ...	3,934	1,206	...	...	9	...	...	...	...	...	...	...
	Others ...	1,183	364	9	78	57	7	...	...	...	1	...	...
	B—Vernaculars of other Asiatic Countries and Africa Total.	3,664	2,458	946	453	263	346	1	...	...	...	...	...
	Persian ...	3,615	2,415	939	452	259	346	1	...	...	...	...	...
	Others ...	49	43	7	1	4	...	...	...	...	...	...	...
	C—European Languages Total.	6,428	1,473	253	51	12	6	...	...	...	...	...	...
	English ...	6,396	1,456	252	50	8	6	...	...	...	...	...	...
	Others ...	32	17	1	1	4	...	...	...	...	...	...	...
Hazara ...	Total ...	358,193	311,924	7,567	3,876	7,149	3,805	1	...	189	18	150	4
	A—Indian Vernaculars Total.	358,025	311,800	7,566	3,875	7,147	3,805	1	...	189	18	150	4
	A (1)—Vernaculars of the N.-W. F. P. Total.	346,842	308,365	7,499	3,787	6,521	3,722	1	...	167	18	150	4
	Pashto ...	17,169	12,206	...	...	6,310	3,544	...	...	28	...	2	...
	Lahnda ...	329,339	295,929	7,481	3,783	...	...	1	...	139	17	148	4
	Kashmiri ...	75	21	6	1	8	5	...	...	...	...	...	...
	Kohistani ...	56	23	10	3	38	15	...	...	...	...	...	...
	Gujuri ...	203	186	2	...	165	158	...	...	...	1	...	...
	A (2)—Other Indian Vernaculars Total.	11,183	3,435	67	88	626	83	...	...	22	...	...	...
	Punjabi ...	3,897	1,539	23	58	460	48	...	...	22	...	...	..
	Hindustani ...	366	261	...	...	6	1	...	...	...	...	...	...
	Urdu ...	3,096	384	44	20	130	31	...	...	...	...	...	...
	Hindi ...	4	2	...	...	...	...	...	...	...	...	...	...
	Naipali (Gorkha ...	3,733	1,200	...	...	...	...	...	...	...	...	...	...
	Others ...	87	49	...	10	30	3	...	...	...	...	...	...

TABLE XV

Part II—Bilingualism

languages

Punjabi		Hindustani		Urdu		Hindi		Naipali		Bengali		Persian		Arabic		Turkish		English		Others	
Males	Females	Males	Females	Males	Females	Males	Females	Males	Females	Males	Females	Males	Females	Males	Females	Males	Females	Males	Females	Males	Females
15	16	17	18	19	20	21	22	23	24	25	26	27	28	29	30	31	32	33	34	35	36
1,487	577	1,150	210	9,843	1,052	94	13	34	...	4	...	1,475	64	81	29	1	...	2,458	365	61	13
...	...	1,150	210	9,150	950	92	13	34	...	...	...	837	22	64	24	...	...	1,766	213	44	8
534	296	...	...	...	...	...	...	...	...	...	...	502	6	...	...	...	...	237	63	...	...
725	185	...	...	...	...	...	...	...	...	2	...	106	36	16	5	...	...	337	58	6	...
101	95	...	...	267	7	...	...	...	...	...	...	9	...	..	...	...	...	41	6	...	...
50	1	...	...	112	35	...	...	...	...	...	...	...	...	...	...	...	...	23	...	2	...
77	...	...	...	314	60	2	...	...	...	2	...	21	...	1	...	1	...	54	25	9	5
100	12	...	...	500	330	...	...	...	...	...	...	2	1	18	2	...	...	101	9	...	...
100	12	...	...	494	325	...	...	...	...	...	...	...	...	18	2	...	...	101	9	...	...
...	...	...	...	6	5	...	...	...	...	...	...	2	1	...	...	...	...	...	...	...	...
21	27	...	...	884	443	...	...	3	...	...	...	2	2	...	...	...	...	1	2	8	2
21	27	...	...	881	442	...	...	3	...	...	...	2	2	...	...	...	...	...	...	8	2
...	...	...	...	3	1	...	...	...	...	...	...	...	...	...	...	...	...	1	2	...	...
1,104	159	...	...	4,809	2,209	...	...	11	...	...	...	37	1	37	...	...	...	282	10	1	9
1,094	157	...	...	4,756	2,177	...	...	8	...	...	...	35	...	34	...	...	...	282	10	1	9
1,074	148	...	...	3,937	1,981	...	...	4	...	...	...	29	...	33	...	...	...	194	5	1	1
30	4	...	..	241	21	...	...	...	...	...	...	18	...	20	...	...	...	42	3	...	...
1,043	142	...	...	3,656	1,948	...	...	4	...	...	...	11	...	13	...	...	...	151	1	1	1
1	2	...	...	40	12	...	...	...	...	...	...	...	...	...	...	...	...	1	1	...	...
...	...	...	...	...	...	...	...	...	...	...	...	...	...	...	...	...	...	...	...	...	...
...	...	...	...	...	...	...	...	...	...	...	...	...	...	...	...	...	...	...	...	...	...
20	9	...	...	819	196	...	...	4	...	...	...	6	...	1	...	...	...	88	5	...	8
...	...	...	...	778	161	...	...	4	...	...	...	3	...	1	...	...	...	64	...	...	8
4	1	...	...	...	...	...	...	...	...	...	...	...	...	...	...	...	...	5	1	...	...
14	7	...	...	...	...	...	...	...	...	...	...	3	...	...	...	...	...	19	...	...	...
...	...	...	...	...	...	...	...	...	...	...	...	...	...	...	...	...	...	...	...	...	...
...	1	...	...	14	29	...	...	...	...	...	...	...	...	...	...	...	...	...	...	...	...
2	...	...	...	27	6	...	...	...	...	...	...	...	...	...	...	...	...	...	4	...	...

TABLE XV

Part II—Bilingualism

Area of Bilingualism	Mother tongue	Number of persons speaking mother tongue		Subsidiary									
				Pashto		Lahnda		Kashmiri		Kohistani		Gujuri	
		Males	Females	Males	Females	Males	Females	Males	Females	Males	Females	Males	Females
1	2	3	4	5	6	7	8	9	10	11	12	13	14
Hazara—*concld.*	B—Vernaculars of other Asiatic Countries and Africa Total.	23	11	...	1	2	...	...	...	...	...	...	...
	Persian ...	18	6	...	1	2	...	...	...	...	...	...	...
	Others ...	5	5	...	...	...	...	...	...	...	...	...	...
	C—European Languages Total.	145	113	1	...	...	...	...	...	...	...	...	...
	English ...	144	113	1	...	...	...	...	...	...	...	...	...
	Others ...	1	...	...	...	...	...	...	...	...	...	...	...
Peshawar ...	Total ...	538,146	436,175	25,547	11,314	11,003	6,905	...	...	2	216	...	137
	A—Indian Vernaculars Total.	530,674	433,727	24,557	10,876	10,769	6,642	...	...	2	216	...	137
	A (1)—Vernaculars of N.-W. F. P. Total.	492,552	418,489	19,779	9,521	8,651	5,201	...	...	2	...	...	137
	Pashto ...	414,339	367,434	...	...	8,448	5,143	...	...	2	...	...	137
	Lahnda ...	76,862	50,327	19,683	9,442	...	...	...	...	...	...	...	...
	Kashmiri ...	1,188	389	38	7	195	24	...	...	...	..	...	...
	Kohistani ...	57	238	28	34	...	34	...	...	...	...	...	...
	Gujuri ...	106	101	30	38	8	...	...	...	...	...	...	...
	A (2)—Other Indian Vernaculars Total.	38,122	15,238	4,778	1,355	2,118	1,441	...	...	...	216	...	...
	Punjabi ...	29,408	11,397	3,720	997	1,601	714	...	...	...	215	...	...
	Hindustani ...	2,966	1,705	596	119	15	275	...	...	...	...	...	...
	Urdu ...	3,776	1,377	353	170	497	452	...	...	...	...	...	...
	Hindi ...	1,380	594	105	2	...	...	...	...	...	...	...	...
	Naipali (Gorkhali) ...	26	...	...	...	...	...	...	...	...	...	...	...
	Others ...	566	165	4	67	5	...	...	...	...	1	..	...
	B—Vernaculars of other Asiatic Countries and Africa Total.	2,538	1,493	782	400	234	262	...	...	...	...	...	...
	Persian ...	2,496	1,456	775	400	230	262	...	...	...	...	...	...
	Others ...	42	37	7	...	4	...	...	...	...	...	...	...
	C—European Languages Total.	4,934	955	208	38	...	1	...	...	...	...	...	...
	English ...	4,916	948	208	38	...	1	...	...	...	...	...	...
	Others ...	18	7	...	...	...	...	...	...	...	...	...	...

TABLE XV

Part II—Bilingualism

...languages

Punjabi		Hindustani		Urdu		Hindi		Naipali		Bengali		Persian		Arabic		Turkish		English		Others	
Males	Females	Males	Females	Males	Females	Males	Females	Males	Females	Males	Females	Males	Females	Males	Females	Males	Females	Males	Females	Males	Females
15	16	17	18	19	20	21	22	23	24	25	26	27	28	29	30	31	32	33	34	35	36
...	...	...	...	9	3	...	...	...	...	...	...	...	...	3	..	...	...	...	...	...	...
...	...	...	...	9	3	...	...	...	..	...	...	..	...	3	...	...	...	...	...	...	...
...	...	...	...	...	...	...	...	...	...	...	...	...	...	...	...	...	...	...	...	...	...
10	2	...	...	44	29	...	...	3	...	...	...	2	1	...	...	...	...	...	...	...	...
10	2	...	...	44	29	...	...	3	...	...	...	2	1	...	...	...	...	...	...	...	...
...	...	...	...	...	...	...	...	...	...	...	...	...	...	...	...	...	...	...	...	...	...
5,386	1,525	3,251	770	12,589	3,404	...	...	...	...	...	...	3,279	598	375	142	7	...	3,811	850	21	...
5,363	1,492	3,251	770	11,622	2,901	...	...	...	...	...	...	3,277	596	361	142	7	...	3,718	846	21	...
4,267	971	2,101	560	7,741	2,266	...	...	...	...	...	...	1,951	558	341	113	6	...	2,271	512	...	...
1,216	170	...	...	4,468	1,031	...	...	...	...	...	...	1,060	144	281	54	6	...	1,102	58	...	...
2,785	775	2,101	560	3,020	1,206	...	...	...	...	...	...	889	412	60	59	...	...	1,135	454	...	...
266	5	...	...	253	29	...	...	...	...	...	...	1	2	...	...	...	...	34	...	...	...
...	21	...	...	...	...	...	...	...	...	...	...	1	...	...	...	...	...	...	...	...	...
...	...	...	...	...	...	...	...	...	...	...	...	...	...	...	...	...	...	...	...	...	...
1,096	521	1,150	210	3,881	635	...	...	...	...	...	...	1,326	38	20	29	1	...	1,447	334	21	...
...	...	1,150	210	3,563	601	...	...	...	...	...	...	728	18	15	24	...	...	903	205	21	...
525	295	...	...	...	...	...	...	...	...	...	...	502	6	...	...	...	..	230	62	...	...
414	133	...	...	...	...	...	...	...	...	...	...	66	14	5	5	...	...	253	45	...	...
95	93	...	...	157	6	...	...	...	...	...	...	9	...	...	...	...	...	34	6	...	...
23	...	...	...	1	...	...	...	...	...	...	...	...	...	...	...	...	...	...	...	...	...
39	...	...	...	160	28	...	...	...	...	...	...	21	...	...	...	1	...	27	16	...	...
16	11	...	...	404	237	...	...	...	...	...	...	2	1	14	...	...	...	93	3	...	...
16	11	...	...	399	232	...	...	...	...	...	...	...	...	14	...	...	...	93	3	...	...
...	...	...	...	5	5	...	...	...	...	...	...	2	1	...	...	...	...	...	...	...	...
7	22	...	...	563	266	...	...	...	...	...	...	...	1	...	...	...	...	...	1	...	...
7	22	...	...	563	265	...	...	..	...	...	...	...	1	...	...	...	...	...	...	...	...
...	...	...	...	...	1	...	...	...	...	...	...	...	...	...	...	...	...	...	1	...	...

TABLE XV

Part II—Bilingualism

Area of Bilingualism	Mother tongue	Number of persons speaking mother tongue		Subsidiary									
				Pashto		Lahnda		Kashmiri		Kohistani		Gujuri	
		Males	Females	Males	Females	Males	Females	Males	Females	Males	Females	Males	Females
1	2	3	4	5	6	7	8	9	10	11	12	13	14
Kohat ...	Total ...	126,210	110,063	6,749	6,221	4,789	1,753	...	...	...	...	...	...
	A.—Indian Vernaculars Total.	125,271	109,783	6,667	6,172	4,782	1,673	...	...	...	...	...	...
	A.—Vernaculars of the N.-W. F. P. Total.	115,249	106,844	5,914	6,032	2,918	1,496	...	...	...	...	...	...
	Pashto ...	96,344	89,955	...	...	2,910	1,496	...	...	...	...	...	...
	Lahnda ...	18,866	16,889	5,914	60,32	...	...	...	...	...	...	...	...
	Kashmiri ...	39	...	...	...	8	...	...	...	...	...	...	...
	Kohistani ...	...	...	...	...	...	...	...	...	...	...	...	...
	Gujuri ...	...	...	...	...	...	...	...	...	...	...	...	...
	A (2).—Other Indian Vernaculars Total.	10,022	2,939	753	140	1,864	177	...	...	...	...	...	...
	Punjabi ...	8,594	2,483	591	68	1,705	171	...	...	...	...	...	...
	Hindustani ...	11	...	...	...	...	...	...	...	...	...	...	...
	Urdu ...	1,159	364	128	34	150	6	...	...	...	...	...	...
	Hindi ...	91	85	34	38	...	...	...	...	...	...	...	...
	Naipali (Gorkhali) ...	99	...	...	...	5	...	...	...	...	...	...	...
	Others ...	68	7	...	...	4	...	...	...	...	...	...	...
	B—Vernaculars of other Asiatic Countries and Africa Total.	234	129	74	44	1	80	...	...	...	...	...	...
	Persian ...	234	129	74	44	1	80	...	...	...	...	...	...
	Others ...	...	...	...	...	...	...	...	...	...	...	...	...
	C—European Languages Total.	705	151	8	5	6	...	...	...	...	...	...	...
	English ...	696	143	7	4	2	...	...	...	...	...	...	...
	Others ...	9	8	1	1	4	...	...	...	...	...	...	...
Bannu ...	Total ...	145,163	125,138	8,511	3,275	1,920	408	...	...	...	...	...	...
	A—Indian Vernaculars Total.	144,712	125,019	8,504	3,274	1,917	408	...	...	...	...	...	...
	A (1)—Vernaculars of the N.-W. F. P. Total.	138,568	123,429	8,156	3,223	1,607	332	...	...	...	...	...	...
	Pashto ...	121,438	106,943	...	...	1,599	332	...	...	...	...	...	...
	Lahnda ...	17,076	16,471	8,154	3,221	...	...	...	...	...	...	...	...
	Kashmiri ...	54	15	2	2	8	...	...	...	...	...	...	...
	Kohistani ...	...	...	...	...	...	...	...	...	...	...	...	...
	Gujuri ...	...	...	...	...	...	...	...	...	...	...	...	...

TABLE XV

Part II—Bilingualism

languages

Punjabi		Hindustani		Urdu		Hindi		Naipali		Bengali		Persian		Arabic		Turkish		English		Others	
Males	Females	Males	Females	Males	Females	Males	Females	Males	Females	Males	Females	Males	Females	Males	Females	Males	Females	Males	Females	Males	Females
15	16	17	18	19	20	21	22	23	24	25	26	27	28	29	30	31	32	33	34	35	36
2,554	183	...	...	6,607	364	...	...	...	...	2	...	476	52	68	8	...	...	1,495	21	9	4
2,553	182	...	...	6,517	262	...	...	...	...	2	...	476	52	67	8	...	...	1,488	14	1	2
2,314	149	...	...	3,878	216	...	...	...	...	...	...	391	50	55	8	...	...	821	5	...	...
903	46	...	...	1,826	102	...	...	...	...	...	...	295	43	55	6	...	...	449	1	...	...
1,407	103	...	...	2,046	114	...	...	...	...	...	...	96	7	...	2	...	...	372	4	...	...
4	...	...	...	6	...	...	...	...	...	...	...	...	...	...	...	...	...	...	...	...	...
...	...	...	...	...	...	...	...	...	...	...	...	...	...	...	...	...	...	...	...	...	...
...	...	...	...	...	...	...	...	...	...	...	...	...	...	...	...	...	...	...	...	...	...
239	33	...	...	2,639	46	...	...	...	...	2	...	85	2	12	...	...	...	667	9	1	2
...	...	...	...	2,561	43	...	...	...	...	...	...	57	...	9	...	...	...	604	1	...	...
...	...	...	...	...	...	...	...	...	...	...	...	...	...	...	...	...	...	...	...	...	...
96	33	...	...	...	...	...	...	...	...	2	...	28	2	3	...	...	...	29	6	...	...
...	...	...	...	24	1	...	...	...	...	...	...	...	...	...	...	...	...	1	...	...	...
27	...	...	...	31	...	...	...	...	...	...	...	...	...	...	...	...	...	21	...	...	...
16	...	...	...	23	2	...	...	...	...	...	...	...	...	...	...	...	...	12	2	1	2
...	...	...	...	23	80	...	...	...	...	...	...	...	...	1	...	...	...	6	6	...	...
...	...	...	...	23	80	...	...	...	...	...	...	...	...	1	...	...	...	6	6	...	...
...	...	...	...	...	...	...	...	...	...	...	...	...	...	...	...	...	...	...	...	...	...
1	1	...	...	67	22	...	...	...	...	...	...	...	...	...	...	...	...	1	1	8	2
1	1	...	...	64	22	...	...	...	...	...	...	...	...	...	...	...	...	...	...	8	2
...	...	...	...	3	...	...	...	...	...	...	...	...	...	...	...	...	...	1	1	...	...
338	112	...	...	3,359	230	148	51	73	...	...	...	147	7	93	3	...	...	426	15	33	3
337	111	...	...	3,318	215	148	51	73	...	...	...	147	7	93	3	...	...	426	15	33	3
274	104	...	...	1,698	68	54	38	43	...	...	...	125	1	68	3	...	...	274	5	1	...
72	10	...	...	925	29	...	...	...	...	...	...	113	1	66	...	...	...	130	1	...	...
202	91	...	...	765	37	54	38	43	...	...	...	11	...	2	3	...	...	143	4	1	...
	3	...	...	8	2	...	...	...	...	...	...	1	...	...	...	...	...	1	...	...	...
	...	...	...	...	...	...	...	...	...	...	...	...	...	...	...	...	...	...	...	...	...
	...	...	...	...	...	...	...	...	...	...	...	...	...	...	...	...	...	...	...	...	...

TABLE XV

Part II—Bilingualism

Area of Bilingualism	Mother tongue	Number of persons speaking mother tongue		Subsidiary									
				Pashto		Lahnda		Kashmiri		Kohistani		Gujuri	
		Males	Females	Males	Females	Males	Females	Males	Females	Males	Females	Males	Females
1	2	3	4	5	6	7	8	9	10	11	12	13	14
Bannu—*concld.*	A (2)—Other Indian Vernaculars Total.	6,144	1,590	348	51	310	76	...	...	...	...	...	...
	Punjabi ...	5,077	1,190	268	17	277	60	...	...	...	...	...	...
	Hindustani ...	341	93	3	...	10	...	...	...	...	...	...	...
	Urdu ...	331	142	54	13	15	16	...	...	...	...	...	...
	Hindi ...	152	122	20	20	...	...	...	...	...	...	...	...
	Naipali (Gorkhali) ...	75	6	...	...	4	...	...	...	...	...	...	...
	Others ...	168	37	3	1	4	...	...	...	...	...	...	...
	B—Vernaculars of other Asiatic Countries and Africa Total.	12	1	5	...	3	...	...	...	...	...	...	...
	Persian ...	12	1	5	...	3	...	...	...	...	...	...	...
	Others ...	...	...	...	...	...	...	...	...	...	...	...	...
	C—European Languages Total.	439	118	2	1	...	...	...	...	...	...	...	...
	English ...	439	117	2	1	...	...	...	...	...	...	...	...
	Others ...	...	1	...	...	...	...	...	...	...	...	...	...
Dera Ismail Khan.	Total ...	148,106	125,958	7,239	3,273	3,724	1,634	35	...	...	...	...	...
	A—Indian Vernaculars Total.	147,044	124,998	7 120	3,258	3,695	1,625	34	...	...	...	...	...
	A (1)—Vernaculars of the N.-W. F. P. Total	143,257	123,519	6,716	3,228	2,895	1,496	34	...	...	...	...	...
	Pashto ...	28,138	25,505	...	...	2,880	1,496	...	...	...	...	...	...
	Lahnda ...	115,101	98,014	6,715	3,228	...	...	34	...	...	...	...	...
	Kashmiri ...	15	..	1	...	15	...	...	...	...	...	...	...
	Kohistani ...	3	...	...	...	...	...	...	...	...	...	...	...
	Gujuri ...	...	...	...	...	...	...	...	...	...	...		
	A (2)—Other Indian Vernaculars Total.	3,787	1,479	404	30	800	129	...	...	...	...	...	...
	Punjabi ...	3,250	1,196	350	14	707	97	...	...	...	...	...	...
	Hindustani ...	2	17	...	...	...	...	...	...	...	...	...	...
	Urdu ...	239	159	52	16	79	28	...	...	...	...	...	...
	Hindi ...	1	1	...	...	...	...	...	...	...	...	...	...
	Naipali (Gorkhali) ...	1	...	...	...	...	...	...	...	...	...	...	...
	Others ...	294	106	2	...	14	4	...	...	...	...	...	...

TABLE XV

Part II—Bilingualism

languages

Punjabi		Hindustani		Urdu		Hindi		Naipali		Bengali		Persian		Arabic		Turkish		English		Others	
Males	Females	Males	Females	Males	Females	Males	Females	Males	Females	Males	Females	Males	Females	Males	Females	Males	Females	Males	Females	Males	Females
15	16	17	18	19	20	21	22	23	24	25	26	27	28	29	30	31	32	33	34	35	36
63	7	...	...	1,620	147	94	13	30	...	...	...	22	6	25	...	...	...	152	10	32	3
..	...	...	...	1,437	125	92	13	30	...	...	...	17	2	24	...	...	...	128	3	23	...
5	...	...	...	...	...	...	...	...	...	...	...	...	...	...	...	...	...	...	...	...	...
39	5	...	...	...	..	...	...	...	...	...	...	5	4	...	...	...	...	12	4	...	...
6	2	...	...	86	...	...	...	...	...	...	...	...	...	...	...	...	...	6	...	...	...
...	...	...	...	65	6	...	...	..	...	...	...	...	...	...	...	..	...	2	...	2	...
13	...	...	...	32	16	2	...	...	...	...	...	...	...	1	...	...	...	4	3	7	3
...	...	...	...	9	1	...	...	...	...	...	...	...	...	...	...	...	...	...	...	...	...
...	...	...	...	9	1	...	...	...	...	...	...	...	...	...	...	...	...	...	...	...	...
...	...	...	...	...	...	...	...	...	...	...	...	...	...	...	...	...	...	...	...	...	...
1	1	...	...	32	14	...	...	...	...	...	...	...	...	...	...	...	...	...	...	...	...
1	1	...	...	32	14	...	...	...	...	...	...	...	...	...	...	...	...	...	...	...	...
...	...	...	...	...	...	...	...	...	...	...	...	...	...	...	...	...	...	...	...	...	...
4,335	355	...	...	5,822	477	...	...	...	...	12	1	666	75	139	26	...	...	693	11	20	2
4,249	353	...	...	5,589	356	...	...	...	...	12	1	666	75	139	24	...	...	691	11	20	2
4,180	346	...	...	4,705	328	...	...	...	...	10	1	630	57	116	24	...	...	587	4	13	2
2,409	46	...	...	1,018	102	...	...	...	...	3	...	171	43	77	6	...	...	99	1	...	...
1,771	300	...	...	3,687	226	...	...	...	...	7	1	457	14	39	18	...	...	488	3	13	2
...	...	...	...	...	...	...	...	...	...	...	...	2	...	...	...	...	...	...	...	...	...
...	...	...	...	...	...	...	...	...	...	...	...	...	...	...	...	...	...	...	...	...	...
...	...	...	...	...	...	...	...	...	...	...	...	...	..	...	...	..	...	...	...	...	...
69	7	...	...	884	28	...	...	...	...	2	...	36	18	23	...	...	...	104	7	7	...
...	...	...	...	811	20	...	...	...	...	...	...	32	2	15	...	...	...	67	4	...	...
...	...	...	...	...	...	...	...	...	...	...	...	...	...	...	...	...	...	2	...	...	...
62	7	...	...	...	...	...	...	...	...	...	...	4	16	8	...	...	...	24	3	6	...
...	...	...	...	...	...	...	...	...	...	...	...	...	...	...	...	...	...	...	...	...	...
...	...	...	...	1	...	...	...	...	...	...	...	...	...	...	...	...	...	...	...	...	...
7	...	...	...	72	8	...	...	...	...	2	...	...	...	...	...	...	...	11	...	1	...

TABLE XV

Part II—Bilingualism

Area of Bilingualism	Mother tongue	Number of persons speaking mother tongue		Subsidiary									
				Pashto		Lahnda		Kashmiri		Kohistani		Gujuri	
		Males	Females	Males	Females	Males	Females	Males	Females	Males	Females	Males	Females
1	2	3	4	5	6	7	8	9	10	11	12	13	14
Dera Ismail Khan—*concld.*	B- Vernaculars of other Asiatic countries and Africa Total.	857	824	85	8	23	4	1	...	..	..	...	...
	Persian ...	855	823	85	7	23	4	1	...	..		.	...
	Others ...	2	1	...	1	...	...	...	...	...	..	...	...
	C- European Languages Total	205	13[illegible]	34	7	6	5	...	...	...		..	..
	English ...	201	135	34	7	6	5	...	...	...		..	...
	Others ...	4	1	...	...	...	...	...	...	...	...	..	...
Trans-Frontier Posts	Total ...	44,635	1,816	1,054	56	5,915	86	...	...	..			...
	A- Indian Vernaculars Total.	40,624	1,663	897	37	5,907	69	...	...	..			...
	A (1)- -Vernaculars of the N. W. F. P. Total.	12,174	1,086	267	34	799	28	...	...		..		...
	Pashto	10,06[illegible]	95[illegible]	...	...	[illegible]05	27	...	...	...	...	...	...
	Lahnda	1,655	128	266	34	...	...	...	...	...	...	...	...
	Kashmiri ...	448	5	1	...	94	1	...	...	...	...	...	...
	Kohistani ...	11	...	...	...	...	...	...	...	...	...	..	...
	Gujur ...	...	...	...	...	...	...	...	...	...	...	...	...
	A (2)- -Other Indian Vernaculars Total.	28,450	577	630	3	5,108	41	...	...	..	...	...	...
	Punjabi ...	18,203	492	222	3	4,094	41	...	...	...	...	...	..
	Hindustani ...	1,132	24	100	...	201	...	...	...	...	...	...	...
	Urdu ...	1,593	31	269	...	360	...	...	...	...	..		...
	Hindi ...	1,711	30	...	...	...	...	...	...	...	...	...	...
	Naipali (Gorkhali) ...	4,591	...	5	...	108	...	...	...	...	...	...	...
	Others ...	1,220	...	34	...	255	...	...	...	...	...	..	...
	B—Vernaculars of other Asiatic Countries and Africa Total.	210	140	110	19	8	17	...	...	...	...	...	..
	Persian ...	210	140	110	19	8	17	...	...	...	...	...	...
	Others ...	...	...	...	...	...	...	...	...	...	...	...	...
	C—European languages Total.	3,801	13	47	...	...	...	...	...	...	...	...	...
	English ...	3,800	13	47	...	...	...	...	...	...	...	...	...
	Others ...	1	...	...	...	...	...	...	...	...	...	...	...

TABLE XV

Part II—Bilingualism

languages

Punjabi		Hindustani		Urdu		Hindi		Naipali		Bengali		Persian		Arabic		Turkish		English		Others	
Males	Females	Males	Females	Males	Females	Males	Females	Males	Females	Males	Females	Males	Females	Males	Females	Males	Females	Males	Females	Males	Females
15	16	17	18	19	20	21	22	23	24	25	26	27	28	29	30	31	32	33	34	35	36
84	1	...	...	55	9	...	...	...	...	...	...	...	...	...	2	...	...	2	...	...	...
84	1	...	...	54	9	...	...	...	...	..	...	...	...	...	2	..	...	2	...	...	...
...	...	...	...	1	...	...	...	...	...	...	...	...	...	...	...	...	...	...	...	...	...
2	1	...	...	178	112	...	...	...	...	...	...	...	...	...	...	...	...	...	...	...	...
2	1	...	...	178	112	...	...	...	...	...	...	...	...	...	...	...	...	...	..	...	...
...	...	...	...	...	...	..	...	...	...	...	...	...	...	...	...	...	...	...	...	...	...
1,760	68	521	...	5,793	53	28	...	...	...	...	...	213	3	15	...	...	...	1,049	10	6	...
1,741	67	521	...	5,095	46	28	...	...	..	...	...	213	3	15	...	...	...	1,045	10	6	...
617	56	...	..	1,708	17	...	..	...	...	...	...	159	3	7	...	...	...	352	3	...	...
323	32	...	...	,283	7	...	...	...	...	...	...	122	3	7	...	...	...	207	2	...	...
283	22	...	...	285	10	...	...	...	...	...	...	35	...	...	...	...	...	144	1	...	...
11	2	...	...	140	...	...	...	...	...	...	...	2	...	...	...	...	...	1	...	...	...
...	...	...	...	...	...	...	...	...	...	...	...	...	...	...	...	...	...	...	...	...	...
...	...	...	...	...	...	...	...	...	...	...	...	...	...	...	...	...	...	...	...	...	...
1,124	11	521	...	3,387	29	28	...	...	...	...	...	54	...	8	...	...	...	693	7	6	...
...	...	521	...	2,830	29	...	...	...	...	...	...	32	...	5	...	...	...	573	2	...	...
14	...	...	...	...	...	...	...	...	...	...	...	10	...	...	...	...	...	29	...	...	...
160	11	...	...	...	...	...	...	...	...	...	...	12	...	2	...	...	...	50	5	...	...
75	...	...	...	171	...	...	...	...	...	...	...	...	...	...	...	...	...	24	...	...	...
82	...	...	...	150	...	...	...	...	...	...	...	...	...	...	...	...	...	4	...	...	...
54	...	...	...	230	...	28	...	...	...	...	...	...	...	1	...	...	...	13	...	6	...
19	1	...	...	16	1	...	...	...	...	...	...	...	...	...	...	...	...	3	...	...	...
19	1	...	...	16	1	...	...	...	...	...	...	...	...	...	...	...	...	3	...	...	...
...	...	...	...	...	...	...	...	...	...	...	...	...	...	...	...	...	...	...	...	...	...
...	...	...	...	682	6	...	...	...	...	...	...	...	...	...	...	...	...	1	...	...	...
...	...	...	...	681	6	...	...	...	...	...	...	...	...	...	...	...	...	...	...	...	...
...	...	...	...	1	...	...	...	...	...	...	...	...	...	...	...	...	...	1	...	...	...

TABLE XVI

Religion

1. The statement below gives details of Christian sects :—

Sects				Persons	Males	Females
Roman Catholics	...	...	...	1,578	1,214	364
Syrians	...	...	...	...	...	...
Others	...	...	...	14,921	11,998	2,923
		Total	...	16,499	13,212	3,287

2. The statement below gives details of those persons who returned religions other than those specified in this table and shows the religions into which they were thrown :—

District or agency	Religion returned	Persons	Males	Females	Religion into which thrown
Hazara	Mehtar ...	52	29	23	Hindus.
Peshawar	Mehtar ...	488	303	185	Do.
Do.	Balmiki ...	233	133	100	Do.
Do.	Poorbi ...	2	1	1	Do.
Do.	Ramdasi ...	90	54	36	Do.
Do.	Untouchable ...		8	1	Do.
Dera Ismail Khan ...	Balmiki ...	164	85	79	Do.
Do.	Sindhi ...	4	3	1	Sikhs.
Do.	Untouchable ...	24	20	4	Hindus.
Bannu and Kohat ...	...	...	...	...	...
Districts ...	...	066	636	430	
Malakand	Mehtar ...	3	3	...	Hindus.
Khyber	Mehtar and Balmiki...	86	86	...	Do.
Kurram	...	...	...	...	...
North Waziristan ...	Mehtar ...	4	4	...	Hindus.
South Waziristan ...	Mehtar and Balmiki ...	74	74	...	Do.
Tribal Area Dera Ismail Khan ...	Mehtar and Untouchable ...	16	16	...	Do
Agencies and Tribal Area ...	...	183	183	...	
Grand total ...	...	1,249	819	430	

TABLE XVI

Religion

District or Agency	Population: Persons	Population: Males	Population: Females	Muslims: Persons	Muslims: Males	Muslims: Females	Brahmanic: Persons	Brahmanic: Males	Brahmanic: Females
1	2	3	4	5	6	7	8	9	10
N. W. F. Province (Districts and Trans-Frontier posts).	2,471,527	1,360,453	1,111,074	2,250,389	1,218,234	1,032,155	148,839	93,667	55,172
Districts ...	2,425,076	1,315,818	1,109,258	2,227,303	1,196,120	1,031,183	135,198	80,481	54,717
Hazara ...	670,117	358,193	311,924	636,794	338,082	298,712	24,543	15,056	9,487
Peshawar ...	974,321	538,146	436,175	898,683	489,650	409,033	41,334	25,841	15,493
Kohat ...	236,273	126,210	110,063	218,445	114,487	103,958	12,861	8,199	4,662
Bannu ...	270,301	145,163	125,138	237,674	126,671	111,003	25,611	14,163	11,448
Dera Ismail Khan ...	274,064	148,106	125,958	235,707	127,230	108,477	30,849	17,222	13,627
Agencies and Tribal Areas (population of posts only).	46,451	44,635	1,816	23,086	22,114	972	13,641	13,186	455
Agencies									
Malakand (Dir, Swat and Chitral).	3,390	2,928	462	1,672	1,436	236	1,254	1,113	141
Khyber ...	16,516	16,452	64	5,223	5,193	30	6,004	5,995	9
Kurram ...	4,832	3,682	1,150	3,627	3,016	611	605	336	269
North Waziristan ...	13,282	13,154	128	6,707	6,622	85	4,418	4, 54	34
South Waziristan	6,713	6,711	2	4,282	4,282	...	,239	1 237	2
Tribal area under the Political control of the Deputy Commissioner of Dera Ismail Khan.	1,718	1,708	10	1,575	1,565	10	121	121	...

		Persons
Parsis	...	1
† Includes Parsis	...	59
Jews	...	11
Buddhists	...	2
‡ Includes Parsis	...	2
Buddhists	...	1

TABLE XVI

Religion

Hindus						Sikhs			Christians			Others		
Aryas			Total Hindus											
Persons	Males	Females	Persons	Males	Females	Persons	Males	Females	Persons	Males	Females	Persons	Males	Females
11	12	13	14	15	16	17	18	19	20	21	22	23	24	25
7,789	3,885	3,904	156,628	97,552	59,076	47,935	31,409	16,526	16,499	13,212	3,287	76	46	30
7,779	3,877	3,902	142,977	84,358	58,619	42,510	26,284	16,226	12,213	9,013	3,200	73	43	30
717	405	312	25,260	15,461	9,799	7,630	4,393	3,237	432	256	176	* 1	1	...
987	660	327	42,321	26,501	15,820	24,271	15,211	9,060	8,974	6,742	2,232	† 72	42	30
532	305	227	13,393	8,504	4,889	3,249	2,292	957	1,186	927	259	...	...	...
570	365	205	26,181	14,528	11,653	5,482	3,278	2,204	964	686	278	...	...	...
4,973	2,142	2,831	35,822	19,364	16,458	1,878	1,110	768	657	402	255	...	...	...
10	8	2	13,651	13,194	457	5,425	5,125	300	4,286	4,199	87	‡ 3	3	...
10	8	2	1,264	1,121	143	324	272	52	130	99	31	...	...	...
...	...	...	6,004	5,995	9	2,883	2,883	...	2,406	2,381	25	...	...	...
...	...	...	605	336	269	492	252	240	108	78	30	...	...	...
...	...	...	4,418	4,384	34	705	697	8	1,451	1,450	1	1	1	...
...	...	...	1,239	1,237	2	1,012	1,012	...	178	178	...	2	2	...
...	...	...	121	121	...	9	9	...	13	13	...	...	...	...

Males	Females
1	...
29	30
11	...
2	...
2	...
1	...

TABLE XVII

Caste, Tribe, Race or Nationality.

1. This table does not include figures for Europeans and Anglo-Indians, details of whom are available in Table XIX.

2. Owing to the necessity for economy, sorting and tabulation were limited to those castes and Pathan tribes, tabulated in 1921, which were distinctly recorded in the schedules. All other and unspecified castes were left unsorted, and are grouped together under the head "Others" at the end of the table.

TABLE XVII

Caste, Tribe, Race or Nationality

Caste and Religion	N. W. F. P.			Districts			Hazara		
	Persons	Males	Females	Persons	Males	Females	Persons	Males	Females
1	2	3	4	5	6	7	8	9	10
All castes (excluding Europeans and Anglo-Indians).	2,459,790	1,350,232	1,109,558	2,417,129	1,309,374	1,107,755	669,869	358,055	311,814
ARAIN (*Muslim*) ...	6,550	3,824	2,726	6,480	3,759	2,721	132	37	95
ARORA	61,402	34,576	26,826	60,283	33,662	26,621	2,372	1,329	1,043
Hindu	54,490	30,327	24,163	53,753	29,765	23,988	2,036	1,141	805
Sikh	6,912	4,249	2,663	6,530	3,897	2,633	336	188	148
AWAN (*Muslim*)	283,171	154,943	128,228	280,995	152,803	128,192	106,931	55,851	51,080
BAGHBAN (*Muslim*) ...	28,433	15,266	13,167	28,422	15,255	13,167	25	8	17
BALUCH (*Muslim*) ...	37,199	19,969	17,230	37,145	19,915	17,230	166	84	82
BHATIA	6,632	3,161	3,471	6,533	3,070	3,463	262	124	138
Hindu	6,047	2,834	[illegible]	5,948	[illegible]	[illegible]	193	[illegible]	103
Sikh	585	327	258	585	327	258	69	34	[illegible]
BHATIARA	5,042	2,952	2,090	4,998	2,908	2,090	18	14	4
Muslim	4,999	2,921	2,078	4,986	[illegible]	2,078	18	14	4
Hindu	42	31	11	11	...	11	...	...	...
Sikh	1	...	1	1	...	1	...	...	..
BRAHMAN	17,200	10,723	6,477	15,379	9,935	6,444	4,999	2,792	2,207
Hindu	15,281	[illegible]	[illegible]	14,508	8,848	5,660	3,306	[illegible]	[illegible]
Sikh	1,919	[illegible]	784	[illegible]	1,087	784	1,663	[illegible]	[illegible]
CHAMAR	2,918	1,749	1,169	2,901	1,732	1,169	120	84	36
Muslim	2,680	1,557	1,123	2,663	1,540	[illegible]	18	[illegible]	36
Hindu	227	184	43	227	18	43	2	2	...
Sikh	11	8	3	11	8	3	...	..	...
CHUHRA	9,285	6,380	2,905	8,444	5,612	2,832	1,189	750	439
Muslim	[illegible]	1,546	810	[illegible]	[illegible]	[illegible]	[illegible]	[illegible]	42
Hindu	5,783	4,082	1,701	5,241	[illegible]	[illegible]	38	28	
Sikh	150	83	67	147	[illegible]	67	2	2	...
Christian	996	669	327	723	[illegible]	265	7	4	3
DARZI	2,193	1,396	797	2,177	1,380	797	846	502	344
Muslim	2,180	1,384	796	2,164	[illegible]	[illegible]	846	502	344
Hindu	12	11	1	12	11	1	...	..	...
Sikh	1	1	...	1	1	...	...	...	...
DHOBI	11,870	6,431	5,439	11,669	6,240	5,429	2,418	1,252	1,166
Muslim	11,202	6,020	5,182	11,113	[illegible]	[illegible]	2,387	1,231	[illegible]
Hindu	667	410	257	555	298	257	30	2	
Sikh	1	1	...	1	1	...	1	1	...
DHUND (*Muslim*) ...	39,487	20,599	18,888	39,322	20,434	18,888	38,983	20,200	783
GAKHAR	7,309	4,200	3,109	7,098	3,990	3,108	6,045	3,181	2,864
Muslim	7,243	4,153	3,090	7,032	[illegible]	[illegible]	[illegible]	[illegible]	[illegible]
Hindu	66	47	19	66	47	1	28	[illegible]	5
GUJAR	121,510	66,223	55,287	121,170	65,889	55,281	98,599	53,598	[illegible]
Muslim	121,367	66,139	55,228	121,027	65,805	55,222	[illegible]	[illegible]	[illegible]
Hindu	132	75	57	132	75	57	...	...	...
Sikh	11	9	2	11		2	..	...	...
GURKHA	7,971	7,040	931	4,565	3,634	931	4,173	3,315	858
Hindu	7,969	7,038	931	4,563	3,632	93[illegible]	[illegible]	[illegible]	858
Sikh	2	2	...	2	2	..	...	...	..
JAT	76,327	44,369	31,958	73,919	41,969	31,950	353	313	40
Muslim	71,111	39,401	[illegible]	[illegible]	[illegible]	31,703	58	27	31
Hindu	1,562	1,466	[illegible]	906	[illegible]	96	[illegible]	9	4
Sikh	3,654	3,502	152	2,226	[illegible]	151	282	277	5

TABLE XVII

Caste, Tribe, Race or Nationality

Peshawar			Kohat			Bannu			Dera Ismail Khan			Trans-Frontier Posts		
Persons	Males	Females	Persons	Males	Females	Persons	Males	Females	Persons	Males	Females	Persons	Males	Females
11	12	13	14	15	16	17	18	19	20	21	22	23	24	25
968,326	533,153	435,173	235,436	125,524	109,912	269,775	144,740	125,035	273,723	147,902	125,821	42,661	40,858	1,803
360	86	274	38	28	10	1,468	776	692	4,482	2,832	1,650	70	65	5
9,182	5,212	3,970	6,108	2,981	3,127	17,610	10,999	6,611	25,011	13,141	11,870	1,119	914	205
6,231	3,583	2,648	5,971	2,892	3,079	14,964	9,288	5,676	24,551	12,861	11,690	737	562	175
2,951	1,629	1,322	137	89	48	2,646	1,711	935	460	280	180	382	352	30
134,237	75,433	58,804	19,891	10,543	9,348	13,972	7,556	6,416	5,964	3,420	2,544	2,176	2,140	36
26,531	14,256	12,275	442	228	214	1,414	753	661	10	10	...	11	11	...
326	196	130	237	152	85	797	557	240	35,619	18,926	16,693	54	54	...
396	229	167	14	14	...	3,202	1,390	1,812	2,659	1,313	1,346	99	91	8
117	74	43	8	8	...	2,974	1,261	1,713	2,656	1,310	1,346	99	91	8
279	155	124	6	6	...	228	129	99	3	3	...	...	...	...
3,928	2,339	1,589	480	250	230	467	242	225	105	63	42	44	44	...
3,916	2,339	1,577	480	250	230	467	242	225	105	63	42	13	13	...
11	...	11	...	...	...	...	...	...	...	...	...	31	31	...
1	...	1	...	...	...	...	...	...	...	...	...	...	...	...
7,474	4,755	2,719	836	528	308	1,111	727	384	1,959	1,133	826	821	788	33
7,330	4,630	2,700	827	520	307	1,094	714	380	1,951	1,125	826	773	740	33
144	125	19	9	8	1	17	13	4	8	8	...	48	48	...
1,335	745	590	224	127	97	866	563	303	356	213	143	17	17	...
1,105	561	544	218	121	97	866	563	303	356	213	143	17	17	...
219	176	43	6	6	...	...	...	...	...	...	...	...	...	...
11	8	3	...	...	...	...	...	...	...	...	...	...	...	...
5,284	3,423	1,861	515	320	195	826	582	244	630	537	93	841	768	73
547	281	266	31	25	6	318	210	108	295	291	4	23	23	...
4,208	2,812	1,396	415	263	152	410	301	109	170	147	23	542	531	11
59	30	29	69	32	37	15	14	1	2	2	...	3	3	...
470	300	170	...	...	...	83	57	26	163	97	66	273	211	62
1,198	821	377	112	53	59	6	4	2	15	...	15	16	16	...
1,185	809	376	112	53	59	6	4	2	15	...	15	16	16	...
12	11	1	...	...	...	...	...	...	...	...	...	...	...	...
1	1	...	...	...	...	...	...	...	...	...	...	...	...	...
8,046	4,303	3,743	952	523	429	103	65	38	150	97	53	201	191	10
7,611	4,087	3,524	878	473	405	94	60	34	143	90	53	89	79	10
435	216	219	74	50	24	9	5	4	7	7	...	112	112	...
...	...	...	...	...	...	...	...	...	...	...	...	...	...	...
263	169	94	50	42	8	26	23	3	...	...	...	165	165	...
571	389	182	259	213	46	154	151	3	69	56	13	211	210	1
558	376	182	259	213	46	153	151	2	45	45	...	211	210	1
13	13	...	...	...	...	1	...	1	24	11	13	...	...	...
22,099	11,950	10,149	284	204	80	52	37	15	136	100	36	340	334	6
21,967	11,875	10,092	277	199	78	50	35	15	134	98	36	340	334	6
121	66	55	7	5	2	2	2	...	2	2	...	...	...	...
11	9	2	...	...	...	...	...	...	...	...	...	...	...	...
296	237	59	35	28	7	43	43	...	18	11	7	3,406	3,406	...
296	237	59	35	28	7	42	42	...	17	10	7	3,406	3,406	...
...	...	...	...	...	...	1	1	...	1	1	...	...	...	...
2,463	2,189	274	719	638	81	7,060	3,939	3,121	63,324	34,890	28,434	2,408	2,400	8
740	612	128	87	77	10	6,625	3,525	3,100	63,277	34,843	28,434	324	317	7
622	564	58	238	205	33	20	19	1	13	13	...	656	656	...
1,101	1,013	88	394	356	38	415	395	20	34	34	...	1,428	1,427	1

TABLE XVII

Caste, Tribe, Race or Nationality

Caste and Religion	N. W. F. P.			Districts			Hazara		
	Persons	Males	Females	Persons	Males	Females	Persons	Males	Females
1	2	3	4	5	6	7	8	9	10
JHINWAR	1,142	751	391	1,108	717	391	773	440	333
Muslim	778	435	343	778	435	343	758	426	332
Hindu	307	267	40	285	245	40	10	9	1
Sikh	57	49	8	35	27	8	5	5	...
JOLAHA ...	40,099	21,413	18,686	40,055	21,370	18,675	13,564	7,13[illegible]	6,428
Muslim	40,030	21,382	18,648	39,986	21,339	18,647	13,564	7,13[illegible]	6,428
Hindu	69	31	38	69	31	38	...	...	...
KARAL (*Muslim*) ...	27,202	14,542	12,660	27,185	14,525	12,660	27,117	14,470	12,647
KASHMIRI	21,912	11,974	9,938	21,704	11,776	9,928	13,218	7,031	6,[illegible]87
Muslim	21,902	11,972	9,930	21,694	11,774	9,920	13,218	7,031	6,187
Hindu	2	1	1	2	1	1	...	...	...
Sikh	8	1	7	8	1	7	...	...	...
KHATRI	35,046	19,947	15,099	33,804	18,842	14,962	9,376	5,253	4,123
Hindu	32,791	18,590	14,201	31,759	17,683	14,076	8,8[illegible]	4,16[illegible]	3,[illegible]
Sikh	2,255	1,357	898	2,045	1,159	886	486	28[illegible]	197
KHOJA (*Muslim*) ...	5,031	2,841	2,190	4,986	2,798	2,188	934	478	456
KUMHAR	23,202	12,307	10,895	23,109	12,214	10,895	5,060	2,739	2,321
Muslim	22,924	12,102	10,822	22,901	12,079	10,822	5,04[illegible]	2,7[illegible]	[illegible]
Hindu	261	195	66	191	125	66	13	3	
Sikh	17	10	7	17	10	7	6	5	1
LOHAR	29,093	15,470	13,623	28,968	15,351	13,617	9,600	5,110	4,490
Muslim	29,043	15,425	13,618	28,918	15,306	13,612	9,593	5,[illegible]03	4,4[illegible]
Hindu	45	40	5	45	40	5	7	7	...
Sikh	5	5	...	5	5	...	...	...	...
MACHHI	4,143	2,405	1,738	4,130	2,392	1,738	...	...	...
Muslim	4,137	2,401	1,736	4,124	2,388	1,736	...	...	...
Hindu	6	4	2	6	4	2	...	...	...
MALIAR (*Muslim*) ...	6,652	3,819	2,833	6,622	3,789	2,833	5,204	2,929	2,275
MALLAH (*Muslim*) ...	6,578	4,008	2,570	6,578	4,008	2,570	250	122	128
MIRASI (with DUM) ...	10,896	5,861	5,035	10,869	5,834	5,035	1,799	982	817
Muslim	10,892	5,861	5,031	10,865	5,834	5,031	1,7[illegible]9	[illegible]82	81[illegible]
Hindu	4	...	4	4	...	4	...	...	...
MISHWANI (*Muslim*) ...	6,085	3,175	2,910	6,084	3,175	2,909	5,361	2,804	2,557
MOCHI	26,759	14,244	12,515	26,628	14,113	12,515	9,086	4,774	4,312
Muslim	26,604	14,130	12,474	26,473	13,999	12,474	9,082	4,771	4,311
Hindu	155	114	41	155	114	41	4	3	1
MOGHAL (*Muslim*) ...	16,597	9,550	7,047	16,047	9,024	7,023	11,843	6,475	5,368
NAI	27,242	14,690	12,552	27,178	14,631	12,547	7,176	3,640	3,536
Muslim	2[illegible],091	14,556	12,535	27,027	14,497	12,530	7,173	3,637	3,536
Hindu	129	118	11	129	118	11	3	3	...
Sikh	22	16	6	22	16	6	...	...	...
PARACHA with BANJARA (*Muslim*) ...	8,279	4,293	3,986	8,259	4,280	3,979	185	109	76
PATHAN (*Muslim*) ...	916,630	491,585	425,045	905,122	480,667	424,455	54,544	29,840	24,704
Afridi	11,417	6,757	4,660	10,759	6,101	4,658	57	55	[illegible]
Bangash	35,387	19,020	16,36[illegible]	34,738	18,374	16,364	1[illegible]9	106	3
Bannuchi	43,064	22,986	20,078	43,007	22,938	20,0[illegible]	8	8	...
Bhittani	9,539	4,654	4,885	9,429	4,544	4,885	7	[illegible]	...
Daudzai	343	202	141	328	192	136	...	...	...
Dilazak	4,784	2,347	2,437	4,765	2,328	2,437	906	679	227
Durrani	4,515	2,228	2,287	4,496	2,209	2,287	81	38	43
Gadun (Jadun) ...	22,372	11,476	10,896	22,372	11,476	10,896	19,070	9,[illegible]52	9,318
Gandapur	8,162	4,292	3,870	8,148	4,278	3,870	...	...	...
Ghilzai	3,391	2,191	1,200	3,311	2,111	1,200	10	9	1

TABLE XVII

Caste, Tribe, Race or Nationality

Peshawar			Kohat			Bannu			Dera Ismail Khan			Trans-Frontier Posts		
Persons	Males	Females	Persons	Males	Females	Persons	Males	Females	Persons	Males	Females	Persons	Males	Females
11	12	13	14	15	16	17	18	19	20	21	22	23	24	25
263	215	48	58	48	10	14	14	...	...	...	...	34	34	...
9	6	3	11	3	8	...	...	...	...	...	...	...	...	...
227	189	38	34	33	1	14	14	...	...	...	...	22	22	...
27	20	7	13	12	1	...	...	...	...	...	...	12	12	...
18,625	9,505	9,120	4,944	2,911	2,033	2,074	1,334	740	848	484	364	44	43	1
18,606	9,494	9,112	4,931	2,898	2,033	2,069	1,329	740	816	482	334	44	43	1
19	11	8	13	13	...	5	5	...	32	2	30	...	...	...
31	28	3	27	23	4	10	4	6	...	...	...	17	17	...
8,056	4,442	3,614	232	126	106	79	63	16	119	114	5	208	198	10
8,048	4,442	3,606	231	125	106	78	62	16	119	114	5	208	198	10
1	...	1	...	...	...	1	1	...	...	...	...	...	...	...
7	...	7	1	1	...	...	...	...	...	...	...	...	...	...
14,516	8,384	6,132	1,209	752	457	5,039	2,198	2,841	3,664	2,255	1,409	1,242	1,105	137
13,285	7,732	5,553	1,101	686	415	4,856	2,073	2,783	3,627	2,228	1,399	1,032	907	125
1,231	652	579	108	66	42	183	125	58	37	27	10	210	198	12
2,812	1,525	1,287	5	4	1	59	41	18	1,176	750	426	45	43	2
9,832	5,104	4,728	1,749	941	808	2,993	1,551	1,442	3,475	1,879	1,596	93	93	...
9,821	5,096	4,725	1,708	900	808	2,899	1,498	1,401	3,432	1,854	1,578	23	23	...
11	8	3	41	41	...	83	48	35	43	25	18	70	70	...
...	...	...	...	...	...	11	5	6	...	...	...	...	...	...
10,283	5,569	4,714	1,978	1,001	977	4,840	2,557	2,283	2,267	1,114	1,153	125	119	6
10,248	5,539	4,709	1,971	994	977	4,839	2,556	2,283	2,267	1,114	1,153	125	119	6
31	26	5	7	7	...	...	...	...	...	...	...	...	...	...
4	4	...	...	...	...	1	1	...	...	...	...	...	...	...
52	47	5	19	16	3	291	275	16	3,768	2,054	1,714	13	13	...
46	43	3	19	16	3	291	275	16	3,768	2,054	1,714	13	13	...
6	4	2	...	...	...	...	...	...	...	...	...	...	...	...
764	489	275	608	325	283	5	5	...	41	41	...	30	30	...
3,330	2,081	1,249	59	49	10	...	...	...	2,939	1,756	1,183	...	...	...
4,527	2,426	2,101	319	165	154	2,660	1,414	1,246	1,564	847	717	27	27	...
4,526	2,426	2,100	316	165	151	2,660	1,414	1,246	1,564	847	717	27	27	...
1	...	1	3	...	3	...	...	...	...	...	...	...	...	...
695	343	352	28	28	...	...	...	...	...	...	...	1	...	1
8,732	4,497	4,235	1,912	1,021	891	1,852	914	938	5,046	2,907	2,139	131	131	...
8,672	4,464	4,208	1,866	977	889	1,807	880	927	5,046	2,907	2,139	131	131	...
60	33	27	46	44	2	45	34	11	...	...	...	...	...	...
3,461	2,033	1,428	378	263	115	130	88	42	235	165	70	550	526	24
11,203	6,217	4,986	3,942	2,051	1,891	2,178	1,223	955	2,679	1,500	1,179	64	59	5
11,109	6,137	4,972	3,918	2,030	1,888	2,160	1,205	955	2,667	1,488	1,179	64	59	5
82	71	11	16	16	...	16	16	...	12	12	...	...	...	...
12	9	3	8	5	3	2	2	...	...	...	...	...	...	...
4,776	2,463	2,313	2,208	1,129	1,079	1,058	553	505	32	26	6	20	13	7
473,738	252,558	221,180	148,098	76,583	71,515	159,737	84,642	75,095	69,005	37,044	31,961	11,508	10,918	590
5,024	2,852	2,172	5,269	2,815	2,454	115	90	25	294	289	5	658	656	2
214	199	15	34,248	17,994	16,254	19	17	2	58	58	...	649	646	3
9	1	8	78	38	40	42,825	22,852	19,973	87	39	48	57	48	9
75	47	28	...	...	...	2 547	1,333	1,214	6,800	3,157	3,643	110	110	...
323	187	136	5	5	...	...	...	...	...	...	...	15	10	5
3,859	1,649	2,210	...	...	...	...	...	...	...	...	...	19	19	...
4,298	2,087	2,211	53	28	25	9	6	3	55	50	5	19	19	...
3,283	1,715	1,568	2	2	...	7	7	...	10	...	10	...	...	...
5	...	5	...	...	...	31	18	13	8,112	4,260	3,852	14	14	...
1,855	1,218	637	1,191	717	474	27	21	6	228	146	82	80	80	...

TABLE VII

Caste, Tribe, Race or Nationality

Caste and Religion	N. W. F. P.			Districts			Hazara		
	Persons	Males	Females	Persons	Males	Females	Persons	Males	Females
1	2	3	4	5	6	7	8	9	10
Gigiani	10,372	3,853	6,519	10,367	3,848	6,519	...	...	...
Khalil	8,392	3,728	4,664	8,377	3,714	4,663	...	...	...
Khattak	160,379	81,422	78,957	158,253	79,307	78,946	140	94	46
Marwat	82,593	43,199	39,394	82,527	43,137	39,390	1	...	1
Mohammadzai ...	33,460	17,477	15,983	33,371	17,388	15,983	8	5	3
Mohmand	63,508	32,077	31,431	63,139	31,710	31,429	33	13	20
Orakzai	9,623	5,308	4,315	9,093	4,778	4,315	1	1	...
Tarin	1,208	812	396	1,208	812	396	935	659	276
Turi	1,802	1,786	16	68	59	9	...	...	...
Ustrana	2,633	1,447	1,186	2,633	1,447	1,186	...	...	...
Utman Khel ...	9,260	5,145	4,115	9,191	5,076	4,115	585	303	282
Wazir	32,822	17,365	15,457	32,659	17,202	15,457	...	...	...
Yusafzai	134,067	72,691	61,376	133,737	72,368	61,369	321	189	132
Zadran	319	184	135	319	184	135	...	...	...
Other Pathan ...	223,218	128,938	94,280	218,827	125,086	93,741	32,182	17,922	14,260
PENJARA (*Muslim*) ...	2,573	1,974	599	2,573	1,974	599	49	42	17
QASSAB	11,549	5,960	5,589	11,534	5,945	5,589	284	153	131
Muslim	11,539	5,956	5,583	11,524	5,941	5,583	284	153	131
Hindu	10	4	6	10	4	6	...	...	...
Sikh	..	...	...	...	...	...	...	...	...
QURESHI (*Muslim*) ...	27,489	14,871	12,618	27,211	14,619	12,592	6,415	3,430	2,985
RAJPUT	18,557	13,652	4,905	14,681	9,798	4,883	5,882	3,273	2,609
Muslim	11,506	7,946	3,560	9,435	5,892	3,543	5,016	2,661	2,355
Hindu	6,457	5,281	1,176	4,754	3,583	1,171	689	525	164
Sikh	594	425	169	492	323	169	177	87	90
RANGREZ	5,708	2,950	2,758	5,703	2,945	2,758	30	23	7
Muslim	5,705	2,947	2,758	5,700	2,942	2,758	27	20	7
Sikh	3	3	...	3	3	...	3	3	...
SARARA (*Muslim*) ...	9,984	5,249	4,735	9,984	5,249	4,735	9,984	5,249	4,735
SAYAD (*Muslim*) ...	82,312	42,834	39,478	81,972	42,509	39,463	27,629	14,363	13,266
SHEIKH (*Muslim*) ...	13,572	7,813	5,759	13,046	7,321	5,725	2,455	1,218	1,237
SONAR	9,558	5,272	4,286	9,532	5,246	4,286	458	277	181
Muslim	8,379	4,564	3,815	8,368	4,553	3,815	383	223	160
Hindu	1,030	612	418	1,015	597	418	44	26	18
Sikh	149	96	53	149	96	53	31	28	3
SWATHI (*Muslim*) ...	46,560	25,410	21,150	46,556	25,407	21,149	44,511	24,236	20,275
TANAOLI (*Muslim*) ...	86,075	45,414	40,661	86,003	45,342	40,661	83,417	43,953	39,464
TARKHAN	45,163	24,306	20,857	45,088	24,231	20,857	10,203	5,461	4,742
Muslim	45,113	24,263	20,850	45,038	24,188	20,850	10,201	5,459	4,742
Hindu	25	23	2	25	23	2	2	2	...
Sikh	25	20	5	25	20	5	...	...	...
TELI	7,179	3,846	3,333	7,174	3,841	3,333	2,811	1,498	1,313
Muslim	7,175	3,842	3,333	7,170	3,837	3,333	2,811	1,498	1,313
Hindu	4	4	...	4	4	...	...	...	...
Sikh	...	...	...	..	...	...	...	...	...
TURK (*Muslim*) ...	5,285	3,044	2,241	5,277	3,036	2,241	4,486	2,297	2,189
OTHERS	151,139	90,961	60,178	139,859	80,218	59,641	28,534	14,826	13,708
Muslim	92,689	52,308	40,381	89,328	49,115	40,213	18,038	8,738	9,300
Hindu	23,055	16,175	6,880	18,602	11,822	6,780	5,779	3,432	2,347
Sikh	31,533	20,110	11,443	28,313	17,127	11,186	4,539	2,541	1,998
Christian	3,766	2,322	1,444	3,543	2,111	1,432	177	114	63
Parsi	63	33	30	61	31	30	1	1	...
Buddhist	2	2	...	1	1	...	...	...	...
Jew	11	11	...	11	11	...	...	...	...

TABLE XVII

Caste, Tribe, Race or Nationality

Peshawar			Kohat			Bannu			Dera Ismail Khan			Trans-Frontier Posts		
Persons	Males	Females	Persons	Males	Females	Persons	Males	Females	Persons	Males	Females	Persons	Males	Females
11	12	13	14	15	16	17	18	19	20	21	22	23	24	25
10,274	3,756	6,518	9	8	1	...	...	...	84	84	...	5	5	...
8,222	3.576	4,646	13	11	2	43	43	...	99	84	15	15	14	1
64,907	31,774	33,133	86,543	43,495	43,048	6,392	3,680	2,712	271	264	7	2,126	2,115	11
...	...	...	15	7	8	68,458	35,364	33,094	14,053	7,766	6,287	66	62	4
33,275	17,335	15,940	68	37	31	...	...	...	20	11	9	89	89	...
62,727	31,428	31,299	265	195	70	86	46	40	28	28	...	369	367	2
789	568	221	8,252	4,158	4,094	3	3	...	48	48	...	530	530	...
209	109	100	3	...	3	2	2	...	59	42	17	...	...	...
64	55	9	3	3	...	...	...	...	1	1	...	1,734	1,727	7
...	...	...	...	...	...	6	6	...	2,627	1,441	1,186	...	...	...
8,593	4,764	3,829	9	5	4	4	4	...	...	...	...	69	69	...
44	40	4	873	567	306	30,892	16,034	14,858	850	561	289	163	163	...
132,760	71,665	61,095	411	323	88	191	146	45	54	45	9	330	323	7
24	21	3	25	17	8	269	145	124	1	1	...	...	...	...
132,905	77,512	55,393	10,763	6,158	4,605	7,811	4,825	2,986	35,166	18,669	16,497	4,391	3,852	539
2,066	1,575	491	266	242	24	87	42	45	105	83	22	...	...	...
6,766	3,452	3,314	2,007	1,089	918	1,124	603	521	1,353	648	705	15	15	...
6,756	3,448	3,308	2,007	1,089	918	1,124	603	521	1,353	648	705	15	15	...
10	4	6	...	...	...	...	...	...	...	...	...	...	...	...
...	...	...	...	...	...	...	...	...	...	...	...	...	...	...
6,035	3,423	2,612	5,080	2,703	2,377	7,958	4,170	3,788	1,723	893	830	278	252	26
4,893	3,736	1,157	1,592	1,355	237	1 546	846	700	768	588	180	3.876	3,854	22
2,663	1,797	866	919	746	173	454	377	77	383	311	72	2,071	2,054	17
2,023	1,772	251	660	600	60	1,080	461	619	302	225	77	1,703	1698	5
207	167	40	13	9	4	12	8	4	83	52	31	102	102	...
330	204	126	178	103	75	2,957	1,497	1,460	2,208	1,118	1,090	5	5	...
330	204	126	178	103	75	2,957	1,497	1,460	2,208	1,118	1,090	5	5	...
...	...	...	...	...	...	...	...	...	...	...	...	...	...	...
...	...	...	...	...	...	...	...	...	...	...	...	...	...	...
25,373	13,700	11,673	10,816	5,484	5,332	11,808	6,040	5,768	6,346	2,922	3,424	340	325	15
6,176	3,519	2,657	1,162	664	498	407	281	126	2,846	1,639	1,207	526	492	34
4,191	2,318	1,873	1,094	623	471	2,541	1,368	1,173	1,248	660	588	26	26	...
3 996	2,190	1,806	904	508	396	2,277	1,213	1,064	808	419	389	11	11	...
181	120	61	171	108	63	246	144	102	373	199	174	15	15	...
14	8	6	19	7	12	18	11	7	67	42	25	...	...	...
1,951	1,095	856	46	28	18	1	1	...	47	47	...	4	3	1
2,486	1,325	1,161	41	37	4	12	...	12	47	27	20	72	72	...
17,101	9,384	7,717	6,843	3,672	3,171	5,611	2,923	2,688	5,330	2,791	2,539	75	75	...
17,067	9,353	7,714	6,835	3,666	3,169	5,605	2,919	2,686	5,330	2,791	2,539	75	75	...
15	15	...	4	4	...	4	2	2	...	...	...	...	...	...
19	16	3	4	2	2	2	2	...	...	...	...	...	...	...
3,966	2,100	1,866	157	101	56	38	20	18	202	122	80	5	5	...
3.965	2,099	1,866	156	100	56	36	18	18	202	122	80	5	5	...
1	1	...	1	1	...	2	2	...	...	...	...	...	...	...
...	...	...	...	...	...	...	...	...	...	...	...	...	...	...
758	715	43	6	6	...	1	...	1	26	18	8	8	8	...
86,549	51,949	34,600	7,179	5,109	2,070	3,488	1,666	1,822	14,109	6,668	7,441	11,280	10,743	537
59,023	34,960	24,063	647	195	452	889	503	386	10,731	4,719	6,012	3,361	3.193	168
6,753	4,133	2,620	3,715	2,974	741	313	96	217	2,042	1,187	855	4,453	4,353	100
18,192	11,365	6,827	2,468	1,699	769	1,931	861	1,070	1,183	661	522	3,240	2,983	257
2,509	1,449	1,060	349	241	108	355	206	149	153	101	52	223	211	12
60	30	30	...	...	...	...	...	...	...	...	...	2	2	...
1	1	...	...	...	...	...	...	...	...	...	...	1	1	...
11	11	...	...	...	...	...	...	...	...	...	...	...	...	...

TABLE XIX

European and Allied Races and Anglo-Indians by Race and Age.

This table is divided into two parts. Part A., shows the distribution by Race and Age for the five settled Districts and Trans-Frontier Posts. Part B., gives details for Peshawar City (Municipality).

TABLE XIX

European and Allied Races and Anglo-Indians by Race and Age

(a) European and Allied Races (Including Armenians)

Province, State or Agency	Total			(a) British Subjects											
				All ages			0—13		14—16		17—23		24—33	
	Persons	Males	Females	Persons	Males	Females	Males	Females	Males	Females	Males	Females	Males	Females
1	2	3	4	5	6	7	8	9	10	11	12	13	14	15
A.—N. W. F. P. ...	11,737	10,221	1,516	11,543	10,116	1,427	464	433	37	30	3,518	123	4,896	432
Districts ...	7,947	6,444	1,503	7,764	6,344	1,420	463	432	28	30	2,039	122	2,929	428
Hazara ...	248	138	110	247	137	110	39	30	1	3	15	5	36	32
Peshawar ...	5,995	4,993	1,002	5,848	4,911	937	(a) 330	(b) 304	19	18	1,717	80	2,273	289
Kohat ...	837	686	151	815	673	142	25	36	5	3	173	13	353	45
Bannu ...	526	423	103	520	420	100	33	24	2	2	110	7	191	27
Dera Ismail Khan ...	341	204	137	334	203	131	36	38	1	4	24	17	76	35
Trans-Frontier Posts...	3,790	3,777	13	3,779	3,772	7	1	1	9	...	1,479	1	1,967	4
B—Peshawar City (Municipality).	9	6	3	8	5	3	(a) 3	(b) 3	...	...	...	...	1	...

(a) Includes 3 Armenians. | (b) Includes 3 Armenians.

(b) Anglo-Indians

Province, State or Agency	All ages			0—3		4—6		7—13		14—16	
	Persons	Males	Females	Males	Females	Males	Females	Males	Females	Males	Females
1	39	40	41	42	43	44	45	46	47	48	49
A.—N. W. F. P.	161	97	64	6	9	7	4	12	11	6	4
Districts	150	92	58	6	7	5	4	10	9	6	4
Hazara	1	1	...	...	...	...	...	...	...	...	...
Peshawar	129	75	54	6	7	5	4	10	8	5	4
Kohat	16	13	3	...	...	...	...	...	1	1	...
Bannu	4	3	1	...	...	...	...	...	...	...	...
Dera Ismail Khan	...	...	...	...	...	...	...	...	...	...	...
Trans-Frontier-Posts ...	11	5	6	...	2	2	...	2	2	...	...
B.—Peshawar City (Municipality) ...	...	...	...	...	...	...	...	...	...	...	...

TABLE XIX

European and Allied Races and Anglo-Indians by Race and Age

(*a*) European and Allied Races (Including Armenians)

(*a*) British Subjects						(*b*) Others																
34—43		44—53		54 & over		All ages			0—13		14—16		17—23		24—33		34—43		44—53		54 & over	
Males	Females	Males	Females	Males	Females	Persons	Males	Females	Males	Females	Males	Females	Males	Females	Males	Females	Males	Females	Males	Females	Males	Females
16	17	18	19	20	21	22	23	24	25	26	27	28	29	30	31	32	33	34	35	36	37	38
916	293	254	85	31	31	33	8	25	1	1	...	...	...	2	3	10	3	7	...	5	1	...
659	293	197	84	29	31	33	8	25	1	1	...	...	...	2	3	10	3	7	...	5	1	...
35	23	9	9	2	8	...	...	...	...	...	...	...	...	...	...	...	...	...	...	...	...	...
434	(*c*) 180	115	52	23	14	18	7	11	1	...	...	...	...	1	2	4	(*d*) 3	3	...	3	1	...
86	30	30	9	1	6	6	...	6	...	...	...	...	...	1	...	2	...	2	...	1	...	...
63	31	21	9	...	...	2	...	2	...	...	...	...	...	...	...	...	...	2	...	...	...	...
41	29	22	5	3	3	7	1	6	...	1	...	...	...	...	1	4	...	...	...	1	...	...
257	...	57	1	2	...	...	...	...	...	...	...	...	...	...	...	...	...	...	...	...	...	...
...	...	...	...	1	...	1	1	...	...	...	...	...	...	...	...	...	(*d*) 1	...	...	...	...	...

(*c*) Includes 1 Armenian. | (*d*) Includes 1 Armenian.

(*b*) Anglo Indians

17—19		20—29		30—39		40—49		50—59		60—69		70 & over	
Males	Females	Males	Females	Males	Females	Males	Females	Males	Females	Males	Females	Males	Females
50	51	52	53	54	55	56	57	58	59	60	61	62	63
7	7	18	14	23	8	12	4	5	2	1	...	...	1
7	7	18	14	22	7	12	4	5	2	1	...	...	...
...	...	...	...	1	...	...	...	...	...	...	...	...	...
3	7	14	12	17	6	9	4	5	2	1	...	...	...
4	...	4	1	4	1	...	...	...	...	...	...	...	...
...	...	...	1	...	...	3	...	...	...	...	...	...	..
...	...	...	...	...	...	...	...	...	...	...	...	...	...
...	...	...	...	1	1	...	...	...	...	...	...	...	1
...	...	...	...	...	...	...	...	...	...	...	...	...	...

TABLE XX

Summary figures for districts

This table contains a summary of the detailed statistics given in Table I, II, XVI and Provincial Table I.

TABLE XX

Summary figures for districts

Serial No.	District	Area in square miles	Population 1931: Persons	Population 1931: Males	Population 1931: Females	Population 1921	Percentage of variation: 1921—31	Percentage of variation: 1911—21	Number of persons per square mile in 1931	Number of persons per square mile in 1921	Muslim: Males	Muslim: Females	Hindu: Males	Hindu: Females	Sikh: Males	Sikh: Females	Christian: Males	Christian: Females	Others: Males	Others: Females
1	2	3	4	5	6	7	8	9	10	11	12	13	14	15	16	17	18	19	20	21
	North West Frontier Province (districts)...	13,518	2,425,076	1,315,818	1,109,258	2,2[illegible]1,340	+ 7·7	+ 2·5	179	1[illegible]7	1,195,120	1,031,183	84,3[illegible]8	58,[illegible]19	26,284	16,226	9,013	3,200	43	30
1	Hazara ...	3,009	670,117	358,1[illegible]3	311,924	622,349	+ 7·7	+ 3·2	223	208	338,082	298,712	15,461	9,799	4,393	3,237	256	176	1	...
2	Peshawar ...	2,637	974,321	538,145	[illegible]36,175	[illegible]07,[illegible]67	+ [illegible]	+ 4·9	369	348	48[illegible],65[illegible]	409,033	26 501	15,820	15,211	9,060	6,742	2,232	42	30
3	Kohat ...	2,703	236,273	126,21[illegible]	110 063	2[illegible]4,123	+ 10·3	− 3·8	88	[illegible]9	114,487	103,958	8,504	4,889	2,2[illegible]2	957	927	259	...	...
4	Bannu ...	1,698	270,30[illegible]	145,163	125,138	246,734	+ 9·6	−[illegible]3	159	148	126,671	111,003	14,528	11,653	3,278	2,204	686	278	...	...
5	Dera Ismail Khan ...	3,47[illegible]	274,064	148,106	125,958	260,767	+ 5·1	+ 1·8	79	75	127,230	[illegible]8,477	19,364	16 458	1,11[illegible]	768	402	255	...	...

PROVINCIAL TABLE I

Area and Population by Tahsils

The figures of area are those communicated by the Survey of India. Such areas as adjoin tribal boundaries are only approximate.

PROVINCIAL TABLE I

Area and Population of Tahsils

Tahsils	Area in square miles	Number of		Number of occupied houses	Population				Percentage of variation		Number of persons per square mile in 1931
		Towns	Villages		1931			1921 both sexes	1921 to 1931	1911 to 1921	
					Persons	Males	Females				
1	2	3	4	5	6	7	8	9	10	11	12
N. W. F. Province (Districts) ..	13,518	26	2,830	486,876	2,425,075	1,315,818	1,109,258	2,251,340	+7·7	+2·5	179
Hazara District	3,009	6	927	144,233	670,117	358,193	311,924	622,349	+7·7	+3·2	223
Mansehra	1,449	2	242	40,803	208,660	113,205	95,455	200,879	+3·8	+2·1	144
Abbottabad	699	3	355	53,972	253,779	135,878	117,901	232,034	+9·4	+5·0	363
Haripur	651	1	302	41,230	169,735	88,724	81,011	161,981	+4·8	+2·7	261
Amb	174	...	16	6,693	31,299	16,718	14,581	21,754	+43·9	+7·6	180
Phulra	36	...	12	1,535	6,644	3,668	2,976	5,701	+16·5	−22·4	185
Peshawar District ...	2,637	11	846	190,174	974,321	538,146	436,175	907,367	+7·4	+4·9	369
Peshawar	455	2	253	53,457	278,947	160,675	118,272	263,228	+5·9	+·6	613
Charsadda	383	3	189	29,938	177,860	96,850	81,010	164,438	+8·2	+3·4	464
Mardan	623	2	162	42,460	198,561	107,159	91,402	171,642	+15·7	+11·9	319
Swabi	471	...	104	33,622	158,411	83,681	74,730	159,242	−0·5	+3·6	336
Nowshera	705	4	138	30,697	160,542	89,781	70,761	148,817	+7·9	+8·5	228
Kohat District	2,703	2	281	44,151	236,273	126,210	110,063	214,123	+10·3	−3·8	87
Kohat	745	2	81	16,243	88,310	49,597	38,713	77,171	+14·4	+4·1	119
Teri	1,533	...	157	18,762	103,011	51,990	51,021	92,237	+11·7	−11·7	67
Hangu	425	...	43	9,146	44,952	24,623	20,329	44,715	+0·5	+1·5	106
Bannu District	1,698	3	380	49,763	270,301	145,163	125,138	246,734	+9·6	−1·3	159
Bannu	462	2	230	29,928	161,882	88,931	72,951	142,535	+13·6	+0·2	350
Marwat	1,236	1	150	19,835	108,419	56,232	52,187	104,199	+4·1	−3·3	88
Dera Ismail Khan District ...	3,471	4	396	58,555	274,064	148,106	125,958	260,767	+5·1	+1·8	79
Dera Ismail Khan	1,736	2	247	37,090	171,019	91,807	79,212	156,017	+9·6	+1·7	99
Tank	646	1	76	10,426	51,194	29,169	22,025	59,637	−14·2	+25·6	79
Kulachi	1,089	1	73	11,039	51,851	27,130	24,721	45,113	+14·9	−18·3	48

PROVINCIAL TABLE II

Population of Districts and Tahsils by Religion and Literacy

1. The figures in columns 14, 15, 18, 19, 22, 23, 26, 27, 30, 31, 34 and 35 have been taken from the village tables, and show details by tahsils of the entries in Imperial Table XVI. The distribution of persons who returned religions other than those specified in this table is given on the title page of Imperial Table XVI.

2. The depressed classes in columns 10 and 11 comprise Hindu Chuhras and Chamars only.

PROVINCIAL TABLE II

Population of Districts and Tahsils by Religion and Literacy

Districts and tahsils	Hindus											
	Brahmans				Other Hindus				Depressed classes			
	Number of persons		Number literate		Number of persons		Number literate		Number of persons		Number literate	
	Male	Females	Males	Females	Males	Females	Males	Females	Males	Females	Males	Females
1	2	3	4	5	6	7	8	9	10	11	12	13
N. W. F. P. Districts.	8,848	5,660	3,978	1,084	71,775	51,223	26,578	3,771	3,735	1,733	183	14
Hazara District ...	1,859	1,447	602	90	13,572	8,342	5,923	480	30	10	3	4
Mansehra ...	263	175	111	39	2,154	1,700	622	45	13	3	2	3
Abbottabad ...	1,159	917	321	43	7,664	3,630	4,306	294	6	2	1	...
Haripur ...	433	351	169	7	3,447	2,774	913	138	6	5	...	1
Amb ...	1	1	...	...	283	224	72	1	...	...	...	...
Phulera ...	3	3	1	1	24	14	10	2	5	...	...	...
Peshawar District	4,630	2,700	2,239	815	18,883	11,681	6,689	1,291	2,988	1,439	110	9
Peshawar ...	3,830	2,294	1,961	767	10,630	6,019	3,978	805	569	196	54	8
Charsadda ...	105	67	17	4	1,164	807	408	58	...	2	...	...
Mardan ...	246	125	78	17	3,303	2,121	1,232	287	81	65	...	...
Swabi ...	68	48	13	5	726	584	127	9	...	...	...	...
Nowshera ...	381	166	170	22	3,060	2,150	944	132	2,338	1,176	56	1
Kohat District ...	520	307	249	43	7,715	4,430	2,946	356	269	152	19	...
Kohat ...	306	175	169	37	4,620	2,127	2,317	338	245	142	18	...
Teri ...	60	47	13	5	1,401	1,279	217	12	1	...	...	...
Hangu ...	154	85	67	1	1,694	1,024	412	16	23	10	1	...
Bannu District ...	714	380	327	29	13,513	11,154	3,781	147	301	109	24	...
Bannu ...	583	305	278	27	9,285	7,406	2,740	17	301	109	24	...
Marwat ...	131	75	49	2	4,228	3,958	1,041	130	...	...	...	...
Dera Ismail Khan District.	1,125	825	561	107	18,092	15,609	7,239	1,487	147	23	27	1
Dera Ismail Khan ...	773	597	369	92	12,888	11,664	4,539	1,121	37	23	4	1
Tank ...	165	60	123	15	3,045	1,731	1,850	191	108	...	22	...
Kulachi ...	187	169	69	...	2,159	2,214	850	175	2	...	1	...

PROVINCIAL TABLE II

Population of Districts and Tahsils by Religion and Literacy

Muslims				Sikhs				Christians				Parsis			
Number of persons		Number literate		Number of persons		Number literate		Number of persons		Number literate		Number of persons		Number literate	
Males	Females	Males	Females	Males	Females	Males	Females	Males	Females	Males	Females	Males	Females	Males	Females
14	15	16	17	18	19	20	21	22	23	24	25	26	27	28	29
1,195,120	1,031,183	42,110	2,385	26,284	15,226	9,549	2,592	9,013	3,200	6,637	1,445	30	30	18	16
338,082	298,712	8,854	400	4,393	3,237	1,079	207	256	175	150	107	1	...	...	...
110,177	93,197	3,098	112	589	377	82	12	9	3	9	3	...	...	...	...
124,171	111,283	3,556	207	2,671	1,928	684	155	206	141	129	94	1	...	...	...
83,697	76,933	2,089	75	1,102	917	298	39	39	31	10	9	...	...	...	...
16,402	14,340	85	2	30	15	14	1	2	1	2	1	...	...	...	...
3,635	2,959	26	4	1	...	1	...	...	...	...	...	...	...	...	...
489,650	409,033	21,340	1,478	15,211	9,060	5,625	1,555	6,742	2,232	5,125	941	29	30	18	16
135,896	104,746	11,346	1,018	6,221	3,515	3,283	1,055	3,502	1,489	2,357	638	14	13	13	11
94,509	79,461	1,250	68	1,013	640	298	62	59	33	13	3	...	...	...	...
100,403	86,777	3,137	163	2,995	2,179	912	239	131	135	41	63	...	...	...	...
81,240	72,689	1,430	16	1,632	1,398	269	29	15	11	4	2	...	...	...	...
77,602	65,360	4,177	213	3,350	1,328	863	170	3,035	564	2,710	235	15	17	5	5
114,487	103,958	4,216	186	2,292	957	963	231	927	259	705	135	...	...	...	...
42,080	35,328	2,870	177	1,481	703	665	225	865	238	677	129	...	...	...	...
50,494	49,685	787	7	23	4	5	...	11	6	2	...	...	...	...	...
21,913	18,945	559	2	788	250	293	6	51	15	27	7	...	...	...	...
125,671	111,003	2,887	72	3,278	2,204	1,390	471	685	278	463	105	...	...	...	...
75,059	63,093	2,086	56	3,019	1,960	1,299	427	684	278	462	105	...	...	...	...
51,612	47,910	801	16	259	244	91	44	2	...	1	...	...	...	...	...
127,230	108,477	4,813	250	1,110	768	492	128	402	255	193	155	...	...	...	...
77,229	66,330	2,706	208	540	354	177	65	340	244	151	152	...	...	...	...
25.425	20,014	1,045	8	365	209	214	47	61	11	42	4	...	...	...	...
24,576	22,133	1,062	34	205	205	101	16	1	...	...	...	...	...	...	...

PROVINCIAL TABLE II

Population by Districts and Tahsils by Religion and Literacy

Districts and tahsils	Jews: Number of persons: Males	Jews: Number of persons: Females	Jews: Number literate: Males	Jews: Number literate: Females	Buddhists: Number of persons: Males	Buddhists: Number of persons: Females	Buddhists: Number literate: Males	Buddhists: Number literate: Females	Number literate: Aged 0-15: Males	Number literate: Aged 0-15: Females	Number literate: Aged 15—20: Males	Number literate: Aged 15—20: Females	Number literate: Aged 20 and over: Males	Number literate: Aged 20 and over: Females	Literate in English: Males	Literate in English: Females	Remarks
1	30	31	32	33	34	35	36	37	38	39	40	41	42	43	44	45	46
N.-W. F. P. Districts.	11	...	5	...	2	...	...	...	11,332	2,815	13,367	1,998	64,359	6,495	23,921	1,795	
Hazara District	...	...	...	...	...	...	...	...	2,155	319	2,694	218	11,762	751	1,819	141	
Mansehra ...	...	...	...	...	...	...	...	...	640	61	607	37	2,677	116	320	11	
Abbottabad ...	...	...	...	...	...	...	...	...	979	180	1,621	133	6,397	480	1,041	119	
Haripur ...	...	...	...	...	...	...	...	...	522	78	448	45	2,509	146	438	10	
Amb ...	...	...	...	...	...	...	...	...	7	...	11	1	155	4	9	...	
Phulera ...	...	...	...	...	...	...	...	...	7	...	7	2	24	5	11	1	
Peshawar District.	11	...	5	...	2	...	...	...	5,245	1,537	5,967	1,123	29,939	3,445	14,239	1,163	
Peshawar ...	11	...	5	...	2	...	...	...	2,500	1,124	2,727	787	17,770	2,391	8,573	841	
Charsadda ...	...	...	...	...	...	...	...	...	250	46	243	29	1,493	120	234	1	
Mardan ...	...	...	...	...	...	...	...	...	546	146	1,516	186	3,338	437	1,911	64	
Swabi ...	...	...	...	...	...	...	...	...	414	27	362	13	1,067	21	118	2	
Nowshera ...	...	...	...	...	...	...	...	...	1,535	194	1,119	108	6,271	476	3,403	255	
Kohat District	...	...	...	...	...	...	...	...	942	244	1,376	170	6,781	548	3,235	156	
Kohat ...	...	...	...	...	...	...	...	...	787	231	1,109	161	4,820	514	2,976	148	
Teri ...	...	...	...	...	...	...	...	...	82	5	79	4	863	15	54	...	
Hangu ...	...	...	...	...	...	...	...	...	73	8	188	5	1,098	19	205	8	
Bannu District	...	...	...	...	...	...	...	...	1,177	67	1,317	104	6,378	653	1,558	145	
Bannu ...	...	...	...	...	...	...	...	...	805	34	1,030	40	5,054	558	1,344	145	
Marwat ...	...	...	...	...	...	...	...	...	372	33	287	64	1,324	95	224	1	
Dera Ismail Khan District	...	...	...	...	...	...	...	...	1,813	648	2,013	383	9,499	1,098	3,060	190	
Dera Ismail Khan	...	...	...	...	...	...	...	...	1,255	497	1,242	281	5,449	861	2,302	146	
Tank ...	...	...	...	...	...	...	...	...	236	69	467	51	2,593	145	497	44	
Kulachi ...	...	...	...	...	...	...	...	...	322	82	304	51	1,457	92	261	...	

PROVINCIAL TABLE III

Pathan Sub-Tribes by Tahsils

This table, which appears for the first time at this Census, shows details by Tahsils of the Pathan tribes given in Imperial Table XVII.

PROVINCIAL TABLE III

Pathan Sub-Tribes by Tahsils

District and Tahsil	Pathan			Afridi			Bangash			Bannuchi		
	Persons	Males	Females	Persons	Males	Females	Persons	Males	Females	Persons	Males	Females
1	2	3	4	5	6	7	8	9	10	11	12	13
North-West Frontier Province (Districts)	905 122	480,667	424,455	10,759	6,101	4,658	34,738	18,374	16,364	43,007	22,938	20.069
Hazara District ...	54,544	29,840	24,704	57	55	2	199	106	93	8	8	...
Mansehra	9,460	4,825	4.635	...	...	...	...	...	...	...	...	...
Abbottabad	24,923	12,971	11,952	45	43	2	...	...	...	...	...	...
Haripur	18,746	11,227	7,519	12	12	...	2	2	...	8	8	...
Amb	1,264	732	532	...	...	...	197	104	93	...	...	...
Phulra	151	85	66	...	...	...	...	...	...	...	...	...
Peshawar District ...	473,738	252,558	221,180	5,024	2,852	2,172	214	199	15	9	1	8
Peshawar	95,781	53,922	41,859	2,762	1.429	1,333	123	114	9	9	1	8
Charsadda	94,915	52,162	42,753	372	245	127	38	33	5	...	...	...
Mardan	119,890	64,035	55,855	1,166	632	534	...	...	...	...	...	...
Swabi	80,684	41,491	39,193	69	49	20	39	39	...	...	...	...
Nowshera	82,468	40,948	41,520	655	497	158	14	13	1	...	...	...
Kohat District	148,098	76,583	71,515	5,269	2,815	2,454	34,248	17,994	16,254	78	38	40
Kohat	39,469	21,247	18,222	4,387	2,303	2,084	16,308	8,400	7,908	10	7	3
Teri	77,760	38,996	38,764	289	169	120	180	113	67	44	11	33
Hangu	30,869	16,340	14,529	593	343	250	17,760	9,481	8,279	24	20	4
Bannu District	159,737	84,642	75,095	115	90	25	19	17	2	42,825	22,852	19,973
Bannu	87,288	47,343	39,945	99	76	23	19	17	2	42,727	22,786	19,941
Lakki (Marwat)	72,449	37,299	35,150	16	14	2	...	...	...	98	66	32
Dera Ismail Khan District ...	69,005	37,044	31,961	294	289	5	58	58	...	87	39	48
Dera Ismail Khan	25,794	13,401	12,393	19	14	5	..	...	...	45	2	43
Tank	26,630	15,022	11,608	237	237	...	54	54	...	39	34	5
Kulachi	16,581	8,621	7,960	38	38	...	4	4	...	3	3	...

PROVINCIAL TABLE III

Pathan Sub-Tribes by Tahsils

Bhittani			Daudzai			Dilazak			Durrani			Gadun			Gandapur		
Persons	Males	Females	Persons	Males	Females	Persons	Males	Females	Persons	Males	Females	Persons	Males	Females	Persons	Males	Females
14	15		17	18	19	20	21	22	23	24	25	26	27	28	29	30	31
9,429	4,544	4,885	328	192	136	4,765	2,328	2,437	4,496	2,209	2,287	22,372	11,476	10,896	8,148	4,278	3,870
7	7	...	...	...	...	906	679	227	81	38	43	19,070	9,752	9,318	...	...	...
7	7	...	...	...	...	98	50	48	22	13	9	337	193	144	...	...	...
...	...	...	...	...	...	111	79	32	3	1	2	17,539	8,946	8,593	...	...	...
...	...	...	...	...	...	697	550	147	56	24	32	1,189	609	580	...	...	...
...	...	...	...	...	...	...	...	...	...	...	...	5	4	1	...	...	...
...	...	...	...	...	...	...	...	...	...	...	...	...	...	...	...	...	...
75	47	28	323	187	136	3,859	1,649	2,210	4,298	2,087	2,211	3,283	1,715	1,568	5	...	5
69	41	28	316	187	129	384	168	216	1,180	583	597	2	2	...	5	...	5
...	...	...	7	...	7	1,769	576	1,193	2,267	1,016	1,251	...	...	...	...	...	...
6	6	...	...	...	...	67	32	35	57	46	11	123	66	57	...	...	...
...	...	...	...	...	...	747	412	335	214	116	98	3,157	1,646	1,511	...	...	...
...	...	...	...	...	...	892	461	431	580	326	254	1	1	...	...	...	...
...	...	...	5	5	...	...	...	...	53	28	25	2	2	...	...	...	...
...	...	...	4	4	...	...	...	...	53	28	25	2	2	...	...	...	...
...	...	...	1	1	...	...	...	...	...	...	...	...	...	...	...	...	...
...	...	...	...	...	...	...	...	...	...	...	...	...	...	...	...	...	...
2,547	1,333	1,214	...	...	...	...	...	...	9	6	3	7	7	...	31	18	13
179	124	55	...	...	...	...	...	...	9	6	3	7	7	...	17	10	7
2,368	1,209	1,159	...	...	...	...	...	...	...	...	...	...	...	...	14	8	6
6,800	3,157	3,643	...	...	...	...	...	...	55	50	5	10	...	10	8,112	4,260	3,852
83	8	75	...	...	...	...	...	...	9	8	1	10	...	10	992	739	253
6,697	3,129	3,568	...	...	...	...	...	...	35	31	4	...	...	...	675	394	281
20	20	...	...	...	...	...	...	...	11	11	...	...	...	...	6,445	3,127	3,318

PROVINCIAL TABLE III

Pathan Sub-Tribes by Tahsils

District and Tahsil	Ghilzai			Gigiani			Khattack			Khalil		
	Persons	Males	Females	Persons	Males	Females	Persons	Males	Females	Persons	Males	Females
1	32	33	34	35	36	37	38	39	40	41	42	43
North-West Frontier Province (Districts).	3,311	2,111	1,200	10,367	3,848	6,519	158,253	79,307	78,945	8,377	3,714	4,663
Hazara District	10	9	1	...	...	...	140	94	46	...	...	...
Mansehra	6	5	1	...	...	...	88	48	40	...	...	...
Abbottabad	1	1	...	...	...	...	24	23	1	...	...	...
Haripur ...	3	3	...	...	...	...	17	12	5	...	...	...
Amb	...	...	...	...	...	...	7	7	...	...	...	...
Phulra ...	...	...	...	...	...	...	4	4	...	...	...	...
Peshawar District ...	1,855	1,218	637	10,274	3,756	6,518	64,907	31,774	33,133	8,222	3,575	4,646
Peshawar	351	223	128	207	19	88	1,148	820	328	7,673	3,282	4,391
Charsadda	1,114	695	419	10,066	3,636	6,430	3,401	2,442	959	56	121	35
Mardan	60	28	32	...	...	...	15,771	7,097	7,774	...	...	...
Swabi	...	...	...	...	...	...	[illegible]	6,048	[illegible]	...	...	...
Nowshera	330	272	58	1	1	...	31,511	14,467	17,044	393	173	220
Kohat District	1,191	717	474	9	8	1	86,543	43,495	43,048	13	11	2
Kohat	1,079	633	446	7	7	...	8,350	4,320	4,030	9	9	...
Teri	27	21	6	...	...	...	76,697	38,325	38,372	...	...	...
Hangu	85	63	22	2	1	1	1,496	850	646	4	2	2
Bannu District	27	21	6	...	...	...	6,392	3,680	2,712	43	43	...
Bannu	27	21	6	...	...	...	4,939	2,900	2,039	43	43	...
Lakki (Marwat)	...	...	...	...	...	...	1,453	780	673	...	...	...
Dera Ismail Khan District ..	228	146	82	84	84	...	271	264	7	99	84	15
Dera Ismail Khan	228	146	82	65	65	...	80	73	7	44	29	15
Tank	...	...	...	...	...	...	145	145	...	54	54	...
Kulachi	...	...	...	19	19	...	46	46	...	1	1	...

PROVINCIAL TABLE III

Pathan Sub-Tribes by Tahsils

Marwat			Mohmand			Mohmandzai			Orakzai			Tarin		
Persons	Males	Females	Persons	Males	Females	Persons	Males	Females	Persons	Males	Females	Persons	Males	Females
44	45	46	47	48	49	50	51	52	53	54	55	56	57	58
82,527	43,137	39,390	63,139	31,710	31,429	33,371	17,388	15,983	9,093	4,778	4,315	1,208	812	396
1	...	1	33	13	20	8	5	3	1	1	...	935	659	276
...	...	...	15	6	9	8	5	3	1	1	...	6	3	3
...	...	...	...	...	...	...	...	...	...	...	...	39	3	36
1	...	1	18	7	11	...	...	...	...	...	...	890	653	237
...	...	...	...	...	...	...	...	...	...	...	...	...	...	...
...	...	...	...	...	...	...	...	...	...	...	...	...	...	...
...	...	...	62,727	31,428	31,299	33,275	17,335	15,940	789	568	221	209	109	100
...	...	...	18,180	9,405	8,775	752	472	280	471	250	221	...	...	...
...	...	...	18,438	8,073	10,365	19,254	10,889	8,365	318	318	...	...	...	...
...	...	...	24,152	12,846	11,306	47	25	22	...	...	...	...	...	...
...	...	...	339	171	168	...	...	...	...	...	...	14	12	2
...	...	...	1,618	933	685	13,222	5,949	7,273	...	...	...	195	97	98
15	7	8	265	195	70	68	37	31	8,252	4,158	4,094	3	...	3
9	7	2	65	43	22	63	35	28	202	191	11	3	...	3
6	...	6	40	40	...	...	...	...	5	3	2	...	...	...
...	...	...	160	112	48	5	2	3	8,045	3,964	4,081	...	...	...
68,458	35,364	33,094	86	4[illegible]	40	...	...	...	3	3	...	2	2	...
2,985	1,729	1,256	82	44	38	...	...	...	3	3	...	...	...	...
65,473	33,635	31,838	4	2	2	...	...	...	...	...	...	2	2	...
14,053	7,766	6,287	28	28	...	20	11	9	48	48	...	59	42	17
7,843	4,075	3,768	3	3	...	19	10	9	...	...	...	12	...	12
5,359	3,195	2,164	25	25	...	...	...	...	48	48	...	40	35	5
851	496	355	...	...	...	1	1	...	...	...	...	7	7	...

PROVINCIAL TABLE III

Pathan Sub-Tribes by Tahsils

District and Tahsil	Turi			Ustrana			Utman Khel			Wazir	
	Persons	Males	Females	Persons	Males	Females	Persons	Males	Females	Persons	Males
1	59	60	61	62	63	64	65	66	67	68	69
North-West Frontier Province (Districts).	68	59	9	2,633	1,447	1,185	9,191	5,076	4,115	32,659	17,202
Hazara District ...	...	...	...	...	...	...	585	303	282	...	...
Mansehra	...	...	...	...	...	...	72	39	33	...	...
Abbottabad	...	...	...	...	...	...	...	...	...	...	...
Haripur	...	...	...	...	...	...	509	262	247	...	...
Amb	...	...	...	...	...	...	4	2	2	...	...
Phulra	...	...	...	...	...	...	...	...	...	...	...
Peshawar District ...	64	55	9	...	...	...	8,593	4,764	3,829	44	40
Peshawar	63	54	9	...	...	...	332	192	140	40	40
Charsadda	...	...	...	...	...	...	2,272	1,494	778	4	...
Mardan	1	1	...	...	...	...	5,974	3,066	2,[illegible]08	...	...
Swabi	...	...	...	...	...	...	...	...	...	...	...
Nowshera	...	...	...	...	...	...	15	12	3	...	...
Kohat District ...	3	3	...	...	...	...	9	5	4	873	5[illegible]7
Kohat	3	3	...	...	...	...	9	5	4	39	39
Teri	...	...		...	...	...	...	...	...	266	206
Hangu	...	...	...	...	...	...	...	...	...	568	322
Bannu District ...	...	...	...	6	6	...	4	4	...	30,892	16,034
Bannu	...	...	...	6	6	...	4	4	...	30,351	15,800
Lakki (Marwat) ...	...	...	...	...	...	...	...	...	...	541	234
Dera Ismail Khan District ...	1	1	...	2,627	1,441	1,186	...	...	...	850	561
Dera Ismail Khan ...	...	...	...	249	241	8	...	...	...	51	1
Tank	...	...	...	1	1	...	...	...	...	797	558
Kulachi	1	1	...	2,377	1,199	1,178	...	...	...	2	2

PROVINCIAL TABLE III

Pathan Sub-Tribes by Tahsils

	Yusafzai			Zadran			Other Pathans		
Females	Persons	Males	Females	Persons	Males	Females	Persons	Males	Females
70	71	72	73	74	75	76	77	78	79
15,457	133,737	72,368	61,369	319	184	135	218,827	125,086	93,741
...	321	189	132	...	...	...	32,182	17,922	14,260
...	81	46	35	...	...	...	8,719	4,409	4,310
...	50	46	4	...	...	...	7,111	3,829	3 282
...	166	84	82	...	...	...	15,178	9,001	6,177
...	18	10	8	...	...	...	1,033	605	428
...	6	3	3	...	...	...	141	78	63
4	132,760	71,665	61,095	24	21	3	132,905	77,512	55,393
...	547	405	142	7	4	3	60,860	36,131	24,729
4	1,656	1,184	472	...	...	...	33,783	21,440	12,343
...	65,656	36,097	29,559	...	...	...	6,810	3,193	3,617
...	63,204	32,971	30,233	...	...	...	125	27	98
...	1,697	1,008	689	17	17	...	31,327	16,721	14,606
306	411	323	88	25	17	8	10,763	6,158	4,605
...	356	288	68	7	5	2	8,504	4,918	3,586
60	43	27	16	13	7	6	149	73	76
246	12	8	4	5	5	...	2,110	1,167	943
14,858	191	146	45	269	145	124	7,811	4,825	2,986
14,551	129	105	24	266	144	122	5,396	3,518	1,878
307	62	41	21	3	1	2	2,415	1,307	1,108
289	54	45	9	1	1	...	35,166	18,669	16,497
50	25	19	6	...	...	...	16,017	7,968	8,049
239	15	12	3	...	...	...	12,319	7,070	5,339
...	14	14	...	1	1	...	6,740	3,631	3,109

APPENDICES

APPENDIX I

Social Map (opposite page 186)

District	Sub-Division	Population	Proportion per cent. Muslim	Hindu	Sikh	Others
Hazara ...	Mansehra	208,660	97·5	2·1	0·4	...
	Feudal Tanawal ...	37,943	98·4	1·5	0·1	...
	Abbottabad	423,514	93·5	4·8	1·6	0·1
Peshawar ...	Peshawar (including Charsadda) ...	456,807	90·8	5·6	2·5	1·1
	Nowshera	160,542	89·0	5·8	2·9	2·3
	Mardan	256,972	95·5	2·1	2·3	0·1
Kohat ...	Kohat	191,321	92·8	5·4	1·2	0·6
	Hangu	44,952	90·9	6·7	2·3	0·1
Bannu ...	Bannu	270,301	87·9	9·7	2·0	0·4
Dera Ismail Khan ...	Dera Ismail Khan ...	222,870	85·4	13·8	0·6	0·2
	Tank	51,194	88·8	10·0	1·1	0·1

Note.—The only classes to be held "depressed" are Chuhras and Chamars. These are not separately shown in the social map, because they form an infinitesimal proportion of the total population in each sub-division.

The following table shows the number of *Chuhras* and *Chamars* enumerated in the five districts of the Province :—

	Muslim	Hindu	Sikh	Christian	Total
Chuhras	2,333	5,241	147	723	8,444
Chamars	2,663	227	11	...	2,901

Linguistic Map (opposite page 174)—Statement No. 1

District	Total population	Number speaking: Pashto as mother tongue	Lahnda as mother tongue	Other languages as mother tongue	Pashto as subsidiary to Lahnda	Lahnda as subsidiary to Pashto
Hazara	670,117	29,375	625,268	15,474	11,264	9,854
Peshawar	974,321	781,773	127,189	65,359	29,125	13,591
Kohat	236,273	186,299	35,755	14,219	21,946	4,406
Bannu	270,301	228,381	33,547	8,136	11,375	1,931
Dera Ismail Khan ..	274,064	53,643	213,115	7,306	9,943	4,376

Linguistic Map—Statement No. 2

District	Number per *mille* (all speakers) speaking: Pashto as mother tongue	Lahnda as mother tongue	Other languages as mother tongue	Pashto as subsidiary to Lahnda	Lahnda as subsidiary to Pashto
Hazara	44	933	23	18	335
Peshawar	802	131	67	37	107
Kohat	789	151	60	64	123
Bannu	846	124	30	50	58
Dera Ismail Khan	196	778	26	185	21

APPENDIX II

OVERCROWDING IN PESHAWAR CITY.

An attempt has been made for the first time in the present Census to obtain statistics of over-crowding in Peshawar City. The results of the inquiries made are shown in the table on the following page. The results are unfortunately valueless for the purpose for which they were intended. The figures for areas of circles were not obtainable, and those for charges do not show boundaries nor indicate the amount of waste land or the number of unoccupied buildings within the area of the charge. The instructions with regard to the numbering of census houses separately from structural houses were, moreover, issued too late to be observed, and there is no information available to show either the number of families living in a house, or the number of rooms which each family occupies. It may be stated as a result of local inquiries made that pressure of population on accommodation is less in Muhammadan than in Hindu quarters of the city. The reason for this is that the *purdah* system among Muhammadans makes it impossible for more than one family to occupy one house, however many rooms and storeys the house may have. Thus a two-storeyed house of seven rooms if situated in a Muhammadan quarter will only accommodate one family, whereas the same house in a Hindu quarter might accommodate four or five families. The result of this is that there is no serious overcrowding in Muhammadan quarters of the City, nor in the city as a whole ; there is, however, serious congestion in the Hindu quarters. These facts are not reflected in the figures reproduced in the table. Andarshahr ward is occupied almost exclusively by Hindus, and is extremely overcrowded ; Karimpura is crowded, but not so densely as Andarshahr ; Chauk Nasir Khan is an almost exclusively Muhammadan quarter, and is not in the least overcrowded. Yet the figures for Andarshahr and Chauk Nasir Khan give almost the same density, being approximately 206 and 190 persons per acre respectively, while the figure for Karimpura, which ought to be lower than Assyia and higher than Chauk Nasir Khan is roughly 295. Lahori contains a large number of Muhammadans of the poorer classes and is undoubtedly more overcrowded than Chauk Nasir Khan ; yet its figure is only 150.

The table on the two following pages is therefore of little value for the present inquiry, but may perhaps be of use for comparison with those to be recorded at the next Census.

Statement showing overcrowding in

Name of ward	Number of charge	Number of circle	Area in acres	Population — Total — Persons	Total — Males	Total — Females	Muslims — Males	Muslims — Females	Hindus — Males	Hindus — Females	Sikhs — Males	Sikhs — Females
1	2	3	4	5	6	7	8	9	10	11	12	13
Peshawar City (Municipality)	...	...	Not available	87,440	50,151	37,289	39,915	29,978	6,781	4,813	2,992	2,158
Assiya ...	5	1	Not available	5,272	2,828	2,444	1,708	1,536	627	530	493	378
		2		4,791	2,704	2,087	1,979	1,537	592	462	131	85
		3		6,419	3,404	3,015	3,125	2,746	102	81	177	188
		4		2,279	1,506	773	1,318	647	15	6	9	2
Total Charge No. 5	...	...	109·93	18,761	10,442	8,319	8,130	6,466	1,336	1,079	810	653
Jahangir Pura ...	6	5	Not available	4,997	2,946	2,051	2,771	1,883	157	138	5	5
		6		2,730	1,633	1,097	1,490	1,084	95	5	46	8
		7		4,683	2,784	1,899	2,726	1,852	22	12	...	...
Total Charge No. 6	...	...	69·52	12,410	7,363	5,047	6,987	4,819	274	155	51	13
Chauk Nasir Khan ...	7	8	Not available	3,292	1,785	1 507	1,785	1,507	...	...	...	...
		9		3,568	1,962	1,606	1,846	1.517	2	...	113	89
		10		3,092	1,742	1,350	1,739	1,359	3	...	...	...
Total Charge No. 7	...	...	52·32	9.952	5,489	4,463	5,370	4,374	5	...	113	89
Gunj ...	8	11	Not available	2,639	1,444	1,195	1,399	1,149	25	27	20	19
		12		3,634	1.966	1,668	1,667	1,402	175	159	124	107
		13		3,974	2,157	1,817	2,132	1,817	25	...	...	...
Total Charge No. 8	...	...	64·03	10,247	5.567	4,680	5,198	4,368	225	186	144	126
Lahori ...	9	14	Not available	3.099	1,686	1,413	1671	1,404	1	...	...	...
		15		3,154	1,791	1,363	1,744	1,344	32	9	15	10
		16		3,828	2,345	1,483	2,056	1.342	129	45	46	24
Total Charge No. 9	...	...	65·54	10,081	5,822	4.259	5,471	4,090	162	54	61	34
Karimpura ...	10	17	Not available	4,179	2,299	1,880	1,049	882	521	385	729	613
		18		4,214	2,438	1,776	857	629	1,273	926	308	221
		19		4,781	2,632	2,149	1,771	1,477	701	563	160	109
Total Charge No. 10	...	...	44·47	13,174	7,369	5,805	3,677	2,988	2,495	1,874	1,197	943
Andarshahr ...	11	20	Not available	2,943	1.938	1,005	533	118	1,166	763	238	124
		21		1,318	875	443	272	132	469	262	134	49
		22		2,167	1,220	947	866	675	302	257	52	15
Total Charge No. 11	...	...	31·06	6,428	4,033	2,395	1,671	925	1,937	1,282	424	188
Extra Rural Areas ...	12	23	Not available	3,145	1,835	1,310	1,817	1,304	11	...	2	1
		24		2,482	1,699	783	1,182	491	309	158	180	112
		25		760	532	228	412	153	27	25	10	...
Total Charge No. 12	...	...	Not available.	6,387	4,066	2,321	3,411	1,948	347	183	192	112

the Peshawar City (Municipality)

Christians: Males	Christians: Females	Others: Males	Others: Females	Density per acre	Proportion of females per 1,000 males	Number of occupied structural houses	Number of persons per occupied structural house	Number of commensal families	Average number of persons in family
14	15	16	17	18	19	20	21	22	23
452	340	11	...	Not available	744	14,639	6·0	18,209	4·8
...	...	...	...	Not available	864	735	7·2	1,054	5·0
2	3	...	...		772	747	6·4	987	4·9
...	...	...	...		886	937	6·9	1,241	5·2
156	118	8	...		513	503	4·5	553	4·1
158	121	8	...	170·66	797	2,922	6·4	3,835	4·9
43	25	...	...	Not available	696	799	6·3	1,023	4·9
1	...	1	...		678	565	4·8	596	4·6
36	35	...	...		682	794	5·9	852	5·5
50	60	1	...	178·51	685	2,158	5·8	2,465	5·0
...	...	...	...	Not available	844	485	6·8	578	5·7
...	...	1	...		819	561	6·4	586	6·1
...	...	...	...		773	521	5·9	5[illegible]8	5·2
...	...	1	...	190·21	813	1,567	6·4	1,762	5·6
...	...	...	...	Not available	828	478	5·3	603	4·4
...	...	...	...		848	639	5·7	745	4·9
...	...	...	...		842	661	6·0	793	5·0
...	...	...	...	160·02	841	1,778	5·8	2,141	4·8
14	9	...	...	Not available	838	601	5·2	674	4·6
...	...	...	...		761	534	5·9	623	5·1
114	72	...	...		632	647	5·9	825	4·7
128	81	...	...	153·81	732	1,782	5·7	2,120	4·8
...	...	...	...	Not available	818	607	6·9	858	4·9
	...	...	...		728	634	6·7	770	5·5
...	...	...	...		816	797	6·0	954	5·0
...	...	...	...	296·24	788	2,038	6·5	2,582	5·1
...	...	1	...	Not available	519	511	5·8	782	3·8
	...	...	...		506	209	6·3	283	4·7
...	...	...	...		776	372	5·8	474	4·6
...	...	1	...	206·96	594	1,092	5·9	1,539	4·2
5	5	...	...	Not available	714	700	4·5	821	3·8
28	23	...	...		461	417	6·0	701	3·5
8[illegible]	50	...	...		429	185	4·1	243	3·1
116	78	...	...	Not available	571	1,302	4·9	1,765	3·6

APPENDIX III

THE QUESTION OF "DEPRESSED CLASSES".

For the first time in the present Census instructions have been received the writing of an appendix on "Depressed Classes". The intended scope of this appendix is indicated by the definition "untouchable Hindus and any other classes which are under some special social disability", which was adopted at a conference of Census Superintendents.

The term "depressed classes" even in the light of this definition can not be rightly applied in this Province to any class of person. There are, no doubt, persons who are regarded as unclean, but this is by virtue of their employment and manner of life rather than on account of their birth, and they are so regarded and treated by persons of all religions, not only by Brahmans and other caste Hindus. It is obvious that such employments as scavenging or the dressing and treatment of raw skins are dirty employments, and that unless the persons concerned take steps to keep both themselves and their clothing clean when they are away from their work, they will themselves become consistently unclean and, as a consequence, liable to contaminate and infect those with whom they come in contact. Since such persons do not as a rule in this Province take any steps to render or keep themselves clean, it follows that they are as a general rule avoided by persons whose occupations and habits are more sanitary. Further, since the following of these professions is to a great extent hereditary and confined to certain castes, it follows that such castes come to be regarded, as a general rule, as something to be avoided. There is nothing objectionable to most people in a 'Chuhra' or 'Chamar' in clean clothes and in a healthy and sanitary condition, but since most 'Chuhras' are not in clean clothes, and most 'Chamars' working in raw skins are extremely filthy and smelly, there is a prejudice against their presence in general society. It is only in this sense that there are any depressed classes in this Province.

In these circumstances it is difficult to offer any reliable statistics. The figures in the margin show the number of persons of all religions who have been entered as 'Chuhras' and the number of Muslims, Hindus and Sikhs who were recorded as 'Chamars' working in raw skins. Chamars not shown as working in raw skins have not been included, since the name is frequently used in this Province to cover cobblers and other workers in leather. The total of 'Chuhras' includes all those who returned their caste as Sweeper, *Chuhra*, *Bhangi*, *Khakrob*, *Mazhabi Sikh*, *Musali*, *Shah Khel*, *Mehtar*, *Lalbegi* or *Balmiki*. So far as can be ascertained this includes all those in the Province who perform scavenging work.

	Persons	Males	Females
Chuhra ...	8 444	5,612	2,832
Muslim ...	2,333	1,523	810
Hindu ..	5,241	3,551	1,690
Sikh ...	147	80	67
Christian ...	723	458	265
Chamar ...	2,901	1,732	1,169
Muslim ...	2,663	1,540	1,123
Hindu ...	227	184	43
Sikh ...	11	8	3

The social disabilities from which 'depressed classes' are generally supposed to suffer include exclusion from temples, prohibition from the use of wells and other common sources of drinking water, and exclusion from schools. These disabilities, so far as they are imposed on grounds of religion, are practically non-existent in this Province. As a general rule the class under reference is too poor and ignorant and too much occupied by its employment to have any desire to enter a temple; where this was not the case its entry into temples was to some extent unpopular at the time of the taking of the census, but since 1932 it is stated that no objection is as a rule raised, provided the person seeking entry is clean of body and in clean clothes, i. e., provided there is no sanitary or medical reason to the contrary. The problem of the prohibition of access to sources of drinking water has never existed in the Province at all. With regard to schools, the figures for general literacy and for literacy in English, discussed in paragraphs 233 to 235 of the Report, show that no exclusion is enforced. Literacy among Pathan males in the districts of the Province is 48 per *mille* and among Awans 67 per *mille*, while among *Chuhras* it is 98 per *mille*. In the case of females there is higher proportion of literacy among Chuhras than among any of the selected Muslim caste for which figures were extracted. No special provision for the education of *Chuhras* is made except for one C. M. S. Mission School for Punjabi Christian Sweepers in Dera Ismail Khan and one Arya Hindu High School. Their backwardess, like all their other disabilitles, is due more to economic than to social causes.

This appendix contributes little or nothing to the study of the problem of the depressed classes of India, but so also does this Province contribute little or nothing to the existence of the problem.

APPENDIX IV

OCCUPATIONS RETURNED

This Appendix is divided into two parts :—

Part I.—List of occupations as classed in the Imperial Table X by groups.

Part II.—An alphabetical index of occupations actually found in the Census Schedules with the numbers of groups in which they are classified.

APPENDIX IV—

PART I.—

Group No.	Occupation: Urdu	Occupation: English
1	پٹی دار	Pattidar
	لگان لینے والا	Rent receiver, (in money or kind)
	مالک اراضی	Land holder (non-cultivating) Proprietor (landed estate)
	زمیندار	Land owner
3	ملازم و مینیجر کورٹ آف وارڈس	Court of Wards Managers and employees
	افسر محکمہ زراعت	Director of Agriculture
	قانونگوے	Kanungo
	ملازمین زمینداری	Estate Agents and managers
	عملہ بندوبست	Settlement Officer and employees
4	لگان جمع کرنے والا	Rent Collector
	کلرک و محرر وغیرہ	Moharrirs and clerks of owners of landed estates
	بخشی یا ناظر	Rent Collectors and Managers
5	مالک خود کاشت	Cultivating owner, land holder (cultivating)
6	مزارعہ خود کاشت	Cultivating Tenant, farmer cultivator (tenant)
	لگان دہندہ مزارعہ	Rent payer (cultivator)
7	زراعتی مزدور (چوکار)	Agricultural labourer
	محافظ فصل	Crop watcher
	رکھوالا (کھٹہ)	Crop watcher
	کھا پانی	Water watchman (private)
	کھیتوں میں مزدوری کرنے والا	Field labourer
	ہالی	Ploughman
	خوشہ چین	Gleaner
	فصل کی کٹائی کرنیوالا	Reaper
7	اناج برسانے والا صاف کرنے والا	Winnower (grain)
	ملازم فارم	Farm servant
16	مالی-باغبان	Gardener
	پھول اور میوے بونے والا	Flower and fruit grower
	سبز ترکاریاں و مرچ بونے والا	Chilli and vegetable grower
17	افسر جنگلات	Forest officer
	رینجر	Ranger
	گارڈ جنگل	Guard
	ملازمت جنگل ہر قسم	Forest service
18	لکڑی چیرنے اور کاٹنے والا	Wood cutter
	لکڑی کا کوئلہ جلانے والا	Charcoal burner
	جلانے کی لکڑی جمع کرنے والا	Fire wood collector
19	درختوں کا چھلکا جمع کرنے والا	Bark collector
	جنگل کی پیداوار جمع کرنے والا	Forest produce collector
	ایندھن جمع کرنے والا	Fuel collector
	گھسیارہ	Grass cutter
	شہد جمع کرنے والا	Honey collector
21	مویشی یا بھینس پالنے اور رکھنے والا	Cattle and buffalo breeder and keeper
	دودھ والا	Milkman

Occupations returned

List of Occupations

Group No.	Occupation	
	Urdu	English
	گوالا	Cowherd
	ملازمان ڈائری فارم	Dairy farm servant
22	باربرداری کے مویشی پالنے اور رکھنے والا	Breeder and keeper of transport animals
	گدھا خچر اونٹ گھوڑا پالنے والا	Ass,-mule,-camel, or horse-breeder
	چابک سوار	Horse-trainer
	بھیڑ بکری رکھنے والا	Sheep and goat breeder
	آجڑی	Sheep breeder
	چروال	Grazier
23	چرواہا	Herdsman
	گڈریہ	Shepherd
	کتے پالنے والا	Dog breeder
27	ماہی گیر	Fisherman
	مچھلی کا شکار کرنیوالا	Do
28	شکاری	Hunter
	چڑی مار	Bird catcher
	کیڑے مکوڑے پکڑنے والا	Vermin catcher
	سانپ پکڑنے والا	Snake catcher
39	چونے کا پتھر نکالنے والا	Lime quarrier
40	نمک نکالنے والا	Salt miner
	شورہ نکالنے والا	Saltpetre extractor
41	سجی نکالنے والا	Alkali preparer
	سجی بنانے والا	Carbonate of soda extractor
42	روئی صاف کرنے والا	Cotton cleaner
	نداف-پینجا-پنجارہ	Cotton ginner, presser

Group No.	Occupation	
	Urdu	English
	روئی کی مشین کا مالک و کام کرنے والے	Cotton ginning mills, owners and workmen, e to
43	جولاہا-پاولی-بافندہ	Cotton weaver
	روئی کاتنا	Cotton spinning
	دھاگہ بنانے والا	Thread maker
	روئی کاتنے اور کپڑا بننے کی مشین کے مالکان و کام کرنے والے	Cotton spinning and weaving mills (owners, workmen, etc.)
	فیتہ بنانے والا	Tape maker
	دری باف	Carpet weaver (cotton)
	سریش لگانے والا	Sizer
	تانا بننے والا	Warper
	نوار باف	Nawar maker
44	بوریا باف	Bag (gunny) weaver and maker
	چٹائی بنانے والا	Mat maker
45	مچھلی کا جال بنانے والا	Fish-net maker
	رسہ وٹ	Rope maker
	رسی بنانے والا	String maker
	وان بنانے والا	String-bedstead maker
46	اون کا کپڑا بننے والا	Weaver (wool)
	نمدہ بنانے والا	Blanket weaver
	غالیچہ بنانے والا	Carpet maker
	شالباف	Shawl weaver
	اون کے پٹو و کمبل بنانے والا	Weaver of woollen blankets
	اون اٹیرنے والا	Wool winder
	اون کاتنے والا	Wool spinner

Group No.	Occupation	
	Urdu	English
47	ریشم کا کپڑا بننے والا	Silk weaver
	ریشم گر	Silk spinner
	ریشم کی تار بنانے والا	Silk thread maker
49	رنگریز چھیمبا و للاری۔ ٹھپلگر	Dyer and cloth printer
	کپڑا رنگنے والا	Cloth dyer
	ریشے دار تاروں کو کو صاف کرنے والا	Bleacher of textiles
50	لیس بنانے والا	Lace maker
	گوٹہ و کناری بنانے والا	Do
	جھالر بنانے والا	Fringes maker
	ریشم کی ڈوری بنانے والا	Silk braid maker
51	زین ساز	Saddle maker
	ساز بنانے والا	Harness maker
	سراج	Saddler
	یخدان بنانے والا	Leather box maker (Yakhdan)
	چمڑے کے ڈول بنانے والا	Bucket (leather) maker
	مشک بنے والا	Water-bag (leather) maker
	چمڑے کی اشیا بنانے والا	Leather articles maker
	چمرنگ چمڑا رنگنے والا	Dyer (leather)
	کپے بنانے والا	Ghee-pot (leather) maker
53	چوڑی گر	Bangles maker
	سیپ کی چیزیں بنانے والا	Shell, worker in
	سینگ اور ہڈی کی چیزیں بنانے والا	Horn and bone, worker in

Group No.	Occupation	
	Urdu	English
54	آرا کش	Sawyer
55	ترکھان کاریگر	Carpenter
	خرادی	Turner
	لکڑی کے صندوق بنانے والا	Wooden box maker
	کنگھی بنانے والا	Loom comb maker
	نجار	Joiner
56	بانس کی چیزیں بنانے والا	Worker in bamboo articles
	ٹوکری بنانے والا	Basket maker
	جھاڑو بنانے والا	Broom maker
	چک ساز	Chik (screen) maker
	چھج بنانے والا	Leather winnowing fan maker
	بورز گر	Mat maker
	پنکھا بنانے والا	Fan (leaf) maker
	پتوں کی چیزیں بنانیوالا	Leaves, worker in
59	لوہار-آہنگر	Blacksmith
	آلات کشاورزی بنانے والا	Maker of implements (agricultural)
	آہنی اشیاء بنانے والا	Maker of iron articles
	آہنی ٹرنک بنانے والا	Maker of steel trunks
	چاقو ساز و تیز کرنے والا	Knife-maker and grinder
	سان کھینچنے والا	Grindstone turner
	قفل بنانے والا	Lock maker
	نعل بند	Farrier
60	مس گر	Coppersmith
	تانبے کے برتن بنانے والا	do
	پیتل کے برتن بنانے والا ٹھٹھیار	Worker in brass and bell metals

Occupations returned

List of Occupations

Group No.	Occupation	
	Urdu	English
61	ٹین کے برتن بنانے والا	Maker of tin utensils
	ٹینفل گر-قلعی گر	Tinner
	ٹین کے ٹرنک بنانے والا	Maker of tin trunks
63	کلال- کمہار- مٹی کے برتن بنانے والا	Potter
	کل گر	Do
64	اینٹ بنانے والا خشت ساز	Brick maker
	مالکان و مزدوران بھٹہ	Proprietors and workers (brick kiln)
65	شیشہ کی چوڑی بنانے والا	Bangles (glass) maker
	شیشے کے برتن بنانے والا	Glass ware maker
	مٹی کے بت بنانے والا	Image (earthen) maker
	شیشہ گر	Mirror maker
66	آتشبازی بنانے والا	Fire-work maker
	بارود و دارو گر	Do
67	برف و سوڈا واٹر کی مشین کے مالکان و مزدوران	Proprietor and worker in Aerated water and ice factory
68	تیلی	Oil presser
	کولہو چلانے والا	Do
	گھانی چلانے والا	Do
70	عرق نکالنے والا	Arak (perfume) preparer
	عطار	Atar preparer (rose water preparer)
	صابن ساز	Soap maker
	ویکس کلوتھ بنانے والا	Wax-cloth maker
	رنگ ساز، رنگ بنانے والا	Paint manufacturer
	سرمہ بنانے والا	Eye powder (surma) maker
	سیاہی بنانے والا	Ink maker
71	چکی پیسنے والا	Flour grinder
	آٹا پیسنے والا	Do
	جندر چلانیوالا جندروئی	Water mill worker
	مالک و مزدور کارخانہ جندر	Proprietors and workmen of flour mills
	شالی کٹ	Rice pounder
	مزدوران جندر	Water mill workers
72	چاول بھوننا	Rice parcher
	دانہ بھوننا	Grain parcher
73	بکر قصائی	Butcher
	جھٹکئی	Jhat kai (butcher)
	بڑ قصائی	Butcher (beef)
74	مصری پتاسہ بنانیوالا	Candy and patasha maker
	گڑ اور شکر بنانیوالا	Makers of sugar molasses and Gur
75	پاپڑ وڑی بنانیوالا	Papar ware maker
	مٹھائی بنانیوالا	Sweet-meat maker
	حلوائی	Confectioner
	ملائی کلفی بنانیوالا	Ice cream maker
	اچار چٹنی بنانیوالا	Condiment maker
77	مالک شراب	Brewery (owners, workers etc.)
78	تمباکو بنانیوالا	Manufacturers of tobacco
	نسوار بنانیوالا	Snuff manufacturer
80	گانجا بنانیوالا	Manufacturers of ganja
81	جھبور-ماچھی مہرہ	Baker and cook
	نانبائی-نان فروش	Bread seller (cook shop keeper)

APPENDIX IV—

PART I—

Group No.	Occupation	
	Urdu	English
	بسکٹ وغیرہ بنانیوالا	Biscuit factory (owners workmen etc.)
	کیک بنانیوالا	Cake maker
	پنیر ساز	Cheese maker
	مکھن بنانیوالا	Butter maker
	گھی بنانیوالا	Ghee preparer
82	موچی	Shoe maker
	بوٹ بنانیوالا	Boot maker
	چمار	Shoe maker
	چپلی بنانیوالا	Sandal (chapli) maker
	کفش دوز	Shoe maker
83	درزی	Tailor
	رفو گر	Darner
83	پوستین دوز	Postin maker
	طلا چڑھانے والا	Embroiderer in gold lace
	کشیدہ نکالنے والا	Embroiderer in lace
	گوٹہ چڑھانے والا	Embroiderer in lace
	میدا کاری کرنیوالا	Embroiderer
84	ٹوپی و کلاہ ساز	Cap and kullah maker
	کلاہ دوز	Cap and hat maker
	چھتری چھاتہ مرمت کرنیوالا	Umbrella maker and repairer
85	دھوبی-دھوبا	Washerman
	پرانی اشیاء رنگنے والا	Dyer of used articles
	کندی گر	Cloth celenderer
86	حجام	Barber
	حجامت بنانا	Barber
	سر مونڈنا	Barber

Group No.	Occupation	
	Urdu	English
	نائی	Barber
	بال کی ٹوپی بنانیوالا	Wig maker
87	حمام والا	Owner and employee of bath house
88	گاڑی کو رنگ کرنیوالا	Carriage painter
	بچوں کی گاڑی بنانیوالا	Cabinet maker
	فرنیچر بنانیوالا	Furniture maker and workman
	لیمپ بنانیوالا	Lamp maker
	پردہ بنانیوالا	Screen maker
89	خیمہ بنانیوالا	Tent maker
	چار پائی بنانیوالا	Bed stead (of any material) maker
	بسترہ بنانیوالا	Bedding maker
	گدیلہ بنانیوالا	Cushion maker
	گھر کا سامان بنانیوالا	Upholsterer
90	چونا بنانے و جلانیوالا	Lime burner
	سیمنٹ کا کام کرنیوالا	Cement worker
	ٹوبا-کنواں صاف کرنیوالا	Well sinker
	سنگ تراش	Stone cutter and dresser
	راج	Mason
	گلکار	Mason
	اینٹ لیجانے والا	Brick carrier
	پرت نویس رنگساز	Painter
	معمار و ٹھیکیدار عمارت	Builder (building contractor)
	سرخی بنانیوالا	Surkhi pounder
	سفیدی کرنیوالا	White washer
91	مستری بائیسکل	Persons engaged in making and repairing cycles
	مستری موٹر-موٹر سائیکل	Persons engaged in making and repairing motor vehicles

Occupations returned

List of Occupations

Group No.	Occupation	
	Urdu	English
92	گاڑی چھکڑا پالکی بنانیوالا	Carriage, cart, Palki etc. makers
	گاڑی کا پہیہ بنانیوالا	Wheel maker and wheel wright
93	کشتی بنانے و مرمت کرنے والا	Boat maker and repairer
94	بجلی گھر میں کام کرنیوالا	Worker in electricity power house
95	ملازم پرنٹنگ پریس	Worker in printing press
	جلد ساز	Book binder
96	باجہ بنانیوالا	Harmonium maker
	رباب ساز	Guitar maker
	طبلہ-ڈھول-نقارچہ بنانے و مرمت کرنے والا	Drum maker, repairer
97	گھڑی ساز	Clock and watch maker
	سامان جراحی وغیرہ بنانیوالا	Maker of surgical or scientific instruments etc.
98	زرگر-سنار-سونار	Goldsmith
	کندی ساز	Worker in precious stones
	جڑت کرنیوالا	Jewel setter
	نیاریہ	Gold smith dust washer
99	کھلونے بنانیوالا	Toy maker
	پنجرہ بنانے والا	Cage maker
	گلدستہ بنانیوالا	Garland maker
	حقہ بنانیوالا	Hukka (pipe) maker
	پتنگ بنانیوالا	Kite maker
	تصویر کی چوکھٹ بنانیوالا	Picture frame maker

Group No.	Occupation	
	Urdu	English
100	بھنگی-مہتر چوڑا خاکروب-مصلی	Sweeper or scavanger
	ٹھیکیدار مٹی و خاکشورہ	Dust contractor
	ٹھیکیدار گندگی و میلہ	Refuse contractor
	گوبر جمع کرنیوالا	Cow-dung gatherer
	کھاد جمع کرنیوالا	Manure contractor
102	ملاح-موہانہ	Boatman
	مالکان کشتی و مزدوران	Boat owner and employee
	کشتی کا رسہ کھینچنے والا	Tow-man
103	ملازمت پبلک ورکس نہر	Irrigation Department service
	ملازمت نہر ماسوائے مزدور	Person employed (other than labourers) on rivers and canals
104	مزدور نہر	Labourers employed on canals and river
105	پل کا چپڑاسی	Bridge peon
	سڑک کا اورسیر	Road overseer
	سڑک کا ٹھیکیدار	Contractor for road works
	پل کا محصول لینے والا	Toll collector, bridge
	ملازمت پارکماسٹری	P. W. D. Service
106	سڑک پر پتھر توڑنے والا	Breaker of stones for road
	قلی سڑک	Road cooly
107	موٹر ڈرائیور اور منیجر	Motor car driver and Manager
108	تانگہ ایجنٹ	Tanga agent
	گاڑی بان	Tum-tum driver
	کوچوان تانگہ والا	Tanga driver

APPENDIX IV—

PART I—

Group No.	Occupation	
	Urdu	English
	ریڑا-یکہ چلانیوالا	Ekka driver
108	ریڑا چھکڑا چلانے والا	Bullock cart driver
	بگی والا	Hackney carriage driver
109	کہار	Dooly bearer
	ڈولی اٹھانے والا	Dooly bearer
	پالکی یا چوپہال بردار	Palki bearer
110	گدھے کی باربرداری والا	Ass driver
	بیل کا مالک و بوجھہ لادنے والا	Ox driver
	اونٹ و خچر چلانے والا	Camel and mule driver
	ٹٹو لادنے والا	Pack horse driver
	کرایہ کش	Owners of pack animals
111	کشتی سے سامان اتارنے والا	Unloader of boats
	بارکش	Porter
	پیغام رسان	Messenger
112	ملازم ریلوے ماسوائے قلی	Railway employees of all kinds (other than coolies)
	ٹھیکدار ریلوے	Railway Contractor
113	قلی ریلوے	Railway cooly
	ریلوے گاڑی سے اسباب اوتارنے والا	Porter
	مستری ریلوے	Railway Mistri
	بھشتی ریلوے	Water carrier, Railway
114	ملازم ڈاکخانہ و تار گھر و ٹیلیفون	Post office, Telegraph and Telephone service
115	ملازم و مینیجر بنک	Bank managers and other employees
	ایجنٹ انشورنس	Exchange and insurance agents

Group No.	Occupation	
	Urdu	English
	ساہوکار	Money lender
	صراف و دلال	Money changer and broker
116	کمیشن ایجنٹ	Commission agent
	نیلام کرنے والا	Auctioneer
	دلال ہنڈوی	Bill broker
	دھڑ وائی	Weighman
	گھروں کا ایجنٹ	House agent
	کمیشن ایجنٹ	Commission Agent
117	بزاز	Cloth seller (cotton and silk)
	سوت بیچنے وا	Thread and yarn seller
	ریشم فروش	Trader in silk
	کٹ پیس فروش	Cut piece goods dealer
	رسی فروش	Rope seller
	روئی فروش	Cotton dealer
	وان فروش	String-bedstead seller
	بوری کا سوداگر	Dealer in gunny bags
118	سوداگر چرم	Trader in skins, leather and hides
	مشک اور بوقہ فروش	Trader in bucket and water bags (leather)
	بگی کا سامان فروش	Harness seller
	ہڈی کا سوداگر	Trader in bones
	جانوروں کے پروں کا کاروبار کرنے والا	Trader in furs and feathers
	یخدان فروش	Yakhdan seller
119	سوداگر چوب-لکڑی	Trader in timber
	لکڑی کا بورہ فروش	Sawdust seller

Occupations returned

List of Occupations

Group No.	Occupation	
	Urdu	English
120	دنداسہ اور درختوں کے چھالکے فروش	Trader in barks
121	سوداگر بانس	Trader in bamboos
	توکریاں فروخت کرنے والا	Basket seller
123	پیتل فروش	Brass metal seller
	ہر قسم کا سامان زراعتی فروخت کرنے والا	Implement seller
	لوہا فروش	Ironmonger
	چھری-چاقو فروش	Knife seller
	سینے کی مشین بیچنے والا	Sewing-machine seller
	ٹین فروش	Tin dealer
	ہتھیار فروش	Fire-arms seller
124	اینٹ و کھپریل کا سوداگر	Trader in bricks and tiles
	مٹی کے برتن بیچنے والا	Trader in pottery
125	رنگ فروش - وارنش فروش	Dye and paint seller
	بنجارہ	Pedlar
	دوائی فروش	Chemist and druggist
	مٹی کا تیل بیچنے والا	Kerosine oil seller
	پیٹرول کا سوداگر	Trader in petroleum
	شورہ قلمی فروش	Saltpetre seller
126	ٹھیکدار آبکاری و شراب	Wine vendor
	ملازمت آبکاری	Abkari service
	برف بیچنے والا	Ice seller
	خودہ فروش	Liquor seller
	ولایتی پانی کی دوکان	Aerated water seller
127	قہوہ خانے والا	Tea seller
	ملازم ڈاک بنگلہ	Dâk-bungalow employee

Group No.	Occupation	
	Urdu	English
	ہوٹل کا ملازم و مینیجر	Manager, owner or employee of hotels
	چوکیدار-مالک-ٹھیکدار سرائے	Owner, contractor or employee of Sarais
	کبابی	Roast-meat seller
128	بوتلوں وغیرہ کی پھیری والا	Hawker of drinks and food stuffs
129	آٹا فروش	Flour seller
	غلہ فروش	Grain seller
	چاول فروش	Rice seller
	دوکان کریانہ	Grocer
	لون تیل کی دوکان والا	Oil, salt dealer
	دوکاندار گھی کھچڑی	Ghee, rice etc. dealer
	دال فروش	Pulse dealer
130	مٹھائی فروش	Dealer in sweet-meats
	دوکاندار شربت	Molasses seller
	شہد فروش	Honey seller
	شکر گڑ فروش	Gur and sugar seller
131	انڈے فروش	Egg seller
	مکھن فروش	Butter seller
	گھی فروش	Ghee seller
	پنیر فروش	Cheese seller
	دودھ دہی والا	Milk and Curd seller
32	بکری فروش	Goat dealer
	دنبہ فروش	Sheep dealer
	کبوتر-تیتر-بٹیر فروش	Pigeon, partridge, quail etc. seller
133	سبز گھاس و چارہ فروش	Grass and fodder seller
	چوکر فروش	Bran dealer
	سوکھی گھاس بیچنے والا	Hay seller
134	پان فروش	Betel leaf seller

APPENDIX IV—

PART I—

Group No.	Occupation — Urdu	Occupation — English
	خوراک کے پرندہ بیچنے والا	Bird seller
	مچھلی فروش	Fish dealer
	میوہ فروش	(ruit seller
	پنساری	Grocer
	اچار فروش	Pickle seller
	سوکھی چائے فروش	Green tea grocer
	سبزی فروش	Vegetable seller
135	تمباکو فروش	Tobacco seller
	نسوار فروش	Snuff seller
136	ٹھیکیدار افیون	Opium contractor
137	بھنگ چرس فروخت کرنے والا	Bhang and charas seller
138	عطر فروش	Perfume seller
	جوتی فروش	Shoe seller
	بوٹ فروش	Boot seller
	ٹوپی و کلاہ فروش	Dealer in caps
	بساطی	Trader in socks, umbrellas and other articles of dress and the toilet
	کنگھی فروش	Comb seller
	سرمہ فروش	Antimony seller
	کناری فروش	Lace seller
	صابن فروش	Soap seller
	گودڑی فروش	Old-clothes dealer
	ریشم فروش	Silk seller
	کباڑی	Second-hand goods and furniture vendor
139	بسترہ فروش	Trader in bedding
	چارپائی بیچنے والا	Dealer in bedsteads
	کمبل وغیرہ فروخت کرنے والا	Blanket seller

Group No.	Occupation — Urdu	Occupation — English
	قالین فروش	Trader in carpets
	پردہ فروش	Curtain seller
	فرنیچر فروش	Trader in furniture
	پھوڑ فروش	Mat seller
	خیمہ فروش	Tent seller
140	مس وغیرہ کے برتن فروخت کرنے والا	Utensil (cooking) seller etc.
	انیمل کے برتن فروخت کرنے والا	Enamelled-utensils seller
	شیشے و لیمپ فروخت کرنے والا	Dealer in glass-ware
	بساط منیاری والا	Haberdasher
141	عمارت کے سامان کی تجارت کرنے والا	Trader in building material
	چونا فروش	Lime dealer
	سرخی فروش	Surkhi seller
142	بائیسکل فروش	Dealer in bicycles
	موٹر سائیکل فروش	,, Motor cycles
	موٹر فروش	,, motors
143	سوداگر پہیہ گاڑی	Dealer in wheels of carts
	گاڑی و ریڑے فروخت کرنے والا	Dealer in carts and carriages
144	خچر و گدھے کی سوداگری کرنے والا	Dealer in mules and asses
	اونٹ و گھوڑے کی سوداگری کرنے والا	Dealer in camels and horses
	بیل کا سوداگر	Dealer in cattle
	دلال مویشیاں و اسپان	Broker of sales of animals
145	لکڑی کا کوئلہ فروخت کرنے والا	Dealer in charcoal

Occupations returned

List of Occupations

Group No.	Occupation — Urdu	Occupation — English
	ایجنٹ کوئلہ	Coal merchant
	لکڑی بیچنے والا	Fire-wood seller
	اوپلے فروخت کرنے والا	Seller of cowdung
146	سامان جراحی فروش	Dealers in optical instruments
	گھڑی فروش	Dealer in clocks
147	موتی بیچنے والا	Dealer in bead necklaces
	پنجرہ فروش	Cage seller
	پنکھا فروش	Fan seller
	مصنوعی پھول فروخت کرنے والا	Seller of artificial flowers
	کھیلنے کے سامان فروخت کرنے والا	Dealer in toys, small articles
	سامان شکار فروخت کرنے والا	Dealer in hunting and fishing tackle
148	اشتہار جاری کرنے والا	Publisher
	کھلونے، بچوں کے باجے فروخت کرنے والا	Dealer in musical instruments and curiosities
	اخبار فروش	News paper seller
	کتب فروش	Book seller
	کاغذ سیاہی فروش	Paper and ink seller
	تصویریں بیچنے والا	Dealer in pictures
	سٹیشنری کا سوداگر	Stationer
149	ردی کاغذ فروش	Dealer in waste-paper
	کباڑ فروش	Dealer in refuse
	چیتھڑے فروش	Dealer in rags
150	بنیا	Bania
	عام دوکاندار	Shopkeeper unspecified
	متفرق تجارت	Trader unspecified
151	چھابڑی فروش	Itinerant trader

Group No.	Occupation — Urdu	Occupation — English
	پھیری والا	Hawker
152	اسٹامپ فروش	Stamp vendor
153	ملازمت فوج شاہی ہر قسم	Army (imperial)
154	فوجی ملازمت ریاست ہائے ہندوستانی	Army (Indian states)
155	ملازمت بحری	Navy or Merchant Service
156	ملازمت ہوائی جہاز	Air Force
157	ملازمت پولیس	Police
158	چوکیدار دیہہ	Village watchman
159	عام ملازمت سرکار سول حیل	Service of the State, general
160	ملازمت ہندوستانی و بیرونی ریاستہائے	Service of Indian and Foreign States
161	ملازمت ڈسٹرکٹ بورڈ	District Board Service
	ملازمت کمیٹی	Municipal and other local service
	بتی جلانے والا	Lamp-lighter
162	پٹواری	Patwari
	ملازمت دیہہ	Village Official
	لمبردار	Lambardar
163	پادری	Priest, clergyman
	پنڈت	Minister
	واعظ	Religious preacher
164	شکرانہ خور	Receiver of alms
	امام مسجد	Priest of a mosque
	مذہبی درس گاہ میں رہنے والا	Religious mendicant
	فقیر	Faqir
	سادھو درویش	Sadhu, monk
165	انجیل پڑھنے والا	Bible reader

APPENDIX IV—

PART I—

Group No.	Occupation: Urdu	Occupation: English
	گورو	Spiritual guide
	مہنت	Pandit
166	ملازم گرجا	Church servant
	خادم مسجد	Mosque attendant
	مسان جلانے والا	Service at a burning ground
	ملازم قبرستان	Service at burials
	قبر کند	Grave digger
	ملازم دھرم سال	Servant in Dharm-sala
	ملازم مشن	Mission Servant
	مجاور	Shrine-keeper
167	ایجنٹ وکلا	Law agent
	وکیل	Lawyer of any kind
	قاضی	Expounder of Muslim law
168	کلرک وکلا	Lawyer's clerk
	عرائض نویس	Petition writer
169	ملازمت ڈاکٹری	Medical service
	ڈاکٹر	Doctor
	میڈیکل افسر	Civil Surgeon
	دوکان دار ڈاکٹری	Registered medical practitioner
	آنکھوں کا ڈاکٹر	Oculist / Eye Doctor
170	حکیم یونانی	Physician
	بزاری حکیم	Quack-doctor
	دانتوں اور کانوں کے کیڑے نکالنے والا	Extractor of worms from tooth or ear
171	دندان ساز	Dentists
172	ملازم اشرم یتیم خانہ	Servant in an asylum
	کمپونڈر	Compounder

Group No.	Occupation: Urdu	Occupation: English
	دایہ	Mid-wife
	ٹیکہ لگانے والا	Vaccinator
	جونک لگانے والا	Applier of leeches
	ہسپتال کی دایہ و نرس	Nurse
173	ملازمت وٹیرینری	Veterinary service
	سلوتری	Veterinary surgeon
	نعل بند	Farrier (cattle)
174	جملہ استادان	Teacher of any kind
	پروفیسر	Professor of any kind
	سکول ماسٹر	School master
	انسپکٹر مدارس	Inspector of schools
175	چپراسی سکول	School attendant
	کلرک و دیگر ادنیٰ ملازمان محکمہ تعلیم	Clerk or servant connected with education
176	معمولی منشی	Public scribe
	خطوط نویس	Letter writer
	ٹائپ کرنیوالا	Typist
	اسٹامپ نویس	Stamp-writer
	وثیقہ نویس	Bond-writer
177	ملازمت انجنیری (غیر سرکاری)	Engineering service (not Government).
	معمار	Architect
	نقشہ نویس	Draughtsman
	بندوبست کے جریب کش	Chainman of Settlement operations
178	مصنف	Author
	ایڈیٹر اخبار	Editor
	رسالہ نویس	Journalist
	فوٹو گرافر	Photographer
	شاعر	Poet

Occupations returned

List of Occupations

Group No.	Occupation — Urdu	Occupation — English
179	پتھر کے بت بنانیوالا	Sculptor
	ڈرائنگ کے اوستاد	Drawing-master
	مصور	Artist
	نقاش	Painter
180	جوتشی	Fortune-teller
		Astronomer
181		Astrologer
	جادو گر	Wizard, magician
182	ایکٹر	Actor
	باجہ بجانے والا	Bandsman, musician
	ناچنے والے-طوائف	Bandsman, musician, dancer, dancing girl
	باجے کا اوستاد	Music teacher
	مالکان و کارکنان تھیٹر	Theatre managers, employees, other than performers
	ہجڑے	Eunuch
183	ملازم چڑیا گھر	Zoological-garden employees
	کرکٹ و پولو کلب وغیرہ کے منیجران و کام کرنیوالے	Managers and employees of places of public entertainments
	ملازمت گھوڑ دوڑ	Race course
	ملازمت لائبریری	Servant in a library
	سوسائٹی و کلب گھر کے ملازم	Employee of societies and clubs
184	بازیگر-نٹ	Acrobat and tumbler
	ریچھ-بندر وغیرہ نچانے والا	Keeper of performing bear, monkey, or other wild animal

Group No.	Occupation — Urdu	Occupation — English
	مداری	Exhibitor of curiosities
	بازیگر-ساحر	Juggler, conjurer
	مدح خوان	Reciter
	پہلوان	Wrestler
	ماندری	Snake charmer
185	پنشنر (ہر قسم)	Pensioners
	وظیفہ خور	Scholarship holder
	کرایہ خور	Rent receiver (houses)
186	موٹر ڈرائیور نجی	Private motor driver
	کلینر نجی	Private motor cleaner
187	آیا	Ayah
	ملازم و نوکر نجی	Private domestic service
	بہشتی-ماشکی-سقہ	Water carrier
	سائیس	Syce
	باورچی	Cook
	خانساماں	,,
	کوچوان	Coachman
	خادمہ	Maid-servant
	خدمتگار	Servant
188	متفرق کاروبار سوداگری ٹھیکیداری	Manufacturer businessman, or contractor otherwise unspecified
189	حساب لکھنے والا خزانچی وغیرہ (نجی)	Cashier, accountant, clerk etc., in unspecified offices and factories, and shops
190	مشینوں کا کام کرنیوالا جس کا ذکر نہیں ہوا	Mechanic, otherwise unspecified
191	عام قلی-مزدور	Labourer, workman, otherwise unspecified

APPENDIX IV—Occupations returned

PART I—List of Occupations

Group No.	Occupation		Group No	Occupation	
	Urdu	English		Urdu	English
192	پوجاری وغیرہ	Pujari (Hindu priest)	195	دیگر غیر تشریح شدہ کارخانہ ھائے —	Other unclassified non - productive industries
	قیدی وغیرہ	Inmate of jail		دیوالیہ	Bankrupt
	یتیم خانہ کے رہنے والے	Inmate of asylums, alms-house etc.		جوا کھیلنے والا	Gambler
193	گدا گر	Beggar, vagrant		جوار گر	"
194	کنجریاں	Prostitute			
	دلالہ	Procurer			

PART II

APPENDIX—

PART II— Alphabetical

Occupation	Group number
A	
Accountant (Bank)	115
Accountant (Commercial)	189
Accountant (District Board)	161
Accountant (in Government Offices)	159
Accountant (Military)	153
Accountant (Mission Establishment)	166
Accountant (Municipal)	161
Accountant (Public Works Department)	103
Accountant (Railway)	112
Accountant (Village service)	162
Accounts Writer	189
Acharjya (Hindu Priest)	181
Acrobat	184
Actor	182
Administrative establishment (Air Force)	156
Administrative Establishment (Medical)	169
Administrative Establishment (Military)	153
Administrative Establishment (Education)	174
Administrative Establishment (Engineering and Survey).	177
Advocate	167
Aerated Water Factory (owners, workmen etc.)	67
Agent (of Bank)	115
Agent (Carting)	108
Agent (Commercial)	116
Agent (Insurance)	115
Agent (Law)	167
Agent (Motor Transport)	107
Agent (Railway)	112
Agent (Sugar press)	123
Agent (Warehouse)	116
A—contd.	
Agriculture, Director of—	3
Agriculture, Staff of Director of—	4
Agricultural Chemist	180
Agricultural Expert	180
Agricultural implement maker	59
Agricultural labourer	7
Aide de-Camp	153
Alabaster worker	65
Allowance drawn from Mission Boarding Fund	185
Allowance drawn from relatives	185
Aloes (resin) preparer	70
Alta (paint) dealer	125
Alta (paint) maker	70
Aluminium, worker in	61
Ammunition-factory, worker in	66
Ammunition maker	65
Ammunition seller	125
Amulet maker...	99
Amulet seller	147
Analyst	180
Animal catcher	28
Animal stuffer	99
Animal (trained), exhibitor of—	184
Animal seller	125
Appraiser (Customs house)	159
Apprentice (District Board)	161
Apprentice (Government Office)	159
Apprentice (pleader's)	167
Apprentice (Printing Press)	95
Apprentice (shop)	189
Arak (perfume) preparer	70
Arak (perfume) seller	138

Occupations returned

Index of Occupations

Occupation	Group number	Occupation	Group number
A—contd.		**A—concld.**	
Arboricultural Expert ...	180	Auditor (Railway) ...	112
Archæological Officer ...	180	Aviator (Military) ...	156
Architect	177	Ayah	187
Army Doctor	169		
Army Officer, non-commissioned officer and private (Imperial Army)	153	**B**	
Army Officer, non-commissioned officer and private (Indian State)	154	Bag (canvas) maker ...	45
Army Officer, non-commissioned officer and private (in civil employ)	159	Bag (gunny) maker ...	44
		Bag (leather) maker ...	51
Army Officer, non-commissioned officer and private (retired)	185	Bailiff (Municipal) ...	161
		Baker	81
Artisan (unspecified) ...	191	Bakhar (Ferment) preparer ...	64
Artist	179	Bakhar (Ferment) seller ...	128
Ashes, seller of— ...	149	Ballast, labourer carrying ...	113
Ass breeder	22	Bamboo articles, maker of— ...	56
Ass dealer	144	Bamboo seller ...	139
Ass (pack) owner, driver ...	110	Bandmaster (Military) ...	153
Assessor (Income Tax) ...	159	Bandmaster (non-Military) ...	182
Assessor (Municipal) ...	161	Bandsman (Imperial Force) ...	153
Assistant (Commercial) ...	189	Bandsman (not Military) ...	182
Assistant Commissioner ...	159	Bangles (glass), maker of— ...	65
Assistant Magistrate ...	159	Bangles (conch shell), maker of— ...	53
Assistant Surgeon ...	169	Bangles (gold and silver), maker of—	93
Astrologer	181	Bangles (other or unspecified materials), maker of—	93
Astronomer	180		
Asylum, inmate of— ...	192	Bangles (all kinds), seller of— ...	147
Asylum service ...	172	Baniya	150
Atar (of roses) preparer ...	70	Banker	115
Atar (of roses) seller ...	138	Banker's agent, employee ...	115
Attorney	167	Barber	86
		Bard	184
Auctioneer	116	Bar keeper, bar-man ...	127
Auditor	115	Bark collector ...	19
Auditor (Government) ...	159	Bark seller	129

Occupation	Group number	Occupation	Group number
B—contd.		**B**—contd.	
Barrister ...	167	Biscuit factory (owners, workmen, etc.)	81
Basket maker ...	56	Biscuit maker ...	81
Basket seller ...	121	Bishop ...	163
Bath house (owners, employees, etc.)	87	Blacksmith ...	59
Bead maker ...	98	Blacksmith's servant ...	59
Bead seller ...	147	Blanket seller ...	139
Bear dancer ...	184	Blanket weaver ...	46
Bearer (Church) ...	166	Bleacher of textiles ...	49
Bearer (domestic) ...	187	Boarding house keeper ...	127
Bearer (palki) ...	109	Boat builder, painter, repairer ...	93
Bedstead (of any material), maker ...	89	Boat man, boat owner ...	02
Bedstead (of any material), seller ...	139	Boat seller ...	'43
Beggar (other than religious) ...	193	Boats, unloader of ...	111
Beggar (religious) ...	164	Body guard ...	153
Bellows, blower of blacksmith's ...	59	Boiler Inspector ...	159
Bell metal, seller of— ...	123	Boiler maker ...	59
Bell metal, worker in— ...	60	Bone black, manufacturer of— ...	53
Bell metal, utensils, maker and repairer of—	60	Bone seller ...	118
Bell metal, utensils seller ...	140	Bone, worker in— ...	53
Bell ringer (church) ...	166	Bonnet maker ...	84
Belt marker (dress) ...	84	Book agent ...	148
Belting maker (for machinery) ...	45	Book binder ...	95
Bench clerk ...	159	Book keeper (unspecified) ...	189
Betel leaf seller ...	134	Book maker (horse racing)	183
Bhagavat reader ...	165	Book publisher, seller ...	148
Bhang preparer ...	80	Boot maker ...	82
Bhang seller ...	137	Boot seller ...	138
Bhisti, (water carrier) ...	187	Bottle seller ...	140
Bible reader ...	165	Box (leather) maker ...	51
Bicycle dealer ...	142	Box (tin) maker .	61
Bicycle maker, repairer ...	91	Box (wood) maker ...	55
Bird catcher ...	28	Braid (all kinds) seller ...	117
Bird seller ...	134	Brakeman ...	112

Occupations returned—continued

Index of Occupations—*continued*

Occupation	Group number
B—contd.	
Bran dealer ...	133
Brass foundry (owners, workmen, etc.)	60
Brass, seller of— ...	123
Brass utensils maker, repairer of— ...	60
Brass utensils, seller of— ...	140
Brass, worker in— ...	60
Brewery (owners, workmen, etc.) ...	77
Brick burner ...	64
Brick carrier, layer ...	90
Brick maker, moulder ...	64
Brick pounder ...	90
Brick seller ...	124
Brick and tile factory (owners, workmen, etc.)	64
Bridge, peon attached to— ...	105
Bristles, seller of— ...	118
Broker, (shares and stocks) ...	116
Broker (unspecified) ...	116
Broker's agent ...	116
Broom maker ...	56
Broom seller ...	140
Brush seller ...	138
Bucket (leather) maker ...	51
Bucket (wooden) maker ...	55
Buffalo herdsman ...	21
Buffalo keeper ...	21
Bugler (Imperial Army) ...	153
Bugler (other than military) ...	182
Builder (building contractor) ...	90
Building contractor ...	90
Building material, trader in— ...	141
Bullock cart driver, owner ...	108
Bullock dealer, hirer ...	144
B—concld.	
Bullock (pack) driver, owner ..	110
Bungalow repairer ...	90
Burial ground or burning ghat service	166
Burning ghat Brahman ...	166
Business man (unspecified) ...	188
Butcher ...	73
Butler ...	187
Butter maker ...	81
Butter seller ...	131
C	
Cabinet maker ...	88
Cafe, manager, etc. ...	127
Cage maker ...	99
Cage seller ...	147
Cake maker ...	81
Call man (Telegraph and Telephone)	114
Camel attenda ...	22
Camel breeder ...	22
Camel dealer ...	144
Camel driver ...	110
Camel (pack) owner ...	110
Can (tin) maker ...	61
Canal labourer ...	104
Canal service (including construction)	103
Cantonment Magistrate ...	159
Canvas seller ...	117
Cap maker, binder ...	84
Cap seller ...	138
Capitalist ...	185
Captain (Imperial Army) ...	153
Carbonate of soda (sajji) extractor ...	41

APPENDIX—

PART II—Alphabetical

Occupation	Group number
C—contd.	
Carpenter ...	55
Carpentry works (owners, workmen, etc.)	55
Carpet seller ..	43
Carpet weaver (cotton) ...	43
Carpet weaver (wool) ...	46
Carriage builder ...	92
Carriage (Railway) examiner ...	112
Carriage (Railway) workshop (managers, workmen, etc.)	112
Carriage painter ...	88
Carriage seller ...	143
Carriage wheel maker ...	92
Carriage wheel seller ...	143
Carrier (carrying agency) ...	108
Carrier (porter) ...	111
Cart driver, owner ...	108
Cart maker, repairer ...	92
Cart seller ...	143
Carter (Municipal) ...	161
Carting Agent ...	108
Carver (wood and ebony) ...	55
Cashier (Bank) ...	115
Cashier (Coal Depôt) ...	145
Cashier (Government) ...	159
Cashier (Municipal) ...	161
Cashier (Railway) ...	112
Cashier (unspecified) ...	189
Catamite ...	194
Catechist ...	165
Cattle breeder ...	21
Cattle dealer ...	144
Cattle farrier ...	173
Cattle herdsman ...	21
Cattle skinner ...	51
Chain (copper) maker ...	60
Chain (gold and silver) maker ...	98
Chain (iron) maker ...	59
Chainman ...	177
Chair maker ...	59
Chairman, Municipality ...	161
Chamar ...	39
Chandler ...	154
Chaplain ...	165
Chaprasi (Canal service) ...	103
Chaprasi (Cantonment) ...	161
Chaprasi (District Board) ...	161
Chaprasi (Education Department) ...	175
Chaprasi (Forest) ...	17
Chaprasi (Government) ...	159
Chaprasi (Municipality) ...	161
Chaprasi (Post or Telegraph) ...	124
Chaprasi (School) ...	175
Chaprasi (Shop) ...	189
Chaprasi (unspecified) ...	111
Charas seller ...	137
Charcoal burner ...	18
Charcoal dealer ...	145
Charcoal-cake maker ...	18
Charcoal cake seller ...	145
Chaudri (of coolies, etc.) ...	108
Chaukidar (Circuit house) ...	159
Chaukidar (Dâk Bungallow) ...	127
Chaukidar (District Board) ...	161
Chaukidar (Government Office) ...	159

Occupations returned—continued

Index of Occupations—continued

Occupation	Group number
C—contd.	
Chaukidar (Graveyard) ...	166
Chaukidar (Lodging-house) ...	127
Chaukidar (Municipality) ...	161
Chaukidar (private) ...	187
Chaukidar (Railway) ...	112
Chaukidar (Village) ...	158
Cheese maker ...	81
Cheese-seller ...	131
Chemical products, dealer in— ...	125
Chemist (dealers in drugs) ...	125
Chemist (dispensing) ...	125
Chess-board maker ...	99
Chief Commissioner ...	159
Chikan-work maker ...	50
Chikan-workseller ...	138
Chilli seller ...	134
Chimney builder ...	90
Chira preparer ...	72
Chocolate maker ...	75
Church service ...	166
Cigar, cigarette maker ...	78
Cigar, cigarette seller ...	135
Circuit house servant ...	127
Circumciser ...	166
Circus manager or servant (not performer)	183
Circus performer ...	184
Civil officer ...	159
Civil service ...	159
Civil Surgeon ...	169
Clergyman ...	163
Clerk (articled) ...	168
Clerk (Bank) ...	115
C—contd.	
Clerk (Canal) ...	103
Clerk (Broker's) ...	116
Clerk (Cantonment) ...	161
Clerk (Customs) ...	159
Clerk (District Board) ...	161
Clerk (Education) ...	175
Clerk (Forest Department) ...	17
Clerk (Government) ...	159
Clerk (Hotel) ...	127
Clerk (Insurance Office) ...	115
Clerk in Holy Orders ...	163
Clerk (landed estate ...	4
Clerk (of learned, charitable societies, clubs, etc.)	183
Clerk (Lawyer's) ...	168
Clerk (Mercantile) ...	189
Clerk (Military Department) ...	153
Clerk (Municipality) ...	161
Clerk (Post office) ...	114
Clerk (Printing Press) ...	95
Clerk (Railway) ...	112
Clerk (Survey office) ...	177
Clerk (Telegraph) ...	114
Clerk (unspecified, shops, etc.) ...	189
Clock maker, repairer ...	97
Clock seller ...	146
Cloth dyer, printer ...	49
Cloth seller ...	117
Cloth washer ...	85
Cloth weaver (cotton) ...	43
Cloth weaver (silk) ...	47
Cloth weaver (wool) ...	46
Clothes (old) dealer ...	13[illegible]

Occupation	Group number	Occupation	Group number
C—contd.		**C—contd.**	
Clothing (ready-made), dealer in— ...	138	Concubine ...	195
Club, service in residential ...	127	Condiment dealer ...	130
Club, service in Polo, Cricket etc. ...	183	Conjuror ...	184
Coachman (private) ...	187	Conservancy cooly ...	100
Coachman (of public conveyance) ...	108	Conservancy Inspector ...	161
Coal broker ...	116	Conservator of Forests ...	17
Coal dealer, agent ...	145	Constable ...	157
Cobbler ...	82	Contractor, Building ...	90
Cocoanut seller ...	134	Contractor, for coolies ...	116
Cocoanut fibre rope maker ...	45	Contractor for railway works ...	112
Cocoon dealer ...	117	Contractor for road works ...	105
Cocoon winder ...	47	Contractor unspecified ...	188
Coffee roaster ...	81	Controller (Government Department)	159
Coffee stall keeper ...	127	*Convict in Jail or Reformatory* ...	192
Coke burner (at gas works) ...	94	Cook (domestic) ...	187
Collar maker ...	84	Cook (in hotel) ...	127
Collecting clerk (unspecified) ...	189	Cooly (ballast) ...	113
Collector (Deputy) ...	159	Cooly (Municipal) ...	161
Collector (Income tax) ...	159	Cooly (Public Works Department) ...	106
Collector of a District ...	159	Cooly (Railway) ...	113
Collector (Municipal) ...	161	Cooly (Road) ...	106
College Hostel staff ...	175	Cooly (Telegraph) ...	114
Colonel (Imperial Army) ...	153	Cooly (unspecified) ...	191
Comb maker ...	87	Cooly Depôt, clerk in ...	160
Comb seller ...	138	Cord manufacturer ...	45
Commercial traveller ...	116	Cotton cloth calenderer ...	49
Commissariat farm establishment ...	21	Cotton carpet seller ...	139
Commission Agent ...	116	Cotton weaver	43
Composer (music) ...	182	Cotton carder, cleaner ...	42
Compositor Printing Press) ...	95	Cotton cloth seller ...	117
Compounder (Hospital) ...	172	Cotton dyer, fuller ...	49
Conch shell bangle maker ...	53	Cotton ginner ...	42
Concrete worker in— ...	90		

Occupations returned—continued

Index of Occupations—continued

Occupation	Group number
C—contd.	
Cotton ginning mills (owners, workmen, etc.)	42
Coton présser ...	42
Cotton Pressing mills (owners, workmen, etc.)	42
Cotton (raw) dealer ...	117
Cotton sizer ...	43
Cotton spinner ...	43
Cotton thread seller ...	117
Cotton weaver ...	43
Cotton weaving mills (owners, workmen, etc.)	43
Country paper maker ...	70
Country paper seller ...	148
Country spirit distiller. ...	77
Country spirit seller ...	126
Court of Wards manager and employees	3
Cow-dung gatherer ...	100
Cow-dung seller ...	145
Cowherd ...	21
Crèam seller ...	131
Crockery, dealer in— ...	140
Crockery maker of— ...	65
Crop watcher ...	7
Crushed food seller ...	133
Crystal ware manufacturer ...	65
Crystal seller ...	142
Cultivator (of own land) ...	5
Cultivator (tenant) ...	6
Curd seller ...	131
Curiosity dealer ...	148
Currier ...	51
Curtain maker ...	89
C—concld.	
Curtain seller ...	139
Cushion maker ...	89
Cushion seller ...	139
Custom House Officer ...	159
D	
Daffadar (Forest) ...	17
Daffadar (Police) ...	157
Dak runner ...	114
Dancer, dancing girl ...	182
Dargah, inmate of— ...	164
Darner ...	83
Daroga (Customs) ...	159
Daroga (Municipal) ...	161
Daroga (Police) ...	157
Daroga (Salt Department) ...	159
Darzi ...	83
Date mat maker ...	56
Day labourer ...	191
Dead bodies, burner of— ...	166
Delivery agent ...	111
Dentist ...	171
Deputy Collector, Commissioner ...	159
Detective ...	157
Devotee ...	164
Director of Criminal Intelligence ...	157
Director of Public Instruction ...	174
Director of Public Information ...	159
Dispensary service ...	172
Distillery (owners, workmen, etc) ...	77
Distillery Expert ...	159
Distributor (Press) ...	95

Occupation	Group number	Occupation	Group number
D—concld.		**E**—contd.	
Diviner ...	181	Earring seller ...	146
Doctor ...	169	Earth worker ...	106
Dog boy ...	187	Earthen pot (pipe bowl, etc.,) maker	63
Dog breeder ...	23	Earthen toy maker ...	99
Dog seller ...	152	Earthen ware articles. Seller of— ...	124
Domestic service ...	187	Editor ...	178
Doorkeeper (private) ...	187	Education Department (employee) ...	174 and 175
Doorkeeper (Railway) ...	112		
Doorkeeper (shop) ...	189	Egg dealer ...	131
Draper ...	138	Ekka driver, owner ...	108
Draughtsman ...	177	Ekka maker ...	92
Drawing master ...	174	Ekka seller ...	143
Dredger, service in— ...	104	Electric light works, employee in—...	94
Dresser (in hospital) ...	172	Embroidery maker ...	50
Dressmaker ...	83	Enamelled cup, plate, etc., seller ...	140
Dress (ready made) seller ...	138	Endowment (educational, etc.,) holder	185
Driver (motor vehicles plying for hire)	107	Engine driver (factory, etc.) ...	150
Driver (private motors) ...	186	Engine driver (Railway) ...	112
Driver (Engine—on Railway) ...	112	Engine driver (Steamer) ...	102
Drummer (military) ...	153	Engineer (Civil, Executive) ...	103
Drummer (other than military) ...	182	Engineer (District) ...	161
Drum-maker repairer ...	96	Engineer (Electrical) ...	94
Drum-seller ...	148	Engineer (Military, Royal) ...	153
Dust contractor ...	100	Engineer (Municipal) ...	161
Dye seller ...	125	Engineer (Railway) ...	112
Dyer (leather) ...	51	Engineering workshop (owners, workmen, etc.)	59
Dyer (of textiles) ...	49	Engraver ...	95
Dyer (of used articles) ...	85	Engravings. Dealer in— ...	148
		Excavator ...	90
E		Exchange agent ...	115
Ear borer .	87	Exchange broker ...	115
Earring maker ...	98		

Occupations returned—**continued**

Index of Occupations—**continued**

Occupation	Group number	Occupation	Group number
E—concld.		**F—contd.**	
Excise Inspector, peons, etc. ...	159	Firewood seller ...	145
Excise Lessee's servant ...	126	Firework maker ...	66
Executive Engineer ...	103	Firework seller ...	125
Executive Officer (Cantonment) ...	159	Fish cage maker ...	99
Exhibitor of curiosities, wild animals	184	Fish cage seller ...	147
		Fish dealer ...	134
Explosives, dealer in— ...	125	Fisherman ...	27
Exporter (of goods) ...	116	Fish net maker ...	45
Eye doctor (occulist) ...	169	Fish net seller ...	147
Eye powder (surma) maker ...	70	Fitter (electric light or gas works) ...	94
Eye powder (surma) seller ...	138	Fitter (Railway) ...	112
		Fitter (unspecified) ...	190
F		Flour grinder ...	71
Fakir ...	164	Flour mill (owners, workmen, etc.)	71
Fan maker ...	99		
Fan (leaf) maker ...	56	Flour seller ...	129
Fan seller ...	147	Flower (artificial) maker ...	99
Farm servant ...	7	Flower (artificial) seller ...	147
Farmer (cultivator) ...	6	Follower (Imperial Army) ...	153
Farrier ...	173	Footman ...	187
Feathers, collector of— ...	28	Forest officer, clerk, ranger, guard, etc. ...	17
Feathers, dealer in— ...	118		
Ferryman ...	102	Forest produce collector ...	19
Fibre (raw) dealer in— ...	117	Fortune teller ...	181
Fibre bag maker ...	45	*Fringes, maker of—* ...	50
Fibre bag seller ...	139	Fruit seller ...	134
Field labourer, watcher ...	7	Fruit tree grower, grafter, watcher ...	16
File maker ...	59	Fuel collector ...	19
Fire arms seller of— ...	123	Fuel seller ...	145
Fireman (Fire engine) ...	161	Fund holder ...	185
Fireman (Railway) ...	112	Funeral service, taker of gifts, etc. ...	166
Fireman (unspecified) ...	190	Fur, hunter of animals for their— ...	28
Firewood collector ...	18	Fur, dealer in— ...	118

Occupation	Group number
F—concld.	
Furniture factory (owners, workmen, etc.)	88
Furniture maker, polisher, varnisher ...	88
Furniture seller ..	139
G	
Gaiter maker ...	84
Gaiter seller ...	138
Gambler ...	195
Games, seller of bats, racquets, balls, etc. for—	147
Gangman (of railway coolies) ...	112
Ganja preparer ..	80
Ganja seller ...	137
Garden fruits, seller of— ...	134
Gardener ...	16
Garlic seller ...	134
Gas fiter ...	94
Gas lighter (Municipal) ...	161
Gas works (managers, workmen, etc.)	94
Gateman (Railway) ...	112
German silver, worker in— ...	61
Ghee pot (leather) maker ...	51
Ghee pot seller ...	131
Gilder ...	98
Glass (looking) maker ...	65
Glass (looking) seller ...	140
Glassware, maker of— ...	65
Glassware, seller of— ...	140
Glazier ...	90
Gleaner ...	7
Glove maker ...	87
Goat breeder ...	23
G—contd.	
Goat butcher ..	73
Goat dealer ...	132
Goat herd ...	23
Gold beater, burnisher ...	98
Gold dealer ...	146
Gold wire drawer ...	98
Gold, worker in— ...	98
Goldsmith's dust washer ...	98
Governess ...	174
Government officers of all grades ...	159
Grain broker, dealer ...	129
Grain gleaner ...	7
Grain grinder, husker ...	71
Grain lender ...	129
Grain parcher ...	72
Grain (parched) seller of— ...	129
Grain weigher, measurer ...	116
Grass cutter ...	19
Grass seller ...	133
Grave digger ...	166
Gravel digger ...	41
Greengrocer ...	134
Grindstone maker, mender ...	90
Grindstone seller ..	152
Grocer ...	134
Groom (Livery stable) ...	108
Groom (private) ...	187
Guard (Forest) ...	17
Guard (Jail) ...	159
Guard (Railway) ...	112
Guard (Temple) ...	166
Gum collector ..	19

Occupations returned—continued

Index of Occupations—continued

Occupation	Group number
G—concld.	
Gum seller ...	125
Gun seller ...	123
Gunner (Military) ...	153
Gunny-bag seller ...	117
Gur, maker of— ...	74
Gur seller ...	130
Guru (spiritual guide) ...	165
Gymnastic master ...	174
H	
Haberdasher ...	138
Hackney-carriage hirer ...	108
Hair, dealer in— ...	117
Hair dresser, plucker ...	86
Hakim (Judicial officer) ...	159
Hakim (Physician) ...	170
Hammerman ...	59
Hammerman in Railway Workshop ...	112
Hardware, maker of— ...	59
Hardware, seller of— ...	140
Harness maker ...	51
Harness seller ...	118
Hat maker ...	84
Hat seller ...	118
Havildar (Military) ...	153
Havildar (Police) ...	157
Hay seller ...	133
Hawker ...	151
Head Constable ...	157
Headman of village ...	162
Health Officer ...	169
Herbalist ...	170
Herdsman ...	23
H—concld.	
Hides, dealer in— ...	118
Hides, curer of— ...	51
Hing (asafoetida) dealer ...	125
Hodman ...	90
Hoe dealer ...	123
Homaeopathic practitioner ...	170
Honey collector ...	19
Honey seller ...	130
Horn dealer ...	118
Horoscope caster ...	181
Horse breeder, trainer ...	22
Horse dealer ...	144
Horse shoe maker ...	59
Horse trainer (for racing) ...	183
Hosier ...	138
Hosiery, maker of— ...	84
Hospital assistant ...	169
Hospital service ...	172
Hotel keeper, manager, etc. ...	127
House agent ...	116
House builder, repairer, tiler ...	90
House owner ...	185
Hukka bearer ...	187
Hukka maker ...	99
Hukka seller ...	147
Hunter ...	28
Huntsman ...	183
I	
Ice Factories (owners, workmen, etc.)	67
Ice maker ...	67
Ice cream maker ...	75
Ice seller ...	126

APPENDIX—

PART II—Alphabetical

Occupation	Group number	Occupation	Group number
I—contd.		**I—concld.**	
Image (earthen) maker ...	65	Iron, worker in— ...	59
Image (of all kinds) seller ...	147	Irrigation Department employees ...	103
Implement (agricultural) maker ...	59		
Implement (agricultural) seller ...	123	**J**	
Income from investments ...	185	Jailor, Jail Warder (Government) ...	159
Income tax assessor ...	159	Jamadar (Army) ...	153
Indian Civil Service ...	159	Jamadar (Police) ...	157
Informer ...	157	Jobber (stock, etc.) ...	115
Ink seller ...	148	Jockey	183
Ink man, printing press ...	95	Joiner	55
Ink pot maker ...	99	Journalist	178
Inn keeper ...	127	Judge	159
Inspector (Local works) ...	177	Juggler	184
Inspector (Permanent-way) ...	112	**K**	
Inspector (Police) ...	157	Kanúngo	3
Inspector (Postal) ...	114	Kazi	167
Inspector (Railway) ...	112	Kennel man	28
Inspector (Salt) ...	159	Kerosine oil dealer ...	125
Inspector (School) ...	174	Keyman (Railway) ...	112
Inspector (Traffic) ...	112	Khansama (private) ...	187
Inspector (Vaccination) ...	172	Khansama (Hotel, Dâk Bungalow) ...	127
Inspectress (Schools) ...	174	Kite maker	99
Inspector-General of Civil Hospitals	169	Kite seller	147
Inspector-General of Police ...	157	Knife grinder, maker ...	59
Inspector-General of Prisons ...	159	Knife seller	123
Instrument (musical) maker ..	96	Koran reader	165
Instrument (musical) seller ...	148	Kuth (Sassurea Lappa) gatherer ...	19
Insurance agent ...	115		
Interpreter (Court) ...	168	**L**	
Iron dealer	123	Lac articles, maker of— ...	99
Ironmonger	123	Lac articles, seller of— ...	148
Iron (old) seller ...	123	Lac dealer	125
Iron rivet maker ...	59	Lac dye maker ...	70

Occupations returned—**continued**

Index of Occupations—**continued**

Occupation	Group number
L—contd.	
Lac manufacturer ...	70
Lace maker	50
Lace seller	138
Lamp maker	88
Lamp seller	140
Lamp lighter (Municipal) ...	161
Lamp man (Railway) ...	112
Landholder (cultivating) ...	5
Landholder (non-cultivating) ...	1
Latrine cleaner ...	100
Law Agent, Lawyer ...	167
Lawyer's clerk ...	168
Lead seller	123
Lead, worker in— ...	61
Leadsman	102
Leaf plate maker ...	56
Leaf plate seller ...	121
Leather articles, maker of— ...	51
Leather articles, seller of— ...	118
Leather curer... ...	51
Leather dealer ...	118
Leather dyer	51
Leather factory (owners, workmen, etc.)	51
Leather stamper ...	51
Leather tanner ...	51
Leaves, worker in— ...	56
Lecturer	174
Legal Remembrancer ...	159
Lemonade seller ...	126
Letter carrier (private) ...	111
Library Service ...	183
Lieutenant (Army) ...	153
Lime, dealer in— ...	141
L—concld.	
Lime-kiln labourer ...	90
Lime-stone burner ...	90
Lime quarrier	39
Lime seller	141
Lineman (Railway) ...	112
Lineman (Telegraph) ...	114
Lingam maker ...	99
Lingam seller	147
Liquor dealer	126
Liquor distiller ...	77
Literary institution, service in— ...	183
Lithographer	95
Litho-press owner ...	95
Livery stable keeper ...	144
Load carrier	111
Local Board Road Overseer ...	105
Local Board service ...	161
Lock keeper (canal) ...	103
Locksmith	59
Lodging-house keeper ...	127
Loom, loom-comb maker ...	55
M	
Magician	181
Magistrate (all grades) ...	159
Magistrate (Cantonment) ...	159
Mahabrahman ...	166
Maid servant	187
Mail carriage contractor, manager ...	107
Major (Army) ...	153
Manager (Bank) ...	115
Manager (Hotel) ...	127
Manager (unspecified) ...	188

Occupation	Group number
M—contd.	
Manure collector ...	100
Manure seller	149
Marker (billiard) ...	183
Marker (rifle range) ...	153
Mason	90
Masseur	172
Mat maker (bamboo, cane or leaf) ...	56
Mat maker (cotton) ...	43
Mat maker (wool) ...	46
Mat seller ...	139
Match factory (owners, workmen etc.)	66
Match seller ...	125
Matron (hospital, etc.) ...	170
Mechanic	190
Medical practitioner (Licensed) ...	169
Medical practitioner (unlicensed) (Kabiraj, Hakim, etc.) ...	170
Medicine seller ...	125
Member, Board of Revenue ...	159
Mendicant (not religious) ...	193
Mendicant (religious) ...	164
Menial (domestic) ...	187
Menial (unspecified) ...	191
Merchant (unspecified) ...	150
Messenger	111
Metals, dealer in— ...	123
Metallurgist	180
Meteorologist	180
Mica, worker in— ...	65
Midwife	172
Military administrative establishment ...	153
Military bandsman ...	153
Military Officer under political training	159
Military Police ...	157
M—contd.	
Military service (all kinds, Government)	153
Military service (Indian States) ...	154
Milkman, milkmaid ...	21
Milk (condensed) manufacturer ...	81
Milk seller	131
Milliner	83
Millinery, seller of— ...	138
Millstone maker, mender ...	90
Millstone seller ...	152
Mimic	184
Mineral water factory (owners, workmen, etc.)	67
Mission catechist ...	165
Mission pensioner ...	185
Mission service ...	166
Missionary doctor ...	169
Molasses preparer ...	74
Molasses seller ...	130
Monastery, inmate of— ...	164
Money-lender, changer, tester ...	115
Money-lender's agent ...	115
Monk	164
Monkey dancer ...	184
Mosaic seller	147
Mosaic worker ...	65
Mosque attendant ...	166
Motor-car maker, repairer ...	91
Motor-car seller ...	142
Mounte-bank	184
Muharrir (Road) ...	15
Mukhtiar	167
Mule breeder	22
Mule dealer	144
Mule (pack) owner, driver ...	110

Occupations returned—continued

Index of Occupations—continued

Occupation	Group number
M—concld.	
Municipal Secretary ...	161
Municipal service ...	161
Munsiff	159
Museum (officer and staff) ...	183
Mushroom grower ...	16
Music composer ...	182
Music, dealer in— ...	148
Music teacher ...	182
Musical instrument maker, repairer ...	96
Musical instrument player ...	182
Musical instrument seller, hirer ...	148
Musician	182
Muslin maker... ...	43
Muslin seller	117
Mustard oil dealer ...	134
Mustard manufacturer, presse ...	68
Mustard seed dealer ...	129
N	
Naik (Imperial Army) ...	153
Naik (Military Police) ...	157
Nail maker	59
Naturalist (Man of science) ...	180
Naturalist (taxidermist) ...	99
Nautch girl	182
Navy service (all kinds) ...	155
Nazir (Government) ...	159
Necklace maker ...	98
Necklace seller ...	146
Necromancer	181
Net maker, weaver ...	45
Newar weaver ...	43
Newspaper manager, proprietor, etc....	178
Newspaper vendor ...	148
N—concld.	
Nickel dealer	123
Nickel, worker in— ...	61
Night-soil remover ...	100
Nomad (hunting) ...	28
Nomad (keeping camels and asses)...	22
Nomad (keeping cattle) ...	21
Nomad (keeping sheep) ...	23
Notary public	167
Nun	164
Nurse (child's) ...	187
Nurse (hospital, sick nurse) ...	172
Nurseryman	16
O	
Oculist	169
Officer (Civil) of Imperial Government	
Officer (Education) ...	174
Officer (Forest) ...	17
Officer Inspecting (Medical) ...	169
Officer (Military) ...	153
Officer (Non-Commissioned) ...	153
Officer (Police) ...	157
Officer (Post and Telegraph) ...	114
Officer (Public Works Departmet	103, 105, 112
Officer (Railway) ...	112
Official Assignee ...	167
Oil-cake seller ...	133
Oil (Hair) seller ...	138
Oilman (Railway) ...	112
Oilman (unspecified) ...	191
Oil mill (owners, workmen, etc.) ...	68
Oil presser, refiner ...	63 & 69
Oil press (iron) maker ...	59

Occupation	Group number
O—concld.	
Oil press(wood) ...	55
Oil seller	134
Opium vendor	136
Optical instruments maker ...	97
Optical instruments seller ...	146
Optician	97
Orchard keeper ...	16
Order supplier	116
Orderly (Military) ...	153
Orderly (Police) ...	157
Organist	182
Ornament (jewellery) maker ...	98
Ornament seller ...	146
Orphanage, inmate of— ...	192
Overseer (Conservancy) ...	100
Overseer (District Board) ...	177
Overseer (Municipal) ...	161
Overseer (Post Office) ...	114
Overseer (Public Works Department)	103, 105 & 112
Overseer (Railway) ...	112
Overseer (Road) ...	105
Overseer (unspecified) ...	189
P	
Pachwai seller ...	126
Paint manufacturer ...	70
Painter (Artist) ...	179
Painter (boat) ...	93
Painter (carriage) ...	88
Painter (house) ...	90
Palki-bearer, owner ...	109
Palki maker ...	92

Occupation	Group number
P—contd.	
Palki seller ...	143
Palm leaf, worker in— ...	56
Pan (betel leaf) seller ...	130
Panda (pilgrim conductor) ...	166
Panda's servant ...	166
Pandit (school) ...	174
Paper hanger ...	90
Paper maker ...	70
Paper seller ...	148
Paper (waste) dealer ...	149
Paper box maker ...	95
Parched rice seller ...	129
Parchment maker ...	51
Pasham worker ...	46
Paste-board manufacturer ...	70
Pastor ...	163
Patent stone manufacturer ...	90
Patshala teacher ...	174
Patwari ...	162
Pawnbroker ...	115
Pedlar ...	151
Pen (metal) maker ...	59
Pen (metal) seller ...	148
Pensioner (all kinds) ...	185
Perfume preparer ...	70
Perfume seller ...	138
Periodicals, seller of— ...	148
Petition writer ...	168
Petroleum dealer ...	125
Pewt[illegible] ewellery maker ...	98
Pewter seller ...	146
Pewter, worker in— ...	61
Photo [illegible] ...	95

Occupations returned —continued

Index of Occupations—continued

Occupation	Group number	Occupation	Group number
P—contd.		**P—contd.**	
Photographer ...	178	Pony (pack) owner, driver ...	110
Photographic apparatus seller ...	146	Porcelain factory (owners, workmen, etc.)	65
Physician ...	169 & 170	Porcelain manufacturer ...	65
Pickle seller ...	134	Porcelain seller ...	140
Picture dealer ...	148	Porter ...	111
Picture frame maker ...	99	Portmanteau seller ...	118
Picture frame seller ...	148	Portrait painter ...	179
Piece-goods dealer ...	117	Postmaster General ...	114
Pigeon dealer ...	132	Post Office service (all grades) ...	114
Pilgrim conductor ...	166	Potato seller ...	134
Pilot ...	103	Pottery ware maker (potter) ...	63
Pimp ...	194	Pottery ware seller ...	140
Pincushion maker ...	99	Poultry seller ...	132
Pipe (earthen) maker ...	63	Pound keeper ...	152
Pipe (iron) maker ...	59	Powder (tooth) maker ...	70
Pitch dealer ...	125	Powder (tooth) seller ...	138
Pitch worker, melter ...	70	Preacher ...	165
Pith, worker in— ...	56	Preceptor (Religious) ...	163
Planer ...	55	Press (printing) proprietor ...	95
Plasterer ...	90	Preventive officer ...	159
Pleader ...	167	Priest ...	163
Plinth maker ...	90	Principal of a college ...	174
Ploughman	7	Print dealer ..	148
Plough maker ...	59	Printer ...	95
Plough seller ...	123	Printing press (owners, workmen, etc.)	95
Plumber ...	90	Printing (Government) Superintendent	95
Podder (money tester) (Government)	159	Prisoner (all kinds) ...	192
Podder (money tester) (private) ...	115	Private means ...	185
Poe ...	178	Private tutor ...	174
Pointsman (Railway) ...	112	Procurer ...	194
Police (all grades of police officers and men).	157	Professor ...	174
Political Officer ...	159	Proof reader ...	95
		Proprietor (of house, etc.) ...	185

APPENDIX—

PART II—Alphabetical

Occupation	Group number	Occupation	number
P—concld.		**R—contd.**	
Proprietor (landed estate) ...	1	Railway service of all kinds (other than above)	112
Prostitute ...	194	Railway workshop(owners, workmen, etc.)	112
Protector of emigrants ...	159	Ranger (Forest) ...	17
Public entertainment places of, (owners, managers, etc.)	183	Razor maker ...	59
Public entertainment, places of, persons employed in	183	Reader (religious service) ...	165
Public entertainment, places of, scribes	176	Receiver (appointed by court) ...	116
Public Works Department Officers ...	159	Reciter ...	184
Publishers ...	148	Reed seller ...	122
Pujari (temple) ...	166	Refreshment room keeper ...	127
Pumpman (Railway) ...	112	Refuse matter, dealer in— ...	149
Punkha puller ...	187	Registrar (Education) ...	175
Puppet dancer ...	184	Registrar (Government) ...	159
Purohit ...	163	Religious mendicant ...	164
Purse maker ...	99	Religious student supported by teacher.	164
Purser ...	102	Rent collector (agricultural land) ...	4
		Rent collector (municipal) ...	161
Q		Rent collector (unspecified) ...	189
Quack doctor ...	170	Rent payer (cultivator) ...	6
Quicksilver, dealer in— ...	123	Rent receiver (agricultural) ...	1
Quicksilver, worker in— ...	61	Rent receiver (house rent) ...	185
Quinologist ...	180	Reporter (Newspaper) ...	178
		Resin preparer ...	70
R		Resin seller ...	125
Race course service ...	183	Restaurant (owners, managers, etc.)	127
Rag dealer ...	149	Rest house (owners, managers, etc.)	127
Rag gatherer ...	100	Revenue Agent ...	167
Railway cooly or porter or water carrier, all kinds	113	Rice (cooked) seller ...	127
Railway doctor ...	169	Rice winnower ...	71
Railway mail service ...	114	Rider (Jockey) ...	183
Railway police ...	157	Rider (private) ...	187
Railway sweeper ...	100	Ring (ornament) maker ...	98

Occupations returnd—continued

Index of Occupations—continued

Occupation	Group number
R—concld.	
Ring seller ...	146
Ring for well (earthen) maker ...	64
Ring for well (earthen) seller ...	124
Road, breaker of stone for— ...	106
Road labourer ...	106
Road (Sarkar, contractor) ...	103
Rope maker ...	45
Rope seller ...	117
Rope works (owners, workmen, etc.)	45
Rosary maker ...	99
Rosary seller ...	147
Rose-water preparer ...	70
Rose-water seller ...	138
Rubber stamp maker ...	99
Rubber stamp seller ...	148
S	
Saddle-cloth maker, embroiderer ...	50
Saddle-cloth seller ...	117
Saddler ...	51
Saddlery, dealer in— ...	118
Sadhu (religious mendicant) ...	164
Sajji (carbonate of soda) refiner ...	70
Salesman (unspecified) ...	189
Saltpetre extractor ...	40
Saltpetre refiner ...	70
Saltpetre seller ...	125
Salt preparer, miner, extractor ...	40
Salt seller ...	134
Sanitary Inspector (Government) ...	159
Sanitary Inspector (Municipal). ...	161
Sawyer ...	54
Scabbard maker ...	51
S—contd.	
Scavenger ...	100
Scholarship holder ..	18
School Inspector, master ...	17
Scissors maker ...	59
Scissors seller ...	123
Screen maker ...	88
Screen maker (bamboo) ...	56
Screen seller ...	139
Scripture reader ...	165
Secretary (Government) ...	159
Section holder, press ...	95
Section writer (Government) ...	159
Section writer (unspecified) ...	176
Seed (garden) seller ...	147
Sepoy (Military) ...	153
Sepoy (Indian State) ...	154
Sepoy (Police) ...	157
Serai (owners, managers, etc.) ...	127
Sergeant (Military) ...	153
Sergeant (Police) ...	157
Servant (groom, coachman, dog-boy, etc.)	187
Servant (in-door, e. g., cook, bearer, water carrier)	187
Servant (in trade or industry unspecified).	189
Service in residential clubs ...	127
Service in charitable, etc. societies	183
Service in turf, polo-club, etc. ...	183
Sewing-machine maker, repairer ...	59
Sewing-machine seller ...	123
Shares and other property (not land) income from—	185
Shaver (barber) ...	86

APPENDIX—

PART II—Alphabetical

Occupation	Group number	Occupation	Group number
S—contd.		**S—contd.**	
Shawl dealer ...	138	Slate, worker in— ...	90
Shawl weaver ...	46	Slaughterer ...	73
Sheep breeder, grazier ...	23	Snake catcher ...	28
Sheep dealer ...	132	Snake charmer ...	184
Shell bangle maker ...	53	Snuff manufacturer ...	78
Shell bangle seller ...	147	Snuff seller ...	135
Shell burner (for lime) ...	90	Soap factory (owners, workmen, etc.)	70
Shell dealer ...	118	Soap seller ...	138
Shell, worker in— ...	53	Sock maker ...	84
Shepherd ...	23	Sock seller ...	138
Shikari ...	28	Soda-Water Factory (owners, workmen, etc.) ...	67
Shoe maker (any material) ...	82	Soda-water seller ...	126
Shoe seller ...	138	Soldier (Imperial Army) ...	153
Shop boy, girl (unspecified) ...	189	Soldier (Indian State) ...	154
Shop-keeper (unspecified) ...	150	Solicitor ...	167
Shop-keeper's clerk, servant ...	189	Spade maker ...	98
Shorthand writer ...	176	Spade seller ...	123
Shunter (Railway) ...	112	Spangle maker ...	98
Signaller (Railway) ...	112	Spangle seller ...	147
Signaller (Telegraph) ...	114	Spear maker ...	58
Signboard painter ...	90	Spectacle maker ...	97
Silk braid maker ...	50	Spectacle seller ...	146
Silk carder, spiner ...	47	Spice dealer ...	130
Silk weaver ...	47	Spiritual guide ...	165
Silk cloth seller ...	117	Stamp vendor ...	152
Silk dyer ...	49	Starch manufacturer ...	70
Silk lace maker ...	50	Stationer ...	148
Silk lace seller ...	138	Station Master (Railway) ...	112
Silver (braid) maker ...	50	Stenographer ...	176
Silver, dealer in— ...	146	Stone breaker for roads ...	106
Silver wire drawer ...	98	Stone mason, sawyer, worker ...	90
Silver, worker in— ...	98	Straw, dealer in— ...	136
Singer ...	182	Straw, worker in— ...	56

Occupations returned—continued

Index of Occupations—continued

Occupation	Group number	Occupation	Group number
S—concld.		T—contd.	
String maker ...	45	Tanner ...	51
Sub-Registrar ...	159	Tannery (owners, workmen, etc.) ...	51
Subadar (Imperial Army) ...	153	Tape maker ...	43
Subadar (Indian State) ...	154	Tax collector (Municipal) ...	161
Sugarcane presser ...	74	Taxidermist ...	99
Sugarcane press hirer, seller ...	123	Tea, dealer in— ...	143
Sugar factory (owners, workmen, etc.)	74	Teacher (of music and dancing) ...	182
		Teacher (of Drawing) ...	179
Sugar refiner ...	74	Teacher (all others) ...	174
Sugar seller ...	130	Telegraph and telephone service (all grades).	114
Superintendent Jail ...	159	Temple, inmate of— ...	164
Superintendent Market, Octroi ...	161	Temple service ...	166
Superintendent Veterinary Department.	173	Tenant (cultivator) ...	6
Surgeon (wherever employed) ...	169	Tennis Court service ...	183
Surki dealer ...	141	Tent maker ...	89
Surki pounder ...	90	Tent seller ...	130
Surma (eye powder) maker ...	70	Thana office ...	157
Surma (eye powder) seller ...	138	Thatch dealer ...	122
Survey office employe ...	177	Thatcher ...	56
Surveyor (Railway) ...	112	Theatre performer ...	182
Surveyor (Road) ...	105	Theatre manager, employees other then performers.	183
Surveyor (others) ...	177	Thought reader ...	181
Sweeper ...	100	Thread maker ...	43
Sweeping contractor ...	100	Thread (silk) maker ...	47
Sweetmeat maker ...	75	Thread (sacred) seller ...	147
Sweetmeat seller ...	130	Ticket Collector (Railway) ...	112
T		Tiles, dealer in— ...	124
Tahsildar (Government) ...	159	Tiles, maker of— ...	64
Tailor ...	83	Tiler ...	90
Talc worker ...	65	Timber dealer ...	119
Tallow manufacturer ...	70	Tin, dealer in— ...	123
Tallow seller ...	125	Tin, worker in— ...	61

Occupation		Group number	Occupation		Group number
T—concld.			**U**		
Tinsmith	...	61	Udasin (religious mendicant)	...	164
Tobacco manufacturer	...	78	Umbrella maker, repairer	...	84
Tobacco seller, tobacconist	...	135	Umbrella (of all material) seller	...	138
Toddy seller	...	126	Underwriter	...	115
Toilet articles, dealer in—	...	138	Uniform maker	..	83
Toll collector (bridge)	...	105	Utensil (brass, copper, etc.) maker, repairer.		60
Toll collector (canal)	...	103	Utensil (earthen) maker, repairer	...	63
Tomb keeper	..	166	Utensil (iron) maker, repairer	...	98
Tool maker, grinder	...	59	Utensil (glass) maker, repairer	...	65
Tool seller	...	123	Utensil (porcelain) maker, repairer	...	65
Tooth powder maker	...	70	Utensil (soap stone, etc.) maker, repairer.		65
Tooth powder seller	...	138	Utensil (tin, aluminum) maker, repairer		61
Tow maker	...	45	Utensil (cooking, etc.) seller	...	140
Towman (boat)	...	102			
Toy maker	...	99	**V**		
Toy seller	...	147	Vaccination Inspector, Vaccinator	...	172
Trader, itinerant	...	151	Vagabond, Vagrant	...	193
Trader, tradesman (unspecified)	...	150	Vakil	...	167
Traffic Inspector (Railway)	...	112	Varnish, dealer in—	..	125
Trainer of race horses	...	183	Vegetable seller	...	134
Translator (Government)	.	159	Veterinary Surgeon	...	173
Trollyman (Railway)	...	112	Village Headman, servant	...	162
Trumpeter	...	182			
Trunk (leather) maker	...	51	**W**		
Trunk (steel) maker	...	59	Waggon unloader	...	113
Trunk (tin) maker	...	61	Waiter (Hotel, etc.)	...	127
Trustee of Temple	...	166	Walking-stick maker	...	84
Tumbler (acrobat)	...	184	Warder (Jail)	...	159
Turmeric dealer	...	130	Warehouse (owners and employees)	...	116
Turner	...	55	Warrant Officer (Army)	...	153
Tutor	...	174	Washerman	...	85
Twine manufacturer	.	45	Waste, dealer in—	.	149

Occupation returned—**concluded**

Index of Occupations—concluded

Occupation	Group number
W—contd.	
Watchman (over crops) ...	7
Watch-maker, repairer ...	97
Watch seller ...	118
Water-bag (mashk) maker ...	51
Water-bag (mashk) seller ...	118
Water carrier (domestic) ...	187
Water carrier (Railway) ...	113
Water carrier (unspecified) ...	187
Water seller ...	128
Water Works (Managers, workmen, etc.)	161
Wax-cloth manufacturer ...	7[illegible]
Way Inspector (Railway) ...	112
Weaver (cotton) ...	43
Weaver (other fibres) ...	45
Weaver (silk) ...	47
Weaver (wool) ...	46
Weighman (unspecified) ...	116
Well-bag (leather) maker ...	51
Well-bag (leather) seller ...	118
Well sinker, engineer ...	90
Wheel (carriage) maker ...	92
Wheel (carriage) seller ...	143
Wheelrwight ...	92
Whipper-in ...	183
Whitewasher ...	90
Wholesale dealer (otherwise unspecified).	150
Wicker-work maker ...	56
Wig maker ...	86
Wig seller ...	126
Wig-shop service ...	126
Wire (gold and silver) drawer ...	98

Occupation	Group number
W—concld	
Witch, wizard ...	181
Wood carver (cabinet work) ...	88
Wood cutter ...	18
Wood sawyer ...	54
Wood seller ...	119
Wood seller (for fuel) ...	145
Wood turner, etc. ...	55
Wood, worker in— ...	55
Wool, woollen goods, dealer in— ...	117
Wool carder, knitter, spinner ...	46
Wool dyer ...	49
Wool weaver ...	46
Wreath (artificial) maker ...	99
Wreath (artificial) seller ...	147
Wrestler ...	184
X	
Xylophone maker ...	96
Y	
Yarn (cotton) beater, reeler, etc. ...	43
Yarn (cotton and wool) seller ...	117
Yarn (wool) beater, reeler, etc. ...	46
Z	
Zamindar ...	1
Zamindari service (Estate Agents and Managers).	3

INDEX

TO

PART I—REPORT

PARA.

A

Accretions to the urban area since 1881 ... 54
Accuracy of the earlier Censuses ... 17
Accuracy of the enumeration, general ... 9
Actual and natural population ... 116
Administrative and Political Divisions ... 3
Afridi blockade 80
Age distribution of population ... 87
Age groups of certain castes ... 96
Age, reference to statistics ... 85
Age, reference to Sundbarge's theory ... 89
Age, unreliability of returns ... 86
Agricultural castes ... 323
Agricultural conditions ... 27
Agriculture and allied occupations ... 188
Agror 257
Ahl-i-Hadis 294, 298
Ahmadis 294
Ahmadis and other sects ... 298
Amb State 38, 50
Anand Marriage Act ... 320
Anglican Communion ... 314
Anglo-Indian 317
Anglo-Indians and Europeans ... 205
Arabic 277
Arains 323
Area by districts 11
Area mortgaged, redeemed and sold ... 35
Area of the North-West Frontier Province 2
Area, population and density, reference to statistics 10
Army 193
Aroras 116, 132, 202, 233, 235, 329
Aryan Sub-family 252
Arya Samaj 307, 320
Attar 320
Awan 116, 132, 202, 233, 235, 325

B

Baghbans 323
Balochis 262
Baluchis 251
Barbers ... ... 320—323
Beggars 199
Bengalis 275
Bhatiaras ... ... 320—323
Bhogarmang Valley ... 23
Bilingualism ... ... 278—281
Birth-place and migration statistics ... 64
Birth-rate 98
Birth variations 99
Blindness ... ... 163—170
Boatmen and palki-bearers ... 323
Brahman 116, 132, 202, 233, 235, 317, 323
Building industry ... 190
Butchers 323

C

Canadians 317
Cantonment population ... 57
Carpenters 323
Castes and tribes localised ... 332
Castes classified by hereditary occupation 322
Castes—reference to ethnographical glossary 333

C—concld.

Caste, race and nationality—Caste system not rigid in the Province ... 320
Castes, etc.—Division by tribes ... 321
Castes, etc.—Reference to statistics ... 3, 316
Castes, etc.—Variations ... 331
Ceramics 190
Chadar-andazi 121
Chamar 132, 202, 233, 235, 323
Changes of area 4
Chinese 277
Chishtis 294
Cholera 24
Christians 313
Christians and literacy ... 222
Christians—variations and sects ... 314
Chuhra 116, 132, 202, 233, 235, 236, 323
City, definition of 48
Civil condition ... ... 120—140
Civil-Disobedience ... 21
Communications 35
Conditions of the decade 1921—31 ... 18, 21
Confectioners and grain-parchers ... 323
Congress 21
Co-operative Credit Societies ... 31
Cotton-spinning 190
Crime 199
Cultivation (its extension) ... 29
Cultivators 323
Cultivators and cattle rearers ... 323

D

Dardic languages 263
Darzis 323
Deaf-mutism ... ... 159—162
Death-rate 100
Death-rate, incidence ... 102
Death-rate in other countries ... 102
Death variations 101
Deghani 255
Density (comparison with countries outside India) 13
Density and over-crowding in Peshawar City 61
Density of cultivated area ... 14
Density of districts ... 14
Density of tahsils ... 15
Dera Ismail Khan 38
Derawali 254, 270
Description of North-West Frontier Province 1
Dhobis 323
Dhunds 331
Distribution of Pathans ... 324
Distribution of population by age-groups 87, 93
Distribution of rural population ... 63
Distribution of total population ... 122
Distribution of urban population by religion 59
District-to-district migration ... 173
Domestic service 197
Dums 320

E

Early marriages by caste ... 132
Earners and others ... 182
Economic position of the agriculturist ... 30
Educated unemployment ... 177, 206

	PARA.
E—concld.	
Education among females ...	248
Education, expenditure on ...	245
Edwardes College	247
English	276
Eranian Branch	252
Europeans and Anglo-Indians and their occupations	203
Excess of male births ...	109
Excess of males in India ...	104
Extension of cultivation ...	29
Extraction of mineral wealth ...	189
F	
Feudal Tanawal	23, 37, 50, 63, 98
Fevers, mortality from ..	25
Fishermen, boatmen and palki-bearers ...	323
Frontier Enquiry Committee of 1922 ...	21
Frontier Constabulary	193
Frontier Corps	193
G	
Goanese	317
Gold and silver-smiths ...	323
Gomal and Zhob passes ...	78
Gorkhali or Naipali ...	274
Grierson, Sir George ..	252, 256, 263, 265
Growth of population 1911—1921 ...	19
Growth of population of towns since 1881	53
Growth of urban population ...	52
Gujar	116, 132, 202, 233, 235, 323, 337
Gujrati	275
Gujuri	271, 272
Gurkhali	274
H	
Halwai	320
Haripur Central Jail ...	35, 159
Hazara	38
Hazara (Insanity)	153
Higher education	247
Hijrat movement	18
Hindi	254, 266, 271, 273
Hindko	251, 260, 270
Hindu population... ...	299, 305
Hindus and literacy ...	223, 229, 244
Hindustani	254, 266, 271, 273
Holi	303
House, definition of— ...	43
Houses and size of families ...	44
I	
Immigration compared with emigration	74
Immigration—direction of main currents	75
Immigration figures of two censuses compared	80
Immigration from Peshawar rural area to Peshawar City	62
Immigration from the West ...	76, 77
Industrial development ...	34
Industry, decline in ...	190
Infant mortality	110
Infirmities	143—150
Influenza epidemic... ...	9, 18
Inmates of alms-houses ...	199
Inmates of asylums ...	199
Inmates of jails	199
Insanity	150—158
Islamia College	247
Ismaili	294—298
J	
Jamrud	35
Japanese	277
Jat	116, 132, 202, 233, 235, 326
Jatatar	257
Jatki	253, 254
Jhatkai	323
Jhinwar ...	323
Joint Stock Companies ...	32
Jolaha	323
K	
Kabul	78, 261
Kabul River Canal ...	17, 29
Kafir Language	255
Kagan Valley	7, 23, 98
Kahar	320
Kanjar	320
Karewa	121
Kashatriya (Caste)... ...	317
Kashmiri	263
Keshdharis	303
Kharadi	320
Khassadars	21
Khatri	116, 132, 202, 233, 235
Khattak	324
Khyber Pass	78
Khyber Railway ...	21, 35
Konsh, Bhogarmang and Kagan Valleys	23, 257
Kohati	254, 270
Kohistan	251, 263, 264
Kumhari	323
Kurram	209
Kutana	323
L	
Lady Reading Hospital ...	35
Lahnda	4, 253, 265
Landha and Punjabi ...	266—270
Landi Khana	35
Language	250—277
Languages of other families ...	273
Leather workers ...	321
Legislative Assembly ...	26
Leprosy	171—175
Linguistic Surveys ...	252, 250
Literacy	207—249
Lohar	320, 323
Lower Swat Canal... ...	17, 29
M	
Machhis	323
Mahsud	2, 18, 325
Malak (Jurist)	294
Malakand	209
Malandri Tract	4, 37
Males, excess of	104
Maliaras	323
Mallahs	323
Marathi	275
Marriage Statistics ...	124—132
Marwat	324
Mean age	94, 95
Migration	82
Migration between Asiatic Countries ...	83
Migration between the Province and other parts of India ...	82
Migration, general figures ...	70
Migration, outside Asia ...	84
Migration, other extra provincial ...	81
Mirasi	323
Mochi	323
Moghal	320
Mohmand	324
Momandzai	324
Mortality from fevers ...	25

PARA.

M—concld.

Movement of population ... 36
Mulki 270
Mullahs 195
Multani 253
Muslim population... ... 287-290
Muslims and literacy ... 224, 228, 243
Mussalli 323

N

Nais 323
Nanak Panthis 306
Naqshbandis 294
Nathia Galli 35
Natural and actual population of sexes ... 117
Natural Divisions 5
Nepali 274
Non-Synchronous areas ... 7
Normal and natural population ... 8
North-West dry area ... 5
Nowshera-Dargai Railway ... 35

O

Occupation 178-205
Oil pressers 323
Ormuri 255
Other extra-Provincial migration considered 81
Other Indo-European Languages of India 275
Over-crowding and density in Peshawar City 61

P

Pahari 270
Pakhli plain 257
Palki-bearers 323
Pashto 251-260
Pashto-Comparison with figures of Linguistic Survey ... 256
Pashto-Comparison with 1921 ... 259
Pashto, distribution of ... 255
Pashto in the districts ... 257
Pashto-speakers, females ... 260
Pashto-speakers, general decline in proportion 260
Pashto, variation by districts ... 258
Pashto, variation in proportion by districts 260
Pathans 116, 132, 202, 233, 235, 320
Pathans, increase in numbers ... 325
Penjara 323
Pensioners 196
Persian 261
Persons living on their income ... 196
Peshawar City 60
Peshawar City, density and over-crowding 61, 82
Peshawari 254, 270
Phulra State 38, 50
Plague epidemic 26
Police 193
Political and Administrative Divisions ... 3
Polygamy and its extent in the Province 142
Population, meaning of the term ... 6
Population of Cantonments ... 57
Population, movement ... 36
Potters 323
Powindah 8, 37, 78
Priests and devotees ... 323
Prices and wages 28
Professions and liberal arts ... 195
Prostitutes 199
Public wealth 24
Public administration ... 194
Public force 193
Punjab 82, 135
Punjabi 253, 254, 265, 266, 270, 271
Purdah 204

Q

Qadiris 294
Qassab 323
Qazilbash 261

PARA

R

Rafee, Mr. M. A., Industrial Survey by— 34
Raj (masons) 323
Rangila Rasool case, reference to ... 21
Rangrez 323
Razmak 21
Religion ... ... 282—314
Religion in towns 58
Roman Catholics 314
Roshania 297
Royal Air Force 193
Rural and urban population compared ... 49
Rural population and its distribution ... 193

S

Sahjdharis 303
Sala-i-am 320
Sanatan Dharam 305
Sayad 116, 132, 202, 233, 235, 320, 323, 328
Season and Crops Report ... 18
Sex proportions in towns ... 56, 107
Shafi 294
Shamsi Sect 308
Sheikh 320
Shia ... ... 294—297
Shyok Dam 35
Sikh population ... ... 310—312
Sikhs and literacy 223
Simon Commission ... 21
Singers and dancers ... 323
Singh Sabha 320
Size of families 44
Sizing 190
Soharwardis 294
Sonar 323
Statistics of Primary and Secondary education 246
Sudra 317
Sundbarge, theory ... ... 89—91
Sunni 294
Swathi 116, 132, 202, 233, 235, 330
Swat State 37
Sweeper 323
Sweeper Sects 309

T

Tailor 323
Tamil 277
Tanaoli 116, 132, 202, 233, 235, 330
Tanaoli (language) 254, 270
Tangi 53
Tarbela 257
Tarkhan 323
Telis 323
Telugu 277
Textiles 190
Tirah 297
Town, definition of— ... 47
Towns 50
Trade 33, 190, 192
Traders and pedlars . 323
Transport 190, 191
Turis 297
Turizuna 297
Turkish 277, 317
Types of migration ... 67

U

Undefined occupations ... 198
Unemployment among educated ... 177, 206
Unproductive occupations ... 199
Upper Swat Canal 17, 29
Urban and rural population compared ... 49
Urban population and its distribution ... 51
Urdu 254, 266, 271, 273

V

Vaishnavas 306
Vaishya and Sudra (Castes) ... 317

PARA.

V—concld.

Vedic Bharatri Intermediate College ... 247
Village, definition of ... 46
Vital statistics 22, 97
Vital statistics, system of registration ... 23

W

Wage Census 28
Wages and prices 28
Wahabis ... 298
Washermen 323
Wazir 18, 21, 325
Waziristan 21, 28, 37, 209

PARA

W—concld.

Weavers, carders and dyers ... 323
Weaving ... ...
Western Punjabi 254, 27
Widowed-variations by religion ... 142
Widows and Widowers ... 5.

Y

Yusafzai 324

Z

Zhob and Gomal Passes ... 78

GP&SO-NWFP—1067CS—750—2-6-33—(29)